big cat diary Leopard

Jonathan and Angela Scott

To Pam Savage, for her many kindnesses.

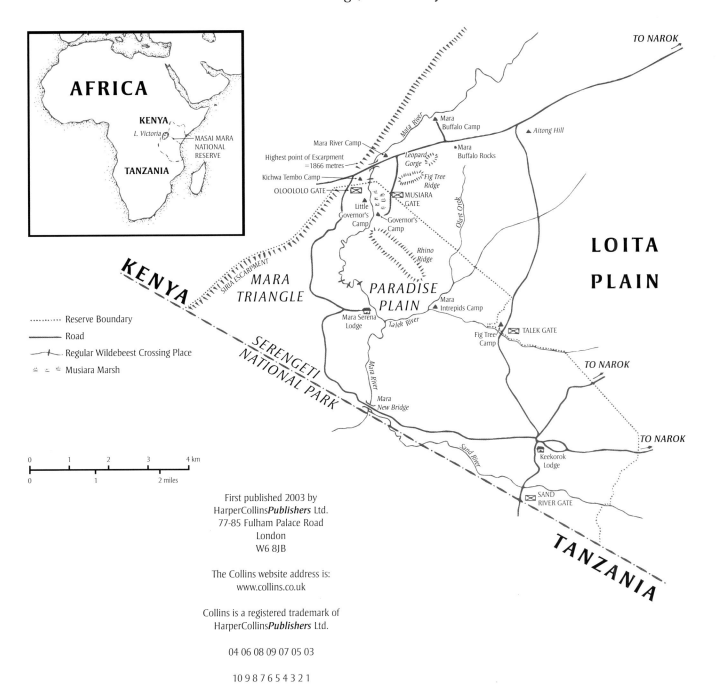

AFRICA

KENYA

L. Victoria

MASAI MARA
NATIONAL
RESERVE

TANZANIA

TO NAROK

Mara River Camp

Mara
Buffalo Camp

Aitong Hill

Highest point of Escarpment
=1866 metres

Leopard
Gorge

Mara
Buffalo Rocks

Kichwa Tembo Camp

Fig Tree
Ridge

OLOOLOLO GATE

MUSIARA
GATE

Little
Governor's
Camp

Governor's
Camp

KENYA

SIRIA ESCARPMENT

MARA
TRIANGLE

Rhino
Ridge

Olare Orok

LOITA

PLAIN

PARADISE
PLAIN

Mara
Intrepids Camp

SERENGETI
NATIONAL PARK

Mara Serena
Lodge

Talek River

Fig Tree
Camp

TALEK GATE

TO NAROK

.... Reserve Boundary

——— Road

Regular Wildebeest Crossing Place

Musiara Marsh

Mara River

Mara
New Bridge

Sand River

TO NAROK

Keekorok
Lodge

| 0 | 1 | 2 | 3 | 4 km |

| 0 | 1 | | 2 miles | |

SAND
RIVER GATE

TANZANIA

First published 2003 by
HarperCollins*Publishers* Ltd.
77-85 Fulham Palace Road
London
W6 8JB

The Collins website address is:
www.collins.co.uk

Collins is a registered trademark of
HarperCollins*Publishers* Ltd.

04 06 08 09 07 05 03

10 9 8 7 6 5 4 3 2 1

© 2003 Jonathan and Angela Scott

ISBN 0 00 7146671

Edited by Caroline Taggart
Designed by Liz Brown

Colour reproduction by Colourscan, Singapore
Printed and bound in Great Britain by Butler & Tanner Ltd, Frome and London

Contents

Introduction

Hawks for sunlight; owls for half-light; but for the night, cats, wild cats.

Doris Lessing: On Cats

When *Big Cat Diary* was first commissioned in 1996, we imagined it would be a one-off, stand-alone series. Surely a follow-up that again featured lions, leopards and cheetahs in the Masai Mara in Kenya would seem repetitive. 'Not another lion hunt or wildebeest river crossing,' we could hear people groaning. But we were wrong. The response to the first series was so positive that in September 1998 we returned to the Mara to film a second.

The challenge was to make it feel different. We would still concentrate most of our efforts on finding and filming the three big cats, but would also include material on some of the Mara's other resident characters, such as the spotted hyenas, jackals and elephants. We knew that people identified strongly with the

The best times to look for predators are dawn and dusk. The Mara is an ideal place to view big cats, due to the open, rolling terrain.

individual cats, so we wanted to provide as much continuity as possible. By returning to the Musiara Marsh area in the northern Mara we felt confident we could find the cats we had filmed in the previous series. As in the first series, co-presenter Simon King followed the cheetahs, I searched for leopards, and we both covered the lions.

Because Angie and I live in Kenya and spend long periods of time on safari as wildlife photographers in the area surrounding Musiara Marsh, we are in the ideal position to help keep track of our animal stars between series, relying heavily on the co-operation of our friends among the drivers and guides at the various camps

A lioness stares out across Musiara Marsh, the heart of the Marsh Pride's dry-season territory.

Half-Tail and Zawadi when she was nine months old, walking along Fig Tree Ridge early one morning, looking for a place to lie-up for the day.

and lodges. Drivers from Governor's Camp (which is situated in the Musiara area) keep a daily game record, noting which lions, leopards and cheetahs they have seen, what they killed and any other interesting details. Over the years they have named key geographical features, creating an unofficial 'map' that everyone who knows the area understands, making it relatively simple to guide vehicles to a sighting of lions or a leopard. Whenever we visit the Mara we meet the drivers and go through the game record, catching up on all the news. My association with the Mara's big cats goes back over 25 years, to the time when Brian Jackman and I wrote a book entitled *The Marsh Lions*, detailing the life of a pride whose territory centres on Musiara Marsh and about which Angie and I have kept records ever since.

When you see a pride of lions slumped in the shade of an acacia tree, an amorphous mass of tawny hides intertwined in friendly union, it seems impossible to distinguish one from another.

Over time Angie and I have learned to recognize each cat as an individual, marked out by its unique character and physical presence. But in order to be absolutely certain who is who, we rely on the lion's whisker-spot pattern, which remains constant throughout its life. Though we know each lion by name – Notch, Scar, Brown Mane, Khali – we generally avoid using these names on *Big Cat Diary*. To the audience one lion looks much the same as the next – at times they do to us, too – so naming them all would simply add to the confusion. Instead we focus on the story of the pride, and in this respect the Marsh Lions have provided a sense of continuity, playing a leading role in each of the four series filmed to date.

The spotted cats have proved somewhat easier to identify for the audience, particularly the leopards. Half-Tail, our all-time favourite, became an instant star of the first series, her short stumpy tail simply adding to her character. Leopards are normally shy and retiring, spending much

of their time hidden from view, so being able to work with Half-Tail was a joy, in marked contrast to my first years in the Mara, when it was virtually impossible to see a leopard. For as long as Half-Tail was alive we could almost guarantee finding her somewhere among the acacia country surrounding Leopard Gorge and Fig Tree Ridge, to the north-east of the Marsh. During that first series, Half-Tail was accompanied by a seven-month-old cub whom the drivers named Zawadi, meaning 'gift' in Swahili (to the television audience she is known as Shadow, though I always think of her as Zawadi). A leopard with a young cub ensured that there was plenty of activity for us to film, and as these were the only leopards we featured there was never any doubt as to who they were.

In 1996 Simon had two female cheetahs to work with, each with young cubs. He named the adults Fundi (the specialist) and Kidogo (the small one). Two years later the cheetah story became even easier to tell. For many years the drivers and safari guides had kept track of a female they had named Queen, due to her regal bearing. Queen didn't have cubs when we filmed the first series, but she must have given birth a few months later, because by the time we returned she was accompanied by three large cubs. Simon preferred the name Amber to Queen, acknowledging her beautiful amber eyes. Though each cheetah has a unique pattern of spots there was never any chance of mistaking Amber. She was so relaxed around vehicles that she often leapt up onto the bonnet. There was nothing playful or pet-like about her behaviour – she simply treated vehicles as just one more termite mound, an aerial perch from which to peruse her surroundings. Amber's cubs soon learned to be equally fearless of vehicles, though they preferred to jump up onto the spare tyres on the back of the cars and then hop up onto the roof, much to the delight of visitors, who were treated to a unique close-up view of these beautiful creatures.

As filming of the second series drew to a close we once again found ourselves wondering if there would be another. It brought back memories of the time when Brian Jackman and I were working on *The Marsh Lions*, and people kept asking us why we were producing yet another book on lions. Surely Joy Adamson's landmark tale *Born Free*, narrating the story of Elsa the lioness in the wilds of Kenya, had said all there was to say. And if it hadn't, then what about George Schaller's treatise *The Serengeti Lion*, for anyone looking for a more scientific text? But big cats have a universal appeal that cuts across generations, and I can think of nowhere easier to film them than the Masai Mara. Not only are the lions, leopards and

Every cheetah can be distinguished by the rings and spots on its tail and its individual coat markings. Amber also had a distinctive nick out of her right ear.

cheetahs extremely habituated to vehicles, making them easy to approach, but the mix of open grassy plains and acacia woodlands provides excellent visibility in which to find them. It is the perfect filming location.

One thing was certain, without the continued support of *Animal Planet*, our American co-producers, who provide a sizeable part of the budget, the series would not be recommissioned. But the feedback from American audiences was as enthusiastic as elsewhere, prompting *Animal Planet* to go for a third series. So, early in September 2000, the *Big Cat Diary* team once again gathered at a private tented camp along the banks of the Mara River just a few kilometres north of Governor's Camp. This time, though, things were to be very different.

The Mara usually receives some rain in even the bleakest of dry seasons, but not this year. We barely recognized the location of the previous series. On that occasion our tented camp had been hit by a ferocious gale, dumping one of our soundmen's tents into the middle of the river – clothes, books, mobile phone, the lot. But now

Amber would regularly jump up onto the bonnet of cars for an unimpeded view across the plains.

An adult hippo intimidating a young male who had encroached on his bend of the river.
Bull hippos sometimes kill each other in territorial disputes, inflicting gaping wounds with
their awesome canine tusks and peg-like lower incisors.

Kenya was suffering its third year of drought. What a transformation! Nomadic pastoralists throughout the country had lost tens of thousands of head of cattle by the time we started filming. Dust devils ripped across the plains, sucking the earth from the parched land. The pastoralists had no option but to encroach into game reserves and national parks – even private ranchland – in their search for food and water, inevitably bringing them into conflict with park authorities and landowners. Politicians pleaded with game managers to exercise tolerance during the people's time of need. At night we could hear the sounds of cowbells tinkling deep within the reserve as the Masai herded their cattle into the sanctuary. And each morning vultures filled the ashen sky, wheeling overhead, as others plummeted to the ground to feast on yet another carcass.

Ironically the drought made for spectacular filming, as all the predators were assured of plenty of food. Added to this, dry years are always the best ones to view the migration of wildebeest and zebras. As the dry easterly winds whip across the southern Serengeti at the end of the rainy season in late May and early June, the wildebeest nation turns its back on the stinging wind and moves rapidly to the north and west. The dryer the year the greater the spectacle, with the animals leaving the plains en masse. The Mara is situated in the highest rainfall area in the ecosystem, offering water and grazing during the long dry season that lasts until the onset of the short rains in mid-October. This is as far north as the herds travel – beyond lies settlement, agriculture, fences all the way to the shores of Lake Victoria. As the rains replenish the Serengeti grasslands and fill the muddy

alkaline pools with water in October and November, the wildebeest head south again to their ancestral calving grounds on the short-grass plains.

In times of drought more than half a million wildebeest flood into the Mara at the beginning of the dry season. Some of the bulls are in the first flush of the annual rut, and from the air the wildebeest look like an army of ants, the females clustered into dense knots around the territorial males, with large herds of bachelors loitering on the fringes, peacefully feeding. It is for this reason that we always choose the middle of the dry season – the months of September and October – to film *Big Cat Diary*, relying on the wildebeest and zebras – and fires – to knock down the long grass and make it easier for us to find predators.

The migration is all-pervasive. Within days the grass is gone, forcing the elephants to seek out the acacia woodlands to the north of the reserve where Half-Tail and Zawadi can be found. The presence of the migration helps to guarantee plenty of action, particularly at favoured river-crossing sites, to which the herds return year after year, gathering in their thousands to cross the river to find better grazing. The wildebeest and zebras – sometimes even the Thomson's gazelles – must brave the giant crocodiles that pilot up and down the river in search of prey. And if they survive the crocodiles there is always the threat posed by prides of lions lying in ambush or the occasional leopard that sneaks out of the thickets to snatch a wildebeest calf or zebra foal as it struggles to clamber up the riverbank. Year after year, Angie and I make our annual pilgrimage to the Mara River. No matter how many times we have witnessed the spectacle before, the noise, dust and mayhem are irresistible.

While filming the first series of *Big Cat Diary* we struggled to deliver exciting footage of the Marsh Lions. The pride mostly killed at night, and for much of our stay there were no cubs to entertain us during the daytime, or they were too young

The Topi Plains males who took over the Marsh Pride territory in 2000.

to film, tucked away in the croton thickets along the Bila Shaka Lugga, the intermittent watercourse at the heart of the pride's territory. Two years later we had better luck, with a large crèche of cubs, but

everything changed in late 1999 when Scruffy, one of the two pride males, and two of the five lionesses were killed by Masai pastoralists. Scruffy's death precipitated a take-over of the pride territory by two blond-maned males from the neighbouring Topi Plains Pride to the east. The Topi Plains males were quick to exploit the weakness, terrorizing Scruffy's companion Scar, and prompting a split in the pride. Though two of the adult females stayed and eventually mated with the invaders, the eleven subadults left their birthplace along the Bila Shaka Lugga and retreated to the Marsh to escape the threat posed by these new males.

The young Marsh Lions and an older female called Bump Nose, who was the mother of three of them, spent the dry season hunting around the Marsh. Scar did his best to keep out of harm's way, somehow managing to avoid outright war with the Topi Plains males and scavenging from kills made by the younger generation. While Simon watched the Marsh Lions, I kept an eye on the Ridge Pride, who live to

Up to 600,000 wildebeest migrate from the Serengeti in Tanzania to the Masai Mara during the dry season, which begins in early June and continues through to mid-October.

the south of the Musiara area. They provided us with one of the real characters of the third series, a cub named Solo who was easy for people to identify, being the only baby in the pride.

All our worries about how we were going to find enough new material to film proved unfounded. The Marsh Lions were particularly active, partly due to the wealth of hunting opportunities Musiara Marsh offers in the dry season, but also as a consequence of having so many subadults eager to try out their fledgling hunting skills – and so many mouths to feed. Nothing was too big for the subadults and they often hunted during daylight. We filmed them attempting to ambush (with varying degrees of success) hippos, buffaloes, wildebeest, zebras and warthogs. All the young lions had to do was bury

themselves in the dense reedbeds at the heart of the Marsh and wait. Sooner or later, throngs of wildebeest and zebras would file down from the high country to the north and the rolling plains to the east, slaking their thirst at the spring-fed waters. And with the hippos and buffaloes very prone to the ravages of drought – and outnumbered by the massed feeding herds of wildebeest – there were many times when these heavyweights found themselves in a life-or-death struggle with the lions.

There was plenty of action with the cheetahs, too, even though Amber's three cubs – a female and two males – had left their mother shortly after we finished filming the second series, and were fully grown. Though they were now wandering widely together, Angie and I occasionally found the two young males. They seemed

strangely wary of vehicles, unlike their sister Kike (Swahili for 'young female') who had lost none of her tameness and still regularly climbed onto vehicles. Simon spent much of his time following Amber, who was by now the oldest female in the area. He also tracked the movements of an adult male known as Nick, due to the prominent nick in his ear, the current territory-holder on the Musiara side of the river.

Kike had settled in an area to the south-east of Musiara Marsh and could often be found hunting around the eastern edge of Rhino Ridge and the plains surrounding Mara Intrepids tented camp. Simon and cameraman Warren Samuels filmed some wonderful footage of a violent spat between Kike and Nick that left the larger male with blood dripping from his nose. Such

Half-Tail disappeared in early 1999. This was the last occasion that I saw her – accompanied by her sixth litter of cubs.

aggressive encounters between widely dispersed individuals often have the desired effect and within a day or so prompt the female to come into season.

Leopards were an entirely different story. In 1999 an event of major significance had left Angie and me feeling utterly desolate and prompted us to return to the Mara during September to film a brief up-date. Earlier in the year Half-Tail had disappeared. We had followed the life of this charismatic cat since she first emerged along Fig Tree Ridge and Leopard Gorge in 1990, and as I said she had been a star of the first series of *Big Cat Diary*. By the time we filmed the second, her daughter Zawadi was fully independent, and at two and a half years old would soon mate and give birth to her first cubs. Half-Tail was nursing her sixth litter at the time and had moved further north, burying herself in an area of acacia woodlands and rocky tree-spotted hills closer to the Mara River. I remember thinking on the occasions we found her that she had finally started to show signs of age. She was now eleven, old by Mara leopard standards. Even so we managed to capture some wonderful footage of her and her two cubs. Meanwhile, Zawadi regularly entertained us with her playful antics, proving to be just as much of a character as her mother.

The events leading to Half-Tail's death remain something of a mystery. It is said that she was caught up in a wire snare set by herdsmen as she crawled through a hole in the thornbush stockade enclosing a temporary cattle boma. Apparently she had taken a goat or a sheep the previous night, and paid the price for her persistence. It was a sad end for a unique creature who had given pleasure to millions of viewers. But a leopard can be a real menace to stockmen, a murdering thief to their way of thinking, a silent hunter that visits in the dead of night.

Despite Half-Tail's absence, we found plenty to film when we returned for series three in 2000. As we had expected, Zawadi

Zawadi with her daughter Safi, aged three months. Zawadi is snarling at a hyena that she has seen approaching her along Fig Tree Ridge.

had given birth in Leopard Gorge shortly after we filmed the update in September 1999. But the two cubs lived for barely two weeks, tracked down and eaten by hyenas. Then as the sun rose on the morning of 1 January 2000 Angie, our son David and I could hardly believe our good fortune as we sat and watched Zawadi carry a half-eaten impala carcass back to where she had hidden her second litter – a male and female – along Fig Tree Ridge. It is tough raising leopard cubs in the Mara with so many lions and hyenas to compete with: within six months lions managed to kill the more adventurous male cub. Nevertheless, Zawadi and Safi, as we named her daughter – it's a Swahili term

of approval meaning a combination of 'clean' and 'nice' – provided us with many wonderful moments, spending much of their time to the north of Leopard Gorge in the area that Half-Tail used to roam.

When it was decided to film a fourth series of *Big Cat Diary* in 2002 I wondered how on earth we could compete with the kind of scenes we had filmed two years earlier. Droughts of that magnitude come along only once every five to ten years, and with people now talking about the possibility of an El Niño, I had visions of it being really wet. I imagined acres of long grass greeting us at the end of the rainy season, which in turn was likely to yield a dismal migration – and very tough times trying to find the cats. Fortunately I was wrong. What made the fourth series different was cubs – lots of them. All three big cats had youngsters for us to film – something that had been missing from the earlier series.

Angie and I travelled down to the Mara a few days before the crew assembled to catch up with what had been happening. Angie had already been networking with our friends at the various camps and lodges, who had provided us with almost daily updates on the movements of the Marsh Lions and Zawadi, who was by now heavily pregnant again. Bump Nose, one of the five original Marsh lionesses, had disappeared, leaving just two of the older generation, Khali and Notch. Meanwhile, Red – one of the Marsh Sisters, a small group of lionesses exiled from the Marsh Pride some years earlier – had been speared by the Masai after she killed a calf, leaving her companions Gimpy and Go-Kat to fend for themselves. Fortunately the Marsh Pride itself had a new generation of seven young females to bolster their number – the subadults who had featured so prominently in series three.

A few weeks before we arrived in the Mara, Angie received a report from Governor's Camp that a cheetah had given birth to five cubs along the Bila Shaka Lugga. This is the traditional birthplace of the Marsh Lions' cubs and one of the few places out on the plains where the lions can still find shade in the heat of the day. In the past whenever a cheetah has tried to raise a litter in the vicinity she has failed. Sooner or later one or more of the lions happens to look up and see her, recognizing by her behaviour that she has cubs and immediately moving in to investigate. If the cubs are small they are doomed, and so it proved in this instance. We were told that one of the Marsh Lions' new pride males was the culprit and that the cheetah mother was Amber's daughter, Kike. We had hoped that for the first time on *Big Cat Diary* we would be able to feature a cheetah with small cubs. But it would not be Kike.

In recent years cheetah numbers have plummeted in the northern Mara, especially beyond the reserve boundary. A few years ago, driving through this area early in the morning was guaranteed to yield at least one cheetah, often several. With plenty of gazelles and impalas – and fewer lions and hyenas than within the reserve – it was ideal cheetah country, and the sight of a cheetah hunting, often in the company of up to five fluff-ball cubs, was the highlight of any game drive. In those days there were more than 60 adult cheetahs living in and around the Mara, and we always assumed that those outside the reserve thrived here due to the presence of the Masai, who provided a powerful deterrent to lions and hyenas, the cheetah's main competitors. With these larger predators seeking the safety of cover during the daytime, the cheetahs could hunt and move about with their cubs in relative safety. Cheetahs are timid cats and no threat to the Masai, rarely

Warriors (*Ilmurran*) of the Kisongo Masai in northern Tanzania dancing in celebration at becoming junior elders during the colourful ceremony called *Eunoto*.

Notch (left) and her sister Khali, part of the original group of five Marsh lionesses we filmed in 1996. Notch is acting submissively as she greets her sister, who is nursing young cubs.

attempting to take livestock, and the fact that they do not scavenge renders them immune to the effects of the poison that the herdsmen sometimes employ to rid the area of predators, lacing a carcass with toxic cattle-dip.

Today the Masai are more sedentary and more numerous, bringing ever greater numbers of cattle, sheep and goats into the area surrounding the Mara Reserve. The grass is cropped short year round, leaving little cover for cheetahs to den or to provide camouflage for newly emerging cubs.

The plains around Aitong and the wooded thickets to the north of Leopard Gorge were traditionally Amber's hunting grounds. Nobody was sure how old she was, though some people thought she might be as much as 12 – almost unimaginably old by wild cheetah standards. This time when we asked after her, the drivers said that they had lost track of her in recent months and thought she had probably died. It is impossible not to feel sad when an old friend – which these cats are to us – dies or is injured. Just like Half-Tail, Amber was a huge part of our

lives: it was always so good to seek either of them out and to spend time in their company. Both cats were such distinctive characters that at first we couldn't quite believe they had gone. Even though Amber ranged widely from Paradise Plain in the south all the way to the Aitong Plains in the north-east, sooner or later she would reappear, in the same way that Half-Tail would vanish for months at a time during the long rains, submerging herself in a shroud of long red-oat grass. Then one day we would find her again, lying among the lichen-covered rocks in Leopard Gorge or feasting on a kill in a sausage tree on top of Observation Hill. But though we searched for Amber in all her old haunts there was no sign of her, and we were forced to accept that she had gone for good.

So for the first time on *Big Cat Diary*, Simon and his camera crew crossed the Mara River to search for cheetahs in that part of the reserve situated on the west of the river – the Mara Triangle. Angie and I love the Triangle; scenically it is stunning country. We were married there in 1992, on a high bluff on top of the Siria Escarpment, overlooking the Mara River. The escarpment

forms the western boundary of the reserve, one side of the 520 km² (200 sq. mile) triangle of land enclosed by the river to the east and the Kenya–Tanzania border to the south, which separates the Masai Mara from the vast Serengeti National Park. In 1995 control of the reserve was divided between the Narok County Council to the east of the river and Trans-Mara County Council to the west. A management company known as the Mara Conservancy is now responsible for running the Triangle on behalf of the Trans-Mara County Council and has made a welcome and positive impact on road maintenance, visitor surveillance and revenue collection. Since the Mara Conservancy took over more than 1,000 wire snares have been recovered and nearly 200 people arrested, sending a clear warning to meat hunters that the Triangle is no longer poachers' country.

From the first day they set foot in the Triangle, Simon and his crew were in cheetah paradise. They quickly discovered two females, each with three cubs, as well as a male, all hunting within a few kilometres of each other, barely half an hour's drive from Little Governor's Camp,

Balanites woodland is a feature of the Mara Triangle, where cheetahs are thriving, partly because there are fewer lions and hyenas.

where the film cars were stationed overnight. Simon concentrated on the female with the younger cubs, which were about three months old when filming commenced. He called the female Honey. Sometimes the two cheetah mothers were within sight of each other, though typically these solitary cats kept their distance and simply avoided each other rather than needlessly fighting over turf. There were nail-biting confrontations with lions, and as filming came to a close Simon and the cheetah crew managed to film a dramatic encounter between Honey and her cubs and the territorial male.

Meanwhile on the other side of the river, a new presenter, Saba Douglas-Hamilton, joined us to watch over the Marsh Lions. At first we thought this would be a relatively easy assignment for Saba, but things soon got complicated with three of the lionesses giving birth to cubs within weeks of each other along the Bila Shaka Lugga, while other members of the pride concentrated

their activity around the Marsh. It is quite normal for lionesses in the same pride to come into season at the same time, particularly after a takeover, when any young cubs sired by the previous males are invariably killed by the newcomers. The best way for lionesses to raise their cubs is

as part of a crèche and mothers of young born within a few weeks of each other bring their cubs together as soon as they are old enough to emerge from the dense cover of their hiding place.

This was an exciting time in the history of the Marsh Lions. Angie and I were fascinated to see the way in which the young females from the group of eleven subadults who had retreated to the Marsh two years earlier had returned to the Bila Shaka Lugga as adults and mated with the new Marsh males from the Topi Plains. As sleek young four-year-olds, their lives had come full circle; they were back where they had been born, raising their own cubs.

Now they were faced with a different problem. The Marsh Pride's territory has always supported a finite number of lions, and in all the time we have watched them the pride has averaged between four and six lionesses. With the two oldest, Notch and Khali, now joined by six younger female relatives, and with ten young cubs to feed as well as the two pride males, it seemed inevitable that there would not be enough food for the whole pride once the migration deserted the Marsh for the Serengeti, unless they took to hunting buffaloes. I suspect that when we return for the next series, much will have changed in the Musiara area.

The 1,500 elephants living in and around the Masai Mara are a potent force for change in the landscape, contributing to the present shift from woodland to grassland.

The biggest surprise during the last series was finding Solo, the lion cub who had kept us enthralled with his antics throughout series three. Solo was the only survivor of a litter of four born to the oldest lioness in the Ridge Pride. He was full of character, a tough little cub whose only playmates were many months older than he was. I felt sure that, come the rainy season, Solo would find it impossible to compete with all those hungry mouths (there were more than 20 lions in the Ridge Pride) and would be bullied out of his share at any kills. But I obviously hadn't taken into account Solo's tenacious character. He had been raised in the white-hot cauldron of competition where no quarter is sought or given. The two magnificent old pride males had long since been chased from the pride and were probably dead by now, but there was Solo, bossing around his older relatives as if he owned the place.

Solo's mother had died since the last series, and three of the other adult females were heavily pregnant, possibly due to the arrival of two four-year-old males who had appeared with the migration and may have come from the Serengeti. This group was tentatively forming a new pride, though the males and females were rarely seen together. The rest of the pride roamed around the fringes of the riverine forest to the south of Governor's Camp without males to protect them, doing their best to avoid conflict with the Marsh Pride, who were numerically far stronger. The Ridge Pride now consisted of four young males of just over three years of age, and their two sisters – Solo's one-time playmates. Accompanying them was an old female whom we named Gimpy, a brave, defiant old lioness who aggressively defended her younger relatives – hence the damaged front leg that earned her her name.

Sharing the same area and wandering even further afield were Solo and his three-year-old male companion, the youngest of the older generation of cubs. These two itinerant males had formed a strong bond

Young male lions become nomadic when they are two to three years old, and must compete with the more numerous hyenas for food.

that would continue throughout their lives – if they survived the next two years as nomads. They were in endless conflict with their older relatives, disputing kills and scrapping over living space. It was a stark reminder of just how tough life can be for lions during this transitional time. Many never make it. Lacking a territory of their own, Solo and his chum were forced to keep on the move. As long as the wildebeest remained in the area, providing easy pickings for all the predators, they could find enough to eat, though it often meant warring with members of the local hyena clans, who were always ready to dispute ownership of a kill with young lions such as these.

Who knows where Solo will be in two years' time? By then he will be in the first flush of adulthood, and if he and his companion survive they will be ready to stake their claim to a pride territory somewhere in the Mara–Serengeti.

Events such as I have described are the daily fare of game drives in the Masai Mara, which over time have provided us with an

insight into the lives of the most charismatic animals. There is always something new or interesting to discover, and I never tire of watching lions hunting or playing – or even just lying there doing nothing at all. I have always maintained that my favourite creature is the one that Angie and I happen to be following at the time – be it wild dogs, lions or leopards. But there is something special about leopards which sets them apart and which I hope will become apparent in the pages of this book. This story is not only about the African leopard, nor just about the particular leopards that Angie and I have come to know over the years – Chui, the Mara Buffalo female, Half-Tail and Zawadi. It is an attempt – as was *Big Cat Diary: Lion* (the first book in this series of three) – to look at Africa's big cats from a broader perspective. We examine the findings of the latest field research and conservation initiatives, which in the case of the leopard stretch far beyond the African continent. The leopard is the world's most adaptable and widespread large cat. Long may it remain so.

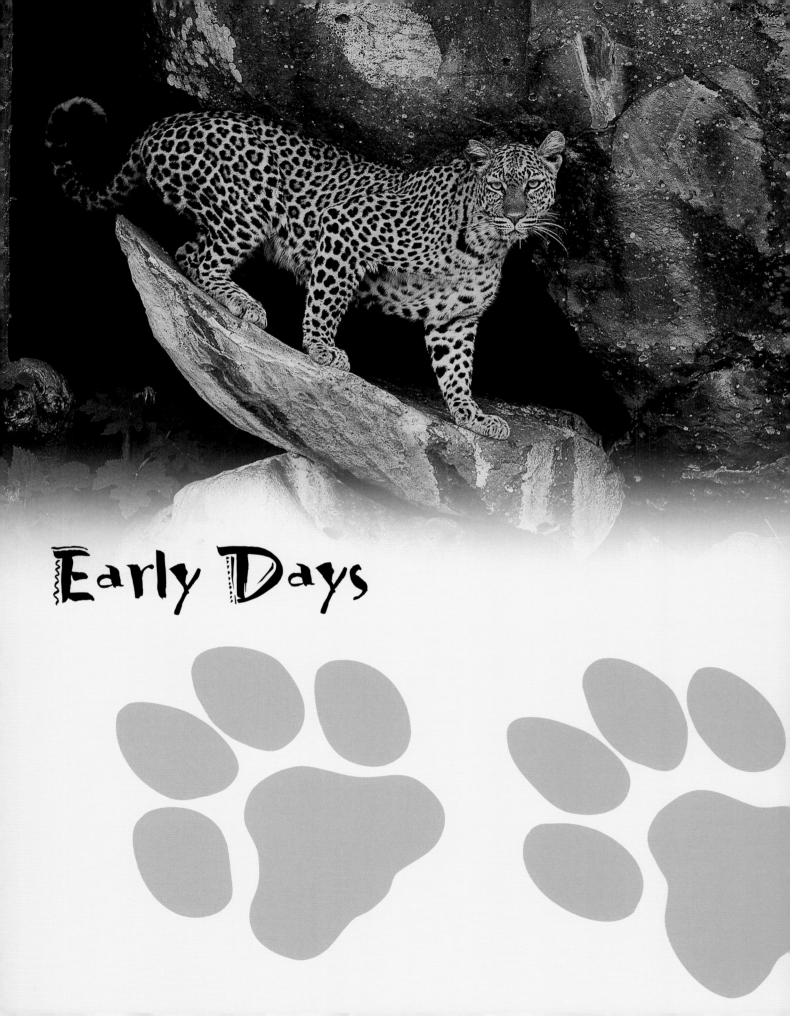

Early Days

Chui with a young impala. Impalas are a favourite prey of leopards wherever the two species occur together.

'Even before I first set foot in Africa ten years ago, I knew which of the wild animals I most wanted to see. It was the leopard that embodied my idea of Africa: an animal of supreme grace and agility, a hunter of the dark concealed in a spotted coat.

When I was a small child on a Berkshire farm, the annual visit to Regent's Park Zoo was the highlight of my year. I still remember standing spellbound in front of a barren enclosure as a huge male leopard padded up and down. Occasionally it would pause and stare at me through pale green eyes before setting off again on its endless journey. Surely this must be "the cat that walked by himself", I thought, equally convinced that Rudyard Kipling really did know the secret of "How the Leopard got his spots". But I knew if I wanted to learn more about leopards then I would have to journey to Africa.'

I wrote those words 20 years ago in the introduction to my book The Leopard's Tale. It had taken me six years of living in the Masai Mara to complete the book: that was how difficult it was in the 1970s to find a leopard that you could watch, let alone photograph.

I first visited the Mara in 1974 on a four-month overland trip from London to Johannesburg. In those days the Mara was little more than a stopover en route to the great Serengeti National Park in Tanzania or on the way back to Nairobi. There was time for only a single game drive, but that was enough. I knew even then that I wanted to return – the Mara is a predator's paradise.

When I arrived in South Africa at the end of my trip, I happened to pick up a copy of the Rand Daily Mail. It was one of those defining moments, a stroke of luck that helped determine that I stay on in Africa, rather than continuing my travels by boat from Cape Town to Sydney in Australia. An article by Dr Theodore Bailey had caught my eye. Bailey had just begun his study of leopards in the Kruger National Park, a massive tract of wooded savanna in the Transvaal Lowveld that stretches along

South Africa's eastern boundary, bordering Mozambique. The Kruger is 320 km (200 miles) from north to south and 65 km (40 miles) from east to west at its widest, an area of 19,485 km² (7,800 sq. miles). At the time it received 360,000 tourists annually.

The article was accompanied by pictures of Bailey tracking his study animals using radio-telemetry, a technique that was in its infancy. Here was somebody doing what I wanted to do, spending their time in the bush watching big cats. I immediately wrote to Bailey and asked him if he needed an assistant. He didn't. His wife was able to offer whatever support he needed, and besides if I was serious about studying predators I should continue my studies at university as a postgraduate student (I had told him I had a first degree in zoology). I appreciated the fact that he replied at all – I imagine he must have been inundated with requests such as mine.

Following Bailey's advice I then applied to the Pretoria Mammal Research Institute, who generously offered me the chance to study predators in Zimbabwe for my Masters degree. But I felt uncomfortable accepting the offer when the majority of South Africans were still disenfranchised by the apartheid system. That was the closest I ever came to becoming a scientist. The only options left to me if I wanted to work with wildlife were to become a safari guide, or to

develop my interest in wildlife art. Apart from the article on the leopard project, the Rand Daily Mail had other reasons to inspire me. The newspaper was running a series of articles about wildlife written by Sue Hart, a veterinary surgeon who once helped George Adamson patch up one of his beloved lions and who writes with poetic passion about wild Africa. But it was the beautiful stippled pen-and-ink sketches by Lee Voight that caught my attention. I had always loved to draw and had dabbled with pointillism (or stippling) at university to illustrate my honours thesis. The detail and range of tones that you can produce with a graphic pen are outstanding. Hart and Voight had published a collection of their work in book form, which I duly rushed out and bought – along with a set of Rotring pens and reams of art paper.

For the next two years I managed to find temporary work in Botswana with various wildlife-related projects, before heading back to Kenya to make the Mara my home. I based myself at Mara River Camp, which in those days was owned by legendary paleontologist Richard Leakey and wildlife filmmaker Alan Root. The deal was that I received free board and lodging in return for keeping an eye on the camp and acting as the in-house naturalist. This would allow me the chance to explore the Mara while taking guests on game drives; at the same

Leopards are secretive creatures, preferring to remain hidden among thickets and rocky outcrops to avoid being detecting by potential prey or by other predators.

time I could develop my interest in animal behaviour and wildlife illustration. By then my first set of pen-and-ink drawings had been published as prints, and within a couple of years I had earned enough from my art work to buy a Toyota Landcruiser. This brought me the freedom at last to go out on my own and get serious about my new passion – wildlife photography.

Though I had abandoned any ideas I might have had of continuing my studies as a zoologist, my academic training never left me. To this day, I still meticulously record whatever I see when I am in the bush. I have a pile of notebooks in my study in Nairobi filled with drawings and details of the animals I encountered, dating back to the time when I first arrived in the Mara.

Big cats have always featured prominently in these journals. There were plenty of lions for me to watch. Cheetahs too were relatively easy to track down in those days, and there was one female with three large cubs who treated vehicles just as Amber and her offspring would do years later – jumping onto spare wheels, clambering over roof hatches and generally enjoying themselves. It was unusual to come back from a game drive without having seen at least one of these elegant cats. Leopards were quite another matter. Neither lions nor cheetahs make a point of hiding themselves away, often appearing in open country and easy to approach. My failure to find a leopard just heightened my appetite for discovering all that I could about the most elusive of Africa's big cats.

I had seen my first leopard in the Serengeti during the overland trip, a glorious male shrouded in golden grass resting at the base of a yellow-barked acacia tree. We waited for him to rouse himself and climb back up into the tree to feast on the half-eaten impala that he had stored safely out of reach of lions and hyenas, 6m (20ft) up in the air. But leopards have a different sense of time from humans. This one was in no hurry to provide us with a better view of his spotted coat.

After I settled in the Mara I was not to see a leopard for many months, even though I was now living in some of the best leopard country in Africa. The problem, of course, was that stunningly beautiful coat. Concerns for the plight of spotted cats worldwide were first voiced in the 1960s, leading to various countries imposing voluntary bans on the trade in leopard skins. In 1972 the United States classified the leopard as an endangered species throughout its entire range, and the International Union for the Conservation of Nature (IUCN) listed five subspecies of leopards as rare or endangered. A report by Norman Myers published in 1974 on the status of leopards and cheetahs for the IUCN and World Wildlife Fund estimated that during the 1960s as many as 50,000 leopards were being killed each year in Africa to supply the seemingly endless demand for fur coats. In 1968 and 1969 alone fur brokers in the United States imported the skins of more than 17,000 leopards, and in 1980 Europe imported nearly half a million skins of medium-sized and small cats such as clouded leopards

Though food, water and cover are the basic requirements of life for most species, leopards are so adaptable that they can live virtually anywhere. They have the widest distribution of any cat, ranging far beyond the African continent. Leopards are still found in parts of Israel, the Near and Middle East, Iran, Pakistan, India, much of South-East Asia and the Malaysian archipelago, north over the Himalayas through Tibet, southern China and into Siberia. The pattern of spots and rosettes on their coats mimics the dapple of leafy shade, a geometric abstraction that helps to mirror the background, merging the leopard with its surroundings. Even a scarcity of cover can be overcome – the leopard simply confines itself to the hours of darkness. It has proved itself a master of living close to human habitation, something that is impossible for lions or cheetahs.

Leopards can go without drinking water for long periods, remaining primarily nocturnal in very dry areas.

and ocelots. Thankfully many countries are now members of the Convention on International Trade in Endangered Species (CITES), which banned the sale of leopard skins in 1975. Some of the smaller species have not been so fortunate.

Big cats in areas such as the Mara and Serengeti – national game reserves and parks – had already enjoyed protection from all forms of hunting for many years by the time these figures were published. In fact the 1960s had seen the dawning of a new awareness about the way wild animals lived and behaved, and leading conservationists such as Professor Bernhard Grzimek (author of *Serengeti Shall Not Die*, which became not only a successful book but also an Oscar-winning film) had encouraged tourism to parks and reserves as a way of helping to pay for conservation and promoting concern for the fate of wildlife. Gradually the word safari began to take on a new meaning. Visitors now came armed with cameras rather than guns. It

didn't take long for the wild animals to become habituated to people in vehicles, and places such as the tree-lined Seronera Valley in Serengeti were famous the world over as *the* place to see leopards. Tour leaders and drivers could pretty much guarantee that at some point on your safari they would be able to show you a leopard. I remember admiring a photograph of a magnificent male whose territory overlapped parts of the Seronera Valley, standing profiled in a fever tree. The guides named him 'Good as Gold', as a tribute to his co-operative nature.

That all changed as the demand for skins increased and the price that traders were willing to pay for a leopard skin skyrocketed. Visitors to Governor's Camp in the Masai Mara suddenly found that the handful of leopards who could be approached at close quarters had vanished; so too did Good as Gold. It wasn't just the skin trade. Prior to the ban on trophy-hunting in Kenya in early 1977, leopards

Zawadi with a Thomson's gazelle kill – another of the leopard's favourite prey.

were being baited and killed illegally in and around the reserve. By the time I arrived at Mara River Camp in 1977, it was impossible to find a leopard who would tolerate close observation, and during my first year there I saw a leopard on only two occasions – fleeting glimpses of a spotted coat melting away among the acacia thickets.

But leopards are adaptable creatures. Given the chance they will bounce back and repopulate an area, particularly if lion and hyena numbers are low, and provided they are left in peace by man – their greatest enemy. In time I was able to unravel some of the mysteries of how these beautiful creatures live in the wild.

Leopards are most commonly associated with some type of forest cover from tropical rainforests to savanna woodlands, and inhabit rocky hills and mountainous terrain up to elevations of 5,000m (16,250ft) or more. They reach their highest densities in forested regions, and in parts of West Africa and tropical Asia they live in forests where the mean annual rainfall is well over 2,000mm (80in). Temperature does not seem to be a major influence on distribution: leopards are capable of moulding their behaviour to the blistering heat of semi-arid areas as easily as to the bitter winters of colder regions. Though they do not occur in true deserts such as

the Sahara, they can live in areas with virtually no rainfall, going for long periods without drinking. But cats have very few sweat glands and rely on panting to help regulate their body temperature. In dry habitats such as the Kalahari in southern Africa, leopards are active only during the cooler hours and do most of their hunting at night so as not to overstress themselves, relying on the blood and body fluids of their prey to meet their moisture requirements, and at times eating fruit such as tsama melons and wild cucumbers.

As if to prove the point about their adaptability, the frozen remains of a leopard lie entombed near the summit of Mount Kilimanjaro, some 5,800m (19,000ft) above the African plains, and in China and Russia leopards at times endure subfreezing temperatures, growing a thicker coat to counteract the cold. But they are not as well adapted to snowy climes as their relative the snow leopard, which has thick cushions of fur between its pads to insulate its feet in winter and to help spread its weight like a snowshoe.

The leopard's adaptability to a wide variety of habitats goes hand in hand with its catholic taste in food – 92 prey species are recorded in sub-Saharan Africa. Nothing is too small for a hungry leopard, and they will take insects such as dung beetles, reptiles, birds' eggs and nestlings, as well as small mammals and carrion – even humans – though those living in game-rich sanctuaries such as the Mara–Serengeti gain most of their sustenance from impalas or gazelles. There is even a record of a leopard killing a full-grown male eland – Africa's largest antelope, which can weigh up to 900kg (1,980lb). The leopard is the cat for all seasons.

Despite its adaptability, there is no doubt that the leopard's distribution and numbers have diminished in recent times. Fossils dating back to 1.5–2 million years ago (mya) hint at a greater range – leopard remains have been found in Pleistocene deposits in Europe, the Middle East, India,

Male leopards are immensely powerful creatures, 30–50 per cent heavier than females. Older males develop a dewlap of loose skin down the throat which often extends along the belly.

further north in Asia than today, as well as on the island of Sumatra, and of course in Africa. The leopard of those times was certainly equal in size to recent forms, and specimens from Java and Palestine were somewhat larger.

There is sufficient variation in the leopard's coat markings and colour from one region to another for some taxonomists to assign them to different subspecies. Jonathan Kingdon, in his wonderful treatise on the evolution of East African mammals, has a colourful illustration showing the skins of leopards from a variety of regions: Ethiopia, Ruwenzori, Zambia, Somalia, the Cape, Zanzibar (now thought to be extinct) and Mount Elgon in Kenya. Leopards from the Democratic Republic of the Congo are said to be consistently small and greenish in comparison to other populations, while those from Anatolia, Lebanon and Iraq are described as consistently large, tan and with markings quite distinctive from those of northern Iran. In a paper written in 1932 by Pocock, savanna leopards were described as

rufous to ochraceous; desert leopards as pale cream to yellow-brown, with those from cooler regions being more grey; rainforest leopards a dark, deep gold and high-mountain leopards even darker.

Colour variations such as these led to over 30 subspecies of leopards being described in the 1950s, but recent work using molecular biology points to only six geographically isolated groups – the African, central Asian, Indian, Sri Lankan, Javan and east Asian – and says that only eight subspecies should be recognized. The 12 African subspecies are now lumped together as *Panthera pardus pardus* (the so-called North African leopard, although its range is actually south of the Sahara from West Africa to Eritrea). The six subspecies from Central Asia are now known as *P. p. saxicolor* (the Persian leopard), the Arabian leopard as *P. p. nimr*, the Sri Lankan as *P. p. kotiya* (the top predator on the island), the Javan as *P. p. melas* (also top predator since the Javan tiger went extinct in the 1970s), the South China as *P. p. delacouri*, the North China as

P. p. japonensis and the Amur or Far Eastern leopard as *P. p. orientalis*.

Black or melanistic leopards, with coats that are so heavily pigmented that they appear black – a feature caused by a recessive gene – gave rise to considerable confusion when they were first observed and were thought to be a different species – the fabled black panther immortalized in Rudyard Kipling's stories. They are not. The rosettes can be seen patterning the dark coat in reflected light. Leopards from humid forested areas tend to have darker coats and melanistic individuals are more common in these areas and in mountainous regions. They are found more often in Asia than Africa – though a black leopard was recently seen in an area bordering the Masai Mara. In the dense forests of the Malay Peninsula, up to 50 per cent of the leopards are said to be black. This seems to follow the assumption that dark colouring in mammals occurs more frequently in warm, humid regions, though in the case of the jaguar, which also has a melanistic form, this may not be so.

Male and female leopards do not differ in any great respect, unlike the more social lions, where males have a mane and are instantly recognizable from the smaller females – when you live together it is more important to be able to distinguish males from females. Male leopards are certainly considerably bigger and more powerful than females, in some cases weighing up to 50 per cent more, and with broader heads and heavier muzzles. Both sexes have massive skulls to allow for the attachment of strong jaw muscles. Older males often develop a pronounced dewlap – a loose flap of skin under the throat, sometimes running along the stomach. But coat markings and coat colour are similar. Leopards of both sexes vary greatly in size according to area, probably because of prey availability and the fact that it is advantageous to be larger in colder conditions, in order to reduce heat loss, and in more open terrain where you are likely to be hunting larger prey. This is also the case with the jaguar – the largest individuals live in less forested habitats.

In most parts of East and Southern Africa male leopards weigh in at 60–65kg (130–145lb), with females averaging 40–45kg (88–100lb). Males of more than 70kg (150lb) in weight and 2.3m (7ft 6in) in length including the tail are considered exceptionally large. There is a photograph in Jay Mellon's book *African Hunter* that I will always remember – it shows a 93kg (205lb) male leopard shot by a client of professional hunter Tony France on the dense forested slopes of Mount Kenya. This is a huge animal almost the size of a lioness, though if it had recently gorged itself this might account for up to 20 per cent of its weight. A number of people have recorded seeing large leopards in the Aberdare Forest and Mount Kenya regions,

perhaps because of a high density of medium-sized prey such as bushbuck, less competition from other predators – and plenty of trees in which to stash kills. Leopards from the Cape Province in South Africa are much smaller, with males averaging just over 30kg (65lb) and females around 20kg (45lb) – an adaptation no doubt to their prey, which is limited to smaller fare such as rock hyrax and the occasional klipspringer.

Of the five big cats lumped together in the genus *Panthera*, and sometimes referred to as roaring cats, the leopard and the somewhat larger and stockier jaguar are the most similar in appearance, and both produce a cough-like roar. Though the African leopard generally has smaller, more numerous rosettes than the jaguar and normally lacks spots within the rosettes, some Asian leopards have larger rosettes, superficially similar to those of the jaguar, making it difficult to distinguish one skin from another at times. Though the leopard's skull is similar to the tiger's, the skeleton is more like the jaguar's, with relatively short legs better suited to tree-climbing, and it is likely that the leopard and jaguar are the most closely related of the pantherine cats. The fact that young lions show a similar pattern of rosettes to the leopard and jaguar, which may even be present along the margins of the belly and upper legs in adult lions, together with the ability to utter a structured series of roars, or 'roaring

proper', not found in the tiger or snow leopard (which some people argue should not be included in *Panthera* – it does not roar, among other things) hints at a close relationship for all three cats. In all probability the ancestor of the lion was a spotted cat that lived in more densely forested habitat.

Though the early history of the genus *Panthera* is not well known, the work of molecular biologists such as Stephen O'Brien and his co-workers supports the idea that the pantherine cats evolved into distinct species more recently than other groups, probably within the last two million years. But at present the fossil evidence does not support this. Attempts to clarify the evolution and classification of cats have been the subject of long and bitter debate, though most taxonomists now agree that there are 36 species (at most 39).

One of the biggest stumbling blocks to sorting out the relationship between the species has been the very nature of cats. Though varying in size, coat pattern, colouring and social behaviour, cats are strikingly similar in shape and design, from the mighty tiger to the pint-sized domestic cat. All cats stalk, chase and then pounce on their prey (though as a coursing predator the cheetah might be considered an exception to this). The anatomy of the skull with its short face and binocular vision, the long stabbing canines, scissor-like carnassials and feet armed with retractable claws are

Half-Tail stretching before setting off to hunt. Leopards are consummate stalkers, creeping to within a few metres of their prey before rushing forward and pouncing.

Serval cats, distinguished by their large ears and short tails, favour long-grass areas and marshland. They locate their prey primarily by hearing and then pounce on it, holding it down with their forepaws and killing it with a bite to the neck or head.

The older of the Topi Plains males returning to cover early one morning. Male lions are warriors and will fight to defend their territory against other coalitions of males. Most die a violent death, killed by other lions or hyenas, wounded by buffaloes, shot by trophy-hunters or killed by livestock-owners when they attempt to take cattle.

similar throughout the family, reflecting the supple build of the specialist hunter.

Cats in all their varied forms are grouped into a single family called the Felidae. The so-called 'true cats', those with conical canines, belong to the subfamilies Felinae and Pantherinae, while the sabre-toothed cats with their flattened and elongated upper canines are grouped in the subfamily Machairodontinae. The Felinae include Africa's smallest cat, the black-footed cat, weighing just 1.5–2.5kg (3–5lb), as well as the mountain lion or cougar with males weighing up to 100kg (220lb), while the Pantherinae include the various species of lynx (of which the caracal is one), as well the largest of all cats such as the lion and tiger. Being large predators they reside at the top of the food chain, and for this reason are far scarcer than their prey: in

order to survive, any animal must be outnumbered or outweighed by its food source. This is one of the reasons that cats are poorly represented in the fossil record – antelopes and zebras will always outnumber the predators that feed on them.

The first of the modern or true cats is thought to have been *Proailurus*, an example of which, *Proailurus lemanensis*, was found in deposits at Saint-Gerard-le-Puy, France, dating back to the Oligocene, 30 mya. *Proailurus* had more teeth than today's cats and stood about 38cm (15in) at the shoulder, half the height of a male leopard in his prime. Its skeleton suggests that it was similar in shape to the living fossa of Madagascar and, though slightly larger, was probably just as adept at climbing and jumping from branch to branch. In the New World the earliest known cat is a proailurine, found in Nebraskan Miocene deposits from around 16 mya. *Proailurus*' likely Miocene descendent was *Pseudaelurus* – a cat about the size of a large lynx – which emerged about 20 mya. *Pseudaelurus* is thought to be ancestral to the modern, living and fossil conical-toothed species of true cats, and to the now extinct sabre-toothed species known as machairodonts. Most of the known felids are confined to the past 10 million years, though we lack any clear idea of the immediate ancestry of the living species or the precise pattern of relationships between them.

Species that have been separated for a long time show a greater divergence in their DNA, and on this basis Stephen O'Brien and his colleagues initially divided the cat family into three distinct lineages. Around 12 mya the seven species of small South American cats such as the margay and ocelot branched off, followed 8–10 mya by the wild cat lineage (from which the domestic cat evolved), numbering six species. Finally, 4–6 mya the *Panthera* lineage branched off. Its 24 species include members of both the subfamilies Felinae and Pantherinae. This group boasts an array

of medium-sized and large cats, together with members of the genus *Panthera* – the lion, tiger, leopard and jaguar, commonly referred to as the big cats – as well as two fossil species, *Panthera gombaszoegensis* (the European jaguar) and *P. shaubi* (a cat the size of a small leopard or very large lynx). The most recent development in this group occurred 1.8–3.8 mya, leading to a

More than 200,000 zebras migrate through the Mara–Serengeti ecosystem, often arriving first in the long-grass areas at the end of the rainy season. They have a potentially lethal kick and can crush a lion's skull or break its jaw.

split between the lynxes and the large cats of the genus *Panthera*.

That was the state of our knowledge until ten years ago. But the latest information brought together in Mel and Fiona Sunquist's outstanding reference work *Wild Cats of the World* points to eight major cat lineages rather than three. The domestic cat lineage and that of the small cats of South America remain the same, while the *Panthera* lineage has undergone further revision and now comprises just six species: jaguar, tiger, lion, leopard, snow leopard and clouded leopard. Of these, the clouded leopard was the first to diverge from the ancestral line, followed by the snow leopard, with the lion, tiger, jaguar and leopard diverging more recently, 2–3 mya. The remaining 18 species are reclassified into a further five major lineages, with the origins of the serval, marbled cat, rusty-spotted cat and manui something of a mystery. The puma and closely related jaguarundi are grouped with the cheetah. Fossil evidence proves that cheetahs occurred in North America as far back as 2–3 mya, and they are thought to

Infant baboons begin to ride jockey-style from the age of about five weeks. The black coat they are born with gradually turns to a uniform light brown by the time they are four to six months old.

have diverged from their common ancestor 8.25 mya. The closely related leopard cat, fishing cat and flat-headed cat of South-East Asia diverged from a common ancestor only 3.95 mya, making them one of the most recent lineages. The Eurasian and Canada lynx share an older ancestor with the bobcat, and form a separate lineage with the Iberian lynx. The desert lynx or caracal and the African golden cat share a common ancestor 4.85 mya ago, sufficient to warrant their own lineage. The bay cat lineage also contains just two species, the bay cat and Asiatic golden cat, believed to have diverged from a common ancestor 4.9–5.3 mya.

It seems strange to think that there were once lions, leopards, jaguars and cheetahs in Europe, with the cheetah being the first to appear in the fossil record some 2.1 mya years ago in France. The European jaguar is recorded in Italy at around 1.6 mya ago, and it is particularly well represented in

England at the middle Pleistocene site of Westbury-sub-Mendip, just to the south of Bristol, home of the BBC Natural History Unit. It seems to have been a larger animal than the New World jaguar, *Panthera onca*. The leopard makes its first appearance in the fossil record in Europe around 0.9 mya at Vallonnet in the south of France, though the only place where it is well represented is the Italian cave site of Equi. This patchy fossil record is probably more to do with the leopard's solitary and secretive nature than with any accurate representation of its distribution and abundance.

At one time the leopard inhabited an area equivalent in size to that occupied by the tiger and lion combined, though it does not appear to have crossed into North America, where another secretive and solitary species, the mountain lion, *Puma concolor*, intermediate in size between the leopard and the jaguar, occupies the same ecological niche. The lion first appears in

Europe at Isernia in Italy, around 0.7 mya, and then becomes fairly common across most of Europe.

It has long been believed that a jaguar-like ancestor of the genus *Panthera* evolved some 2 million years ago in Eurasia and spread over Africa, Europe, southern and northern Asia and North America, later giving rise to the living species. One possibility is that the ancestral leopard then became extinct throughout the world except for Africa, with the modern leopard later spreading out of Africa again. But fossil remains of leopards and lions found at the famous archaeological site of Laetoli in Tanzania, where Mary Leakey discovered man's ancient footprints, date back 3.5 million years, pointing to an African genesis, and certainly in the lightly wooded savannas of East Africa 2 mya, the leopard would have included australopithecine hominids among its prey. John Cavalo, who studied leopards in the Serengeti in the

1980s, believes that while leopards were indeed predators of our early ancestors, the latter in turn no doubt climbed up into trees to scavenge animal flesh and marrow from the leopard's larder. Fossil evidence from South Africa attests to leopard predation on both early hominids and baboons 1–2 mya. One fossil skull of a juvenile australopithecine bears two small holes that match the lower canines of a leopard skull found in the same site.

Ancient and isolated, the African continent of around 3.2 mya provided a rich mosaic of habitats, allowing most species to survive changes in the environment. This is in sharp contrast to Europe, Asia and North America, where shifting climatic conditions had a marked effect on the native flora and fauna, leading to the extinction of many species. At some point the unknown ancestor of the larger pantherine cats evolved. It would have had both the strength and the agility to chase and overpower large agile prey like wildebeest and zebras – creatures that were too nimble for the sabre-toothed cats and too strong for the smaller pantherines. A number of modern carnivores appear at fossil sites, first in eastern and later in southern Africa, including the lion, leopard, cheetah and spotted hyena. For the next 2 million years, these species lived side by side with the old order of sabre-toothed and false sabre-toothed cats such as *Homotherium*, *Megantereon* and *Dinofelis*, during which time the forests and woodlands of eastern Africa were transformed into bush and savanna, and the Sahara Desert became a permanent feature.

For a while the sabre-toothed cats and light-heavyweight pantherines were both able to find sufficient prey to feed on. But 1.5 mya Africa's climate began to grow colder and the mega-herbivores on which the sabre-tooths had relied disappeared. As their prey dwindled and competition with man became ever more intense, these cats vanished. It was the turn of the pantherines to dominate the predator hierarchy, with

large, agile cats such as the lion, which can sprint at 60kph (nearly 40mph) and weigh up to 200kg (440lb), leading the way. Gone was the dentition that had been so successful in the era of huge, thick-skinned herbivores such as the mammoth and rhino. Instead of slashing and wounding their prey with dagger-like canines, lions, leopards and cheetahs strangled their prey by clamping their jaws over its throat or, in the case of lions, by biting over the mouth and nose of large prey such as a buffalo to suffocate it. Of the modern pantherines, the clouded leopard (it is not a leopard) of South-East Asia, weighing up to 30kg (65lb) and about the size of a small leopard, is the only living cat with teeth that come anywhere near to rivalling those of the sabre-toothed cats. It has canines measuring up to 44mm (1.7in), which it uses to kill wild pigs. The clouded leopard is thought to be an evolutionary link between big and smaller cats, though little is known about these reclusive carnivores. Their climbing skills put even the agile leopard to shame; they possess ankle joints that can swivel, allowing them to climb underneath

the branches of trees, hang by their hind feet and descend head first, whereas a leopard is sometimes forced to come down backwards if a tree-trunk is tall and vertical. Clouded leopards are hunted for their distinctive fur, their large teeth and even for their bones, which are believed by some to have healing powers; like many of the world's spotted cats it is threatened by man's activities.

The migratory movements of humans from Africa to Europe and then onwards around the world were mirrored by the patterns of dispersal of lions, leopards and hyenas. Early humans would have competed with these predators for food, at times scavenging from their kills. But when our genus *Homo* arose, humans began to dominate the others in a way not seen before, hunting and foraging in groups. The development of weapons to protect our puny bodies – first clubs fashioned from wood and bone, then spears and poisoned arrows, and finally guns – spelt the beginning of the end for the large predators. But the secretive leopard has survived man's onslaught better than most.

Half-Tail (before she lost her tail) carrying a male Thomson's gazelle to cover.

The Elusive Leopard

The mere mention of the word leopard inspires thoughts of a cat that remains hidden, the reluctant star of the show whose allure is only magnified by its desire to remain in the shadows. It is not by chance that the leopard wears a coat of spots and rosettes, allowing it to merge with the sunlight and shadow of the forest canopy. It is a question of survival. Leopards are designed to be invisible to enemies and prey alike. They must employ the utmost stealth to stalk within touching distance of their prey, before engaging in a short chase and a pounce, ending with their long canine teeth clamped around the victim's throat. The leopard that makes itself visible is the leopard that is shot by a trophy-hunter or killed by a poacher; the leopard that reveals its hiding place is the leopard that loses the chance of catching prey, and risks conflict with lions and hyenas. There is little that a leopard doesn't view as a potential meal, prompting alarm calls to ring out from all directions when it is on the move, warning every creature in the vicinity to be on the alert. Little wonder that leopards prefer to remain hidden for much of the time.

I can remember many years ago spotting a leopard slinking away from the base of a fig tree where it had been hurriedly trying to remove the stomach from a freshly killed impala so that it could hoist its catch to safety. I drove forward a short distance and then stopped in the hope that it might reappear, scanning the bushes with my binoculars. But hard as I tried I could not see it, until I realized that it was crouched just a metre or so from my car, buried amid a tangle of grass and thorn branches. It lay there, watchful, barely visible, pale green eyes – or were they yellow? – fixed on my vehicle, relying on the fact that I would not see it as long as it remained motionless. I carefully backed away, then sat and watched through my binoculars from a distance of 100m (330 ft) or more. Gradually the leopard relaxed, then crawled back, snake-like, to the impala and carried on plucking the fur from the carcass. I stayed there all day, forgoing breakfast and lunch, waiting to see if the leopard would succeed in treeing its kill before the sharp noses of the hyenas picked up the scent of fresh meat.

Half-Tail anxiously looking around as she tries to hide a freshly killed male impala, weighing considerably more than she does. Hyenas stole the kill before she could haul it into a tree.

Zawadi resting in one of her favourite fig trees. Not all leopards spend much time in trees, but Zawadi invariably seeks out a suitable branch to rest on in the middle of the day.

In those days nothing was more important to me than spending time with a leopard.

When Norman Myers published his report on spotted cats and the fur trade in 1974, he noted that leopards were still abundant in only five of the 40-something countries south of the Sahara, and were holding their own in 15 others. A year later, Cynthia Moss produced a book called *Portraits in the Wild: Animal Behaviour in East Africa*, a highly readable account of the findings of field biologists, giving an up-to-date picture of each species' social organization, behaviour and general ecology. This was just the book I needed now that I was acting as a driver-guide at Mara River Camp. In the section on Africa's big cats, lions warranted 28 pages, cheetahs 21 pages and leopards just 13, highlighting how little was known about leopards at that time. In fact there had not been a single scientific paper published dealing exclusively with the ecology or behaviour of free-ranging leopards in Africa. The only book that I could find devoted entirely to

leopards was Turnbull-Kemp's *The Leopard*, published in 1960, which was filled with interesting snippets on the leopard in history, hunting, man-eating and in captivity. But it contained little information on the behaviour of wild leopards – there simply wasn't any.

At that time, the Serengeti was the only park or reserve in Africa where leopards could readily be seen without the aid of baits set in artificial light. George Schaller, who studied lions in the Serengeti from 1966 to 1969, watched leopards whenever he could, but even though a number of leopards in his study area tolerated vehicles, they all too easily melted into cover when they became active, making them difficult to see or follow. It was for reasons such as this that Ted Bailey decided to employ the relatively new technique of radio-telemetry to help him track leopards on a regular basis in Kruger National Park in South Africa.

The beauty of radio-telemetry is that you can study certain aspects of the behaviour

and ecology of shy and elusive species in their natural habitat without having to see them. Bailey had been one of the pioneers of radio-telemetry in the 1960s, when it was used to track mountain lions and bobcats in Idaho in the United States, in order to document territorialism and its function in the regulation of these populations. First Bailey had to catch the leopards, using metal box-traps with a single sliding door. These had to be positioned 1–3m (3–10ft) above the ground in trees to prevent hyenas and lions from entering them. The traps were baited with portions of carcasses from annual culling operations – part of Kruger's management policy to regulate the numbers of species such as buffaloes, elephants, hippos and impalas. The trap was sprung when an animal stepped on a foot release at the back of the cage, causing the door to slide shut.

Bailey found that the leopards favoured riverine forests and montane habitat, with seasonal rivers being ideal as they attracted

Chui with Light and Dark. Leopards use the white underside of the tip of their tail as a signal. A mother leopard often holds her tail curled high when moving with her cubs, making it easier for them to follow her.

prey and provided good cover. The best location for traps was along riverbanks, near tributary streams or bordering firebreak roads. Leopards had more difficulty capturing prey in the dry season when there was less vegetation, increasing the chances that they would try to obtain meat from traps. During the latter half of the wet season (January and February), when newborn prey was abundant, they showed less interest in the traps.

Mothers with dependent cubs were very wary and Bailey never captured one. Other females trapped for the first time were more intent than males on escaping or attacking when approached, and were generally more aggressive and vocal.

Once a leopard had been trapped it was darted and anaesthetized, then fitted with a collar large enough to house a radio, batteries and aerial, but still weighing only 565–680gm (1¼–1½lb). Each animal was weighed, measured and fitted with neck- and ear-tags; they were then released again and their daily movements and prey recorded. Some people bridled at seeing animals with collars and ear-tags, objecting to what they considered unnecessary interference in the lives of wild creatures in a protected area. But in those days there was little alternative if scientists were to find out more about how leopards survived in the wild.

The range of radio transmitters has improved over the years; depending on terrain the signal may be audible on headphones from several kilometres (perhaps 3–4 miles) away and up to 65km (40 miles) from the air; along with the development of satellite collars, this has opened up a whole new world to scientists. But in the '70s, radio reception was no more than 1.5–2.5km (1–1½ miles) from a vehicle and 15km (9 miles) from the air, and most radio fixes were taken within 1–2km (⅔– 1⅓ miles). Collars functioned for anything from six months to a year, whereas today batteries last for up to three years. Over the course of his two-year study Bailey drove 54,475km (34,046 miles) in his search for leopards, an average of 2,270km (1,419 miles) a month.

The first questions Bailey considered were how leopards spaced themselves and what size of area they needed. He also wanted to determine the frequency with which they killed large prey, their overall impact on prey populations and the number of impalas needed to support a given population (impalas were already known to be the leopard's principal prey in the Kruger). He captured a total of 30 leopards and was able to pinpoint their location by telemetry on 2,500 occasions, though he actually saw them only 100 times. Matters were complicated by the fact that during the day leopards often do very little other than rest in that typically nonchalant, cat-like way of theirs, lying up in a tree or under a bush, or curled up in the darkened recess of a cave, stretched out, eyes tightly shut, chin resting across their forepaw, apparently oblivious to what is going on around them. As I was to find out, the best chance of recording leopard behaviour is to find a habituated female with young cubs, when daytime activity is far more common.

While Bailey was busy radio-collaring leopards in Kruger, Patrick Hamilton, a young graduate student from the University of Nairobi, was setting about answering the same kinds of questions in Tsavo West National Park in Kenya. Hamilton employed a former poacher turned tracker for the anti-poaching unit to help him locate leopards. Elui Nthengi could find a leopard where nobody else would try; he could read the spoor that another man might not even be able to discern among the rocky outcrops and dry riverbeds in Tsavo. He could age and sex a leopard from a single pawprint, and tell you how long ago it passed this way and where it was going. Elui knew the habits of the wild creatures so well that he could even hazard a guess as to what it was going to do next, headed perhaps for a favourite waterhole or resting place, or on the track of prey.

Hamilton and Elui walked the 250 km² (100 sq. mile) study area and decided on

Half-Tail. Leopards regularly scent-mark fallen trees, rocky outcrops and bushes. First they 'read' any messages left by other leopards, then overmark the place with their own scent.

the best places to position bait to attract the leopards. Once a leopard had begun to feed, they moved the bait into a large metal box-trap. When they caught a leopard it was moved to a special wooden box designed to make it easier to inject it with an immobilizing drug. Hamilton would gingerly grasp the leopard's tail, drawing it far enough out of the box to inject it rather than trying to pierce the rump or shoulder. Within 15 minutes the leopard was drowsy enough to be removed from the box and collared. Photographs of its spot pattern were taken and various measurements recorded. The leopard would then be watched over until it had fully recovered, to prevent other predators from attacking and injuring it.

At one time Hamilton had seven different leopards radio-collared, each transmitting on a different frequency. But though he was able to track them with an aerial mounted on his Land-Rover he rarely saw them; the Tsavo leopards appeared much shyer than those in Kruger, probably because they are exposed to far fewer visitors. Of the 12 leopards that Hamilton trapped, only one was a female, though he saw a number of other females in the study area. Like Bailey, Hamilton found females to be far warier than males, and he never saw cubs. In fact the leopards were so timid that Hamilton recorded very little behaviour during his two-and-a-half-year study. He could, however, plot their movements on a map and determine how far they wandered and the extent of their home range or territory.

Both scientists noted a similar pattern in the way that male and female leopards divided up an area and used it. There appeared to be a degree of fluidity to the system. A home range might vary seasonally according to prey availability and what other leopards in the area were doing. It was maintained by subtle forms of communication such as scent-marking, scraping the ground, claw-marking trees and calling.

Both male and female leopards mark their home range by spraying, arching their tail high and squirting a stream of urine against a prominent scent-post.

Because most cats are solitary and actively avoid each other as adults, much of the information they convey to one another is by long-distance communication. Scent-marking is probably the most important of these, leaving messages that last far longer than the sound of a call. It is highly economic in that it may last for days, weeks or even months, and leaves a clear message without having to be delivered face to face, with the risk of conflict that that would entail. Though we cannot be sure exactly what a scent message tells the recipient, it seems likely that it helps to identify individuals, signal how recently they were there, whether they were young or old, male or female, and whether or not a female was in oestrus. Interestingly, young males did not seem to be unduly deterred by the scent of a big male, probably because they were either his sons and/or were not yet sexually active and unlikely to be seen as a threat.

All leopards seem to be attracted to the same kinds of prominences that serve as scent-posts: bushes, tree-stumps, overhanging branches and rocky boulders that they sniff for signs of scent before marking them. Laying down scent not only helps to communicate information to other leopards, it also has an important part to play in making an individual feel at home. As I write this at home in my study, I have just watched our cat Geronimo examining a new object– a slender box over 2m (7ft) long containing a slide-projection screen. He walked alongside it, sniffing it, rubbing his face along it and taking particular interest in its pointed ends – perfect spots to smell for signs of scent and to mark with

Zawadi relaxes in a giant fig tree overlooking Leopard Gorge – perfect leopard country. This is one of her favourite daytime resting places, with an uninterrupted view of the surrounding area.

glands situated at the corner of his mouth. If he wasn't neutered he would have sprayed it too. It was as if he were saying, 'No other cat has been here – good – I'll leave my scent and make this new feature part of my home.' All cats familiarize themselves in this way with objects in their area – be they boxes or fallen trees – incorporating them into their spatial map. The familiarity brings a sense of well-being that is probably a prerequisite for successful breeding.

Calling is another important way in which leopards advertise themselves. In Kruger adult males often called at night after scent-marking and scraping, scuffing their hind feet to leave a visible mark in the earth, using every available means to make their presence known. Leopards call when they are stationary and at times when they are walking. On flat, densely vegetated terrain in the wet season a leopard's call may be audible over no more than 1km (⅔ mile), but in the dry season on a sparsely vegetated ridge above the Sand River it could be heard from three times that distance. According to Bailey's study, the pattern of calls varied, with females giving more strokes per call, more calls per period with longer intervals between calls, and longer total call periods. Most calling occurred around dawn and dusk. The leopards seemed to be signalling their presence at the onset of their evening activity, just before they began moving around, and again when they were about to stop to rest for the day, though they have been heard calling at all hours. Not surprisingly leopards did not call near den sites or kills – locations they wanted to remain secret – but called more often when travelling well-used routes such as firebreak roads, where they might expect to encounter an adjacent territory-holder or another leopard passing through the area. Hyenas are attracted to the call of a leopard and may investigate or even follow one to try to parasitize its kills – another good reason not to call at a kill site or den.

On hearing a call a leopard may respond by joining the caller, by ignoring or avoiding it, or by answering. Females call more often when they are in oestrus, and when looking for a mate may immediately move in the direction of a male's call. In Kruger leopards called most frequently between April and June (the dry season), and least between August and January (the rainy season). This seemed to be due to seasonal changes in their environment. Calls should carry further during dry seasons when vegetation is at a minimum, and scent-marks should remain most pungent during the wet season, when high humidity reduces evaporation of scent. Hence leopards called more frequently when few scent-marks were observed and scent-marked more frequently when calling was minimal. Because leopards are such elusive and stealthy creatures, calling helps to prevent unexpected encounters, acting as an early-warning system that allows them to keep a distance, and it is probably significant that adult leopards spend most of their time 1–3km (⅔–2 miles) apart – the distance that a call can carry.

Male leopards sometimes 'duet', with both parties calling and answering, usually ending with one of them moving away to avoid confrontation. Bailey never heard subadult males calling, though they are capable of doing so by the time they are a year and a half old. Young males learn the whereabouts of territorial males by listening to their calls and taking the appropriate avoidance action. At this age they aren't yet ready to become players in the territory game, so tend to keep a low profile; adult residents find it difficult to know where subadults are if they do not call or scent-mark. Young females do not begin calling until they are 24 to 30 months old and ready to mate.

Hamilton found that adult male leopards had large territories, averaging 36 km² (14 sq. miles) and ranging from 18 to 63 km² (7–25 sq. miles), while in Kruger, Bailey found the average male territory in

Chui sheltering among the croton thickets along Dik-Dik Lugga. These seasonal watercourses provide ideal cover for a hunting leopard or a mother with small cubs.

also relied on small kills such as dikdiks, hares, hyraxes and various game birds, including guinea fowls and francolins. They tended to feed on the ground rather than hauling kills up into trees, no doubt because there was less likelihood of interference from lions and hyenas, which are less numerous here than they are in Mara–Serengeti. Like leopards everywhere, those in Tsavo readily killed and ate other predators, with jackals, servals, bat-eared foxes, caracals, wild cats, civets and genets all featuring on their menu.

A few years after I came to live in the Mara, an American television producer showed me some footage of Ted Bailey's study. There were some extraordinary images of the capture and radio-collaring of leopards, and one scene stays firmly in my mind – that of a leopard jumping to the ground, then springing back into the air like an acrobat and attacking the cage, as if to say, 'Take that!' Bailey describes the incident in his book *The African Leopard*:

Once an infuriated female leopard appeared to attack on release. When the trap door was opened, she attacked the upraised door, biting and clawing, but fell 1m (3ft) to the ground. She then leaped 2m (6ft 6in) up to the trap, scratched and bit the door again, and rushed a nearby vehicle. When she was 3m (10ft) away, however, she fled into nearby cover.

It was a potent reminder of just how dangerous a cornered leopard can be – far more aggressive and unpredictable than a lion, always ready to defend itself and prepared to attack at the slightest provocation.

Once one begins to understand what is important to a leopard – the basic requirements for life – it is easier to know where to start looking for them. By now I realized that a leopard's favourite areas had to provide good cover, such as rocky

two habitat zones to be 28 and 76 km² (11 and 30 sq. miles) respectively. The single female that Hamilton managed to radio-collar occupied a home range of 16 km² (6.25 sq. miles), very similar to Bailey's findings: the range of the single radio-collared female in one of his study areas was 18 km² (7 sq. miles), while four females in the other area averaged 15 km² (6 sq. miles). Figures for both males and females in the Mara–Serengeti are similar to this, though in some parts of Africa where prey is scarce home ranges can occupy more than 450 km² (176 sq. miles).

According to Bailey's study, not only were the ranges of adult male leopards much larger than those of females, they usually overlapped the home range of anything from one to six females. Males seemed to be trying to hold as much land as they could adequately defend against other males to enable them to breed with as many females as possible. To do this a male must try to deter others from settling in the area, and will fight if necessary. However there is often a degree of overlap around the edges of male territories, which may allow them to reach high densities where there is enough prey to sustain them all.

Female leopards spend most of their adult life either pregnant or in the company of dependent cubs – though they often leave the cubs to their own devices. Their primary needs are a reliable supply of food, and a number of safe hiding places in which to leave small cubs when they are away hunting. But this doesn't always mean excluding other adult females from the area. In fact the home ranges of many adult females appear to overlap to a greater or lesser degree, though not because they are more social than males – they still generally make a point of avoiding other adults, regardless of sex. Avoiding that part of a home range currently occupied by another adult helps reduce competition over food. If leopards were to share hunting grounds, they would find either that prey would be hiding or that it would be ultra-alert, and too many leopards hunting in the same area would lessen the chance of any one of them obtaining a meal.

Impalas are the leopard's commonest prey in Tsavo, Kruger and much of the Mara–Serengeti. But the Tsavo leopards

outcrops and hilly country where they could melt away at the first sight of danger. In the Mara, leopards often hunt along the intermittent watercourses or luggas that attract prey to pools of water, with the green and orange leaves of the croton thickets providing the perfect hiding place, though as everywhere the size of their home range varies according to the nature of the terrain and how much prey it can support. A defining moment in my quest to find a leopard was when I learned about a place called Leopard Gorge.

I'm not sure who gave the gorge its name. Perhaps it was Joseph Rotich, the Kipsigis guide at Mara River Camp, who became my mentor in all things concerning leopards – and ensured that I found my way safely back to camp each evening. Joseph was the keeper of secrets. He knew exactly what kind of country leopards preferred and where to look for them at a time when even the briefest glimpse of a leopard was more than a reward for all the hours – weeks even – of searching. Joseph was Bwana Chui – Mr Leopard – and it is hard to describe the kudos that this gave him among the other drivers. It was a good day when Joseph was in your area. He would always have something new to share.

The acacia woodland surrounding Fig Tree Ridge and Leopard Gorge is perfect leopard country. It is divided up into blocks by a series of luggas, offering a maze of cover and escape routes, with plenty of trees for a leopard confronted by lions to clamber into. There are similar woodland areas elsewhere in the Mara, but nowhere so full of character as the rocky cliffs of Fig Tree Ridge and the fortress-style architecture of Leopard Gorge. The gorge itself is concealed from view – a narrow cleft in a hillside beyond the ridge. It is so well hidden that you realize it is there only when you are almost on top of it. From it you have an unimpeded 360-degree view across the Mara. To the south you can see all the way to Musiara Marsh, and with a good pair of binoculars can pick out the tawny shapes of lions resting on a termite mound. To the north your gaze wanders past Leopard Lugga and over rising ground towards Big Wood and Military Thicket, onwards to the place where Half-Tail spent the last years of her life. To the east lie the northern extension of the Bila Shaka Lugga and Observation Hill, and further east still are Mara Buffalo Rocks, a massive rocky fortress that is another favourite leopard haunt. Across the river to the west you see the blue knife-edge of the Siria Escarpment, where Angie and I were married, a rugged strip of country that runs all the way to the Serengeti, topped by ancient fig trees and bisected by densely wooded valleys where the meat-poachers sometimes camp.

Having spent most of the day in the shade of this giant fig tree overlooking Leopard Gorge, Zawadi gets up and stretches at dusk, preparing to set off on her evening hunt.

Kisongo Masai dancing during the closing day of the *Eunoto* ceremony, when warriors have their heads shaved and become junior elders. They may now marry and own cattle.

To me Joseph was a sage, a fund of the kind of knowledge not found in the books that I was reading, the dry stuff of scientific papers detailing the extent of a leopard's home range or describing what percentage of their diet was made up of impalas. No, Joseph was dealing with the real, flesh-and-blood creature. He had for many years been a driver for filmmakers Alan and Joan Root and knew every inch of the Mara. Like George Adamson – Bwana Simba or Mr Lion – Joseph had learned to think like his quarry. He not only knew the best places to look for a leopard at first light, but also understood the way they responded when approached by a vehicle, was familiar with their favourite hiding places. He realized, and made me realize, that if you wanted to watch leopards you needed to be patient – as patient as the leopard itself.

Leopard Gorge and the rocky outcrop to its west known as Fig Tree Ridge lie beyond the Mara Reserve boundary. This land belongs to the Masai – as does the reserve itself, which is held in trust on their behalf by the Kenya Government. In the 1970s the land surrounding the Mara was owned on a communal basis, divided into large group ranches that were owned collectively by a number of families. All that has now changed. The group ranches are being subdivided and individual title given to the people. Conservationists worry that some of the land will be sold to agriculturalists and ploughed up, that fences will divide the land and that wildlife will disappear as the Masai adopt a more sedentary lifestyle. If, as seems inevitable, this happens, the Masai will lose the opportunity to capitalize on some of the finest game country in Africa; a priceless heritage will be destroyed in exchange for a pittance compared to its true value.

In the old days, the leopards living in these northern ranchlands actually benefited from the Masai's pastoral lifestyle. There are fewer lions and hyenas living outside the reserve, where they have to compete with the pastoralists for living space, and for as long as there are plenty of impalas and Thomson's gazelles in the area, leopards have little reason to take livestock.

Leopard Gorge and Fig Tree Ridge fall within an area designated for photographic safaris, not trophy-hunting. But that didn't stop the killing in the bad old days. Leopards were shot illegally by unscrupulous trophy-hunters sanctioned by corrupt officials, and by poachers eager to earn the price of another spotted coat. Little wonder that it was so hard to find a leopard when I first came to live at Mara River Camp. At least Joseph knew where to look. He told me that there was nowhere better to start than Leopard Gorge and Fig

Tree Ridge. This was very different country to Musiara Marsh and the Bila Shaka Lugga where we searched for lions. That is open country, bounded by riverine forest in the west and rolling plains to the east, dissected by the narrow intermittent watercourse known as Bila Shaka Lugga, which is shaded by dense croton thickets and the occasional tree or clump of woodland. Here the Marsh Lions could invariably be found, exuding the confidence that their size and numbers allowed them. Occasionally – if you were very lucky – someone might report seeing a leopard skulking among the forested river's edge or in the densest part of the lugga.

But as you travelled north beyond the Musiara entrance gate, the country changed. Where before you could see a predator moving about from a couple of kilometres or more, now the country crowded in around you, a mosaic of tightly packed acacia bushes and elegant eleaodendron trees, leaving just enough space for you to squeeze through in a Toyota Landcruiser, the long thorns snagging and scraping against your paintwork. Here there were more trees of every description, giant figs and euphorbias hugging the rim of Fig Tree Ridge, as well as sweet-smelling, crimson-flowered kigelia – the sausage trees with their huge cream-coloured pods. At night I would lie in my tent dreaming of the day when I might find a leopard resting in one of these trees and photograph it. Occasionally I would awake to the sound of a leopard's distinctive rasping call. But I was to wait six years before being able to achieve my ambition.

On our walks up the Siria Escarpment, Angie and I would often see fresh signs of leopards – claw marks gouged deep into the bark of a tree, or tufts of fur plucked from a kill before the leopard began to eat. I would sometimes climb into one of the fig trees and lie along a massive limb, looking out over the Mara 300m (1,000ft) below me, imaging myself to be the leopard that just hours earlier had lain here, smelling

the musky scent it had sprayed against the tree trunk as it passed on its way.

A number of leopards shared this area. That I knew from listening to Joseph. Finding a leopard was a gift Joseph could bestow on a safari that few other people could match in those days. In fact the other drivers made a point of tracking Joseph down when he was in residence to find out what he had seen. Joseph guarded his secrets carefully. If he knew that a particular driver wasn't respectful in his approach to wildlife he kept his information to himself. But if the driver was careful in the way he went about his business, then Joseph would tell him what he had seen, cautioning him to *chunga* – to be careful not to disturb the leopard. He hated to see a mob of vehicles crowding any of the big cats and never allowed his clients to talk loudly in their presence. Joseph could silence people simply by raising his finger to his lips, or touching the leg of someone standing out of the roof hatch. They would know from his expression to sit down and keep quiet, that being in the presence of a leopard was something special and worthy of respect.

It took me a while to find my way unerringly to Leopard Gorge, but in time I came to recognize the clump of trees guarding its western entrance. It made little

difference to my success in seeing a leopard, though. Meanwhile, Joseph regaled me with tales of the resident female – a big leopard with a coat the colour of burnished oak. The male whose territory overlapped hers was himself a huge animal, with the massive head so typical of an adult male leopard, a pronounced, dog-like muzzle and a heavy dewlap of skin around his throat. He was instantly recognizable due to his opaque wall-eye. This gave him a particularly fierce look, adding to his presence and magnifying the intensity of the stare from his one good eye. I saw him only on a handful of occasions. But that was all one could hope for in those days, a brief glimpse simply increasing the excitement that leopards inspired in me.

The turning point in my love affair with leopards came one morning in July 1978 when Joseph told me that a female had been sighted with two small cubs in the Leopard Gorge area. It seemed certain that this must be the shy creature on whom I had yet to set eyes. Her cubs were occasionally spotted peering from the entrance to one of the many caves in the gorge. Joseph thought they must be about four months old. Eventually, after many days of searching, my luck changed and I had my first glimpse of the cubs as they

The Mara Buffalo female – Chui's mother. This is one of the few photographs I managed to take of this shy leopard.

Chui's younger sister watching a hyena emerge from a cave at Mara Buffalo Rocks. Leopards and hyenas use this area as a resting place and to hide their young.

reached for my camera, but the movement was too much for them and they bolted for the gorge.

I would not see the mother again for five years, though I knew she was still in the area. Joseph would occasionally find her, and every so often I would see one or other of the cubs, a male and a female. The female cub I named Chui, which is Swahili for leopard. She was the first of a new generation of leopards that had no reason to fear people in vehicles, and would in the years to come allow me an intimate glimpse of her life.

Chui mated for the first time when she was two and a half years old, and in January 1981 gave birth to two cubs in a cave hidden away in the middle of a huge rocky fortress at the eastern entrance to Leopard Gorge – the same place that Zawadi would use as the hiding place for her third litter some 20 years later. I never managed to discover the sex of Chui's cubs, though one was lighter in colour than the other. They were about ten weeks old when Joseph first found them, and for a while the two of us skulked around the vicinity of the gorge whenever we could, trying not to precipitate a flood of vehicles that would almost certainly have forced the mother to move the cubs.

In the end our caution was of little consequence. Members of the Gorge Pride discovered Chui's hiding place, sniffing at the entrance to the cave and prowling around the rocks in the most menacing manner. Fortunately Chui must have sensed the danger and moved her cubs before any harm could come to them.

I saw them one last time towards the end of the long rains in the middle of May, when they were six months old. From the upper reaches of a diospyros tree along Leopard Lugga, not far from the gorge, they stared down at me with a mixture of curiosity and wariness. Shortly afterwards a lioness surprised Chui and her cubs along this same lugga, forcing them to seek the safety of the treetops. Though Chui and

crouched over the carcass of a wildebeest calf their mother had killed. The calf was too heavy for her to hoist into the leafy crown of the nearby eleaodendron tree, so she had left it on the ground. After opening the carcass and feeding from it for a while, she must have called her cubs and led them to the kill.

As I drove along the top of the gorge she watched me from her hiding place high up

in the tree – ideally positioned to detect the approach of danger. I had no clue as to her whereabouts until I saw a blur of spots descending the trunk of the tree and disappearing into the gorge 30m (100ft) away. The cubs ignored their mother's sudden departure – they were far less nervous of vehicles than she was. I sat watching them, their faces bloody from feasting. I never took my eyes off them as I

one of the cubs managed to escape into the trees, the other reacted a fraction too late and was trapped in a thicket and killed.

This was the first of many incidents that made me realize how dangerous lions are to leopards of all ages. I never discovered if the remaining cub survived to adulthood, though I think it probably did, as the next time Chui gave birth was two and a half years later.

I was lying flat on my back in England recovering from a back operation when the moment I had been waiting for arrived unexpectedly one September morning in 1983. A friend wrote to say that two leopards had given birth to cubs within 6.5km (4 miles) of each other. If anything was destined to speed up my recovery this was it. The two leopards turned out to be Chui and her mother – the shy female I later named the Mara Buffalo female. She had given birth to a male and a female cub early in the year, choosing as her den site the Mara Buffalo Rocks – hence her name. Six months later Chui produced two male cubs in a cave along Fig Tree Ridge.

At last I was able to watch a leopard on a regular basis. I would drive to Fig Tree Ridge at dawn each morning and stay there until darkness drove me back to camp. There were times, after all the tourists had left, when Chui would emerge from one of her favourite fig trees or walk out of the lugga, calling her cubs to join her and making the many hours I had spent cramped in my vehicle more than worthwhile.

I named Chui's cubs Light and Dark, acknowledging the colour of their coats, though I soon discovered that they had personalities as different as their markings. Light was somewhat nervous and timid, while Dark was bold and adventurous and generally dominated his brother when play became rough or there was a dispute over food. All that changed when the cubs were

Light and Dark playing at the Cub Caves – a perfect location to hide young cubs.

Dark at six months old. He was bolder and more inquisitive than his brother Light.

about four months old and Dark hurt himself in a fall, badly wrenching and spraining one of his back legs. This was a devastating injury and at times Chui was forced to carry the crippled cub in her mouth. For all their marvellous climbing ability, even adult leopards occasionally tumble from trees. Although they normally land safely on their padded paws, they do sometimes sustain injuries – more often to

their face and jaw than to their shock-absorbent limbs. After his accident, Dark was no longer able to dominate Light. Suddenly the tables were turned and it was Light's turn to gain the upper hand, providing a graphic example of how life's uncertainties can mould and change the individual. I wrote about the incident in *The Leopard's Tale*:

It was pathetic to watch as Dark tried to follow his mother. Every step seemed to cause him pain and Light just would not leave him alone. He pounced on his helpless brother and wrestled him to the ground, holding him down by biting him in the neck and throat. Weakened by his injury, Dark's only defence was to lie as still as possible, waiting for his brother to tire of the game. But the moment he tried to crawl forward to reach Chui's teats, the movement stimulated Light even further – just like a cat playing with an injured mouse.

It was noticeable that Light had at last started to lose some of his shyness. He was full of playfulness, chasing up and down in the croton bushes and pestering Dark. Light seemed instilled with a new source of energy, leaping and exploding into the air like a jack-in-a-box. It was difficult to know if this new-found confidence and vigour was a consequence of Dark's injury or just the natural process of Light's own development. Whichever it was, Light exploited to the full the opportunity to dominate Dark whilst his brother was less than a hundred per cent fit. "

Two weeks later I watched as Chui returned from one of her hunting excursions with the hindquarters of a freshly killed impala fawn clasped firmly in her jaws. She called the cubs from their hiding place along Fig Tree Ridge, and both immediately emerged and ran towards her, with Dark still noticeably limping. The minute Chui dropped the kill, Dark grabbed it and carried it into the bushes; he was thinner than his brother and hadn't eaten for a number of days. Meanwhile, Light was forced to content himself with a suckle and a lick from his mother. When he tried to approach his brother, Dark turned on him, chasing after him on his three good legs and bowling him over. Chui tried to intervene, but the cubs rolled away from her. Over and over they tumbled, biting and clawing, neither giving way, until they finally broke apart. Dark rushed back to the kill, protectively straddling it and threatening both his relatives not to come any closer.

But it wasn't over yet. After Dark had fed for a while, his tummy bulging with meat, he walked over to Light and in a friendly gesture rubbed against his brother's head. But Light was only interested in the remains of the kill, trying to slide surreptitiously past his brother. Seeing this, Dark quickly moved back to the meat, then just as quickly moved away again. Light took his chance and this time when Dark tried to return he had lost the initiative. Now the food was Light's possession and he quickly leapt forward to defend it. The brothers fought fiercely for nearly a minute in a manner that I had never observed amongst lion cubs, whose quarrels were usually resolved as soon as they started, or cheetahs, who never behaved in this manner at a kill. The leopard is a creature apart.

Distinguishing individual cubs – both physically and in terms of their temperaments – is much easier with leopards than with lions or cheetahs. Lionesses in the same pride often breed at the same time, particularly when new pride males have killed any young cubs, prompting the females to come into oestrus again. This means that there may be a dozen or more cubs of a similar age being raised communally in a crèche. The fact that lionesses often allow their relatives' cubs to suckle from them, and that small cubs all look so similar, makes it very difficult to identify and keep track of individuals among the crèche until they are six months or older. Cheetahs may have up to eight cubs in a litter, so although each has a different pattern of rings and spots on its tail as well as different spot markings on its face and body, it can take time to sort out which individual is which. In contrast, leopards normally have only two cubs, occasionally three, and each cub quickly establishes a teat order, making it relatively easy to tell them apart, particularly if one is male and one is female. The spot markings are useful too – Zawadi, for instance, is easy to recognize because of the row of five identical spots beneath her right eye. The fact that leopard cubs are often very different in character also helps distinguish one from another. They may be shy or bold, cautious or adventurous, some quickly becoming relaxed with vehicles while others, such as Zawadi's daughter Safi, remain wary and nervous throughout their lives.

Dark and Light at five months, waiting for their mother to return from hunting.

Chui in her prime at six years old. She was the first
leopard that I was able to observe closely.

The Paradise Female

Following Chui and her cubs was the highlight of those early years living in the Mara. It was the fulfilment of all that I had hoped for. I dreaded the moment when it might end – and sure enough, when Light and Dark were six months old, Chui moved away from Fig Tree Ridge. Despite all our efforts we failed to find her new hiding place. But finally, after six years of waiting, I had sufficient photographs to illustrate their story.

Having completed *The Leopard's Tale* I spent much of the next few years in Tanzania, documenting the story of the wildebeest migration as it moved back and forth between the Serengeti's southern plains and the Masai Mara. This enabled me to fulfil another of my ambitions – watching packs of wild dogs when they paused long enough from their nomadic wanderings to establish a den and breed.

Even though months might pass when I was unable to visit the Mara and my old haunts around Musiara Marsh and Leopard Gorge, I kept in close contact with what was happening in the lives of key animal characters in these areas. I still held out hope that Chui would reappear and that I would have the chance to follow her when she had her next litter of cubs.

But she didn't. It wasn't until almost two years later that I had word of her again. In October 1985 friends told me that a leopard with three cubs had been seen in Leopard Gorge. She was rather shy, though the cubs were old enough occasionally to venture forth from their hiding place in one of the caves. They were about three months old, the same age as Light and Dark had been when I first saw them. I immediately went in search of the leopards, and sure enough one morning found the cubs playing on a slab of rock halfway along the gorge – close to where Chui and her brother had been born in 1978. As the sun soared higher into the sky the cubs retreated again to their rocky hideaway. I stayed, hoping that sooner or later their mother would return.

Light greeting his mother in typical cat fashion, pushing his head and body under her throat and winding his tail around her neck, wafting his scent in her face.

Later that afternoon I heard the piercing alarm call of a bush hyrax, and turned to see a leopard walking cautiously along the top of the gorge. She paused to drink from a rocky depression where rainwater had collected, and I studied her through my binoculars, wondering who she might be. Perhaps it was Chui's younger sister, one of the two cubs born to the Mara Buffalo female in late 1982, who would by now be nearly three years old. But this leopard was older than that, thicker set and with one or two black spots on her pink nose. I'm not sure why I didn't immediately recognize her as Chui – perhaps because she appeared so wary, even though I was nowhere near her, on the far side of the gorge.

At one point she turned towards me, bared her teeth and hissed, telling me to keep my distance. I moved back and watched as she continued on her way. She was behaving just as I would have expected a leopard with young cubs to behave, stopping every so often to look around, checking to make sure that she hadn't been seen by lions or hyenas, anxious not to reveal the hiding place of her young. As she drew nearer I could just make out the soft puffing sound she often used to let her family know that she was home. Instantly three cubs appeared on the top of the rocks above the cave where they had been waiting patiently. They greeted their mother in a frenzy of excitement, pushing up under her chin and winding themselves sinuously around her chest and legs as she licked them. Then she lay down, making a point of not letting them suckle. Perhaps she had made a kill and would lead them to it later, but for the moment she seemed content to rest, while the cubs busied themselves scrambling about in the bushes that sprouted from the top of the rocks, biting and playing with one another.

I still didn't realize that this was Chui. Only many months later while looking through some photographs taken that morning did I pick up a copy of *The Leopard's Tale* and compare the spot markings of this leopard with Chui's – they

The Mara Buffalo Female's year-old cubs in 1984. By this age male cubs (left) are noticeably bigger and heavier than their sisters.

were identical. I was overjoyed at the thought of this chance meeting with my old friend, who by now was seven years old and in her prime – this was her third litter of cubs. I had sometimes wondered if she had been killed, and had often dreamed of seeing her again and perhaps finding out what had happened to Light and Dark. Watching Chui with her new litter convinced me that Light and Dark must have survived – at least to the point where they were old enough to become independent from their mother. The timing was perfect. They had been born in June 1983, two years before the arrival of these three cubs. Eighteen months to two years is the typical interval between litters for a leopard if the youngsters survive.

Any ideas that I might have had of repeating my success in following Chui and her new litter soon evaporated. She and her cubs were seen once more a few days later at the Cub Caves along Fig Tree Ridge, the same site where she had spent so much time with Light and Dark. Looking back on that period I now realize that Chui probably simply moved further to the north or east, seeking sanctuary in the area that Half-Tail and Zawadi ended up using – the rocky hideaways beyond Mara River airstrip. Very few tourist vehicles bothered to search

here. There was so much to be seen in the Musiara area and its surrounds that there was little need for drivers to invest time patrolling country that others rarely frequented: part of the key to a successful game drive is to tap into the network of information provided by other vehicles.

I did, however, occasionally manage to catch up with Chui's younger brother and sister. The female could sometimes be found between Mara Buffalo Rocks and Fig Tree Ridge, an area she shared with her mother and sister, as well as wandering further to the north where some years later she succeeded in raising a single cub. Her brother developed into a magnificent young male. On one occasion I watched him feeding on a full-grown female topi, which weighed in the region of 110kg (240lb) – double his weight – that he had dragged into a thick patch of croton. The carcass was too big to haul into a tree, and anyway there wasn't a suitable tree close at hand, so he feasted on the ground until he looked fit to burst. At one point he was surprised by a group of young lions who must have smelt the kill, or heard him methodically gnawing through the rib-ends, and sneaked up on him. The lions were two-year-olds, large enough to kill a leopard – but he was saved by a driver from Mara

Buffalo Camp, who launched his vehicle straight at the lions, scattering them and giving the male time to escape.

That was very much the way things were for the next four years – an occasional glimpse of a leopard with days or even weeks between sightings. Nevertheless, a number of leopards scattered through the Mara had become accustomed to vehicles, though there was no guarantee that you would find them. The Talek River, a tributary of the Mara, was a favourite place to search, offering plenty of cover for a hunting leopard; so too were the dense thickets and rocky hills on the southern reaches of Paradise Plain near the wildebeest river-crossing sites. Leopards were also sometimes seen along the Siria Escarpment or in the riverine thickets bordering the Mara River. But trying to keep track of a leopard is a painstaking business, and few people have the time or inclination to go out doggedly each day and cover every inch of a home range. Nowhere was there a leopard that could offer the kind of opportunities we had enjoyed with Chui.

Then one day word began to spread that a new leopard was being seen around Fig Tree Ridge and Leopard Gorge, a leopard you could watch if you could find her – a leopard like Chui. I could hardly wait to see who this 'new' leopard might be. By all accounts she was one of two cubs who had been born in a rocky outcrop to the south of Governor's Camp and whose mother occupied a home range bordering the southern reaches of Paradise Plain. If this was true then she had moved 20km (12 miles) from her normal haunts, which at the time I found surprising. Young females often remain in the area where they are born, just as Chui had done, overlapping part of their mother's home range or establishing themselves close by. But a move of 20km (12 miles) is not beyond the realms of possibility – male leopards sometimes make a journey of that distance in a single night as they move around their territory, and young leopards of both sexes must sometimes seek new areas if they are to breed successfully. However, Fig Tree Ridge and Leopard Gorge – Chui's old haunts – were such prime leopard habitat that I would not have thought that a stranger to the area would find much room available. I looked forward to finding out more about this new leopard, whom the drivers at Governor's Camp had named the Paradise female.

There was one other leopard whom we occasionally saw skulking around the area, a shy female who in April 1990 had given birth to two cubs – a male and female – in the Cub Caves along Fig Tree Ridge. I don't know what happened to the female cub, but, unlike his mother, the male became quite tolerant of being viewed. I felt certain that this older leopard couldn't be the Paradise female's mother. Any leopard as relaxed around vehicles as she was must have grown up in the presence of a mother with a similar attitude. But then I thought about how shy the Mara Buffalo female had been compared to her daughter Chui.

Regardless of where she came from or who her mother was, everyone agreed that the Paradise female was something special. Even Chui had never been as amenable as this. The Paradise female was about two and a half years old when I first saw her in early 1990, a normal age for a leopard to produce her first litter. She had recently mated with the territorial male, and we all anxiously awaited the arrival of her cubs.

Sadly, it is not unusual for any cat to lose its first litter, and the Paradise female proved to be no exception. She was seen one morning emerging from a thicket to the east of Leopard Gorge, looking very distressed. She was plainly no longer pregnant, but no sign was ever seen of any cubs. As I wrote at the time:

Perhaps her cubs had been stillborn, or she had chosen her den unwisely: it is not uncommon for cats and dogs to fail to raise their first litter due to

Half-Tail (before she lost her tail) rests in a balanites tree early one morning. A Thomson's gazelle kill is stashed safely out of sight in the tree beside her.

inexperience. Lions or hyenas – even baboons – would certainly penalize the slightest error in judgement on the part of a mother leopard who failed to conceal her newborn cubs carefully.

Surprisingly, perhaps, baboons can be a real menace to leopards, particularly females

with young cubs. It has often been said that baboons are the favourite prey of leopards, and certainly leopards do kill baboons at times. But in all my years of watching leopards I have rarely seen one with a baboon kill and have come to have a healthy respect for the monkeys' ability to look after themselves in their dealings with leopards – at least during daylight hours.

Adult male baboons weigh 27kg (60lb) or more – some as much as 45kg (100lb), equal to a leopard the size of the Paradise female. Most monkeys spend their lives in trees, only occasionally foraging on the ground, but baboons are unusual in that they spend much of their time searching for food on the open savannas or among the acacia thickets, eating a wide variety of vegetable matter, particularly short green grass and ripe fruits such as figs, as well as grubs and termite alates, birds' eggs and nestlings; adult male baboons also sometimes kill and eat young gazelles, impalas and hares. At the first sign of danger, baboons emit a loud bark, immediately attracting the attention of troop members, who respond either by taking avoidance action or by rallying to counter the threat. The big males quickly challenge a predator such as a leopard, ganging up on it and chasing it away. This mobbing behaviour is highly effective in ensuring that the leopard hunts elsewhere, allowing the baboons to continue feeding in relative safety.

A large male baboon is a bold, brave and dangerous adversary, confident in its ability to scare off a leopard – particularly the smaller females. I watched numerous hostile encounters between Chui and baboons from the Fig Tree Troop, who included Fig Tree Ridge and Leopard Gorge in their home range. The giant fig trees provided the perfect roost for the troop when they were in the area, and every few days they would return to the ridge and take up residence at their chosen sleeping place. They knew all about Chui, and made a point of harassing her throughout the six months that she stayed at the Cub Caves with Light and Dark. Eventually an uneasy truce developed, ensuring that neither baboons nor leopards sustained injury, though there were a few close calls. Many was the time that Chui was caught in the open and had to run for one of the caves – though it often seemed as if the baboons did not actually want to lay hands on her. Safely inside the cave, Chui would hiss and snarl at the mob, forced to endure the taunts of the younger males, who were always quick to exploit the situation.

On one memorable occasion members of the troop joined Chui in the top of one of her favourite fig trees, nonchalantly plucking ripe figs from among the branches, forcing her to retreat to the topmost limbs and tuck her legs beneath her. Eventually she lost her nerve – or had simply had enough – charging down past the baboons, who fled screaming and chattering as she streaked past them and disappeared into the Cub Caves.

In 1992, something happened that was to mark the Paradise female out for the rest of her life. She lost her tail. Nobody knows for certain how this happened – baboons have to be high on the list of potential assailants, though it may have been the

Male baboons weigh 30–35 kg (66–77 lb), almost as much as most female leopards. This yawn is really a threat, exposing dagger-like canines.

On one occasion the young male leopard I sometimes happened upon in the area found himself cornered by baboons in Leopard Gorge. He lay on a rock watching as the baboons moved closer, and then instead of disappearing into one of the caves took up a position crouched in a clump of long grass.

I could barely see him as he flattened himself against the ground, but the baboons were not to be denied the satisfaction of forcing him to flee. They crowded onto the rocks above him, becoming more and more agitated and vociferous as their number swelled – the sounds of their barks and screams rising in an intimidating crescendo. Surely the young male must give ground and run for safety. But he wasn't moving. Sometimes a leopard will hold its ground simply so as not to provoke a chase, ready to defend itself if it must, but hoping that the danger will fade away. Not this time. One of the big male baboons jumped down into the grass no more than a metre or so from the young leopard, thumb-sized canines bared right in his face, shrieking and grunting as loudly as he could. The leopard responded with an explosive cough, prompting the baboon to leap high into the air, giving him time to turn and disappear from view. He was lucky; baboons have been known to kill leopards, even adult males.

Chui sheltering from baboons. In the Mara leopards do everything possible to avoid confrontation with these powerful monkeys.

result of a scrap with another cat. Female leopards do sometimes fight with a rival over turf, though the lack of visible injuries to most of the females I have watched (they look far less battered than many lionesses) indicates that fighting is uncommon and rarely life-threatening. That said, the consequences of being forced to leave an area can be serious. Wounds to the rump and tail are a common feature of cat fights, with the combatants slashing and biting at one another, particularly when a solitary individual is forced to face off against more than one rival, as happens when lions corner an adversary. While one lion confronts its opponent head on, others try to get in behind it to inflict maximum injury to its exposed hindquarters. If the Paradise female's wound was the result of a fight with lions, then she was lucky to escape with her life. Lions are ruthlessly efficient in inflicting damage on their competitors and kill cheetahs and leopards whenever the chance arises.

I could easily envisage how baboons might have surprised the Paradise female,

having photographed a previous incident when she was forced to flee from a gang of them. On another occasion I had seen her race for her life along the top of Leopard Gorge, pursued by two or three large males, one of whom reached out and grabbed at her tail and rump, forcing her to flip on to her back to defend herself, before slithering to safety among the rocks.

Friends sent me photographs of the Paradise female after her injury. Her beautiful spotted tail had been left hanging limply like a broken branch, almost severed in two. Eventually two-thirds of her tail were lost and from that day onwards she became know as Half-Tail. But if she suffered any undue consequences it was never apparent. She continued to hunt and

Half-Tail being chased by male baboons. Although she reached the safety of a thicket, this may have been how she lost part of her tail.

A year-old male leopard with a Thomson's gazelle that his mother had killed. At this age young leopards are also beginning to hunt small prey for themselves.

enables them to keep a constant check on the sexual readiness of the females living in their area, and helps to ensure that they are in a position to drive away any wandering males who might find an oestrus female before they do. This is vital from the male's point of view, as a female on heat is promiscuous and liable to mate with any male of her choosing; in areas where males have overlapping territories a female may end up mating with two or three males in one oestrus. But as biologist Luke Hunter pointed out to me, mating with more than one male probably helps to confuse paternity, lessening the chance that a male might try to harm any cubs produced from the liaison.

Normally subadult males have little opportunity to mate until they acquire a territory of their own at around three to four years of age. Prior to this they wisely adopt a low profile, rarely scent-marking or calling and thereby reducing the chance of a hostile reception from the territory-holder (who may be their father) and giving themselves the opportunity to stay in their natal range for as long as possible. But sometimes they have little choice in the matter, as happened when Half-Tail lost her first litter. Unknown to her, the territorial male had recently been killed by Masai herdsmen in retaliation for an attack on a herdboy. This caused a temporary vacuum, and Half-Tail was unable to find a suitable mate in her normal range. One day we found her in Leopard Gorge, attempting to mate with the young male leopard born to

climb trees with all her old athleticism, and her cubs found her stumpy tail just as irresistible a plaything as it was when it was still intact.

Half-Tail provided us with the opportunity to observe a female leopard throughout her adult life. She produced six litters – 14 cubs in all – and raised three cubs to adulthood. When she wasn't pregnant or accompanied by cubs she would come into oestrus every 20 to 50 days until she conceived again, with oestrus lasting anything from a few days to a week and a gestation period of 90–105 days.

Cats are induced ovulators, releasing an egg only once mating commences, an adaptation to the solitary existence that most male and female cats lead. Induced ovulation allows time for a female and male to find each other before the female ovulates. A female on heat becomes restless, ranging more widely as she searches for a mate, scent-marking and calling frequently, often pausing to rub her head and face against rocky promontories and bushes, sometimes rolling on the ground. The fact that male leopards move around their territories relatively rapidly – in some cases every four or five days –

The young male was killed by lions from the Gorge Pride when he was 18 months old.

the shy female who shared part of the same area. Half-Tail must have linked up with the male and was now trying to seduce him. At one point she mounted him, biting the skin on his nape and thrusting with her hindquarters. Both leopards sniffed and sprayed, each intrigued by the other's scent. But the male wasn't yet sexually mature – the earliest instance of a male mating successfully is at two years of age – and so Half-Tail failed to become pregnant. That was the closest the young male ever got to siring cubs. A few months later he was killed by members of the Gorge Pride, when a vehicle flushed him from cover, revealing his hiding place to the lions resting nearby.

In prime leopard habitat there is rarely a vacuum for long. There is nearly always a reservoir of male leopards – young or old – ready to capitalize on a vacant territory, and in time a new male took over the territory and mated with Half-Tail. Both Bailey and Hamilton noted that although young male leopards sometimes made exploratory forays well beyond their natal area, they often returned, at least until they were almost adult. But when a vacancy occurred it was invariably a leopard from outside the area who took over. The ownership of male territories seemed generally to be quite stable, with established males maintaining their ranges for a number of years, though not as long as resident females.

Half-Tail was five years old when she gave birth to her second litter along Fig Tree Ridge on 3 November 1992. Three cubs were seen initially, though one of them is thought to have been killed by a lion, possibly the second one too. The third, a female, survived. The German photographer Fritz Polking was so entranced by her that he named her Beauty.

It was just like old times, reminding me of days spent watching Chui with Light and Dark. After a gap of nearly ten years, here at last was another leopard with a cub whom we could observe and photograph on a daily basis, at least for as long as she remained in one locality. In my experience leopard cubs are at their most photogenic

Half-Tail and Beauty early one morning near Leopard Gorge.

*L*eopard cubs weigh 430–1000g (1–2lb) at birth and their eyes open in their second week. They begin to scramble around in bushes and onto tree stumps from the time they are about six weeks old, and by three months they can climb up into most trees, which often proves to be a life-saving ploy. A mother leopard sometimes brings small prey or a part of a carcass back to where she has left her cubs, though at two months they pick at the meat rather than really eating it and still prefer to suckle when they can. But by the time they are three months old they really begin to tuck in, and are old enough to be led to a kill (some females start to bring their cubs to a kill from as early as eight weeks). Once the carcass is finished the female often moves the cubs to a new lair before setting off to hunt again, unless she has the luxury of a place like Fig Tree Ridge or Leopard Gorge that offers longer stays if needed. Cubs are virtually weaned at four months and their mother becomes increasingly reluctant to let them suckle, baring her teeth and hissing her disapproval, refusing to roll onto her side despite their noisy protests. The cubs still try to suckle for another month or so, though they probably gain very little milk by this stage, just the comfort of lying close to their mother and making contact with her. By now she may be absent for two or three days at a time, reaffirming her claim to her home range and searching for food. If she has been unsuccessful then she may move with the cubs to a new area before setting off to hunt again. The introduction to a solitary existence starts early.

Light and Dark at four months old feasting on a warthog piglet. Cubs do not like to share food, usually taking it in turns to feed.

between the ages of six weeks and six months. This is certainly the best time to photograph them with their mother – with lots of lovely greetings and play sessions.

It is not uncommon for a leopard to move her cubs on an almost daily basis during the first few weeks of their lives, in an attempt to prevent their scent from building up and attracting predators. Leopards have a very distinctive scent and any passing lion or hyena would be able to tell that one was in residence – as would smaller predators such as mongooses and civets, who would certainly be capable of killing young cubs. Hyenas in particular have such a well-developed sense of smell and are such inquisitive creatures that they would soon notice if a leopard remained in the same place for any length of time. Both Fig Tree Ridge and Leopard Gorge have

long found favour with lions and hyenas as well as leopards, providing birthplaces for their own young and cool resting places to lie up in the heat of the day. Today Leopard Gorge is like hyena city, as Zawadi found to her cost when trying to raise a litter here in August 2002. All it took was one risky move to a cave with a wide open mouth. Attracted by the smell of a Thomson's gazelle kill that Zawadi had stashed in a nearby tree, the hyenas must have tracked her to the place where she had left her cubs, who were less than a month old. Though she managed to carry one of the cubs to safety, the other two perished. Anything that disturbs a mother leopard's equilibrium is liable to prompt her to move her cubs – whether it be discovery by vehicles, people moving through the area on foot or predators.

Angie and I were able to watch Half-Tail and Beauty for a number of weeks in the early part of 1993. By then they had become localized around a series of three low hills near the northern end of Ngorbop Lugga, close to where the Masai had speared the old male leopard and where the young male had been killed by the Gorge Pride in 1991. The rocky, bush-covered hills and nearby lugga offered numerous escape routes for mother and cub when the inevitable confrontations with lions, hyenas and baboons occurred. There was plenty of prey here too, with herds of Thomson's gazelles and impalas always somewhere within view, as well as smaller fare such as dikdiks and hares.

We would try to reach the three hills each morning before sun-up, scouring the rocks and bushes for any signs of movement, listening for the tell-tale yelping barks of black-backed jackals that might signal that a leopard was afoot, and glassing the surrounding plains for indications that the herds of prey were in any way disturbed. Often there was nothing – nothing except for the sound of a hyena whooping or the distant roaring of lions. As the sun began to edge towards the horizon, white-bellied bustards competed with coqui francolins, uttering harsh grating calls that marked their position out on the plains or among the acacia woodlands, contrasting sharply with the liquid notes of white-browed robin chats invisible among the dense undergrowth of the lugga.

There is a chill to the morning air in Africa. A leopard who has been active during the night may still be huddled, scrunched up for warmth among the bushes or on a rocky ledge – better still, tucked away in a cave, emerging only to warm itself briefly once the sun is up before disappearing from view again. We quickly learned that just because we couldn't see Half-Tail or Beauty – however hard we looked – it didn't mean that they weren't there. If we simply revisited the same places time and again, sooner or later one of them would appear. By now Beauty was six months old, could easily climb the tallest tree and was used to being left on her own for long periods. Beauty was confident enough to show herself to vehicles – or at least to ignore them and continue her normal routine. For a leopard of this age this means becoming more and more involved with its immediate environment, stalking small prey such as lizards and birds, watching larger prey that might pass by, even creeping up on animals such as buffaloes and elephants that sometimes passed through the thickets where Beauty spent her days.

With no siblings to play with, Beauty was forced to amuse herself, wiling away the many hours – days even – when her mother was absent. She invented all manner of games with sticks, rocks and

Light perched on top of a dead tree he had clambered up in order to chase a tawny eagle. Leopard cubs are inquisitive and are used to being left to their own devices.

animal droppings, leaping into the air to launch attacks on plants and bushes, clasping them between her over-sized forepaws and collapsing onto her back, scampering up and down trees, chewing on twigs and dabbing at pebbles and elephant droppings. Sometimes she would whip herself into such a frenzy that she reminded us of a hyperactive child, performing somersaults, twists – anything was possible. Slow-moving creatures such as pangolins and porcupines were particularly attractive, though porcupines are something that leopards have to learn to treat with caution. Beauty loved nothing better than when a tortoise blundered into view, a harmless

Dark, aged five months, playing with a leopard tortoise along Fig Tree Ridge.

'rock' that could be gnawed or up-ended, forcing her to wrinkle her nose and curl her lip in an exaggerated grimace or flehmen face as the tortoise responded to the shock by releasing a stream of foul-smelling liquid from its cloaca. The best moments were when Half-Tail eventually returned from her wanderings. After the mandatory greeting session between mother and cub with Beauty sinuously rubbing her head and flank against her mother, a period of grooming would give way to play-fighting, which both leopards clearly relished. This was a chance for us to witness, close up, the extraordinary athleticism, speed of reflex and agility that leopards possess. They are just so quick.

Most leopards become semi-independent by the time they are a year to a year and a half old. By this stage their mother is likely to be pregnant again. It has

Dark and Light at six months, play-fighting. At this age cubs often wrestle and practise the killing bite that they will use on prey.

always been assumed that lions, leopards and cheetahs – perhaps all cats – do not come into oestrus as long as they have dependent cubs. Yet females do usually mate again before their cubs become independent, and where leopards are concerned the arrival of a new litter normally puts an end to further contact

with or provision of food for the older offspring. Kate Nicholls and Pieter Kat, who for the past few years have conducted lion research in the Okavango Delta in Botswana, question the assumption that big cats remain anoestrus while they have cubs, believing that, in the case of lions at least, females continue to cycle but that those

with dependent cubs simply avoid mating when they are in season, rather than not cycling at all. Support for their work comes from faecal analysis, allowing traces of reproductive hormones to be monitored on a regular basis without the need to anaesthetize and take blood samples.

Whatever the case may be, an interval of 18 months to two years between litters seems to be fairly normal for leopards, though Half-Tail proved the exception to this, lending further credence to Nicholls' and Kat's work. When Beauty was barely ten months old Half-Tail mated again, and three months later gave birth to her fourth litter. By this stage Beauty was already catching small prey such as hares and impala fawns that she found 'lying out' in concealment among the acacia thickets, and like all young leopards she invested considerable time and effort in searching for food. But she was still too young to survive on her own, and for the next few months regularly sought out her mother, feeding from her kills and at times playing and interacting peacefully with her younger brother and sister.

Fritz Polking was able to spend weeks at a time with Half-Tail and her two new two cubs – a male called Mang'aa (Kikuyu for 'the one that doesn't care', in reference to his bold and nonchalant nature) and a female called Taratibu (Swahili for 'pretty') – during this extraordinary period. Although he often saw Beauty with her mother's new family, it was evident that Half-Tail was firmly in control of the situation, snarling and grunting when she wanted her older daughter to keep her distance, ready to intervene if play became too rough, while still holding out a life-line for as long as Beauty needed access to kills. Beauty was even seen to allow the younger cubs to feed from a kill she had made herself.

All cats have the innate ability to stalk, rush and pounce – this is evident whether you are watching a domestic kitten stalking a ball of wool, a cheetah cub creeping up on a bird or a young leopard chasing an

agama lizard. What is lacking in the youngsters is the knowledge of which prey is the most suitable to hunt, and how to overpower it once it has been caught – it takes time to learn how to apply an effective killing bite without injuring yourself. This is one reason why young cats remain dependent on their mothers for such a long time. Nevertheless, when it comes to living by their wits and finding a

meal, the solitary leopard is a master of the art of killing – in marked contrast to the more social lion. A two-year-old lion is still only a fledgling hunter, and without the help of its pride mates might well starve – it certainly would if it found itself on its own any younger than this. Not so the leopard. By the age of two it will have been independent for a number of months, killing both small and large prey unaided.

Half-Tail inciting Beauty to play with her. She seemed to enjoy play sessions as much as her cubs did.

Just how different the three species of big cats are is highlighted in words I wrote while watching Half-Tail in the early 1990s, when she was still known as the Paradise female:

"Within a kilometre of where I sit are eight lions, a mother cheetah accompanied by a year-old cub, and the Paradise female. For the moment all the cats are resting. But how different they are. The Gorge Pride lie sprawled nonchalantly around the base of an acacia bush. Three young cubs wrestle among the giant paws of one of the lionesses, a huge creature. The cubs are relaxed and confident, basking in the powerful presence of their mother. A few hundred metres away, the cheetah female looks constantly about her, responding nervously to the slightest hint of danger, anxious for the safety of the sole survivor of her litter of five cubs. Meanwhile, the leopard, all fluid grace, skulks unseen between them, living out her secret life."

The character and way of life of Africa's three big cats have been moulded by competition for food and living space. Each cat is uniquely suited to its own lifestyle, superbly adapted to catching its prey and surviving among so many other predators. Between them, lions, leopards and cheetahs exhibit the full range of cat behaviour – the heavyweight social cat, the solitary opportunist and the fleet-footed specialist. Together they paint a vivid picture of power and beauty, reminding us why man has deified and worshipped cats in all their many forms since the dawn of time.

Mang'aa (left) and Taratibu, Half-Tail's third litter. Taratibu was killed when she was a year old. Mang'aa survived to maturity and, like most male leopards, moved away from his natal area to seek a territory elsewhere.

Life of a Leopard

While I was trying to follow Chui in the late 1970s and early '80s I made a point of keeping up to date with any articles or photographic essays published on leopards. The work of Bailey and Hamilton had given me an invaluable insight into how many leopards lived in a particular area, the size of their home ranges and how frequently (or infrequently) they made contact with one another. But I had always longed for a more intimate view, a sense of the real animal. It was only when someone happened to mention the existence of a private game sanctuary called Londolozi, in South Africa, that I realized there were other people beginning to watch leopards on a daily basis, gradually piecing together a clearer picture of how these enigmatic creatures live. I was intrigued.

Londolozi is part of the wilderness area known as the Sabi Sand Game Reserve, an association of privately owned game sanctuaries covering an area of 650 km² (250 sq. miles) and situated along the western boundary of the Kruger National Park, where Ted Bailey had conducted his leopard research. Many of these properties started life as cattle ranches, and as in the Kruger of the early days their owners took a dim view of predators in every shape and form, applying a ruthless predator-control programme, particularly against lions, hyenas and wild dogs. Leopards and cheetahs felt the brunt of this campaign, too. In those days all predators were considered vermin, to be eradicated to make way for agriculture and livestock ranching. Wilderness was rapidly replaced by large tracts of farmland. Game – as wildlife was commonly called in those days – was either to be eaten, in the case of antelope, or used for financial gain in the form of biltong, hides, ivory and rhino horn. In 1927 Harry Kirkman was employed as warden of the Transvaal Consolidated Land and Exploration Company (TCC), which then owned most of what is today known as the Sabi Sand Complex. The TCC was engaged in cattle-

A Thomson's gazelle carcass hanging from a tree. In the 1970s this was often the only clue I would have to a leopard's presence.

ranching and Kirkman's job was to eradicate predators, particularly lions, that strayed into the area from Kruger. In six years he killed over 400 of them.

Fortunately, attitudes have changed over the intervening decades, to the extent that in 1993 all fences were removed between the Kruger and the Sabi Sand Complex, as well as other similar private reserves such as Timbavati, Klaseries, Umbabat and Manyeleti, allowing the unimpeded movement of game throughout the whole area. An even more visionary approach is now being applied with the creation of TransFrontier parks, huge wilderness areas that have no boundaries. The fence separating Kruger from sanctuaries along the shared border with Mozambique and Zimbabwe is being taken down, allowing the resumption of the traditional east-west migration of species such as zebras, wildebeest and elephants over the whole of this huge natural ecosystem. But the lawlessness currently being witnessed in Zimbabwe has decimated wildlife populations within the country, raising concerns about the long-term viability of such cross-border initiatives.

Meanwhile, the brothers John and Dave Varty, who own Londolozi, had a dream.

They wanted to create a wildlife paradise, to return the land that they had inherited from their father in 1969 to its natural state. Inspired by the work of ecologist Ken Tinley they set about developing the property, which had previously been farmed and hunted, as an ecotourism project. They were going to give the land back to the animals, encouraging tourism through the development of three small luxury camps, and ploughing back some of the revenue into the local community to help them meet their development needs.

In those early days John and Dave took their visitors out in battered old Land-rovers, with a local Shangaan game-tracker seated on the bonnet of the car to search the ground ahead. Once they had located something of interest – rhino, lion, elephant – John or Dave and a tracker would leave the vehicle and set off on foot, armed with a high-powered rifle as back-up. If they were successful in finding what they were searching for they would return to the vehicle and drive closer so that the guests could have the best possible view.

More than anything, it was the chance of seeing a leopard that people wanted – not least the Vartys themselves. They were well aware that Londolozi was ideal leopard country: 130km² (50 sq. miles) of dense woodland enveloping a mosaic of open spaces, criss-crossed by dongas – the dry riverbeds with sandy bottoms and dense thickets on their banks where a leopard might give birth to cubs and find cover to hunt. But in those days the leopards were painfully shy.

Today both Londolozi and neighbouring Mala Mala pride themselves on being able to show their guests the 'big five' – lion, leopard, elephant, rhino and buffalo – so revered by trophy hunters. Years of painstakingly tracking generations of leopards from vehicles and on foot have eventually created a population that can be approached at close quarters in a vehicle, which is highly desirable in the thickly bushed environment of the Sabi Sand

Half-Tail and Beauty. Mother leopards are always on the look-out for possible danger – from lions, hyenas or humans on foot.

Reserve. To this day the rangers keep detailed records on the different leopards in their area, building up a comprehensive library of photographs of each individual so that they can recognize them again whenever they are relocated. All sightings and any interesting behaviour are recorded in a game record book. This has enabled the staff to map out the home ranges of individual leopards, and to follow the patterns of dispersal of subadults as they leave their mother and begin to carve out an existence for themselves.

Night game drives have always been particularly popular with visitors to Londolozi. They rely on the skills of the trackers, who sit perched on the rear of the vehicles with a spotlight, throwing an arc of light into the darkness and picking out all manner of nocturnal creatures – tiny Scops owls, genets, bushbabies, civets – that are almost impossible to see during the day. And in the back of everyone's mind in the early days was the hope that they might – just might – have the chance of seeing a leopard. 'Always there but never seen, it moved like a ghost in the night, making its kills, leaving its drag-

marks and footprints and calling hauntingly into the darkness,' was how wildlife photographer Lex Hess described the situation. Hess went to work as a ranger at Londolozi in 1976, but it would be another three years before he could realize his dream of watching and photographing leopards on a regular basis.

That moment came in September 1979, when one of the trackers picked up the glint of two pairs of eyes shining back at him from the topmost branches of a tree, in an area where the tracker and ranger had seen leopard prints earlier in the day. At first they thought the two small spotted creatures must be genets. Then it dawned on them that they were staring into the eyes of two leopard cubs. They could hardly believe their luck. From that day onwards the rangers and trackers carefully pieced together a picture of the mother leopard's movements. Initially she was very shy and they saw little more than her tracks. Every few days she would move her cubs, and each time she did so the rangers and trackers were able to pin down the new location and spend time with the cubs. Gradually the Mother leopard, as she became known, began to relax and within six months she had lost her fear of vehicles. It is thought that she was about three years old when she was first sighted, so it seems likely that the two cubs perched in the tree were her first litter. So began an extraordinary story that helped to establish Londolozi as the place to visit if you wanted the best chance of seeing a leopard.

Not long after this a friend sent me an illustrated article about the leopards at Londolozi. Here was what I had been hoping to record – leopards mating, a mother with cubs, adults fighting – the kind of thing that you just didn't see in the Mara in those days – unless your name was Bwana Chui – let alone photograph. I was able to keep track of events at Londolozi through the newsletter they circulated to friends and clients, giving regular updates on what was happening with their leopards.

By 1991 Lex Hess had managed to collect enough material to publish his magnificent book *The Leopards of Londolozi*, which documented the story of the Mother leopard and her offspring. The book is a treasure-trove of anecdotes and data, liberally illustrated with Hess's beautiful portraits of the leopard and its world. Much of the behaviour recorded by Hess and the other rangers mirrored what we had been observing in the Mara, first with Chui and the Mara Buffalo female, and then with Half-Tail and her cubs. Similar patterns emerged, reinforcing our ideas of how leopards lived in the wild. But even more exciting were the many insights that were new to Angie and me.

One of the biggest limitations of our work in the Mara has always been that we only watch leopards during the daytime; we never go on night game drives. Even if we were allowed to drive at night it would prove difficult to follow leopards. The Mara's black-cotton soils and haphazard system of tracks do not lend themselves to the tracker's craft, unlike the sandy roads at Londolozi which the leopards often use as convenient travel routes and scent-posts, and which are a great bonus in hunting down these elusive creatures. With the Mara being a National Game Reserve rather than private property one isn't as free to do as one wants, and night game drives in and around the Mara are discouraged. The anti-poaching unit and security personnel have enough on their hands trying to control poaching, without wasting their time worrying about vehicles driving around at night looking for leopards. But just as Hess found at Londolozi, we have discovered leopards are far more active during the day than was previously thought – and this is particularly true of a female with cubs. Eventually we found many opportunities to observe their behaviour during daylight.

In areas where there is plenty of prey, female leopards spend around 80 per cent of their adult lives caring for cubs, and the majority of the rest of their time pregnant. Between 1979 and 1989, the Mother leopard gave birth to nine litters, most of which could be observed from the time they were about two months old. One rarely sees cubs younger than this, so it is almost impossible to know exactly how many cubs are born in each litter, though leopards have been known to have up to six in captivity. In our experience two cubs – occasionally three – seems to be the norm, and five of the Mother leopard's litters numbered two cubs each. Two of her litters had only one cub, and one disappeared before they could be counted or sexed. Of 14 litters known to me in the Mara, only four contained three cubs as far as I could tell – the rest had two. Even if a female gives birth to three cubs, it is rare for her to raise them all to maturity; it may sometimes be that one is a weakling who fails to survive the first few days. As far as is known the Mother leopard produced only one litter of three cubs during this period, and when she did, two of them were killed by lions when they were about four months old.

Leopards give birth at any time of the year, though there is some evidence to show that in certain areas they breed seasonally. Situated astride the Equator, Kenya experiences two wet and two dry seasons each year. This is a different weather pattern from southern Africa, where there are just two distinct seasons – a dry winter from April to October, and a wet summer from November to March. Many southern African birds and mammals give birth in midsummer, between December and February. Bailey's data from Kruger appears to point to a peak in leopards mating and giving birth, though this is based on observation of only six litters. He found that most courtship occurred during the late dry season from July to September (49 per cent), coinciding with the greatest concentration of impalas; only 9 per cent occurred in the wet season, from January to March. The peak in mating obviously produced a peak in leopard

A mother leopard with three cubs aged about six to eight weeks. All three survived to independence, a significant achievement in the Mara.

births some three months later, between October and December/January. This meant that more cubs were born during the early wet season than at any other period, matching the pattern of impala births. Five of the six leopard litters observed were born during the early wet season, and three of these were in December. At this time there is plenty of good cover – vital for a mother with tiny cubs – and the young impala are easy to catch and ideal for bringing back to the place where she has left small cubs. More leopards died and showed poor condition during the dry season, suggesting that hunting was more difficult at this time of the year when there was the least cover to help them in stalking their prey.

Bailey recorded no leopard births in the winter months, which tallies with the more recent findings of wildlife filmmakers Dale Hancock and Kim Wolhuter in the adjoining Mala Mala reserve. All seven litters produced during their filming were born between September and February. But if this does point to a significant peak in breeding, how is such a thing brought about? Would a leopard's lower nutritional levels and poorer body condition mean she had less chance of becoming pregnant if

the season wasn't right? Might she even abort or miscarry her foetuses?

In the Mara I have recorded 14 litters of cubs from five females. Cubs were born in every month except February, March and May, but most leopards gave birth in the long dry season of July to October, and at the beginning of the short rainy season that lasts from mid-October to December. Only one litter was recorded in the long rainy season from March to the end of May. It certainly seems to benefit a leopard female if her cubs are born around the time of the short rains, as this is when many of the prey animals also have their young, and a mother leopard often targets warthog piglets and impala calves during this period. This is also the time when the wildebeest and zebra migration is in the Mara, ensuring that there is plenty of food for the hyenas and lions, helping to reduce competition for the smaller prey that leopards hunt.

Scientists working with the Serengeti Lion Project have noted a seasonal peak in breeding and in births, which is thought to be tied to the lionesses' nutritional state and related to the movements of one of their main prey species – the wildebeest. Though lionesses give birth at any time of

Half-Tail hauling a freshly killed impala into the safety of a fig tree. Her daughter Zawadi had been feeding on the ground until hyenas began to arrive.

when the migration is in the area. There may be a similar peak in the Mara coinciding with the period when the migration is in the northern part of the ecosystem – June to October.

In Londolozi, Hess found that all the leopard females he observed became very secretive just before giving birth, seeking out places that are either hidden from view or particularly secure, such as a cave or crevices in a rocky outcrop or overhang, or in a dense thicket. A termite mound covered with vegetation, the depression

the year, there is a peak in the Serengeti between March and July. This may be partly because when the wildebeest return to the Serengeti in November and December there is an upsurge in pride takeovers due to the influx of nomadic males that follow the herds. Lionesses also tend to reach peak physical condition during this period because food is abundant, and this prompts them to come into season more often, regardless of pride takeovers. Hence most pregnancies or suckling of small cubs occur

Plains zebras congregating at a waterhole during the dry season. When there is little moisture in the grass, wildebeest and zebras must drink almost daily.

beneath a hollow fallen log or the holes in the roots of a tree were also popular hiding places – anywhere, in fact, that a cub can crawl into when its mother departs. In the Kalahari leopard cubs are often born in aardvark burrows, and stay there or under bushes during their mother's absence; adults also use burrows as daytime resting places as a way of avoiding the Kalahari's intense heat. Just how important a secure hiding place is was illustrated when a hyena came sniffing around the hollow base of a tree where a mother leopard had hidden

her young cub. The hyena was unable to extricate the cub, which spat and hissed in defiance. Eventually the hyena moved off.

One fortunate group of visitors to Leopard Gorge witnessed Half-Tail's daughter Zawadi giving birth to her third litter in 2001, by which time Safi, the only survivor of her previous litter, was nearly two years old. Guided by Shieni Ropiara from Kichwa Tembo Camp, George McKnight and Christine Hart were with two other couples on a morning game drive and had already enjoyed dawn encounters with

elephants and lions. But what happened at around midday on 28 September was a once-in-a-lifetime experience for all of them. Shieni had heard over his radio that Zawadi had been seen in the area, and as Christine wrote:

Shieni knew the most likely lair and positioned our vehicle on the bank

Wildebeest leaving the plains and heading for one of the river-crossing sites along the Mara River.

Zawadi with a three-week-old cub in Leopard Gorge. She has produced nine cubs in all, of which only one – Safi – has survived.

Like all cats, mother leopards carry cubs in their mouth up to the time that they are about eight weeks old. Young cubs have dark coats with tightly packed spots.

Zawadi suckling Safi and her brother along Fig Tree Ridge – her second litter of cubs.

opposite two boulders which framed the entrance. From a distance of about 25m (80ft), we were able to look downwards into the small cave and get our first glimpse of Zawadi…. As we watched through binoculars and marvelled at her beauty, Zawadi got up, turned around and became more visible. Then to our astonishment she began to give birth. As the sac emerged she doubled round to help it out, and we watched spellbound as she worked to free the cub. About 20 minutes later the procedure was repeated, though this time Zawadi, possibly aware that she had an audience, moved so the delivery of the second cub was not so clearly seen. But the post-natal attention and the subsequent release of the cub were well observed.

Though Zawadi remained at the gorge for the next month, no-one saw the cubs again, and she eventually left the area. The cubs can't have survived, because three and a half months later she was seen mating in the gorge, though this time she failed to become pregnant. Not until the following August – eleven months after she had been seen giving birth – did she produce another litter. Once again she chose the gorge as their birthplace.

For the first few days after her cubs are born a mother leopard spends the majority of her time with them, providing them with warmth and milk. When she does go hunting she remains very localized in her movements, returning every few hours to suckle the cubs, and every so often transfer them to a new location, sometimes no more than 100m (330ft) away, often less. We watched Zawadi move her fourth litter eight times in two weeks as she worked her way from one end of Leopard Gorge to the other – a distance of no more than 300m (1,000ft). At Londolozi the longest time a mother spent with young cubs at the same den was 16 days, prior to which she moved them every five days on average. But as we had seen with Chui and her mother years earlier, leopards adapt their behaviour to suit local conditions, and if they feel secure at one particular location they may stay there for months.

Zawadi lost two of that fourth litter during her stay in the gorge, and when she moved the third cub, then aged about four weeks, to a new area we were fascinated to see where her new hiding place might be. She travelled a total of 6km (4 miles) due north, carrying the cub in her mouth and eventually hiding it among the roots of a fallen tree on a rocky hillside known as Moses Rock. This was the same area that we had often found her with her daughter Safi the previous year, and the same area that her mother Half-Tail had used in 1998 when rearing her sixth and final litter.

Moses Rock is an ideal location, with lots of trees and thickets as well as jumbles of rock that make a series of nooks and crannies in which to hide small cubs. When a fire set by Masai pastoralists rampaged through the area in September 2002, we were concerned that Zawadi's cub might perish, but fortunately the fire burned around the fallen tree, and as it turned out Zawadi had already moved the youngster to a cluster of rocks higher up the hillside.

Some time later I explored Moses Rock on foot, and had a chance to see exactly where Zawadi had hidden her cub. Beneath the fallen tree were a number of small passageways among the decaying roots and jumble of rocks, just big enough for a cub to crawl into. Zawadi used to leave the cub while she went off hunting, calling whenever she returned with a guttural arragh-grunt or by making a puffing sound, and soon enough the cub would emerge from its hiding place to suckle and be groomed. The second lair was a cub-sized crevice among rocks which became progressively narrower, making it almost impossible for a predator to extract a cub, though a venomous snake such as a puff

adder might have been able to enter and aim a deadly strike at it. Though I had always thought of Leopard Gorge and Fig Tree Ridge as ideal birthplaces, it was evident that there were many other areas offering a multitude of safe retreats, even though they were nothing like as photogenic – in fact they were a nightmare for anyone hoping to photograph a leopard with cubs. But then no doubt a leopard would like that.

Africa's three big cats adopt different strategies to minimize the risk to their young offspring – particularly in a place such as the Mara where there are so many predators. A cheetah mother must defend and feed her cubs on her own, just like a leopard – but the similarities end there. Cheetahs generally range over such large areas in their search for prey that cubs begin to follow their mother as soon as they are six to seven weeks old, and from then on remain with her; their rapidly maturing mobility is adapted to this requirement, which allows the mother the freedom to hunt wherever prey is most easily available. This is vital in the Serengeti and parts of the Mara, where a cheetah's main prey is the Thomson's gazelle – a migratory species. To keep track of the gazelles' movements a mother cheetah may have to undertake lengthy journeys, so life becomes far easier once her cubs can follow. In fact she may even abandon small cubs when they are still at a den if she is forced to commute too far – with a gestation period of just three months, it is better for her to try again when conditions may be more favourable.

Many cheetah cubs don't survive the first few months, which is no doubt why cheetahs produce larger litters than the other big cats – five or more is not unusual. In the 1980s scientists in the Serengeti became concerned about reports that litter sizes seemed to be diminishing, and wondered if this might be a consequence of low levels of genetic diversity – Africa's cheetah population is very inbred. What

they found instead was that cheetah cubs are highly vulnerable to predation, and that only 5 per cent reach maturity in places like the Serengeti, where lions and hyenas are responsible for 70 per cent of the losses.

When a mother cheetah hunts, young cubs tend to sit and watch, waiting for her to bring a gazelle or impala fawn back to them or to call them with that high-pitched, bird-like whistle that carries across the plains and prompts them to rush towards her, eager to begin feeding. If danger threatens in the form of lions or hyenas a cheetah's only choice is to try and distract these larger predators, rushing towards them growling and hissing, slapping at the ground with her forepaws, hair bristling, teeth bared, veering off only when she is almost on top of them and using her greater speed to try to lead them away while the cubs escape.

Meanwhile, lion cubs are able to enjoy the benefits of the pride system. By being raised as part of a crèche, they are provided with the best start in life – suckled, fed and protected communally by the lionesses. Once they are old enough to be introduced to the rest of the pride – at around eight weeks – they can be brought into the open and led to wherever a kill has been made. Thereafter they spend much of their time with other members of the pride. Though lionesses often leave their cubs among cover when they go off hunting, this proves increasingly difficult once the cubs are six to nine months old. By that age they often insist on following along behind the lionesses as they move about, and sometimes try to stalk up on prey – in the process ruining many a hunting opportunity for the adults, but gaining valuable practice in how, when and what to hunt. Lion cubs tend to rest together – as do cheetahs – and the close bonds that they establish with siblings of a similar age is vital to their well-being as adults, forging relationships that bind groups of males and groups of females together for life.

Leopards take a much more furtive approach to raising their cubs, shielding them from view during the first few months and then leaving them to their own devices for much of the time.

Like all young cats, leopard cubs are very inquisitive. They are attracted by movement, and from the earliest age will stalk and pounce. It is difficult to ascertain how much they gain from watching their mother, as she often hunts alone and needs to remain hidden from view to creep close to her prey. But she will sometimes bring small creatures that are not yet dead back to the cubs, allowing them to practise a killing bite. If there is more than one cub they will play together for hours at a time, and many of their games revolve around behaviour patterns that they will need to have mastered by the time they become independent – stalking, pouncing, biting, fighting, escaping from attack and learning to deal with the complexities of how to kill various animals. Nonetheless, cubs frequently seek out their own resting places from an early age, as if they prefer their own company – a way of being that typifies all leopards.

One cub is often dominant over the other, either because one is a male and with age becomes bigger and stronger, or simply because one is tougher in temperament. Regardless of this, leopards retain their curiosity for the first two years of life and remain very cubbish and playful in character. But once they settle down and have cubs of their own or have to defend a territory, life seems to take on a more serious aspect and they may abandon their relaxed demeanour.

Thomson's gazelles are the cheetah's main prey in the Mara–Serengeti.

Because so much of what leopards do is hidden from view it is hard to gauge at what age they make their first kills, though in general it seems to be at around six to nine months. Occasionally a leopard may

A mother cheetah must be constantly vigilant due to the threat posed to her cubs and herself by other predators.
Cheetahs regularly use termite mounds as vantage points to look for prey or keep an eye out for danger.

Six-week-old lion cubs from the Marsh Pride. At this age a lioness usually keeps her cubs hidden, introducing them to the rest of the pride when they are eight weeks old.

have the opportunity to kill earlier than this – we witnessed a three-month-old male cub of Zawadi's sneak into a crevice along Fig Tree Ridge and emerge with a young hyrax while on a walkabout with his mother and sister. A day or so after this we saw Zawadi patiently stalk a hare that was crouched motionless among a tangle of vegetation beneath a fallen acacia bush. When she was close enough, she darted forward and pounced on it, grabbing it by the neck. Instead of killing it she carefully carried it back along the top of the ridge to where she had left the cubs, then dropped it – still alive – in front of them. They immediately grabbed it and mauled it before launching into a brief but vicious

tussle over possession, which the slightly larger male won. When young cubs fight like this their mother is quick to intervene, biting down on them until they stop squabbling, or snatching the kill away and repositioning it in a tree. Apart from playing the role of peacemaker and preventing her cubs from injuring one another, she may also be anxious to stifle the noise the youngsters are making, which might attract the unwanted attention of other predators.

Despite the need to remain concealed, a mother leopard will at times encourage her cubs to take the initiative. Hess watched a female leading her offspring to a burrow where warthogs had taken refuge, and then

hold back as the cubs tried to kill the piglets. On another occasion a mother leopard caught an adult impala by the hindquarters and let her cub jump onto it before releasing it. The antelope immediately shook itself free and bounded away, leaving the cub looking perplexed and causing the mother to rush after the impala and dispatch it with a throat-hold. Once the impala was dead the cub stalked, pounced and then bit it in the throat. It is apparent from these observations how vital this period of trial and error is in allowing cubs the chance to refine their hunting and killing skills. Without their mother there to intervene, they could easily be hurt or fail to find food. Even so, the fledgling hunters

Zawadi pouncing on a hare she has surprised among a tangle of grass. Female and subadult leopards invest considerable time searching for small prey such as this.

do not always have things their own way. A banded mongoose managed to save its life by biting a cub that attacked it, forcing the predator onto the defensive and giving itself time to escape.

By one year of age a leopard has its full complement of permanent teeth, though the canines do not reach their maximum length until they are a year and a half to two years old. This may have some bearing on when they become able to kill larger prey. Full independence often seems to coincide with this transition, though as we have seen the arrival of a new litter of cubs may be the main factor in finally terminating contact between a mother and her young, and Beauty was killing full-grown Thomson's gazelles by the time she was a year old.

At Mala Mala a young male known as the Mlowathi male gained independence from his mother at around 14 months. Not long after this he was observed attacking a full-grown male warthog, struggling to subdue it for 25 minutes in a noisy battle as he vainly tried to transfer his hold from the pig's head to its throat. The pig was too big

for the leopard to drag into a tree and inevitably its blood-curdling squeals attracted a pride of nine lions, forcing the smaller cat to flee for his life. At around the same time he managed to find and kill a bushbuck fawn, biting it in the head. Male cubs are substantially bigger and stronger than their sisters by this age, allowing them

to catch and overpower larger prey. Hess mentions an eleven-month-old male killing a young male impala and using the throat-hold expertly. By this age he was also attempting to kill warthog piglets and was quick to learn that mother pigs will bravely defend their young against predators the size of leopards and cheetahs.

Young leopards often chase vervet monkeys from tree to tree, something that adult leopards generally do not bother doing, though I once saw Half-Tail eating a vervet that she had killed. The young female at Mala Mala on whom Dale Hancock and Kim Wolhuter focused most of their attention was particularly quick and adept at harassing vervets, intimidating them to the point where they would freeze in terror and cling trembling to the branches, unable to move. Tjellers, as she was known, would then catch one with little effort, plucking it from the tree and worrying it in a mock attack, but never killing it. By contrast a young male in the same reserve, known as the Hogvaal male, tended to target far larger prey. Full of the exuberance of youth, coupled with the added size, strength and boldness that characterize male leopards, he stalked giraffe, adult kudu and wildebeest – even

Zawadi carrying a live hare back to her three-month-old cubs, allowing them the chance to practise their hunting skills on it.

Among the more obvious targets for young leopards are small prey such as mice, hares, mongooses, francolins – creatures that are easy to overpower and unlikely to injure them. One male cub at Londolozi killed a full-grown civet weighing 10kg (22lb) when he was eight months old and weighed about 15–20kg (33–44lb), and then played with it but did not eat it. In the next three weeks he and his sister killed a monkey, a banded mongoose, a scrub hare and a francolin, kills that their mother's previous litters had not started to make until they were between nine and eleven months. Small prey such as this is often dispatched with a bite to the head or neck, which is typical of the

way small cats kill; there is no need to apply the bite to the throat favoured by all three big cats. Lions sometimes use a suffocating hold over the nose and mouth when the prey is a really large animal such as a buffalo, and a female leopard attacking a topi cow with a broken leg – far bigger prey than she would have attempted to kill had the antelope been healthy – used a similar hold, but the topi managed to struggle free and escape.

Zawadi and Safi in 2000. Safi was nearly one year old at the time and had killed (and partially eaten) a white tailed mongoose.

regularly trying his luck with a herd of buffaloes that would quickly turn on him and force him to seek refuge in the nearest tree. Not content with making kills the size of a young zebra, he attacked an adult kudu, jumping on to its back like a lion hunting a buffalo, and forcing the antelope to collapse under his weight.

The road to independence exacts a heavy price, and the mortality rate for subadult leopards is nearly twice that of adults. Not only does it take time for hunting skills to

be refined, but to breed successfully a leopard must establish a territory of its own. In areas such as the Mara–Serengeti and the Kruger good leopard habitat is going to be occupied, and the best hunting grounds are liable to be aggressively defended by resident adults. Under such competitive conditions a young leopard could easily find itself having to fight for a permanent home or to remain in a less productive area, where the chances of finding food and mating opportunities were

greatly reduced. Hardly surprisingly, quite a number of young and old or injured leopards either die of starvation or are forced into taking livestock or killing dogs around settlements, and are shot or poisoned in retaliation.

Silent Assassin

Leopards are the quintessential stalking cat, creeping closer to their prey than lions or cheetahs would ever attempt. The cheetah hunts in the open and has the blinding burst of speed that allows it to run down its prey; the lion is a stalker but targets larger prey that is generally slower off the mark than an impala or gazelle, and will continue to pursue its quarry in open country if it feels there is a chance of overhauling it in the first few hundred metres. But a leopard cannot afford to hunt in the open where it might be caught out by lions or hyenas. It is a creature of the thickets and forests, bounding forward and overpowering its victim only when it is almost on top of it. A leopard will always stalk that extra metre rather than launching itself forward and missing its prey. Stealth – and a quiet kill – are essential if it isn't to attract unwanted attention from its larger competitors. This is why a leopard moves away quickly once it has been seen and the alarm calls are ringing in its ears, signalling to all and sundry that a predator is about.

Dale Hancock and Kim Wolhuter followed leopards at Mala Mala day and night for several years – Wolhuter is now a permanent resident – and Hancock wrote a book about their experiences. They soon discovered that although Tjellers, in typical cat fashion, rested for much of the time, she adopted a fairly predictable routine at night, with three peaks in activity. When she had a kill safely stashed in a tree she tended to stay in the vicinity until it was finished, alternating rest periods in the tree or on the ground with bouts of feeding and grooming, though she sometimes went to drink at the nearest source of water. This was similar to the routine that Zawadi adopted when she had a kill. At other times Tjellers would generally start hunting at sunset and continue for a few hours until about 10 p.m., after which she would rest wherever she was until around 1 a.m. Then she would move off again and continue prowling. If she were still unsuccessful she would rest for a few hours until just before first light, and then try one more time. This dawn patrol often lasted for as long as it remained cool enough to move about comfortably. During the winter when the weather was cool and dry, and Tjellers was

Half-Tail watching a female impala, having already ambushed her fawn 'lying out' in a thicket and carried it into the acacia bush.

To watch a leopard hunting is sublime, a mixture of grace, suppleness and power, using sight, hearing and smell to track their prey. They will sit and listen, sniff the air, perhaps climbing into a tree or onto a termite mound for a better view of their surroundings. Occasionally they will abandon their cautious, methodical approach and run like a cheetah in a fast sprint to overhaul an easy target such as an impala fawn or warthog piglet. They may even sit up on their haunches mongoose-style to peer over the long grass, something that you never see a lion or cheetah doing, probably because leopards spend much more of their time in dense cover than lions or cheetahs. Though cats do not have such an acute sense of smell as wild dogs, jackals or hyenas, they are quite capable of following the scent trails left by prey – or other leopards, or their enemies. Camouflage and patience are precious advantages. A leopard will watch the direction in which its prey is moving and

Chui stalking impalas. Leopards use every available patch of cover to creep closer to their prey, and where cover is sparse they can always wait until dark.

then circle ahead to intercept it, often lying in wait, adjusting its position where necessary; a deadly game of hide and seek. It may stalk, be seen, move away and then stalk the same prey all over again. A stalk of an hour or more is not unusual, with a leopard sometimes noting the direction of prey from a vantage point in a tree or from a ridge top, and only later moving off in that direction, sniffing the ground, picking up the sounds of its quarry and monitoring its route as it heads off in pursuit.

really determined to find food, she might remain active until midday. If she was nursing cubs, she often returned to them during rest periods.

With small prey such as grass rats, I have seen Half-Tail and Zawadi perform an agile, high-arching pounce like a serval or jackal, landing with forepaws right on top of the victim concealed in the grass. And there is no craftier cat to meet the challenge of crossing open terrain, flattening itself against the ground, legs bent beneath it, snaking forward, then disappearing into a lugga for concealment, peering from behind a termite mound or even using a vehicle to screen itself from view. Lex Hess watched one leopard chase a herd of impala in the open, driving them towards the cover of a thicket. Finding themselves

blocked by a wall of bush, some of the impalas turned back, straight into the outstretched paws of the leopard. Who knows if this was strategy or opportunism?

Leopards are known for their predilection for dogs – domestic and wild – and they can be the bane of a dog-lover's life, sneaking around villages at night and waylaying any dog that is foolish enough to think it is safe to close its eyes. Nothing is too big or too small when it comes to hunting down a dog – or a cat, for that matter. Many years ago, when we were living at Kichwa Tembo camp, a leopard was seen trotting off with Esmerelda, our favourite domestic cat, in its mouth. A reputation for fierceness means nothing to a leopard, as a priest living in the Mara region discovered when his full-grown

rottweiler was taken by a leopard without uttering a sound. More recently, our Nairobi neighbours Frank and Dolcie Howitt had the tranquillity of an evening stroll shattered when a leopard burst from a bush and snatched one of their dogs, a Jack Russell terrier. But it takes more than a leopard to keep Frank and Dolcie from their walk, and besides, they presumed that the leopard was just passing through. A day or so later, however, it struck again. This time, Frank, who is built like a solid English oak, managed to scare it off, leaving one terrified labrador in need of a patchwork of stitches. The leopard was later trapped and moved by the Kenya Wildlife Service.

Among wild canids, jackals feature regularly on the list of species killed by leopards, which is no doubt the reason why these foxy creatures act with such alarm at the sight or smell of the big cat. In fact black-backed jackals can be a real pest for a leopard, while bringing joy to leopard enthusiasts such as ourselves, uttering incessant, high-pitched barks the minute they see our spotted friend, and in the process pointing us in the right direction. Zawadi would sometimes show her irritation when mobbed by jackals, appearing as if she wanted to trick them into coming just a little closer. Every prey animal knows its 'flight distance' – how close it is safe to approach, based on its ability to turn and outrun a predator if necessary. Zawadi would suddenly lie down and roll on her back, almost playfully, enticing the jackals to come closer, then spring to her feet and chase after them at a fast gallop. But jackals are almost as crafty as leopards, and can dart and jink with incredible agility, though they do miscalculate at times and end up in the leopard's jaws. When they establish a den in a termite mound, as they tend to do each September in the Mara, they are particularly wary of revealing their hiding place to a leopard, and have even more reason to want to escort it off the property.

Even guinea fowl will race after a leopard among the acacia thickets, looking like motorized tea-cosies, clucking and churring in alarm. The leopard knows that the game is up and quickly finds a new place to conceal itself.

In the olden days, artists often depicted a leopard ambushing its prey from the concealment of a tree, leaping from the branches directly onto its victim. Though this rarely happens, filmmaker Richard Matthews did manage to capture just such a sequence in the Mara in 1985, when a female leopard jumped onto the back of a zebra foal and then killed it. Normally a leopard that spots potential prey from a tree quickly descends and then stalks or runs to get into a good position to ambush it. From the ground it has far more options in responding to what the prey might do,

Beauty leaping from a tree after being chased and harassed by a male cheetah.

and it must be rare for a leopard to find itself in a position to jump directly onto prey from a tree-top, though it may leap to the ground and then pounce. The slightest movement in the tree is likely to give a split-second warning to the prey, which is usually capable of outdistancing a leopard.

Subadult leopards, and sometimes adult females, invest a considerable amount of energy in stalking small prey– particularly hares and hyrax – as they move about their territory, and will target the young of many species, including impala fawns, warthog piglets and wildebeest calves. Females of larger species such as wildebeest and topi will defend their young from attack by hyenas, wild dogs, cheetahs and leopards, something they wouldn't risk doing with lions. Angie and I once witnessed Half-Tail

launch a lightning attack on a two-month-old wildebeest calf that had been born months after the peak calving season in the Serengeti, making it an obvious target (most wildebeest calves are born within a few weeks of each other, providing a glut of prey for the predators but giving an individual, protected by the vast numbers of the herds, the best chance of survival). The cow wildebeest was running through the acacia thickets along the top of Fig Tree Ridge with her calf pressed close to her side, not far from where Half-Tail had left her cubs. Half-Tail grabbed the calf, prompting the mother to turn and charge her. But Half-Tail was too quick and experienced, summoning all her considerable strength to hoist herself and the calf into the nearest bush. The cow flailed away at the bush with her sharp, curved horns, but to no avail, and she soon gave up and ran off, leaving Half-Tail to drag the calf to one of the fig trees, providing food for her and the cubs for the next two or three days.

Adult warthogs are even more dangerous than an irate wildebeest mother, though all the big cats prey heavily on warthog piglets and sometimes lie in ambush at the entrance of a burrow waiting for the pigs to leave or enter. Leopards have even been observed entering a burrow and dragging a piglet out, and Half-Tail was once seen catching three piglets at a burrow. Having eaten two of them she set off for where young Zawadi was waiting along Fig Tree Ridge, carrying

the third piglet in her mouth. But she never got that far. A hyena forced her to seek shelter in a tree, where the temptation to eat the pig herself was too much for her. A mother warthog will invariably challenge a leopard if her piglets are attacked, whipping round and charging the predator, sometimes thumping into it and bowling it over, slashing with her razor-sharp lower tusks. Many a leopard has been forced to drop the piglet and flee to save itself from injury. Even lions have received gaping wounds from an altercation with a large warthog, though the pig usually ends up being overpowered and killed, particularly if a second lion arrives on the scene.

Leopards often bite small prey such as young warthogs in the back of the neck or

head. But when they target larger animals, many of which – such as impalas and Thomson's gazelles – have sharp horns, they have to adopt the easiest way of overpowering prey with the least risk of injury, avoiding the horns and flailing hooves by pinning the animal to the ground with a bite to the throat. This technique employs the leopard's long canines to good effect, sometimes hastening death through loss of blood as well as strangulation. In Londolozi three-quarters of the leopards' prey is made up of just three species: impalas, duikers and warthogs, with the majority of kills being impalas, the most abundant large mammal in the area. Monkeys, bushbucks and hares are also regularly taken, and smaller prey

Half-Tail carrying a wildebeest calf to the safety of a fig tree. A kill of this size would normally last her for two or three days.

Wildebeest watching Zawadi, who is signalling by her posture and the way she is arching her tail that she is not hunting.

Half-Tail with a warthog piglet. All the large predators in the Mara kill warthog piglets, which are born in September/October, at the beginning of the short rains.

includes mice, tree squirrels, spring hares, rock monitors, leopard tortoises and birds, with francolins, red-billed wood hoopoes, hornbills, quails and korhaans featuring among them. One young leopard in the Mara killed a succession of white storks, 'naïve' winter migrants from Eastern Europe, taking six in a ten-day period and carefully plucking them before eating.

This wide range of prey underlines what a versatile and opportunistic hunter the leopard is, far more so than lions or cheetahs. The majority of their kills weigh less than 50kg (110lb), though they have been known to kill animals far in excess of their own weight. On one occasion Half-Tail, who weighed about 40kg (90lb), killed a full-grown Coke's hartebeest weighing 125kg (275lb), and a male leopard in the Mara attacked an adult bull wildebeest with a broken leg. It weighed about 225kg (500lb) and the leopard suffocated it only

after a long struggle. But kills as large as this are unusual, particularly in areas where there are lots of other predators that might steal the leopard's meal.

In fact there is little that a leopard won't kill when it is hungry – one large male at Lewa Wildlife Conservancy in Kenya is known to have killed a month-old rhino calf and stored it in a fig tree. Not even snakes are immune. A leopard at Mala Mala was seen playing a crafty game with a python, having been attracted by the distress calls of a duiker the snake had just caught. The leopard watched as the python coiled itself around its victim and suffocated it. When the leopard approached, the python struck out aggressively and the cat backed off. But as soon as the python had swallowed the duiker, the leopard walked up and clouted the snake on the head, forcing it to disgorge its prey, with which the leopard promptly ran away.

Crocodiles are quite a different proposition and have been known to leave the safety of the river to steal a leopard's kill; even lions sometimes lose kills to crocodiles when the wildebeest and zebra cross the Mara River, ending up in a tug of war with one or more crocodiles. Crocodiles are known to have killed and eaten adult leopards that ventured into the water, though a leopard will kill a small crocodile for food. They may even fish for their supper, snagging catfish from shallow water with their claws, something that Angie and I witnessed a young lioness doing in the Okavango Delta in Botswana.

Though the leopard is a consummate predator, superbly adapted to a killing way of life, it too has to face the threat of predation. Many leopard cubs die before they are a year old, particularly in areas where leopards, lions and hyenas occur together. Cubs that are too small – or too

Safi at three months, seeking refuge in a dead tree. The ability to climb trees from an early age is often the difference between life and death for leopard cubs when confronted by lions or hyenas.

slow – to climb trees are often unable to take other evasive action. Mortality in Londolozi and Mala Mala averaged 50–60 per cent, and in the Mara, which has one of the highest densities of lions and hyenas in Africa – one lion per 3 km² (1.1 sq. miles) and one hyena per km² (⅓ sq. mile) – the survival rate is even lower. Half-Tail and Zawadi both lost 80 per cent of their cubs.

All of the large predators compete with one another for food, though competition is reduced by the fact that lions tend to take larger prey than leopards, killing adult wildebeest, zebras and buffaloes, while leopards generally take only the young of these species and prefer medium-sized ungulates such as impalas and gazelles. Both lions and leopards are primarily

nocturnal, but leopards are also quite often active during the daytime when most lions and hyenas have sought shade and are sleeping or resting.

Of all the leopard's competitors, hyenas probably have the greatest impact in terms of food, certainly in the Mara. Hyenas are so adaptable and have such remarkable senses of smell and hearing that they are often able to steal food from a leopard before it can get a carcass into a tree. Although they generally kill larger prey, they also take young and sometimes adult impalas and gazelles – two of the leopard's most important food sources. Hyenas will seek out young leopards and kill them if they are not well protected in the first few months of their life, but they rarely attack healthy adults.

A Marsh lioness stalking. Lions kill leopards of all ages, hunting them down whenever they get the chance.

Lions, on the other hand, are more likely to kill leopards than to deprive them of much food; although they will certainly attempt to steal a leopard's kill if they spot it wedged in a tree that is easy to climb, they mostly fail to detect a well-concealed larder. Lions rarely eat other predators that they have killed, though one pride did take a small portion of meat from the carcass of an adult male leopard they ambushed in the Mara. The leopard had fled in panic out of a tree after being surrounded by tourist vehicles, and charged straight at the lions. Cornered, it never had any hope of escape;

it was promptly overpowered and strangled.

Half-Tail almost lost her life to lions while preoccupied with eating a hare on the ground. Alerted to the possibility of a meal by the strident alarm calls of a pair of jackals, two lionesses left the shade of a croton thicket where they had been resting and ran to investigate. The moment the lionesses saw Half-Tail crouched over her kill, they began to stalk her. Fortunately the leopard saw them at the last moment and bounded into the topmost branches of a sturdy fig tree, where she devoured the rest of her kill, with barely a glance towards her adversaries. Such incidents must be commonplace to a leopard, for whom keeping out of trouble is a way of life.

Rangers at Londolozi and Mala Mala witnessed lions killing leopard cubs on a number of occasions. In one incident a group of lions picked up the scent of where a mother leopard had left her offspring hidden in a donga. They immediately veered off and surprised the youngsters, with a young male leading the chase. Though one of the cubs managed to escape into the bush, the other was too slow and was caught. With a growl the male lion bit the cub, then shook it several times before dropping it on the ground and biting it again. The other lions rushed to the scene and took it in turns to bite and shake the cub, before moving off to investigate the scent of a dead impala that the Mother leopard had killed.

Lions are bullies and they deal with leopards as ruthlessly as they would an adversary of their own or any other species. Wild dogs are particularly vulnerable, especially when a pack is moving through bush country with young puppies and is easy to ambush, with the lions killing as many of their smaller opponents as they can. Male lions seem even more belligerent towards other predators than lionesses, partly perhaps because they are so much larger and can more easily intimidate rivals, and also because they rely on scavenging from kills made by lionesses or by stealing

Beauty snarling with displeasure, having been chased into a tree by a male cheetah.
Sometimes a leopard is forced to sit up in a tree all day after fleeing from lions.

from other predators. Though lionesses do kill hyenas, leopards and cheetahs at times, they don't seem to have quite the same unforgiving streak as males.

Leopards are far more unpredictable and volatile than lions. Dale Hancock found that at Mala Mala a leopard would let a human pass close by, crouching concealed in the grass, but if the person happened to notice the leopard it might prompt an immediate charge. Lions confronted by a human on foot tend to mock-charge; if you hold your ground they will normally back off. Leopards will charge, and then charge again, forcing you to give ground. Under such frightening circumstances there seems to be some disagreement as to whether to make or avoid eye contact. In a cat's world staring is an act of aggression, averting your eyes an act of submission. Most people would agree that backing off – rather than turning and running – is the best option, though your legs may say otherwise.

There have been instances when a leopard has been so quick and agile that it managed to escape when challenged by a lion, squirming free from beneath the larger adversary. On another occasion a leopard charged a lioness, pulling up only a metre or so from her face, hissing defensively. The lioness was so surprised by this gutsy display that she backed off, and the leopard was able to flee. Small, fierce creatures can be frightening, particularly members of the cat family with their repertoire of explosive spits and coughs. There is no doubt that a cat's dagger-like canines and razor-sharp claws are reason enough not to fight unnecessarily, regardless of the size of your opponent. Nonetheless, lions normally manage to put the fear of God into a leopard, causing it to empty its bladder with the stress of confrontation even when safely perched in the top of a tree. In fact a leopard has only to hear lions roaring nearby to make a hasty retreat, and if it

picks up their scent it sniffs the ground, carefully examining the spot, then moves away in the opposite direction.

Fortunately for leopards, lions are far clumsier climbers, though in one incident a lioness pursued a leopard cub into a tree, prompting the terrified youngster to fall to the ground where it was mauled to death by a second lioness. Half-Tail's daughter Taratibu was killed by a lioness when she was a year old, although her mother and brother escaped into the trees.

The response of a mother leopard on finding a dead cub is the same as we have witnessed with a lioness. She sniffs at it, licking and grooming it briefly before picking it up and carrying it around. Then she settles down to feed on the lifeless body, sometimes storing her grizzly find in a tree. Every so often she calls, using both the short, abrupt, rather guttural arragh-grunt that mother leopards use to summon their cubs from their hiding place, as well as

Hyenas have acute hearing and sense of smell, and keep a watchful eye on vulture activity, which helps lead them to kills made by other predators.

the more robust and far-carrying contact call that all adults employ to let others know of their whereabouts. This process of wandering and calling may go on for a number of days, occasionally up to a week. This is not as pointless as it might seem. A mother leopard often leaves her cubs on their own for days at a time, and sometimes they move away from their hiding place. Under these circumstances, calling and searching have survival value.

Though lions are a far greater threat to leopards of all ages than hyenas, the latter are still the bane of a leopard's life. It is often a race against time for a leopard to stash its kill in a tree before the hyenas come running, and over the years we have witnessed countless interactions between the two predators – mostly to the leopards' disadvantage. Whereas it takes up to four hyenas to force a lioness to abandon her kill, even a single hyena is usually sufficient to intimidate a leopard into relinquishing its food. For all its legendary ferocity, a leopard simply cannot afford the risk of being injured in a brawl with a hyena – particularly a female hyena, who is bigger than her male counterpart and outweighs a female leopard by 10–30kg (20–65lb).

Hyenas are incredibly powerful creatures, with bone-crushing jaws, thick muscular necks to rival a leopard's, and a matt of coarse hair that helps protect them from bites and cuts. They are quick to resort to violence if a leopard resists their attempts to steal its kill, biting the cat's rump, neck or leg to force it to drop the carcass, though if a leopard has cubs close at hand she will certainly try to defend them from attack. One female was observed to charge an overly inquisitive hyena and bite it in the rump, sending it packing – but the moment two more hyenas arrived she wisely leapt into the tree where she had stashed her kill.

I once saw Chui engage in a violent tug of war with a hyena over the remains of an impala kill that Dark had dropped out of a tree and then tried to drag away. The hyena rushed forward, ignoring Chui's hiss of warning. Dark quickly abandoned the kill and scrambled up the nearest tree. But having waited patiently until her cubs had eaten their fill, Chui was not about to surrender her meal so easily.

The situation quickly turned into the animal equivalent of a bar-room brawl. I never saw Chui quite so determined, the

gathering darkness seeming to increase her aggressiveness. She charged, clawing at the hyena and sinking her dagger-like canines into his neck as he attempted to snatch the impala away. For a moment he seethed and writhed on the ground with Chui, both animals struggling ferociously for possession of the carcass. Neither dared to release their grip so as to bite the other, for fear of losing the prize altogether.

Finally, summoning all her considerable strength, Chui wrenched the kill and the hyena towards the euclea tree where the impala had originally hung. Inch by inch she forced him to follow. Eventually it was the hyena who let go, biting savagely at Chui's back leg. She did not even pause, ignoring the pain. Sensing that the battle was nearly lost, the hyena lunged forwards again, locking his powerful teeth around the impala's trailing back leg. Still Chui pulled and tugged, hauling herself closer and closer to the base of the tree. Suddenly she felt the weight release behind her as the hyena toppled backwards in an untidy heap, the impala's leg still clenched between his teeth. Chui scrambled into the tree – she was too tired to leap – leaving the hyena to race away with a portion of meat. On this occasion she had managed to turn the tables on a member of the Fig Tree Clan.

The relationship between leopards and hyenas is complex, and often has a history, with individuals of each species responding according to past experiences. Both leopards and hyenas mark out territories, so the resident leopards and the local hyena clan get to know one another and respond to one another on the basis of individual strengths and weaknesses. This is apparent in the manner in which a leopard may immediately give way to a particularly large hyena, though not all meetings are aggressive. If a leopard is resting on the ground and there is no food to contest, it often simply lies still, allowing a hyena to approach. Though hyenas have excellent vision, they rely heavily on their acute sense of smell. They tend to approach a leopard from down wind, heads bobbing as they assess the situation, making sure that there is nothing more dangerous – such as lions – in the vicinity. If the leopard has made a kill, the hyena will cock its tail and rush in with an intimidating growl to steal the food, whooping for reinforcements only if it can't manage on its own. I once saw a large female hyena charge straight at Half-Tail as she stood at the base of an acacia bush, barrelling into her with a hefty body check and putting her on the defensive, though her kill was already safely stashed 4.5m (15ft) above the ground.

Even if there is no food to contest, the hyena may still come within centimetres of the leopard's face to see if it has been eating and, if so, back-track in an attempt to pin down the location of the kill. Sometimes the leopard keeps its cool, not even bothering to growl or hiss, but if it feels threatened it twists its ears down,

revealing the black and white stripes on the backs. Mouth ajar, black lips emphasizing the long white canines, it crouches like a coiled spring. But hyenas seem singularly unimpressed by such menacing looks – they have seen it all before and know exactly how far they can go. At this point, with no food to garner, the hyena may sniff around for the leopard's droppings and eat them. Hyenas sometimes trail a leopard or a pack of wild dogs, and may even lie up close to where these predators are resting, waiting for them to set off on a hunt and then rushing in to steal the spoils.

Though female leopards rarely put up much resistance when confronted by a hyena, male leopards are larger, more aggressive and less likely to be intimidated, growling rather than hissing at hyenas and more than able to hold their own in a one-on-one encounter. The problem is that it is hard to defend a kill and eat from it at the

Chui with an impala kill stashed safely out of the reach of hyenas.

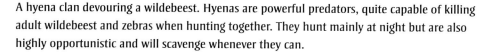

A hyena clan devouring a wildebeest. Hyenas are powerful predators, quite capable of killing adult wildebeest and zebras when hunting together. They hunt mainly at night but are also highly opportunistic and will scavenge whenever they can.

same time, and there are occasions when a leopard and a hyena may feed together on a carcass, though the minute other hyenas arrive it is time for the leopard to leave. Male leopards are more likely than females to stay in the vicinity of a kill that has been stolen from them, sometimes managing to rush in at the right moment and retrieve part of it. Otherwise the best solution is to move off quickly and hunt again.

Personality as well as size has a part to play in how predators respond to one another; degree of hunger, too, with some individuals being much more aggressive and liable to attack or to defend their property. At least two hyenas were killed by a male leopard during Bailey's study in Kruger; one was stashed in a tree, while the other was eaten on the ground. The same male was seen to attack two hyenas who tried to scavenge from a warthog he had killed, but they escaped without injury. On another occasion a large male leopard attacked and strangled a full-grown male cheetah weighing 45kg (100lb) and then

Half-Tail was completely relaxed around vehicles and quite unperturbed – it seemed – by the hustle and bustle of visitors on safari.

hoisted the carcass into a tree; a similar incident has been reported in the Serengeti.

Sometimes the tables are turned. I once saw a large male cheetah chase Beauty into a tree when she was almost fully grown. She looked most put out, snarling and grunting at the cheetah, who stared up at her and then lay down a short distance away. When Beauty climbed down from the tree the cheetah immediately charged, chasing her up a rocky hillside, where she escaped into a thicket.

It is rare to see a leopard in poor condition in the Mara, though this could be because an old or ailing leopard would soon be killed by lions or hyenas. In all the time I have spent there I have never seen a sick leopard, though I have found a number of adult cheetahs in poor condition, often due to a disease known as sarcoptic mange. Mange is caused by a tiny mite that eats away at the skin, causing the victim to scratch itself continually, tearing out the fur and opening up flesh wounds that become infected with bacteria. It is often these secondary infections that are fatal. The skin mites themselves are not usually a problem as long as the animal stays healthy. Bailey noted that mange was a significant factor in leopard mortality in the Kruger, and Lex Hess describes the Londolozi rangers being faced with the dilemma of whether or not to intervene when a leopard was suffering from mange, which is easy to treat with the right prescription.

In this instance it was a subadult who had been struggling to find sufficient food while trying to stay out of trouble with the resident adult leopards. Before the area was opened up to tourism her illness would have passed unnoticed. Is it right to offer a helping hand when your action may simply be putting other leopards under pressure? In the end the rangers decided not to interfere. The youngster then wandered onto the Mala Mala property, where she was promptly treated and recovered.

Any environmental stress such as a shortage of food during a particularly dry

winter or an increase in lion and hyena numbers may cause a rise in the animal's cortisone levels, suppressing the immune system and allowing the mites to multiply. Mange seems to be one of nature's means of controlling cat populations, and leopards at times also succumb to diseases such as anthrax, canine distemper and rabies.

There is currently a male leopard at the Nairobi Orphanage who was captured as an adult in 1985, when he was at least three years old. He must therefore be over 20 now and is somewhat arthritic; he no longer climbs into trees to rest, and has difficulty chewing his food, though he is otherwise very much alive. Half-Tail was 11or 12 years old when she died, and was fortunate to have lived as long as she did, surviving being shot in the face with an arrow by a Masai herdsman in 1997. At the time she was accompanied by a male, and one of them took a sheep or a goat, incurring the wrath of its owner. The arrow went through Half-Tail's nose and penetrated her palate, leaving a metal tip exposed and lacerating her tongue whenever she tried to close her mouth. Fortunately, drivers from Governor's Camp discovered her and one of them watched over her throughout the night, until a vet from the Kenya Wildlife Service could anaesthetize her and remove the arrow.

Though a wild leopard might be considered old by the time it is ten, in Londolozi and Mala Mala a number of animals have exceeded this lifespan – the Mother leopard lived for 14 years, and her daughter a year or so longer. But this is exceptional, particularly in areas where the slightest miscalculation in hunting large or dangerous prey – or a confrontation with a more powerful predator – could leave a leopard severely injured or dead.

Half-Tail taking a kill to safety having been disturbed by an eagle. She hid it in a croton thicket, but next morning it had gone, so she probably lost it during the night to hyenas.

The Territorial Imperative

Male leopards are impressive-looking creatures, exuding a raw muscular power. I have seen so few adult males that even now whenever I happen upon one it reminds me of the old days when finding any leopard made my heart race.

During the first few years of Lex Hess's stay at Londolozi, adult male leopards seemed as shy around vehicles as those in the Mara did, and we both waited for the time when one of the male cubs that we had been able to watch would eventually settle somewhere in the area, allowing us to get a better idea of their behaviour. Today there are adult males in both our old stamping grounds who are very relaxed around vehicles, particularly in the area near Mara Intrepids Camp, which puts out bait, giving visitors the chance to watch leopards at night and helping to habituate them. The reason so many of our observations have been of females with cubs is partly that female offspring often settle as adults in an area adjacent to their mother and in some cases overlap her home range, giving birth to their cubs in favoured places that we have come to know.

Once a female leopard has established a territory she seldom strays far, living there until her death or until she is displaced by a younger rival. She demarcates the area by laying down her individual scent, reading the messages left by other passing leopards, sniffing around the bushes, fallen trees and rocks, then rubbing her face, head and body against a bush or tree before turning and spraying urine tainted with scent from her anal glands. She knows every nook and cranny of her home range, and may even choose to give birth in the same place where she herself was born. It is hardly surprising that young leopards are so reluctant to leave their natal range, or that a translocated leopard often heads straight home again after being released, regardless of the distance it must travel.

A leopard's solitary and independent nature is evident from an early age. A young lion or cheetah takes care not to

Beauty examining an interesting scent – perhaps the spot where another leopard or predator has urinated or raked its feet on the ground, leaving scent from its paws.

become separated from its companions, and if it does get left behind or lost it becomes very agitated and calls out in distress. Leopards are much more self-possessed; from the time they are barely a few months old, they grow accustomed to stopping and investigating their environment, sometimes becoming separated from their mother and siblings in the process. When this happens the leopard cub simply settles down somewhere safe – in a cave, under a bush or in a tree – and then waits for its mother to come back and find it. This independent mien increases month by month, initially driven as much by the natural way of being of a leopard as by the mother's wish to weaken the ties of kinship.

By the time a leopard is one year old it is spending the majority of its time on its own, and the changing relationship between parent and young is reinforced by the mother's increasing hostility towards her offspring. At first this is no more than a degree of impatience when the cubs try to greet her. She will bare her dagger-like canines, hiss and snarl or grunt, signalling

Half-Tail and Zawadi claw-marking the bark of an acacia tree. This helps keep their claws sharp and leaves a visible mark that other leopards can read.

that she wants to be left alone – a mixture of 'I want some peace and quiet' and 'Time to grow up and fend for yourself', in response to a cub's overt displays of affection or pestering to be fed. The bond is further weakened as a mother gradually stops leading her cub to kills, though if the young leopard is really struggling to find sufficient prey it may still be allowed to feed with her. The difference is that where before the mother would come and find her cubs, as they grow older the onus is more and more on them to find her – and kill for themselves.

A female leopard usually mates and become pregnant some months before she finally abandons her cubs. The changes that occur in the latter stages of pregnancy as she becomes even more secretive and wants to be left on her own no doubt help to put an end to contact between a mother and her previous litter, though, as we saw with Half-Tail and Beauty, there are no absolutes – a young leopard may still occasionally make contact with its mother up to the age of 20 months or more.

While watching Chui's mother, the Mara Buffalo female, with her two cubs in 1983, I was able to observe a marked difference in the development of the two sexes. I wrote at the time:

By the time the cubs were a year old the young male had abandoned Mara Buffalo Rocks as a resting place. He acted in a much more independent manner than his sister, who seemed to require a closer relationship with their mother. The male, being larger, stronger and faster, was probably better equipped to supplement the food that he still sometimes obtained from his mother's kills and he was already killing smaller game. Perhaps when only one cub is being reared, a male cub can maintain a closer association with his mother for a longer period. But in these particular circumstances there was just not enough food to go round.

On the few occasions that I was able to find the Mara Buffalo female she was still often accompanied by her daughter, at least up to the time the youngster was 14 months old. I was unable to tell what role she had played in establishing her son's more independent ways, though I noticed wounds on his back that could have been caused by a fight with another leopard.

All this is very different from the way a cheetah mother deals with her subadult offspring. There is no gradual severing of the familial bond and little sign of aggression between mother and cubs for as long as they remain together. Separation for a cheetah family normally occurs when the cubs are 14–18 months old. One day the mother simply walks away – or the cubs do. After this it is unusual for the family to make contact again, though the cubs stay together for the next few months, with female cubs then splitting off on their own and male cubs staying together for life.

Perhaps the mother's lack of aggression reflects the different land-tenure systems that cheetahs and leopards operate. Cheetah females do not defend a territory, roaming so widely – up to 800km^2 (300 sq. miles) in the Serengeti – that it would be impossible to do so. They are much more nomadic than leopards, probably due to their preference for Thomson's gazelles, which are migratory. Gaining the occasional meal from their mother once they have branched out on their own is just not an option for young cheetahs, which is perhaps why they stay with their siblings for a few months, providing them with greater vigilance against other predators and a greater chance of one of them making a kill that can then be shared.

I have never seen young cheetahs engage in real cat-fights the way leopards do over food. Sharing rather than fighting is the norm for a cheetah mother and her cubs. Time is of the essence, and there is no advantage to be gained in each waiting their turn; cheetahs cannot store kills in trees and must eat quickly and move on

The Mara Buffalo Female and her 14-month-old daughter. Daughters often end up sharing part of their mother's home range, though as adults the two leopards avoid each other.

before vultures attract hyenas or lions to the scene. Cubs occasionally compete for position by manoeuvring with their bodies or holding tight to a scrap of meat or skin and engaging in a tug of war, but a bit of low-intensity growling or churring is about as aggressive as it gets, with one or other of the cubs simply giving way or running off with a leg bone.

Lex Hess followed one young male leopard forced onto the path to independence by his mother's aggression. Rejected by her and finding it hard to obtain sufficient food for himself, he began to hang around camp and occasionally stole meat from the staff. A few weeks later he was seen trying to make contact with his mother again. She was moving, calling and scent-marking, as if she was looking for a mate. Her son was 500m (⅓ mile) away; he stopped and listened when she called and then moved towards the sound, replying with his own call and the single guttural grunt used by cubs when they are searching for their mother. Although the female chose to ignore her son's overtures, the young male picked up her scent, following in her footsteps and responding to her call whenever she gave one. At one point he was within 100m (330ft) of her, but she simply kept moving and then stopped calling. Eventually he lost her scent trail and began hanging around camp again.

Despite his tender years the young male managed to find enough food to survive

Safi greets her mother Zawadi, who responds with a discouraging snarl. This is a non-damaging way in which a mother leopard pushes her offspring towards independence.

over the next few months. At 15 months he killed a warthog piglet after a noisy confrontation with the sow. Unknown to him, his mother was only 50m (160ft) away with a kill of her own and accompanied by a new litter of cubs. Alerted by the commotion, she came to investigate, watching as the young male strangled the piglet at the base of a tree. When he looked up again he found his mother sitting

watching him. The two leopards glared at each other, the male growling quietly, the mother staring back at him. Then she crouched down facing her son, holding her ground as every so often he advanced towards her, snarling. After a few minutes she got up and moved back to where she had left her cubs. This is so cat-like, the disdain for other cats, the dislike of strangers, the sizing up of the opposition,

Subadult and young adult leopards of both sexes form a separate part of the leopard population, each with its own home range. This may initially overlap not only their mother's range but also part of their father's. Depending on the area, an adult female may be prepared to share part of her home range with her daughter as she reaches adulthood, and the daughter may be able to expand her range into that of another female (who may also be a relative). But there are bound to be times when there isn't sufficient room for this to happen, particularly if a female has already raised one or more daughters to adulthood. Under these circumstances the young female is going to have to move away, as happened with Half-Tail when she became

independent, or fight for possession with a resident, regardless of whether that is her mother, sister or an unrelated adult.

Young leopards who have dispersed (or are in the process of dispersing) from their natal range and are still searching for a place to settle have been described as 'floaters'. The males among them are usually forced to wander further afield as they mature and are hard to keep track of. If they survive – and many do not – they establish themselves in a vacant area or on the fringe of existing territories, where they may eventually be able to carve out a niche for themselves. Though the sex ratio at birth is one to one, among the adult population it is closer to one male to two females.

Zawadi looking out across her home range not far from Moses Rock, with the Siria Escarpment looming in the background. Zawadi – like Half-Tail before her – lives outside the Mara Reserve boundary, among the Masai pastoralists.

the prickly antipathy, the desire to attack and drive the intruder away tempered by the threat of those dangerous teeth and claws that can inflict such terrible injuries.

Next afternoon the young male went for a drink and then called. Hess was surprised to hear such a young leopard announcing his presence so boldly, and wondered if he was trying to locate his mother again. Having satisfied his thirst the leopard walked back up the bank, but as he crested the rise his ears went back and he bared his teeth in a snarl, flattening his body against the ground. At that moment a large male charged over the top of the bank in an intimidating display and attacked him. Both leopards tumbled down towards the water; as they reached the bottom the younger male managed to slip out from beneath his more powerful opponent and fled. The older male followed him for a while, but

Mature male lions seem less likely to attack youngsters who do not yet boast a well-developed mane. But once the nomads are four years old and begin to challenge the established order by scent-marking and roaring, there is no denying their intentions and resident pride males will defend their territory fiercely. Likewise with leopards. Older males will generally tolerate the younger generation until they are almost ready to breed, and refrain from seriously injuring a subadult, acknowledging signs of submission such as the younger male flipping onto his side and exposing his vulnerable throat.

Though serious fights are probably rare, both Patrick Hamilton and Ted Bailey found evidence of conflict when examining the leopards they had trapped and radio-collared. Some had open wounds where they had been bitten and clawed, others were scarred and showed signs of old injuries, with damage to ears, nose and eyes. Males certainly do occasionally fight tooth and nail, gladiatorial contests in which the participants rear up onto their hind legs just as male lions and tigers do, slashing and biting, breaking off and then returning to the fray until one has had enough and runs off. Injuries from a leopard's claws are more likely to cause flesh wounds; the greatest danger is of being bitten in the neck, throat or spine by those 6cm (2½in) canines. Dr Luke Hunter, who is currently studying leopards in Phinda Resource Reserve in South Africa, recently wrote to tell me that one of his males was killed by a four-year-old newcomer who surprised him sleeping and killed him without a struggle by a single throat bite.

A serious fight has to be over something worth fighting for, and for males that is generally control of a territory and the access to breeding females that this brings. The greatest stability comes when males have held their territories for some time, getting to know their neighbours as 'dear enemies', recognizing that they can live alongside one another if both respect the other's rights of tenure and in general keep to their own patch. But if there is any weakness or significant difference in size between males, then one may gradually take advantage of that fact – just as a larger or more experienced male lion tends to dominate a smaller or younger one in a coalition. And a female in oestrus is always likely to provoke conflict between any males in her vicinity.

Hancock and Wolhuter felt that battles for territory were often wars of attrition. They were able to follow the changing fortunes of a leopard known as the Flockfield male who settled as an adult to the south of the territories of two resident males, the Jakkalsdraai and Mlowathi males. In time the core of the Flockfield's territory shifted by over 40km (25 miles), due to pressure from his neighbours. Over a two-week period in 1994 the Flockfield and Jakkalsdraai males met regularly along their common boundary, which they marked by scuffing their hind feet, raking up the ground and claw-marking certain trees to leave a visible sign that other leopards would recognize. The two males would walk along the western bank of Boomer's Crossing, each trying to intimidate the other into backing down, parading shoulder to shoulder, salivating profusely with a mixture of pent-up aggression and fear. It was like two boxers standing eyeball to eyeball, each desperate to gain a psychological advantage. The moment one male got ahead of the other, he would attempt to move across his rival's path, prompting the other to run and try to cut him off. If either stopped they would both lower their hindquarters and scrape-mark, then roll onto their backs and rub their heads on the ground. But it never escalated beyond this show of force, as if each male was saying, 'Look how big and powerful I am, why don't you just push off before you get hurt?'

Whatever was 'said' between the two males, the message finally forced the older

next morning the youngster was back in the same area, none the worse for wear, though over the next two months he began to wander further and further afield.

In many ways young male leopards live a similar life to nomadic lions who are too young to claim a territory of their own and must roam around trying to keep out of harm's way until they are fully grown.

Flockfield male to concede the advantage and relinquish another small chunk of his territory. In other words, he was acknowledging that the Jakkalsdraai male was in the ascendancy, and would win if it came to a fight. The Flockfield male was never again seen so far north, veering off to the east for the Kruger Park whenever he reached Boomer's Crossing during his regular three-to-four-day border patrols. Eventually he spent all his time in the large plot of dense uncharted bushveld in the Kruger, and at 14 years old was still somewhere out there by the time Hancock and Wolhuter finished filming – though perhaps no longer in prime territory.

One question that is yet to be resolved is 'To what degree are female leopards territorial?' Adult females generally show little evidence of injuries from conflict with other leopards. But there is no doubt that they will chase and fight with a rival when necessary, actively defending their home range even if it isn't their exclusive preserve. As we have seen, young male leopards often mirror their mother's home range when they first become independent, and apart from competition over food pose no threat to their mother by continuing to use the area. But once young females reach breeding age, it would seem to be in their mother's interest to drive them out. However, the degree to which females adhere to this convention varies from region to region and is probably related to a number of factors – the density of the leopard population, food supply and competition with other predators.

Observers at Mala Mala and Londolozi have witnessed several encounters between mothers and daughters that provide an insight into how adult female relatives adjust to sharing parts of the same area. One incident was particularly savage and ended only when the younger female fell from a tree in which the encounter with her mother took place. Though still somewhat smaller than her mother, the daughter put up a spirited defence on being attacked.

Lex Hess describes an interaction between the Mother leopard and her subadult daughter, at a time when the Mother had two eleven-month-old cubs. She was bringing her cubs to the place where she had stashed an impala in a tree, only to find that her older daughter had discovered the kill and was already feeding. The female cub approached the tree aggressively, baring her teeth at her big sister in a throaty snarl. The older sibling snarled back; both leopards stared at each other, hissing loudly. The stand-off lasted for ten minutes, until the cub could no longer contain herself and with a loud growl rushed at her sister, springing into the tree to attack her – spurred on, no doubt, by the sense that this was her food and her territory. Finding herself on the defensive, the older sister leapt some 7m (23ft) to the ground.

The Mother leopard, who had been watching all this time, rushed forward and nipped her older daughter in the base of the tail as she turned and bounded off, ensuring that she continued on her way. The following day, the Mother was seen moving around the same area, calling and repeatedly scent-marking, probably as a result of the intrusion, though she may have been looking for a mate. The normal avoidance mechanisms had broken down and needed to be reinforced. There were no further sightings of the young female, and the Mother safely chaperoned her cubs to independence, abandoning them once they were 15 months old. Three months later she gave birth again.

In general, though, interactions between mothers and daughters are not particularly serious or damaging – a brief spat, a chase perhaps, and then it is over. In most cases females with overlapping home ranges simply avoid one another, as is illustrated by the story of another female and her daughter at Londolozi. The daughter had just failed in her attempt to ambush a herd of impala, prompting them to snort loudly in alarm. Her mother was 200m (650ft)

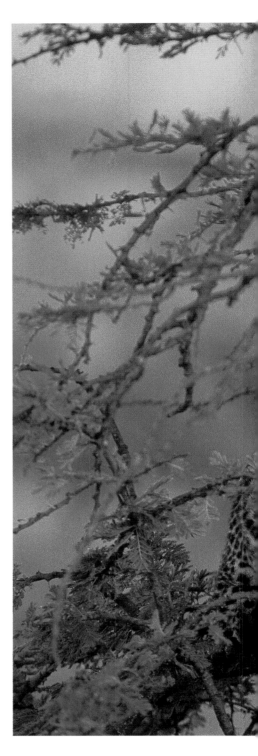

away at the time and, on hearing the impala, began to call, alerting her daughter to the fact that she was in the area. The young female immediately stopped and looked in the direction of the call, then walked a few metres and scraped vigorously with her hind feet before turning 90 degrees and walking away, pausing every so

Half-Tail and Zawadi. Half-Tail raised two daughters to maturity:
Beauty, who was born in 1992, and Zawadi, in 1996.

often to spray-mark bushes. The mother then moved in the opposite direction. Neither leopard showed any inclination to engage in a chase, perhaps because they were near the shared boundary of their adjacent territories. The mother had recently started to shift her activity further north, allowing her daughter to establish herself as a permanent resident in the southern part of her former range, something we witnessed Half-Tail do as Zawadi matured. Having a relative as a neighbour, someone whose habits you know and with whom you have a shared history, is likely to be less volatile than accommodating an unknown leopard. In fact relatedness may be the reason for allowing young females to acquire a home

Zawadi suckling Safi, aged three months, on a termite mound. Leopards, like cheetahs and lions, often climb onto termite mounds for a good look round, particularly when the grass is long.

range nearby, and only by sharing at times is this possible.

The degree of tolerance shown between females is no doubt modified by the stage in their breeding cycle they are in. A mother about to give birth or with young cubs is likely to be less tolerant of intrusions, particularly when she is confined with her offspring to a relatively small part of her range, and females with young cubs are fiercely aggressive when threatened. But if a female does not constantly mark her home range it may give a younger animal or a transient adult the impression that the area is unoccupied. This might help to explain why mother leopards leave their cubs for considerable lengths of time from a young age – it is not just to hunt.

Tjellers, the female whom Hancock and Wolhuter followed, stayed very close to her den site for five days after she gave birth, then set off on a boundary patrol. She soon came across the scent of another female – the adjacent territory-holder – who had large cubs. Tjellers paused to sniff at the

ground, rolled on her back and then trotted forward, uttering a few harsh grunts and pausing briefly to listen as the intruders disappeared into the nearby lugga. There was a brief commotion as she flushed the other female from cover and chased her for 150m (500ft) before catching up with her. A brief but vicious fight took place before the females broke free and stood face to face 2m (6ft) apart, growling. Both were wounded and neither seemed keen to renew hostilities as they headed north, side by side, in the same way that male territory-holders sometimes walk parallel to one another in a boundary dispute. At one point they paused to scrape and roll on the ground, then the mother of the older cubs called to them to join her. But they were too scared to emerge from their hiding place among the bushes, and the females continued on their way, shoulder to shoulder, salivating with the stress of the encounter.

Eventually they lay down to rest 5m (16ft) apart. Ten minutes later Tjellers got to her feet and mock-charged her opponent,

who refused to give ground. After another 20 minutes, she too stood up and headed back in the direction she had come from, pausing every so often to scrape the ground with her hind feet – something that lionesses often do after an encounter with intruders or a battle with hyenas over food; it seems to boost their confidence and assert their claim to the area. Once the other female was safely on her way, Tjellers went and rolled where her adversary had marked, following her tracks for a while to confirm that she had gone.

It is evident from these illustrations that adult leopards do meet at times, and must become familiar with their neighbours, constantly assessing their strengths and weaknesses. The way a leopard behaves and how aggressively it is prepared to defend itself and its territory is modified to some degree by where the encounter takes place. The closer a leopard is to its core area – the heart of its home range – the more likely it is to fight to defend its right to that area, and the more likely a trespasser is to flee rather than stand its ground. Only when another leopard is determined to take over an area from the resident is there likely to be a serious fight.

There also seems to be a different approach to defending a home range according to whether you are male or female, as there is with lions. A male lion generally has only a short tenure as a territory-holder. His life is about maximizing breeding opportunities, and there is no time to waste. Males have been known to fight to the death in defence of their territory – or in trying to acquire one. Lionesses also defend their territory, which is passed down from one generation of females to another and is primarily a hunting ground and somewhere offering suitable hiding places for cubs – as it is for female leopards. With lions, disputes with other groups of females over territory are not quite as urgent or as viciously contested as those between rival males, though lionesses do sometimes kill a non-pride member. But generally they are long-term wars, rather than one-off battles, and this often seems to be the case with female leopards too.

One can see how the land-use system employed by solitary cats, whereby adult females tolerate their female offspring settling down in an adjacent area or even sharing part of their home range or hiving off a portion of it for themselves, allows the young females the best chance of finding living space and breeding. This could under the right circumstances evolve into an even more social way of life, with mother and daughter sharing the responsibility of raising their cubs, hunting together and defending their kills against hyenas. Which may be what gave rise to the pride system that characterizes lion society in prey-rich, savanna-type country.

The fact that many young female leopards establish themselves in or near their own natal area does pose the problem of inbreeding, with the potential for a father mating with his daughter. Hancock witnessed such an incident with one of

Tjellers' offspring. Lion society is organized in such a way that it is rare for fathers to mate with their own daughters. Lionesses don't normally breed successfully until they are in their fourth year, by which time the pride males will almost certainly have been forced out and replaced by new males to whom the females are unlikely to be related. Male leopards don't start breeding (even though they may already be sexually mature) until they have acquired a territory, by which time they are probably a minimum of three years old. In an area where competition is fierce, a territory-holder may have been displaced by the time his daughter is ready to breed, and it is also possible that most females end up settling within adjacent male territories or simply avoid mating with their father and seek out a male from an adjoining territory.

Until recently the accepted view was that apart from the few days a male and female leopard spend together when mating, they rarely meet up – in fact they avoid each other. But the years of observation at Londolozi and Mala Mala have given us a different leopard from the solitary cat described in the past. We now know that males and females living in overlapping ranges do at times meet, often without much sign of hostility, though there have been instances of males killing females. Some encounters could even be described as friendly, in as much as the leopards did not fight, nor did they seem unduly concerned by one another's presence. This is similar to reports of male and female tigers sometimes associating at a kill, or a mother socializing briefly with the father of her cubs, and they with him.

In addition to communicating by body language, cats use certain calls to reduce the possibility of aggression and signal to one another that their intentions are amicable. One such call is known as prusten or, less formally, chuffling, which I feel conveys a better sense of a sound that seems to have a touch of playfulness about it. Whatever you choose to call it, it is a

series of sharp, explosive puffing sounds like loud sniffing, made by blowing sharply through the nostrils with the mouth closed. I first heard this sound in 1983 while watching Chui summon Light and Dark from their hiding place along Fig Tree Ridge. It is a quiet and intimate call, perfect for not arousing the attention of predators; Chui often seemed to prefer to chuffle rather than use the short, sharp, rather gruff and guttural arragh-grunt that is the most commonly used contact call between a mother leopard and her cubs. The arragh-grunt is louder, and therefore more appropriate when a mother is actively searching for her cubs, unsure of their precise location; it can be modified in pitch and loudness. Though Chui often chuffled when her cubs were small, I never heard Half-Tail call in this manner, nor have I often heard Zawadi use it – both preferred the arragh-grunt.

Clouded leopards chuffle in friendly close-contact situations, as do tigers, jaguars and snow leopards. It is an integral part of the tiger's greeting behaviour, described as 'the forced exhalation of air through the nostrils and mouth, which results in a fluttering action of the lips'. Tigresses are said to chuffle most often when maintaining contact with their young, and both sexes chuffle during courtship and mating. I have never heard cheetahs or lions use this sound as a greeting, though in their book *Wild Cats of the World* Mel and Fiona Sunquist mention that 'leopards, along with lions, have a vocalization called puffing, which is analogous to the prusten of tigers, jaguars, clouded leopards, and snow leopards'. Puffing is said to be mainly articulated through the nose, though I am not convinced that, in the case of leopards at least, the sound they are making isn't chuffling or prusten. Hancock and Wolhuter heard adult leopards chuffling on a number of occasions during friendly encounters, helping to reduce tension between individuals who spend most of their time on their own.

Chui with Dark when he was three or four months old. Cubs will grizzle to be fed and, though they start eating meat from the age of seven or eight weeks, continue to suckle for the first three or four months – sometimes longer, particularly if food is scarce.

Hancock and Wolhuter once recorded the Jakkalsdraai male announcing his arrival by chuffling and being greeted in a friendly manner by Tjellers, who was accompanied by two small cubs. One might have expected her to jump up and react aggressively to the sudden arrival of a male, but the fact that she was familiar with this one and that he was probably the father of her cubs no doubt influenced her response. In fact if she had reacted aggressively she might have prompted him to attack her and her family. In any case the cubs scattered when the male let out a grunt, but he never appeared to pose a threat to them. On another occasion when the same adults sensed each other's presence they both started to chuffle – a friendly duet of reassurance analogous to 'Don't panic, everything is all right, I am not about to attack.' This is a vital form of communication between such well-armed individuals and reinforces the idea that while leopards may be primarily solitary,

they are not as antisocial as was previously thought. They learn to recognize the individual scent, call, physical bearing and temperament of other leopards in their area, and respond accordingly.

Hancock also witnessed the Jakkalsdraai male sniffing nose to nose with Tjellers after they had chuffled. The male then climbed into the tree where Tjellers had stored her kill. There was no dispute over possession of the food; the leopards simply adopted their normal feeding routine whereby one feeds alone before giving up its position to another. In this instance the cubs, who were already up in the tree, bit at their father's flank and tail as he gorged himself without provoking a violent response. This doesn't mean to say that males aren't sometimes harsh in their treatment of cubs – or so it might appear to human eyes – snarling and cuffing the youngsters when they want to be left in peace. Male lions often respond in a similarly rough fashion when young cubs

try to extend a perfunctory greeting into a play session. But even though a male might grunt out a warning, show his massive canines and bite down on the cubs to stop them bothering him, this doesn't inflict serious damage – though I have never forgotten seeing a pride male savagely attack an 18-month-old cub who was trying to hold on to a wildebeest calf that the male wanted for himself. A single bite left the cub writhing in agony, and I never saw it again. But that dispute was about food at a time when all the pride members were hungry and no quarter was given – even to their own offspring.

Like male lions, individual leopards react differently according to their age, health and temperament. The Jakkalsdraai male seemed to be particularly tolerant of Tjellers' cubs. He was seen with them on a number of occasions, and once when she had a single cub of just a few weeks old the male tracked mother and cub to their lair. Tjellers watched him approach as she lay suckling and immediately began to chuffle, prompting the male to break into a trot. The cub stopped suckling and rolled more than walked towards the male, who veered off and pushed under a bush, possibly because he was nervous that Tjellers might react aggressively towards him in the presence of such a small cub.

Lex Hess also observed a 'friendly' meeting between a male leopard and a female with two young cubs. The adults greeted, rubbing heads and intertwining their tails, then moved off together. The female was in the process of leading her cubs to a kill, and later all four leopards lay up in the tree where the carcass had been stashed, taking it in turns to feed, while a hyena waited below for any titbits. There was no sign of aggression between the leopards, underlining the theory that the reaction of one individual to another depends very much on prior experience and specific circumstances, exhibiting a degree of flexibility that makes generalizations difficult. In this instance the male remained with the female and her cubs, sharing the kill for another day, while the hyena was eventually rewarded for its persistence when the entire ribcage fell to the ground.

Some of these interactions may have been prompted by the male's desire to obtain an easy meal, which would mirror the way male lions often parasitize kills made by lionesses within their pride territory as part of the price the females pay for the males' protecting them and their cubs from the dangers posed by outsiders. The Jakkalsdraai male seemed to make a point of tracking down females in his area, checking on their sexual status and feeding on any kills they might have made – this may well be the norm for territorial males. Males sometimes even leave a partially eaten carcass to go walkabout, something a female would rarely do. Tjellers was observed taking the Jakkalsdraai male on a wild-goose chase one evening when he was trying to accompany her as she led her cubs to where she had stashed her kill. This

Chui resting at the Cub Caves with Dark and Light when they were three or four months old. By this age the cubs were old enough to be led to kills, though when Chui made a small kill she often brought it back to their hiding place for them to feed on.

prompted her to move off in the opposite direction, leading the male around her territory until he gave up. Only then did Tjellers return to finish her meal in peace.

I am convinced that there is much still to be discovered about these enigmatic cats, and that with the help of new forms of tracking devices, night-vision binoculars, image intensifiers and infrared cameras, a far more complex world will be revealed of how leopards conduct their lives.

Taratibu and Mang'aa play-fighting. At five months Mang'aa (right) was already bigger and stronger than his sister and could dominate her in this kind of situation when play became rough.

Natural-Born Killers

Male leopards are able to monitor the sexual readiness of females in their territories by analysing their scent. All cats have an organ in the roof of their mouth known as the organ of Jacobsen, which has two pit-like openings behind the front incisors. When a male comes across the scent-mark left by a female he draws back his upper lip in a grimace, sucking in a stream of air that passes over the depressions, allowing the hormone content to be analysed. If the female is coming in to season he will follow her scent trail in the hopes of mating with her.

It is a rare and exciting experience to witness leopards mating, and we were fortunate to be able to film such an event during the first series of *Big Cat Diary*: we discovered Beauty with a male on a rocky hill overlooking the upper reaches of the Bila Shaka Lugga. A leopard in oestrus is a mixture of solicitousness and aggression, and her initial response to a male may be tempered or exacerbated by previous contacts. This may lead to a degree of conflict with the female turning and rebuffing the male each time he approaches. But that generally doesn't last long. Watching Beauty consorting with her mate, we got the impression that she was the one taking the initiative. It was almost comical at times to see the seductive manner in which she approached the male, moving rapidly towards him from her

resting place in the grass a few metres away. She paced around him, changing position so quickly that at first he looked somewhat bemused. I described the occasion in *Mara–Serengeti: A Photographer's Paradise*:

When we first discovered the mating couple they were secluded in a patch of thick croton bush on top of a rocky hill bordering the northern end of the Bila Shaka Lugga. The male was huge – he looked almost twice the size of Beauty – with a dark coat and floppy tip to his spotted tail. Beauty was in

the height of oestrus, and so hyped up that she could hardly keep still for more than a minute or so at a time. She slunk towards the male, whipping round and shoving her hindquarters provocatively in his face before sitting on his head for good measure, pushing up under his chin and nudging him into a sitting position. Then she darted forward and crouched, ears laid back, growling. No sooner had the male mounted her than he reached sharply forward and gaped across her neck,

Half-Tail making a flehmen face. This is the way all cats analyse scent, drawing an odour into their mouths and testing it.

Zawadi yawning. A leopard's long canines are used to grasp and kill its prey.

Beauty, aged six months, resting in a tree along the Ngorbop Lugga. She settled to the east of her natal home range, but continued to share part of the area with her mother.

towards us, the last of the light golden on her spotted coat.

Angie and I stayed with the courting couple until it was dark, hoping that we might hear them call. It was one of those evenings when the sun sets against inky-black clouds, casting deep shadows across the long golden grass. Every so often one of the leopards would sit up, or they would mate, moving closer and closer to where we had parked. We felt like voyeurs, deriving intense pleasure from such a rare moment, watching these two solitary creatures drawn together briefly, virtual strangers rubbing up against one another in the most intimate fashion."

Mating leopards show little interest in food, though like lions they will take advantage of any prey that wanders within range. On the one occasion that mating leopards were seen to make a kill, they abandoned their food before it was finished and resumed their meanderings. Other people who have observed leopards mating have commented on how the male often leaps to one side after ejaculating, sometimes vaulting right over the female's head in an attempt to avoid her turning and slapping him. Lionesses sometimes act in a similarly aggressive manner after mating, perhaps because a cat's penis has tiny, backward-pointing spines that are thought to help stimulate ovulation in some way, perhaps by roughening the wall of the vagina.

That was the first time I had seen Beauty for more than two and a half years. By then she was four years old, so there was a chance that she had already had one litter and was ready to mate again. But nobody had reported seeing her with cubs, so it was possible that she had yet to raise any. Once she became independent Beauty was never the same carefree, trusting leopard that she had been in the company of her mother. She came to resent the intrusion of vehicles into her life. It was all too apparent that she

exposing his long dagger-like canines. As Beauty rumbled – a low, deep growl – he let out a high-pitched gurgling noise, a most unexpected and extraordinary throaty explosion of stuttering, quite unlike the sound made by a mating lion.

A pattern quickly became apparent. Every 50 minutes or so, Beauty would initiate another bout of mating, the act itself lasting no more than ten seconds, with intervals of only a few minutes before another coupling,

repeated four or five times in all – then silence as both cats lay flat in the long grass, hidden from view. One evening a few weeks later we found the pair mating again. Beauty must have failed to conceive and come back into oestrus. They had been seen together in Leopard Gorge and by the time we arrived had moved to a hillside covered with long grass. The area was a minefield of concealed rocks, but we were able to inch forward; at one point Beauty came

wanted to be left alone and would charge any car that came too close – and many did. Beauty chose to retreat into that secret world that many leopards inhabit, unseen by humans for much of their lives. Some time later I was told that she had been seen with cubs, though I have never again been able to track her down myself. If she is still alive she would be ten years old – old by leopard standards.

Dale Hancock and Kim Wolhuter were able to observe an interesting sequence of events when Tjellers came into season some ten months after giving birth to her previous litter and mated with the Jakkalsdraai male. When the courting couple came across Tjellers' cubs, the two youngsters fled at the sounds of mating. Tjellers failed to conceive, perhaps because she was not yet ready to become a mother again or because the chances of a female conceiving are fairly poor – Bailey gives a figure of just 15 per cent for the likelihood that a female will become pregnant from any one mating session, mirroring the low conception rate – 20 per cent – reported for lions.

A month later Tjellers mated again with the same male, and again failed to conceive. These monthly mating sessions continued over the next few months and lasted for up to six days, until finally a second male was heard calling to the north-west. Tjellers almost immediately set off in his direction. The Jakkalsdraai male tried to head her off, prompting her to crouch down and hiss at him defensively. Little by little she managed to move towards the other male, with the Jakkalsdraai following her, until eventually she crossed out of her home range. They were now on the boundary of the Jakkalsdraai's territory and suddenly found themselves face to face with the Mlowathi male. Tjellers immediately acted submissively, though it didn't prevent the male from attacking her.

The Mlowathi male then chased the Jakkalsdraai back to his territory, both of them calling repeatedly. Tjellers followed

the Mlowathi male into his territory, though by now she was far from home. For as long as she remained with the male she would be safe from attack, but once she had finished mating she would have to negotiate a way home alone, hoping to avoid contact with any resident females in the area. This mating too proved unsuccessful, and a month later she mated with the Jakkalsdraai male again and produced a single cub. All this had taken nearly a year, by which time the cubs from her previous litter were 21 months old and capable of looking after themselves.

Research in India provides insights into the life of another solitary big cat, the tiger, indicating that fights between males are most likely to occur when a female is in oestrus and males transgress the normal limits of their territories in an attempt to mate. Male tigers have much shorter reproductive lives than females, anything from seven months to six years with an average of just under three years, half that of females. Male tigers who lost their territories within their first year of residency did not manage to sire any offspring – none that survived, at least.

In another study two female tigers bred successfully for many years until they were eventually ousted from their territories, and though they survived to the ages of 13½ and 15½ years respectively, neither managed to breed again having lost the security of a home range. It is evident that, as with leopards, a stable system of land tenure yields greater breeding success for territory-holders. Up to 90 per cent of tiger cubs in this study survived when there were no takeovers, but when resident males died or lost their territories, widespread infanticide reduced cub survival to 30 per cent. In Bandhavgarh, where the male tiger population is less numerous than in most other reserves, challenges are infrequent, and a male called Charger held a territory for ten years and lived to the age of 17 – far older than might otherwise have been expected.

When people first began to report incidents of infanticide among lions it was thought to be an aberrant form of behaviour. But it has since been reported in tigers and leopards, and can be viewed as normal – imperative even. Infanticide by a new male territory-holder helps to ensure that he has the best chance not only of siring cubs, but of remaining in the area long enough to provide a stable environment in which they can grow up: it takes a minimum of two years from conception for tigers and leopards to become independent. Infanticide simply speeds up the process of change, wiping the genetic slate clean by obliterating the offspring of the previous territory-holder, and in the process reducing competition for food from the offspring of other males.

Infanticide is found mainly among rodents and carnivores, but is also relatively common in many primate societies. Indian langurs and gorillas lose up to 30 per cent of their young to males impatient to breed, and losses of as high as 60 per cent have been reported in red howler monkeys in South America. The prevalence of infanticide seems to be exacerbated by the

Half-Tail coaxing Beauty from under a safari vehicle. Big cats in the Mara become so used to vehicles that they virtually ignore them.

Lions, being social, adopt a different strategy to rearing cubs from that employed by leopards and tigers. Male lions spend a considerable amount of time in the company of the lionesses in their pride (though this may vary from area to area), gaining food from any kills the lionesses make, and often remaining close to lionesses with cubs – their cubs – particularly when these are small and at their most vulnerable. This helps ensure that strange males do not have the opportunity to kill them. Leopards do not live like this. Instead of investing time and energy in staying close to a female and her cubs and possibly compromising her ability to hunt successfully, a male leopard spends most of his time – when not sleeping or resting – patrolling his territory, laying down a web of scent-marks and scrapes along its boundaries, as well as calling and at times making himself conspicuous to let any potential rivals know that the area is already under management. This means covering his territory on a regular basis, sometimes travelling 10 km (6 miles) or more in a night in an attempt to deter any rival from settling in the area. Even so, infanticide is a real threat for small cubs. Any time a territorial male dies or is displaced, the new territory-holder will certainly try to hunt down and kill any cubs too young to escape.

The elder of the Topi Plains males mating with Mama Lugga, one of the Marsh Lionesses, after taking over her pride.

long period of dependency of the young of these species and their need to remain constantly with their mothers, making it relatively easy for males to identify which females are not currently receptive to breeding. Under these circumstances it would make sense for a male to stay with any female with whom he has consorted to

The Topi Plains male guards Mama Lugga to prevent any rivals from approaching and mating with her.

protect his offspring against infanticide by new males – and to help deter any other predator from attacking his young. The fearsome canines of many monkeys probably evolved as weapons to intimidate rivals in the race to breed, with the added benefit of being highly effective as a defence against predators.

Whenever a male lion finds a female in season he immediately begins to follow her, staying within a metre or so to prevent any other male from gaining access to her. His coalition partners must wait their turn – sometimes after two or three days the first male loses interest in the female, enabling one of the others to mate with her. This seemingly promiscuous behaviour on the part of the female may be essential to the well-being of any cubs born to the pride after a takeover. If the males have mated with a number of different lionesses in the

pride and sometimes with the same female(s) as their coalition partners, none of them can be sure who has fathered any cubs that are born. This helps ensure that the males provide equal support in defending the cubs and do not try to kill them – they all act in a paternal way. In all probability every male lion who manages to take over a pride has been a cub-killer at some point in his life, and probably so have most male leopards – they have no option if they are to fulfil their sexual imperative and sire as many cubs as possible during their tenure as territory-holders.

I had seen male lions indulge in infanticide, but never thought I would encounter it with leopards. Then one morning towards the end of 1997 Angie and I witnessed just such an incident in Leopard Gorge. We were working on an American television series called *Wild*

Cubs from the Marsh pride trying to suckle from their mother on a termite mound.

Things, which was very much a forerunner of the 'actuality' style that *Big Cat Diary* was developing, relying on presenters to bring to life the excitement and wonder of spending time with wild animals in exotic locations. In July, when Zawadi was a year and a half old, Half-Tail had mated again, and in early October had given birth to her fifth litter. By this stage there was little or no contact between the two leopards, though their home ranges overlapped considerably. When Angie and I heard that Half-Tail had cubs we decided to head to the Mara with a *Wild Things* film crew.

On arrival we tracked down our friend Enoch Isanya, one of the driver-guides at Mara River Camp. Over the past few years Enoch had spent months at a time following Half-Tail and her various litters as a guide to Fritz Polking, who had recently written a book on the Mara's most famous leopard. The previous evening Enoch had seen Half-Tail carrying a tiny cub from one cave to another and felt certain that there was another cub in there as well. We were excited at the prospect of some excellent filming opportunities with both Half-Tail and Zawadi, who had been seen around Observation Hill 1km (⅔ mile) to the east of Leopard Gorge.

A ten-week-old cub playing with its mother's tail. Cubs love to play with their mother's tail – indeed, any twitching tail tip is irresistible.

The following morning we found Half-Tail in the gorge, relaxed as ever, pausing to spray her scent against the bumper of one of the vehicles, then using another as cover to scrutinize a herd of impalas. She moved carefully, checking for hares among the tangles of grass at the base of acacia trees that had been felled by passing elephants, sniffing and spraying bushes and boulders, leaving a scent trail that would tell other leopards she was in residence and that they should avoid the area.

That evening we were told that Half-Tail had killed a Thomson's gazelle on Observation Hill and had stashed it in a tree. But when we arrived at the spot the

following morning we found Zawadi feasting on the kill. Perhaps the driver had been mistaken and it had been the younger female all the time, or perhaps Zawadi had found her mother's kill and taken possession of it while she was preoccupied with suckling her new cubs back at the gorge. Leopards are not averse to scavenging, and as we have seen male leopards sometimes feed from a kill made by a female in his territory. But generally adult females give each other a wide berth, and stay close to a kill until it is finished.

The following morning we drove back to Leopard Gorge in the hope of finding Half-Tail, but none of us was prepared for what happened next. Our support vehicle had spotted a leopard in the gorge and called us on the radio. When we arrived we saw immediately that it wasn't Half-Tail. This leopard was shy and had a tail. In fact it was a young male with a pink nose and unmarked ears – he was in perfect condition. At first I thought it might be Mang'aa, Half-Tail's son, who was almost four years old by now and still occasionally seen in the area, though mostly further to the west. But this leopard was not as dark as Mang'aa, nor as relaxed around vehicles. He had a pale-coloured coat and certainly wasn't the male we had seen mating with Beauty the previous year, who we imagined had also fathered Half-Tail's latest litter.

Angie and I felt distinctly uneasy. The male looked nervous and was obviously in the process of investigating the area, almost certainly searching for where Half-Tail had hidden her cubs. Though the scent trail that Half-Tail had lain down around the gorge would serve to deter other adult females from using the area, her only defence against other males was the presence of a territorial male. Was this young male the new territory-holder? Had he managed to chase the older incumbent away, and was he now searching for mating opportunities of his own? Perhaps the territory-holder had been killed or died, opening the door to newcomers. To add to the mystery,

A young male leopard prowling around the entrance to Leopard Gorge, searching for Half-Tail's latest litter.

another vehicle found two dead bush hyrax, their fur partially plucked, lying on a rock at the base of the gorge near where Half-Tail's cubs were hidden. Had she sensed the presence of the male earlier in the morning and quickly moved away, abandoning her meal?

Every so often the young male paused to sniff the rocks, silently continuing his search, wary perhaps of a surprise encounter with the old female. Suddenly he dropped down behind one of the boulders and disappeared into a clump of long grass shielding the mouth of a cave. Moments later he reappeared with a tiny cub in his mouth, clasping it around the waist like a cat with a mouse. There was blood on the neck of the lifeless body. He dropped the cub behind the rock face, then entered the cave again and re-emerged with a second cub. Later he checked the cave for a third time, but there were no more cubs for him to kill. We imagined he ate the little corpses before continuing along the top of the gorge.

We spotted Half-Tail resting in a tree about 200m (⅛ mile) away. Had she seen the male prowling around the top of the gorge?

She certainly must have seen the two young lions that appeared on the scene an hour or so later. The male leopard did and, after watching them approach for a while, wisely slunk away.

Later, Half-Tail returned to the gorge. She could obviously smell the male long before she reached the place where she had left her cubs. At one point she leapt aside

as she crept around the rocks, appearing fearful. She did not enter the cave but, having carefully sniffed around the vicinity, continued towards a giant fig tree that stands like a sentinel above the west rim of the gorge. What she didn't realize was that the male leopard had seen her coming and was crouching among the rocks. A violent confrontation must then have taken place, because the next thing we saw was Half-Tail bounding up the trunk of the fig tree, taking refuge among the topmost branches. The male chased after her, and before I had time to move the vehicle one of the leopards toppled backwards out of the tree in a shower of leaves and twigs – a fall of more than 6m (20ft). Surely it must have been Half-Tail. But no – it was Half-Tail who climbed down the broad trunk of the fig tree, hissing out a warning to the male to move on. We gave a silent cheer for the gutsy female as the young male skulked off, followed at a distance by Half-Tail, limping on a bloodied forepaw.

Half-Tail resting in a tree within view of Leopard Gorge, a few hundred metres from where the male was killing her cubs. It is hard for a female to challenge a male – they are so much bigger and stronger.

The young male emerges with one of the cubs which he had already bitten in the neck and killed. Both cubs were killed in this fashion and probably eaten.

We stayed with Half-Tail for most of the rest of the day. She lay among the blackened stubble on the flank of the gorge, spittle drooling from her lips. She seemed anxious and distressed, but made no attempt to return to the place where she had last left her cubs, as if she knew that they had gone.

The father of Half-Tail's cubs would certainly have vigorously contested the presence of this young adult male, fighting if necessary to drive him away. But a male's territory is large, and he can't be everywhere at once. Other males are bound to slip through at times, and young ones wander widely when searching for a place to settle. Sooner or later, every territory-holder must face the challenge posed by younger, fitter males. Killing cubs is a natural part of the cycle by which males win and lose the rights to a breeding territory. If ever a creature was designed to sniff out the place where a mother leopard has hidden her cubs, it is another leopard.

A few weeks later a friend reported seeing Half-Tail mating with a large male in a patch of forest just above the spring that feeds Musiara Marsh. At one point she followed him across the Mara River, but returned a day or so later. By the time we began filming the second series of *Big Cat Diary* in early September 1998, she had given birth to her sixth litter and had moved further north, forced perhaps to relinquish Leopard Gorge and Fig Tree Ridge to Zawadi.

If the young male who had killed Half-Tail's previous litter did succeed in establishing himself in the area, he certainly wasn't the only one to have access to Fig Tree Ridge and Leopard Gorge: during the filming of our third series in 2000 we were fortunate to be able to catch glimpses of another adult male, and this one was unmistakable. Droopy Jaw, as he became known, was distinguished by an old injury or deformity to his lower jaw that had left the front half (between his back teeth and

Wildbeest streaming over the ridge leading to Musiara Marsh. They can always find water here during the dry season, though the Marsh Lions regularly lie in wait for them among the reedbeds.

his canines) drooping whenever his mouth was ajar. I doubt if he would have lived had he been born with such a pronounced deformity, so perhaps a zebra foal had lashed out and kicked him as he attempted to pull it down, and he had somehow survived while it healed. One thing was not in dispute – he was in perfect health now, proving just how resourceful and tough leopards are: the injury didn't prevent him from killing or eating.

On one occasion we filmed Droopy Jaw ambushing a wildebeest calf in Leopard Gorge. He was a wily character, waiting until he spotted a calf and then rushing to intercept the herd as it picked its way down a narrow pathway, knowing exactly the right moment to launch his charge up the slope. It was noticeable studying the videotape later that he had to maintain his grip on the calf's throat for longer than one might otherwise have expected, presumably because he couldn't bring his lower canines into play to apply the normal vice-like stranglehold to its full extent. He was seen successfully adopting the same strategy on a number of occasions to kill wildebeest calves, though the hyenas sometimes managed to steal his partially eaten meals before he could drag the remains into a tree.

If in fact Droopy Jaw was the new territory-holder, Zawadi was highly suspicious of his intentions. We saw her engaging him in a violent cat-fight one morning when he surprised her with Safi, who was then a year old: he suddenly dropped from his hiding place in the dense crown of a tree on Moses Rock and confronted mother and daughter. This made me suspect that Safi was not his cub – or perhaps he was checking if Zawadi was ready to mate. But Zawadi was taking no chances and briefly fought with Droopy Jaw, then moved parallel to him, blocking his path to give Safi time to escape. Neither adult seemed to want to risk unnecessary injury, and after two such scraps involving lots of grunting and snarling, Zawadi forced the male to move on. She then back-

Zawadi resting on a termite mound near Moses Rock. She still returns to Leopard Gorge and Fig Tree Ridge, where she was born, to have her own cubs.

tracked to the place where Safi had disappeared, and spent the rest of the day in a state of some anxiety. We waited with her. As the sky darkened she called repeatedly – not the loud, long-distance contact call, but the guttural 'arragh-grunt'. Eventually, having hidden herself away in a thicket, Safi reappeared and joined her mother.

A few days later we filmed Zawadi calling, perched conspicuously on top of a termite mound, and wondered if she was looking for her daughter or trying to locate a mate. I was mesmerized to see Zawadi making her contact call at such close range – she was only metres from our vehicle. Just as a lion puts maximum effort into roaring, so too does a leopard, lowering its head and stretching out its neck, forcing the air bellows-like from its lungs, sides heaving with the effort. Each time Zawadi finished a series of eight or ten calls, she listened intently. She obviously expected or hoped for an answer, or for Safi to find her. It was around this time that we saw Safi scent-mark for the first time, so perhaps this was an indication that she intended to try to stay on in the area.

There was no sign of Droopy Jaw while we were working on series four, though that didn't mean that he wasn't still in the area. But during the last few weeks of filming we managed to track down another adult male. One of our game-spotters had caught sight of a large male leopard hiding in a patch of forest to the east of Leopard Gorge. A week earlier we had finally caught up with Safi again in this same area. She was now three years old and ready to become a mother herself, but she had never been as comfortable with vehicles as Zawadi and was only occasionally seen.

When I arrived at the place where the male was hidden, I could just make out part of his long spotted tail and a patch of coat among the dense foliage of a tree. In situations like this you are left wondering how on earth anyone ever finds a leopard, and thinking of the countless times you

Zawadi and Safi resting on a termite mound. At the time of writing, Safi is in her fourth year. She shares part of her mother's home range and should soon give birth to her first litter of cubs.

must have driven past one, searching, searching, yet finding nothing to suggest that the leopard was there all the time, watching you from its hiding place as you continued on your way.

Moments later the leopard suddenly peered out at us from the canopy before hurrying down the tree and disappearing from view. That was the last we would see of him, I thought – but then a mother warthog emerged from her burrow at the edge of the lugga and trotted straight towards where the leopard must have been watching. The male couldn't resist the chance of a kill and reappeared, even though he looked as if he had already eaten a huge meal. But the warthog was having none of it – turning at the last minute and confronting the male, she stopped him in his tracks and forced him to abandon the hunt. This time I got a good look at him through my binoculars. The minute I had him in my sights I knew that it was the male that Angie and I had watched kill Half-Tail's cubs in Leopard Gorge, almost exactly five years earlier. He had that same russet-ginger coat and dog-like face. More importantly, when I leafed through the identification album that our son David had compiled for us, there he was – the same spot pattern – everything matched.

It was ironic to think that this was probably the male who had recently been seen mating with Safi, Half-Tail's grand-daughter. Had he been displaced by Droopy Jaw or did the two males' territories overlap? With males being so difficult to observe I couldn't be sure if just one male patrolled Half-Tail's old home range and also included the overlapping home ranges of her daughters Beauty and Zawadi within his territory, an area of more than 60 km² (22 sq. miles). It was certainly possible. That is the fascination in trying to follow the lives of these beautiful, enigmatic creatures. There are always new questions to try to answer.

Zawadi searching for prey from the top of an acacia tree. It is amazing how leopards are able to clamber around in these trees without constantly getting thorns in their feet.

The World of Cats

The leopard is a solitary and secretive inhabitant of thickets, an animal of darkness. These characteristics have been both its salvation and its doom. By remaining out of sight, it has been able to survive near dense human habitation, areas from which other large cats have long vanished. But, whereas the lion invokes good will by displaying its indolent, seemingly carefree nature, the leopard conveys visions of a nocturnal marauder, of a cold, detached personality. Friendliness leads to friendliness. By virtue of its being so withdrawn the leopard has received little sympathy from man and now desperately needs it. Persecuted for its lovely hide, it maintains only a precarious foothold where it was formerly abundant. Every woman who needs to satisfy her vanity with a leopard-skin coat should first contemplate the exquisite beauty of this cat in repose.

George Schaller
Serengeti: Kingdom of Predators

The lion, tiger, and leopard are no longer simply emblems on flags and signet rings. They are flesh-and-blood creatures with a past and a present, as are the secretive mountain lion and jaguar of the Americas. Myths have been replaced with fact. We know what diseases lions and leopards suffer from, what parasites infect them, and we can supplement the findings of field studies with a wealth of information gleaned from research on cats in zoos and safari parks. There is even a Cat Specialist Group, part of the Species Survival Commission (SSC) of the World Conservation Union (IUCN), which helps to monitor the status of cats worldwide and publishes a twice-yearly newsletter, *Cat News*.

Radio-telemetry and its even more modern cousins the satellite collar and computer-chip implants mean that cats, and many other animals from polar bears to humpback whales, can now be tracked as they journey over vast areas – 1000km (625 miles) or more in the case of whales. Elsewhere camera traps, triggered automatically by the subject treading on a pressure pad or breaking an infrared beam, have proved highly successful in establishing the numbers of tigers and jaguars in forest reserves where it is difficult to radio-track individuals. Such traps would be a relatively cost-effective way of obtaining data on leopard densities in Africa's tropical rainforests, where little is known about their numbers.

Trying to come up with realistic figures for the world's total leopard population has proved difficult. Nobody knows how many leopards exist in most areas where they are protected, let alone on private land or country by country. Ironically the leopard is abundant enough to be considered a pest in some parts of its range, although it is critically endangered in others. This has prompted heated debate between those who favour seeing it utilized, either as a hunting trophy or for trade in its spotted coat, and those who remind us that before these activities were banned they had a serious impact on many leopard populations. When I arrived in Africa in 1974 all leopards were listed as vulnerable

Safi and her brother at three months old. Leopard cubs are very playful, amusing themselves for hours while their mother is away hunting or patrolling her range.

Translocating giraffes from a game ranch in Namibia to a sanctuary in South Africa. Southern African countries apply a 'use it or lose it' policy to game management on private land, and game-ranching and trophy-hunting are lucrative industries

by the IUCN and continued to be so until I published my first book, *The Marsh Lions*, in 1982, by which time a new generation of leopards was just beginning to show itself. During this period all international trade in leopards was banned. There is no question that the depredations of the skin trade put the worldwide leopard population at risk – in 1969 it was estimated that 50,000 leopards were killed every year in Africa alone to supply the fur trade.

Since 1983, the Central African Republic, Ethiopia, Kenya (where hunting has been banned since 1977), Tanzania, Malawi, Zambia, Zimbabwe, Botswana, Mozambique, Namibia and South Africa have all been entitled to provide export quotas for leopards hunted as trophies, and as such the trophies may be imported into the United States. However, leopards are still classified by the United States as endangered throughout the rest of their historic range – the remainder of Africa, Asia Minor, India, South-East Asia, China, Malaya and Indonesia – and commercial trade in all leopard products is banned under Appendix 1 of the Convention on the International Trade in Endangered Species

(CITES). (Appendix 1 lists animals 'that are threatened with extinction and that are or may be affected by international commercial trade'.) Thankfully the trade in leopard skins experienced a remarkable decline in the 1970s, prompted in part by a highly effective advertising campaign that helped to make wearing a leopard-skin coat in public an anathema. But recently there has been a worrying trend among the young rich to sanction the wearing of a fur coat as chic, and certain countries such as Germany, Japan and parts of South America have never lost their appetite for this particular 'fashion'. The memorable '70s catchphrase 'It takes the skins of 20 dumb animals to make a fur coat, but only one dumb bitch to wear it' remains etched in my consciousness.

There are people who argue that hunting and trade are justifiable on the basis that they can serve conservation efforts by generating revenue from wildlife. Tanzania, for example, currently earns more foreign exchange from trophy-hunting than from wildlife-based tourism. And in many parts of Africa the sale of skins of leopards who had killed livestock and were then shot,

provided a degree of compensation for the livestock owners. Loss of this form of recompense prompted some ranchers to try to eradicate all predators. But the re-opening of trade is always likely to pose serious problems for the authorities. This has certainly proved the case with ivory. How do you control consumptive utilization so that the age-old abuses of the system don't come back to haunt you, particularly in countries in East and southern Africa where a well-developed tourist industry thrives on the ability to show visitors big cats? Wildlife-based tourism is still the mainstay of Kenya's conservation ethos, while most southern African countries prefer to follow the 'use it or lose it' philosophy, where game-ranching and trophy-hunting compete with wildlife tourism for the tourist dollar.

A compromise is probably the only way forward, and the hunting of leopards as trophies – distasteful as it may be – may continue to be viewed as sound management practice, provided proper quotas are established and honoured. But opening up the trade in skins would seem to be asking for trouble.

In the 1970s South Africa was believed to have the greatest number of fur dealers in Africa and acted as a convenient conduit to world markets for skins from elsewhere on the continent. Many of the skins were obtained illegally, with prices averaging $250–300 between 1966 and 1972, with a high of $680. In his book *The African Leopard*, Ted Bailey maintains that 'any relaxation of existing regulations or amendments that might create loopholes in those regulations should be considered with extreme caution; such loopholes in those regulations might once again trigger a dramatic increase in the numbers of leopards illegally killed for their skins.'

Supporters of consumptive utilization on a sustainable basis might disagree. Dr Anthony Hall-Martin, Director: Research and Development of the National Parks Board of South Africa, says, 'The only really honest argument against the harvesting of African leopard skins is the possibility that an open market may conceivably represent a threat to leopards in Asia – where they are threatened.' Hall-Martin feels that under the right circumstances, and if rigorously controlled, trophy-hunting should still be permitted. Referring to southern African countries he says, 'In these arid southern savannas, the hunting industry has evolved into a paying partner of the cattle industry. One of the prizes remains the leopard, Africa's ultimate spotted cat, and a trophy leopard will add up to US$4,000 on top of daily rates. This ends up giving the leopard a significant cash value. There is considerable incentive, therefore, to maintain breeding populations of leopards to service the hunting industry. The extermination of leopards as a result of trophy-hunting is most unlikely.'

If this attitude is going to prevail, quotas based on scientific studies will be needed to ensure that areas are not overhunted, and both quotas and ethical hunting practices will have to be rigorously enforced. For example, taking too many adult male leopards year after year from the same area may encourage a continual influx of new males, making it difficult for resident females to breed successfully. Loss of established territory-holders opens the door to newcomers eager to begin breeding – and they are liable to kill any young cubs.

Another worry arises from the barbaric practices that have crept into the hunting industry in recent times. A business known as canned hunting has sprung up in certain southern African countries, notably South Africa, where in particular lions – not wild lions, but lions bred in captivity – are released into large enclosures for trophy-hunting purposes. In one well-publicized incident the lion was drugged beforehand to make the job of killing it as easy as possible for the client. To preserve the 'trophy', the lion sometimes endures an agonizing death, shot in the back or abdomen to ensure that the head and

mane are undamaged, rather than being dispatched with a brain shot. To add to this, leopards are sometimes hunted with dogs, chased until they take refuge in a tree and then shot either with a rifle or with bows and arrows. The popularity of this kind of leopard-hunting has perhaps been increased by the ban on hunting mountain lions with dogs in the United States. Fortunately, an international outcry prompted by an exposé on television and in the print media is leading to these kinds of practices being banned in South Africa.

The expansion of the human population and its livestock over vast parts of Africa's woodlands and savannas is the greatest threat to both leopards and lions, particularly due to the loss of their natural prey. Ranchers often eliminate wild game in an attempt to reduce competition for valuable grazing and browse, leaving large predators little choice but to kill stock. The fact that leopards are creatures of habit, frequenting well-used paths and scent-posts, makes individuals easier to eradicate than might be thought. Even a creature as

adept at living close to humans as the leopard has little chance of survival once it incurs man's wrath and is faced with a lethal combination of traps, poison (organochlorine pesticides are a cheap and easily available poison) and guns.

Though we can be certain that there are many more leopards in Africa than the combined total for lions (maximum of 30,000, possibly as few as 20,000) and cheetahs (12–15,000) – and that as a species it is not currently in danger of extinction – various attempts to estimate how many leopards survive in the wild have failed to establish an accurate figure. Under intense lobbying from the powerful trophy-hunting industry, which was anxious to see the leopard downlisted as an endangered species, in 1987 CITES commissioned two scientists to provide population estimates for the 38 African countries where leopards were still known to exist. By then I had written *The Leopard's Tale* and was working in the Serengeti on a book on wild dogs. I met the two scientists concerned – Rowan Martin of the Zimbabwe Department of

Elephants enjoying a mud wallow at the spring feeding Musiara Marsh.
Mud helps elephants to keep cool and is a perfect skin conditioner.

National Parks and Wildlife Management and Tom de Meulenaer, a Belgian biologist – somewhere out in the vastness of the short-grass plains. They had developed a computer model to help them answer the question that everyone was asking. By feeding in information on rainfall and habitat country by country, they felt it should be possible to calculate the abundance of suitable prey, and from that extrapolate the number of leopards each area could sustain. By this process they estimated the leopard population for sub-Saharan Africa to be 714,105. But when they presented their findings to the Secretariat of CITES, who in turn asked for comments from experts, it caused a furore. One of the biggest weaknesses of the study

was that it had been apparent for some time that certain areas which had previously supported healthy leopard populations no longer did so, and Martin and de Meulenaer's calculations did not take this into account. If the figure of 700,000 were true, it would have been sufficient to warrant moving the leopard from the endangered list to threatened, prompting the easing of protective measures such as the international ban on trade in leopard skins.

Fortunately, the general consensus among field biologists who had studied leopards in Africa was that there might be less than half the number that Martin and de Meulenaer suggested – 350,000 leopards – leading CITES to reject any

change in protective measures for the species. Interestingly, Viv Wilson, who studied duikers in the Central African Republic, which has always been thought to represent good leopard habitat, maintained that in this particular instance 'there was no relationship whatsoever between leopard densities, habitat and rainfall. The rainfall in the area is at least 1,524mm (60in) a year; there are hundreds of square kilometres of ideal leopard habitat, large numbers of blue duiker; and yet leopard numbers are very low.' The reason for the paucity of leopards was that they had been virtually exterminated many years earlier and were only just beginning to recover.

In South Africa, where Martin and de Meulenaer gave an estimate of 23,472

Half-Tail resting in a giant fig tree along Fig Tree Ridge. A leopard without cubs spends much of the day resting and sleeping, waiting until it is cool before setting off to hunt or patrol its home range.

leopards, one reviewer suggested that fewer than 3,000 leopards survived, and Ted Bailey felt that even this figure could be too high, taking into account that his estimate for the vast protected area of the Kruger National Park was only about 700.

There is no doubt that there are still many leopards in Africa: in some areas they are extremely common. But equally there is no question that their range is shrinking worldwide, with the vast majority occurring in sub-Saharan Africa. The fact that so many subspecies have been described over the years attests both to how wide-ranging the leopard is and to how fragmented and isolated some of the populations have become. They are still found scattered across North Africa, Arabia and through Central Asia to the Far East. But while African and South Asian leopards are numerous, the other subspecies occur in small or geographically isolated populations, most of which are at risk.

Little is known about the status of the leopard in much of Asia. We do know that by the mid-1970s it was still abundant in the larger forests of India and Nepal and in the Alborz Mountains of Iran, and that it was present in the Karchat Hills of Pakistan. Its numbers have been greatly reduced throughout China, and in Sri Lanka they are on the decline outside parks and reserves. The Barbary leopard of North Africa clings on in the Central Atlas Mountains and forests of Oulmes in Morocco, but is separated from other leopard populations by hundreds or perhaps thousands of kilometres, and the Zanzibar leopard *Panthera pardus adersi* is almost certainly extinct. The Anatolian leopard is on the brink, with only a few scattered individuals recorded in south-western Turkey, and leopards in the deserts of southern Israel are faring little better. The most northern subspecies, the Amur or Far Eastern leopard (also known as the Korean leopard), *P. p. japonensis*, is now largely confined to several reserves in North Korea and the Maritime Territory of Russia

Chui with a young impala at dawn, waiting for hyenas to retire to a shady spot, so she can carry her kill back to her cubs.

and numbers fewer than 100 individuals. That means that there are fewer Amur leopards in the wild than in the world's zoos. The largest single population numbers about 30 and a recovery plan awaits the support of federal and regional governments in China and Russia.

The struggle of isolated leopard populations to survive is illustrated by recent attempts to protect what is probably physically the smallest of all leopard subspecies, *Panthera pardus nimr*, the Arabian leopard – or nimr, as it is known locally. The Arabian leopard once occurred throughout the mountains of southern Arabia, where its small size and pale coat with small, widely spaced spots are adaptations to the bare, rocky areas in which it lives. It is now highly endangered due to hunting and loss of habitat to livestock, and by 1990 had become locally extinct in most areas, mainly due to persecution by man. It still occurs in Saudi Arabia, Yemen, Oman and possibly the United Arab Emirates, though the distribution is scattered around the edges

of the Arabian peninsula, with a remnant population thought to exist on the eastern shore of the Dead Sea and in the Negev Desert. Genetic studies have resulted in a proposal that the Arabian leopard should be grouped with seven other subspecies in western Asia as *Panthera pardus saxicolor*, the North Persian leopard. However, area specialists maintain that the Arabian leopard is distinctive, and in the light of new genetic findings its subspecies status has been restored on the basis that populations 'appear to have been isolated for quite a long time, accumulating multiple diagnostic sites that distinguish it from any other subspecies'.

Whatever its classification, it is certain that the Arabian leopard faces a litany of woes, many of which feature on the résumés of other vulnerable cat species: loss of natural prey due to hunting and competition from livestock for grazing; dwindling habitat due to the spread of settlements, tree-cutting and road-building. Add to this the value of the leopard as a hunting trophy or for the price of its skin, as well as the antipathy of man to predators in general, and you have an animal that is trapped, shot and poisoned at every opportunity. Estimates of its surviving population range from around 80 to 250 individuals, with the Yemen home to the bulk of them – though this is probably no more than a good guess. CITES rates the Arabian leopard as Critically Endangered, a status it shares with the Amur and Anatolian subspecies.

The priority for those concerned with the survival of the Arabian leopard is to get base-line information on its distribution and ecology; so far only Oman has a field programme in place using camera traps and satellite telemetry. Photographing the last Arabian leopards has been the ambition of David Willis, a talented Australian artist living in Oman with whom Angie and I became friends during his many visits to the Masai Mara. Like us, David and his family are passionate about wildlife and loved nothing better than to try to catch up with Half-Tail or one of her offspring. David had told me about his quest to photograph the Arabian leopard, a task that made my attempts to record the lives of these secretive creatures in the Mara pale by

Honey with a cub aged three or four months. A hyena killed one of this cub's brothers in a dispute at a kill – the young cheetah did not move away fast enough when challenged.

Lionesses often form a crèche of similar-aged cubs, the most efficient way to raise them.

comparison. His search began in 1991, a year or so after Half-Tail made her first appearance along Fig Tree Ridge and Leopard Gorge. David knew that the Arabian leopard had all but disappeared from the north of Oman, and decided to concentrate his efforts in the high mountain known as Jabal Samhan, one of the most remote areas in the country, where in 1985 four leopards had been trapped to help establish the first captive-breeding centre for Omani mammals. Years later these same animals were used to support a second captive-breeding programme in the Emirate of Sharjah.

On his first week-long safari to Jabal Samhan, David saw ibex, fox and hyrax – his quarry's prey – but no leopard. But he did see signs – scrapes and droppings –

prompting him to return to Jabal Samhan each winter for the next four years. Realizing that photographing a leopard using ordinary techniques was almost impossible, David decided to adopt the methods employed by field biologist Rodney Jackson with snow leopards in the Himalayas. Jackson had finally captured a snow leopard on film using a camera trap activated by a pressure plate. David, ever resourceful and innovative, set about making his own camera trap with solar-powered flash, and installed it on an ibex trail in early 1995. When he retrieved the film three months later he had seven photos of leopards.

David was then joined by biologist Andrew Spalton, who used camera traps and examined leopard scats to try to estimate how many leopards there were, where they moved, what they fed on and if they were breeding successfully. The area they had chosen for their study comprised a system of deep, dry gorges or wadis that twisted and turned through the high mountains, intersected by ancient pathways used since pre-Islamic times by camel caravans that came in search of the much-prized Arabian frankincense – the resin of the *Boswellia sacra* tree. Conditions here are extreme, the land high, hot (in excess of 45°C/113°F in summer) and hyper-arid: by 1995 there had been no rain for six years.

On their second trip together in 1997, Spalton and Willis covered 200km (120 miles) of trails and wadi beds in their search for leopards and suitable sites for camera traps. Occasionally they found scrapes, often containing scats, located under overhangs or at prominent points on trails, left by leopards as a way of marking their home ranges or territories. By analysing hairs in the scats they were able (with help from researchers at the University of Aberdeen) to confirm that the leopards were preying on Nubian ibex, rock hyrax, Arabian gazelle, porcupine and Arabian red-legged partridge. This confirmed the general assumption that

Leopards merge with dappled light so effectively that they can be almost impossible to spot until they move.

leopards prefer to prey on medium-sized ungulates, taking smaller prey to supplement their diet when necessary. Much to their relief, Spalton and Willis found no sign in the scats of camel or goat remains – the domestic stock kept by the local people.

Spalton mounted his camera traps (using infrared beams as a trigger) in old ammunition boxes to prevent loss or damage to his equipment being caused by leopards rubbing their cheeks against the

traps as a form of scent-marking or by striped hyenas chewing the infrared transmitter units. Over the next three years Spalton, often with Willis, hiked into Jabal Samhan every two to three months to service the camera traps. The fact that they rarely got more than one shot per camera per month indicated that leopards were present in low numbers and lived in very large home ranges, so that an individual patrolling its territory passed a given spot only rarely. However, the same

Zawadi on the alert for prey – note the row of five distinct spots below her right eye, making her easy to identify.

camera had sometimes taken pictures of both males and females, leading Spalton to deduce that the two sexes occupied overlapping home ranges and avoided one another by using common routes at different times. When Spalton finally removed the traps in November 2000 he had lost cameras to hyenas, rainfall and the effects of monsoon cloud, but had captured more than 200 photographs of his elusive quarry. Not once had he actually seen a leopard.

Buoyed by his success, Spalton got permission to fit global positioning system (GPS) collars, which employ satellites to fix each collared leopard's position. It took seven weeks to capture four leopards (and an Arabian wolf), with a further two leopards caught in early 2002. The smallest, a female, weighed just 17kg (37lb), while the largest was a male of 33 kg (73lb) – nearly double the weight of the female, but still only half that of a full-grown African male. Spalton found that in general the Arabian leopard grows no bigger than 1.3m (4ft 3in) in length from head to tail base, whereas African leopards reach 1.8 m (5ft 10in). The GPS collars weighed 300g (just over 10oz) and were programmed to drop off some months later, allowing location data to be downloaded.

For the moment leopards in the Jabal Samhan Nature Reserve and its southern escarpment seem secure, with a team of rangers patrolling the reserve; conflict with local people is minimal. The hunting and capture of leopards is illegal in Oman, though the collapse of the reintroduced Arabian oryx population in the late 1990s has proved a salutary lesson, which should help to ensure that nothing is taken for granted.

In recent years the main focus of leopard conservation in the Arabian region has been in fostering a captive-breeding programme to act as a safeguard for a viable wild population. But as Andrew Spalton says, 'In Oman, in situ conservation efforts must carry on – for once the leopard has gone from the wild, there will be no return.' By the time the Breeding Centre for Endangered Arabian Wildlife was founded by Sheikh Sultan bin Mohammed al Qassimi, Ruler of Sharjah, in 1996, the population of Arabian leopards had already dipped well below the recommended threshold for a captive-breeding programme to be implemented. After long negotiations seven leopards which had been held in captivity in the Yemen for several years were included in the programme, and by the end of 2001 the project totalled 33 leopards (15 males and 18 females), of which half were wild-caught animals to help boost genetic variability. In the Yemen private collectors are willing to pay huge sums of money for a live leopard, and there are a considerable number of such collectors within the Arabian region, raising further anxiety over the wild population, even though such trade is illegal in all the countries concerned.

Once a population drops below a certain level things can become critical, not least because of the effect of inbreeding. One such population, the subspecies *Panthera pardus jarvisi*, was identified in the Judaean Desert and Negev Hills of Israel. In this instance the population had become so unbalanced that there were too many males competing for breeding rights with too few females. Competition among the males was so intense that they continually killed any offspring, and in one instance a male called Hordos killed his mother's two three-month-old cubs. He then mated with his mother and she produced a single male cub which was in turn killed by Hordos' father.

Chui with Light and Dark, providing tourists with the opportunity of a lifetime to watch a mother leopard and her cubs.

In fact both females in this population mated with their own sons, and when one died all the adult males were competing for breeding rights with one female. Between 1984 and 1989, not one cub survived to adulthood, primarily due to the impact of infanticide.

The extreme pressure on this small population was also evident in other ways. An adult female, defeated in a fight with a younger rival, was intimidated into relinquishing most of her territory and moving out with her young son. This older female was seen some time later expelling her nine-month-old daughter from her natal home range. After she became independent the daughter temporarily assumed a substantial part of her mother's range, but was then chased away again by her mother and was never seen in the Judaean Desert again. This highlights the difficulties that small isolated populations face. Denied adequate space and a stable population, the chances of individuals breeding successfully are greatly reduced, leading to an increase in infanticide and inbreeding. Youngsters may be driven away by their mother, long before they are really able to fend for themselves. All these factors combine to produce a precipitous decline in the population.

The Sri Lankan leopard *Panthera pardus kotiya* is another subspecies that has only recently begun to be studied. At the

Zawadi's first litter. Safi (right) is nearing maturity at the time of writing, but her brother was killed by lions when he was six months old.

Zawadi stretching and yawning – typical of a leopard about to become active – at dusk along Leopard Gorge.

beginning of the 20th century the leopard was widespread throughout Sri Lanka (or Ceylon as it then was), and even though the forest cover has since been reduced by more than half, leopards still occur in most of the national parks and in many areas where large tracts of forest and scrub jungle remain. Though no proper census has ever taken place, estimates range from 300–600 leopards, based on prey densities for particular habitats. I first became aware of Sri Lanka's leopard population years ago because the cats were often active during the daytime, making it the perfect area to try to photograph them. As the top predator on the island, leopards do not suffer from competition with tigers, lions or hyenas, and so are free to roam at will, day or night. Though there are scavengers such as sloth bears, mugger crocodiles, wild boars, jackals, mongooses and monitor lizards, these rarely seem to pose a problem, and leopards usually drag kills away from roads and into thick cover, rather than needing to store them in trees. The Sri Lankan leopard is said to be generally larger than other leopards, and to tackle larger prey, perhaps partly due to this lack of

competition from other predators. Its preferred prey is the chital or spotted deer, but it will sometimes tackle almost full-grown buffaloes, as well as small animals such as hares and rats, birds, monitor lizards, pangolins and porcupines.

Studies in Yala National Park suggest that female leopards in Sri Lanka have very small home ranges with considerable overlap, and they are said to be 'more social and tolerant of each other' than leopards observed elsewhere. Smaller home ranges may be related to the plentiful supply of food and the absence of other large predators, allowing the leopards to exist at higher densities. As reported for other leopard populations, males sometimes scavenge from kills made by females, and in one instance a large male fed from a female's kill in her presence and allowed her cub to feed alongside him. Of concern are reports of increasing numbers of leopard skins being seized around Yala and other parts of Sri Lanka, coupled with the demand for leopard bone – a substitute for tiger bone in traditional medicine. Under-funded and under-staffed, the Department of Wildlife struggles to offer adequate protection to the remaining leopards, and poachers rarely receive heavy penalties, often justifying their actions on the grounds that they are protecting their livestock. As everywhere, loss and fragmentation of the leopard's habitat point to an uncertain future, and without detailed scientific research it is impossible to offer proper management.

Angie and I returned to the Mara in early 2003, just before finishing this book. In the intervening months, our friend Paul Goldstein had sent us photographs of two of the leading characters from past series of *Big Cat Diary*. One of them was Amber's daughter Kike, who until now had failed to raise any cubs. Twice she had given birth along the Bila Shaka Lugga, and on both occasions the Marsh Pride had found the den and killed her cubs when they were just

a few weeks old. Kike gave birth for the third time in mid-December 2002, again choosing the Bila Shaka Lugga as a den site. Paul had counted four cubs, and Kike was fortunate in that the Mara had been receiving plenty of rain – not only was the grass long by the time she gave birth, but the soggy conditions prompted the Marsh Pride, who appeared to be prospering, to abandon the heartland of their territory temporarily, following the herds of topis and zebras to the higher ground further east. By the time we saw Kike she had lost one of her cubs, which were now four and a half months old, and had moved with them to an area where we had so often seen her in the past, between Mara Intrepids Camp and Rhino Ridge. Perhaps now that the young cheetahs were old enough to follow their mother they might have a better chance of surviving.

Paul also sent me a photograph of a leopard he had seen close to Leopard Gorge. It was Zawadi's daughter Safi, whom I have yet to see as an adult. As for Zawadi, she was found mating with a shy male at the entrance to Leopard Gorge in late February, and a few days later was spotted around Moses Rock, one of her favourite locations since Half-Tail died and left the area vacant. With a fifth series of *Big Cat Diary* planned for later this year, we are hopeful that by then she will be accompanied by her fifth litter. Zawadi is true to her name, which means gift in Swahili – just as her mother Half-Tail before her had been a gift to everyone who wanted to see wild leopards.

I have often thought about Half-Tail while writing this book, and Angie and I agree that she was a unique character, a wild animal blessed – from our perspective at least – with a temperament that allowed her to accommodate the endless procession of vehicles that searched for her each day in their hope of seeing a leopard. True, everyone wants to see lions and cheetahs too, but finding a leopard adds a different element to a game drive, something

Zawadi with Safi, aged about three months, in early 2000. Leopard cubs start to follow their mother from the age of about eight weeks.

indescribably exciting, the cat of cats. Half-Tail allowed us to indulge that moment of discovery, the knowledge that we were in the presence of a creature whose essence is sublime. Gone were the years of fleeting glimpses of a spotted coat vanishing among cover, the longing to snatch even one good photograph that could be savoured. Here was a leopard who allowed you the chance to absorb her beauty, her secret ways and liquid movements. Half-Tail gave us all of that, and something else besides.

It was one of those mornings when everything just falls into place; an early start full of hope, searching all the familiar places, and then suddenly there she was, right where we hoped she would be, lying

relaxed along a wide branch of one of the giant fig trees that sprout from the cliff face of Fig Tree Ridge. Even with a leopard as obliging as Half-Tail you never took her presence for granted. Having found her, I had to head back to camp, leaving Angie to keep an eye on her in case she moved off to hunt. When I returned a few hours later, she had gone, though Angie was parked in exactly the same spot where I had left her. 'Where's Half-Tail?' I asked. Angie pointed to the side of her car. I backed away until I could just make out Half-Tail wedged in the shade beneath the vehicle, totally trusting.

Vehicles were such a part of Half-Tail's existence that she took them for granted, using them when it suited her as shade or as a blind to hunt from or to scent-mark as

a moveable part of her home range. Angie had never been so close to a wild leopard before and, finding herself alone with no other vehicle to break the spell, she relished the moment, gazing at the sheen of Half-Tail's spotted coat, the brightness of her golden eyes, the length of her long white whiskers. Occasionally Half-Tail looked up, calm and assured, certain, it seemed, that nothing untoward would happen.

As the sun dropped behind a low bank of clouds, she slipped out from beneath the vehicle and stood for a moment, then lowered her forequarters and stretched, a cavernous yawn revealing ivory-coloured teeth. Then she walked away without so much as a backward glance and disappeared from view among the rocks.

The World of Cats *119*

Gazetteer of big cat safari destinations

Setting out on a safari to Africa is the high point of many people's lives. For some it will be a journey of just a few weeks; for others it may mean the beginning of a new life, as it was for me when I left London in 1974 and joined a group of other young people travelling overland through Africa.

Most people who come on safari have high expectations, built on visions of wildlife captured in books or on television programmes such as *Big Cat Diary*. But these images can be deceptive, often relying on months or even years of waiting for the right moment, capturing events that happen only rarely. Consequently, when people arrive in the Mara they often expect – rather than hope – to see a leopard lounging in a tree in Leopard Gorge, to experience the thrill of having a cheetah jump on the bonnet of their car, or to watch lions pulling down a buffalo. But there are no guarantees about what you see on safari – just the promise that the experience will change you forever.

The biggest lesson Angie and I learned on our recent safari through southern Africa was to throw away our expectations and enjoy whatever came our way. We had chosen destinations that we hoped would give us the best chance of seeing big cats. Some were famous for leopards or cheetahs, others places where all the big cats were said to be on view. Not all of them lived up to their reputation, not because it was undeserved, but because what we had hoped to see had happened yesterday or last week.

Due to time considerations we visited Namibia, Botswana, Zimbabwe, Zambia and South Africa in one continuous safari in the space of six weeks. The changing seasons can have a huge influence on what you see or don't see, so make sure you are travelling at the right time of the year for each destination when you plan your itinerary. If a place is 'good' for big cats, that implies that there's plenty for them to eat – the antelopes, gazelles, zebras and buffaloes on which they depend. By comparison with these prey species, predators are in the minority, so in looking for them you are guaranteed to find plenty of other animals to feast your eyes on. A safari is so much more than finding big cats. Nevertheless we have chosen places where we have experienced the best big cat watching. Our list is by no means exhaustive. There are many other areas out there waiting to be explored. Though leopards are the focus of this book we have included all three big cats in this review. The Insight guide *African Safari* and the Lonely Planet guides to *Watching Wildlife in East Africa* and *Southern Africa* are a mine of information for safari travellers.

Recommended destinations

Masai Mara National Reserve, Kenya

(1,510 km²/583 sq. miles)

This is one of the best places to see all three big cats, particularly lions. The rainy seasons are mid-October through to December (short rains) and April to June (long rains). The grass is at its longest after the long rains, making it more difficult to find predators, though you are virtually guaranteed to see lions at any time of year. The migration of wildebeest and

zebras usually arrives in June or July, with most of the herds returning to the Serengeti by the end of October.

September through to the end of March is our favourite time in the Mara, as the long grass retreats under a wave of animals. The best time to witness the great herds crossing the Mara River is from August to October – so September is a good bet, but no two years are the same. Even when the wildebeest and zebras depart the Mara it is still a beautiful place to visit, and with the grass short (and green during the rains of October–November) it is easier to find predators. The drier the year the better the predator viewing; the grass and bush are eaten back and stripped bare, making it easier to get around and see what is on offer.

The Mara is a birder's paradise, with more than 500 species. For accommodation, try Governor's Camp, Mara Intrepids or Mara River Camp. The Mara Triangle to the west of the river is excellent for cheetahs, though they are found throughout the reserve, and Little Governor's Camp, Olonana and Serena Lodge are among the best places to stay in the Triangle. If you prefer a private tented camp, East African Wildlife Safaris and Abercrombie and Kent are among a number of safari outfitters offering this option in Kenya.

Samburu National Reserve, Kenya

(104 km²/40 sq. miles)

One of the smaller reserves, but what a gem, providing a taste of northern Kenya, with excellent bird life. Any safari to Kenya should include a visit to Samburu. The scenery makes a wonderful contrast to the lush, rolling plains of the Mara, with stark rocky outcrops, dry bush country with towering termite mounds, and the palm-fringed Ewaso Nyiro River. To the south of the river lies Buffalo Springs National Reserve, which is equally good.

The dry seasons are best in Samburu, with plenty of activity around the river and large herds of elephants emerging from the forests to drink and cross. There are Grevy's zebras, gerenuks and reticulated giraffes – dry-country species that you don't find in the Mara.

Samburu and Buffalo Springs are famous for their leopards, and some of the camps and lodges put out bait in the evenings to attract nocturnal visitors. But you are quite likely to see leopards here during the day. There are lions and cheetahs, too, and wild dogs are occasionally seen. Among the best places to stay are Larsens tented camp and Samburu Serena Lodge.

Serengeti National Park, Tanzania

(14,763 km²/5,700 sq. miles)

The Serengeti would be worth a visit even if it didn't have any wildlife. The fact that it does – in the kind of abundance found in few other places – makes this one of our top five wildlife destinations worldwide.

The sheer expanse of the Serengeti plains, particularly in the rainy season when the massed herds of wildebeest and zebras darken the grasslands, is a sight to behold, with lions, hyenas and cheetahs all in attendance. The wildebeest cows give birth to their calves between January and March, so February is a good time to visit. The wildebeest leave the plains and head for the woodlands and water at the beginning of the dry season towards the end of May, streaming in their thousands through the spectacular Moru Kopjes. The more marked the transition between wet and dry seasons, the more dramatic the exodus from the plains. This is when the wildebeest begin their rut, and it is well worth heading for the Seronera area in the centre of the park, which has always been one of Africa's top leopard haunts. They frequently lie up among tall stands of yellow-barked acacia trees along the Seronera Valley or slump contentedly along the broad beam of a sausage tree. Seronera is also a good place to look for lions and cheetahs.

The rugged northern woodlands around Lobo are another good place to visit when the great herds are passing through in the dry season (June–October). Among the best places to stay when the herds are massed on the southern plains are Ndutu Lodge, overlooking Lake Lagarja, and Kusini Camp; with Serengeti Sopa Lodge within easy reach of Moru, Serengeti Serena Lodge a good base in the centre of the park, and Klein's Camp for the Lobo area.

Ngorongoro Crater, Tanzania

(260 km²/100 sq. miles)

The eighth wonder of the world, and certainly worth stopping for two nights, not only for its unique geological features and stunning views, but also as home to some striking black-maned lions. You will be lucky to see cheetahs here, though you might catch sight of a leopard among the forests. The crater is an excellent place to view the endangered black rhino, with the ink-blue backdrop of the crater wall making the perfect scene-setter for wildlife photography. The birdlife is excellent, and the magnificent bull elephants with their long ivory tusks are always a favourite. If you are a keen photographer, or just want to get the best out of your stay, be sure to take a picnic breakfast as well as lunch. The misty morning atmosphere and chances of finding lions on the move make it well worth being out early.

Of the three lodges, Sopa Lodge provides the easiest access to the crater floor, while Ngorongoro Serena Lodge offers 75 rooms, all with crater views. If you just want luxury and fine food, it might almost be worth spending the day in your room, with a view to match, at the Ngorongoro Crater Lodge.

Selous Game Reserve, Tanzania

(43,000 km²/16,600 sq. miles)

Tanzania's southern wilderness is the place to take a walking safari in East Africa. This is 'old' Africa, wild bush country that harbours more than 100,000 buffaloes, nearly 60,000 elephants, the highest density of wild dogs anywhere in Africa and probably the largest single population of lions – with fewer tourists watching them. Even though the lions are not as numerous or as easy to see as in places such as the Mara and Serengeti, a visit to one of the tented camps along the Rufiji River is an ideal starting point for a walking safari. A boat trip along the river to watch giant crocodiles, large pods of hippos and elephants is a must, or you could simply take time out back at camp, to catch up with identifying some of the more than 440 species of birds.

Among the best of the camps are Sand Rivers Selous (particularly for those wanting to walk) and Selous Safari Camp (formerly known as Mbuyuni tented camp). A safari combining a visit to Selous and Ruaha National Park, and either Mahale Mountains or Gombe National Park to see chimpanzees, would be a great adventure away from the hustle and bustle of Tanzania's northern tourist circuit. But if it is easy wildlife watching that you want and your first fix of Africa, then Serengeti, Ngorongoro and Tarangire (1,360km²/525sq. miles), with its magnificent baobabs, large herds of elephants, excellent birdlife and a good chance of seeing lions and leopards, are hard to beat.

South Luangwa National Park, Zambia

(9,050 km²/3,500 sq miles)

Known locally as the Valley, this is where Norman Carr, one of Africa's most experienced safari guides, pioneered walking safaris. The Luangwa River dominates the park, providing a cooling and tranquil element. With the camps and lodges situated along the riverbanks, you can spend hours at a time watching the various animals coming to drink from the veranda of your tent – elephants, buffaloes, pukus, waterbucks, even lions and leopards. The best game-viewing is during winter (May–August) and the dry, hot months from September to November. Game concentrations tend to increase as the dry season progresses, but so too does the temperature. The rains (November–April) are excellent for birding, though most of the lodges and camps close at this time. The density of leopards is exceptional and lions are frequently seen. We visited in September, and during a night game drive – a highlight of any visit to Luangwa – saw one of the leopards that helped to make this area famous. Apart from looking for big cats, we spent many hours photographing elephants drinking and crossing the river, and enjoyed close-up views of the spectacular colonies of carmine bee-eaters that nest in the sandy banks.

There are a number of outfitters offering walking safaris, but Robin Pope Safaris is consistently recommended. The ideal time is probably late June to late September, for a five-day walk with a top guide, staying at mobile tented camps deep in the bush. Robin and Joe Pope also run three of the best permanent camps in the Valley: Nsefu, Tena Tena and Nkwali. A walking safari – even if only for a morning – is a must.

Kafue National Park, Zambia

(22,480 km²/8,680 sq. miles)

The second largest national park in Africa, comprising vast tracts of woodland and savanna bisected by the Kafue River. Surprisingly few people visit Kafue, considering that it is home to large herds of elephants, buffaloes, lions and leopards, and is renowned for its diversity of antelopes, with floodplains brimming with thousands of red lechwes and glimpses of magnificent sables and roans. There are cheetahs and wild dogs here, too, with large prides of lions hunting buffaloes on the Busanga Plain in the north. The animals tend to concentrate around water between July and October, with Busanga best between August and October.

There are only a handful of lodges, adding to the sense of wilderness. Among the best are Ntemwa and Busanga Bush camps, situated in the middle of the plains where lions are often seen; Lufupa Camp is well located for game drives and bush walks, with the chance of seeing leopard on night game drives.

Mana Pools National Park, Zimbabwe

(2,200 km²/850 sq. miles]

It is hard to think of Zimbabwe without planning a visit to the spectacular Victoria Falls and overnighting at the grand Victoria Falls Hotel. This is the place to take a canoe safari down the mighty Zambezi River, which forms the northern boundary of Mana Pools National Park. Hippos, crocodiles, elephants and buffaloes are all easily seen here. Mana is a likely spot to see lions, as is Matusadona National Park, which stretches up from the shores of Lake Kariba, and both offer the chance to walk or canoe, an exciting alternative to being driven around the African bush. John Stevens was one of the pioneers of canoe safaris and is one of Africa's top guides, specializing in walking and canoeing safaris, during which guests stay in mobile tented camps. Musangu and Muchichiri are two pleasant riverside lodges offering permanent accommodation, with Wilderness Safaris' Rukomechi and Chikwenya camps also highly recommended.

If you visit Lake Kariba, then Sanyati Lodge is among the best – you can relax, enjoy the lake and strike out on game drives, walks or fishing trips.

Moremi Game Reserve, Botswana

(3,900 km²/1,505 sq. miles)

The Okavango Delta is a huge oasis, an inland delta of wooded islands and papyrus swamps, whose crystal-clear waters disappear among the Kalahari sands. The delta rivals the Serengeti and Masai Mara as a wildlife spectacle, with excellent lion- and leopard-viewing, and a good chance of seeing cheetahs and wild dogs. The combination of water and wildlife is hard to beat, and the big-game viewing and birding opportunities are virtually limitless. The Moremi Reserve encompasses almost one third of the delta, and includes Chief's Island. The autumn/winter dry season (April–September) is best for wildlife viewing. There is an excellent chance of seeing wild dogs in June and July when they abandon their nomadic wandering for a few months and establish a den. Game-viewing reaches a peak during September and October, when animals congregate around permanent water, though temperatures can be high.

Many lodges close during the rainy season (December–March). There is a huge selection of camps and lodges to choose from, but among the best are Chief's Camp in the Mombo area, and Wilderness Safari's camps, Mombo and Little Mombo.

A visit to the Okavango Delta also offers the possibility of walking safaris, horseback safaris, even elephant-back safaris at Randall Moore's Abu's Camp, and a chance to walk with Doug Groves's elephants at Stanley's Camp. In the north, and bordering Namibia, Chobe National Park (11,700 km²/4,520 sq. miles) is home to large prides of lions and huge herds of buffaloes, and offers river trips to watch elephants crossing the Chobe River. In the west of the park, the Linyanti Marsh and Savuti areas are famous for their lion-viewing, though it can be very seasonal. Chobe is a good place to visit en route to Victoria Falls, stopping over at Chobe Chilwero Lodge.

Okonjima and the Africat Foundation, Namibia

(135 km²/52 sq. miles)

Namibia is home to more cheetahs than any other African country, with perhaps 3,000 of these elegant cats. But 90 per cent are found on private ranchland, where they often run into conflict with ranchers. Lise Hanssen and her team at the Africat Foundation have dedicated themselves to working with ranchers to lessen conflict with predators, removing animals that are trapped and might otherwise be shot or poisoned. They work mainly with cheetahs and leopards, but also with servals, caracals and the occasional lion, supporting a number of research and education projects.

The Hanssens have turned the family home at Okonjima ranch into comfortable guest accommodation, providing visitors with the chance to visit the Africat Foundation and meet some of the cheetahs. Photographers will find plenty of interest here, and a visit to the leopard blind in the evening is an experience not to be missed.

The Cheetah Conservation Fund (CCF), Otjiwarongo, Namibia

CCF was the brainchild of Laurie Marker and Daniel Kraus, and is dedicated to the long-term survival of the cheetah through research and education. Laurie and her team are at the hub of cheetah conservation and, like the Africat Foundation, work closely with ranchers, providing a home for orphaned cheetahs trapped on ranchland. CCF has pioneered the use of guard dogs to help farmers reduce stock losses to predators, and has placed well over 120 Anatolian Shepherd dogs with farmers. Where possible wild-caught adult cheetahs are relocated. The excellent Visitor Education Centre at CCF is open to the public.

To see wild cheetahs in Namibia, the best option is to visit Etosha National Park (22,270 km²/8,600 sq. miles). Natural springs and artificial waterholes (such as the Okaukuejo waterhole) dotted along the southern edge of the stark Etosha Pan at the heart of the park provide the focal point for game-viewing, attracting large numbers of animals, such as wildebeest, zebras, springboks, gemsboks and elands. Though all three big cats are found here, there is no guarantee that you will see them. If big cats are the priority and time is short then perhaps this is not the place for you; otherwise it is memorable.

Namib-Naukluft Park, Namibia

(49,754 km²/19,210 sq. miles)

This enormous wilderness stretches from Luderitz in the south to Swakopmund in the north. Not the place to see big cats, but as a safari destination it is a world apart, a vast moonscape with towering dunes, which are transformed when the summer rains come – if they come – in December to February. The extraordinary creeping welwitschia plants are endemic to the Namib and can live for more than 2,000 years. Sossusvlei Mountain Lodge in the adjoining Namib Rand Nature Reserve, and Wilderness Sossusvlei Camp are among the best, offering a variety of activities including day trips to the towering dunes of Sossusvlei. There is even a star-gazing safari with the help of a giant telescope at Mountain Lodge – not to be missed.

Kruger National Park, South Africa

(19,480 km²/7,520 sq. miles)

This is South Africa's premier national park, with more mammal and bird species than any other park in the country. All of the 'big five' can be found here – lions, leopards, buffaloes, rhinos and elephants – as well as cheetahs and wild dogs, with the southern area of the park offering the greatest variety of landscape and the best game-viewing. The one big limitation has always been that you are confined to tarmac roads. However, the parks authorities have recently put out to tender a number of private concessions, where off-road driving and walking safaris from small camps and lodges will add a whole new dimension to a safari in Kruger. Game-viewing is best during winter (May–October), when animals concentrate at water sources. The rainy season is from October to March.

Sabi Sands Game Reserve, South Africa (including Londolozi and Mala Mala)

(650 km²/250 sq. miles)

There are a number of private game reserves clustered along the western boundary of the Kruger that are no longer separated from it by fencing. These offer excellent opportunities for big cat enthusiasts, and are particularly worth a visit if your passion is leopards. The most famous is Londolozi (130km²/50sq. miles), which has been transformed by John and Dave Varty since they took over the lodge in the early 1970s and restored the area to its former glory. Also well worth a visit is Mala Mala – both of these virtually guarantee leopard sightings. When we visited Londolozi we saw three different leopards on five separate occasions, as well as three magnificent male lions and plenty of cubs, white rhinos, elephants and two glorious kudu bulls.

Night game drives are a feature at all the lodges, and a good way to see leopards, though the rangers work hard to track them down during daytime as well, with off-the-road driving the norm. Cheetahs and wild dogs are not uncommonly seen. Ngala, Sabi Sabi, Singita and Idube lodges are all recommended.

Phinda Resource Reserve, South Africa

(180 km²/70 sq. miles)

Lions and cheetahs have been introduced to this private game reserve, and it is certainly a good place to photograph them – particularly cheetahs, which are almost guaranteed. But getting a clear view of them usually depends on being able to drive off-road, and this is restricted after annual burning, so be sure to check first. All the 'big five' are here, and leopards are quite often seen. Winter (May–October) is the dry season and the best time for clear sightings. Accommodation is in four luxury lodges. Phinda offers a number of extensions. You can opt to walk in search of black rhino in the adjacent Mkuzi Game Reserve, dive on the east coast coral reefs or fly over Greater St Lucia Wetland Park.

Further Information:

Websites

African National Parks
HYPERLINK
http://www.newafrica.com/nationalparks/
Africat (Lise Hanssen's project)
HYPERLINK http://www.africat.org/
Cheetah Conservation Fund
(Laurie Marker's project)
HYPERLINK http://www.cheetah.org
Big Cats Online
dialspace.dial.pipex.com/agarman/bco/ver4.htm
Big Cat Research
www.bigcats.com/
IUCN Cat Specialist Group
lynx.uio.no/catfolk
The Lion Research Centre (lions of the Serengeti
and Ngorongoro Crater)
HYPERLINK http://www.lionresearch.org
Friends of Conservation
(conservation body involved in the Mara)
HYPERLINK http://www.foc-uk.com

Tour Operators

Abercrombie and Kent
(East and southern Africa)
HYPERLINK http://www.abercrombiekent.co.uk
Afro Ventures (East and southern Africa)
HYPERLINK http://www.afroventures.com
Conservation Corporation Africa
(East and southern Africa)
HYPERLINK http://www.ccafrica.com
East African Wildlife Safaris (Kenya)
HYPERLINK mailto:eaws@kenyaweb.com
Gibb's Farm Safaris (Tanzania)
HYPERLINK mailto:ndutugibbs@nabari.co.tz
John Stevens Safaris
(Zimbabwe canoe/walking safaris)
HYPERLINK mailto:bushlife@hare.iafrica.com
Okavango Tours and Safaris
(Botswana)
HYPERLINK http://www.okavango.com
Richard Bonham Safaris
(Tanzania – Selous specialist)
HYPERLINK
mailto:Bonham.Luke@swiftkenya.com
Robin Pope Safaris
(Zambia – Luangwa Valley specialist)
HYPERLINK mailto:popesaf@zamnet.zm
Wilderness Safaris
(southern Africa specialists)
HYPERLINK mailto:outposts@usa.net
Governor's Camp
(Kenya/Masai Mara tented camps)
HYPERLINK mailto:info@governorscamp.com
Worldwide Journeys and Expeditions
(African safari specialists)
www.worldwidejourneys.co.uk

Bibliography

It would have been impossible to write this book without leaning heavily on the work of other authors. We're particularly grateful to Luke Hunter, who was incredibly generous with his time, providing us with invaluable information on Africa's big cats, as well as many contacts among predator researchers working in southern Africa. Here in Nairobi, Judith Rudnai kindly shared her excellent library of books and articles with us. Thanks are also due to Gus Mills at Kruger Park in South Africa for his fund of knowledge on Africa's large predators and providing copies of scientific articles; Lise Hanssen of the Africat Foundation (thank you, Lise, for sending copies of Flip Stander's excellent leopard papers) and the Hanssen family at Okonjima in Namibia, who were helpful and welcoming. So too were Laurie Marker and everyone at the Cheetah Conservation Fund. Our Nairobi neighbours, Esmund Bradley-Martin and his wife Chryssee, were a mine of information on matters relating to wildlife conservation, and generously allowed us access to back issues of *Cat News*, the newsletter of the Species Survival Commission (IUCN), which I would recommend highly to anyone with a passion for the world's wild cats.

Ted Bailey's book *The African Leopard* is essential reading for leopard enthusiasts, and the accounts of leopard behaviour written by Lex Hess (formerly a ranger at Londolozi), and filmmakers Dale Hancock and Kim Wolhuter at Mala Mala provided us with many insights. We are only too well aware of the dangers of interpreting the work of others, particularly when trying to present information gleaned from scientific papers in a 'popular' way. Accordingly, while we are indebted to the following authors, they remain blameless for any inaccuracies in our text, and we apologize for the inevitable simplifications in interpreting their work.

Adamson, J. *Born Free: the full story*, Pan Books: London 2000
Ames, E. A *Glimpse of Eden*, Collins: London 1968
Bailey, T.N. *The African Leopard: ecology and behavior of a solitary felid*, Columbia University Press: New York 1993
Bertram, B.C.R. *Pride of Lions*, J.M.Dent: London 1978
————— *Lions*, Colin Baxter Photography: Grantown-on-Spey 1998
Bothma, J du P. and Walker, C. *Larger Carnivores of the African Savannas*, J. L. van Schaik Publishers: Pretoria 1999
Estes, R.D. T*he Behavior Guide to African Mammals: including hoofed mammals, carnivores, primates*, University of California Press: Oxford, England 1991
Grzimek, B., & Grzimek, M. *Serengeti Shall Not Die*, Hamish Hamilton: London 1960
Hall-Martin, A, & Bosman, P. *Cats of Africa*, Swan Hill Press, an imprint of Airlife Publishing: Shrewsbury 1997
Hancock, D. *A Time with Leopards*, Black Eagle Publishing: Cape Town 2000
Hess, L. *The Leopards of Londolozi*, Struik, Winchester, an imprint of Struik Publishers (Pty) Ltd: Cape Town 1991
Hunter, L.T.B. 'The Quintessential Cat.' *Africa: environment and wildlife*. Vol. 7 (2): 32-41 1999
————— 'Fighting tooth and claw: the future of Africa's magnificent cats.' *Africa Geographic*. Vol. 9 (5): 46-56 2001
Jackman, B.J. 'Cat-watching, Africa: lions, leopards and cheetahs: where to see them', *BBC Wildlife*, Vol.19, No.2 2001
Jackman, B.J., & Scott, J.P. *The Marsh Lions*, Elm Tree Books: London 1982
—————*The Big Cat Diary*, BBC Books: London 1996
Jackson, P. (ed) *Cat News*, the newsletter of the Species Survival Commission (IUCN) No.36 Spring 2002 and No.37 Autumn 2002
Jordan, W. *Leopard*, Hodder Wayland, an imprint of Hodders Children's Books 2001
Kingdon, J. *East African Mammals: an atlas of evolution in Africa*, Vol.3, part A (Carnivores), Academic Press: London 1977
Kumara, J. 'Island Leopard (Sri Lanka)', *BBC Wildlife*, Dec 2001
Macdonald, D. *The Velvet Claw: a natural history of the carnivores*, BBC Books: London 1992
Mellon, J. *African Hunter*, Cassell: London 1975
Mills, G., & Harvey, M. *African Predators*, Struik Publishers: South Africa 2001
Moss, C. *Portraits in the Wild: animal behaviour in East Africa*, Elm Tree Books: London 1989
Myers, N. 1973. 'The spotted cats and the fur trade' in R. L. Eaton, ed., *The World's Cats. Vol. 1, Ecology and Conservation*, pp. 276–326. Winston, OR: World Wildlife Safari
—————1976. 'The leopard *Panthera pardus* in Africa'. IUCN monogr. no. 5
Neff, N.A. *The Big Cats: the paintings of Guy Coheleach*, Harry N. Abrams: New York 1982
Nowell, K., & Jackson, P. *Wild Cats: status survey and conservation action plan*, IUCN/SSC Cat Specialist Group, IUCN: Gland, Switzerland.
Pocock, R. I. 'The Leopards of Africa'. *Proc. Zool. Soc.* London, 543 1932
Schaller, G.B. *The Serengeti Lion: a study of predator-prey relations*, University of Chicago Press: Chicago 1972
—————*Serengeti: a kingdom of predators*, Collins: London 1973

Scott, J.P. *The Leopard's Tale*, Elm Tree Books: London 1985

——————*The Great Migration*, Elm Tree Books: London 1988

——————*Painted Wolves: wild dogs of the Serengeti–Mara*, Hamish Hamilton: London 1991

——————*Kingdom of Lions*, Kyle Cathie: London 1992

——————*Dawn to Dusk: a safari through Africa's wild places*, BBC Books: in association with Kyle Cathie: London 1996

——————*Jonathan Scott's Safari Guide to East African Animals (revised and updated by Angela Scott)*, Kensta: Nairobi 1997

——————*Jonathan Scott's Safari Guide to East African Birds (revised and updated by Angela Scott)*, Kensta: Nairobi 1997

Scott, J. P., & Scott, A. 'Death on the rocks (infanticide in leopards)', *BBC Wildlife*, Vol.16 No.4 April 1998

——————*Mara–Serengeti: a photographer's paradise*, Fountain Press: London 2000

——————*Big Cat Diary: Lion*, HarperCollins: London 2002

Seidensticker, J., & Lumpkin, S. (eds) *Great Cats: majestic creatures of the wild*, Merehurst, by arrangement with Weldon Owen

Shales, M. *African Safari*, Discovery Communications: 2000

Spalton, A. 'Chasing the leopard's tale (Arabian leopards)', *BBC Wildlife*, August 2002

Stander, P. E. 'The ecology of asociality in Namibian leopards'. *J. Zool.*, London, 242, 343-364 1997

Stander, P. E. 'Field age determination of leopards by tooth wear'. *Afr. J. Ecol.* Vol 35 May 1997

Sunquist, M, and Sunquist, F. *Wild Cats of the World*, University of Chicago Press: Chicago and London 2002

Turnbull-Kemp, P. *The Leopard*, Howard Timmins: Cape Town 1967

Turner, A., & Anton, M. *The Big Cats and their Fossil Relatives: an illustrated guide to their evolution and natural history*, Columbia University Press: New York 1997

Uphyrkina, O et al. 'Phylogenetics, genome diversity and origin of modern leopards'. *Molecular Ecology* 10: 2617-2633. 2001

Acknowledgements

We have received such generous support from so many individuals and companies that it is possible to mention only a few of them here.

We would like to thank the governments of Kenya and Tanzania for allowing us to live and work in the Serengeti–Mara, and to acknowledge the assistance of Tanzania National Parks, and both the Narok and Trans Mara County Councils, who administer the Masai Mara National Game Reserve. Over the years Senior Wardens John Naiguran, Simon Makallah, Michael Koikai, Stephen Minis and James Sindiyo in the Mara, and David Babu and Bernard Maregesi in the Serengeti have all been helpful and supportive of our projects, as have Brian Heath and Jonny Baxendale of the Mara Conservancy (Mara Triangle).

Thanks to everyone involved in *Big Cat Diary* (BCD), both here in Kenya and at the Natural History Unit (NHU) in Bristol. To 'field commander' Keith Scholey and series producer Fiona Pitcher, for supporting the idea of this series of books, and to Keith and his wife Liz, and Robin and Elin Hellier, for welcoming us into their homes whenever we visit the NHU. The success of BCD relies on people working together, and as much as anyone Mandy Knight, production manager of series 1 to 4, epitomizes the combination of professionalism and big-heartedness which makes working on BCD such a privilege and pleasure.

Rosamund Kidmund-Cox, editor of *BBC Wildlife* magazine, has been a good friend and great supporter of our work over the years, and helped us believe that there was room for yet more books on Africa's big cats.

Myles Archibald at HarperCollins commissioned this series of three titles featuring Africa's big cats, beginning with *Lion* (we are now hard at work on the final book *Cheetah*). Myles' enthusiasm for the project helped to spur us on. Helen Brocklehurst, our editor at HarperCollins, has been a pleasure to work with, full of optimism and new ideas, and Liz Brown, our designer, managed to add her own brand of creative flare in record time.

Caroline Taggart has edited all but one of our books, but even someone as unflappable as Caroline realized that once again she was going to have to call on all her considerable editing skills – and an uncanny ability to make her authors feel that anything is possible – if we were to complete *Leopard* on time. Thank you again.

Mike Shaw, who was for many years our literary agent at Curtis Brown, always provided a safe pair of hands and we wish him a long and happy retirement. His former assistant Jonathan Pegg has agreed to take on the role of our agent and has been wonderfully supportive, managing our affairs with great charm and professionalism.

Our wildlife photographs are held by three picture libraries: NHPA, ImageState and Getty Images. Tim Harris and his team at NHPA generously allowed us to rifle the leopard files at short notice for this book, as did Diana Leppard at ImageState and Helen Gilks at the Nature Picture Library who hold some of Angie's pictures.

Both Angie and I have family living overseas who have been an unfailing source of help and encouragement. Now that my sister Caroline has moved from England to sunny Portugal, my brother Clive and his wife Judith have kindly inherited the boxes of books and slides that used to live at Caroline's house in Inkpen. Angie's mother Joy still lives in England but sadly hasn't enjoyed the best of health recently, and her brother David and wife Mishi now live in France. Her cousin Richard Thornton, his wife Gay and their daughter Bridget and husband Bill kindly found space for more of our possessions at short notice. We miss them all.

Pam Savage and Michael Skinner have taken us under their wing these past few years, offering advice and reassurance when needed, and allowing us the freedom of their home in London. It is difficult to know how to thank friends like that adequately, though dedicating this book to Pam will perhaps go some small way towards recording our gratitude to her for many kindnesses over the years. Cissy and David Walker have been equally forthcoming with their generosity and good fellowship.

Frank and Dolcie Howitt continue to be the best of neighbours to us here in Nairobi, and are very dear friends.

Many other people have provided us with a second home during our visits to England over the years, particularly Pippa and Ian Stewart-Hunter in London, Brian and Annabelle Jackman in Dorset, Dr Michael and Sue Budden in Buckinghamshire, Ken and Lois Kuhle and Martin and Avril Freeth in London, and Charles and Lindsay Dewhurst in West Sussex, who have been such caring and generous guardians to our son David during his schooldays in England. They are all wonderful hosts and friends who put up with our comings and goings with admirable tolerance.

We have shared some remarkable times with our good friends Neil and Joyce Silverman in Africa, Antarctica and their beautiful home in Florida. They have helped us in many ways over the years, and are always there when we need them.

Carole Wyman has been a loyal and generous friend to Angie since they met in Kenya many years ago, and is godmother to our son David. Carol is an individual of rare qualities, and our only regret is that we see so little of her and her husband Karma.

Jock Anderson of East African Wildlife Safaris continues to be a great friend to our family. He gave me the chance to live at Mara River Camp 27 years ago, a gift of such magnitude that I shall never forget his role in making it possible. Stephen Masika, Jock's office messenger, still keeps track of correspondence and renews licences for us with unfailing efficiency.

Aris, Justin and Dominic Grammaticus have been generous in allowing us to base ourselves at Governor's Camp, and Pat and Patrick Beresford and their staff at Governor's Workshop somehow manage to keep us on the road, regardless of the damage we inflict on our Toyota Landcruiser.

Finally, we would like to acknowledge the invaluable help of Shigeru Ito of Toyota East Africa, Allan Walmsley, formerly of Lonrho Motors East Africa, Canon Camera Division (UK), John Buckley and Anna Nzomo at Air Kenya, Mehmood and Shaun Quraishy at Spectrum Colour Lab (Nairobi), Pankaj Patel of Fuji Kenya, Jan Mohamed of Serena Hotels and David Leung, the Canon Camera specialist at Goodmayes Road, Ilford (UK), all of whom make life in the bush tenable through their ongoing support.

We are truly fortunate in being able to follow our passion as a career. But the joy that this brings pales alongside the inspiration and love we derive from our children Alia and David. May their lives be equally blessed.

Index

Page numbers in *italic* refer to illustrations

THE
RELIGIONS
BOOK

THE RELIGIONS BOOK

LONDON, NEW YORK, MELBOURNE, MUNICH, AND DELHI

DK LONDON

SENIOR EDITORS
Gareth Jones, Georgina Palffy

PROJECT ART EDITOR
Katie Cavanagh

JACKET DESIGNER
Laura Brim

JACKET EDITOR
Manisha Majithia

JACKET DESIGN
DEVELOPMENT MANAGER
Sophia MTT

MANAGING ART EDITOR
Lee Griffiths

MANAGING EDITOR
Stephanie Farrow

ILLUSTRATIONS
James Graham

PRODUCTION EDITOR
Lucy Sims

PRODUCTION CONTROLLER
Mandy Inness

original styling by
STUDIO8 DESIGN

produced for DK by
COBALT ID

ART EDITORS
Darren Bland, Paul Reid

EDITORS
Louise Abbott, Diana Loxley,
Alison Sturgeon, Sarah Tomley,
Marek Walisiewicz

DK DELHI

MANAGING EDITOR
Pakshalika Jayaprakash

SENIOR EDITOR
Monica Saigal

EDITOR
Tanya Desai

MANAGING ART EDITOR
Arunesh Talapatra

SENIOR ART EDITOR
Anis Sayyed

ART EDITOR
Neha Wahi

ASSISTANT ART EDITORS
Astha Singh, Namita Bansal,
Gazal Roongta, Ankita Mukherjee

PICTURE RESEARCHER
Surya Sankash Sarangi

DTP MANAGER/CTS
Balwant Singh

DTP DESIGNERS
Bimlesh Tiwary, Rajesh Singh

First published in Great Britain in
2013 by Dorling Kindersley Limited,
80 Strand, London, WC2R 0RL
Penguin Group (UK)

2 4 6 8 10 9 7 5 3 1
001 - 192329 - Aug/2013

Copyright © 2013
Dorling Kindersley Limited

A CIP catalogue record for this
book is available from
the British Library.

ISBN: 978-1-4093-2491-1

Printed and bound in Hong Kong
by Hung Hing

**Discover more at
www.dk.com**

CONTRIBUTORS

SHULAMIT AMBALU

Rabbi Shulamit Ambalu MA studied at Leo Baeck College, London, where she was ordained in 2004 and now lectures in Pastoral Care and Rabbinic Literature.

MICHAEL COOGAN

One of the leading biblical scholars in the United States, Michael Coogan is Director of Publications for the Harvard Semitic Museum and Lecturer on the Old Testament/Hebrew Bible at Harvard Divinity School. Among his many works are *The Old Testament: A Historical and Literary Introduction* and *The Illustrated Guide to World Religions*.

EVE LEVAVI FEINSTEIN

Dr Eve Levavi Feinstein is a writer, editor, and tutor in Palo Alto, California. She holds a PhD on the Hebrew Bible from Harvard University, and is the author of *Sexual Pollution in the Hebrew Bible*, as well as articles for *Jewish Ideas Daily* and other publications.

PAUL FREEDMAN

Rabbi Paul Freedman studied Physics at Bristol University and Education at Cambridge. Following a career in teaching, he gained rabbinic ordination and an MA in Hebrew and Jewish studies at Leo Baeck College, London.

NEIL PHILIP

Neil Philip is the author of numerous books on mythology and folklore, including the Dorling Kindersley *Companion Guide to Mythology* (with Philip Wilkinson), *The Great Mystery: Myths of Native America*, and the *Penguin Book of English Folktales*. Dr Philip studied at the universities of Oxford and London, and is currently an independent writer and scholar.

ANDREW STOBART

The Rev Dr Andrew Stobart is a Methodist minister. He studied Christian theology to doctoral level at the London School of Theology and Durham and Aberdeen universities, and has taught and written in the areas of theology, Church history, and the Bible, contributing to Dorling Kindersley's *The Illustrated Bible*.

MEL THOMPSON

Dr Mel Thompson BD, M.Phil, PhD, A.K.C. was formerly a teacher, lecturer, and examiner in Religious Studies, and now writes on philosophy, religion, and ethics. Author of more than 30 books, including *Understand Eastern Philosophy*, he blogs on issues of religious belief, and runs the "Philosophy and Ethics" website at www.philosophyandethics.com.

CHARLES TIESZEN

Dr Charles Tieszen completed his doctorate at the University of Birmingham, where he focused on medieval encounters between Muslims and Christians. He is currently a researcher and adjunct professor of Islamic studies, specializing in topics related to Islam, Christian–Muslim relations, and religious freedom.

MARCUS WEEKS

A writer and musician, Marcus Weeks studied philosophy and worked as a teacher before embarking on a career as an author. He has contributed to many books on the arts, popular sciences, and ideas, including the Dorling Kindersley title *The Philosophy Book*.

CONTENTS

HINDUISM
FROM 1700 BCE

BUDDHISM
FROM 6TH CENTURY BCE

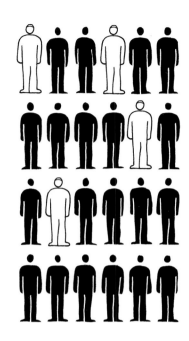

JUDAISM
FROM 2000 BCE

CHRISTIANITY
FROM 1ST CENTURY CE

ISLAM
FROM 610 CE

MODERN RELIGIONS
FROM 15TH CENTURY

INTRODU

CTION

There is no simple definition of the concept of religion that fully articulates all its dimensions. Encompassing spiritual, personal, and social elements, this phenomenon is however, ubiquitous, appearing in every culture, from prehistory to the modern day – as evidenced in the cave paintings and elaborate burial customs of our distant ancestors, and the continuing quest for a spiritual goal to life.

For Palaeolithic people – and indeed for much of human history – religion provided a way of understanding and influencing powerful natural phenomena. Weather and the seasons, creation, life, death and the afterlife, and the structure of the cosmos were all subject to religious explanations that invoked controlling gods, or a realm outside the visible, inhabited by deities and mythical creatures. Religion provided a means to communicate with these gods, through ritual and prayer, and these practices – when shared by members of a community – helped to cement social groups, enforce hierarchies, and provide a deep sense of collective identity.

As societies became more complex, their belief systems grew with them and religion was increasingly deployed as a political tool. Military conquests were often followed by the assimilation of the pantheon of the defeated people by the victors; and kingdoms and empires were often supported by their deities and priestly classes.

A personal god

Religion met many of the needs of early people and provided templates by which they could organize their lives – through rites, rituals, and taboos. It also gave them a means by which they could visualize their place in the cosmos. Could religion therefore be explained as a purely social artefact? Many would argue that it is much more. Over the centuries, people have defied opposition to their faiths, suffering persecution or death to defend their right to worship their god or gods. And even today, when the world is arguably more materialistic than ever before, more than three-quarters of its population consider themselves to hold some form of religious belief. Religion would seem to be a necessary part of human existence, as important to life as the ability to use language. Whether it is a matter of intense personal experience – an inner awareness of the divine – or a way of finding significance and meaning, and providing a starting point for all of life's endeavours, it appears to be fundamental at a personal, as well as a social, level.

Beginnings

We know about the religions of the earliest societies from the relics they left behind and from the stories of later civilizations. In addition, isolated tribes in remote places, such as the Amazonian forest in South America, the Indonesian islands, and parts of Africa, still practise religions that are thought to have remained largely unchanged for millennia. These primal religions often feature a belief in a unity between nature and the spirit, linking people inextricably with the environment.

All men have need of the gods.
Homer

As the early religions evolved, their ceremonies and cosmologies became increasingly sophisticated. Primal religions of the nomadic and semi-nomadic peoples of prehistory gave way to the religions of the ancient and, in turn, of the classical civilizations. Their beliefs are now often dismissed as "mythology", but many elements of these ancient narrative traditions persist in today's faiths. Religions continued to adapt, old beliefs were absorbed into the religions of the society that succeeded them, and new faiths emerged with different observances and rituals.

Ancient to modern
It is hard to pinpoint the time when many religions began, not least because their roots lie in prehistory and the sources that describe their origins may date from much later times. However, it is thought that the oldest surviving religion today is Hinduism; it is rooted in the folk religions of the Indian subcontinent, which were brought together in the writing of the Vedas as early as the 13th century BCE. From this Vedic tradition came not only the pluralistic religion we now know as Hinduism, but also Jainism, Buddhism, and, later, Sikhism, which emerged in the 15th century.

Meanwhile, other belief systems were developing in the East. From the 17th century BCE, the Chinese dynasties established their nation states and empires. There emerged traditional folk religions and ancestor worship that were later incorporated into the more philosophical belief systems of Daoism and Confucianism.

In the eastern Mediterranean, ancient Egyptian and Babylonian religions were still being practised when the emerging city-states of Greece and Rome developed their own mythologies and pantheons of gods. Further east, Zoroastrianism – the first major known monotheistic religion – had already been established in Persia, and Judaism had emerged as the first of the Abrahamic religions, followed by Christianity and Islam.

Many religions recognized the particular significance of one or more individuals as founders of the faith: they may have been embodiments of God, such as Jesus or Krishna, or recipients of special divine revelation, such as Moses and Muhammad.

The religions of the modern world continued to evolve with advances in society, sometimes reluctantly, and often by dividing into branches. Some apparently new religions began to appear, especially in the 19th and 20th centuries, but these invariably bore the traces of the faiths that had come before.

Elements of religion
Human history has seen the rise and fall of countless religions, each with its own distinct beliefs, rituals, and mythology. Although some are similar and considered to be branches of a larger tradition, there are many contrasting and contradictory belief systems.

Some religions, for example, have a number of gods, while others, especially the more modern major faiths, are monotheistic;

There is no use disguising the fact, our religious needs are the deepest. There is no peace until they are satisfied and contented.
**Isaac Hecker,
Roman Catholic priest**

and there are major differences of opinion between religions on such matters as the afterlife. We can, however, identify certain elements common to almost all religions, in order to examine the similarities and differences between them. These aspects – the ways in which the beliefs and practices of a religion are manifested – are what the British writer and philosopher of religion Ninian Smart called the "dimensions of religion".

Perhaps the most obvious elements we can use to identify and compare religions are the observances of a faith. These include such activities as prayer, pilgrimage, meditation, feasting and fasting, dress, and of course ceremonies and rituals. Also evident are the physical aspects of a religion, the artefacts, relics, places of worship and holy places. Less apparent is the subjective element of the religion – its mystical and emotional aspects, and how a believer experiences the religion in achieving ecstasy, enlightenment, or inner peace, for example, or establishing a personal relationship with the divine.

Another feature of most religions is the mythology, or narrative, that accompanies them. This can be a simple oral tradition of stories, or a more sophisticated set of scriptures, but often includes a creation story and a history of the gods, saints, or prophets, with parables that illustrate and reinforce the beliefs of the religion. Every existing faith has a collection of sacred texts that articulates its central ideals and narrates the history of the tradition. These texts, which in many cases are considered to be have been passed directly from the deity, are used in worship and education.

In many religions, alongside this narrative, is a more sophisticated and systematic element, which explains the philosophy and doctrine of the religion, and lays out its distinctive theology. Some of these

What religion a man shall have is a historical accident, quite as much as what language he shall speak.
George Santayana, Spanish philosopher

ancillary texts have themselves acquired canonical status. There is also often an ethical element, with rules of conduct and taboos, and a social element that defines the institutions of the religion and of the society it is associated with. Such rules are typically concise – the Ten Commandments of Judaism and Christianity, or the Noble Eightfold Path of Buddhism, for example.

Religion and morality
The idea of good and evil is also fundamental to many faiths, and religion often has a function of offering moral guidance to society. The major religions differ in their definitions of what constitutes a "good life" – and the line between moral philosophy and religion is far from clear in belief systems such as Confucianism and Buddhism – but certain basic moral codes have emerged that are almost universal. Religious taboos, commandments, and so on not only ensure that the will of the God or gods is obeyed, but also form a framework for society and its laws to enable people to live peaceably together. The spiritual leadership, which in many religions was given by prophets with divine guidance, was passed on to a priesthood. This became an

essential part of many communities, and in some religions has wielded considerable political power.

Death and the afterlife

Most religions address the central human concern of death with the promise of some kind of continued existence, or afterlife. In Eastern traditions, such as Hinduism, the soul is believed to be reincarnated after death in a new physical form, while other faiths hold that the soul is judged after death and resides in a non-physical heaven or hell. The goal of achieving freedom from the cycle of death and rebirth, or achieving immortality encourages believers to follow the rules of their faith.

All religions, arts and sciences are branches of the same tree.
Albert Einstein

Conflict and history

Just as religions have created cohesion within societies, they have often been the source – or the banner – of conflict between them. Although all the major traditions hold peace as an essential virtue, they may also make provision for the use of force in certain circumstances, for example, to defend their faith or to extend their reach. Religion has provided an excuse for hostility between powers throughout history. While tolerance is also considered a virtue, heretics and infidels have often been persecuted for their beliefs, and religion has been the pretext for attempted genocides such as the Holocaust.

Challenges to faith

Faced with the negative aspects of religious belief and equipped with the tools of humanist philosophy and science, a number of thinkers have questioned the very validity of religion. There were, they argued, logical and consistent cosmologies based on reason rather than faith – in effect, religions had become irrelevant in the modern world. New philosophies, such as Marxism-Leninism considered religions to be a negative force on human development, and, as

a result, there arose Communist states that were explicitly atheistic and anti-religious.

New directions

Responding to societal change and scientific advance, some of the older religions have adapted or divided into several branches. Others have steadfastly rejected what they see as a heretical progress in an increasingly rational, materialistic, and godless world; fundamentalist movements in Christianity, Islam, and Judaism have gained many followers who reject the liberal values of the modern world.

At the same time, many people recognize a lack of spirituality in modern society, and have turned to charismatic denominations of the major religions, or to the many new religious movements that have appeared in the past 200 years.

Others, influenced by the New Age movement of the late 20th century, have rediscovered ancient beliefs, or sought the exoticism of traditional religions with no connection to the modern world. Nevertheless, the major religions of the world continue to grow and, even today, very few countries in the world can be seen as truly secular societies. ∎

PRIMAL BELIEFS

FROM PREHISTORY

Primal religions – so-called because they came first – were practised by people throughout the world and are key to the development of all modern religions. Some are still active today.

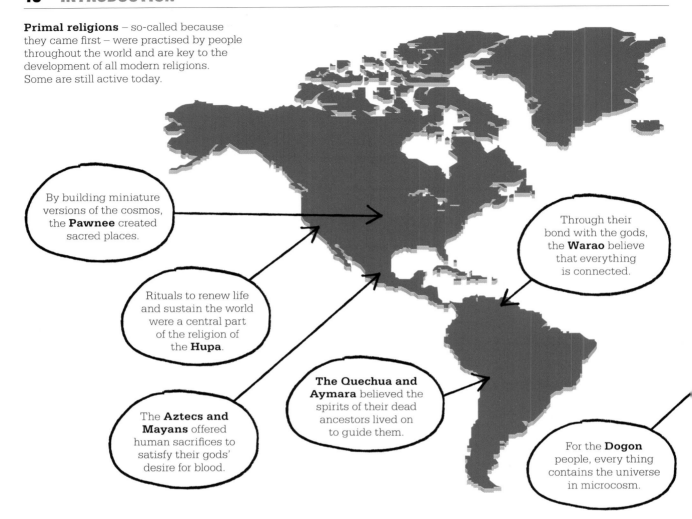

By building miniature versions of the cosmos, the **Pawnee** created sacred places.

Through their bond with the gods, the **Warao** believe that everything is connected.

Rituals to renew life and sustain the world were a central part of the religion of the **Hupa**.

The Quechua and Aymara believed the spirits of their dead ancestors lived on to guide them.

The **Aztecs and Mayans** offered human sacrifices to satisfy their gods' desire for blood.

For the **Dogon** people, every thing contains the universe in microcosm.

O ur early hunter-gatherer ancestors considered the natural world to have a supernatural quality. For some, this was expressed in a belief that animals, plants, objects, and forces of nature possess a spirit, in the same way that people do. In this animistic view of the world, humans are seen as a part of nature, not separate from it, and to live in harmony with it, must show respect to the spirits.

Many early peoples sought to explain the world in terms of deities associated with particular natural phenomena. The rising of the sun each day, for example, might be seen as a release from the darkness of the night, controlled by a sun god; similarly, natural cycles such as the phases of the moon and the seasons – vital to these people's way of life – were assigned their own deities. As well as creating a cosmology to account for the workings of the universe, most cultures also incorporated some form of creation story into their belief system. Often this was in the form of an analogy with human reproduction, in which a mother goddess gave birth to the world, which was in some cases fathered by another god. Sometimes these parental deities were personified as animals, or natural features such as rivers or the sea, or in the form of mother earth and father sky.

Rites and rituals

The belief systems of most primal religions incorporated some form of afterlife, one that was typically related to the existence of a realm separate from the physical world – a place of gods and mythical creatures – to which the spirits

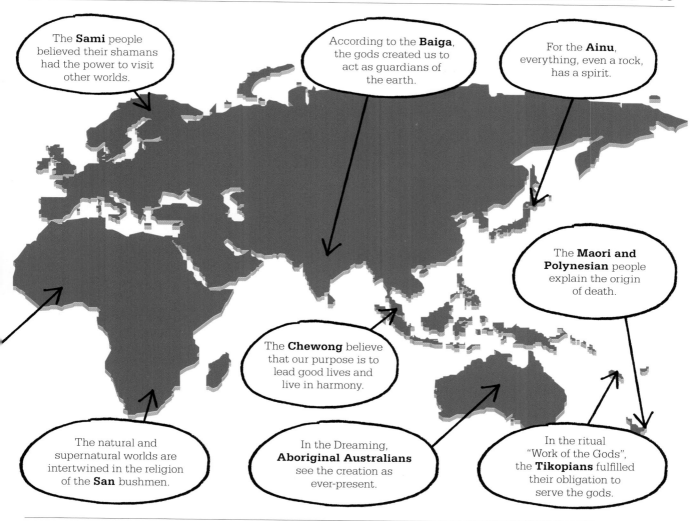

The **Sami** people believed their shamans had the power to visit other worlds.

According to the **Baiga**, the gods created us to act as guardians of the earth.

For the **Ainu**, everything, even a rock, has a spirit.

The **Maori and Polynesian** people explain the origin of death.

The **Chewong** believe that our purpose is to lead good lives and live in harmony.

The natural and supernatural worlds are intertwined in the religion of the **San** bushmen.

In the Dreaming, **Aboriginal Australians** see the creation as ever-present.

In the ritual "Work of the Gods", the **Tikopians** fulfilled their obligation to serve the gods.

of the dead would travel. In some religions, it was thought possible to communicate with this other realm and contact the ancestral spirits for guidance. A particular class of holy person – the shaman or "medicine man" – was able to journey there and derive mystical healing powers from contact with, and sometimes possession by, the spirits.

Early peoples also marked life's rites of passage; these, along with the changing of the seasons, developed into rituals associated with the spirits and the deities. The idea of pleasing the gods to ensure good fortune in hunting or farming inspired rituals of worship, and, in some cultures, sacrifices to offer life to the gods in return for the life they had given to humans.

Symbolism also played a key role in the religious practices of early cultures. Masks, charms, idols, and amulets were used in ceremonies, and spirits were believed to occupy them. Certain areas were thought to have religious significance, and some communities set aside holy places and sacred burial grounds, while others made buildings or villages in the image of the cosmos. A few of these primal religions survive to the present day among dwindling numbers of tribespeople around the world untouched by Western civilization. Some attempts have been made to revive them by indigenous peoples who are trying to re-establish lost cultures. Although their belief systems may seem at first glance to be primitive to modern eyes, traces of them can still be seen in the major religions that have evolved in the modern world, or in the "New Age" search for spirituality. ∎

UNSEEN FORCES ARE AT WORK

MAKING SENSE OF THE WORLD

IN CONTEXT

KEY BELIEVERS
/Xam San

WHEN AND WHERE
**From prehistory,
sub-Saharan Africa**

AFTER
44,000 BCE Tools almost
identical to those used by
modern San are abandoned
in a cave in KwaZulu–Natal.

19th century German
linguist Wilhelm Bleek sets
down many of the ancestral
stories of the San.

20th century Government-
sponsored programmes are
set up to encourage San
peoples to switch from hunter-
gathering to settled farming.

1994 San leader and healer
Dawid Kruiper takes the
growing campaign for San
rights and land claims to
the United Nations.

T he question of why human
beings first develop the
idea of a world beyond
the visible one in which we live
is complex. Motivated by an urge
to make sense of the world around
them – particularly the dangers
and misfortunes they faced, and
how the necessities of life were
provided – people in early societies
sought explanations in a realm
that was invisible to them, but
had an influence over their lives.

The idea of a spirit world is
also associated with notions of
sleep and death, and the interface
between these and consciousness,
which can be likened to the natural
phenomenon of night and day.

See also: Animism in early societies 24–25 ▪ The power of the shaman 26–31 ▪ Created for a purpose 32 ▪ Living the Way of the Gods 82–85 ▪ A rational world 92–99

In this "twilight zone" between sleep and waking, life and death, light and dark, lie the dreams, hallucinations, and states of altered consciousness that suggest that the visible, tangible world is not the only one, and that another, supernatural world also exists – and has a connection with our own. It is easy to imagine how the inhabitants of this other world were thought to influence not only our own minds and actions, but also to inhabit the bodies of animals and even inanimate objects, and to cause the natural phenomena affecting our lives.

A meeting of worlds

The figures of humans, animals, and human-animal hybrids in Palaeolithic cave paintings are often decorated with patterns that are now thought to represent the involuntary "back-of-the-retina" patterns known as entoptic phenomena – visual effects such as dots, grids, zigzags, and wavy lines, which appear between waking and sleep, or between vision and hallucination. The paintings

themselves represent a permeable veil between the physical and the spirit worlds.

It is impossible to ask the Palaeolithic hunter-gatherers of Europe about the beliefs and rituals that lie behind their cave paintings, but in the 19th century it was still possible to record the cultural and religious beliefs of the /Xam of southern Africa, a now-extinct clan of San hunter-gatherers who made cave paintings reminiscent of those of the Stone Age, for similar reasons. The spiritual life of the /Xam San offered a living parallel to the religious ideas archaeologists have attributed to early modern humans. Even the "clicks" of the /Xam San language (represented »

Since prehistoric times, the San have renewed their rock paintings, transmitting the stories and ideas they depict down the generations.

The Storm Bird blows his wind into the chests of man and beast, and without this wind we would not be able to breathe.
African fable

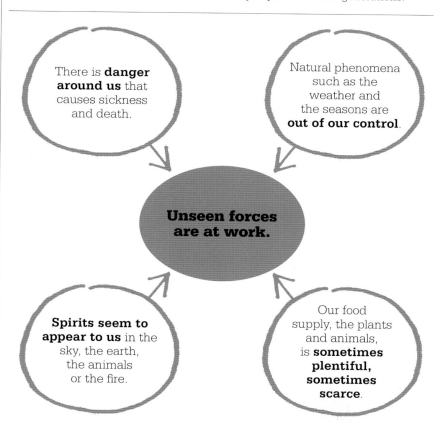

There is **danger around us** that causes sickness and death.

Natural phenomena such as the weather and the seasons are **out of our control**.

Unseen forces are at work.

Spirits seem to appear to us in the sky, the earth, the animals or the fire.

Our food supply, the plants and animals, is **sometimes plentiful, sometimes scarce**.

by marks such as "/", indicating a dental click rather like a tut of disapproval), are thought to survive from humankind's earliest speech.

Levels of the cosmos

The mythology of all San peoples is modelled closely on their local environment and on the idea that there are both natural and supernatural realms that are deeply intertwined. In their three-tiered world, spirit realms lie both above and below the middle, or natural, world in which humans live; each is accessible to the other, and whatever happens in one directly affects what happens in the other. Humans with special powers could visit the upper or sky realm, and travel underwater and underground in the lower spirit realm.

For the /Xam San, the world above was inhabited by the creator and trickster deity /Kaggen (also known as Mantis) and his family. They shared this world with an abundance of game animals, and with the spirits of the dead, including the spirits of the Early Race – a community of hybrid animal-humans, with powers to

shape, transform, and create. The /Xam believed that these beings were the first to inhabit the earth.

Elemental forces

In /Xam myth, elements of the natural environment were given supernatural significance or personified as spirits. Supernatural figures could take the form of the animals they shared their lands with, such as the eland (a type of antelope), the meerkat, and the praying mantis. The creator /Kaggen, who dreamed the world into being, usually took human form but could transform into almost anything, most often a praying mantis or an eland. While he was the protector of game animals, he would sometimes transform himself into one in order to be killed and feed the people.

The people of the Early Race were regarded with awe and respect, but not worshipped. Not even /Kaggen the Mantis was prayed to, although a San shaman such as //Kabbo (see box, facing page) might hope to intercede with /Kaggen to ensure a successful hunt. Because /Kaggen is a

> My mother told me that the girl [of the Early Race] put her hands in the wood ash and threw it into the sky, to become the Milky Way.
> **African fable**

trickster, many of the myths surrounding him and his family are comic rather than reverent; even the key myth of the creation of the first eland includes a scene in which an ineffectual /Kaggen is beaten up by a family of meerkats.

Important elemental forces and celestial bodies also became characters in stories that explained how they came to be, and why they behave in the way that they do. The children of the Early Race, for example, threw the sleeping sun up into the sky, so that the light that shone from his armpit would illuminate the world. It was a girl from the Early Race who made the stars by throwing the ashes of a fire into the sky of the Milky Way. Rain was not thought of as a natural phenomenon, but as a large animal. A fierce thunderstorm was a rain-bull, and a gentle rain was a rain-cow. Special people who had the power to summon the rain, such as //Kabbo, would make a supernatural journey to a full

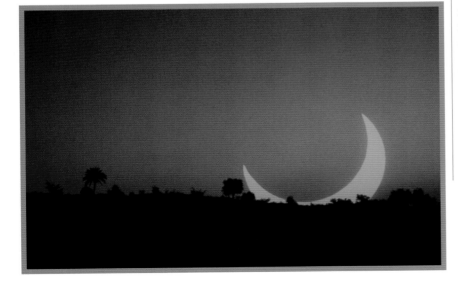

Natural phenomena such as eclipses, possibly never before seen by any living member of the San, might be explained through tales passed down in their rich oral tradition.

> A long time ago,
> the baboons were little
> men just like us,
> but more mischievous
> and quarrelsome.
> **African fable**

waterhole to summon a rain-cow, and then bring it back through the sky to the place in need of water. There he would "kill" the rain-cow so that its blood and milk fell down as rain on the earth.

Rain was a vital necessity in the arid desert landscape in which the /Xam lived. It was essential to replenish the widely scattered waterholes that they moved between, and which were linked to each other by a complex web of story and myth, known as *kukummi* and similar to the Dreamings of the Australian Aborigines (pp.34–35).

Entering other worlds

Many aspects of the natural world described in /Xam stories feature the interaction of the supernatural beings with humans – how they have an interest in this world, and how humans can, in turn, act to influence and please them. All San peoples believe that the spirit realms are accessible, in altered states of consciousness, to those who have a supernatural potency, known as *!gi*, imparted to humans and animals by their creator. The trance dance is the key religious ritual in which the San

can use this power to access the spirit world, via trance, and launch their essential selves up through the top of their heads and into the spirit world. There, they may plead for the lives of the sick, and return with healing power so that they can drive out the arrows of disease fired by the dead from the other world.

The /Xam offered prayers to the moon and stars to give them access to spiritual power, as well as good luck in hunting. When /Xam people entered a state of altered consciousness, it was believed that they were temporarily dead, and that their hearts had become stars. Humans and the stars were so intimately linked that when a person actually died, "the star feels that our heart falls over [and] the star falls down on account of it. For the stars know the time at which we die."

After death, the links in /Xam belief between the worlds of human experience, of spirits, and of natural phenomena become even more apparent. The hair of a deceased person was believed to transform into clouds, which then shelter

Ascribing "human" traits to animals – for example, the inquisitiveness of the meerkat – is a mainstay of early myth, around which stories are woven about how the world came to be as it is.

humans from the heat of the sun. Death was described in elemental terms: the "wind" that exists inside every human being was said to blow away their footprints when they died, making the transition between the world of the living and the world of the dead a decisive one. If the footprints remained, "it would seem as if we still lived". ∎

Kabbo's dream-life

Much of the information we have about /Xam San beliefs comes from a man named //Kabbo, who in the 1870s was one of several /Xam San released from prison into the custody of Dr Wilhelm Bleek, who wished to learn their language and study their culture. They had been jailed for crimes such as stealing a sheep to feed their starving families. //Kabbo spoke of "his" waterholes, between which his family would move in the arid desert of the central Cape Colony, camping some way from the water so as not to frighten off the animals that came to drink the brackish water. Wilhelm Bleek said of him: "This gentle old soul appeared lost in a dream-life of his own", and in fact the name //Kabbo means "dream". The god /Kaggen was said to have dreamed the world into being, and //Kabbo had a special relationship with him; as a /Kaggen-ka !kwi, a "mantis's man" he was able to enter a dream state to exercise powers such as rain-making, healing, and hunting magic.

EVEN A ROCK HAS A SPIRIT

ANIMISM IN EARLY SOCIETIES

IN CONTEXT

KEY BELIEVERS
Ainu

WHERE
Hokkaido, Japan

BEFORE
10,000–300 BCE Neolithic
Jomon people – remote
ancestors of the Ainu –
live in Hokkaido, probably
worshipping clan deities.

600–1000 CE Okhotsk hunter-
gatherer people occupy coastal
Hokkaido. Some of their ritual
practices, such as bear worship,
are seen later in the Ainu.

700–1200 Okhotsk culture
blends with that of the
Satsumon to create the Ainu.

AFTER
1899–1997 The Ainu are
forced to assimilate into
Japanese culture; many Ainu
religious practices are banned.

2008 The Ainu are officially
recognized as an indigenous
people with a distinct culture.

Everything in the world **has a spirit**.

Even human beings are **simply containers** for a spirit.

Spirits are **immortal**.

The most important spirits are **the gods**.

Ceremonies, songs, and offerings give the gods status in the other world.

If we treat the gods well, **they will provide us with food**.

The word "Ainu" means "human being", and refers to the indigenous population of Japan, now living mainly on the island of Hokkaido. The Ainu have close cultural ties with other inhabitants of the north Pacific Rim – Siberian peoples (such as the Chukchi, Koryak, and Yupik) and the Inuit of Canada and Alaska. These peoples share, in particular, an animistic view of the world, in which every being and object that exists has a spirit that can act, speak, and walk by itself. They also believe that the spiritual and physical worlds are separated by only a thin, permeable membrane.

The Ainu consider the body to be simply a container for the spirit; after death, the spirit passes out of the mouth and nostrils, and arrives in the next world to be reborn as a *kamuy*, a word meaning both "god" and "spirit". When the *kamuy* dies in the next world, it is reborn in this one. It will always reincarnate in the same species and gender – a man will always be a man, for example.

Kamuy can be animals, plants, minerals, geographical or natural phenomena, or even tools and utensils produced by humans. Because all spirits, even those of

See also: Living the Way of the Gods 82–85 ■ Devotion through puja 114–15

An Ainu chief performs a ceremony to honour the spirit of a slaughtered bear as it returns to the divine world, in a photograph taken in 1946.

inanimate objects, are considered immortal, after death a person's house may be burned, to ensure that his or her *kamuy* will have a home in the other world; their tools and implements may also be broken (to release the spirits inside) and buried with the body, for use again in the next world.

The power of words

Some *kamuy* have roles in both the supernatural and human worlds. Kotan-kor-kamuy, for example, is the creator god, but he is also the god of the village, and may manifest himself on earth as a long-eared owl.

Humans and *kamuy* have a close relationship – so close that *kamuy* have been described as "gods you can argue with". The *kamuy* can be prayed to, using special carved prayer sticks, but the ritual relationship is based more on mutual respect and correct behaviour than on worship. If someone has angered a god by carelessness or disrespect, they must conduct a ceremony to express their remorse. If, however, a person has treated a god with due respect and performed all the appropriate rituals, yet still receives bad luck, the Ainu can ask the fire goddess, Fuchi, to compel that god to apologize and make recompense.

In Ainu belief, even words are spirits, and the use of words is one of the gifts that humans have that gods and things do not. Words can be used to make bargains with both gods and things, and also to give pleasure to the gods. For example, the Ainu epic songs known as *kamuy yukar*, or "songs of the gods", are sung in the first person, from the perspective of *kamuy* rather than humans, and it is said the *kamuy* take delight in watching humans dance and sing the songs of the gods. ■

I also continue forever to hover behind the humans and always watch over the land of the humans.
Song of the Owl God

Spirit-sending rituals

Hunting rituals were central to traditional Ainu life and were used to appease the gods who visited earth disguised as animals. In return for offerings and rituals, the gods left behind the gift of their animal bodies.

After killing and eating a bear, the Ainu would perform the *iyomante* spirit-sending ritual. The spirit of the bear – revered as the mountain-bear god Kimun-kamuy – was entertained with food, wine, dance, and song. Arrows were fired into the air to aid Kimun-kamuy's return to the divine world, where he would invite other gods to share the gifts of sake, salmon, and sacred carved willow sticks with which he had been honoured on earth.

An *iwakte* spirit-sending ceremony was also held for broken tools and objects that had come to the end of their use.

SPECIAL PEOPLE CAN VISIT OTHER WORLDS

THE POWER OF THE SHAMAN

Shamanism describes one of humankind's oldest and most widespread religious practices, based on a belief in spirits who can be influenced by shamans. These shamans, men or women, are believed to be "special people" who possess great power and knowledge. After entering an altered state of consciousness, or trance, they are able to travel to other worlds and interact with the spirits who live there.

Bargaining with the powerful spirits who control these other worlds is often a key aspect of the shaman's activities. For example, the shaman often requests the release of game animals (essential in some traditional societies) from the spirit world into this world, to gain insight into the future, or for remedies to cure the sick. In return, the spirits may ask humans (via the shaman, who acts as an intermediary) to make offerings to them or to observe certain rules and codes of conduct.

Shamans play an important role as healers of the sick; this role emphasizes that their journeys are not simply personal and private, but are undertaken primarily to

We believe in dreams, and we believe that people can live a life apart from real life, a life they can go through in their sleep.
**Nâlungiaq,
a Netsilik woman**

alleviate suffering and hardship in the community. This function is reflected in some of the (now largely obsolete) terms that have been used to describe shamans, such as "witchdoctors" in sub-Saharan Africa and "medicine men" in North America.

In Europe, shamanism was a dominant feature of many societies from around 45,000 years ago up until the modern era. The Vikings, practised a form of shamanic divination known as *seiðr* between

In worlds we cannot see, powerful **supernatural beings control** the supply of game and the weather.

These other worlds are **full of spirits**, too, as both humans and animals have **undying souls**.

These people can **enlist the help of the spirits** to ask for game or good weather for us, or cure us when we are ill.

There are some **special people who can visit the worlds** in which these spirits live.

See also: Making sense of the world 20–23 ▪ Animism in early societies 24–25 ▪ Divining the future 79

the 8th and 11th centuries; and shamanic elements appear in the medieval myths of the Norse god Odin, who hanged himself in an initiation sacrifice on the World Tree (the axis of the universe).

In the 16th and 17th centuries, shamanic traces were evident in the Benandanti spirit-battlers (an agrarian fertility cult) of Friuli, Italy, and in the night-flying "seely wights" (fairy-like nature spirits) of Scotland. In more recent times, the *mazzeri* dream-hunters of Corsica show clear shamanic influence.

Sami shamans

The longest recorded history of shamanism in Europe, however, is in northern Scandinavia, in the area now known as Sápmi (formerly Lapland). Here the Sami people, semi-nomadic reindeer herders and coastal fishers, maintained a fully shamanic religion into the early 18th century, which has been partially revived in recent decades. Their religion can be reconstructed from historical sources as well as

Mankind does not end its existence because sickness or some other accident kills its animal spirit down here on earth. We live on.
Nâlungiaq, a Netsilik woman

from close comparison with related cultures in North Asia and the American Arctic.

Sami shamans, or *noaidi*, could inherit their calling or be chosen directly by the spirits. In some other cultures, those "chosen" to be shamans often experienced a period of intense illness and stress, as well as visionary episodes in which they might be killed and then brought back to life.

Sami shamans had helping spirits in the form of animals, such as wolves, bears, reindeer, or fish, whom they imitated when entering a trance. Shamans are often said to "become" the animal they imitate; this occurs through a process of interior transformation rather than by visible, exterior change.

Three things helped the Sami shaman enter a trance. The first was intense physical deprivation, often achieved by working naked in the freezing Arctic temperatures. The second was the rhythmic beat of the sacred "rune" drum (among similar peoples, such as the Yakut and Buryat, the drum is called

The Sami shaman's drum was used to make contact with the spirit world. Some of these drums survive, although many were burned by Christian missionaries.

the "shaman's horse"); the drum was decorated with images of the world of the gods above, the world of the dead below, and the world inhabited by humans (the earth) – the three realms connected by the World Tree. The third way the shaman was helped to enter a trance was through the ingestion of the psychotropic (mind-altering) fly agaric mushroom (*Amanita muscaria*). After taking the mushroom, the shaman would fall into a trance and become rigid and immobile, as if dead. During this process, male Sami guarded the shaman, while the women sang songs about the tasks to be performed in the upper or lower realms, and songs to help the shaman find his or her way home.

Stories are told of Sami shamans who never returned from the other world, often »

In some Arctic cultures, animals are believed to have spirit guardians who protect them and ensure their wellbeing. Shamans have the power to negotiate with these guardians, on behalf of human beings, for the release of animals from the spirit world into the human world for hunting and fishing.

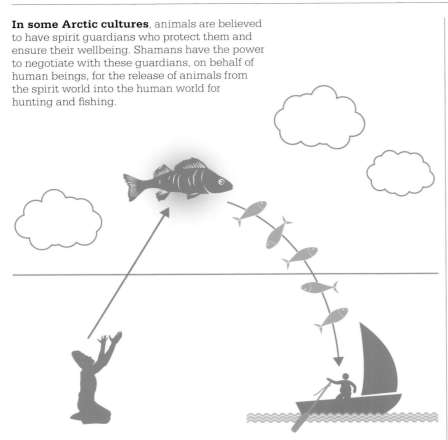

because those responsible for waking them with a spell had forgotten the magic words. One shaman was said to have been lost for three years, until the person acting as his guardian remembered that his soul needed to be recalled from "the coil of the pike's intestine, in the third dark corner". When the relevant words were spoken, the shaman's legs trembled, and he awoke, cursing his guardian.

Communicating with the spirits

Sami shamans were believed to fly to a mountain at the centre of the world (the cosmic axis) before entering the spirit world, either above or below the mountain. They might typically ride on a fish spirit,

be guided by a bird spirit, and protected by a reindeer spirit. A journey to the upper world of Saivo would be undertaken in order to plead for game or for help of some other kind; a journey to the underworld of Jabmeaymo would be made to fetch back the soul of a sick person. This could only be done after the mistress of the underworld had been placated with offerings. The shamans were able to communicate with the spirits in the upper and lower worlds because their shamanic training involved learning the secret language of the spirits.

The Netsilingmiut (Netsilik Inuit) shamans – an Arctic culture, from present-day Canada (west of Hudson Bay) – had similar religious

beliefs to the Sami. As well as subduing storms and acting as healers, they also mediated between the human world and the spirits of the earth, air, and sea. A shamanic seance was always held in subdued light, in a snow hut or a tent. The shaman would summon his helping spirits by singing special songs. After falling into a trance, he would speak in a voice that was not his own – most often in a deep, resonant bass, but sometimes in a shrill falsetto.

While in this trance state, the shaman could send his soul up into the sky to visit Tatqiq, the moon man, who was thought to bring fertility to women and good luck in hunting. If he was pleased with the offerings the shamans made to him, he would reward them with animals. When the moon was not visible in the sky, the Netsilik believed that he had gone hunting for animals to feed the dead.

Into the sky, under the sea
According to one Nitsilik account, one day the great shaman Kukiaq was trying to catch seals from a breathing hole in the ice. He gazed

Everything comes from Nuliayuk – food and clothes, hunger and bad hunting, abundance or lack of caribou, seals, meat, and blubber.
Nâlungiaq, a Netsilik woman

Some Inuit in Gojahaven, northern Canada, have maintained a belief in shamans, who are thought to have a special relationship with the landscape and with the spirits who control it.

upwards and realized that the moon was gradually moving towards him. It hovered above his head and transformed into a whalebone sledge. The driver, Tatqiq, gestured to Kukiaq to join him, and whisked him off to his house in the sky. The entrance of the house moved like a chewing mouth, and in one of the rooms the sun was nursing a baby. Although the moon asked Kukiaq to stay, he was anxious he would not be able to find his was home. So he slid back to earth on a moonbeam, landing safely at the very same breathing hole he had left from.

Sometimes, however, the Netsilik shamans would send their souls down to visit Nuliayuk (also known as Sedna), the mistress of sea and land animals, at the bottom of the ocean. Nuliayuk possessed

the power to either withhold or release the seals on which the Netsilik depended for food and clothing. She therefore had great influence over them. When the Netsilik broke any of her strict taboos, she would imprison the seals. However, if the shamans ventured down to her watery underworld to braid her hair, she was usually appeased and would release the seals into the open sea.

The shamanic tradition of the Netsiliks lasted into the 1930s and 1940s. Within the Netsilik community, only the shamans (or *angatkut*) – who were protected by their own guardian spirits – were unafraid of the dangerous and malevolent spirits that filled the world. A Netsilik shaman might have several helping spirits. For example, the spirits of the shaman Unarâluk were his dead mother and father, the sun, a dog, and a sea scorpion. These spirits informed Unarâluk about what existed on, and beneath, the earth, and in the sea and sky. ∎

Au's mysterious shamanic illumination

The following account of shamanic illumination was given to the Danish explorer Knud Rasmussen by Au, an Iglulik Inuit shaman. Au recalled a period in his life when he sought solitude, was deeply melancholic, and would sometimes weep uncontrollably. Then, one day, a feeling of immense, inexplicable joy overcame him. He explained that in the middle of this fit of pure delight, "I became a shaman, not knowing myself how it came about. But I was a shaman". Thereafter, Au could see and hear in a completely different way: "I had gained my *quamaneq*, my enlightenment ... it was not only I who could see through the darkness of life, but the same light also shone out from me, imperceptible to human beings, but visible to all the spirits of earth and sky and sea, and these now came to me and became my helping spirits."

Knud Rasmussen (1879–1933) spent many years documenting the culture of Arctic peoples during his journeys of exploration.

WHY ARE WE HERE?
CREATED FOR A PURPOSE

IN CONTEXT

KEY BELIEVERS
Baiga

WHEN AND WHERE
From 3000 BCE, Mandla Hills, southeastern Madhya Pradesh, central India

BEFORE
From prehistory The Baiga are thought to share common ancestry with the Australian Aborigines.

AFTER
Mid-19th century British forest officials restrict sacred *bewar* agriculture. Food shortages follow; the Baigas say that the Kali Yuga, the age of darkness, has begun.

1890 A reserve that surrounds eight Baiga villages is demarcated where *bewar* is permitted.

1978 A Baiga development agency is established.

1990s More than 300,000 Baiga live in central India.

The Baiga are one of the indigenous tribal peoples of central India, collectively known as the Adivasis. The Baigas, who call themselves the sons and daughters of Dharti Mata, Mother Earth, believe that they were created to be the guardians of the forest – a task they have carried out since the beginning of time.

In their belief, Bhagavan, the creator, spread the world out flat like a chapati, but it flapped about and would not stay still. The first

You are made of the earth and are lord of the earth, and shall never forsake it. You must guard the earth.
Bhagavan the Creator

man, Nanga Baiga, and the first woman, Nanga Baigin, who were born in the forest from Mother Earth, took four great nails and drove them into the four corners of the earth to steady it. Bhagavan told them that they should take care of the earth to keep the nails in place, promising them a simple but contented life in return.

The Baiga followed the example of Nanga Baiga, hunting freely in the forest and considering themselves lords of the animals. Believing it wrong to tear the body of Mother Earth with a plough, they practised a form of slash-and-burn agriculture known as *bewar* (although always leaving the stump of a saj tree for the gods to dwell in), moving every three years to a new patch of forest. However, 19th-century British officials opposed the Baiga's methods, forcing them to abandon their traditional axe-and-hoe cultivation and take up the hated plough. They were permitted to practise *bewar* only in the reservation of Baiga Chak in the Mandla Hills. ∎

See also: The Dreaming 34–35 ∎ A lifelong bond with the gods 39 ∎ Renewing life through ritual 51

WHY DO WE DIE?

THE ORIGIN OF DEATH

IN CONTEXT

KEY BELIEVERS
Maori

WHEN AND WHERE
From prehistory,
New Zealand

BEFORE
2nd and 3rd millennia BCE
Ancestors of the Polynesian people spread across the Pacific Ocean, possibly from origins in Asia. Their ritual practices and mythology develop independently but retain parallels across this vast region.

Before 1300 CE The Maori people settle in New Zealand.

AFTER
Early 19th century European settlement begins. Some Maori convert to Christianity.

1840 The Treaty of Waitangi formalizes relations between whites and Maori.

Today Around 620,000 Maori are resident in New Zealand.

According to Maori belief, death did not exist at the beginning of the world but was brought into being following an act of incest. In one version of the Maori myth, the forest god Tane grew up between and separated his parents – Rangi, the sky god, and Papa, the earth goddess – because they forced him to live in darkness. He then asked his mother to marry him, but when Papa explained that this could not be, Tane shaped a woman from mud and mated with her.

The result of this union was a beautiful child – Hine-titama. She became Tane's wife, unaware that he was also her father. One day, however, she discovered the terrible truth, and descended in shame to the darkness of Po, the underworld; it was from this moment that humankind's descent to the realm of death began.

When Tane visited his wife, she told him, "Stay in the world of light, and foster our offspring. Let me stay in the world of darkness, and drag our offspring down". She then

The trees, plants, and creatures of the forest were believed by the Maori to be offspring of Tane, the forest god. Before felling a tree they therefore made an offering to the spirits.

became known as Hine-nui-te-po, the goddess of darkness and death. In an attempt to overturn the course of events and regain immortality on behalf of human beings, the trickster hero Maui raped Hine-nui-te-po as she slept, believing that after this act she would die, and that death would also cease to exist. But Hine-nui-te-po awoke during the attack and squeezed Maui to death with her thighs, thereby ensuring that mortality would remain in the world forever. ∎

See also: Preparing for the afterlife 58–59 ▪ Living the Way of the Gods 82–85

ETERNITY IS NOW

THE DREAMING

IN CONTEXT

KEY BELIEVERS
Australian Aborigines

WHEN AND WHERE
From prehistory, Australia

AFTER
8000 BCE The date ascribed
to certain changes to the
Australian landscape in
Aboriginal oral tradition;
this has been supported
by geological evidence.

4000–2000 BCE Aboriginal
rock art depicts the ancestral
beings of the Dreaming; some
experts estimate the earliest
portrayals of the Rainbow
Serpent to be even older, dating
them to some 8,000 years ago.

1872 Uluru is first seen by
a non-Aborigine, Ernest Giles,
who called it "the remarkable
pebble". European settlers give
it the name Ayers Rock in 1873.

1985 The ownership of Uluru
is returned to the Pitjantjatjara
and Yankunytjatjara peoples.

In the Dreaming, the **ancestral beings shaped the land**.

↓

They **embedded their spiritual power** within the land.

↓

The **land is alive** with this power.

↓

The **power** of the Dreaming is **eternal and ever-present**.

↓

We can **access that power** and enter the eternal Now.

I n the Australian Aboriginal
tradition, the time of the
creation was once called the
Dreamtime, but is now referred to
as the Dreaming. This term better
captures the crucial element of
Aboriginal faith – that the creation is
continuous and ongoing, existing in
the real, eternal present, as opposed
to the remote past. It also accords
with the Aboriginal belief that the
Dreaming can be accessed through
acts of ritual, song, dance, and
storytelling, and through physical
media such as sacred objects, or
paintings on sand, rock, bark, the
human body, and even canvas.

Myths of the Dreaming, called
Dreamings, tell of the ancestral
beings, who are known as the

See also: Making sense of the world 20–23 ▪ Created for a purpose 32 ▪ The spirits of the dead live on 36–37 ▪ Living the Way of the Gods 82–85

Uluru holds great spiritual power, according to Aboriginal tradition. It is said to be the heart of the ancestral beings' Songlines, whose signs may still be seen in the great rock's features.

First People or "the eternal ones of the dream", and their role in creation. Aboriginal tradition tells how these beings awake in a primal world that is still malleable and in a state of becoming. They journey across the land, leaving sacred paths known as "Songlines", or "Dreaming tracks", in their wake. As they go, they shape human beings, animals, plants and the landscape, establishing rituals, defining the relationships between things, and changing shape back and forth from animal to human forms. Finally they transform themselves into features of the environment including stars, rocks, watering holes, and trees.

The living land

Dreamings are thus intimately tied to natural features such as hills, rocks, and creeks, as well as the Songlines themselves. Aboriginal peoples revere the topography of Australia as sacred because it offers evidence both of their spiritual ancestors' wanderings, and of their bodies. The Gunwinggu tribe describes the land as being infused with the ancestral beings' *djang* (spiritual power): it is this that gives it its life and its holy power.

This sacred topography converges on Uluru, a sandstone rock formation in the Northern Territory, the centre from which all the Songlines are said to radiate. Uluru is venerated as a great storehouse of *djang*, the navel of the living body of Australia.

Aborigines consider the land to be both their inheritance and responsibility, and so they nurture it, and the Dreamings, accordingly. While they may be mortal, the *djang* of their ancestral beings lives forever, and is forever in the now. ▪

We say *djang*…
That secret place…
Dreaming there.
**Gagudju elder
Big Bill Neidjie**

The origin of Uluru

According to one legend, before the Uluru rock existed, the Kunia, or carpet-snake people, lived there. To the west lived the Windulka, or mulga-seed men, who invited the Kunia to a ceremony. The Kunia men set out, but, after stopping at the Uluru waterhole, they met some Metalungana, or sleepy-lizard women, and forgot about the invitation. The Windulka sent the bell bird Panpanpalana to find the Kunia. The Kunia men told the bird they could no longer attend as they had just got married. Affronted, the Windulka asked their friends the Liru, the poisonous-snake people, to attack the Kunia. During a furious battle, the Liru overcame the Kunia, who surrounded their dying leader, Ungata, and sang themselves to death. In the course of the battle, Uluru was formed. Three rock holes high on Uluru mark the place Ungata bled to death, and the water that spills from them is Ungata's blood. It flows down to fill the pool of the Rainbow Serpent, Wanambi.

OUR ANCESTORS WILL GUIDE US
THE SPIRITS OF THE DEAD LIVE ON

We **inherited the land** from our ancestors.

→

The **spirits of the ancestors** are enshrined in the land.

↓

Both the ancestors and the land must be **fed with blood and fat**.

←

If we do this, the **land will feed us** and the **ancestors will guide us**.

The religion of the Andean highlands can be said to be, in essence, a cult of the dead. This tradition of reverence for the ancestors stretches back to long before the short-lived empire of the Incas – the culture for which the region is best known – and has lasted to the present day.

Just one of many Quechua-speaking Andean peoples, the Incas rose to dominate much of modern-day Peru, Ecuador, and Chile, and parts of Bolivia and Argentina in the 13th century. As they extended their empire, they imposed a culture that in many ways resembled that of the Aztecs of Mesoamerica (pp.40–45), who were their contemporaries. It revolved around worship of their own supreme deity, the sun god.

However, beyond the Inca capital of Cuzco, with its priests, rituals, and golden artefacts, the common people, whom the Incas called the Hatun Runa, persisted with a cult of ancestor-worship and earth-worship that dated back to prehistoric times. This survived the mighty Inca Empire when, in the 16th century, it was utterly destroyed by Spanish conquistadors led by Francisco Pizarro.

See also: Making sense of the world 20–23 ▪ Created for a purpose 32 ▪ Sacrifice and blood offerings 40–45 ▪ Devotion through puja 114–15

People of the mountains

Since before recorded time, Andean peoples have organized themselves into *ayllus,* extended family groups or clans, each attached to a specific territory. Within these groups, they worked the land, shared resources, and worshipped at their *huacas*, or animistic earth shrines. The focus of worship was to pray to the earth to feed them – vital assistance in a mountainous region where farming was a harsh and laborious process. Running parallel to their entreaties to the earth was a belief that, just as the land had nurtured their ancestors, it would, with the intercession of those departed spirits, continue to nourish them.

Each *ayllu* mummified and worshipped the bodies of its dead, believing that the ancestors would help maintain the cosmic order and ensure the fertility of the land and the animals. The bodies were wrapped in weavings and placed in rock mummy shrines (*chullpa machulas*) facing the mountaintop. Once desiccated by the freezing, dry air, the mummies would be paraded around the fields during rituals to make the crops grow. Meanwhile, priests or diviners at the *huacas* and grave shrines offered up coca leaves, blood, and fat, believing that if the spirits of the land and the ancestors were fed, they would in turn feed the people.

An enduring power

In the 17th century, Christian missionaries burned many Andean mummies, to quash what they saw as pagan beliefs. However, some mummies have survived, and the modern Quechua believe them to be the first beings or ancient ones. The *chullpa machulas*, now just niches in the rocks, remain sacred shrines at which contemporary diviners still sprinkle blood and fat, believing this to infuse the sites with life and energy. Some groups, such as the Qollahuayos Indians (see box, below) may burn coca leaves there, wrapped in bundles of llama wool. The graves are believed to retain their power, even without the mummies that once occupied them. The Feast of the Dead, on

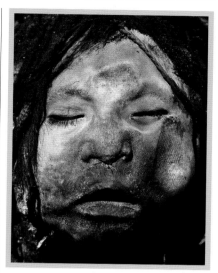

An Inca mummy of a girl who died five hundred years ago is still preserved; the ancestors are revered and have a central role among Andean peoples.

2 November – marking the end of the dry season and the beginning of the rains, when crops can be planted – remains a focus of the Andean year, when the dead are ritually invited to revisit the living, and to take a share of the harvest. ▪

The dead visit us and assist us in our work. They provide many blessings.
Marcelino, Kaatan elder

A mountain and a god

The Kaata of modern Bolivia, who live northeast of Lake Titicaca, form one of nine *ayllus* of the Qollahuayas Indians. The Kaata have a historic reputation as fortune-telling soothsayers; in the 15th century, Kaatan diviners carried the chair of the Inca emperor, an honoured task. The power of these Qollahuaya ritualists was thought to derive from the graves of their ancestors on Mount Kaata. In addition to the ancestral graves on the mountain, Mount Kaata itself is venerated as if it were a human being – a kind of super-ancestor – and is also ascribed physical human attributes. The highlands are regarded as the head, with grasses as hair, a cave for a mouth, and lakes for eyes; the middle region is the torso, with heart and bowels identified; and a pair of ridges on the lowest reaches are the legs. The mountain is a living being that gives the Kaata both sustenance and guidance.

WE SHOULD BE GOOD
LIVING IN HARMONY

IN CONTEXT

KEY BELIEVERS
Chewong

WHEN AND WHERE
From 3000BCE, Peninsular Malaysia.

BEFORE
From prehistory The Chewong are one of the 18 indigenous tribes of Peninsular Malaysia collectively known as the Orang Asli – the "original people". Each tribe has its own language and culture.

AFTER
1930s Europeans first encounter the Chewong; contact with Chinese and other Malay ethnic groups is also very restricted until this time because of the tribe's remote forest location.

From 1950s Chewong come under pressure to assimilate themselves into mainstream Malay society and convert to Islam; many choose to retain their traditional practices.

Most societies have developed a system of morality based on an appeal to notions of human goodness, reinforced by sanctions from religious and social authorites. Very few cultures have existed where ideas such as crime and warfare are unknown, but the few that have been found have been tribal peoples eking out a hunter-gatherer existence in the rain-forest. One such tribe is the Chewong of Peninsular Malaysia, whose first contact with Europeans was in the 1930s. They now number around 350 people.

The Chewong are non-violent and non-competitive; their language has no words for war, fight, crime, or punishment. They believe the first human beings were taught the right way to live by their culture hero Yinlugen Bud – a forest spirit who existed before the first humans. Yinlugen Bud gave the Chewong their most important rule, *maro*, which specifies that food must always be shared. To eat alone is regarded as both dangerous and wrong. Only by looking after the entire population in a spirit of fairness and sharing can the group hope to survive. The Chewong believe that violation of their moral code – by not sharing food, by showing anger at misfortune, by expressing anticipation of pleasure, or by nursing ungratified desires – will have supernatural repercussions such as illness, or physical or psychic attack, either by a tiger, snake, or poisonous millipede, or the *ruwai* or soul of the animal. ∎

Human beings should never eat alone. You must always share with others.
Yinlugen Bud

See also: Created for a purpose 32 ▪ The burden of observance 50 ▪ The Five Great Vows 68–71

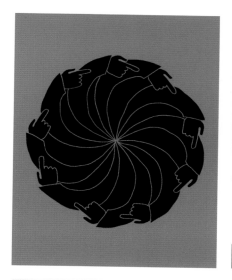

EVERYTHING IS CONNECTED
A LIFELONG BOND WITH THE GODS

Living in the environment of the Orinoco Delta, where the land is divided into countless islands by a network of waterways, the Warao tribe see the world as flat – the earth is just a narrow crust between water and sky. They believe that Hahuba, the Snake of Being – the grandmother of all living things – is coiled around the earth, and that her breathing is the motion of the tides. Their various gods, known as the Ancient Ones, live on sacred mountains at the four corners of the earth, with the Warao living at its very centre. In villages under the particular protection of one of the gods, the temple hut also contains a sacred rock in which the god dwells.

Divine dependence

The Warao gods depend on humans to nourish them with offerings, especially tobacco smoke; in return, the Warao depend on the gods for health and life. This lifelong bond with the gods is established as soon as a baby is born. The child's

In Warao myth, the Bird of Beautiful Plumage is believed to provide supernatural protection to children. A child that dies is said to be claimed as food by spirits of the underworld.

first cry is said to carry across the world to the mountain of Ariawara, the God of Origin, in the east; in return, the god sends back a cry of welcome. Soon after a baby is born, Hahuba, the Snake of Being, sends a balmy breeze to the village, to embrace the new arrival. From that point on, the baby becomes part of the complex balance between natural and supernatural that forms the web of Warao daily life. ∎

See also: The Dreaming 34–35 ∎ The spirits of the dead live on 36–37 ∎ Symbolism made real 46–47 ∎ Man and the cosmos 48–49

THE GODS DESIRE BLOOD

SACRIFICE AND BLOOD OFFERINGS

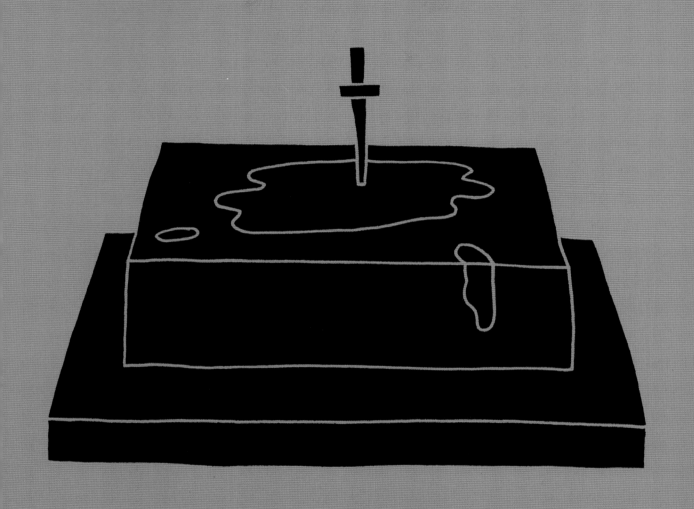

IN CONTEXT

KEY BELIEVERS
Aztec, Maya, and other Mesoamerican peoples

WHEN AND WHERE
3rd–15th century CE, Mexico

BEFORE
From 1000 BCE The Maya civilization begins its slow rise, reaching its peak – the Classic Maya period – between the 3rd and 10th century CE.

From 12th century CE The Aztec empire is established.

AFTER
1519 CE The Aztecs, whose population numbers 20–25 million, are overthrown by Spanish forces under the conquistador Hernán Cortés.

1600 CE Forced conversion to Catholicism and exposure to European diseases destroy the Aztec civilization and reduce the population to around one million.

The sacrifice of animals and humans has been a feature of many religious traditions around the world, but the idea of ritual sacrifice was particularly important to societies in the ancient civilizations of Mesoamerica, notably the Maya and the Aztecs.

The Mesoamerican peoples inhabited the area from present-day central Mexico through to Nicaragua. The Maya civilization (which peaked c.250 CE–900 CE) preceded and then coincided with the Aztec civilization, which reached its height around 1300–1400 CE. Aztec culture drew on the Maya tradition and the two peoples had several deities in common; they went by different names, but shared characteristics.

A reciprocal gift of blood

The Mesoamerican cultures believed that blood sacrifice to their gods was essential to ensure the survival of their worlds, in a tradition of ritual bloodletting that dated back to the first major civilization in Mexico – that of the Olmecs, which flourished between 1500 and 400 BCE. In legends, the gods themselves had made tremendous sacrifices in forming the world, which included shedding their own blood to create humankind; therefore they desired similar sacrifices of blood from humanity in return.

Sacrifice and creation

The power of blood and the necessity of sacrifice are central to the Aztec creation myth. The Aztecs believed that the gods had created and destroyed four earlier eras, or "suns", and that after the destruction of the fourth sun by flood, the god of the wind, Quetzalcoatl, and his trickster brother, Tezcatlipoca, tore the goddess (or god in some versions) Tlaltecuhtli in half to make a new heaven and earth. From her body grew everything necessary for the life of humankind – trees, flowers, grass, fountains, wells, valleys, and mountains. All this caused the goddess terrible agony, and she howled through the night demanding the sacrifice of human hearts to sustain her.

Further cosmic acts of creation followed, all requiring sacrifice or blood offerings. One relief shows

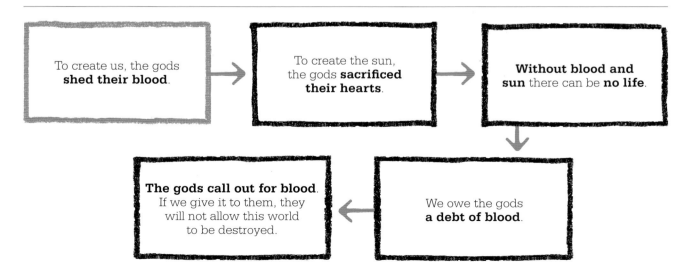

To create us, the gods **shed their blood**.

To create the sun, the gods **sacrificed their hearts**.

Without blood and sun there can be **no life**.

We owe the gods **a debt of blood**.

The gods call out for blood. If we give it to them, they will not allow this world to be destroyed.

See also: Created for a purpose 32 ▪ A lifelong bond with the gods 39 ▪ The burden of observance 50 ▪ Renewing life through ritual 51 ▪ Beliefs for new societies 56–57

You have yet
to take care of bleeding
your ears and passing a
cord through your elbows.
You must worship. This
is your way of giving
thanks before your god.
Tohil, Maya god

Victims of Aztec human sacrifice
were typically prisoners of war, and,
when in combat, Aztec warriors sought
to capture rather than kill in order to
ensure plentiful offerings for the gods.

the first stars being born from blood flowing from Quetzalcoatl's tongue after he had pierced it. Most notably, the creation of the fifth sun required one of the gods to cast himself into a funeral pyre. Two gods, Tecuciztecatl and Nanahuatzin, vied for the honour, both immolating themselves; Nanahuatzin became the sun and Tecuciztecatl the moon. The other gods then offered their hearts in order to make the new sun move across the sky (the offering of hearts is a recurring theme in Mesoamerican myth and ritual).

Humanity's gruesome debt

Both the Maya and the Aztecs were bound to their gods by a blood debt from these acts of creation that could never be repaid. After Quetzalcoatl descended to the underworld and retrieved the bones of former humans (remains from the four previous eras), the gods ground them into a fine meal flour. They let their own blood drip onto the flour to animate it and created a new race of people – people whose hearts could in turn satisfy the gods' own need for blood.

In Mesoamerican myth, each period of 52 years was seen as a cycle, the end of which could spell the end of the world. Human sacrifice could be used to appease the gods and persuade them not to bring an end to the present age – that of the fifth sun. The Maya believed that blood sacrifice was necessary for the sun to rise in the sky every morning.

The Aztecs' sun god, Huitzilopochtli, was locked in an ongoing struggle with darkness and needed to be fortified by blood in order for the sun to continue in its cycle. Thus the continued existence of the Mesoamerican world was seen as extremely tenuous, and in need of constant support through acts of sacrifice.

Bloodletting for the gods took two forms: autosacrifice (self-inflicted bloodletting) and human sacrifice. Both Maya and Aztecs took part in autosacrifice. Mesoamerican nobles had what was seen as the privilege and responsibility to shed their own blood for the gods. This involved piercing their flesh with stingray spines, obsidian knives, and, most often, with the sharp spines of the maguey (agave) plant. Blood was drawn from the ear, shin, knee, elbow, tongue, or foreskin. Autosacrifice »

> And this goddess cried many times in the night desiring the hearts of men to eat.
> **Saying of Aztec goddess Tlaltecuhtli**

> And when his festival was celebrated, captives were slain, washed slaves were slain.
> **Aztec hymn to Huitzilopochtli**

dates back to the Olmec people and continued after the Spanish Conquest of Mexico in 1519. Both men and women of the Maya nobility took part – the men drawing blood from their foreskins, women from their tongues. They collected their offerings on strips of bark paper, which were then burned; through the smoke from these offerings, they communicated with their ancestors and the gods.

Sacrificial rites
Human sacrifice was far more common among the Aztec than the Maya, who performed it only in special circumstances, such as the consecration of a new temple.

Aztec sacrifice usually involved cutting the victim's heart from his body. The heart was believed to be a fragment of the sun's energy – so removing the heart was a means of returning the energy to its source. The victim was typically held by four priests over a stone slab in the temple, while a fifth cut the heart from the body with an obsidian knife, and offered it, still beating, to the gods in a vessel called a *cuauhxicalli*, an "eagle gourd". After the removal of the heart,

the body was rolled down the stairs of the pyramid-shaped temple to the stone terrace at the base. The victim's head was removed and the arms and legs might also be cut off. Skulls were displayed on a skull rack. Depending on the particular god being honoured in the sacrifice, victims might be slain in ritual combat, drowned, shot with arrows, or flayed.

The scale of sacrifice sometimes reached immense proportions: for example, at the re-dedication of the Aztec temple of Huitzilopochtli, at Tenochtitlan, in 1487, around 80,400 victims were said to have been sacrificed to the god, their clotted blood forming great pools in the temple precinct. Even if a more modest estimate of 20,000 victims is accepted, this was still slaughter on a vast scale.

The Aztec ritual year was marked by sacrifices to various gods and goddesses. Although the gods could also be propitiated with

Descendants of the Maya, the Tzotzil people were put to work on the Spanish colonists' estates, and fused their own beliefs with Christian forms of worship in a syncretic religion.

smoke from incense and tobacco, and with food and precious objects, blood was what they really craved.

Rituals and the calendar
The Mesoamerican year lasted 260 days, a calendar observed by both the Mayas and the Aztecs. At the end of each year in Aztec society, a man representing Mictlantecuhtli, the god of the underworld, was sacrificed in the temple named Tlalxicco, "the navel of the world". It is thought that the victim was then eaten by the priests. Just as human flesh sustained the gods, so by consuming a god (embodied in the sacrificial victim) a form of communion could be enacted. Less high-ranking celebrants ate figures made from dough, into which sacrificial blood was mixed. To break apart and consume these dough figures, known as *tzoalli*, was also to commune with the gods.

Such re-enactment of the myths of the gods was a feature of Aztec belief and of annual rituals. During the main festival of Xipe

Tzotzil souls

The Tzotzil religion blends Catholicism with some non-Christian beliefs. The Tzotzil people maintain that everyone has two souls, a *wayjel* and a *ch'ulel*. The *ch'ulel* is an inner soul that is situated in the heart and blood. It is placed in the unborn embryo by the gods. At death, this soul travels to *Katibak,* the land of the dead at the centre of the earth. It stays in *Katibak* for as long as the deceased person had lived; but it lives its life in reverse, gradually returning to infancy, until it can be assigned to a new baby of the opposite sex.

The second soul, the *wayjel*, is an animal spirit companion that is shared with a wild animal, or *chanul,* and kept in an enclosure by the ancestral Tzotzil gods. The human and the animal spirit have a shared fate – so whatever befalls the human is replicated in the animal spirit and vice-versa. The animal spirits include jaguars, ocelots, coyotes, squirrels, and opossums.

Totec, the flayed deity, a priest impersonating the god donned the flayed skin of a sacrificed captive. As the skin tightened and tore away, the impersonator emerged like a fresh shoot growing from the rotting husk of a seed, representing growth and renewal. Other Aztec sacrifices honour the importance of maize, their staple food. Every year, a young girl representing Chicomecoatl, the maize goddess, was sacrificed at harvest time. She was decapitated, her blood poured over a statue of the goddess, and her skin worn by a priest.

Conquest and absorption

When Spanish invader Hernán Cortés and his conquistadors landed in Mexico in 1519, the Aztecs are believed to have mistaken him for the returning god Quetzalcoatl, partly because Cortés' hat resembled the god's distinctive headgear. They sent the Spaniard maize cakes soaked in human blood, but their offering failed to appease the "god", and the Aztec civilization, just four centuries old when Cortés landed, was destroyed by the Spanish.

This Aztec stone sun calendar places a depiction of the sun within a ring of glyphs representing measures of time, reflecting the Aztec preoccupation with the sun.

In contrast, the Maya culture did not suffer the same annihilation, possibly because the Maya were more widely dispersed. In southern Mexico, even today the Tzotzil people, descendants of the Maya, retain many elements of the old culture and religion, including the 260-day calendar.

The Tzotzil religion is a blend of Catholicism and traditional Maya beliefs. The people's homeland, in the highlands of Chiapas in southern Mexico, is dotted with wooden crosses. These do not just reference the Christian crucifix, but are thought to be channels of communication with Yajval Balamil, the lord of the earth, a powerful god who must be placated before any work can be done on the land. In their adaptation of the ancient beliefs, the Tzotzil people associate the sun with the Christian God and the moon with the Virgin Mary, and also worship carvings of Christian saints. ∎

At this feast [to Xipe Totec] they killed all the prisoners, men, women, and children.
Bernadino de Sahagún, General History of the Things of New Spain

WE CAN BUILD A SACRED SPACE
SYMBOLISM MADE REAL

The **world** and we ourselves were **created by Tirawahat**, the expanse of **the heavens**. He told us **the earth is our mother, the sky is our father**.

↓

If we make **our lodges** to **encircle the earth and encompass the sky**, we invite our mother and father to live with us.

↓

If we open our lodges to the east, Tirawahat can enter with the dawning sun. **Our lodges are a miniature version of the cosmos**.

The first sacred spaces of early religions were naturally occurring ones – groves, springs, and caves. However, as worship became more ritualized, the need to define holy places arose, and buildings designed for worship encoded the essential features of each religion.

On the other hand, buildings used for everyday activities often took on cosmic significance in cultures in which religious and daily life were intertwined. This was true of the earth lodges, or ceremonial centres, of the Pawnee, one of the Native American nations of the Great Plains. The Pawnee earth lodge had a sacred architecture, making each lodge a miniature cosmos as Tirawahat, the creator god and chief of all the gods, had prescribed at the beginning of time, after he had made the heavens and earth and brought the first humans into being (see box, facing page).

Four posts held up each earth lodge, one at each corner. These represented four gods, the Stars of the Four Directions, who hold up the heavens in the northeast, northwest, southwest, and southeast. The Pawnee believed that stars had

See also: Making sense of the world 20–23 ▪ Man and the cosmos 48–49 ▪ Living the Way of the Gods 82–85

The earth lodge was a mini-cosmos in the Pawnee tradition, and was constructed accordingly. This Pawnee family stands at an earth lodge entrance at Loup, Nebraska in 1873.

helped Tirawahat create them, and that at the world's end, the Pawnee would become stars.

The entrance to the earth lodge would be in the east, allowing the light of the dawn to enter. A hearth would be positioned in the centre of the lodge, and a small altar of mounded earth in the back (the west). A buffalo skull would be displayed on the altar, which the spirit of Tirawahat was said to occupy when the first rays of sun shone on it in the morning. Through this skull, Tirawahat was said to live and communicate with the people. Sacred star bundles containing objects used for rituals, such as charts of the night sky, hung from a rafter above the skull. These were said to give each village its identity and power.

A world within a world

In winter, a domed sweat lodge would often be constructed inside the earth lodge, creating a second mini-cosmos. These sweat lodges, or steam huts, used for spiritual and healing purposes, were also sacred spaces. The heated stones used inside them were said to be ancestral "grandfathers", and were treated with great reverence. The hot stones were doused in water, and the steam produced was believed to be the breath of the grandfathers.

The first sweat lodge was, according to legend, made by the son of a bundle-keeper, as part of a ritual taught to him by guardian animals. As he performed the ritual he said, "Now we are sitting in darkness as did Tirawahat when he created all things and placed meteors in the heavens for our benefit. The poles that shelter us represent them… When I blow this root upon them you will see a blue flame rise from the stones. This will be a signal for us to pray to Tirawahat and the grandfathers." ▪

The legend of Tirawahat

In Pawnee myth, after the creator god, Tirawahat, had made the sun, moon, stars, heavens, earth, and all things on earth, he spoke. At the sound of his voice a woman appeared. Tirawahat created a man and sent him to the woman. Then he said: "I give you the earth. You shall call the earth 'mother'. The heavens you shall call 'father'… I will now show you how to build a lodge, so that you will not be cold or get wet from the rain." After a time Tirawahat spoke again and asked the man if he knew what the lodge represented. The man did not know. Tirawahat said: "I told you to call the earth 'mother'. The lodge represents her breast. The smoke that escapes from the opening is like the milk that flows from her breast… When you eat the things that are cooked [in the fireplace], it is like sucking a breast, because you eat and grow strong."

Our people were made by the stars. When the time comes for all things to end, our people will turn into small stars.
Young Bull

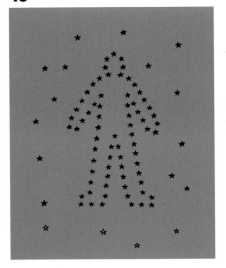

WE ARE IN RHYTHM WITH THE UNIVERSE

MAN AND THE COSMOS

IN CONTEXT

KEY BELIEVERS
Dogon

WHEN AND WHERE
From 15th century CE, Mali, West Africa

BEFORE
From 1500 BCE Similarities in oral myths and knowledge of astronomy suggest that the Dogon's ancestral tribes may have originated in ancient Egypt before migrating to the region of present-day Libya, then Burkina Faso or Guinea.

From 10th century CE Dogon identity evolves in West Africa from a mixture of peoples of earlier tribes, many of whom have fled Islamic persecution.

AFTER
Today The Dogon people number between 400,000 and 800,000. The majority still practise their traditional religion, but significant minorities have converted to Islam and Christianity.

The Dogon people live in the Bandiagara plateau in Mali, West Africa, where they practise a traditional animist religion: for them, all things are endowed with spiritual power. Fundamental to Dogon religious belief is that humankind is the "seed" of the universe, and that the human form echoes both the first moment of creation and the entire created universe. Every Dogon village is therefore laid out in the shape of a human body, and is regarded as a living person.

Sacred and symbolic space

A Dogon village is arranged lying north to south, with the smithy, or forge, at its head and shrines at its feet. This layout reflects the belief that the creator god, Amma, made the world from clay in the form of a woman lying in this position. Everything in the village has an anthropomorphic, or human, equivalent. The women's menstrual huts, to the east and west, are the hands. The family homesteads are the chest. Each of these big homesteads is, in turn, laid out in the plan of a male body, with the kitchen as the head, the large central room as the belly, the arms as two lines of storerooms, the chest as two jars of water, and the penis as the entrance passage. The building reflects the creative power of the male–female twin ancestral beings, the Nommo (see facing page).

The hut of the *hogon*, the Dogon's spiritual leader, is a model of the universe. Every element of the hut's

Masked dancers perform the *dama*, or funeral ritual. This traditional Dogon religious ceremony is designed to guide the souls of the deceased safely into the afterlife.

See also: Symbolism made real 46–47 ▪ The ultimate reality 102–105

The **whole universe** was originally contained in an **egg or seed**.

⬇

Everything that exists **began as a vibration** in this egg.

⬇

The **form of man was prefigured** in the egg, and is also echoed in the form of the universe.

⬇

Everything, from the smallest seed to the expanse of the cosmos, **reflects and expresses everything**.

⬇

A village, or a homestead, or a hat, or a seed, can **contain the whole universe**.

The Nommo

The Nommo are ancestral beings worshipped by the Dogon. They are often described as amphibious, hermaphroditic, fish-like creatures who, acccording to myth, were fathered by the god Amma, when he created the cosmic egg. This egg was said to resemble both the smallest seed cultivated by the Dogon, and the sister star to Sirius – the brightest star in the night sky. Within the egg lay the germ of all things.

In one version of the myth, two sets of male–female twins, the Nommo, were inside the egg waiting to be born so that they could bring order to the world. But the egg was shaken by a vibration and one of the male twins, Yurugu, broke out of it prematurely, creating the earth from his placenta. So Amma sent the three remaining Nommo down to earth, and they established the institutions and rituals necessary for the renewal and continuation of life. But because of Yurugu's premature actions, the world was tainted right from the beginning.

---

decoration and furnishing is laden with symbolism. The *hogon's* movements are attuned to the rhythms of the universe. At dawn he sits facing east, towards the rising sun; he then walks through the homestead following the order of the four cardinal points; and finally at dusk he sits facing west. His pouch is described as "the pouch of the world"; his staff is "the axis of the world".

Cosmic meaning
Even the hogon's clothing represents the world in miniature. His cylindrical headdress, for example, is a woven image of the seven spiral vibrations that shook the cosmic "egg of the world" (see right). During a crisis, the chiefs gather round the headdress; the *hogon* speaks into it and upturns it on the ground, as if the world itself has been turned upside down, ready to be restored to order by the god Amma.

The complex cosmic symbolism of the Dogon reflects outwards from the cosmos, and then back in again to the headdress of the *hogon*, the shell of the world egg. Religion, society, cosmology, mythology, cultivation, daily life – all are intermeshed in every detail, and reflected in every action. ▪

For [the Dogon], social life represents the workings of the universe.
Marcel Griaule, anthropologist

WE EXIST TO SERVE THE GODS
THE BURDEN OF OBSERVANCE

U ntil Christianity arrived in Tikopia in the 1950s, all the residents of this small Pacific island devoted themselves to ritual for two weeks twice a year, as they undertook the "Work of the Gods". At these times, they perfomed duties to propitiate the *atua*, spirits or gods, believing that they, in turn, would ensure plentiful harvests.

The Work of the Gods was a form of worship expressed as a system of trade between human and spirit beings. The Tikopians performed the rituals, and the gods granted the people the necessities of life. Moreover, the religion was structured so that many of the activities undertaken to please the gods – such as repairing canoes, planting and harvesting, and the ritual production of turmeric – were of economic value to the Tikopians. Offerings of food and kava (an intoxicating drink) made to the gods were consumed only "in essence" – leaving the actual food available for human consumption.

Taking part in the Work of the Gods brought status to individuals, and was perceived as a privilege. The rituals involved in this religion also underpinned key social and economic structures, and held Tikopian society together. ∎

A Tikopian man performs a dance with a canoe paddle: ritual dancing and drumming on canoes were part of the Work of the Gods.

See also: Making sense of the world 20–23 ∎ A lifelong bond with the gods 39 ∎ Sacrifice and blood offerings 40–45 ∎ Devotion through puja 114–15

OUR RITUALS SUSTAIN THE WORLD
RENEWING LIFE THROUGH RITUAL

Through their ritual songs and dances, the Hupa tribe of northwestern California believed they could renew the world, or "firm the earth", and revitalize the land to ensure sufficient resources for the coming year. One of their most important world renewal dances, held every autumn, was the White Deerskin Dance. The purpose of the dance was to recreate the actions of the the Kixunai, or First People, the Hupa's mythical predecessors.

By replaying the sacred narrative of the Kixunai, the Hupa hoped to tap into the powers of creation in order to safeguard the health of the people and guarantee abundant stocks of game and fish for the hunting season. During the dance, which lasted 10 days, the elaborately decorated hide of an albino deer – a symbol of great wealth and status – was displayed. Participants paddled along the river in dugout canoes every morning and danced every afternoon and evening, holding deer effigies aloft on poles.

[The Kixunai] painted themselves and danced there one night. The next morning they danced again.
Hupa myth

The First People
The Kixunai were believed by the Hupa to be human in form but extraordinary in character. Whatever the Kixunai did became the predestined custom of the unborn Hupa race. So every detail of Hupa daily life was mapped out by the activities of the First People. According to Hupa belief, the Kixunai later scattered across the ocean, leaving only the mythical being Yimantuwinyai to assist people in their life on earth. ∎

See also: The spirits of the dead live on 36–37 ▪ Beliefs that mirror society 80–81

ANCIENT CLASSIC BELIEFS

FROM 3000 BCE

AND
AL

Tomb inscriptions known as the "**Pyramid Texts**", the oldest known religious writings, suggest an **Ancient Egyptian** belief in an afterlife.

The probable date of the foundation of **Zoroastrianism** in Persia, although this may have been as early as the 18th century BCE.

Ancient Egypt is unified and the **Early Dynastic period** begins. A cult of a divine Pharaoh is established.

The pantheon of Greek mythology evolves in the **Minoan culture** of Crete.

c.3000 BCE   **25TH–24TH CENTURIES**   **1700–1400 BCE**   **c.1200 BCE**

c.3000 BCE   **20TH–16TH CENTURIES**   **c.1600 BCE**   **8TH CENTURY BCE**

Celtic clans spread across much of Europe, each tribe having its own local deities.

In the **First Babylonian Dynasty in Mesopotamia**, a complex mythology is recorded in the Enuma Elish.

Scandinavian peoples begin to make figures of their gods and goddesses, and develop a recognizable **Norse mythology**.

According to legend, **Romulus** usurps his twin brother Remus to found the **city of Rome**.

The earliest civilizations emerged when scattered nomadic tribes began to settle in order to raise crops. Previously localized religious beliefs and practices evolved, and the beliefs of different tribes amalgamated around common deities and mythologies. Complex pantheons emerged, and an often sophisticated body of myths arose from the various strands that had come together, describing the role of the gods and mythical creatures in the workings of the world.

These more formal religions offered explanations for natural phenomena, such as the sun, moon, seasons, weather, and the gods' influence on them. They often included creation stories and tales of the interaction of gods and humans. It is clear from elaborate tombs left by the early civilizations, such as the Egyptians, that belief in an afterlife existed, and that rituals of death and burial played a major part in religion. As people settled in ever bigger communities, temples dedicated to the gods became focal points in the towns and cities.

Civilization also gave rise to various forms of written language, which allowed these stories of gods and creation to be recorded and embellished over the millennia. Religious inscriptions first appeared on the walls of tombs and temples in early civilizations, such as that of Egypt. Elsewhere, distinctive traditions were also taking shape as Indian, Chinese, Japanese, Norse, and Celtic folk religions were incorporated into the belief systems of the emerging nations.

Coalescing faiths

By about 1500 BCE, regional religious traditions were well established in many parts of the world, and new, more advanced, societies arose, requiring more elaborate belief systems. Some new religions also appeared, notably Zoroastrianism, which was arguably the first monotheistic faith, while the foundations of Judaism were also being laid down.

In India, the numerous local religious beliefs were incorporated into the Vedic tradition, based on ancient scriptures called the Vedas. This later became the pluralistic amalgam now known as Hinduism, but alongside this came Jainism, which placed more emphasis on a correct way of life than on the worship of deities, and Buddhism, which was arguably

The Greek poet **Homer** writes the *Iliad* and *Odyssey*, and **Hesiod** writes his *Theogony* (Origin of the Gods).

The Indian sage **Mahavira** establishes the **central tenets of Jainism**.

The classical period of the **Ancient Greek civilization** begins in the eastern Mediterranean.

The **Vikings** flourish, spreading their religion across northern Europe and in Iceland and Greenland.

8TH–7TH CENTURIES BCE   **599–27 BCE**   **5TH–4TH CENTURIES BCE**   **9TH–10TH CENTURIES**

6TH CENTURY BCE   **551 BCE**   **8TH CENTURY CE**   **13TH CENTURY**

The Chinese sage **Laozi** describes the *dao*, the way, and **establishes Daoism** in China.

Confucius, founder of Confucianism, is born in Zou, Lu State, China.

Two collections of **Japanese mythology**, the Kojiki and the Nihon Shoki, are compiled as a resource to support **Shinto** as national religion of Japan.

Icelandic epic poems describing **Norse mythology** are composed and recorded in the *Eddas*.

more a philosophy than a religion, as it concentrated on enlightenment without the need for gods.

This focus on moral philosophy was also prevalent in the religions that evolved in China and Japan. In the ordered society of the great Chinese dynasties, religion and political organization became intertwined. Daoism, proposed by the legendary scholar Laozi, advocated a religious way of life compatible with Chinese society. Confucius built on this to develop a new belief system based on a reinterpretation of respect for the hierarchy, and reinforced by ritual. Latterly, in Japan, traditional religions were unified to create the state religion, Shinto, which showed special reverence to ancestors and encouraged followers to connect with them through ritual practices.

By the 6th century BCE, the Greek city states had been established, and classical Greek civilization was exerting a strong influence on the eastern Mediterranean region. Religion (although the Greeks did not have a specific word for it) was very much a part of life, and, although the gods were believed to live separately from the people, they were imagined to lead remarkably similar lives. The history of the Greek people, as interpreted by Homer in his epic poems, was also the history of their gods. The hierarchy of deities, with their very human lifestyles and tempestuous relationships, mirrored Greek society. As well as offering an explanation for aspects of the world, the deities gave reasons for the vagaries of human behaviour, and with their help it was possible

to divine the future, choose auspicious times for action, and even defeat enemies. Most of the time they existed alongside people, unconcerned with human affairs, but, to keep them happy, the Greeks erected temples, performed rituals, and held regular festivals.

As the early civilizations rose and fell, many of their beliefs faded away, or were incorporated into the religions that replaced them; the pantheon of Greek mythology, for example, was absorbed into Roman mythology, and along with Celtic and other beliefs, into Christianity. Some religions, however, such as that of the Norse, were still practised until the Middle Ages, and others, including Shinto, Jainism, Daoism, and Confucianism, have survived into the modern age. ∎

THERE IS A HIERARCHY OF GODS AND MEN
BELIEFS FOR NEW SOCIETIES

The god **Marduk kills** the goddess **Tiamat** and makes all the other gods accept him as king.

The **Babylonians succeed the Sumerians** and establish the city of Babylon.

He then brings **order to the universe** and creates mankind to serve the gods.

King Hammurabi then claims divine authority for his rule and introduces a code of laws.

Both **Marduk and Hammurabi** assert their supremacy over others by establishing…

…a hierarchy of gods and men.

Mesopotamia, the area of modern Iraq between the Tigris and Euphrates rivers, is often referred to in the West as the "cradle of civilization". It was there that – in the Bronze Age – small communities first evolved into towns and cities.

As these larger settlements grew, so did the need for new social structures, a common culture, and shared beliefs in order to unify the population and reinforce the political system. Religion not only explained natural phenomena but also provided a coherent mythology.

See also: Created for a purpose 32 ▪ Renewing life through ritual 51 ▪ Beliefs that mirror society 80–81 ▪ A rational world 92–99

Images of Babylonian soldiers lined the Ishtar Gate, which led to the city of Babylon. Effigies of gods were paraded from the gate to the city along the Processional Way.

In the 4th millennium BCE, the Sumerian people inhabited the region. The population of Sumer was concentrated in about a dozen city-states; each was ruled by a king, but political power was vested in the high priests of each city's religion. The Sumerians worshipped a pantheon of gods, including Enki, god of water and fertility, and Anu, god of heaven. When the Babylonians began to settle in Mesopotamia in the 3rd millennium BCE, they absorbed the Sumerians and their culture – including some aspects of their mythology – into their own empire. The Babylonian leaders used the Sumerian mythology to reinforce the hierarchy they established, which helped to assert their power over their own people and the supplanted Sumerians.

Babylonian religion
Central to the Babylonian religion was the epic creation story of the Enûma Elish, recorded on seven clay tablets. The sequence of events it relates had largely been adapted from earlier Sumerian mythology, but in this retelling featured Babylonian deities – in particular Marduk, son of the Sumerian god Enki and the rightful heir to Anu. The story tells of Marduk as the leader of a hierarchy of young deities, whose victory over the older gods, including the creator god, Tiamat (see box, right) gave him the power to create and organize the universe, which he ruled from his chosen home of Babylon. The Enûma Elish provided an obvious analogy to the takeover of Sumer and founding of Babylon, but Marduk's ascendancy over the other gods and his ordering of the world also served as a metaphor for the sovereignty of Babylonian kings and their authority to make and enforce laws.

A mark of kingship
To reinforce the idea of Babylonian dominance and to unify the empire, the Enûma Elish was recited and acted out in an annual New Year festival, known as the Akitu, which was held at the time of the spring equinox. This performance did more than mark the calendrical movement from one year to the next; it was a ritualized recreation and re-energizing of the cosmos, which enabled Marduk to settle the destinies of the stars and planets for the year ahead. Both in its mythology and its ritual, the Akitu was fundamentally about legitimizing kingship; it was a public demonstration that the Babylonian monarch held his authority directly from the god. By recreating Marduk's triumph over Tiamat, the centrality of Babylon was also re-affirmed. ▪

The Enûma Elish

The Akitu ritual recreated the creation story of the Enûma Elish. This begins before time, when only Apsu (the freshwater ocean) and Tiamat (the saltwater ocean) exist. Apsu and Tiamat give birth to the primal gods, including Anshar and Kishu, the horizons of the sky and the earth, who themselves beget Anu, the god of the sky, and Ea (the Sumerian Enki), the god of the earth and water. The shouts of the young gods disturb Apsu and Tiamat's peace, so Apsu attempts to destroy them, but is killed by Ea. At the site of this struggle, the god Ea creates a temple for himself, which he names Apsu (after his father), where his son Marduk is born. To avenge her husband, Tiamat wages war on Marduk, and puts her son Qingu in command of her forces. Marduk agrees to fight Tiamat's army, if all the other gods accept him as king, with sovereignty over the universe. Marduk then kills Tiamat and Qingu, and brings order to the universe. From Qingu's blood he creates mankind.

I hereby name it Babylon, home of the great gods. We shall make it the centre of religion.
Marduk, in the Enûma Elish

THE GOOD LIVE FOREVER IN THE KINGDOM OF OSIRIS
PREPARING FOR THE AFTERLIFE

IN CONTEXT

KEY BELIEVERS
Ancient Egyptians

WHEN
2000 BCE–4th century BCE

BEFORE
In predynastic Egypt
Bodies buried in the sand are
preserved by dehydration;
this may have inspired later
mummification practices.

c.2400–2100 BCE Royal tomb
inscriptions at Saqqara – the
Pyramid Texts – suggest belief
in a divine afterlife for the
Egyptian pharaohs, promising
the kings: "You have not died".

c.2100 BCE The first Coffin
Texts – spells inscribed
on the coffins of wealthy men
and women – suggest that
the afterlife is no longer
reserved for royalty.

AFTER
From 4th century BCE The
conquering Greeks adopt some
Egyptian beliefs, especially in
the cult of Isis, wife of Osiris.

We want to **live again after
death**, as the god Osiris did.

If we imitate the
mummification of Osiris by
Anubis, we can **join Osiris**
in the **realm of the dead**.

There, **Osiris will judge us**,
and our hearts will be
weighed against our sins.

If we are **judged
worthy**, we will
enjoy **everlasting life**.

The Ancient Egyptians left
extraordinary tributes to
their dead, such as the
Great Pyramids, huge necropolises,
underground tombs, and fabulous
grave goods and art, but it would
not be true to say that they were
obsessed with death. Instead, they
were preparing for the afterlife.

All their mortuary rituals
of embalming, mummification,
entombment, and remembrance
were aimed at ensuring new life
after death. Egyptians wanted to
live after their death as perfected
beings in Aaru, the "field of reeds",
which was itself a perfected version
of the Egypt they already knew.

Aaru was the domain of Osiris,
lord of the dead. In it, the blessed
dead gathered rich crops of barley
and emmer wheat – abundant
harvests that are joyously depicted
on the walls of Egyptian tombs.

Egyptians believed that a
complete person comprised a
number of elements: the physical
body, the name, the shadow, the
ka (spiritual life force), the *ba*
(personality), and the *akh* (the
perfected being that could enjoy
life in paradise). To ensure life in
paradise, care needed to be taken
of all these constituent parts. The

See also: The origin of death 33 ▪ The spirits of the dead live on 36–37 ▪ Entering into the faith 224–25 ▪ Social holiness and evangelicalism 239 ▪ The ultimate reward for the righteous 279 ▪ Awaiting the Day of Judgment 312–13

Elaborate preparations for safe passage to the next world were at first reserved only for the nobility, as here, but later the promise of rebirth into eternal life was open to all Egyptians.

body had to be preserved by mummification and buried with a set of funerary equipment, including jars containing the internal organs, in rituals that identified the deceased with the god Osiris. Re-enacting the death and resurrection of the god prepared the deceased for the journey to the next world.

Every stage of mummification was accompanied by religious ritual. Embalmers enacted the role of the jackal-headed god, Anubis, who was the protective god of the dead; Anubis invented the mysteries of embalming in order to resurrect the slain Osiris. Embalming spells reassured the deceased: "You will live again, you will live for ever".

The journey of the dead

The preservation of the physical body by mummification was important because it was to the body that the *ka* needed to return for sustenance. If the body was decayed, the *ka* would starve. The *ka* needed to take strength from the body to rejoin the *ba* in the afterlife. Together they created the *akh*, which would have to gain admittance to the afterlife.

The deceased then negotiated the path from this world to the next, and was led by Anubis into the Hall of Two Truths. Here, the heart was weighed in the balance against Ma'at, goddess of truth, symbolized by a feather. If the heart, heavy with sin, outweighed the feather, it would be gobbled up by Ammut, she-monster and devourer of the dead. If the scales balanced, the deceased could proceed to paradise, the gates of which were guarded by Osiris.

Important Egyptians were buried with a "manual": the *Book of the Dead*, or the *Spells for Coming Forth by Day*. This guide taught the dead how to speak, breathe, eat, and drink in the afterlife. It included, crucially, a spell for "not dying again in the realm of the dead". ▪

The death of Osiris

The story of the death and resurrection of Osiris was the foundation myth that offered Egyptians the hope of new life after death – initially just for the king, but for all Egyptians by the Middle Kingdom period.

The god Osiris was said to have been killed by his jealous brother Seth, who cut his body into pieces and scattered them across Egypt. "It is not possible to destroy the body of a god," Seth said, "but I have done so." Osiris's wife Isis and her sister Nephthys gathered up the body, piece by piece, and the god Anubis embalmed it as the first mummy. Isis changed herself into a kite and, hovering over the mummified Osiris, fanned the breath of life back into him for long enough to conceive a child, Horus (who would avenge his father), before Osiris took his place as lord of the underworld.

O my heart...! Do not stand up as a witness against me, do not be opposed to me in the tribunal.
Ancient Egyptian Book of the Dead

THE TRIUMPH OF GOOD OVER EVIL DEPENDS ON HUMANKIND

THE BATTLE BETWEEN GOOD AND EVIL

IN CONTEXT

KEY BELIEVERS
Zoroastrians

WHEN AND WHERE
1400–1200 BCE, Iran (Persia)

BEFORE
From prehistory Many belief systems feature a destructive or mischievous god or spirit who is in opposition to a more benevolent deity.

AFTER
6th century BCE The Persian and Mede empires are unified; Zoroastrianism becomes one of the world's largest religions.

4th century BCE Classical Greek philosophers, including Plato, study with Zoroastrian priests; Aristotle is said to have considered Plato to be a reincarnation of Zoroaster.

10th century CE Zoroastrians migrate from Iran to India to avoid converting to Islam; they become the Parsis, the largest Zoroastrian community today.

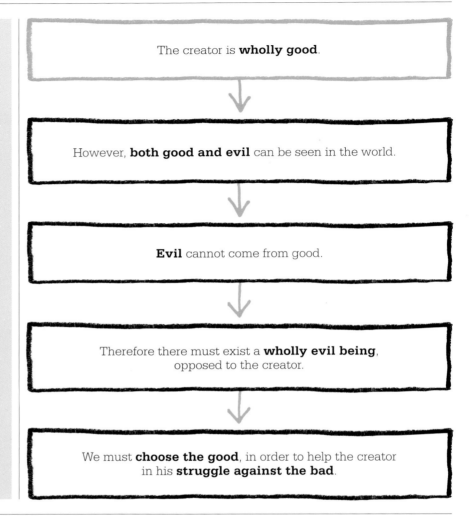

The creator is **wholly good**.

However, **both good and evil** can be seen in the world.

Evil cannot come from good.

Therefore there must exist a **wholly evil being**, opposed to the creator.

We must **choose the good**, in order to help the creator in his **struggle against the bad**.

Zoroastrianism is one of the oldest surviving religions, and one of the first recorded monotheistic faiths. It was founded by the prophet figure Zoroaster in ancient Persia (modern Iran).

Zoroaster's religion developed from the old system of Indo-Iranian gods, which included Ahura Mazda, "lord of wisdom". In Zoroastrianism, Ahura Mazda (sometimes called Ohrmazd) is elevated to become the one supreme god, the wise creator who is the source of all good, and represents order and truth, in opposition to evil and chaos.

Ahura Mazda is assisted by his creations, the Amesha Spenta or "bounteous immortals": six divine spirits. A seventh and less easily definable Spenta is the Spenta Mainyu, who is seen as Mazda's own "bounteous spirit", and the agent of his will.

According to Zoroastrianism, the good Ahura Mazda has been locked in struggle with the evil entity Ahriman (also called Angra Mainyu, or "destructive spirit") since time began. Ahriman and Ahura Mazda are regarded as twin spirits; however, Ahriman is a fallen being,

and cannot be considered Ahura Mazda's equal. Ahura Mazda lives in the light, while his twin lurks in the dark. Their struggle, as evil endlessly attempts to vanquish good, forms the entire body of Zoroastrian mythology.

Ahura Mazda battles with Ahriman using the creative energy of his spirit, Spenta Mainyu; the exact relationship between these three entities remains an unresolved aspect of the religion. Human beings, also Mazda's creation, have an important role in keeping disorder and evil at bay

See also: The end of the world as we know it 86–87 ■ From monolatry to monotheism 176–77 ■ Jesus's message to the world 204–207

> The goodness of the wise Creator can be inferred from the act of creation.
> **Mardan-Farrukh**

by using their free will to do good. Good thoughts, good words, and good deeds support *asha*, the fundamental order of the universe. *Asha* is seen as being constantly at risk from the opposing principle of *druj*, chaos, which feeds on bad thoughts, bad words, and bad deeds. The essential opposition is between creation and uncreation, with evil threatening at all times to undermine the ordered structure of the world.

The birth of Zoroaster, with his destiny to recruit humankind to the fight between good and evil, tipped

the battle in favour of goodness. According to Zoroastrianism, it is good that will ultimately prevail.

A world made by goodness

Zoroastrianism tells that when Ahura Mazda wanted to create a perfect world, he made the Amesha Spenta and a spiritual, invisible world, which included a perfect being. The spiritual nature of this world was intended to foil Ahriman, who tries to attack it nevertheless. Ahura Mazda defeats Ahriman by reciting the holiest Zoroastrian prayer, the Ahunavar, which casts him back into the darkness.

Ahura Mazda then gives material form to his spiritual world. He creates one primal animal (a bull), and his perfect spiritual being becomes a human being, known as Gayomart (meaning mortal or human life). »

The symbol of Zoroastrianism, the Faravahar, is thought to depict a *fravashi*, or guardian angel. These protect the souls of individuals as they struggle against evil.

Zoroaster

It is not known exactly when the prophet Zoroaster (also called Zarathustra) lived, but c.1400–1200 BCE seems likely. Although his teachings draw on early Hindu, texts such as the Rig-Veda, he regarded his religious insights into these texts as visions received directly from God. Zoroaster was already a priest among semi-nomadic, pastoral Iranians on the south Russian steppes when he began to preach the worship of Ahura Mazda. At first he found few followers, but he did convert a local ruler, who made Zoroastrianism the official religion of the Avestan people. However, it was not until the reign of Cyrus the Great, in the 6th century BCE, that the religion spread across the Persian empire.

Key works

4th century BCE Zoroaster's teachings are compiled in the Avesta, including the Gathas, 17 hymns believed to be Zoroaster's own words.
9th century CE The dualistic nature of Zoroastrian philosophy is laid out in detail in his *Analytical Treatise for the Dispelling of Doubts*.

The dissimilarity of good and evil, light and darkness, is not one of function but one of substance... their natures cannot combine and are mutually destructive.
Mardan-Farrukh

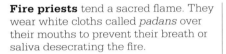

Fire priests tend a sacred flame. They wear white cloths called *padans* over their mouths to prevent their breath or saliva desecrating the fire.

It is not long, however, before Ahriman recovers and renews his attack. He breaks through the sky in a blaze of fire, bringing with him starvation, disease, pain, lust, and death. He also creates demons of his own. Gayomart and the bull ultimately die, but on their deaths, their semen spills on the ground, and is fertilized by the sun. Ahura Mazda sends rain, which brings forth, from the seed of Gayomart, the mother and father of humanity: Mashya and Mashyoi. Meanwhile, the bull's seed gives rise to all the other animals of the world.

Because his perfect creation has been spoiled by Ahriman's destructiveness, Ahura Mazda sets a limit on time, which was previously limitless.

Evil and human will

In Zoroastrianism, all people are born good. The presence of Ahriman, an active principle of evil,

explains why they may be tempted to do wrong. It also explains how evil can exist in the presence of a good god. Zoroastrian texts state: "What is complete and perfect in its goodness cannot produce evil. If it could, then it would not be perfect. If God is perfect in goodness and knowledge, plainly ignorance and evil cannot proceed from him". This is to say that Ahura Mazda cannot be responsible for the presence of evil in the world: the source of this is Ahriman.

The fact that Ahura Mazda has given humankind free will means that every moment of an individual's existence requires a choice to be made between what is right and what is wrong, and that it is our responsibility to choose good over evil.

This focus on moral choice makes Zoroastrianism a religion in which personal responsibility and morality are paramount, not only in conceptual terms but as practised in day-to-day life. Human virtues

One good twin, one evil twin

In Zurvanism, a now-defunct branch of Zoroastrianism, Ahura Mazda is not the sole creator; he and Ahriman are the sons of a pre-existing god, Zurvan ("Time"). This doctrine arose from the reasoning that, if Mazda and Ahriman were twin spirits (as texts said), they needed a progenitor. Zurvan, a neutral, androgynous god, sacrifices 1,000 of his years to create a son. But, as the end of the millennium approaches, Zurvan begins to doubt his power to produce a son. The evil Ahriman is born from his doubt, just as Ahura Mazda is born from his optimism. Zurvan prophesies that his first-born will rule the world. Ahriman forces his way out first, declaring himself Ahura Mazda, but Zurvan is not deceived, saying, "My son is light and fragrant, but you are dark and stinking". And Zurvan weeps to think he has produced such an abomination.

Establish the power of
acts arising from a life
lived with good purpose,
for Mazda and for the lord
whom they made pastor
for the poor.
The Ahunavar Prayer

worthy of, and helpful to, Ahura Mazda include truthfulness, loyalty, tolerance, forgiveness, respect for one's elders, and the keeping of promises. Vices such as anger, arrogance, vengefulness, bad language, and greed are condemned – and not only in this life.

Judgment and salvation

Zoroastrians believe that after death, individuals will be judged twice: once when they die and once at a Last Judgment at the end of time. The two judgments will address, respectively, the individual's morality of thought and his or her morality of action. In both cases, moral failings are punished in hell. However, these punishments are not eternal; they cease when the person corrects their moral failing in the afterlife – which, once successfully accomplished, is followed by the person going to dwell with Ahura Mazda in heaven.

Zoroastrians gather to pray together. This very moral religion is summed up in the old Avestan phrase: *"Humata, Hukhta, Hvarshta"* – "Good thoughts, good words, good deeds".

Zoroastrian teachings tell that as the end of time draws near, the Saoshyant ("saviour") will arise and prepare the world to be made anew, helping Ahura Mazda to destroy Ahriman. People will grow pure and stop eating meat, then milk, plants, and water, until at last they need nothing. When all have chosen good over evil, there will be no more sin, so Az, the demon of lust made by Ahriman, will starve, turning on her creator. Ahura Mazda will cast Ahriman from creation through the hole that Ahriman made when he broke in. It is at this point that time will be at an end.

Saoshyant will then raise the dead, who will pass through a stream of molten metal to burn away their sins. According to Zoroastrianism, the world will begin again, but this time it will be a world everlasting, free of taint.

The use of fire and molten metal as a purifier in the Last Judgment is reflected in the prominence of fire in Zoroastrianism as a symbol of sanctity. It is seen as the purest of the elements. Ahura Mazda is strongly associated with fire and also the sun. For this reason, Zoroastrian temples always keep a fire burning, symbolizing their god's eternal power. Some temple fires have been kept burning for centuries. Believers bring offerings of wood (the only fuel used), and fire priests place these in the flames. Visitors are anointed with ash.

The continuing struggle

The Zoroastrian idea of eternal, opposing forces of good and evil is a form of what philosophy calls "dualism". Another Persian dualistic religion, Manichaeism, was founded by the prophet Mani in the 3rd century CE. Mani felt that his "Religion of Light" completed the teachings of Zoroaster, Buddha, and Christ.

Like Zoroaster, Mani saw the world as an eternal struggle between the forces of good and evil, light and darkness. This was to have a profound effect on Christian thinkers, and influence medieval, heretical Christian cults such as the Paulicians in Armenia, the Bogomils in Bulgaria, and, most famously, the Cathars in France. ∎

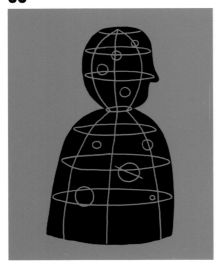

ACCEPT THE WAY OF THE UNIVERSE
ALIGNING THE SELF WITH THE DAO

IN CONTEXT

KEY FIGURE
Laozi

WHEN AND WHERE
6th century BCE, China

BEFORE
7th century BCE In popular Chinese religion, people believe their fate is controlled by deities and practise ancestor worship.

AFTER
6th century BCE Confucius proposes an ethical system in which virtue and respect lead to a just and stable society.

3rd century CE Buddhism, with its focus on the personal journey to enlightenment, first reaches China.

20th century Daoism is banned in China by the Communist regime; this ban is reversed in 1978.

20th century The physical and mental discipline of t'ai chi attracts followers in the West.

The *dao*, or Way, is the **fundamental principle** of the universe.

The *dao* **sustains all things**.

The *dao* **remains unchanged**, while all else flows around it.

We must cease actions that interrupt this flow, and **live simply, in harmony** with nature.

Through meditation and inaction we **accept the Way of the universe**.

The origins of Daoism are rooted in ancient Chinese beliefs concerning nature and harmony, but its first text, attributed to the philosopher Laozi, was written in the 6th century BCE – an unusually active time for ideas that also saw the emergence of Confucianism in China, both Jainism and Buddhism in India, and early Greek philosophy. Laozi's book, the *Daode jing* ("The Way and Its Power") identified the *dao,* or "Way", as the power or principle that underlies and sustains all things and is the source of order in the universe. Following the *dao*, rather than hindering or obstructing it, not only helps to ensure cosmic harmony, but also leads to personal spiritual development and a virtuous, fulfilled, and possibly longer life.

See also: Wisdom lies with the superior man 72–77 ▪ Physical and mental discipline 112–13 ▪ Zen insights that go beyond words 160–63

For life to run smoothly along the Way, we must attune and align ourselves with it, performing only those simple actions that maintain nature's inherent balance.

What it means to follow the *dao* is succinctly expressed in the more modern phrase, "going with the flow".

Action and inaction

The *dao* itself is eternal and unchanging. It is life that eddies and swirls around the *dao* and, to keep to its path, people must detach themselves from material concerns and disruptive emotions such as ambition and anger. They should instead live a peaceful, simple life, acting spontaneously and in harmony with nature, rather than acting on impulses from the self. This is the concept of *wu wei*, or inaction, inherent in the *dao*; as the *Daode jing* says, "the Way never acts, and yet nothing is left undone". In daily life, Laozi placed great emphasis on those virtues that encourage *wu wei*: humility, submissiveness, non-interference, passivity, and detachment.

The wisdom of Laozi came from long contemplation of the nature of the universe and its constituents, which in Chinese philosophy are yin and yang. Yin comprises all that is dark, moist, soft, cold, and feminine; all that is light, dry, hard, warm, and masculine is yang. Everything is made of yin and yang, and harmony is achieved when the two are kept in balance. In Daoism such balance is sought in mind, spirit, and body through practices such as meditation and t'ai chi: physical, mental, and spiritual exercises intended to balance the flow of qi, the life-force, through the body.

Under the rule of the Han dynasty (206 BCE–220 CE), Daoist philosophy became a religion. Its meditative practices were thought to guide adepts to immortality. In the *Daode jing* itself, the notion of immortality is not intended literally. Someone who completely accepts the *dao* reaches a plane above the material, and achieves immortality by detachment. But the statement that, for the sage, "there is no realm of death", was to be taken more literally by followers of the Daoist religion, who believed that actual immortality could be achieved through acceptance of the Way. ∎

My words are very easy to understand and very easy to put into practice, yet no one in the world can understand them or put them into practice.
Laozi

Laozi

The author of the *Daode jing* is said to have been a court archivist for the Zhou emperors who earned the name Laozi (the Old Master) because of his wisdom. The younger sage Kong Fuzi, or Confucius (p.75), is thought to have journeyed to consult him on religious rites. However, almost nothing is known for certain about Laozi. It is possible that he was not a historical figure at all, and that the *Daode jing* is in fact a later compilation of sayings.

According to legend, Laozi disappeared under mysterious circumstances; Confucius himself compared him to a dragon, which can ascend to heaven on the wind. The story goes that on witnessing the decline of the Zhou dynasty, Laozi left court and journeyed west seeking solitude. As he left, a border guard who recognized him asked for a token of his wisdom. Laozi wrote the *Daode jing* for him, and then travelled on, never to be seen in this world again.

Key works

c.6th century BCE *Daode jing* (also known as the *Laozi*).

THE FIVE GREAT VOWS

SELF-DENIAL LEADS TO SPIRITUAL LIBERATION

IN CONTEXT

KEY FIGURE
Mahavira

WHEN AND WHERE
From 6th century BCE, India

BEFORE
From 1000 BCE The concept of samsara, the cycle of death and rebirth, is developed by wandering ascetics of the *shramana* tradition in India.

AFTER
6th century BCE Buddha's enlightenment shows him the way to escape samsara.

From 2nd century BCE In Mahayana Buddhism, bodhisattvas – enlightened humans that remain on earth to help others – are revered.

20th century Jainism is recognized as a legally distinct religion in India, separate from Hinduism.

J ainism is the most ascetic of all Indian religions. Its followers practise self-denial in order to progress towards moksha, release from constant rebirth into this world of suffering. Jainism as we know it was founded by Mahavira, a contemporary of Buddha, in the 6th century BCE. However, Jainism takes a long view of its own historical development: it is said that it has always existed and always will exist. Within the faith, Mahavira is simply regarded as the most recent of 24 enlightened teachers in the current era. Jains believe each era lasts for millions of years and recurs in an infinite cycle of ages. These teachers are called

See also: The four stages of life 106–109 ▪ Escape from the eternal cycle 136–43 ▪ Buddhas and bodhisattvas 152–57 ▪ The ultimate reward for the righteous 279 ▪ The Sikh code of conduct 296–301

Life is an endless **cycle of reincarnation**.

Only by freeing ourselves of the **burden of karma** can we achieve enlightenment, and be liberated from this cycle.

To do this we must **follow the example** of the great teachers who have achieved liberation, such as Mahavira.

The path is set out in the **Five Vows** of non-violence, truth-telling, chastity, not stealing, and non-attachment.

If we follow this path, we too may eventually **achieve enlightenment**.

Images of the *jinas* or *tirthankaras*, the enlightened beings revered in Jainism, are used as devotional objects and as a focus for meditation while prayers and mantras are recited.

jinas, or more commonly, *tirthankaras*: "builders of the ford across the ocean of rebirth". By following the path of self-denial taught by the *tirthankaras*, Jains hope to free their souls from the entanglements of material existence. Without this hope, life is simply a continuous cycle of life, death, and reincarnation.

Personal responsibilty
Jainism does not recognize any deity, placing full responsibility on the actions and conduct of the individual. In order to adhere to a life of self-denial, Jain monks and nuns take what are called the Five Great Vows – non-violence (ahimsa), speaking the truth (satya), celibacy (brahmacharya), not taking what is not willingly offered (asteya), and detachment from people, places, and things

(aparigraha). The most important of these vows is the practice of ahimsa, which extends beyond avoiding violence against human beings to encompass all animals, including the smallest organisms found in water or air. The other four Great Vows equip the monk or nun to follow the life of a wandering mendicant, dedicated to preaching, fasting, worship, and study.

Self-denial is central to Jainism. It is said within the faith that Mahavira himself went naked, having been so deep in thought at the start of his wanderings that he failed to notice when his robe snagged on a thorn bush and was pulled off. But in the 4th century CE, long after Mahivira's death, the extent to which self-denial should be practised caused a schism in Jainism between the Shvetambara ("white-clad") and Digambara

("sky-clad") sects. Shvetambara monks believe that detachment and purity are mental qualities that are unimpeded by wearing a simple robe. However, Digambara monks go naked, believing that the wearing of clothes indicates that »

Having wisdom, Mahavira committed no sin himself, nor did he induce others to do so, nor did he consent to the sins of others.
Akaranga Sutra

The symbol adopted by Jainism is a complex arrangement of elements within an outline that represents the universe: earthly concerns in the lower regions lead up to the abode of celestial beings.

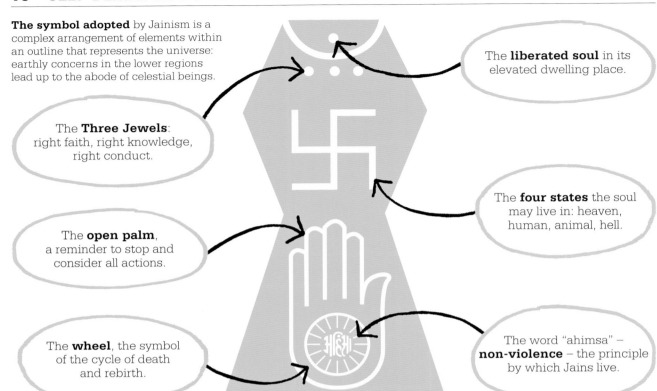

The **liberated soul** in its elevated dwelling place.

The **Three Jewels**: right faith, right knowledge, right conduct.

The **four states** the soul may live in: heaven, human, animal, hell.

The **open palm**, a reminder to stop and consider all actions.

The **wheel**, the symbol of the cycle of death and rebirth.

The word "ahimsa" – **non-violence** – the principle by which Jains live.

a person is not completely detached from sexual feelings and false notions of modesty. Digambara monks may not even carry alms bowls, but must receive food in their cupped hands. Digambaras also believe that liberation from rebirth is not possible for women until they have first been reborn as a man.

Living in the world

Lay Jains do not take the Five Great Vows, but they do take lesser vows that are similar: renouncing violence, vowing not to lie or to steal, embracing chaste sexual behaviour, and avoiding attachment to material things. All Jains are strictly vegetarian, in line with the vow of non-violence, and must not do work that involves the destruction of life. Some Jains will only use flowers that have already

fallen from the plant in their worship, arguing that to cut a living flower is an act of violence. Lay Jains may marry, but are expected to uphold the highest standards of behaviour. In this, as in all things, Jains follow the path of the Three Jewels: right faith, right knowledge, and right conduct.

Sometimes there is said to be a fourth jewel, right penance: atonement for sins is important in Jainism. At the annual festival of Samvatsari, which follows an eight-day period of fasting and abstinence in the monsoon season, a full confession is made to family and friends of the sins of the past year, and vows are taken not to carry grudges into the new year. Meditation is important, too, and Jain daily rituals include 48-minute sessions of meditation, in which

the aim is to be at one with the universe, and to forgive and be forgiven for all transgressions. (Forty-eight minutes – one-thirtieth of a day – is a *mahurta*, a standard unit of time in India often used for ritual purposes.)

Other Jain virtues are: service to others; attention to religious study; disengagement from passion; and politeness and humility. Particular merit is gained by donating food to monks and nuns. All of these practices combine with the self-denial required by even laypersons' vows to reduce the karma (consequences of past deeds) which, the Jains believe, accumulates on the soul as a kind of physical substance. All karma, both good and bad, must be removed to achieve liberation. The idea is to progress gradually along the path of spiritual enlightenment, earning merit little by little, life by life. One of the Jain holy texts, the *Tattvartha Sutra*, sets out a sequence of 14 stages through which the soul must pass to achieve liberation: the first stage is called *mithyadrishti*, in which the soul is in a spiritual slumber; the final, 14th, stage is *ayoga-kevali*, which is populated by souls known as *siddhas*, who have achieved full spiritual liberation. This final stage is beyond the reach of lay Jains.

Forms of devotion

Jains may worship in a temple or at a domestic shrine at home. Jain temples are seen as replicas of the celestial assembly halls where the liberated *tirthankaras* continue their teaching. The adoration and contemplation of images of these *tirthankaras* is thought to bring about inner spiritual transformation. The simplest form of worship, also

Only monastic Jains who have fully embraced a life of austerity and detachment can hope to ascend the 14 steps to spiritual enlightenment.

> I ask pardon of all living creatures. May all of them pardon me. May I have a friendly relationship with all beings.
> **Jain prayer**

found in Hinduism, is called *darshan*, and involves making eye contact with the image of a *tirthankara*, often while reciting a sacred mantra. The fundamental prayer of Jainism is the Navkar, or Namaskar, Mantra. By reciting this mantra, *namo namahar*, the worshipper honours the souls of the liberated and gains inspiration from them in his or her own quest for enlightenment. ∎

Mahavira

The religious reformer Mahavira was born in around 599 BCE in northeast India as Prince Vardhamana, the son of King Siddhartha and Queen Trishala, who is said to have had many auspicious dreams during her pregnancy. According to Jain tradition, Mahavira was placed in the queen's womb by Indra, the king of the Vedic gods. Mahavira was allegedly so dedicated to non-violence that he did not not kick in his mother's womb, in case he caused her pain.

At the age of 30, Prince Vardhamana left the palace to live as an ascetic, renouncing material comfort and devoting himself entirely to meditation. After 12 years he reached enlightenment and then became a great teacher, with the new name of Mahavira. Founding a large community of Jain monks and nuns (traditionally thought to be more than 50,000 in total), he moulded Jainism into its current form. Mahavira died at the age of 72 at the town of Pava in Bihar, India, and is said at this point to have attained moksha (release from the cycle of death and rebirth).

VIRTUE IS NOT SENT FROM HEAVEN

WISDOM LIES WITH THE SUPERIOR MAN

IN CONTEXT

KEY FIGURE
Confucius

WHEN AND WHERE
6th–5th century BCE, China

BEFORE
From 11th century BCE
The Zhou dynasty redirect traditional Chinese ancestor worship towards the concept of a heaven, with the Zhou emperor as its representative.

6th century BCE Laozi proposes acting in accordance with the *dao* (the Way) in order to maintain universal harmony.

AFTER
From 6th century BCE
Confucian ideals of virtue and responsibility inform Zhou imperial rule and the political ideology of later dynasties.

18th century Confucius's meritocratic ideas are admired by Enlightenment thinkers who oppose the absolute authority of Church and State.

onfucius, as he is known in the West, was one of the first thinkers to systematically explore the notion of goodness and whether moral superiority is a divine privilege, or is inherent in humankind and can be cultivated.

Born in the 6th century BCE in Qufu, in modern China's Shandong Province, Confucius was one of a new breed of scholars – in effect, the first civil servants – who became advisors to the Chinese court, rising from the middle classes to positions of power and influence on the strength of their own merit rather than through inheritance. In the rigidly class-stratified society of the day, this presented an anomaly, and it is this anomaly that lies at the heart of Confucius's thought.

The rulers of the reigning Zhou dynasty believed that they were given their authority directly by the gods, under the Mandate of Heaven, and that the quality of *ren* (or *jen*) – humaneness – was an attribute of the ruling classes. Confucius, too, saw heaven as the source of moral order, but he argued that the blessing of heaven was open to all, and that the quality

To govern by virtue, let us compare it to the North Star: it stays in its place, while the myriad stars wait upon it.
The Analects

of *ren* could be acquired by anyone. It is in fact the duty of everyone to cultivate the attributes that make up *ren* – seriousness, generosity, sincerity, diligence, and kindness. To practise these virtues is to uphold the will of heaven.

The *Analects* – sayings and teachings of Confucius collected by his pupils – established a new philosophy of morality in which the superior man, or *junzi* (literally "gentleman"), devotes himself to the acquisition of *ren* for its own sake – he learns for learning's sake, and is good for goodness' sake.

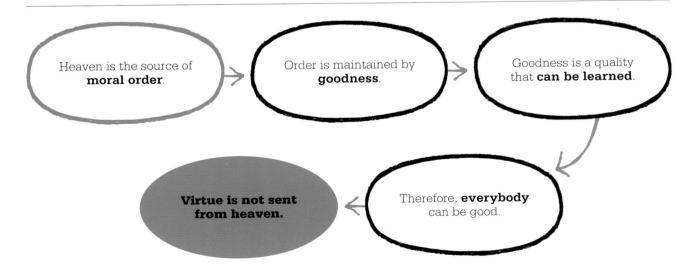

Heaven is the source of **moral order**.

Order is maintained by **goodness**.

Goodness is a quality that **can be learned**.

Therefore, **everybody** can be good.

Virtue is not sent from heaven.

See also: Living in harmony 38 ▪ Aligning the self with the *dao* 66–67
▪ Selfless action 110–11 ▪ Man as a manifestation of God 188

Asked by a student to explain the rules to be followed by the seeker of *ren*, Confucius replied, "One should see nothing improper, hear nothing improper, say nothing improper, do nothing improper".

Confucius was concerned not simply with self-cultivation, but with the relations between people, and the proper way to behave in a family, a community, and a larger society. Confucius himself admitted students of all classes as his disciples, and fundamentally believed that virtue lay in self-cultivation rather than noble birth. Because of the rigidity of the prevailing hierarchy in China's feudal society, Confucius had to find a way to promote individual virtue without calling for a simple meritocracy. He did so by arguing that the virtuous man accepts and understands his place in the social order, and uses his virtue to fulfil his allotted role rather than to transcend it. "The superior man", he said, "does what is proper to the station in which he is; he does not desire to go beyond this".

Attributes of a wise ruler

As for the rulers, Confucius advised that rather than exercising their powers in an arbitrary and unjust way, they should lead by example, and that treating the people with generosity and kindness would encourage virtue, loyalty, and right behaviour. However, in order to govern others, it is necessary first to govern oneself. For Confucius, a humane ruler was defined by his practice of *ren*; without it, he might forfeit the Mandate of Heaven. In many ways Confucius's idea of the perfect ruler echoes Laozi's concept of the *dao*: the less the ruler does, the more is achieved. The ruler is the stable centre around which the activity of the kingdom revolves.

Rulers who took this advice to heart also found themselves in need of advisors and civil servants whose skill and trustworthiness »

Imperial authority in China was expressed through decisive rule that reinforced the notion of a stable power centre; well-advised judgments were less likely to require revision.

Confucius

According to tradition, Confucius was born in 551 BCE in Qufu, in the state of Lu, China. His name was originally Kong Qiu, and only later did he earn the title Kong Fuzi, or "Master Kong". Little is known about his life, except that he was from a well-to-do family, and that as a young man he worked as a servant to support his family after his father died. He nevertheless managed to find time to study, and became an administrator in the Lu court, but when his suggestions to the rulers were ignored he left to concentrate on teaching.

As a teacher he travelled throughout the Chinese empire, returning to Qufu at the end of his life. He died there in 479 BCE. His teaching survives in fragments and sayings passed down orally by his disciples and subsequently collected in the *Analects* and anthologies compiled by Confucian scholars.

Key works

5th century BCE *Analects; Doctrine of the Mean; Great Learning*

The Five Constant Relationships

Sovereign–Subject
Rulers should be benevolent, and subjects loyal.

Father–Son
Parents are to be loving, and children obedient.

Husband–Wife
Husbands are to be good and fair, and wives understanding.

Brother–Brother
Elder siblings are to be gentle, and younger siblings respectful.

Friend–Friend
Older friends are to be considerate, younger friends reverential.

were founded in the Confucian concepts of virtuous behaviour; in 136 BCE the Han dynasty introduced new competitive examinations for the imperial civil service based on meritocratic Confucian ideals. In turn the Chinese concept of heaven acquired a distinctly bureaucratic tone, and by the time of the Song dynasty (960–1279 CE), heaven was seen as a mirror image of the court of the Chinese emperor, with its own emperor and a vast celestial civil service of lesser deities.

Despite his many references to heaven, Confucius did not believe his moral precepts were derived from the gods; instead he found them already existing in the human heart and mind. To this extent, Confucianism is more a humanistic system of moral philosophy than it is a religion; although even today, with some 5–6 million followers, the distinction between the two remains blurred. In Chinese popular religion, Confucius has joined the crowded pantheon of gods, but many of his followers revere him simply as a great teacher and thinker.

Building on ritual

The adoption of Confucianism as a religion stems largely from the fact that Confucius upheld the duty to practise rites and ceremonies that honoured ancestors. This he saw as part of a wider imperative of loyalty to family and friends, and respect for elders – which Confucius defined in what he called the Five Constant Relationships (see left). Reciprocity plays a key role in these relationships, for Confucianism, at its heart, embodies the so-called "Golden Rule": do not do to others what you do not want done to yourself. Confucius believed that by honouring ties of love, loyalty, ritual, and tradition, virtuous thought, virtuous action, and respect, not

Confucius travelled and taught for 12 years, acquiring disciples in much the same way that the contemporary "schools" of philosophy were taking shape in the Ancient Greek world.

only could everybody be good, but society would be bound together in a positive and right-thinking way. By revering the ancestors and performing the correct rites in their honour, humans could maintain a state of harmony between this world and heaven. At the family level, such rites were an echo of those in which the emperors made sacrifices to their ancestors and confirmed the Mandate of Heaven under which they ruled.

> Only he who is possessed of the most complete sincerity that can exist under Heaven can transform.
> **Doctrine of the Mean**

Filial piety remains one of the most important Confucian virtues, and its ties and duties extend beyond death. Sons are expected to make offerings at their parents' graves, and to honour them at shrines in the home that contain "ancestor tablets", in which the spirits of the elders are said to dwell. Even today, the key moment in a Confucian wedding is when the couple bow to the groom's ancestor tablets, thus formally "introducing" the bride to the ancestors of her husband's family in order to secure their blessing.

Confucianism evolves

It was during the Song dynasty that the scholar Zhu Xi (1130–1200 CE) incorporated elements of Daoism and Buddhism into Confucianism, creating an enduring religion that is also known as Neo-Confucianism. Confucius was not the first Chinese sage to contemplate the eternal truths, and Confucius himself claimed to have invented nothing, but merely to have studied the ideas of earlier thinkers, gathering them together in five books, known as the Five Classics. Under the Western Zhou dynasty, from 1050 to 771 BCE, scholars were highly valued at court, and in the 7th century BCE the so-called Hundred Schools of Thought emerged. Confucius lived in a time of philosophical ferment, but also of social change, as the power of the Zhou emperors declined and the whole social order seemed to be under threat. His focus on order and harmony emerged from a genuine concern about potential societal breakdown. The emperors

Respect for elders and ancestors is a core value of Confucianism: these young Chinese students are marking the anniversary of Confucius's birth by honouring his image.

> Hold faithfulness
> and sincerity
> as first principles.
> **The Analects**

> Men's natures are alike,
> it is their habits that
> carry them far apart.
> **The Analects**

of later dynasties such as the Han (206 BCE–220 CE), the Song (960–1279 CE) and the Ming (1368–1644 CE) recognized the value of Confucian ideals in maintaining social order, and Confucianism became the Chinese state religion. It was also a profound influence on daily life and thought into the 20th century, and was attacked during the Cultural Revolution for its social conservatism, but in recent years a New Confucianism has emerged in China, blending Confucian ideas with modern Chinese thinking and Western philosophy. Although Confucius built his philosophy on existing concepts and practices, he was remarkable for his insistence that human beings are naturally good – only needing to be taught and encouraged, to be virtuous – and that this goodness is not confined to the aristocracy. ■

A DIVINE CHILD IS BORN
THE ASSIMILATION OF MYTH

IN CONTEXT

KEY BELIEVERS
**Ancient Minoans
and Myceneans**

WHEN AND WHERE
14th century BCE, Crete

BEFORE
From prehistory Early
settlers, probably from western
Asia, leave evidence of rituals
and worship in caves on Crete.

c.25th century–1420 BCE
Goddesses are a focus of
worship in Minoan Crete;
many are associated with
serpents, birds, or bees.

AFTER
7th century BCE The Greek
poet Hesiod relates the birth
of Zeus to Rhea at Psychro
and his concealment from
the wrath of his father.

5th century BCE The Roman
Republic assimilates the
myths and iconography
of Zeus in its supreme
god, Jupiter or Jove.

Around 1420 BCE, the Minoan civilization of the island of Crete was conquered by the Myceneans from mainland Greece, and as the Greek invaders absorbed the culture of the Minoans, so indigenous Cretan and Greek myth became intertwined. One of the Minoan deities was a great mother goddess, who, in legend, gave birth to a divine son in the Diktaean cave above Psychro. This cave became her holiest shrine and no one, god or man, was permitted to enter. Once a year a fiery glow was said to erupt from the cave, when the blood from the birth of the divine child spilled over.

This child grew into a wondrous beardless youth or *kouros*, a demi-god who was often invoked in hymns to bring fertility and good fortune to humans each year.

The Dorian Greeks, who succeeded the Myceneans, gave the Minoan *kouros* the name of their own supreme god, Zeus, the deity who came to rule the classical Greek pantheon of gods that lived on Mount Olympus. Regarded as the place where Zeus's mother, Rhea, hid her baby from his jealous father, Cronus, the cave became one of ancient Greece's many sacred sites, or shrines.

Rhea may have been one of the names of the original, Minoan, great goddess, but in Greek myth, although she was the mother of gods, Rhea was not considered an Olympian goddess in her own right. Her divine child, on the other hand, was elevated in status to become the highest god of all, the father of all other gods. ∎

The infant Zeus, here painted by Carlo Cignani (1628–1719), was variously described in myth as being nursed by nymphs, a she-goat, or bees that lived in the Diktaean cave.

See also: Symbolism made real 46–47 ▪ Beliefs for new societies 56–57
▪ The power of the great goddess 104

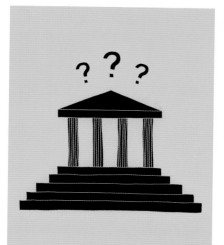

THE ORACLES REVEAL THE WILL OF THE GODS
DIVINING THE FUTURE

IN CONTEXT

KEY BELIEVERS
Ancient Greeks

WHEN AND WHERE
8th century BCE–4th century CE, Greece and the Mediterranean

BEFORE
From 3rd millennium BCE
The temple at Per-Wadjet contains the most renowned oracle in Egypt, that of the snake-headed goddess Wadjet.

c.800 BCE The oracle of Apollo is established at Delphi.

AFTER
From 1st century BCE The *haruspex* is an influential figure in the Roman Empire, using Etruscan divination techniques to interpret the entrails of sacrificed animals.

From 1st century CE The Christian Church condemns divination as a pagan practice; it is forbidden in the biblical Book of Deuteronomy.

The ancient Greeks set great store by divination of the future, and the most valuable and influential sources of prophecy and wise counsel were the oracles, who were almost always women. The oracles would enter a trancelike state, during which the gods "spoke" directly through them. The gods' messages were sometimes unintelligible, but could be interpreted by priests. If offerings were made at the oracles' sanctuaries, or dwelling places (often caves), they would often provide more satisfactory responses.

Oracles could be consulted on any aspect of life, from personal matters, such as love and marriage, to affairs of state. Prophecies could also be used for political ends: Alexander the Great visited the oracle of the Egyptian god Amun after conquering Egypt in 332 BCE, and had his rule legitimized when the oracle recognized him as the "son of Amun". However, the number of oracles was limited, and this, combined with the fact that substantial offerings were often advisable, meant that "personalized" access to the gods became the province of the rich and powerful. A popular alternative was the service offered by seers or soothsayers, who, unlike the oracles, were prepared to travel – particularly useful for Greek armies on the move. These seers interpreted "signs" from the gods by methods such as dream analysis, inferring meaning from chance events, observation of birds, and deducing omens from animal sacrifice. ∎

The Sibyl, with raving lips… reaches over a thousand years with her voice, thanks to the god in her.
Heraclitus

See also: The power of the shaman 26–31 ∎ The African roots of Santeria 304–305 ∎ The Pentecostal Church 336

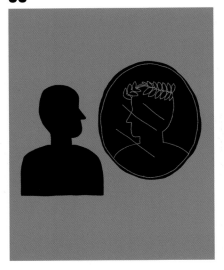

THE GODS ARE JUST LIKE US
BELIEFS THAT MIRROR SOCIETY

IN CONTEXT

KEY BELIEVERS
Ancient Romans

WHEN AND WHERE
8th century BCE, **Rome**

BEFORE
8th–6th centuries BCE
The Greek civilization flowers, with its pantheon of deities.

AFTER
8th century BCE
Rome is founded.

c.509 BCE The Roman monarchy is overthrown and the Republic established.

133–44 BCE Civil wars finally bring an end to the Roman Republic; Julius Caesar is named "dictator for life" before his assassination in 44 BCE.

42 BCE Julius Caesar is deified.

c.335 CE Roman Emperor Constantine I (the Great) converts to Christianity.

391 CE Emperor Theodosius bans the worship of pagan gods.

The gods take an active interest in our **public affairs**.

The gods take an active interest in our **domestic affairs**.

Household gods, **the penates**, reside in our homes and help provide for us.

The gods are just like us

Public leaders **consult the gods** about political decision-making.

Political leaders can be given the status of gods.

Ancestor spirit gods, **the lares**, act as our guardians.

The pantheon of ancient Roman gods was largely adapted from that of other civilizations, notably the Greeks. As the Greek deities had done, the Roman gods lived, loved, and fought their battles in a way that mirrored the lives of mortals and reflected their history. However, whereas the Greeks saw their gods as remote controllers of the universe, the Romans considered them to be an intrinsic part of their lives, and to have

See also: Beliefs for new societies 56–57 ▪ The assimiliation of myth 78
▪ Living the Way of the Gods 82–85

a direct influence on every aspect of existence. They believed that divine aid was key to successful governance, and so worship, ritual, and sacrifice were incorporated into public ceremonies in order to ensure the cooperation of the gods. Public ceremonies also helped to strengthen the authority of the regime, and religious festivals, often involving public holidays and games, contributed to political unity. Religious and state life were interdependent, with priests forming a part of the political elite, and leaders expected to perform religious duties. In time, individual rulers became associated, during their lifetime, with a particular god; some eventually became regarded *as* gods – either by being deified after death or even achieving divine status while they were still alive.

Cults and household gods
Various cults coexisted with the religion of the state. Some were devoted to a particular god – often one outside the conventional pantheon; sometimes the foreign god of a conquered people was

"invited" to take up residence in Rome. For most Roman citizens, however, the local and household gods, the lares and penates, were the ones associated with everyday life. They were so interested in human affairs that their presence was everywhere; they were open to negotiation, and prayers to them often took the form of bargains: "I give so that you will give".

The foundation of religion for the Romans was the family. The paterfamilias – head of the family – was the spiritual leader and moral authority, who held legal rights over the property of the family and was responsible for its members in society. The home was sacred to the Romans, and the heart of the home was the hearth. The spirit of the head of the household presided over all the household gods, including the penates, the deities of the store cupboard, to whom a portion of each meal was offered on the flames of the hearth. ▪

The Roman gods had human characteristics; they are often depicted feasting, sleeping, or engaging in bawdy drunkenness.

The lares
Constituting a bridge between the public and domestic gods, the lares were typically guardian deities, whose function was to protect the livelihood of a particular area. While many homes had a shrine devoted to the local lares, their scope was broader than that of the household penates, and shrines to the neighbourhood lares were often placed at crossroads, a symbol of "home" in its wider sense. The lares are thought to have evolved from earlier cults of hero-ancestors, or the spirits of ancestors buried in farmland, with their role as protectors of agriculture and livestock. In the Roman Republic, they came to be the guardians of businesses, transport, and communication. Lares were closely associated with local communities and everyday public life, and were very much gods of the plebeians (such as soldiers, seafarers, farmers, and traders), rather than of the ruling class of patricians, complementing the major deities of the "state religion".

At Rome as elsewhere, in order to understand the society of the gods, we must not lose sight of the society of men.
Georges Dumézil

RITUAL LINKS US TO OUR PAST

LIVING THE WAY OF THE GODS

Shinto is the indigenous, traditional religion of Japan. Some say that it is not so much a religion as a Japanese way of life, because it is so intrinsically linked to the topography of the land and its history and traditions. Its origins can be traced to prehistoric times in Japan, when animist beliefs, with their respect for nature and natural phenomena, prevailed.

As the universal belief system of an isolated island nation, Shinto had no need to define itself until it was challenged by the arrival of a rival religion, Buddhism, in the 6th century CE. The traditional Japanese beliefs lacked complex intellectual doctrines, allowing

See also: Making sense of the world 20–23 ▪ Animism in early societies 24–25 ▪ Beliefs for new societies 56–57 ▪ Devotion through puja 114–15 ▪ The performance of ritual and repetition 158–59 ▪ Jesus's divine identity 208

Great Japan is the Land of the Gods. Here the Deity of the Sun has handed on her eternal rule.
Account of the Righteous Reigns of the Divine Emperors

The **world was created by the gods** at the beginning of heaven and earth.

It is full of sacred energies, or **kami**.

Some kami are great **creative beings**, some are **natural forces**, some are the **souls of the ancestors**.

The kami **created our nation** and **shaped our culture**.

Rituals honouring the kami link us to our past.

Buddhism and also Confucianism to become influential in Japanese theology and philosophy. In response, the Japanese imperial court consolidated Japan's native beliefs with a name – Shinto – and in the early 8th century, at the request of the Empress Gemmei, the great Shinto texts such as the Kojiki ("Record of Ancient Matters") and Nihon Shoki ("Continuing Chronicles of Japan") were compiled.

These books recorded the oral traditions of Japanese history and myth, alongside the lineage of the Japanese emperors, said to be descended from the gods. They also defined a body of ritual that has remained key to Shinto ever since – perhaps more so than belief. Shinto still permeates every aspect of Japanese life, and its rituals, in which purification plays a key role, are performed in both spiritual and secular situations – for example, to bring success and good fortune to sporting events, new car assembly lines, or construction projects. During these rituals, which carry

a great weight of tradition, sacred beings called kami are prayed to and honoured. The word Shinto literally means "Way of the Divine Beings", and Shinto is known in modern Japanese as *Kami no michi*, the "Way of the Kami".

The essence of everything
The word kami means "that which is hidden" and can be translated as god, spirit, or soul. However, in Shinto belief, the term designates not only a vast range of divinities and spirit beings, but also the "spiritual energy" or "essence" that is found in everything, and which defines that thing: kami are

present, for example, as essences of natural phenomena (such as storms and earthquakes) and the geographical environment (rivers, trees, and waterfalls, for example). Mountains, especially Mount Fuji, are held to be particularly sacred.

As entities, kami include gods, goddesses, and the souls or spirits of family ancestors (*ujigami*) and other, exceptional human beings. Shinto teaches that these kami occupy the same material world as people, rather than existing on a supernatural plane. They respond to prayer and can influence events. However, unlike the divine beings in many other religious traditions, » kami, although godlike, are not omnipotent: they have limitations and are fallible. However, not all kami are good – some can be evil or demonic. But in their more benign aspect, they possess sincerity and a will to truth, or *makoto*, and maintain harmony in the universe through the creative potency known as *musubi*.

Shinto's creator gods

According to the Kojiki, at the creation of the universe, the first three kami emerged. These included the Kamimusubi (divine/high generative force kami), which was too abstract to be a focus of worship. However, after several generations of formless kami, the major Shinto gods appear: Izanagi and Izanami, who created the world, or "invited it into being." Many Shinto myths are devoted to them and to the activities of their offspring, Susanoo, the storm god, Tsukuyomi, the moon god, and Amaterasu, the sun goddess.

The kami represent the creators of Japan, the very land itself (as the spirits of its natural features and natural forces), and those who have gone before – Japanese ancestors. The ritual worship of these sacred beings therefore confirms a powerful connection to Japanese history and tradition.

Shrines and temples

A harmonious relationship between kami and humankind is maintained by praying and making offerings at shrines and temples. On entering a shrine, a ritual of purification is performed. These rituals are central to Shinto, for which ideas of purity and impurity are very important. Shinto does not have a concept of original sin, but rather believes that human beings are born pure, only becoming tainted by impurity later. The sources of impurity are sin (acts within our control) and pollution (things beyond our control, such as disease or contact with death). These impurities, or *tsumi*, need to be ritually purified. Purification rituals may take a variety of forms, but ceremonial hand-washing and mouth-washing sequences are common to most.

Small shrines known as *kami-dona* are found in many Japanese homes, consisting of a small shelf displaying objects used to honour the ancestors and other kami.

As you have blessed the ruler's reign... so I bow down my neck as a cormorant in search of fish to worship you through these abundant offerings on his behalf.
Prayer to Amaterasu

Public temples and shrines may be as large as a village, or as small as a beehive. They are remarkable for their simplicity; many originated as sacred areas around natural objects such as trees, ponds, or rocks. Each Shinto temple has a gateless entrance called a torii, which usually consists of a pair of uprights and a crossbar. Typically, every temple also has a wall where worshippers may post wooden votive tablets that bear a message to the kami, asking, for example, for success in passing an exam or help in finding a suitable marriage partner.

Individual prayers at the worship hall of a Shinto shrine follow a set four-step process, after the initial ritual cleansing. First money is put into an offering box. Next the worshipper makes two deep bows before the shrine, then claps their hands twice, and finally, after concluding prayers, makes

Shinto priests may be male or female; their white-clad assistants, or *miko*, are often the daughters of priests. Traditional costumes emphasize Shinto's connections with Japan's great imperial past.

one last deep bow. In addition to prayer and offerings at shrines, Shinto has celebratory festivals known as *matsuri*, at which the kami are honoured and important points in the agricultural year are marked, such as rice-planting in April. Correctly performed, Shinto followers believe that these rituals enable *wa*, the positive harmony that helps to purify the world and keeps it running smoothly.

Descended from the gods

The most revered Shinto temple is that of Amaterasu, the sun goddess, at Ise, on the Japanese island of Honshu. The simple wooden shrine has been rebuilt every 20 years for the last 1,300 years; the action of renewal is thought to please the kami. Most Japanese people aim to visit Ise at least once in their life.

The emperors of Japan were traditionally regarded as the direct descendants of Amaterasu (the first emperor, Jimmu, who took power in 660 BCE, was said to be her great-great-great-grandson), and this became official doctrine in the 7th and 8th centuries. The codifying of Shinto at this time not only eliminated influences from

Rituals that please and propitiate the gods are among the oldest in history, and still reverently attended to by followers of Shinto. An offering of sushi to a fox-spirit or *kitsune* statue should result in a prayer being carried to Inari, goddess of plenty, and be rewarded with a fine harvest.

Buddhism, but also placed an emphasis on the superior status of the Japanese people in general. This was used, in turn, as the rationale for Japan's political and military ambitions, especially after the Meiji Restoration, which returned imperial rule to Japan in the 19th century.

The emperor and his court were obliged to carry out ceremonies to ensure that the kami watched over Japan and secured its success, a tradition that was maintained until the end of World War II. Shinto's standing in Japan was transformed, however, after the country lost the war and was forced to make

concessions to the Allies. Viewed by the occupying US forces as too militaristic and nationalistic, Shinto was disestablished in 1946, ceasing to be the official state religion. In the same year, Emperor Hirohito renounced his claim to divinity. But while today the emperor is no longer formally regarded as divine, the imperial ceremonies are still viewed as important. Shinto's strong emphasis on order and harmony, its regard for social norms, ritual, and tradition, and its respect for the emperor means that Shinto has maintained its role as the bedrock of conservative Japanese society. ∎

Man by nature is inherently good, and the world in which he lives is good. This is the kami-world. Evil then cannot originate in man or in this world. It is an intruder.
Sokyo Ono

The origins of purification rituals

Purification rituals (*harai*) play a key role in Shinto and are believed to originate in a myth involving Izanami and Izanagi, the two creator gods. The female of this pair, Izanami, is fatally burned while giving birth to the fire god, Kagutsuchi, so she descends to Yomi, the land of the dead. Grief-stricken, Izanagi follows her there, but discovers that she has eaten the food of the underworld and is unable to leave. Izanami begs Izanagi

not to look at her, but he lights a torch and discovers her rotting body crawling with maggots. He flees to the land of the living and bathes in the sea to purify himself. The message of the contaminating influence of the dead is clear: Shinto regards death as the ultimate impurity. For this reason, Shinto priests will not officiate at funerals, which means that most funerals in Japan are Buddhist, whatever the beliefs of the deceased.

THE GODS WILL DIE

THE END OF THE WORLD AS WE KNOW IT

IN CONTEXT

KEY BELIEVERS
Vikings

WHEN AND WHERE
**8th–12th century CE,
Scandinavia**

BEFORE
From prehistory Preserved
"bog bodies" such as Tollund
Man, found in modern
Denmark, suggest ritualized
human sacrifice. A pantheon
of Norse gods – the Aesir, led
by Odin – develops and is
widely worshipped across
northern Europe.

AFTER
13th century As Christianity
spreads across Nordic regions,
Viking beliefs begin to pass
into legend. To preserve them,
the Eddas, poetic compilations
of Norse myth, are compiled.

From 19th century In
Scandinavia and across
northern Europe, Germanic
neopagan movements that
venerate the Aesir are formed.

A sense of doom runs through the Norse mythology of the Vikings, for everything in it leads up to one calamitous moment, in which two gods – Odin, the "all-father", and the trickster, Loki – bring an age-old conflict between the gods and the giants to its terrifying conclusion. This is Ragnarok, the final battle, in which gods will die and the world will be utterly destroyed.

As punishment for having duped Odin's blind son, Hoder, into slaying his brother, Baldr, the "shining prince" of goodness, Loki was chained to three rocks for eternity. As he struggles to

Catastrophe and **violence** will signal the **beginning of the end**.

↓

The **barrier** between the worlds of the living
and the dead **will be breached**.

↓

In a **mighty conflict**, the **gods** themselves **will die**.

↓

In the twilight of the gods, the **whole world** will be **destroyed**.

↓

But a **new world** will arise, with **new hope** for humanity.

See also: Making sense of the world 20–23 ▪ The battle between good and evil 60–65 ▪ Beliefs that mirror society 80–81 ▪ Entering into the faith 224–27 ▪ Awaiting the Day of Judgment 312–13

The gigantic wolf Fenrir, here swallowing Odin, was the offspring of Loki's liaison with a female *jötunn*, one of a race of giants at war with the gods.

free himself, the world will shake; trees will be uprooted, and mountains will fall. Loki will begin to regain his strength, and nature itself will start to go awry: a series of terrible winters, with snow, frost, and biting winds, will soon become constant, with no summer at all. There will be battles everywhere, brother fighting against brother, father against son, until the whole world is ruined. When the chained god finally breaks free, the sky will split open, Loki's monstrous wolf-son Fenrir will swallow the sun, and Loki will lead an army of giants, monsters, and the dead from the underworld, in a ship made from the uncut fingernails of the dead.

Odin's army retaliates
Odin is the god of poetry and magic, but he is also the god of war and battle, and it is from the slain of the battlefield that he assembles his army of dead warriors, the Einherjar, to fight against Loki's underworld horde.

Norse mythology is quite clear, however, that even with this mighty army, the gods are destined to be defeated and destroyed in this conflict. Odin's son, the mighty god Thor, will be killed by the huge serpent Jörmungandr, and Odin will be devoured by Fenrir. Thor's brother Vidar will step forward and rip Fenrir in two by the jawbones, but it will not be enough to save either Odin or creation. The whole world will be destroyed by fire, and will subside beneath the sea.

Yet from this destruction a new world will be born, as a new land rises from the sea. One man and one woman, Lifthrasir and Lif, will survive the destruction. From them a new race of humans will be born. As for the gods, Odin's sons Vidar and Vali, and Thor's sons Modi and Magni, will be the only survivors of the battle. They will be joined by the slain Baldr the beautiful and his blind brother Hoder, who were tricked by Loki – both freed at last from the underworld. ▪

The sun turns black, earth sinks into the sea, the bright stars vanish from the sky.
The Eddas

The Viking heaven

Vikings who died of natural causes faced the dismal prospect of Hel, the cold, damp realm of the dead. Only Vikings chosen to die in battle by Odin's valkyries (a race of warlike, supernatural females), or those selected for sacrifice, could cross the "rainbow bridge" to Asgard, home of the gods. Half of those who had died in battle belonged to the goddess Freyja and went to the meadow, Fólkvangr, to be seated in her hall. Women who died heroic deaths may also have been eligible. The other half of slain warriors belonged to Odin, and they spent the afterlife in Valhalla, the hall of the slain, roofed with shields. There they fought each other all day, but arose unhurt at night to feast on the meat of a magical boar and drink the mead milked from a magical goat. This was to prepare them for the day when they would march from Valhalla to fight for the gods in the final battle of Ragnarok.

Fallen warriors were burned on a pyre, as decreed by Odin. Weapons, food, and tools were burned with them for use in the afterlife.

HINDUIS

FROM 1700 BCE

M

Vedic tradition
begins to develop
in India, with ritual
offerings made
to the gods.

Brahmanic ideas
emerges based on the
concept of Brahman,
the supreme power.

Mahavira becomes
a major figure
in establishing
Jainism.

The poet **Valmiki**
writes the Sanskrit
epic the *Ramayana*.

1700BCE   **6TH CENTURY BCE**   **6TH CENTURY BCE**   **c.500–100**BCE

1200–900BCE   **6TH CENTURY BCE**   **6TH CENTURY BCE**

The **four Vedas** are
written. These are the
oldest Hindu scriptures
and most ancient
Sanskrit texts.

The first of the
Upanishads is
written, offering a
philosophical approach
to religion.

Siddhartha
Gautama, later
known as **Buddha**,
is born into a
Hindu family.

Although Hinduism could arguably be called the oldest of living religions, the term itself is a relatively modern one, which gives a misleading impression of a unified faith with a single set of beliefs and practices. Hinduism can trace its origins to the Iron Age, but it is in fact more a convenient umbrella term covering most of the indigenous religions of the Indian subcontinent. Although these religions share some characteristics, they vary greatly in practice and encompass a wide range of different traditions. In some of these traditions, the faith has remained substantially unchanged since the earliest times.

While more than three-quarters of the population of India identify themselves as "Hindu", today the definition of such a range of loosely connected faiths is as much socio-political as religious. The word "Hindu" (which shares its roots with the name of the River Indus, and of India) essentially means "Indian". It distinguishes the native religions from those introduced to the country, such as Islam, and newer "breakaway" religions such as Jainism and Buddhism.

The difficulty of defining Hinduism was summed up in an Indian High Court ruling in 1995: "… the Hindu religion does not claim any one prophet; it does not worship any one god; it does not subscribe to any one dogma; it does not believe in any one philosophic concept; it does not follow any one set of religious rites or performances; in fact, it does not appear to satisfy the narrow traditional features of

any religion or creed. It may broadly be described as a way of life and nothing more."

Common beliefs
However, certain ideas have remained central to virtually all strands of Hinduism, in particular the notion of samsara (the cycle of birth and rebirth of the atman, the soul) and the associated belief in the possibility of moksha, or release from this endless cycle. The key to achieving moksha is encapsulated in the word dharma, which is variously translated as "virtue", "natural law", "right living", or simply "appropriateness".

Inevitably, this is subject to a number of interpretations, but three main ways of achieving moksha have emerged, collectively known as the *marga*. These are *jnana-marga*

The **Yoga Sutras** – the key texts of Yoga, a school of Hindu philosophy – are compiled.

Adi Shankara establishes the non-dualistic Advaita Vedanta school of Hindu philosophy.

Sri Ramakrishna emerges as a leading figure in the Hindu reform movement.

Mahatma Gandhi combines religion and politics in his peaceful opposition to injustice and discrimination.

2ND CENTURY BCE　　**788–820 CE**　　**1836–86**　　**1869–1948**

2ND CENTURY BCE　　**6TH CENTURY CE**　　**1526**　　**1788–1860**

The *Mahabharata*, including the **Bhagavad-Gita** ("Song of the Lord"), offers role models for Hindus.

Bhakti – a Hindu movement with an emphasis on personal devotion – develops.

The Islamic **Mughal Empire** is founded, ruling parts of India until the arrival of the British Raj in 1858.

The German philosopher **Arthur Schopenhauer** begins to incorporate Indian beliefs into his Idealist philosophy.

(knowledge or insight), *karma-marga* (appropriate action or right behaviour), and *bhakti-marga* (devotion to the gods). The *marga* allow scope for a very wide range of religious practices to suit the different traditions, including a variety of rituals, meditation, yoga, and everyday worship (puja).

Concepts of god

Virtually all branches of Hinduism accept that there is a supreme creator god, Brahma, who with Vishnu (the preserver), and Shiva (the destroyer) form a principal trinity, the Trimurti. However, many traditions have their own pantheons, or add local and personal deities to the mix. Confusingly, even the three major gods (and a lot of the minor ones) often appear in different guises.

And so, while it may seem that Hinduism is a polytheistic religion, in many traditions it is truer to say that adherents have a belief in a Lord God, who is complemented by the many minor deities who have special powers or carry particular responsibilities.

Sacred texts

The different Hindu traditions have all been shaped by the four Vedas, a collection of ancient texts composed between 1200 and 900 BCE. The Brahmanas, commentaries on the Vedas, and later the Upanishads, provided a theoretical underpinning of the religion, while other texts – notably the two Indian epic poems, the *Mahabharata* and the *Ramayana* – expanded on history, mythology, religion, and philosophy.

One of the main characteristics of these Hindu traditions is tolerance. As a consequence of invasion, first by the Greeks under Alexander the Great, and later by Muslims and Christians, Hinduism has adapted and accepted some influences.

However, while some reform movements emerged as a result of colonial influences, collectively labelling these connected religions as Hinduism gave them political clout and a focus for nationalism. This came to a head in the struggle for Indian independence in the 20th century, with Mohandas Gandhi famously advocating the Hindu weapons of non-violent resistance and civil disobedience, and thereafter establishing an independent India in which all religions are not only tolerated but embraced. ∎

THROUGH SACRIFICE WE MAINTAIN THE ORDER OF THE UNIVERSE

A RATIONAL WORLD

IN CONTEXT

KEY SOURCE
The Vedas

WHEN AND WHERE
1500–500 BCE

BEFORE
From prehistory Early beliefs regard events as unpredictable or at the whim of the gods.

1700 BCE Aryan races begin a migration into the Indian subcontinent.

AFTER
6th century BCE The authority of the Brahmin class to perform sacrifices is challenged by both Buddha and Mahavira, founder of the Jain movement.

6th century CE Devotional Hinduism, or bhakti, becomes popular; worshippers make their own offerings in order to develop a personal relationship with the gods, an idea very different from the establishing of order by Vedic sacrifice.

There is, strictly speaking, no single religion that can accurately be called "Hinduism"; this is a modern, Western term for the different religions and spiritual philosophies that have originated within the Indian subcontinent. Nevertheless, there are some basic features of these religious ideas and practices that are shared by the majority of Hindus, and it is these ideas that are grouped together under the umbrella of "Hinduism". In practice, individual Hindus are free to choose which deities they worship, whether they do so at home or at a temple, and how often they take part in religious activities. But they share a common social and religious background that sets Hinduism apart from other belief systems, especially the monotheistic faiths.

In the same way as other religions, however, Hinduism seeks to explain how human life fits into the universal context. Its rituals and practices aim to address three levels of relationship – person to the divine; person to person; and person to him or herself – and how all of these relate in turn to the universal order of all things.

The eternal cosmic order

Dharma, or "right way", is a key term for expressing what Hinduism is about. In its original form, *sanatana dharma*, it may be translated from Sanskrit as "the eternal order of things", "truth", or "reality". It expresses the idea that there is an underlying structure and meaning to the world; beneath the complexity and apparently random nature of events, there are some fundamental principles, and, underpinning these, a single, unchanging reality. These ideas are demonstrated in Hinduism in the hierarchy of gods and goddesses, each of whom expresses particular aspects of a single truth.

The idea of an "eternal order" also has implications both for the individual and for society. Religion is effectively a way of understanding the place of humanity in the world. If the world is capable of being understood, and if it has a definite hierarchy or structure, then, by following that order, a person can live in harmony with the rest of society and with the universe as a whole. A key feature of the forms of religion that came together as Hinduism was that, in following this

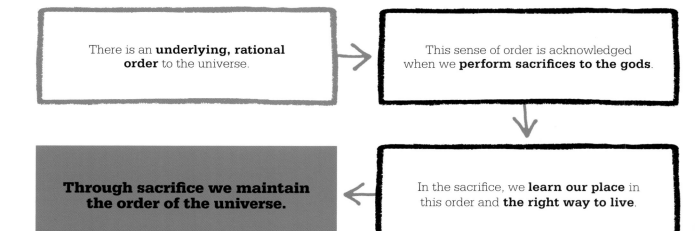

There is an **underlying, rational order** to the universe.

This sense of order is acknowledged when we **perform sacrifices to the gods**.

Through sacrifice we maintain the order of the universe.

In the sacrifice, we **learn our place** in this order and **the right way to live**.

See also: Making sense of the world 20–23 ▪ Sacrifice and blood offerings 40–45 ▪ Man and the cosmos 48–49 ▪ Beliefs for new societies 56–57 ▪ The ultimate reality 102–105

> Hinduism is not just a faith. It is the union of reason and intuition that cannot be defined but is only to be experienced.
> **Radhakrishnan,**
> ***The Bhagavad-Gita***

order, or dharma, a person may be required to perform rituals and make offerings to the gods (a form of sacrifice) that are thought necessary to maintain the sense of order.

Hindu ideas of time

Hindu thought sees time as cyclical, with the universe already having moved through three great cycles. Each of these is said to have taken millions of years; each coming into being and then passing away.

Thinking of time as cyclical has an important consequence for religious thought. In the Western, linear, concept of time it is possible to think of everything as simply the product of something else that preceded it (the law of cause and effect), and it is therefore natural to wonder how the world began. This

By performing rituals in the prescribed way, Hindus believe that they are aligning themselves with the rational ordering of the world and becoming at one with it. The images and actions are richly symbolic.

starting point is the only stage at which linear theories of time require some kind of input from outside the world itself: something has to have been responsible for setting the great train of cause and effect in motion at the beginning of time.

Conversely, in Hindu thought, the ever-turning cycles of time are contrasted with an eternal and unchanging reality called Brahman, which exists in and through everything. Worldly time runs in cycles, but Brahman is timeless, the central force that keeps the cycles moving; it is the eternal reality that stands behind the process of creation and destruction that characterizes the world of human experience.

If the great cycles of time are utterly dependent upon a timeless reality, then the right ordering of this changing world depends on awareness of that reality. This logic gives rise to the idea that one of the aims of religion is to understand and maintain the right ordering of the world.

Religious ritual and order

From perhaps as early as 1700 BCE, and continuing over the next few hundred years, there was a gradual influx of Aryan people from Central Asia into India. They brought with them their pantheon of gods, together with ideas that had parallels with those of the ancient Greeks. The Aryans integrated themselves into the Indus Valley civilization of northern India, an ancient society known to have had its own religious traditions. There is strong evidence to suggest ritual bathing and worship of a great mother goddess (p.100); other artefacts found include cremation urns and a seal depicting a horned, cross-legged deity.

What took place was not a sudden or overwhelming change, but an intermingling of cultures. In terms of religion, what emerged was a tradition of sacrificial worship and ritual that found expression in the hymns of the first great collection of Hindu sacred literature, the Vedas. Within this »

> We concentrate our minds
> upon the most radiant
> light of the Sun god, who
> sustains the Earth, the
> Interspace and the Heavens.
> **Gayatri Mantra,
> the Rig-Veda**

new tradition, religious rituals and sacrifices were considered important because they were thought to maintain the order of the cosmos. They also ensured that participants understood their place within that order and aligned themselves with it.

Sacrifice was the primary rite of the Vedic tradition. It was a symbolic re-enactment of the creation of the world and invoked deities who represented either universal qualities, or different features of the one, true reality. It was through this worship that a human fulfilled the most important of human tasks: forging a link to the divine. The ritual sacrifice was believed not only to provide a connection to the invisible realm, but also to establish the right ordering of things. In exchange for the sacrifice, a human might obtain protection from evil forces and accrue worldly benefits – such as better crops, good weather, robust health, and increased happiness.

"Sacrifice" in this context simply meant making an offering to the gods, generally of food or drink. Fire was an essential part of any sacrificial ritual; fire was thought to exist in both heaven and earth, and thus have a divine power that could reach the gods.

As the Vedic religion developed it became important that the sacrifices were performed by the right people (the Brahmin class) and in exactly the correct form. Details of the hymns to recite and actions to perform were carefully prescribed.

Sacrificial ground needed to be carefully prepared in a particular area as recommended by the ritualistic literature of the Vedas. The texts also specified the right wood needed to light the sacrificial fire, and the type of vessel required to hold the sacrificial offering (*huti*). Priests were expected to feed the sacrificial fire with offerings that might include ghee, cereals, fruits, or flowers, while chanting hymns from the Vedas.

The sacrifice also needed to be performed on an auspicious date. It might be an offering to a particular god or goddess, but especially favoured were Agni, Varuna, and Indra. Agni is the god of fire; his most important role is to manifest as the fire that burns on the sacrificial altar, destroying any demons who may attempt to disrupt the sacrifice. Varuna, the god of the sky, water, and celestial ocean, is also the guardian of *rta* – the cosmic order. He is the most prominent god of the Rig-Veda (the ritual book of the Vedas), responsible for separating night and day. He is believed to have created the waters, to prevent the rivers and oceans from overflowing, and to sustain the universe. Indra, the god of thunder, rain, and war, is known for his indulgence in *soma*, a sacrificial drink (see below); securing his goodwill is considered essential – he is locked in an eternal struggle against the forces of chaos and non-existence, and it is his efforts that separate and support heaven and earth.

Gods as aspects of order
As Hinduism developed, the Aryan gods of the Vedas were joined and, in many cases, superseded by others. Minor Vedic gods were also

The drink of the gods

The ritual drink *soma* appears in the Vedas and the sacred texts of Zoroastrianism, the ancient Persian religion, which, like Hinduism, has its roots in very early Aryan cultures. Produced by pressing the juice from certain plants, it had intoxicating, possibly stimulant and hallucinogenic properties. The Rig-Veda describes it as "King Soma", proclaiming: "We have drunk *soma* and become immortal: we have attained the light, the Gods discovered." It was prepared by priests as an offering to the gods in order that its energizing properties might assist and inspire them, although it seems likely that the priests themselves also partook.

Fly agaric (*Amanita muscari*) or psilocybin mushrooms may have been the source of *soma*; both are common inducers of trance in shamanic rituals. Marijuana and ephedra have also been proposed, the latter for its highly stimulating effects, consistent with descriptions of the god Indra quaffing soma as a preparation for battle.

The dance of Shiva represents the cosmic cycles of creation and destruction, the balance between life and death. Shiva is the destroyer, but also the transformer.

elevated to much more prominent positions. Later Hindu literature contains a huge range of gods and goddesses, reflecting the blending of different traditions and different periods in the history of early Indian religion. From these gods there emerged a ruling triumvirate responsible for the existence, order, and destruction of the universe. These three gods – the Trimurti, or trinity – represent different aspects of reality: Brahma, the creator (not to be confused with Brahman); Vishnu, the protector and guardian of humanity; and Shiva, the destroyer, or, he who balances the forces of creation and destruction.

The god Shiva is often represented, in images and in sculpture, as "Shiva Nataraja", the Lord of the Dance. Shiva's cosmic dance is shown as taking place within a circle of flames, which

You dwell in all beings; you are perfect, all pervading, all powerful and all seeing... You are the Life in all life, yet you are invisible to the human eye.
From a hymn to Vishnu

represents the ongoing process of birth and death. He has four arms: in his upper right hand he holds a drum, whose beat brings about creation, and in his upper left a destructive flame; his lower arms express a rhythmic balance between creation and destruction. His right foot is raised in the dance; his left treads on a demon, representing ignorance. This wild, exuberant figure symbolizes perfect balance in an ever-changing world. Given that time is cyclical, Shiva's destruction of the universe is seen as constructive, in that it paves the way for beneficial change.

The ordering of society

The classification of Indian society into four main groups has, since Vedic times, been based on the concept of dharma, extending the theory of the order and structure of the universe to include the correct ordering of human life and society.

Historically, it is probable that, with the invasion of the light-skinned Aryans, a contrast was established between them and the darker-skinned native inhabitants of India, with the latter being treated as inferior. This led to a social system of four main classes, or varnas, a word meaning "colour".

However, in Hinduism, this historical explanation is overlaid by a mythological account of the origin of the class system. In the Rig Veda there is a hymn to the Divine Person (Purusha) in which the body of a primal human being is sacrificed and divided up to create the four main varnas or classes of people: Brahmin, Kshatriya, Vaishya, and Shudra. Brahmins are members of the priestly class, who are said to have been created from Purusha's mouth. Kshatriya is the military or administrative class, created from Purusha's arms, while »

According to Hindu tradition, the four varnas, or classes, were formed from the various body parts of Purusha, the primal man.

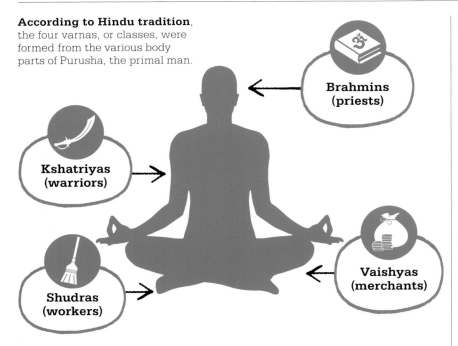

Brahmins (priests)

Kshatriyas (warriors)

Shudras (workers)

Vaishyas (merchants)

All living entities have different characteristics and duties that distinguish them from one another.
Bhavishya Purana

Vaishyas are members of the merchant class, formed from Purusha's thighs. Shudra is the class of the common working people, hewn from Purusha's feet. Because they all come from the single human reality, Purusha, they are interdependent and all have an essential part to play in the ordering of society. Their roles reflect their dharma – their divine duty.

Members of the first three varnas are said to be "twice-born" in a "sacred thread" ritual, the *upanayana*, which marks the person's acceptance of responsibility as a Hindu. The ritual is generally performed when, or soon after, a child turns eight, and has the effect of establishing his or her social position. Below the four varnas are those who find themselves completely outside the class system; formerly called "outcastes" they are now generally referred to as Dalits, meaning "the oppressed".

Class distinctions
The four varnas are sometimes referred to as castes, but that is not strictly accurate. The Indian caste system is based on an equally ancient way of classifying people, broadly in terms of their occupation. There are a very large number of such classes, or *jati*, each with a corresponding social status. The two different approaches seem to have become entangled as Hindu society developed in the later Vedic period (from around 1000 BCE), and the crucial differences between them became blurred.

Under the varna system the different social classes are all essential to to the right ordering of the world; since everyone comes from a single primal human figure, Purusha, everyone depends upon one another. Only the Brahmins were portrayed as a superior class – understandably, given that in the Vedic literature they are the ones empowered and authorized by

tradition to, literally, maintain the sense of order in the universe. By contrast, the caste system was discriminatory, emphasizing separation as being necessary in order to avoid "pollution": higher-caste people began to fear that they would be contaminated by contact with a low-status person. The caste system encouraged social fracturing, with rules forbidding people of different castes to mix together and especially to marry. This divisiveness was recognized in the Constitution of India, drawn up in 1948, which prohibited discrimination against lower castes, although popular prejudice has taken longer to eliminate.

Personal versus social
In the 6th century BCE, wandering teachers within India, such as Buddha and Mahavira, became critical of the formal and class-bound nature of Vedic worship. They welcomed followers from any class, and all were treated equally. These teachers argued for an emphasis on personal insight rather than inherited privilege. They also rejected the authority of the Vedas, and were therefore

branded as "unorthodox". But by around 500 BCE a definite shift in the way religion was viewed throughout Hindu society had taken place. Rather than being seen as a means of maintaining order, it now seemed to offer a way to escape the bondage of physical life by achieving a purely spiritual existence. Seeking liberation from, rather than alignment with, the established order became paramount. And in the centuries that followed, the Hindu tradition embraced the idea of personal devotion as a means of liberation, and worship became a matter more of personal engagement than simply the correct performance of sacrifice. Over time, personal forms of devotion and ritual developed, so much so that shrines became a common feature in people's homes, and a Brahmin was no longer required to enable acts of devotion to take place.

Religion and society

In the Vedic period, religion was focused primarily on the individual finding his or her place within the universe, and within society, and living in the way that had been

Not by birth is one an outcast; not by birth is one a Brahmin. By deed one becomes an outcast, by deed one becomes a Brahmin.
Buddha on the varnas

determined for that individual, according to the varnas; it had, therefore, both a personal and a social dimension, as well as an apparently rational system for prescribing how the personal and social interacted.

This early phase of Hinduism highlights an issue for all religion, namely whether it should be based mainly on the individual, or on society as a whole. Religions are embedded within society, and it is sometimes difficult to distinguish truly "religious" ideas from beliefs and attitudes that arise from the political or cultural milieu within which the religion developed. It is also the case that religious rules and traditions may be used by a ruling elite to maintain their own position.

Even posing the question of whether religion should focus on the individual or society is problematic, for it implies that a personal experience of religion is more valid than the social. ∎

The concept of varna may need redefining in order to be workable in 21st-century India where newly-defined roles and non-traditional careers challenge existing hierarchies.

The sacred literature of Hinduism

Hindu scriptures fall into two categories, distinguished by the names *sruti* and *smriti*. The term *sruti*, which means "that which is heard", is used to describe Vedic literature, which was "heard" by priests and scholars through the process of revelation or of the realization of undoubted truth. This canonical knowledge was then passed down via the oral tradition from one generation of Brahmins to the next.

There are four collections of Vedic hymns, composed over a period of 1,000 years. The first, thought to date back to 1200 BCE, is the Rig-Veda. Associated with these, and also *sruti*, are the Brahmanas, which provide instructions about the performance of ritual; the Aranyakas, which outline discussions on meditation and ritual; and the Upanishads, which provide philosophical interpretations. Vedic *sruti* literature is the ultimate authority for Hindus.

The term *smriti*, which translates as "that which is remembered" is used to describe the remaining Hindu literature, notably the great epic poems, the *Mahabharata* and the *Ramayana*. While not having the same status as *sruti*, because they are not thought to be divinely inspired, these texts are nonetheless important because they are open to interpretation. This significant strand of Indian literature is still hugely influential and includes the Bhagavad-Gita, probably the most popular of all Hindu scriptures.

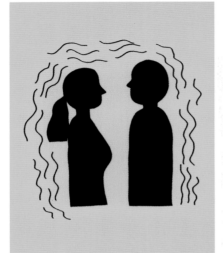

THE DIVINE HAS A FEMALE ASPECT
THE POWER OF THE GREAT GODDESS

IN CONTEXT

KEY TEXTS
The Vedas

WHEN AND WHERE
From 1700 BCE, India

BEFORE
3000 BCE Figurines dating to this time found in the Indus Valley suggest the worship of a fertility goddess.

AFTER
5th–3rd century BCE The Puranas, ancient Hindu texts, celebrate female power, and the goddesses described as consorts of the gods in the Vedas begin to gain their own followings.

300–700 CE Tantric rites use images of coupled male and female deities as a focus for meditation, and Shaktism becomes a fully fledged devotional branch of Hinduism.

c.800 CE Adi Shankara composes Saundaryalahari ("Waves of Beauty"), a hymn to Parvati and her sexual power.

While in many faiths the image of the divine has been mainly masculine, Hinduism has many goddesses, who represent creativity, fertility, or power. The general term for the feminine divine force is Shakti, which means "to be able". Shakti is personified in Maha Devi, the divine mother or "great goddess". She represents the active power of the divine, as well as its nurturing force, and in the Hindu school of Shaktism she is worshipped as the supreme deity. The great goddess takes on many different forms, each expressing particular qualities. In her aspect as consort to Shiva, for example, Shakti may appear as gentle, loving Parvati, but she is also Kali and Durga – terrible and threatening.

The coiled serpent
As well as being the creative power of the divine, Shakti represents the feminine element within the self. Hindus believe that our sexual energy and life force (kundalini) resides like a coiled serpent or

Lakshmi, goddess of good fortune, beauty, and fertility, is the consort of Lord Vishnu. She has four arms and hands, with which she dispenses material and spiritual gifts to devotees.

sleeping goddess at the base of the spine. Awareness and development of this force through yoga can be a form of spiritual release. Sometimes practised physically, more often through meditation, these Tantric rituals are used to enhance the union between a person's male and female elements. ■

See also: Physical and mental discipline 112–13 ▪ Devotion through puja 114–15 ▪ Buddhas and bodhisattvas 152–57 ▪ Shaktism 328

SIT UP CLOSE TO YOUR GURU
HIGHER LEVELS OF TEACHING

IN CONTEXT

KEY SOURCE
The Upanishads

WHEN AND WHERE
6th century BCE, India

BEFORE
From 1200 BCE The Vedas
provide texts and instructions
for rituals used exclusively
by the brahmins, or priests.

AFTER
6th century BCE In India,
travelling teachers, among
them Buddha and Mahavira,
attract their own disciples.

From 1st century BCE Six
distinct schools of Hindu
philosophy, known as the
Darshanas, develop.

800 CE Adi Shankara founds
four famous *mathas*, or
monastery schools, to teach
the ideas of the Upanishads.

1500 CE Sikhism takes its
name from the Sanskrit word
shishya, "student of the guru".

I s it realistic to offer the same
religious teachings and truths
to everyone? In Hinduism
there are different levels at which
the religion can be understood and
followed. Its earliest texts, the
Vedas, and the commentaries on
them that followed, provided the
texts, prayers, and instructions
for the performance of sacrifices
and other public acts of worship.
Later, the epic, often action-packed
stories of the gods, the *Ramayana*
and the *Mahabharata* (p.111),
were used for popular devotion.
But by the 6th century BCE, another
body of literature – the Upanishads
– had developed, offering access,
for the initiated, to a higher plane
of spiritual knowledge.

Difficult concepts
The word "Upanishad" means
"to sit up close", and it applies to
teachings that are restricted to
those who are accepted for religious
study by a guru, or teacher. The
Upanishads focus on abstract
concepts concerning the nature
of the self and of the universe.

In particular, the texts argue
that there is a single universal
reality, Brahman, which can
be known only by thought and
the analysis of experience. The
Upanishads thus added a highly
philosophical dimension to Indian
religious discussion. The idea
of sitting up close to your guru
implies that there are levels
of teaching which, by probing
religious ideas for truths that are
universal and rational, can give
new depth to conventional beliefs. ∎

On Earth, those who
achieve greatness achieve
it through concentration.
The Upanishads

See also: The ultimate reality 102–105 ∎ The self as constantly changing
148–151 ∎ The Protestant Reformation 230–37 ∎ The Darshanas 328

BRAHMAN IS MY SELF WITHIN THE HEART

THE ULTIMATE REALITY

IN CONTEXT

KEY SOURCE
The Upanishads

WHEN AND WHERE
6th century BCE, India

BEFORE
From 2000 BCE The idea of
a soul that can be separated
from the body is present in
some early Indo-European
beliefs, but describes a spirit
that carries the essence of the
individual rather than a soul at
one with an ultimate reality.

AFTER
c.400 BCE Indian philosophy
influences ancient Greek
thinkers. Plato posits a
supreme being from which
all other living beings derive.

1st century Buddhist sage
Nagasena rejects the notion
of a fixed "self", following
Buddha's teaching that all
things exist in a state of flux.

The Upanishads are a series
of philosophical texts, the
earliest of which had been
composed by the 6th century BCE.
They record the highest level of
teachings, reserved for the finely
trained, meditative minds of
Hindu sages or gurus. Their central
concern is the nature of the self; in
effect they argue that to understand
the self is to understand everything.

Western philosophy has
traditionally taken two positions
on the nature of the self. For the
school known as "dualist", the self is
non-physical and distinct from the
body. Whether it is called the soul
or the mind, it is the thinking and
feeling aspect of what we are – the

See also: Animism in early societies 24–25 ▪ Man and the cosmos 48–49 ▪ Seeing with pure consciousness 116–121 ▪ Man as a manifestation of God 188 ▪ Mystical experience in Christianity 238 ▪ Sufism and the mystic tradition 282–83

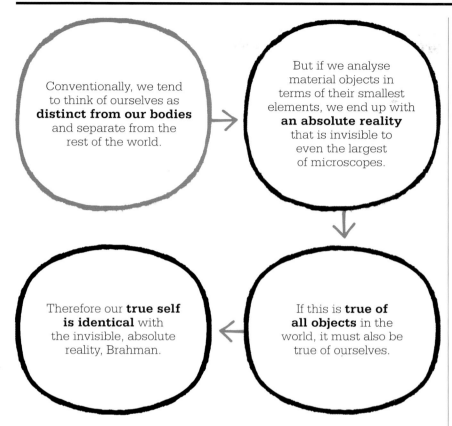

Conventionally, we tend to think of ourselves as **distinct from our bodies** and separate from the rest of the world.

But if we analyse material objects in terms of their smallest elements, we end up with **an absolute reality** that is invisible to even the largest of microscopes.

If this is **true of all objects** in the world, it must also be true of ourselves.

Therefore our **true self is identical** with the invisible, absolute reality, Brahman.

The sage then asks his son to divide one of those seeds, and describe what he sees inside that. The answer is "nothing". The sage then points out that the whole great fig tree is made of just such "nothingness". That is its essence, its soul, its reality. And, the dialogue, concludes "That is you, Svetaketu!"

The statement, "That is you!" (in Sanskrit, "*Tat tvam asi!*"), is probably the most famous in all Hindu philosophy. It rests on the idea that analysis of any apparently solid object will eventually arrive at an invisible essence, present everywhere, which is Brahman. This applies to everything, from a fig to the human self. Beyond the physical and mental aspects of the self, Hinduism says there is something greater, the atman, which can be nothing other than Brahman, the single, absolute reality. There is no distinction between us and this ultimate divine reality. »

"I" that experiences the world. It is this "I" that absorbs sensory data and makes sense of it. Materialists (or physicalists), on the other hand, argue that only physical things exist, therefore "the self" is no more than a way of describing the activity of the brain.

Within Hinduism, however, the Upanishads explored a view that differs from both of these Western approaches. In these texts, the self is described as having three parts: a material body; a more "subtle" body, which is made up of thoughts, feelings, and experiences; and a pure consciousness, called the atman. The atman, it is claimed, is identical with the absolute,

impersonal reality, Brahman. Therefore, although we may experience ourselves as separate, small, and vulnerable individuals, our true selves are actually at one with the fundamental reality of the universe.

The self as "nothing"
The Upanishads express the idea of atman by way of dialogues and images. One of the most famous is from the Chandogya Upanishad. It is a dialogue between the sage Uddalaka Aruni and his son, Svetaketu. The sage asks the boy to bring and cut open a fig. When his father asks him what he sees inside it, the son replies, "Seeds".

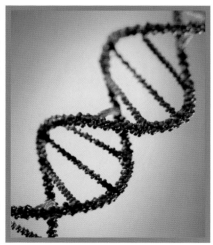

Microscopy has helped science to conclude that an entire human being is made from DNA – but does this include what we think of as our "self"?

An endless cycle of lives is what lies before us, unless we can be released from the suffering of reincarnation through the realization of the true nature of atman or Brahman.

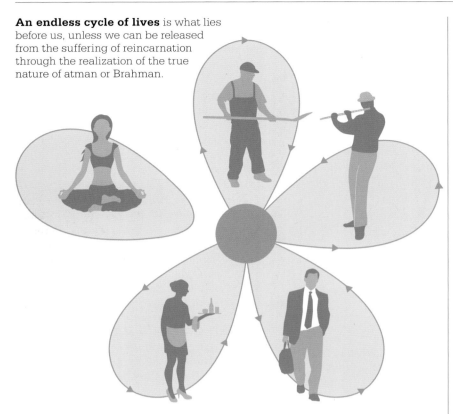

All this is Brahman …
He is my Self
within the heart,
smaller than
a corn of rice …
**Chandogya Upanishad
14th Khanda**

Understanding Brahman

The Upanishad dialogue about the fig seed is followed by a second, which attempts to give us some sense of what Brahman might be like. A bowl of water is brought and the son is asked to taste the liquid from different parts of the bowl. It tastes pure throughout. Salt is then dissolved in the water. Now, although the appearance remains the same, all of the water tastes of salt. In the same way, Brahman, the absolute reality, is unseen but present everywhere.

The Mundaka Upanishad uses a different image for Brahman. Just as thousands of sparks fly from a large fire and then fall back into it, so innumerable beings are created from Brahman, "the imperishable", or "Great One", which is described as unborn, breathless, mindless,

and pure – but bringing forth breath, mind, and all the senses. "Its heart is the whole world. Truly, this is the Inner Self of all."

In this understanding, the way we experience the world through the senses, viewing it as consisting of objects separate from ourselves, is not the absolute truth; there is a reality that underlies and sustains everything, which is invisible and within our innermost self.

Karma and reincarnation

In the earlier Vedic religion, it was believed that the act of offering sacrifices to the gods maintained the sense of order in the universe. The Upanishads internalized that process. They claimed that reality is to be found as an absolutely simple, still point, deep within the self. And that reality is universal,

not individual. Just as making a sacrifice in the correct way was thought to align the self with the universal order, so being aware of Brahman as the true self is to align yourself with reality itself.

Hindus believe that karma (actions) produce consequences – both good and bad – not just in the external world, but also for the person who performs them. Hinduism developed an idea of reincarnation in which the self takes on a succession of bodies over the course of many lifetimes. The form each life takes is determined by karma from the previous life. However, knowledge that "atman is Brahman" can release a person from the constant cycle of birth, death, and rebirth (which is known as samsara). Karma is generated by the actions of the physical body and the "subtle" mental body (such as an individual's thoughts and feelings), but the person who is aware of the atman, and therefore of Brahman, residing deep within the self, will transcend the level of the two "bodies" (physical and "subtle" mental) at which karma operates.

> When many candles
> are kindled from another,
> it is the same flame
> that burns in all candles;
> even so, the one Brahman
> appears to be many.
> **Sage Vasishtha**

Although Hindus hope that, by generating good karma, they will improve their prospects in future lives, there is always the threat that bad karma will lead to them being reborn into a lower caste, or as an animal. However, this is not as important as it first appears, because moving on to another life (good or bad) is not viewed as a final goal in Hinduism. Unlike in monotheistic religions, in which the prospect of life beyond death is a promise to be welcomed, in Hinduism the aim is to be released from the suffering that inevitably arises from living and dying in one life after another.

A conscious intuition

The arguments presented by the Chandogya Upanishad's stories about the fig seeds and the salt water are quite logical. In a sense, they are no more than a scientific analysis of matter, but one that is presented in the language of a pre-scientific age. Today, the equivalent would be to say that everything is comprised of sub-atomic particles, energy, and the fundamental forces.

However, the purpose and implication of the Upanishadic dialogues and modern science are quite different. In the Upanishads, reasoned argument is not an end in itself, but a means of leading a person to an intuition that goes beyond words. The logic of the argument for the identity of atman and Brahman represents no more than the starting point for understanding them. The aim of the Upanishads' teachings is to encourage students to internalize and meditate on the arguments until the reality that they suggest is directly experienced – in a way that goes beyond reason and language. This wordless awareness is said to produce a state of bliss (*ananda*).

It could be argued that a "self" formed by sense experience and reason alone would suffice for the purposes of a human life. This was challenged by the sages who produced the dialogues of the Upanishads. The Katha Upanishad uses a chariot as an analogy of the self. The senses are the chariot's horses and the mind is its driver. But riding in the chariot is the atman. The implication of this image is that, for someone whose whole awareness is limited to reason and sense experience, the onward rush of the chariot is without purpose, since it lacks a passenger who is making the journey. That is what the intuition of the atman restores.

Hinduism does not see gaining consciousness of the atman as easy. It can occur only after other possible identities have been examined and discarded as inadequate. It is not a fact to be learned, but an intuition that can gradually inform a person's conscious awareness. ∎

Death and beyond

If the self, or soul, is non-physical and therefore separable from the physical body, the possibility of surviving death and living on in another form becomes logically possible. Most Western religions see each individual soul as being created at a particular point in time, but capable of living on indefinitely following the death of the body. Hindu thought sees the self as timeless, having no beginning, and identified with the single, undifferentiated reality. This self takes on physical form in a succession of lives, which is the idea of reincarnation. For Western monotheistic religions, the issue is whether the soul is genuinely separable from the body, and how, if separated, it might maintain its identity. For Hindus, the issue is to intuitively grasp that this self and this life are only a part of something much larger, and that the self is one with the fundamental reality of the universe.

> Concealed in the heart
> of all beings is the
> Atman, the Spirit,
> the Self; smaller than the
> smallest atom, greater
> than the vast spaces.
> **Katha Upanishad**

WE LEARN, WE LIVE, WE WITHDRAW, WE DETACH
THE FOUR STAGES OF LIFE

IN CONTEXT

KEY TEXT
The Dharma-shastras

WHEN AND WHERE
5th century BCE, India

BEFORE
From prehistory Many early belief systems have age-related rules and rites of passage.

From 1700 BCE The Vedic religion includes a tradition of ascetic discipline, but emphasizes social duty as the central goal for most people.

6th century BCE As ideas about reincarnation and liberation become more prominent in Hinduism, more people reject society and family life and choose the path of the ascetic.

AFTER
Today The majority of Hindus remain for most of their lives in the "householder" stage.

Implicit in all religions is the notion that there are aims in life, and correct ways of living that might secure these aims. Hinduism proposes that life has several main goals: dharma (right living); the linked concepts of *artha* (wealth) and *kama* (pleasure); and moksha (liberation). The pursuit of dharma – living as duty obliges – keeps a person on the righteous path. The search for wealth and pleasure leads people to learn valuable lessons, as well as producing children, supporting the family, and being in a position to give alms. The final goal, moksha, is a liberation from the concerns and things of the earthly world.

See also: ▪ Self-denial leads to spiritual liberation 68–71 ▪ A rational world 92–99 ▪ Selfless action 110–11 ▪ Finding the Middle Way 130–136 ▪ The purpose of monastic vows 145

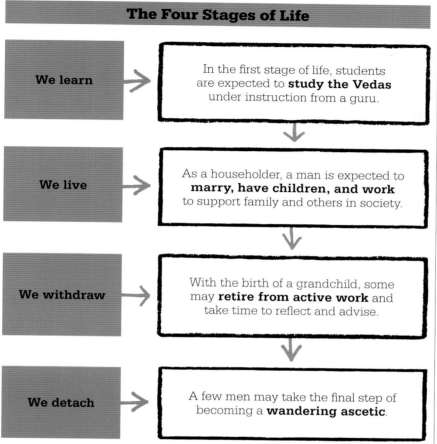

The Four Stages of Life

We learn → In the first stage of life, students are expected to **study the Vedas** under instruction from a guru.

We live → As a householder, a man is expected to **marry, have children, and work** to support family and others in society.

We withdraw → With the birth of a grandchild, some may **retire from active work** and take time to reflect and advise.

We detach → A few men may take the final step of becoming a **wandering ascetic**.

By the 6th century BCE two very different traditions in Indian religion existed. Most people in India followed the Vedic tradition, offering sacrifices to the gods and hoping for a life of wealth and pleasure, moderated by the moral and social principles encoded in dharma. However, others had become attracted to a different lifestyle – that of the wandering ascetic, committed to serious physical and mental discipline in order to achieve spiritual liberation, and shunning both wealth and pleasure. This ascetic tradition, known as *shramana* (a Sanskrit word that translates as something like "to work at austerity") was very influential in the development of both Buddhism and Jainism. The Dharma Sutras – sacred texts on the rules of correct behaviour – suggested that a person who had studied dharma (virtue or "right living") was essentially faced with three possible paths: the continued study of the Vedic texts as the principal goal in life; a life seeking wealth and pleasure; or the renunciation of everything in order to become an ascetic. The last choice was not an uncommon one in Hindu society at this time; the most famous example is that of Buddha, who abandoned his privileged life as prince Siddhartha Gautama, leaving his wife and baby son in order to become a wandering teacher.

However, the position of the followers of the *shramana* tradition – that asceticism was more spiritually valuable than the seeking of *artha* (wealth) and *kama* (pleasure) – placed them in opposition to Vedic tradition. For around a thousand years, the Vedas had been used to teach that seeking material comfort and personal fulfilment were noble goals in life, if correctly pursued. So, was it necessary to choose between such radically different paths? Or might it be possible for a person to enjoy the benefits of all four traditional goals?

Having it all
In about the 5th century BCE, further commentaries on dharma known as shastras offered a new approach: instead of making one final choice, a person might work »

Of Brahmins, Kshatriyas and Vaishyas, as also the Shudras, O Arjuna, the duties are distributed according to the qualities born of their own natures.
The Bhagavad-Gita

> When one renounces all the desires which have arisen in the mind ... and when he himself is content within his own self, then is he called a man of steadfast wisdom.
> **The Bhagavad-Gita**

towards different goals in succession, as they moved through four stages of life, or *ashramas*: student, house-holder, retiree, and renunciate, or ascetic. The correct aims in life, and hence correct behaviour, would not only depend on the individual's varna, or social class (pp.92–99), but would also vary with the stage reached in life.

Not everyone is thought able to travel through these four stages. Women are (usually) excluded, as are Shudras (the labouring class) and those outside the class system (Dalits, or "untouchables"). Only men from the highest three varnas – Brahmins (priests), Kshatriyas (soldiers or protectors of the state), and Vaishyas (merchants and farmers) – undergo the rite, when they are about eight years old, known as the sacred thread ceremony, in which they are "twice born" and begin their journey through life.

Learning and living
The first stage of life is that of the *brahmacharya*, or student. The boy attends a *gurukula* (a school) where he studies Vedic literature with a guru, or teacher. He learns about dharma – right living – in an academic way, together with history, philosophy, law, literature, grammar, and rhetoric. Education traditionally continues until the age of around 25 or 30, and during this stage, as well as showing respect to parents and teachers, students are expected to abstain from sexual activity, sublimating all their energy into their learning.

At the end of his education, a Hindu man is expected to marry and have a family. This is the start of the *grihastha* or "householder" stage, during which every man is expected to be economically active, supporting not just his wife and children, but also elderly relatives. Traditional Indian households often include three or four generations, who pool their income and use a single kitchen. This extended family tends to be organized on hierarchical lines, both for men and women. Householders are also expected to offer support to ascetics.

The householder upholds the duties of his dharma and his varna (class), but, unlike in the other three stages, part of his duty is the pursuit of *artha* (wealth) and *kama* (desire), including sexual pleasure and procreation. To describe this stage of life as one in which wealth and pleasure are the primary goals, however, may give a distorted view of its obligations, for it involves caring for the extended family and offering hospitality.

Withdrawal from the world
The third stage of life of is that of *vanaprastha* – retirement. This traditionally begins with the arrival of the first grandson. Originally, it involved becoming a "forest dweller", opting for a simple life of reflection into which a man could retire with his wife – although, at this stage, ceasing to have sex.

Today it is generally a matter of letting go of overall responsibility for business and financial matters, allowing the next generation to take over, but also having time to study and offer wise advice.

Most Hindus never get beyond the retirement stage to reach that of the ascetic; they are only allowed to enter the fourth stage of life once they have fulfilled all their obligations to their family. This is the point at which the individual sets aside all worldly concerns and ties, and devotes his life to the pursuit of final release (moksha).

A combined formula
The four stages of life combine with a person's class in a single concept that defines morality and lifestyle: *varnashrama-dharma*, literally the right ordering of life (dharma) according to one's class (varna) and stage in life (*ashrama*). As a formula for prescribing "how to live correctly", it is very different to those of other religions, where one

A man measures fabric in his place of business. During the "householder" phase of life a man is expected to pursue wealth and provide for his family and for his extended family.

The various spiritual obligations of Hinduism could seem difficult to fulfil in one lifetime. However, by delineating four separate life phases, each with a different focus, and with specific duties to perform for a limited period, the task seems more achievable.

set of moral commands applies equally to all. It is a moral system that recognizes flexibility and difference in people's circumstances. It also aims to prevent pride in those of the higher classes, who must undergo a disciplined education in order to develop self-detachment and prepare them, mentally, to relinquish their worldly gains and responsibilities in later life. It confers value on the labours of the householder, recognizing that, both economically and practically, those in the second stage of life support everybody else. And it gives dignity to the elderly, with the final letting-go of practical and domestic responsibilities seen as a positive opportunity for spiritual growth.

In the modern world

Until very recent times, the extended family has been the dominant model throughout Hindu society, forming the background against which men lived out the four stages, with their moral and spiritual principles. In this traditional scenario, women do not feature in the first or last stages

of a man's life, and marriage is considered to be a contract between families, rather than a matter of romantic attachment. If a new wife is to be introduced to an extended family home, it is clearly problematic if she is not well suited to the man in terms of dharma, varna, or his *ashrama*. This explains the origins of certain Hindu social attitudes and traditions – for example, the arranged marriage – but many of these now clash with the outlook of some Hindus brought up in a more individualized and secular society.

Hinduism is to a large degree more about practice than belief, and it is closely bound up with ideas about age and class. Western concepts of individual rights and equality do not sit easily alongside some of the early Hindu teachings, and with the Westernization of attitudes, greater social mobility in modern India, and the practice of Hinduism in communities globally, it remains to be seen whether the the "four stages" will remain a viable model for Hindu life. ∎

Moral principles

Hinduism has five broad moral principles: *ahimsa* (not killing), *satya* (speaking the truth), *asteya* (not stealing), *brahmacharya* (sexual continence), and *aparigraha* (not being avaricious). The way each of these is practised depends on the stage of life. For instance, celibacy will not be practised by householders, whose duty it is to have children. These principles define external morality, but there is also a tradition of inner cultivation to practise during all stages of life, which involves the pursuit of five qualities: cleanliness, contentment, pure concentration, group study, and devotion to God. The five qualities reflect the progression from the early Vedic tradition, based on ritual, to a religion of personal spiritual development and devotion, which developed many centuries later.

IT MAY BE YOUR DUTY TO KILL
SELFLESS ACTION

IN CONTEXT

KEY SOURCE
The Bhagavad-Gita

WHEN AND WHERE
2nd century BCE, India

BEFORE
From 1700 BCE Dharma – the right way of living to preserve universal order – is a central feature of early Hindu thought.

6th century BCE Buddha upholds the concept of unselfish action, but teaches that all killing is wrong.

3rd century BCE The Indian emperor Asoka incorporates non-violence and compassion towards all people into his rule.

AFTER
From 15th century Sikhism includes the duty to protect the weak and defend the faith.

19th–20th century Mahatma Gandhi develops the strategy of passive resistance as a non-violent weapon against injustice.

The Bhagavad-Gita is an ancient Hindu scripture about virtue and duty. It tells of a dialogue between Krishna (an incarnation of the supreme god Vishnu) and the warrior-prince Arjuna. Arjuna is about to go into battle against another branch of his family in a dispute over who should rule the kingdom. As a member of the *kshatriya* class (the military or ruling elite), it is his duty is to fight. Yet he despairs of killing some of those on the "other side" – his relatives or those whom he respects as great teachers.

In the opening section of the Gita, Arjuna says that he would rather give up the struggle over the kingdom than be involved in the slaughter. Not only does the idea of killing members of his family and his teachers go against his deepest inclinations, but he also fears that it will have negative consequences, creating bad karma for all involved (in Hinduism, killing a relative is thought to lead to the downfall of a family and rebirth in hell).

Arjuna is caught between two apparently conflicting principles: should he do his duty as a member of the warrior class or avoid the disastrous karmic consequences of killing? Advice comes from his charioteer, who turns out to be none other than the god Krishna.

Krishna tells Arjuna that he should do his duty and fight. The act of killing would only create bad karma if it was done for the wrong reasons – out of hatred or greed, for example. The ideal is for the individual to do his or her duty, whatever it is and however much it goes against personal inclinations, but to do it with selfless motives. Not only will such action not cause harm, but it will be a step towards personal liberation.

Krishna argues that personal motives are what count when considering any type of action.

By fulfilling the obligations he is born with, a person never comes to grief.
Krishna

See also: Living in harmony 38 ▪ A rational world 92–99 ▪ Hinduism in the political age 124–25 ▪ Let kindness and compassion rule 146–47 ▪ Striving in the way of God 278 ▪ The Sikh code of conduct 296–301

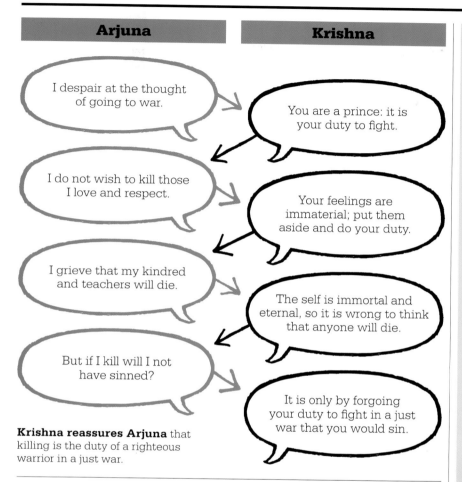

Arjuna	Krishna

I despair at the thought of going to war.

You are a prince: it is your duty to fight.

I do not wish to kill those I love and respect.

Your feelings are immaterial; put them aside and do your duty.

I grieve that my kindred and teachers will die.

The self is immortal and eternal, so it is wrong to think that anyone will die.

But if I kill will I not have sinned?

It is only by forgoing your duty to fight in a just war that you would sin.

Krishna reassures Arjuna that killing is the duty of a righteous warrior in a just war.

The epic poems

The teaching on selfless duty is just one of the themes to be found in the Bhagavad-Gita, a work noted for the beauty of its imagery and language. It is part of the *Mahabharata*, an epic poem that chronicles the rivalry between two branches of one family.

The other great Hindu epic is the *Ramayana*, which tells of the relationship between Prince Rama and his wife Sita, through her kidnap by the demon Ravana. Its narrative, has a wonderful, much-loved cast of characters.

These epics offer a positive view of the brahmins and Vedic sacrifices, and highlight the dire consequences of royal rivalry. They explore moral dilemmas and celebrate human qualities, presenting role models for Hindus to follow. Both epics were created over a long period, probably starting in the 4th or 5th century BCE.

Ravana, the vengeful demon king and villain of the Ramayana, is played by a dancer in a production of the Ramayana in Kerala, Southern India.

He applauds the willingness to act dutifully out of selfless motives, setting aside any selfish preferences. Krishna then gives Arjuna a second reason for going into battle: the self is immortal and passes through a succession of incarnations, so no one is really killed. Only the body dies; the soul will live again in a different body.

A context of change

When the Gita was composed, there were two very different streams of religious thought in India. The older of the two, dating from the early Vedic period, promoted social order and duty as the basis of morality. However, it had been challenged by newer philosophies – particularly the Buddhist and Jain religions – in which "not killing" was the first precept and foundation of morality. This represented a departure from the Vedic class system and its traditional obligations. Arjuna's dilemma reflects that clash of moral priorities, and Krishna's advice is an attempt to maintain class obligations in the face of criticism from philosophies centred on the idea of karma and reincarnation. ∎

THE PRACTICE OF YOGA LEADS TO SPIRITUAL LIBERATION
PHYSICAL AND MENTAL DISCIPLINE

IN CONTEXT

KEY TEXT
The Yoga Sutras

WHEN AND WHERE
2nd century BCE, India

BEFORE
Before 1700 BCE An Indus Valley clay tablet showing a person sitting cross-legged suggests a yoga posture.

1000 BCE Indian Ayurvedic medicine analyses the body and promotes exercise.

6th century BCE Daoism and Buddhism promote mental and physical discipline as aids to harmony and insight.

AFTER
12th century In Japan, Zen Buddhism refines the pursuit of mental stillness and focused thinking.

20th century In the West, yoga becomes popular in a secular context for its physical and mental health benefits.

The Sanskrit word "yoga" is used to describe a range of practices, both physical and mental, which are used to help achieve spiritual insight and escape the limitations of the physical body.

Ideas about yoga are found in the 6th century BCE in the early philosophical Hindu texts known as the Upanishads, and there is a section on yoga in the ancient Sanskrit scripture, the Bhagavad-Gita. The first systematic account of yoga is found in the Yoga Sutras. Some scholars attribute this text to the philosopher Patanjali, who lived in the 2nd century BCE. However, it is now generally agreed that it was written between the 2nd century CE and the 4th century CE by more than one author, and that it includes traditions and practices from earlier periods. The Yoga Sutras comprise a set of techniques to promote mental calmness and concentration, which are deemed necessary for gaining greater insight.

Physical postures and breath control techniques are used in yoga to still both body and mind. More advanced techniques can lead to the attainment of higher consciousness.

Although originally devised for those who had taken an ascetic path, yoga was later developed as a set of practices that could be used by everybody. The physical postures and techniques for breath control are not an end in themselves. They aim to calm the mind and make it singular in its focus – "single-pointed". The mind can only become calm once the senses have been controlled. It is only then that inner freedom and insight may arise.

A path to release
According to the Yoga Sutras, yoga enables the practitioner to avoid mental "afflictions", such as

See also: Aligning the self with the *dao* 66–67 ▪ Seeing with pure consciousness 116–21 ▪ Zen insights that go beyond words 160–63

Both **body and mind must be calm and focused** to be freed from earthly concerns.

↓

Body and mind **influence one another**.

↓   ↓

Thoughts and feelings can affect our **physical wellbeing**.   ↔   Posture and control can promote **mental alertness**.

↓   ↓

Combining both mental and physical discipline with yoga will **help us escape our limitations**.

---

ignorance, ego-centred views, and extremes of emotion. It also offers freedom from the "three poisons" of greed, anger, and delusion (a goal that Buddhism shares).

The Yoga Sutras set out the practice of yoga in eight steps. The first two are preparatory and show the context in which yoga becomes effective. First is the practice of a morality of restraint, particularly of ahimsa (not taking life). The second focuses on personal observances, such as the study of philosophical works and contemplation of a god in order to gain inspiration. The next three steps aim to control the body and senses: adopting physical postures (asanas) to control the body; controlling breathing; and withdrawing attention from the senses. Finally, there are three mental steps: concentrating the mind on a single object; meditating

on that object; and arriving at a state of absorbed concentration. These steps are progressive, leading to the final release from a mundane awareness of self and world, with its mental afflictions, into a higher consciousness.

Today, yoga is widely practised as a healthful physical regime that also promotes inner calm. But it is important to remember that in the context of Hindu religion, the term "yoga" encompasses disciplines and practices not only of posture, but of morality, meditation, knowledge, and devotion, and that taken together, their aim is to release the true self or consciousness (*purusha*) from the entanglements of matter (*prakriti*), thereby restoring it to its natural condition. So, while many in the West think of yoga as a form of physical exercise, for Hindus it is a path to ultimate freedom. ▪

A godless philosophy

Yoga does not require belief in any external deity, but is a natural process of clearing away the entanglements of physical experience, releasing the true self to realize its identity with the absolute. But this makes sense only in the context of the philosophy upon which it is based – Samkhya.

One of the oldest schools of Indian philosophy, Samkhya argues for an absolute dualism of *prakriti* (matter) and *purusha* (pure consciousness). Some philosophies contrast the physical with the mental, but Samkhya sees the mind as a refined form of matter. A person therefore comprises three elements – a physical body, a worldly self (with all its mental activity and sense experience), and a pure and eternal self, which is identified with the eternal *purusha*, and is free and beyond any limitations of time and space.

In Samkhya, rather than devoting the self to any god, the aim is to release the self to appreciate its pure spiritual nature, freed from the limitations of the physical, and the vehicle that is used to achieve this is yoga.

Yoga is the practice of quieting the mind.
Patanjali

WE SPEAK TO THE GODS THROUGH DAILY RITUALS

DEVOTION THROUGH PUJA

IN CONTEXT

KEY MOVEMENT
The development of bhakti

WHEN AND WHERE
6th century CE, India

BEFORE
From prehistory Making
offerings before images of
deities characterizes worship
in many cultures.

From 1700 BCE In Vedic
religion, as in other early
civilizations, a priestly class
performs religious rites on
behalf of the people.

6th century BCE The
Upanishads introduce more
abstract concepts to Hindu
religious thought.

From 2nd century BCE In
Mahayana Buddhism, images
of buddhas and bodhisattvas
(enlightened beings) are used
as devotional aids.

AFTER
15th century Sikh worship
is based on devotional songs.

There has always been
an element of ritual and
worship in Hindu religion.
In the earliest traditions prescribed
by the sacred Vedic texts, it was
vital that sacrifices made at the
sacred fires be performed in
exactly the right way, and solely
by the brahmins or priestly class.
However, in the early centuries CE,
the approach to worship became
less exclusive, and this evolved
into the practice of bhakti (loving
devotion). Temples were built
housing images of the gods, which
could be visited by worshippers,
and gradually, alongside the
priestly rituals connected with
birth, coming of age, marriage, and
death, there developed a tradition
of making personal acts of worship,
or puja, to the deities that was
open to all, irrespective of class.

Honouring the gods
Puja involves making a simple
offering – vegetarian food, incense,
or flowers – before the image of a
god or goddess. It can take place
in a temple or in the home, and the
people performing it often mark
their foreheads with powder or
paste in acknowledgment of the
act of puja and the blessing of

A devotee performs puja by
offering food to the image of a deity,
as if enticing it to eat. Images such
as this are believed to be filled with
the deity's spiritual energy.

the deity that results from it. At the
end of an act of puja, worshippers
may receive any food that has been
offered. The nature of the offering
is less important than the intention
behind the offering. Sometimes it
is enough simply to go to a temple
and look at the image of the deity.

See also: Sacrifice and blood offerings 40–45 ▪ Living the Way of the Gods 82–85 ▪ The Protestant Reformation 230–37 ▪ Devotion to the Sweet Lord 322

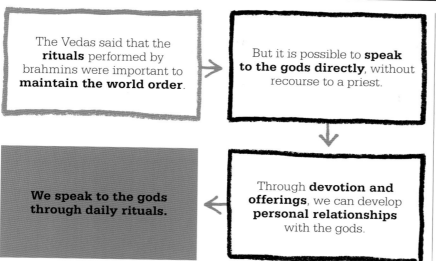

The Vedas said that the **rituals** performed by brahmins were important to **maintain the world order**.

But it is possible to **speak to the gods directly**, without recourse to a priest.

Through **devotion and offerings**, we can develop **personal relationships** with the gods.

We speak to the gods through daily rituals.

Divine love

In worship, the god or goddess (made visible in his or her image, or murti) is seen as a person with whom the worshipper can have a relationship. Through bhakti, the devotee develops an intense emotional bond with a chosen deity; the divine is then seen as dwelling within the heart of the devotee. Bhakti came to dominate Hinduism by the 12th century: temple worship involved singing and dancing, and the relationship between the devotee and his or her god or goddess was likened to a relationship between lovers.

Although practised widely, many forms of bhakti were particularly focused on the god Vishnu (see below left), who is depicted in the great epics of the *Ramayana* and *Mahabharata* as coming down to earth to help humankind in the guise of one of his many avatars (embodiments of a god). The eighth avatar of Vishnu is Krishna, whose followers see bhakti as the highest path towards liberation. ▪

Through puja, people can both pay respects to the gods and ask favours of them. Hindu gods are frequently referred to according to the tasks they perform, such as "Ganesh, remover of obstacles". This enables Hindus to choose the goddess or god most appropriate to the help they need, and to ask them for it through puja. However, puja is not always connected with personal requests and thanksgiving. It may be performed by a large gathering of people at a festival, such as the Durga Puja. This annual, nine-day celebration of the goddess Durga, who embodies the female aspect of divine power, commemorates her slaying of Mahishasura, the terrible buffalo-demon. Devotees make offerings, say prayers, sing hymns, dance, fast, and feast in her honour.

Vishnu's nine forms of worship

In the *Ramayana*, Vishnu, in the form of Rama, describes nine modes of bhakti "guaranteed to reach and please me". "First is *satsang*, or association with love-intoxicated devotees. The second is to develop a taste for hearing my nectar-like stories. The third is service to the guru... Fourth is to sing my communal chorus... Japa or repetition of my Holy name and chanting my bhajans are the fifth expression... To follow scriptural injunctions always, to practise control of the senses, nobility of character and selfless service, these are expressions of the sixth mode of bhakti. Seeing me manifested everywhere in this world and worshipping my saints more than myself is the seventh... To find no fault with anyone and to be contented with one's lot is the eighth... Unreserved surrender with total faith in my strength is the ninth and highest stage."

With hearts filled with love… all should satisfy me frequently with tears of love flowing from their eyes and with voices choked with feelings and with dancing, music, and singing.
The Devi-Gita

THE WORLD IS AN ILLUSION

SEEING WITH PURE CONSCIOUSNESS

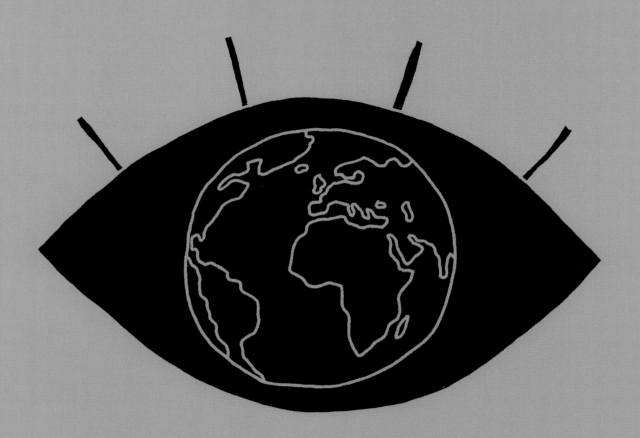

IN CONTEXT

KEY FIGURE
Adi Shankara

WHEN AND WHERE
788–820, India

BEFORE
6th century BCE The Upanishads describe Brahman as the ultimate reality.

4th century BCE The Greek philosopher Plato contrasts the objects of sense experience with reality itself; in some later Platonic thought, this ultimate reality becomes identified with a "transcendent One", or God.

2nd century CE Nagarjuna founds the Madhyamaka school of Buddhist philosophy, which is centred on the key idea of "emptiness".

AFTER
13th century Soto Zen aims to go beyond awareness of the world of sense experience with the development of pure consciousness.

Through the work of the Indian philosopher Adi Shankara, a branch of Hindu philosophy known as Vedanta ("the end of the Vedas") developed in the 9th century. It sought to systematize and explain material found in the ancient scriptures of the Vedas, and to explore the nature of Brahman as discussed in the philosophical works, the Upanishads (the last section of the Vedas).

There are various branches of Vedanta, but the one established by Shankara is called Advaita ("non-dualist") Vedanta. It states that there is only one reality, even if we may experience it in different ways. This "non-dualist" belief lies in contrast to later forms of Vedanta in which the deity assumes a personal role.

Shankara argued that human reason is limited to the objects of sense experience: that is, it is not possible to get outside or beyond the senses to see the world as it really is. Even within the world of experience it is possible to be mistaken, because all sensory knowledge is ambiguous. To use Shankara's example, a coil of rope may be mistake for a snake, or vice versa. Further, an individual may know it is possible to be fooled by what is seen, heard, or touched – but what if the whole enterprise of gathering information from the senses is itself a form of illusion?

An unknowable Brahman?

The Upanishads had taught that there is a single ultimate reality, Brahman, with which the innermost self, the atman, is identified. However, the problem is that Brahman is not an object of sense experience because it is not part of reality (as worldly objects are) – it is reality itself. Ordinary objects can be known because they are distinguished from one another by qualities that the senses can detect. Brahman, by contrast, because it has no physical attributes, cannot be grasped by rational interpretation of what is known through the senses.

So what should be made of the idea of a supreme being, or of the divinities used in religion? There appears to be a profound difference between what the Upanishads have to say in terms

---

Our **knowledge of the world** comes via the **senses**, so it is always liable to error.

We know Brahman – absolute reality – not through our senses but directly, as identical with the **atman, our inner self or soul**.

The world of our conventional knowledge is an illusion.

Absolute reality is not known through the senses.

See also: Higher levels of teaching 101 ▪ The personal quest for truth 144 ▪ The challenge of modernity 240–45 ▪ A faith open to all beliefs 321

The problem for the Advaitin is to solve how from the pure Brahman the impure world of men and things came into existence.
T.M.P. Mahadevan

Brahman is real; the world is an illusory appearance; the so-called soul is Brahman itself, and no other.
Adi Shankara

one sun. How then might Brahman be known? Shankara's answer lies in the identity of Brahman and the atman, the innermost self of pure consciousness. He states that Brahman cannot be known externally, via the senses, but can be known internally, because it is our innermost essence.

Consciousness and knowledge
Shankara proposes that there is a single reality, but two very different ways of understanding it. From the conventional and pragmatic standpoint, we have the world of sense experience, with all its variety. From an absolute standpoint, however, we need to recognize that the experienced world is unreal: it is an illusion. We can therefore only experience the ultimate reality, free from illusion, through an awareness that comes from pure consciousness.

It is possible that Shankara took this idea of the two levels of truth from Buddhism, in which a »

of philosophical argument and what is actually practised in the Vedas, in terms of gods and goddesses that are addressed in worship. How, for example, can Brahman be both personal (knowable) and impersonal (unknowable) at the same time? How, if it is eternal and absolute, can it be described in any way?

Shankara's answer
Shankara attempts to answer these questions by making a distinction between *nirguna* Brahman (unqualified reality), known only through pure consciousness, and *saguna* Brahman (qualified reality), which is more like the traditional idea of a God who exists and acts in the world. Brahman remains the same reality, but can be known in different ways. One means of expressing this is to say that there

is nothing in the world that is not Brahman, as it is the basic reality; however, there is also nothing that is Brahman: there is no separable, knowable object that corresponds to the idea of Brahman. To explain this, Shankara offers the example of the sun shining down on a number of pots, all of which are filled with water: each pot offers its own particular reflection of the light of the sun, and yet there is still only

In Shankara's philosophy, human reason is limited to the information we gather with our senses; a different kind of knowledge, or understanding, is needed to grasp absolute reality.

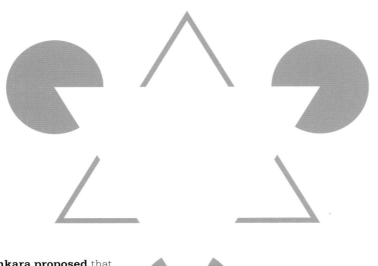

Shankara proposed that the world of the senses is an illusion and that we impose our ideas upon our environment, causing us, for example, to "see" things that may not be present.

This world is transitory. One who has taken birth in it is living as if in a dream.
Nirvana Upanishad

similar distinction was being made at this time between pragmatic and absolute truth. For both Hindu and Buddhist thought, this distinction represented a necessary step in bringing the fundamental philosophical ideas of religion together with actual practice. During the first millennium, religious practice had been moving increasingly towards devotion to various gods and goddesses (or, in the case of Buddhism, different bodhisattva images), each of which was regarded as reflecting a true aspect of reality. For both Hinduism and Buddhism, this was not an attempt to denigrate conventional religion, but to set it in a broader philosophical context.

Not quite an illusion

The most obvious way to describe Shankara's view of the world is that he regards it as an illusion (maya), although his claim is slightly more subtle than that. Shankara suggests there are two levels of "reality", which are both false in some way: the apparent world (which we appear to see and touch around us), and the pragmatic world (which is a view of the world according to our own pre-conceived notions). Whereas the apparent world is derived from our senses' interpretation, the pragmatic world is derived from our minds projecting outwards, imposing our ideas upon our environment (such as organizing a spiky green shape into "a leaf"). However, both of these ideas of the world are incorrect as they are only our representations of the world. So we can say that the world of our experience is an illusion, but not that the world itself – beyond the knowledge given by the senses – is an illusion. The world of the senses is maya (illusion).

This is why Shankara's philosophy is described as "non-dualist"; there are not two different realities – the world and Brahman– but just one.

At the point at which a person gains awareness of the identity of atman (the true self) and Brahman (a single reality), there follows a recognition that the conventional self, as an object among other objects in the world, is partly an illusion. The enlightened awareness is a realization of what we have been all along – the atman of pure consciousness; and compared with this idea, the ever-changing and superficial physical body is relatively unreal.

The gods point the way

The distinction between *nirguna* and *saguna* Brahman (unqualified versus qualified reality), and the contrast between knowledge gained through sense experience, and understanding acquired through pure consciousness, are of fundamental importance – not just for an understanding of Hinduism, but for religion in general.

These distinctions suggest that there are two levels of religion. At a popular level there may be devotion to a chosen deity (as in the bhakti tradition), and the portrayal of gods and goddesses as having particular qualities or acting within the world. However, this devotion is no more than a preliminary step on the path towards knowledge and liberation. Liberation can only be achieved through the mental discipline required for a level of meditation that leads to insight. And that insight, for Shankara, is of a single reality; there is no separate world of the gods. This means that if there is only one reality that is knowable through inner consciousness, then no religious ceremonies are necessary; all a person needs to do is develop insight through the practice of meditation.

It is tempting to say that Shankara promotes philosophy rather than religion, but that would not be strictly true: the quest for an awareness of the unity of atman and Brahman requires disciplines of meditation that are more of a religious exercise than a philosophical questioning. The sort of self-control required for insight is not merely intellectual. Shankara's approach allows

The pure truth of Atman, which is buried under Maya
[…] can be reached by meditation, contemplation, and other spiritual disciplines such as a knower of Brahman may prescribe…
Adi Shankara

him to draw together two very different traditions into a single system: the religious ceremonies of the Vedas and the later commentaries on them; and the mental discipline of the ascetics, who saw themselves as beyond the stage of religious rituals.

Science and reality

Modern scientific theories are based on the premise that the universe comprises of objects, structures, events, and sense experiences that are measurable and knowable. However, such theories – although considered by many to provide a reliable way to understand the world – often reflect only scientists' interpretation of the phenomena they examine and are always open to modification. The world of sense experience, for example, even when explored at the limits of scientific knowledge, is just an approximation of reality, measured through the tools available, as opposed to reality itself.

In addition, the scientific methods used in attempting to discover reality may actually interfere with and influence the nature of what is observed. For instance, the very act of observing and measuring an experiment at quantum level can significantly alter the outcome.

What science may perceive as truth or reality would, in Shankara's philosophy, still be considered an illusion, on the grounds that there are two completely different levels of truth, and that gods and scientific laws alike can only approximate to an ultimate reality beyond both reason and sense experience. Instead, pure consciouness can only be achieved by transcending illusion through meditation. ∎

Adi Shankara

Adi Shankara, the founder of the Advaita Vedanta tradition of Indian philosophy, was born in 788 into a Brahmin family in Kerala, and trained under a guru (teacher) from the age of seven. He later moved to Varanasi, where he gained his first followers, and then to Badrinatha, where, aged only 12, he is believed to have written a commentary on the *Brahma Sutras*.

Shankara became a guru and attracted many followers. He was also instrumental in a revival of Hinduism and establishing a number of monasteries. Shankara died at the age of 32. A number of works, mainly commentaries on the Upanishads, have been attributed to Shankara. His philosophy, which offered a systematic development of the Vedanta tradition in the Upanishads, remains a major contribution to Hindu doctrine.

Key works

8th century *The Brahma Sutra Bhaysa*
8th century *The Crest-Jewel of Discrimination*
8th century *A Thousand Teachings*

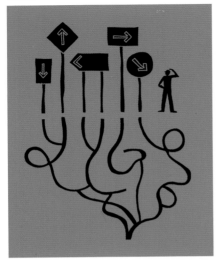

SO MANY FAITHS, SO MANY PATHS
GOD-CONSCIOUSNESS

IN CONTEXT

KEY FIGURE
Sri Ramakrishna

WHEN AND WHERE
19th century, India

BEFORE
From 3rd century BCE As Buddhism spreads, devotional images and practices diversify.

6th century The bhakti tradition in Hinduism accepts that the divine can be worshipped through any number of images.

15th century Guru Nanak, founder of Sikhism, opens his new religion to all who love one God, regardless of class and traditional faith distinctions.

AFTER
20th century Interfaith dialogue becomes common.

20th century A plethora of new religious movements offer a spiritual path open to all, irrespective of cultural and religious background.

Each **person on a spiritual quest** may worship a particular god, or follow a particular path or religion.

But just as the different Hindu gods and goddesses all represent different aspects of Brahman, so **different religions** are all ways to **approach a single spiritual reality**.

It is better to allow each person to **follow their own religion** than try to convert them from one religion to another.

The idea that all religions lead to the same God was put forward by Sri Ramakrishna, a 19th-century mystic who practised bhakti (Hindu religious devotion) and followed the philosophy of Advaita Vedanta, as originally taught by Adi Shankara (p.121) – built around the notion of of a single underlying reality, Brahman, with which the self (atman) is identified. The starting point for Ramakrishna's thinking was the idea that, in meditation, a person comes to appreciate the divine within, and that, to whichever god or goddess they might be devoted, there is only one spiritual reality. Therefore, within Hinduism, each person is free to worship in his or her own way, while recognizing

See also: The ultimate reality 102–105 ▪ Class systems and faith 302–303 ▪ Cao Đài aims to unify all faiths 316 ▪ A faith open to all beliefs 321

We believe not only in universal toleration, but we accept all religions as true.
Swami Vivekananda

that ultimately there is only one "Holy Power" (Brahman). To Ramakrishna, this suggested that it might be possible to experience all religions in just this same, internal or personal way, and therefore all spiritual paths might eventually lead to the same goal.

An inner transformation

What Ramakrishna understood by this is illustrated by his claim that he became a Muslim for a short period. He immersed himself in the teachings of Islam and described the manner in which he performed Islamic prayers, so that, for a time, he felt he really possessed the Muslim faith, and did not even experience any desire to look at Hindu temple images.

The majority of Muslims would not consider this to be a valid experience of Islam, given that he did not engage with its cultural and social practices. However, for Ramakrishna, this entirely internal experience led him to conclude that any inner journey of self discovery will enable a person to identify with what Ramakrishna's disciple Vivekananda would later describe

as the "eternal ideal of the spiritual oneness of the whole universe". For Ramakrishna, if religion means a process of internal transformation, and if God represents the ultimate reality, it follows that, using whatever set of religious ideas are available, an individual can follow a path that is bound to converge with all others who are on a similar quest. Ramakrishna believed that an individual could encounter "the God within" through any religious tradition, and that this transcended any external, cultural, or doctrinal differences between religions. He therefore concluded that a truly religious person should think of all other religions as paths that all lead to the same truth. Rather than attempting to convert people from one religion to another, each person should be encouraged to follow his or her own religion, allowing a natural spiritual convergence to take place. ▪

An imam performs the Muslim call to prayer within the National Cathedral in Washington D.C. during an interfaith service attended by a joint Christian, Jewish, and Muslim congregation.

Sri Ramakrishna

Born Gadadhar Chatterjee into a poor brahmin family in Bengal in 1836, Ramakrishna became a priest in a temple dedicated to Kali just outside Calcutta, where he became well known as a charismatic figure. From an early age, he experienced religious trances, and saw the goddess Kali everywhere, as mother of the universe, even dancing before her image in an ecstatic state.

In 1866 a Hindu Sufi initiated Ramakrishna into Islam. He is said to have followed that faith for a few days, as well as possessing an image of Christ upon which he meditated.

His ideas were spread and given more systematic form by his disciple, Swami Vivekananda (1836–1902), who emphasized that the Hindu religion was not a matter of trying to believe certain doctrines or philosophical propositions, but instead one of entering into an experience. Vivekenanda presented these ideas to the World Parliament of Religions in 1893. He also established the Ramakrishna Movement to promote Sri Ramakrishna's work.

NON-VIOLENCE IS THE WEAPON OF THE STRONG

HINDUISM IN THE POLITICAL AGE

IN CONTEXT

KEY FIGURE
Mahatma Gandhi

WHEN AND WHERE
1869–1948, India

BEFORE
From 6th century BCE
Ahimsa or non-violence is the key ethical principle of the Jain and Buddhist religions.

3rd century BCE The Emperor Asoka converts to Buddhism and initiates social reforms inspired by non-violence.

2nd century BCE The Hindu Bhagavad-Gita explores the dichotomy between ahimsa and the duty of the warrior class to fight in a just war.

AFTER
1964 The Baptist minister Martin Luther King preaches the use of non-violent means to oppose racial inequality in the United States.

It was while working to oppose racial discrimination in South Africa that Gandhi coined the term satyagraha – "holding on to the truth". It was to become the key theme of his campaigns of non-violent civil disobedience, both there and later in India.

Although raised a Hindu, Gandhi was deeply influenced by Jainism, with its emphasis on non-violence and the welfare of all creatures. However, he was opposed to the idea that, in the face of social injustice, a person should simply retire into private spirituality and avoid confrontation. Hinduism had long been divided between those who thought that they should follow their social duty, as determined by their class and stage of life, and those who opted out of society in order to follow an ascetic path of personal religious discipline. Gandhi felt committed to seek political and social justice, while at the same time maintaining the fundamental ascetic value of

---

Inactivity and detachment allow social **injustice** to continue unchecked.

But **violence** only leads to retaliation and further violence, which is **self-defeating**.

Therefore **social and political change** is best achieved through **non-violent protest** and a determination to stand by the **truth**, whatever the consequences.

See also: Self-denial leads to spiritual liberation 68–71 ▪ Selfless action 110–11 ▪ Let kindness and compassion rule 146–47 ▪ Dying for the message 209 ▪ Striving in the way of God 278

> God is truth. The way to truth lies through non-violence.
> **Mahatma Gandhi**

non-violence. He also saw the self-destructiveness and futility of opposing violence with violence.

He believed that an individual could only genuinely seek the truth by discounting his or her social position and self-interest. He therefore argued that the way to oppose injustice was to have the courage and strength to hold on to the truth, whatever the personal consequences – and for him that included years spent in prison. He regarded non-cooperation and civil disobedience as "weapons of truth" that an individual or society should not be afraid to deploy, provided that negotiation had failed. To accept the consequences of our actions is a sign of strength, if accompanied by the moral certainty of the truth.

Love all, hate no one

Gandhi emphasized that ahimsa (non-violence) should be taken in its most positive sense: in other words, that it should mean the cultivation of love towards all, as opposed to simply abstinence from killing. This philosophy had further social and political consequences, since it must entail support for the oppressed. So, for example, Gandhi championed the cause of those who were outside the caste system and called "untouchables" since they were considered to be ritually impure. He regarded "untouchability" as a crime against humanity. It was later outlawed in India. He also argued strongly for religious freedom and against all forms of exploitation.

Unfortunately, the last year of Gandhi's life saw bloodshed and mass displacement as Muslim Pakistan was separated from Hindu India. However, his teachings, notably his legacy of non-violent protest, spread globally, inspiring many of the world's leaders and political movements, including anti-apartheid in South Africa and civil rights movements in the USA, China, and elsewhere. ▪

A lone protestor defies tanks near Tiananmen Square in Beijing, in an image that became a global icon for the principle of passive resistance.

Mohandas Karamchand ("Mahatma") Gandhi

Born in 1869 in Porbandar, India, Mohandas Karamchand Gandhi (known as "Mahatma" or "great-souled") qualified as a lawyer in London. After a brief time back in India, he spent 21 years in South Africa giving legal support to the Indian community, during which time he launched a programme of passive resistance against the compulsory registration and fingerprinting of Indians.

In 1914, he returned to India, where he opposed injustices imposed by the British rulers. During the 1920s, he initiated civil disobedience campaigns for which he was imprisoned for two years. He continued to promote similar campaigns, and suffered a further term in jail. He wanted to see an India free from British rule, in which all its religious groups could have a stake, and when independence was finally agreed in 1947, he opposed the partition of India because it conflicted with his vision of religious unity.

Gandhi was assassinated in Delhi in 1948 by a Hindu fanatic who accused him of being too sympathetic to the needs of the nation's Muslims.

BUDDHIS

FROM 6TH
CENTURY BCE

Siddhartha Gautama (later known as Buddha) is born in northeast India.

The **First Buddhist Council** is held in the year following Buddha's death.

Emperor Asoka of India converts to Buddhism and calls the **Third Buddhist Council**.

A collection of the teachings of Buddha, the **Pali Canon**, is written down in Sri Lanka and forms the basis of **Theravada Buddhism**.

c.563 BCE   **5TH CENTURY** BCE   **3RD CENTURY** BCE   **1ST CENTURY** BCE

5TH CENTURY BCE   **4TH CENTURY** BCE   **3RD CENTURY** BCE   **1ST CENTURY** CE

Different **branches of Buddhism** evolve as the religion spreads across Asia.

The **Second Buddhist Council** is held, resulting in the first schism in Buddhism.

Buddhism spreads to Sri Lanka and Burma, and probably into Central Asia.

Mahayana Buddhism emerges in India, with an emphasis on the bodhisattva ideal.

uddhism is regarded by some as more of a philosophical system than a religion because it does not explicitly involve a god or gods. Its origins are also atypical: its founder, Siddhartha Gautama, the Buddha ("awakened one"), based his teachings not on any mystical vision or appearance, but on conclusions he reached after a long period of experience and thought – enlightenment, rather than revelation. Gautama neither affirmed nor denied the existence of deities, as they were irrelevant to his ideas, but some branches of Buddhism have since become more theistic, even if deities are not central to their practise.

The India in which Gautama grew up was dominated by the Brahmanic religions, and incorporated Hindu belief in the idea of samsara – a soul caught in an eternal circle of birth and rebirth. Buddhism proposed a radically different view of how the cycle could be broken. Instead of relying on Hindu religious practices, such as worship and ritual, Gautama advocated a change of lifestyle; instead of sacred texts giving divine guidance and authority, Buddhism offered its founder's teachings as a starting point for meditation.

Basic tenets

The doctrine of Buddhism was passed by word of mouth, at first to Gautama's immediate group of followers, and then through the teachers of the monastic order that he founded. It was not until the 1st century BCE, hundreds of years after his death, that Gautama's teachings first appeared in written form, in the *Tipitaka*. This was written in Pali, a Sri Lankan dialect, rather than Sanskrit, the language of the scholars. The so-called Pali Canon was followed by commentaries, such as the Mahayana Sutras, which interpreted Buddha's teaching.

What Buddhism lacked in theology, it made up for in its analysis of the reasons a soul might get caught up in samsara; it explored how one could achieve enlightenment and nirvana – the ultimate extinction of desire, aversion, and disillusionment. Gautama explained that the main obstacle to escape from the cycle of samsara was human suffering, caused by desires and attachments that can never be satisfied. He set

The **Mahayana Sutras** are composed.

Vajrayana, or Tantric, Buddhism develops in India, from the Theravada tradition.

Theravada Buddhism spreads from Sri Lanka into **Burma, Thailand**, **Laos, and Cambodia**.

Zen Buddhism emerges in Japan from the Chinese tradition of meditation Buddhism.

1ST–5TH CENTURIES CE   **4TH–5TH CENTURIES**   **11TH–13TH CENTURIES**   **12TH–13TH CENTURIES**

3RD CENTURY CE   **7TH CENTURY**   **12TH CENTURY**   **19TH CENTURY**

Buddhism begins to flourish in **China**.

Mahayana Buddhism is adopted in **Tibet**, with an emphasis on imagery and ritual.

The **decline of Buddhism** accelerates as the Indian subcontinent is invaded by Muslims.

Western philosophers such as **Schopenhauer** begin taking an interest in Indian religions.

out "Four Noble Truths" – the central doctrine of Buddhism – to explain the nature of suffering and how it could be overcome: *dukkha* (the truth of suffering), *samudaya* (the truth of the origin of suffering), *nirodha* (the truth of the ending of suffering), and *magga* (the truth of the path to the ending of suffering). This last Noble Truth alludes to the "Middle Way" – the lifestyle advocated by the Buddha, which is simple in concept but hard to attain.

Spread and diversification

Buddhism spread rapidly from northern India southwards across the subcontinent and northwards into China. Different traditions of Buddhism began to emerge. The two main branches, Theravada and Mahayana, continue to the present day, much along regional lines.

Theravada, with its conservative and austere approach, remained closer to Buddha's original teachings, but became increasingly localized to southern India and especially Sri Lanka. Theravada was revitalized in the 12th century when trade took it into Burma, Thailand, Laos, and Cambodia.

Mahayana Buddhism had a more overtly "religious" following, offering its adherents temples and rituals, as well as rich symbolism and images of the Buddha. Like Theravada, Mahayana also dwindled in India, but it was enthusiastically adopted in Tibet, China, Vietnam, Korea, and Japan. A key element of Mahayana is the concept of religious leaders known as bodhisattvas, who have achieved enlightenment but remain on earth to show the way to others.

Later divisions within these two major traditions also occurred. These gave rise to such contrasting branches as Zen Buddhism, which aims to clear the mind in order to allow spontaneous enlightenment without ritual, scripture, or reasoning; and the various forms of Tibetan Buddhism that are characterized by colourful temples, images, and rituals.

Today, Buddhism is estimated to have more than 500 million adherents, and is considered to be the fourth largest religion in the world (after Christianity, Islam, and Hinduism). However, despite growing Western interest in it as both a religion and a philosophy, it has been in decline since the latter half of the 20th century, falling from its position as the largest single religion in the early 1950s. ∎

FINDING
THE MIDDLE WAY
THE ENLIGHTENMENT OF BUDDHA

IN CONTEXT

KEY FIGURE
Siddhartha Gautama

WHEN AND WHERE
6th century BCE,
northern India

BEFORE
From 1700 BCE A multitude of gods are ritually worshipped in the Vedic religion of northern India.

6th century BCE In China, Daoism and Confucianism present philosophies in which personal spiritual development is cultivated.

6th century BCE Mahavira rejects his destiny as an Indian prince and becomes an extreme ascetic; his teachings form the sacred texts of Jainism.

AFTER
1st century CE The first texts containing Siddhartha Gautama's teachings appear, soon followed by the spread of Buddhism into China.

I n northern India, the 6th century BCE was a time of radical social and political change. There was terrible bloodshed, as local rule by tribal groups gave way to the rise of new kingdoms. Cities were expanding, drawing people away from the simplicity of agricultural village life, and trade was flourishing. At the same time, people were starting to ask fundamental questions about life and the basis of religion.

On the one hand, there was the established Vedic religion, based on sacrifice and the authority of the Vedic texts, to which few outside the brahmin, or priestly class of Indian society, had access. This was a formal and conformist religion; it required obedience to tradition and maintained class differences. On the other hand, many wandering teachers were challenging formal religion. Some of these withdrew from society to practise asceticism (the self-denial of material comforts), opting for simplicity and deprivation as a means of spiritual development. They rejected both physical comfort and social norms, and lived outside the class system. Other wandering teachers followed the Lokayata

Enlightenment came to Siddhartha after meditation beneath the Bodhi Tree. A descendant of the original tree was planted in Bodh Gaya in 288 BCE and is now a site of pilgrimage for Buddhists.

materialist philosophy, rejecting conventional spiritual teachings in favour of a life based on pleasure, in the belief that there is nothing beyond the physical world.

Siddhartha seeks answers

One wealthy man, Siddhartha Gautama, decided, on reaching adulthood, that his comfortable

Siddhartha Gautama

Born in 563 BCE into the ruling family of the Shakya clan of northeast India, Siddhartha Gautama was expected to take a prominent place in society. Brought up in comfort and well educated, he was married at 16 and had a son.

However, at the age of 29, he became dissatisfied with his life and left home, spending years as a religious ascetic. Following an experience he described as "enlightenment", he became a wandering teacher and soon attracted many followers, mainly in the cities of the Ganges Plain.

Siddhartha set up communities of monks and nuns, and also gained a growing number of lay followers. He also engaged in discussions with princely rulers and religious teachers of other faiths. By the time he died, aged 80, Buddhism had become a substantial religious movement.

Key work

29 BCE The Dhammapada, an accessible summary of Buddha's early teachings, forms part of the Pali Canon (p.140).

See also: Aligning the self with the *dao* 66–67 ▪ Self-denial leads to spiritual liberation 68–71 ▪ Wisdom lies with the superior man 72–77 ▪ A rational world 92–99 ▪ A faith open to all beliefs 321

lifestyle was incompatible with his growing awareness of life's hardships and the certainty of death. In addition, material comforts offered no protection from these harsh realities of life. So he embarked on a religious quest to find the origin of suffering, and the answer to it.

For seven years he practised severe asceticism, depriving himself of all but the minimum sustenance, but he found that this did not help him find the knowledge he sought. He therefore abandoned the ascetic life, while remaining determined to discover the cause of suffering. He is said to have gained "enlightenment" (becoming aware of the true nature of reality) during an all-night session of meditation, and this gave him an answer to the problems of suffering, ageing, and death. From that point his followers were to refer to him as Buddha, an honorary title meaning "one who is fully awake" or "the enlightened one".

However many **material comforts** I bring into my life, they **cannot protect me** from the pain of suffering.

⬇

The total **denial of material comforts** and a life of asceticism **does not protect me** from suffering either.

⬇

Each person needs to **find a balanced**, moderately disciplined lifestyle that takes account of their individual circumstances.

⬇

Find the Middle Way.

The Middle Way

Buddha's teaching is known as the "Middle Way". At the most obvious level, this suggests a middle way between the two types of existence that he rejected: the life of luxury, attempting to obtain protection from suffering with material comforts, and that of extreme austerity, denying himself almost everything in pursuit of spiritual growth. The approach or "way" he found involved a moderate amount of discipline in order to live an ethical life, free from indulgence in either sensual pleasures or self-mortification. But Buddha's Middle Way is also set between two other extremes: eternalism (whereby a person's spirit has purpose and lives forever) and nihilism (extreme scepticism in which the value or meaningfulness of everything in life is denied).

Eternalism and nihilism

The Vedic religion, particularly as it was developed in the texts known as the Upanishads (p.105), argued that the true self of every person is the atman, which is eternal and is reincarnated from life to life. The atman is linked to the physical body only temporarily, and is essentially independent of it.

Crucially, the Vedic religion identified this atman with Brahman, the fundamental divine reality that underlies everything. Ordinary things in the world (such as trees, animals, and rocks) are an illusion, known as maya; truth and reality are to be found beyond these physical things. When Buddha rejected the eternal nature of the self, he was rejecting a key feature of Hindu thought and religion.

Buddha also rejected the other extreme – nihilism, which holds that ultimately nothing matters or has any value. Nihilism can be expressed in two ways, both of which were practised during Buddha's lifetime. One way is the path of asceticism: purifying the body by the harshest austerity possible, and rejecting everything that the worldly consider to be of value. This was the path that Buddha had attempted and found wanting. The other way of living out nihilistic beliefs was that taken up in India by followers of the unorthodox Lokayata school of » philosophy: the wholehearted embrace of materialism. Their view was that if everything is simply a temporary arrangement of physical elements, there is no enduring soul that can be influenced by good or bad deeds during life. Furthermore, if there is no life after death, the best policy is to seek as much pleasure as possible in this life.

However, in rejecting these two extremes, Buddha did not simply opt for a "Middle Way" in the sense of a negotiated compromise; rather, his view was based on an insight that is key to understanding the whole of Buddhist teaching: the concept of interconnectedness.

Three marks of existence

Buddha pointed out that all things in life come about as a result of certain causes and conditions; when these cease, the elements that depend upon them will also cease. Nothing, therefore, has a permanent or independent existence. The Sanskrit term for such mutual dependence is *pratitya samutpada*, of which a literal translation might be "things stepping up together". The phrase is sometimes translated as "dependent origination", better to convey the idea that nothing originates in itself – everything is dependent upon prior causes. In other words, we live in a world in which everything is interconnected and nothing is the source of its own being.

This simple but profound observation leads to what are known as the three universal marks of existence. The first is *anicca*: that everything is impermanent and subject to change. We may wish it were not so, but it is.

The Buddha said that the quest for permanence and the certainty of things having a fixed essence leads people to have a general sense of dissatisfaction with life (dukkha), and this constitutes the second mark of existence. Dukkha is sometimes translated as "suffering", but it means more than physical suffering or the inevitability of death – it points to existential frustration. Life does not necessarily provide us with what we want and, at the same time, it contains things, events, and other people that we don't want. Nothing in life gives us complete satisfaction; everything has its limitations.

The third mark of existence is anata: that, because everything is constantly changing, nothing has a fixed self or essence. Conventionally, we see things (such as trees) as separate from one another, and define them on that basis. In reality, however, because everything depends on those elements that bring it about (trees cannot grow without soil, water, and sunlight), nothing can be defined or permanently fixed in the way that our common sense and language supposes.

The idea of interconnectedness, as well as the three marks of existence implied within it, is a matter of observation rather than argument. It is not a statement of how the world should be, simply that this is how it is – and that attempts to deny it are the root cause of our daily frustration.

Buddha's subsequent teaching was shaped by the concept of interconnectedness. By relating dukkha, or dissatisfaction, to the process of change, the concept

Buddhist monks do not cultivate hardship for its own sake; they are expected to eat moderately and depend on the gifts of lay people for their food – a practical example of interdependence.

suggests that there are ways or conditions under which it could be minimized. Buddha explained what these were in the teachings that became known as the Four Noble Truths and the Noble Eightfold Path (pp.136–43).

Applying the Middle Way to daily life

In many practical ways, the spirit of the Middle Way shapes Buddhist practice. For example, some branches of Buddhism emphasize the value of the monastic life, but vows are not taken for life, and many of those who spend either a few months or years as a monk or nun later return to family life (p.145). Similarly, in order not to cause unnecessary suffering, Buddhists aim to be vegetarian. But if it is difficult to obtain a vegetarian diet, or medical conditions suggest that a carnivorous diet is necessary, meat-eating is acceptable. Monks, who rely on gifts of food, are expected to eat whatever they are given. None of this is a matter of compromise; it is the recognition that everything depends on prevailing conditions.

When this exists, that comes to be; with the arising of this, that arises. When this does not exist, that does not come to be; with the cessation of this, that ceases.
Buddha

Just as a flower lives and then dies, Buddha's universal marks of existence hold that everything is impermanent and subject to change (*anicca*). Consequent upon this idea is anata: nothing has a fixed essence, because everything is in constant flux.

The Middle Way also has profound implications for our general understanding of religion, ethics, and philosophy. In practical terms, it argues that the reality of life, with its constant change and the inevitability of old age and death, cannot be permanently avoided either by material security or self-denial. Taken into a person's heart, this view can shape that person's values and ethics, and affect how they choose to live their life.

A flexible philosophy

In terms of religion, Buddhism's denial of the unchanging, eternal self as defined in the Hindu Upanishads was revolutionary. It suggested that life cannot be understood, or its suffering avoided, by conventional religious beliefs. Buddhism – if seen as a religion rather than an ethical philosophy – does not deny the existence of gods, or some form of an eternal soul, but regards them as an unnecessary distraction. When asked if the world was eternal, or whether an enlightened person lived on after death – questions that are often seen to be at the heart of religious belief – Buddha refused to answer. In terms of philosophy, Buddhism argues that knowledge starts from an analysis of experience, rather than abstract speculation. This meant that Buddhism was able to remain undogmatic, flexible, and open to new cultural ideas, while retaining its basic insight. The interconnectedness of all things, experienced in the balance between continuity and change, is the basis upon which Buddhist philosophy is built.

Buddhism's concepts also had psychological significance. By suggesting that the self was not simple and eternal, but complex and subject to change, it became possible for people to explore the self as a non-fixed entity. Moreover, Buddha's invitation to follow the Middle Way was open to all, making Buddhism, despite its lack of interest in a god or gods, an attractive proposition in a society bound by convention and ritual. ∎

THERE CAN BE AN END TO SUFFERING

ESCAPE FROM THE ETERNAL CYCLE

IN CONTEXT

KEY SOURCE
Buddha's first sermon, The Setting in Motion of the Wheel of the Dhamma, and subsequent teachings

WHEN AND WHERE
6th century BCE, India

BEFORE
From prehistory Suffering is often regarded as a punishment from the gods.

From 700 BCE Hindus see suffering as the inescapable result of karma (actions in past or present lives).

AFTER
3rd century BCE The Mauryan emperor Asoka takes practical and political steps to minimize suffering by promoting Buddhist values.

2nd century BCE Nagasena argues that dissatisfaction with life may be overcome by recognizing the insubstantial, changing nature of the self.

T he central aim of Buddha's teaching – the dhamma – is to overcome suffering. Everything that does not contribute to this aim is considered irrelevant. The ideas of Buddhism are not to be taken as ends in themselves, nor are they the result of dispassionate speculation about the nature of the world. They are observations about life and principles that are to be put into practice.

The Noble Truths

The Buddhist dhamma starts with four statements, known as the "Four Noble Truths", which give

> The Blessed One [Buddha] is compassionate and seeks our welfare; he teaches the Dhamma out of compassion.
> **Kinti Sutta**

an overview of the human problem of suffering and solutions for it. The Truths, which are believed to be the subject of the Buddha's first sermon following his enlightenment under the Bodhi Tree, revolve around this issue.

The first of Buddha's Four Noble Truths is dukkha, the truth of suffering. This is the idea that all life involves suffering, which lies at the heart of Buddhist teachings, and was the revelation that began Siddhartha Gautama's long search for truth. Human life, Buddha said, is fragile and always vulnerable. What is more, life is characterized by suffering. The nature of this suffering is very broad, meaning not necessarily intense pain, but also lesser, more widespread feelings of dissatisfaction. It may be the emotional suffering caused by the death of a loved one, an enduring sense that life is somehow pointless or empty, or simply a feeling of being stuck in an unpleasant situation, such as a traffic jam. Dukkha is the feeling that arises in situations that cause stress, discomfort, or dissatisfaction. It makes us feel that we want to be somewhere, or even someone else.

Buddha thought that the search for happiness leads people in the wrong direction. Individuals crave things – sensual pleasure, wealth, power, material possessions – in the hope that these things will make them happy. But the falsity of this thought lies behind samudaya, the Second Noble Truth: that the origin of suffering is craving. Tanha, the Buddhist term for this craving, indicates people's attempts to hold on to what they like, imagining that if only they could have a certain thing and keep it, all their problems would be solved. Tanha can be translated as "thirst", suggesting how natural and essential this craving seems to us. Buddha argued that even so, this craving is counterproductive, leading only to more suffering and unhappiness.

According to Buddha, this craving for things goes beyond material objects and the wish for power – it includes the need to cling to particular views and

People are often moved to tears at funerals and other sad events, but Buddhists regard such suffering as deriving from a mistaken wish to hold on to something or someone.

See also: Aligning the self with the *dao* 66–67 ▪ A rational world 92–99 ▪ Physical and mental discipline 112–13 ▪ The enlightenment of Buddha 130–35 ▪ Sufism and the mystic tradition 282–83 ▪ Tenrikyo and the Joyous Life 310

ideas, rules, and observances, which is equally harmful. In this way, Buddhism takes a radically different view from the majority of religions, which tend to regard people's acceptance of doctrines and religious observances as essential to salvation. While Buddha did not say that such beliefs are harmful in themselves, he warned against clinging to them in the assumption that they will automatically help in the path to overcome suffering.

Finding nirvana

For Buddhists, everything arises from existing conditions. This means that something must cause suffering; and if that cause is removed, suffering will cease. The Second Noble Truth identifies craving as the cause – so Buddha said that if the craving were to stop, the suffering would cease. The Third Noble Truth, *nirodha* (the cessation of suffering and the causes of suffering), refers to the absence of craving. Putting an end to craving does not involve stopping life's normal activities – Buddha himself carried on teaching for 45 years after his enlightenment, and was subject to all the usual problems that afflict human beings. Rather, it refers to a state in which a person understands and deals with life, without the emotional need to crave for it to be other than it is.

With the Third Noble Truth comes a point of peace called, in Sanskrit, nirvana. This is a state beyond craving or desire for anything or anyone. It is not the same as extinction; Buddha was critical of those who tried to escape reality by craving annihilation.

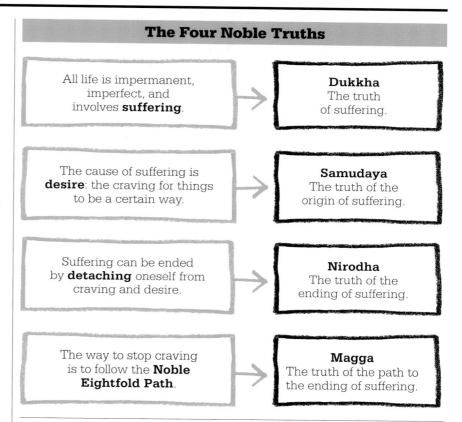

The Four Noble Truths

All life is impermanent, imperfect, and involves **suffering**.
→
Dukkha
The truth of suffering.

The cause of suffering is **desire**: the craving for things to be a certain way.
→
Samudaya
The truth of the origin of suffering.

Suffering can be ended by **detaching** oneself from craving and desire.
→
Nirodha
The truth of the ending of suffering.

The way to stop craving is to follow the **Noble Eightfold Path**.
→
Magga
The truth of the path to the ending of suffering.

Rather, the triple fires of greed, hatred, and illusion – three characteristics that perpetuate human suffering – are "blown out" like a candle. In other words, by letting go of destructive craving, the mind is liberated from suffering and unhappiness. This leads to a state of engaged happiness: a form of happiness that results from good moral conduct.

Unlike everything else, nirvana is not thought to be the result of cause and effect, but stands beyond or outside it. It is said to be permanent and unchanging: whereas everything in the world around us, and we ourselves, are temporary and have arisen because of certain conditions, nirvana is

an unconditioned, uncaused state and is therefore an absolute truth for Buddhists. This blissful state of being is accessible to us on earth and in our lifetimes. Unlike most religions, which encourage people to live a moral life in the present in order to attain happiness in a world beyond this one, Buddhism says that a true end to suffering is possible immediately, in this world.

Buddha himself attained a state of nirvana at the age of 35, and through his teachings sought to show others how to reach this enlightenment. The Fourth Noble Truth describes "the path that leads to the end of suffering". This is *magga*, the Middle Way, also known as the "Noble Eightfold Path". »

Material goods such as shoes may be advertised as "must-have" items, in an attempt to create a desire or craving in us. This desire, which can never be fully satisifed, leads to suffering.

The Noble Eightfold Path

The path to the cessation of suffering is set out as a path of eight steps. However, these need not be taken sequentially as they are eight principles, rather than actions, that allow Buddhists to overcome craving and achieve happiness. The Noble Eightfold Path deals with the three basic aspects of the Buddhist life: wisdom (in the first two steps), virtue (in the next three), and concentration (in the final three).

Wisdom, for Buddha, is made up of two directions in which to turn the mind: "right view" and "right intention". The first of these is important in order to be able to see and identify the cause and cure of suffering, as outlined in the Four Noble Truths. Without a willingness to explore that view, the rest of the path makes little sense. Right intention could equally be described as "right commitment" – it refers to our intention to follow the path,

because a mere understanding of the teaching (without also adopting an intention to act on it) is of no use.

Steps three, four, and five of the path offer practical moral guidelines. Buddhist morality is not about rules to be obeyed, but about creating conditions that facilitate the path towards enlightenment. Step three states that we must use "right speech": avoid telling lies, speaking harshly or cruelly, and listening to or spreading purposeless chatter and malicious gossip. Instead, we must cultivate the opposite: truthful, positive, kindly, and purposeful speech.

Step four says that we must take "right action" by following the five moral "precepts": not to destroy life, not to steal, not to misuse the senses, not to lie, and not to cloud the mind with intoxicants (the last is of particular importance for those who are engaging in the mental training that forms the final

The Pali Canon

In the 400 years after Buddha died, his teachings and the guidelines for monastic life were passed down orally using local languages, rather than Sanskrit, which was the language used in the Hindu scriptures. However, in the 1st century BCE, his teachings were written down in Sri Lanka using a language and script called Pali, which was closely related to the language that Buddha himself spoke. These

texts are collectively referred to as the Pali Canon, and they form the scriptures of the Theravada Buddhist tradition (p.330).

The Pali Canon is also known as the Tipitaka (in Pali) and the Tripitaka (in Sanskrit), meaning "three baskets", as it is divided into three sections: the Vinaya Pitaka, which contains guidance on monastic life; the Sutta Pitaka, a collection of Buddha's sayings and accounts of events in his life; and the Abhidhamma Pitaka, a philosophical analysis of Buddha's teachings.

There are four kinds of clinging: clinging to sensual pleasures, clinging to views, clinging to rules and observances, and clinging to a doctrine of the self.
Sammaditthi Sutta

> There is a Middle Way… which leads to peace, to direct knowledge, to enlightenment, to nirvana. And what is that Middle Way? It is just this Noble Eightfold Path…
> **Buddha**

part of the path). The fifth step also supports an ethical approach, suggesting that we must pursue a "right livelihood". This is the requirement to earn a living in a way that does not go against Buddhist moral principles.

Cultivating right mind

The last three steps advise on how to carry out the right mental training for reaching nirvana. Step six says that "right effort" should be applied. This requires a person to be conscious of and set aside negative or harmful thoughts as they arise, replacing them with their positive equivalent. So, for example, at the beginning of the Dhammapada (the "Verses of the Dhamma"), the Buddha says that those who resent the actions of others, or brood upon injuries sustained in the past, will never become free of hate. Right effort encapsulates the conscious intention to break the cycle of resentment and negative response.

The seventh step tells us to pursue "right mindfulness". It is all too easy for our minds to become distracted, flitting from one thing

to another. An important step in mental discipline is to be fully aware of the present moment and to allow the mind to be quietly focused on just one thing. This is seen in meditation techniques such as "mindfulness of breathing" or "just sitting", which generally form the starting point for training in Buddhist meditation.

The final, eighth, step on the path encourages us to apply "right concentration". The practice of meditation is a crucial aspect of following the Buddhist dhamma. This step recognizes that control of the mind is central to being able to

overcome suffering, since what is being addressed is not physical pain or death itself, but the sense of existential angst that can accompany them. In "insight" meditation, a person may calmly and deliberately contemplate those things that most people try to avoid thinking about, such as death. In a meditation on *metta*, or love, positive thoughts are cultivated towards others, from people we love to those we naturally find most difficult. This exercise encourages benevolence and the development of a more positive set of mental qualities. »

The Noble Eightfold Path, or Middle Way, sets out the eight characteristics that we need to encourage in ourselves to bring an end to our suffering.

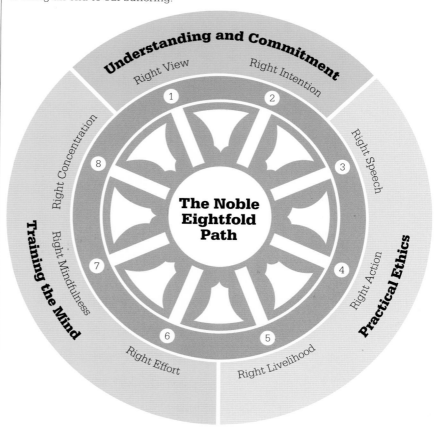

> If lust, anger, and delusion are given up, man aims neither at his own ruin, nor at the ruin of others… and he experiences no mental pain and grief. Thus is nirvana visible in this life.
> **Anguttara Nikaya**

The Noble Eightfold Path offers a programme of self-development. However, Buddhism does not have a set of commands or doctrines to be accepted; instead, it suggests a way to live that will ease suffering. Different people will concentrate on different aspects of the path, depending on their circumstances. In addition, the path itself is not a straight route that begins at step one and ends at step eight. It is not considered necessary to deal with any one of the steps before moving on to another step. The three main aspects of understanding, morality, and meditation may be used to reinforce one another. Some steps, however, such as those that deal with ethical issues, may be important in setting up the conditions in our lives in which meditation can become truly effective.

The Wheel of Life
A key feature of Buddha's teaching is "interconnectedness" (pp.130–35): the idea that everything arises because of pre-existing causes and conditions. The Buddhist path is therefore one that works always with context; it aims to create the conditions that allow angst and suffering to be replaced by contentment and happiness.

This means that if we look at the chain of causes and effects of events in our lives, we can look for the links that might be changed so that our lives can take a different course. If it were not possible to choose differently and alter the outcomes of situations, people's fates and their every action would be absolutely determined, with no escape from suffering. So, although Buddhism takes from Hinduism the idea of karma (that actions have consequences) it does not accept this in any rigid or mechanical sense. There is always an element of choice in our actions.

The Buddhist view of actions and consequences is presented in graphic form in the "Wheel of Life", a complex piece of iconography that depicts suffering and possible ways to overcome it. Everything within the wheel represents the world of samsara – a world of endless rebirth in which all beings are trapped as a consequence of their karmic actions. The wheel itself is held within the jaws of a fearsome demon, who represents death.

In the centre of the wheel are three creatures – a cock, a snake, and a pig – that represent the three poisons: greed, hatred, and ignorance. Buddha saw these as the starting point or root of the "unwholesome" life and thus of human suffering. Surrounding them is a circle filled with human beings either descending or ascending, who pass by a series of realms depicted in the next circle. These realms are those of humans, animals, gods, *asuras* (warlike

The Buddha's teachings on the Four Noble Truths are compared to a physician diagnosing an illness and prescribing a treatment.

The doctor's prescription

The practical aim of Buddhism, much like that of a physician, is to eliminate suffering in the world. The faith's Four Noble Truths can be set out according to the stages involved in medical procedure: the diagnosis, its cause, the fact that suffering will be cured if its cause is removed, and the method of removing the cause.

Buddha described the human condition as being similar to a man who has been wounded by a poisoned arrow but refuses to have the arrow removed until he understands all the details of the arrow and who made it. The man's priority should be to have the arrow removed. Buddha discarded as irrelevant most of the questions posed by Western philosophy, such as speculation about why the world is as it is. Buddhism is therefore seen by some as a therapy rather than a religion: a health-giving regime to be followed, rather than a set of ideas to be believed.

> Finding themselves
> threatened by danger,
> people take refuge in spirits,
> shrines, and sacred trees,
> but these are not
> a true refuge.
> **Dhammapada**

beings constantly doing battle), hungry ghosts, and hell (the lowest of states). The implication is that people can move from one realm to another. It is from the human realm that they may escape to a happier state of existence through the teachings of Buddha.

For those seeking to understand the process by which Buddhists can achieve this – by overcoming suffering – it is the outermost wheel that is the most important. The twelve *nidanas*, or links, in the outer wheel give graphic expression to the interconnectedness that is central to Buddhist teaching. They feature people and buildings, from a blind man (who represents a starting point in total spiritual ignorance) to a house with five windows (representing the mind and senses). There is a crucial opportunity offered between the seventh and eighth *nidanas*, which show a man with an arrow in his eye (representing feelings of pain) and a woman offering a man a drink (feelings leading to craving). It is this link – between the pain or pleasure that comes from contact with the world and the resulting

craving – that is critical. If the link holds, the process of re-becoming (samsara) continues forever. If it can be broken, there is the possibility of escape from the cycle of existence and suffering.

The breaking of the link signals a return to the starting point of Buddha's route to the end of suffering: the ability to engage with life without allowing that experience to generate the craving that arises from attachment and disappointment. And to set up

The Buddhist Wheel of Life represents the universe and the endless cycle of death and rebirth, within which humans are trapped unless they follow the Middle Way.

the conditions to help break that *nidana* link, people should follow the Noble Eightfold Path. Through taking action they may find nirvana. According to Buddhism, there is no god to save humanity, so what people need to cultivate is wisdom rather than faith. ∎

TEST BUDDHA'S WORDS AS ONE WOULD THE QUALITY OF GOLD
THE PERSONAL QUEST FOR TRUTH

IN CONTEXT

KEY SOURCE
The Pali Canon

WHEN AND WHERE
6th century BCE, northern India

BEFORE
From 1000 BCE Traditional Hindu thought is based on Vedic texts and the teachings of the brahmin priests.

6th century BCE Jains and Buddhists reject the Vedas and brahmins as authorities.

AFTER
From 483 BCE For more than four centuries after his death, the teachings of Buddha are passed on by word of mouth among his followers.

29 BCE A written collection of Buddha's teachings and sayings is made at the Fourth Buddhist Council in Sri Lanka.

12th century Zen Buddhists reject the need for authoritative scriptures of any sort.

In most religions, beliefs are based on authority, whether that of a particular leader, a priestly class, or sacred texts. People who accept these beliefs may seek to defend them rationally, while those who feel unable to assent to the beliefs of their culture may be branded as heretics.

Buddhism is different. It pays great respect to Buddha and other religious teachers, and some Buddhist traditions make much of the value of having a teacher with a particular lineage or tradition. However, the faith also values debate and discussion; teachers and intellectual convictions are seen as only a starting point. Buddha argued that people should not take any of his teachings on trust, but should test them out, both rationally and also in terms of personal experience.

Buddhist wisdom is therefore acquired in three stages: from teachers or by reading scriptures; from personal reflection and thought; and as a result of spiritual practice. The third stage generally involves

Accept as completely true only that which is praised by the wise and which you test for yourself and know to be good for yourself and others.
Buddha

meditation, the search for truth and spiritual growth, and putting Buddhist teachings into practice.

Early followers of Buddha achieved enlightenment by seeking understanding of his teaching, not just by believing his word. Buddhism still argues that beliefs should be based on personal conviction and experience, rather than simply trusting external authority. ∎

See also: Wisdom lies with the superior man 72–77 ∎ Buddhas and bodhisattvas 152–57 ∎ Man as a manifestation of God 188

RELIGIOUS DISCIPLINE IS NECESSARY
THE PURPOSE OF MONASTIC VOWS

IN CONTEXT

KEY SOURCE
Early Buddhist Councils

WHEN AND WHERE
From 5th century BCE, northern India

BEFORE
From prehistory Most religions combine spiritual development with awareness of a person's place in society or the religious group.

7th century BCE A new ascetic tradition of extreme self-denial arises in Hinduism.

c.550 BCE Buddha advocates a Middle Way between asceticism and hedonism.

AFTER
From 12th century CE In Japan, Pure Land Buddhism, and Nichiren Buddhism insist that faith in Amida Buddha and chanting, rather than following a particular lifestyle or discipline, are the way to gain enlightenment.

Throughout his life, Buddha had two kinds of followers: monks and householders. The monks were wandering preachers like Buddha at first, but later they settled in monastic communities. Here, they followed disciplines that aimed to benefit their own spiritual progress as well as the community. Householders too could achieve enlightenment, since they practised Buddhism and helped the community of monks.

Young Buddhist monks accept monastic discipline for a short period. In their path towards greater personal and social awareness, they are required to follow some, but not all, monastic rules.

About a hundred years after Buddha died, debates began about how strictly the monastic rules should be obeyed. As Buddhism spread, it developed different traditions, some of which, particularly in China and Japan, placed less emphasis on monastic life. Nevertheless, monasticism remains an important feature of Buddhism, especially in Sri Lanka and Thailand, which follow the Theravada tradition (p.330).

In Buddhism, monastic vows are taken for a limited period, rather than for life. The vows are not an end in themselves, but aim to create conditions that assist Buddhist practice. They are not essential, but helpful, in following the Middle Way. However, individuals must not simply strive for personal enlightenment, because that would be self-defeating, implying a measure of selfishness incompatible with Buddhist teaching. Rather, they must attempt to develop universal compassion and good will, which have a social as well as a personal dimension. ∎

See also: The four stages of life 106–109 ∎ The enlightenment of Buddha 130–35 ∎ Writing the Oral Law 182–83 ∎ Serving God on behalf of others 222–23

RENOUNCE KILLING AND GOOD WILL FOLLOW
LET KINDNESS AND COMPASSION RULE

IN CONTEXT

KEY EVENT
The conversion of Emperor Asoka

WHEN AND WHERE
3rd century BCE, northern India

BEFORE
From 2000 BCE The Vedic religion, then Hinduism, develop the doctrine of ahimsa, or non-violence, but justify war in certain circumstances.

6th century BCE Buddha enjoins his followers to abstain from killing; Mahavira founds Jainism, which forbids the taking of any life.

AFTER
17th century Sikhism allows killing in defence of the oppressed and the faith.

19th century Mohandas Gandhi, raised as a Hindu, adopts non-violence as a political strategy.

If people are killed, their family, relatives, and friends **will suffer**.

↓

Therefore the **good leader abstains from killing** living beings and orders others to do likewise.

↓

He builds a **better society** through cultivating an **attitude of loving kindness** and fostering it in others.

↓

Renounce killing and good will follow.

Buddhism arose out of Hinduism, a faith that had always been ambivalent about killing. On the one hand, Hinduism promoted the principle of ahimsa (not killing); on the other, Hindu society required animal sacrifice, allowed meat-eating, and regarded fighting in a just war as an inescapable duty. Like many other teachers of his day, including Mahavira, founder of the Jain religion, Buddha emphasized the principle of not killing, and it became the first of the Five Precepts, principles that form the ethical basis for those following the Buddhist way of life.

Five rules for living
The Five Precepts forbid the taking of life, stealing, sexual misconduct, lying, and the consumption of mind-dulling intoxicants such as alcohol. Each of these precepts has a positive counterpart, effectively generating five rules relating to things one should do. The first of these is to treat all beings with loving kindness (*metta*); indeed, one of the principal meditation practices in Buddhism is the cultivation of goodwill towards everyone – treating friends,

See also: Living in harmony 38 ▪ Self-denial leads to spiritual liberation 68–71 ▪ Selfless action 110–11 ▪ Hinduism in the political age 124–25 ▪ Dying for the message 209 ▪ The Sikh code of conduct 296–301

If there is one practice
that is sufficient to bring
about buddhahood,
it is the practice of
great compassion.
Dalai Lama

strangers, and even those that one might find difficult with equal care and concern. The broad, positive approach evident in this first rule underpins the other four. Positive goodwill towards others supports the principles of generosity; non-exploitation (the third precept is generally taken to prohibit adultery, rape, and other forms of sexual exploitation); honesty; and the keeping of a clear head to ensure corrrect decisions and actions.

Although the principle of not killing was a key feature of Buddhism from its beginning, the first attempt to apply the principle to the whole of society was made by the Emperor Asoka in the 3rd century BCE. This is evident from the many edicts that he issued, 32 of which have been discovered carved on pillars or rock faces. As well as advocating the avoidance of killing, Asoka promoted support for the poor, the protection of servants, and the establishment of medical centres and veterinary services – all direct expressions of *metta*.

A peaceful ideal

Although there are rare cases of self-harm (as in the suicide of Buddhist monks, who have been known to set themselves alight as an extreme form of political protest), in general Buddhism has never sought to impose its ideas upon society by force, nor has it ever become involved in war.

The principle of not killing suggests that, as an ideal, Buddhists should be vegetarian.

All life is sacred to Buddhist monks. They believe all living beings can exist peacefully side by side, even men and tigers – as demonstrated at the Tiger Temple in Kanchanaburi, Thailand.

However, Buddha's Middle Way (pp.130–135) indicates that self-denial must never be taken to life-threatening extremes, so Buddhists may eat meat and fish if it is deemed necessary for their health, or where there is a shortage of fruit and vegetables (as in the mountains of Tibet). Monks and nuns may eat meat and fish if it is offered to them and has not been killed for their benefit. ▪

The Emperor Asoka

Asoka was born in India in 304 BCE. He was the son of the Mauryan emperor Bindusara and came to the throne of the kingdom of Magadha in 268 BCE, having killed his brothers and other potential rivals in order to secure his position. He embarked on a brutal campaign of expansion, extending his rule to establish an empire that included all but the most southerly part of India.

After one particularly bloody battle, the sight of the dead and the grieving inspired him to pledge never to fight a battle again. He looked for answers in Buddhism and, on finding them, became a fervent convert. His conversion was marked by a dramatic change in attitude: he began to promote Buddhist principles throughout his empire, issuing edicts on moral matters, banning animal sacrifice, and increasing the provision of welfare. He sent missionaries to promote Buddhism abroad, but he also took a positive view of all religions, issuing only moral precepts that would be acceptable to all religious groups within his empire.

WE CANNOT SAY WHAT A PERSON IS

THE SELF AS CONSTANTLY CHANGING

IN CONTEXT

KEY FIGURE
Nagasena

WHEN AND WHERE
1st century CE, India

BEFORE
6th century BCE The Hindu
Upanishads make a distinction
between the physical body, the
"self" made up of thoughts and
experience, and an eternal self.

6th century BCE Buddha
argues that everything is
constantly changing and
nothing has a fixed essence.

AFTER
12th century CE Teachers
of Zen Buddhism distinguish
between the "small mind", or
ego, and the "Buddha-mind".

20th century Existentialist
thinkers, like Buddhists, argue
that individuals shape their
lives through the decisions
they make.

The idea that a human being comprises a physical body and a non-physical self, or soul, is deeply ingrained in almost all religious traditions. It forms the basis of speculation about life after death – whether we survive in some form in heaven or hell, or are reincarnated as the non-physical self takes on a new body. Belief in an immortal soul and in God seem the very essence of religion. Both, however, were rejected by Buddha, who believed we have no fixed self.

The idea that we do not have a permanent self, but are constantly changing, is absolutely central to Buddhist teaching, and sets Buddhism apart from most other

See also: Preparing for the afterlife 58–59 ▪ The ultimate reality 102–105 ▪ Seeing with pure consciousness 116–21
▪ The enlightenment of Buddha 130–35 ▪ Immortality in Christianity 210–11

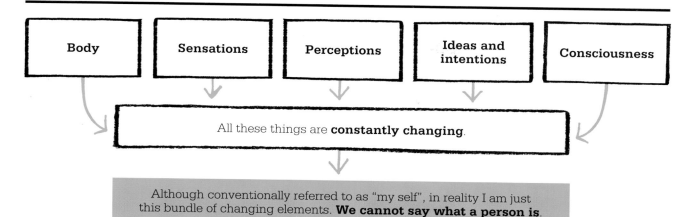

| Body | Sensations | Perceptions | Ideas and intentions | Consciousness |

All these things are **constantly changing**.

Although conventionally referred to as "my self", in reality I am just this bundle of changing elements. **We cannot say what a person is**.

belief systems and philosophies. It is implied by Buddha's teaching of the "Middle Way" (pp.130–35), and also reflects his teaching of the interconnectedness of all things. However, nowhere is the idea of the changing self better illustrated than in *The Questions of King Milinda*, written anonymously in the 1st century CE. This text describes the discussions between a Buddhist sage known as Nagasena, and King Milinda – the Indo-Greek ruler of northwestern India, c.150 BCE.

The monk Nagasena is often referred to as one of the Sixteen (or Eighteen) Arhats, beings who have realized a very high level of spiritual attainment.

Analysing the self
Milinda starts by innocently asking whether the person he is greeting is indeed Nagasena, whereupon Nagasena launches straight into the discussion by stating that although the name "Nagasena" is conventionally used to refer to himself, there is actually nothing that corresponds to it. The word is a designation, a "mere name", because "no real person is here apprehended". In an absolute sense, "Nagasena" does not exist.

Bewildered, the King asks how that can be the case, since Nagasena is clearly standing there in front of him. To answer this, Nagasena uses an analogy. He observes that the King arrived in a chariot, so it is obvious that a chariot exists. But he then starts to analyse the various parts of the chariot: the axle, the wheels, and so on, and asks the King if any of these "are" the chariot – eliciting the answer that they are not.

So where is the chariot, Nagasena asks, if it is not the wheels, or the axle, and so on? Clearly, there is no "chariot" over and above the parts from which it is constructed. "Chariot" is a name applied to the collection of those parts when they are put together to make the vehicle. In the same way, Nagasena argues, there is no fixed or permanent self over and above the various parts of which we are made. "Nagasena" does not represent anything that Milinda could point to. »

I am known as Nagasena. But the word "Nagasena" is only a designation or name in common use. There is no permanent individuality (no soul) involved in the matter.
Nagasena

We think of people as fixed objects. But Nagasena insists that the self is a process of ongoing change, that can no more be pinned down than motion itself.

Like the chariot, "Nagasena" refers to a set of elements that exist in a state of mutual dependence.

Buddhists view the human being as made up of five interdependent *skandhas* (literally, "heaps"). These are: form (our physical body); sensations (information about the world that is constantly fed to us by our senses); perception (our awareness of the world through sensations); and mental formations or impulses (our ongoing flow of ideas, intentions, and thoughts about the things we perceive).

The fifth *skandha* is consciousness: the general sense we have of being alive – including an awareness of the information streaming in from our senses, and of our thoughts, ideas, and emotions.

The key feature of Nagasena's argument is that each of these *skandhas* is constantly changing. This is most obvious in the case of form, or the physical body, as we change from being a baby to an adult through the physical process of ageing. But it is also true of the other four *skandhas*: they too are

in no way fixed. They reflect a constantly changing stream of experience and response as we engage with life. This means that not only is it impossible to point to "Nagasena", it is also impossible to say whether anyone is the same person during the course of one lifetime. Nevertheless, we still have a sense of a person being "the same" over a lifetime, as each of us has a past and a future. Nagasena points out that it is absurd to say he remains "the same" over time, but likewise absurd to say he does not.

In fact, Nagasena insists that the questions themselves are wrong, because they presuppose a fixed self instead of one that is dependent upon the body. In a further example to illustrate the dependency of the self, Nagasena asks Milinda to consider milk, curds, butter, and ghee. These are not the same things, but the three later stages – curds, butter, and ghee – cannot be made unless milk first exists. That is to say that

A meeting of cultures

The meeting between King Milinda and Nagasena occurred in the context of a meeting of cultures. Buddhism had spread to northern India through the teachings of missionaries sent by the Emperor Asoka around 100 years earlier. Meanwhile, the influence of classical Greece was spreading eastward from the Mediterranean, and, when it reached northern India, it was adopted by local rulers (a process known as Hellenization).

Milinda – or Menander, as he is known in Greek – was one such king. He ruled a region known as the Indo-Greek Kingdom – in present-day northwestern India – in the 2nd century BCE, so we may assume that Nagasena lived in that area sometime between the 2nd and 1st century CE.

While evidence of Milinda exists in the form of coins and references by classical writers, we know very little about the philosopher-monk Nagasena. His

only appearance in literature is his dialogue with the King in *The Questions of King Milinda*, a widely respected text in Theravada Buddhism that was written in the 1st century CE. One legend about Nagasena states that while living in Pataliputra (modern-day Patna, India), he created the Emerald Buddha, a jade statue of Buddha clothed in gold, which is now in Wat Phra Kaew, Bangkok, Thailand.

butter only exists because milk exists; it depends on the existence of milk. In the same way, says Nagasena, "do the elements of being join one another in serial succession: one element perishes, another arises, succeeding each other as it were instantaneously."

A category mistake

In the 20th century, the British philosopher Gilbert Ryle attacked the idea that the material body is linked to a non-physical mind. In doing so, he used an argument that is exactly parallel to Nagasena's. A visitor to the city of Oxford who has been shown various colleges, libraries, and so on, asks, "But where is the university?". Ryle claims that there is no university over and above its constituent parts.

Likewise, there is no "mind" that exists separately from the body. People who suppose that there is are making a "category mistake" – where things of one kind are presented as though they belong to another. It is wrong to treat the mind as though it is an object of substance, when "mind" refers to a collection of capacities and dispositions.

What we are today comes from our thoughts of yesterday, and our present thoughts build our life of tomorrow: our life is the creation of our mind.
Buddha

Which of these parts is the chariot? Nagasena would answer that none of them are. Likewise, whatever constitutes "me" cannot be pointed to, but nonetheless continues to affect things in the universe now and in the future.

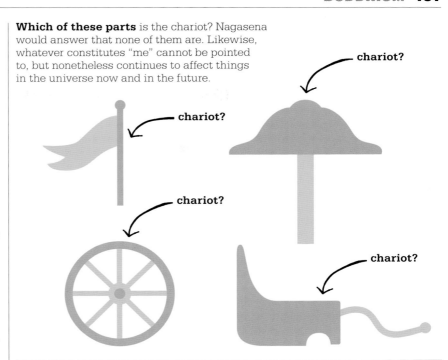

chariot?

chariot?

chariot?

chariot?

Towards the end of the 20th century, and into the 21st, most Western philosophers have argued for a materialist (or physicalist) view of the mind: that "mind" is simply a word that describes brain function. For modern science, there is no "self" over and above the body; the brain performs a complex processing of experience and response, which we think of as our mind, or self.

This differs from Nagasena only in the way that the sage applies a closer analysis of the way in which we experience ourselves as thinking, feeling, and responding beings. As he pointed out to King Milinda, even the fact that we do this does not mean that there is a separate thing called the self.

The other modern philosophy that unwittingly builds on this Buddhist idea is existentialism. It is often summed up in the phrase "existence precedes essence", meaning that we are born and exist before our lives have obtained any

sense of purpose. Existentialism suggests that we shape our lives by the choices we make, and should acknowledge our responsibility for doing so: we are what we choose to do – we do not have an internal "real" self or essence.

Absolute truth

This discussion of the self highlights an important feature of Buddhist teaching: the difference between conventional and absolute truth. In order to function normally, we have to assume a pragmatic or practical approach and refer to objects as though they have a recognizable, permanent, and independent existence.

It would be impossible to communicate if everything had to be described in terms of its constituent parts. Buddhism therefore accepts the need for such conventional truth, but constantly guards against mistaking it for absolute truth. ■

ENLIGHTENMENT HAS MANY FACES

BUDDHAS AND BODHISATTVAS

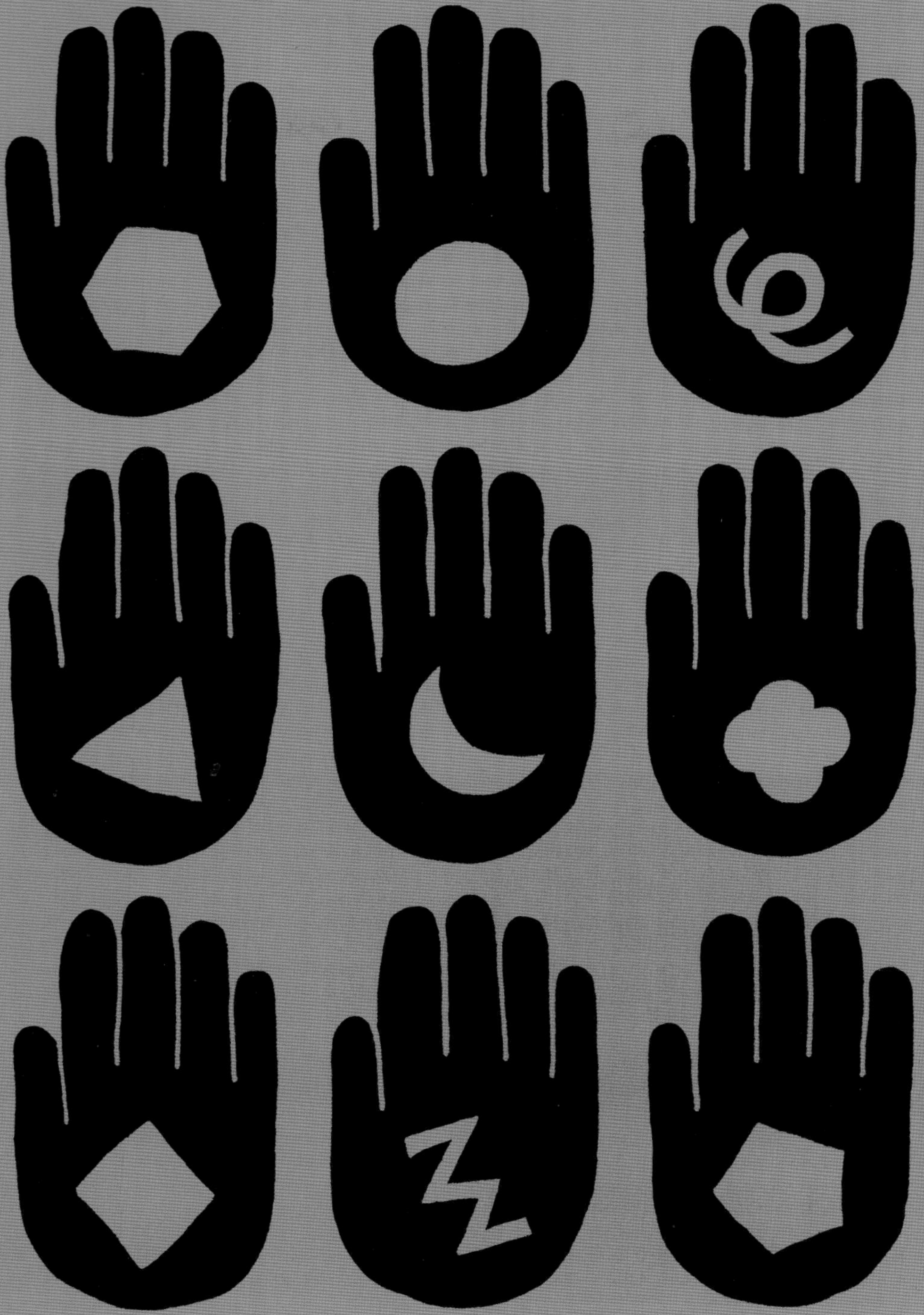

IN CONTEXT

KEY EVENT
The development of Mahayana Buddhism

WHEN AND WHERE
2nd–3rd centuries CE, India

BEFORE
From 1500 BCE The Hindu Vedas refer to many gods and goddesses, each depicting an aspect of nature and life.

From 2nd century BCE Devotional practices become influential in Hinduism.

AFTER
7th century CE Mahayana Buddhism, using elaborate images and ritual, is established in Tibet.

8th century CE Images of Buddhist teachers are used as a source of inspiration, as well as those of buddhas and bodhisattvas. A popular image is that of Padmasambhava, the Precious Guru, who introduced Tantric Buddhism into Tibet.

A bodhisattva is an enlightened being who vows to remain in the world **to help all other creatures**.

Each image of a buddha or bodhisattva represents one or more qualities of **an enlightened mind**.

If we visualize or pay respect to an image, we are helped to **develop the quality** represented by it.

Buddhist images are **aids to spiritual development**, not gods to be worshipped.

Enlightenment has many faces.

The teachings that Buddha encapsulated in his Four Noble Truths and Noble Eightfold Path (pp.136–43) were straightforward and rational. To follow them required mental training and analysis of experience, but did not entail metaphysical speculation (thinking about what does or does not exist), religious ritual, or – at least for the first few centuries – any use of images. However, a modern-day visitor to a Mahayana Buddhist temple in China or Tibet would see many elaborate images and forms of devotional worship.

Buddha figures – of different colours, male and female, some fearsome, others in calm meditation – appear to be the objects of devotion in a way that, to the external observer, appears not unlike devotion to the gods and goddesses of other religions. Since Buddhism still often claims to be rational, how did this imaginative transformation come about, and how is it justified?

The bodhisattva path
Given the general Indian belief in reincarnation, it was not long before people started to speculate about

Buddha's previous lives, and the actions and characteristics he must have displayed in those lives to move towards nirvana. These musings led to the compilation of Jataka tales or "birth stories", involving characters, sometimes human and sometimes animal, that depicted the Buddhist qualities of love, compassion, and wisdom deemed necessary for progress towards enlightenment. In turn, these stories led to the idea of the "bodhisattva": a being who is capable of enlightenment – or of buddhahood – but who chooses

See also: The ultimate reality 102–105 ▪ Physical and mental discipline 112–13 ▪ Seeing with pure consciousness 116–121 ▪ Zen insights that go beyond words 160–63 ▪ Man as a manifestation of God 188

> There has arisen in me the will to win all-knowledge, with all beings for its object, that is to say, for the purpose of setting free the entire world of beings.
> **Sikshasamuccaya**

to remain in the world, continuing to be reborn, in order to benefit all other beings. This idea brought about a remarkable change in the overall view of the Buddhist path. Instead of striving to become an arhat, or "worthy one" (the term used for those of Buddha's followers who have gained enlightenment), it was now possible for Buddhists to dedicate themselves to the more exalted path of becoming, in effect, apprentice buddhas – bodhisattvas who engage with the world out of universal compassion.

The great vehicle
Those who followed this new ideal called it Mahayana, or "great vehicle", in contrast to the earlier tradition, which they described as Hinayana ("small vehicle") and regarded as too narrow in scope. Practitioners of Mahayana believe that it represents a deeper teaching, which was implicit in the original Buddhist dhamma. Its scriptures – notably the Lotus Sutra – present an image of Buddha preaching to beings in a vast universe made up of many world systems, of which this present world is a very small part. Followers of Mahayana argue that the earlier teaching was a necessarily limited version, and that their own was kept hidden for many centuries, awaiting the right conditions to allow it to be preached.

Mahayana Buddhism, although it developed in India, spread north and was established in China and then in Tibet. The earlier tradition still exists as Theravada ("tradition of the elders") Buddhism. It is found today mostly in Thailand, Sri Lanka, and Southeast Asia.

Two bodhisattvas
The earlier tradition, now known as Theravada, recognizes only two bodhisattvas: the incarnation of the historical figure of Buddha (who is also known as Sakyamuni Buddha or Gautama Buddha), and Maitreya, a bodhisattva who will arrive in the future to preach the truth of the dhamma. However, in Mahayana Buddhism, lay people as well as the monastic community are encouraged to reach nirvana and thereafter to become bodhisattvas. Once the possibility of a vast number of bodhisattvas was accepted, each dedicated to the task of universal enlightenment, the floodgates of Buddhist iconography were opened, because these beings could then be imaginatively depicted in order to provide inspiration to others.

Symbolism and images
Each bodhisattva vows to become a buddha (enlightened being) and to lead others towards enlightenment. To do this, they must cultivate six "perfections": generosity, morality, patience, energy, meditation, and wisdom. These qualities are shown in individual bodhisattva images. For example, the quality of wisdom is depicted through the image of Manjushri, a young man holding a lotus (representing the enlightened mind) and brandishing a flaming sword (representing the wisdom with which he cuts through the veil of ignorance).

The most widely venerated of images is that of Avalokiteshvara, the Bodhisattva of Compassion. His name is a Sanskrit word meaning "The Lord who looks down". He looks upon earthly beings as a good father would upon his children, offering them assistance and trying to liberate them from their faults and suffering through his unwavering compassion. »

This thangka, or silk wall-hanging, depicts Tara, who vowed to become a female bodhisattva to show that the difference between male and female is unimportant, as these ideas are illusory.

> May I be an unending treasury for those desperate and forlorn. May I manifest as what they require and wish to have near them.
> **Shantideva**

Buddhists may offer incense or flowers before a buddha image as an act of devotion. This is not worship of a god but respect for an enlightened human being, imaginatively expressed.

Known to Tibetans as Chenrezig, Avalokiteshvara takes on a female form as Kuan Yin in China, and Kannon in Japan. Avalokiteshvara is most commonly depicted as having four arms: two are crossed over his heart, a third holds a lotus flower, and a fourth holds a rosary. The crossed arms symbolize the boddhisattva's compassionate outpouring from his heart to earthly beings. The lotus flower represents enlightenment and pure wisdom, while the rosary symbolizes his desire to liberate earthly beings from their endless cyclical existence. The 14th Dalai Lama (p.159) is traditionally thought of as an incarnation of this Bodhisattva of Compassion.

Not all Mahayana images are elaborate in appearance. Each of the *dhyana* or "meditation" buddhas such as Buddha Amitabha, for example, are depicted sitting cross-legged, wearing a very plain robe, their eyes closed in meditation.

However elaborate or not these images may be, and however far removed they may appear to be from the straightforward teaching of the historical Buddha, they are all taken to represent aspects of enlightenment. They are not gods to be worshipped, although it may be hard to remember this when observing Buddhists paying tribute to them in temples and shrines.

Focuses for meditation

Images of bodhisattvas and buddhas are regarded as aids to spiritual progress. In meditation, a person may become adept at visualizing his or her chosen image, being able to construct it imaginatively at will. So, the practitioner of meditation has an ongoing relationship with a particular image. It is often selected for that purpose, on the advice of a teacher, in order to address a particular quality – represented by the image of a bodhisattva or buddha – that the individual needs or wants to develop. The benefit of such a practice is generally only apparent over a period of time; it is not seen as an automatic process, but one

that requires sustained personal attention to the qualities and ideals that the image represents.

The impermanent mandala

The mandala is another Buddhist image created for the purpose of spiritual development, whether used for meditation or instruction. A mandala is a geometric pattern in which various shapes, letters, and images of buddhas and bodhisattvas are intricately interwoven in a complex image.

The patterns are carefully created out of coloured sand, displayed at festivals, and then destroyed. Their destruction is important because it reinforces the idea that everything is temporary. To attempt to retain the images would encourage clinging and craving, which are counter to Buddhist teachings as they lead to frustration and suffering. It is only through letting go – embracing detachment – that the journey to enlightenment can begin.

Emptiness and buddhas

The Buddhist philosopher Nagarjuna (see facing page) argued that everything is empty

> If you want others to be happy, practise compassion. If you want to be happy, practise compassion.
> **The Dalai Lama**

of inherent existence. By this he meant that nothing in the world, including all living beings, has a "self" or, therefore, an underlying essence (or "inherent existence"). He maintained that this idea was implied by Buddha's original teaching about the concept of interconnectedness (pp.130–35),

which sees earthly items and beings as having no essence (or "own being") because they are all dependent on the prior existence of something else. Given that we ourselves have no independent, underlying essence, the aim of meditation is to see beyond our senses and the ideas we have gained from them, to look directly upon ultimate truth.

Given that the buddhas and bodhisattvas may be conjured up in meditation, this suggests that they are neither substantial (in other words, they do not have a physical embodiment), nor located somewhere else in the universe. Each of the images conjured up is not a representation of a person, but part of the ultimate truth about the person who sits in meditation. The vast array of buddha and bodhisattva images are merely temporary aids to assist a person in recognizing that every individual is a potential Buddha. ∎

Nagarjuna

Nagarjuna is considered the most important Buddhist philosopher after Buddha himself. He was born in the 2nd century CE to a brahmin (priestly) family, probably in southern India. An oracle predicted his early death at the age of eight, so when he was seven, his parents sent him to a monastery to study under the great Buddhist teacher Saraha. It is said that he avoided death by reciting a mantra without interruption on the eve and dawn of his eighth birthday. He then took monastic vows.

Nagarjuna is best known for the teaching of Buddha's Perfection of Wisdom sutras. According to legend, he rescued these from *nagas* (half-worldly spirits), gaining the name Nagarjuna (master of the *nagas*). He also wrote many sutras himself, and founded the Madhyamika ("middle position") school of Buddhist philosophy.

Key works

c.200 CE *Fundamental Verses of the Middle Way; The Treatise on the Great Perfection of Wisdom*

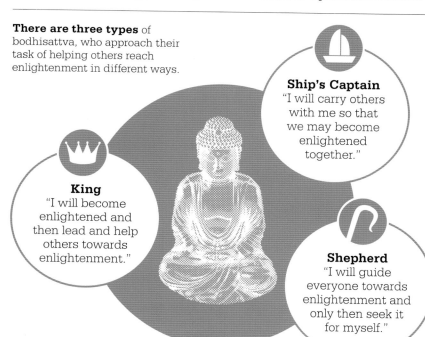

There are three types of bodhisattva, who approach their task of helping others reach enlightenment in different ways.

Ship's Captain "I will carry others with me so that we may become enlightened together."

King "I will become enlightened and then lead and help others towards enlightenment."

Shepherd "I will guide everyone towards enlightenment and only then seek it for myself."

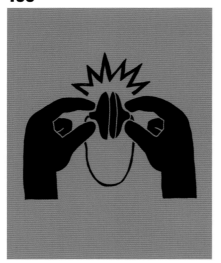

ACT OUT YOUR BELIEFS
THE PERFORMANCE OF RITUAL AND REPETITION

IN CONTEXT

KEY MOVEMENT
Tibetan Buddhism

WHEN AND WHERE
From 8th century CE, Tibet

BEFORE
300 CE Tantric rituals that use dramatic forms to act out spiritual realities start to develop within some branches of Hinduism in India.

4th–5th century CE Yogacara Buddhist philosophy argues that all we know of reality is in fact an interpretation made by the mind; therefore imaginative and symbolic actions are "real" for us.

AFTER
19th century Western Orientalist scholars take an interest in Tantric yoga.

1959 Following the Chinese invasion of Tibet, lamas start teaching Tantric Tibetan Buddhism in other parts of the world, particularly the USA and Europe.

Tibetan Buddhism uses **colourful and imaginative rituals**.

→

These aim to engage the Buddhist **emotionally and physically**, not just intellectually.

↓

This allows the Buddhist to experience what it would feel like to **be enlightened**.

←

Act out your beliefs.

In most forms of Buddhism the rituals are simple (perhaps just making an offering before a Buddha image), whereas Tibetan Buddhism is colourful and dramatic. During worship, monks may chant repeated phrases (mantras), wear striking headdresses, blow horns, and use elaborate hand gestures (mudras) – often while holding small symbolic objects (*vajras*) and bells. Lay Buddhists may also chant, turn prayer wheels, and set out colourful prayer flags. At festivals, there may be dramatic performances and dancing, with huge images on cloth spread out or hung on temple walls, and the creation and destruction of intricate sand patterns, known as mandalas (p.156). How is all of this, which seems so different from the early simplicity of the Buddhist path, explained and justified?

For more than a thousand years, Buddhism and Hinduism co-existed in India and influenced one another. When Padmasambhava, revered as the founder of Tibetan Buddhism, took the religion to Tibet in the

See also: Symbolism made real 46–47 ▪ Living the Way of the Gods 82–85 ▪ Devotion through puja 114–15 ▪ Buddhas and bodhisattvas 152–57 ▪ Sufism and the mystic tradition 282–83 ▪ Devotion to the Sweet Lord 322

early 8th century, it was in a form influenced both by the general Mahayana tradition, which had already spread to China, and by the devotional tradition (bhakti) of Hinduism that had developed in India during the previous centuries. Bhakti involved a more personal and emotional engagement with worship, which was taken a step further in both Hinduism and Buddhism with the development of Tantra.

Tantra involves not just thinking about what will be achieved by spiritual practice, but also a process of "acting out". For instance, rather than simply visualizing an image of a buddha, the practitioner imagines him or herself *as* that buddha. This process of emotional engagement involves the whole person, not just the intellect, encouraging him or her to feel what it would be like to be enlightened.

So, for example, the mudras that are made in Tantric worship are the same as those depicted on the images of buddhas and bodhisattvas. Each of the mudras expresses a particular quality: an open-handed gesture, palm turned outwards, expresses generosity; the "fearless" mudra with the right hand raised as though giving a greeting, a blessing, or even a "stop" sign, is believed to induce a feeling of determination. By making these gestures, a Buddhist imitates the image of the buddha or bodhisattva, and thereby identifies with what it represents. Chanting, mudras, and other aspects of Tantric Buddhism aim to immerse the worshipper in a dramatic expression of what the path towards enlightenment is about, by not just explaining it, but making it feel real.

Personalized rituals

Tantric rituals are performed under the instruction of a teacher, or lama, who selects those that are likely to be of particular value to each individual. In other words, practitioners are given an individualized set of images to visualize, mantras to chant,

Buddhist monks perform a ritual at a northern Indian monastery. The bright clothing and headdresses are intended to engage believers emotionally.

and mudras to perform, depending on their personal inclinations and what they hope to achieve.

Although there are Tantric aspects to publicly accessible forms of Tibetan worship, many Tantric rituals are designed to be performed in private and their details are generally kept secret. But, whether performed in private or public, the feature common to all is that beliefs and values are acted out using esoteric texts and actions. ▪

Tibetan lamas

The Dalai Lama is the 14th in line from Tsongkhapa, who founded the Gelugpa sect of Tibetan Buddhism in the 15th century.

In Mahayana Buddhism, a bodhisattva is someone who remains on earth to help others, perhaps through many lifetimes (p.155). Tibetan Buddhism refines the idea to a *tulku*, or "reincarnate lama" – "lama" being the title given to a senior Buddhist teacher in Tibet. When a great lama dies, it is thought that another will be born to carry on his work. A search is made for the new lama, and the child candidate is expected to identify objects from his past life as a sign that he is indeed the reincarnation. There are hundreds of *tulku*: perhaps the best known is the Dalai Lama, considered the incarnate form of Avalokiteshvara, a bodhisattva of compassion and patron deity of Tibet. While he is regarded as the bodhisattva's latest manifestation, he remains an ordinary human, albeit one with the extraordinary vocation of expressing Avalokiteshvara in today's world.

DISCOVER YOUR BUDDHA NATURE

ZEN INSIGHTS THAT GO BEYOND WORDS

IN CONTEXT

KEY EVENT
**The development
of Zen Buddhism**

WHEN AND WHERE
12th–13th century CE, Japan

BEFORE
6th century BCE The Buddha
teaches meditation leading
to insight and enlightenment.

6th century CE The Buddhist
monk Bodhidharma brings
meditation Buddhism (Ch'an)
to China, and is said to have
instigated martial arts training
at the Shaolin monastery.

AFTER
1950s–1960s Zen ideas
become popular in Western
counterculture, as seen in
the work of the Beat poets and
Robert Pirsig's *Zen and the
Art of Motorcycle Maintenance*.
Many Zen meditation groups
and California's first Zen
monastery are founded.

en and its Chinese
equivalent, Ch'an, simply
mean "meditation". As
a tradition of Buddhist practice,
it is generally regarded as having
been founded by an Indian monk,
Bodhidharma, who brought it to
China in 520 CE, and is credited
with the definition of Zen as "a
direct transmission of awakened
consciousness, outside tradition
and outside scriptures".

This definition highlights the
key features of Zen: it seeks to
allow enlightenment to happen
naturally, as a result of a clearing
of the mind, and does so without
the need for rational argument,
texts, or rituals. In other words,

See also: Aligning the self with the *dao* 66–67 ▪ Sufism and the mystic tradition 282–83 ▪ Life-energy cultivation in Falun Dafa 323

Using words – in prayer, or discussion – **creates clutter in our mind**.

Thinking and reading silently just create more **"words" in our heads**.

When we strive to find answers and insight, our **desire clouds the mind**.

If we are to discover our Buddha nature, we must **empty our minds** of all these things.

With an empty mind, **insight and understanding** will come to us without words.

Nishida Kitaro

The Japanese philosopher Nishida Kitaro (1870–1945) studied both Zen Buddhism and the history of Western philosophy, and tried to express Buddhist insights using Western philosophical terms. He taught at the University of Kyoto from 1910 to 1928, and founded what is known as the Kyoto School of Philosophy.

Nishida argued that pure experience took place before the split between subject and object, self and world – exactly the distinction made by Zen between the ego-based mind and the undifferentiated unity of the Buddha mind (see left). This he compared to the ideas of the German philosopher Immanuel Kant (1724–1804), who distinguished between a person's experience of things (phenomena) and the things themselves (noumena), the latter being unknowable. Nishida even introduced the idea of God as the basis of reality and our "true self", and compared Zen with Heidegger, Aristotle, Bergson, and Hegel.

Key work

1911 *A Study of Good*

it creates the conditions in which a person's mental clutter, which detracts from clarity of the mind, can be replaced by direct insight.

Zen claims to continue a tradition that goes back to the earliest days of Buddhist teachings. There is a story that one day, surrounded by his disciples, the Buddha simply held up a flower, turning it in his hand without speaking. One of the disciples, Kasyapa, smiled; he had seen the point. That wordless insight, it is claimed, was passed down from teacher to disciple for 28 generations to Bodhidharma, who took it to China, from where it spread to Japan. So, rather than being a product of the development of the

two main Buddhist branches, Theravada and Mahayana (p.330), Zen sees itself as having developed independently via a separate line of transmission.

Buddha mind

Central to Buddhism is the idea that existential unhappiness is caused by the illusion that each person has a fixed ego, which is separate from the rest of the world, yet which clings to it, trying to hold on to what changes.

Zen sees this as the small, superficial mind; one that people acquire at birth, then develop, influenced by those around them. However, it holds that people also »

Sitting and meditating is all that is required to achieve enlightenment in Soto Zen. The stilling of the mind dispels the illusion of self.

have a "Buddha mind", freed from egocentric, conceptual thinking. This is innate, but hidden by the clutter of the small mind. People gain nothing by discovering their Buddha mind, they simply recognize what they have had all along.

Zen teacher Dogen said that the true self is not the superficial ego that each person has now, but the "original face" he or she had before they were born and moulded by experience. It is only when people develop their own "faces" that they see themselves as separate entities and become egocentric. Dogen is therefore suggesting that people should strive to recognize who they were before they were conditioned by life and experience.

Zen in Japan
There are two main forms of Zen: Rinzai and Soto. Rinzai Zen was established in Japan in the 12th century by Eisai, and reformed in the 18th century by Hakuin. This school introduced the Zen view that the world is an illusion and that reality is in fact a simple, indivisible unity. Zen has no scriptures or formal teachings; it is an oral teaching, a tradition of meditation passed from teacher to pupil – hence the importance of practising only under the guidance of an experienced teacher.

A key feature of Rinzai Zen, introduced by Hakuin, is the use of koans – unanswerable questions that shatter conventional thinking. Probably the best-known koan is Hakuin's, "What is the sound of one hand clapping?". Those who think they know the answer to a koan should think again, and let go of all preconceived notions. Rationally examining a koan, or a Zen dialogue (a *mondo*) is unlikely to yield great insight, as it is too easy to view it only within the parameters of personal discursive thought. A Zen teacher will try to guard against that happening.

As a result of Zen practice, a person may suddenly experience satori – insight or enlightenment. This is not a one-off or permanent state of enlightenment, but a momentary experience that may be repeated many times. It is said to happen almost as if by accident; it cannot be forced, because wanting to achieve satori is a form of grasping. Zen does not seek to define reality or the nature of satori.

Soto Zen was developed in Japan in the 13th century by the teacher Dogen, who had travelled in China and there encountered a meditation tradition called Ts'ong Tung. His form of meditation is very different from the Rinzai form. Instead of trying to trigger sudden insight, Soto Zen is based on sitting meditation (zazen) and a more gradual process of enlightenment.

Soto considered that religious traditions and rituals could be dispensed with: enlightenment could be achieved simply through the practice of zazen. This involves periods of sitting in an upright, cross-legged position, facing a blank wall, interspersed with reflective walking, known as *kinhin*. In meditation, the mind is cleared of its flow of ideas, so that the process of sitting is exactly what

If you understand the first word of Zen you will know the last word. The last word and the first word: they are not one word.
Mumon

If you meet the Buddha
on the road, kill him!
Zen koan

enlightenment is about. A person does not sit in order to become enlightened; in the act of sitting that person is *already* enlightened. Stilling the mind and clearing away the illusion of a separate self is enlightenment.

Beyond words

In Zen meditation, something is seen, but cannot be described. Careful attention to a piece of calligraphy or raking sand in a garden – both of which are features of Zen practice – can help to free the mind from the constant process of thinking, allowing a person to act in greater harmony with nature. That is why Zen finds expression in many artistic forms, from flower arranging to computer design.

Zen is about creating situations that bring insight, without trying to explain or express it rationally. To try to describe the goal of Zen is to have failed to understand it: Zen aims to set the mind free from content; it is not part of that content. Zen is not studied, it is practised; and if satori or enlightenment is finally achieved, nothing new is known – all that is known is that it is not necessary to know anything. Deliberately full of paradoxes, Zen aims to gradually break down the normal processes of logical thought.

Attempting to explain something is to grasp at it, and that grasping is what the Buddha described as the cause of suffering. In a world where people seek to gain things, to claim knowledge and insight like personal possessions, Zen is the ultimate frustration. Collecting beautiful Zen artefacts could never result in understanding what lies behind their production. Zen is letting go.

In some ways, Zen returns to the earliest phase of Buddhism, before the buddha and bodhisattva images, devotional practices, and revered scriptures. Enlightenment is open to all: indeed, everyone is already enlightened, if only they could recognize it. Zen dispenses with almost everything related to religion and presents itself as a path of insight and understanding that is without religious trappngs.

It is also deliberately anarchic, its stories provocative, and its teachers notoriously challenging. Asked to summarize Buddhism, Bodhidharma is believed to have replied, "Vast emptiness; nothing holy" – not what was expected, but to the point. ■

That wind, banner, and mind are not innately different is what this koan seeks to demonstrate. Externalization is a function of the ego-based mind, not of the undifferentiating Buddha mind.

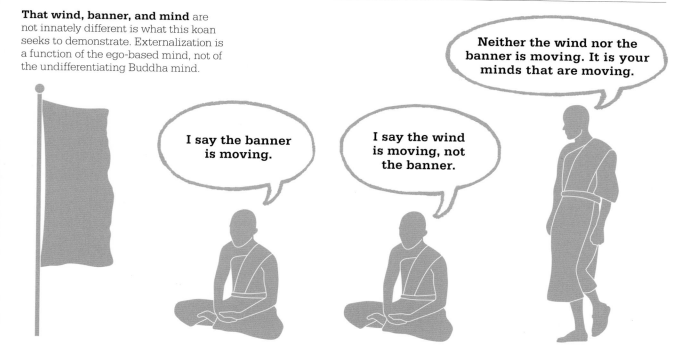

JUDAISM

FROM 2000 BCE

The **era of the Patriarchs**: Abraham, his son Isaac, and grandson Jacob.

King **David** reigns over Israel as God's "anointed" one, or "messiah".

Millions of Jews die in two **revolts against Roman rule**, and are again driven out of Israel.

The **Talmud** is completed. It includes the Mishnah and the Gemara (commentaries on the Mishnah).

The **Zohar**, a key work in the kabbalah (the Jewish mystical movement), is compiled.

c.2000–1500 BCE   **c.1005–965 BCE**   **70 AND 135 CE**   **c.425 CE**   **1250**

c.1300 BCE   **EARLY 6TH CENTURY BCE**   **200 CE**   **900–1200**

Moses leads his people from captivity in Egypt to **Canaan, the Promised Land**, and receives the **Torah**.

Babylon conquers David's kingdom of Israel and in 586 BCE destroys the First Temple of Jerusalem.

A written version of **Jewish Oral Law**, the Mishnah, is compiled.

The **Golden Age of Jewish culture in Spain** burgeons; the philosopher Maimonides writes influential works.

One of the oldest surviving religions, Judaism evolved from the beliefs of the people of Canaan, in the southern Levant region, more than 3,500 years ago, and is closely connected to the history of the Jewish people. The Hebrew Bible, the Tanakh, tells not only the story of God's creation of the world, but also the story of his special relationship with the Jews.

God's agreement, or covenant, with the Jewish people began with God's promise to Abraham that he would be the father of a great people. God told Abraham that his descendants must obey him and adopt the rite of circumcision as a sign of the covenant; in return, God would guide them, protect them, and give them the land of Israel. Abraham was rewarded for his faith with a son, Isaac; he in turn had a son, Jacob, who, the Tanakh relates, was the father of the Twelve Tribes of Israel. Together Abraham, Isaac, and Jacob are known as the Patriarchs – the physical and spiritual ancestors of Judaism.

The Tanakh recounts how Jacob and his descendants were enslaved in Egypt, and then led to freedom by Moses at God's command in the Exodus. As part of Moses's covenant with God, he received the Torah (the Five Books of Moses) on Mount Sinai. Moses took his people back to the Land of Israel, where they settled once again. Later, God appointed David – the anointed one or "messiah" – as king, from which came the belief that a descendant of his, the Messiah, would come to bring in a new age for the Jewish people. David's son, Solomon, built a permanent temple in Jerusalem, symbolising the claim of the Jewish people on the Land of Israel. But twice the Jews were forced from their "Promised Land" and the temple destroyed: first by the Babylonians in the 6th century BCE, and again after they had returned and fallen under Roman rule, in the 1st century CE.

The Diaspora
As a result of foreign rule, the Jewish people became a widespread diaspora. Some Jews, later known as the Sephardim, settled in Spain, Portugal, North Africa, and the Middle East, but the majority, the Ashkenazim, formed communities in Central and Eastern Europe. Inevitably, the geographical separation led to differences in the way Judaism developed between

Revolutions in **France
and America** lead to
Jews being given full
rights and freedom
of religion.

The **Reform,
Orthodox, and
Conservative**
movements
separate.

Theodor Herzl
starts the modern
movement of Zionism
with the publication
of *The Jewish State*.

The **State of Israel**
is founded.

1775, 1789   **19TH CENTURY**   **1896**   **1948**

18TH CENTURY   **LATE 18TH CENTURY**   **1881–1920**   **1938–45**   **1972**

Hasidism is
founded in Eastern
Europe as a
reaction against
the austerity of
legalistic Judaism.

The **Jewish
Enlightenment**
(Haskalah) occurs;
Jews in western Europe
integrate more fully into
their adopted societies.

Thousands of **Jews
are killed** and
millions more
displaced in waves
of **pogroms** in
Russia and Ukraine.

Nazi Germany
persecutes and
executes millions
of Jews in the
Holocaust.

The **first female
rabbi** is ordained
within the Reform
movement.

the groups, and various different religious traditions evolved. In Spain, a Golden Age of Jewish thinking flourished between the 10th and 12th centuries, which produced great philosophers such as Moses Maimonides. This was also the centre, in the Middle Ages, of interest in the more mystical aspects of Judaism, known as kabbalah. In Eastern Europe, a number of the more isolated small Jewish settlements, the shtetls, found that the scholarliness of their religion did little to promote strong community ties, and a more spiritual movement, Hasidism, emerged as a result. In the following centuries, there were further divisions in Judaism, largely over matters of interpretation of Jewish Law. Orthodox Judaism advocated a strict adherence to the Torah, which was considered to be divine in origin, while Reform and Conservative Judaism took a less rigorous approach, regarding the Torah more as a set of guidelines rather than obligations. An issue that divided the different branches of Judaism in the 20th century was the status of women. In spite of the doctrine ruling that Jewish identity is passed down solely through the maternal line, women were not able to play an active part in religious ceremonies until recently.

Oppression and identity
Largely because of their position as displaced immigrants and their distinctive faith, Jews have been widely persecuted throughout their history. In many places, they have been isolated in ghettos, and suffered violent vilification and attacks. From the 18th century on, countries such as the USA and France granted them full rights, and there was a movement towards greater integration. However, this posed a question of identity. Were the Jewish people a religious, ethnic, cultural, or national group? Zionism, which arose in response, pressed for the formation of a Jewish state, and matters were brought to a head in the aftermath of the Holocaust with the formation of the State of Israel in 1948. Today, it is difficult to assess how many followers of Judaism there are, because many who identify themselves as Jewish are not actively religious. However, it is estimated that there are more than 13 million Jewish people in the world, the majority of them living in either North America or Israel. ■

I WILL TAKE YOU AS MY PEOPLE, AND I WILL BE YOUR GOD

GOD'S COVENANT WITH ISRAEL

IN CONTEXT

KEY TEXT
The Torah

WHEN AND WHERE
**c.1000–450 BCE,
the Middle East**

BEFORE
c.1300 BCE Hittite royal treaties provide a model for the Torah's description of the covenant.

AFTER
200–500 CE The Mishnah and Talmud codify the "oral law", or received body of rabbinic learning, and are used to offer further Biblical interpretation and guidance on the covenant.

1948 In the aftermath of World War II, the State of Israel is founded, allowing Jewish people to return to their historical homeland.

1990 US theologian Judith Plaskow urges Jews to reinterpret traditional texts that exclude women from the covenant.

God asked Abraham to **leave his home** and **family**, and go to another land.

If he did so, **God promised** to reward him; this promise became known as **the covenant**

This promise was that as long as Abraham and his descendants obeyed God, **God would protect his descendants** and give them the land of Canaan forever.

"I will take you as my people, and I will be your God."

The covenant, or contract, with God is the central concept of Judaism, and dates back to the beliefs of the Israelites, an ancient Middle Eastern people. In fact, Jews view themselves as bound to God by a series of covenants. The Abrahamic covenant was the first, specifically singling out the Israelites as God's chosen people, while the later Mosaic covenants (mediated by Moses) renewed this initial bond.

The Israelites, sometimes called Hebrews, were a people who occupied part of Canaan, roughly equivalent to modern Israel and Palestine, perhaps as early as the 15th century BCE. In around 1200 BCE, during a period when this part of the world was under Egyptian rule, an inscription was carved that contains the first mention of "Israel" as a people.

In the 6th century BCE, many of the Israelites were forced into exile in Babylonia. During this period of exile, much of the Hebrew, or Jewish, Bible was composed. It sets down the history of the Israelite people and the origin of their religious beliefs.

The first covenant

Like many peoples in the ancient Middle East, the Israelites were polytheists, but worshipped a "national god", one whom they viewed as offering their people particular protection. Jews were later to deem their God's name too holy to pronounce and did not preserve its original vowels, so it became known only by its four consonants: YHWH (probably pronounced "Yahweh"). YHWH was also known by several other names, including El and Elohim, meaning "God".

See also: Animism in early societies 24–25 ▪ Sacrifice and blood offerings 40–45 ▪ The burden of observance 50 ▪ A challenge to the covenant 198

According to the Book of Genesis, the first of the five books of the Torah (the first section of the Hebrew Bible), it was by God's decree that the Israelites first settled in Canaan. He called on a man, Abraham, born in the Mesopotamian city-state of Ur (in modern-day Iraq) and commanded him to travel to a place named Canaan, which was to become the Israelite homeland. The Torah recounts that in Canaan, God established a covenant with Abraham, which took a similar form to a type of royal grant that kings of the time handed out to loyal subordinates. It stipulated that, as a reward for Abraham's loyalty, God would grant him many descendants who would inherit the land. As a sign of this compact, Abraham and all the male members of his household were circumcised. To this day,

Abraham's loyalty was tested when God asked him to sacrifice his son Isaac. However, at the last moment, God sent an angel to stop Abraham, as shown in this 18th-century painting.

Jewish boys are circumcised on the eighth day after their birth as a sign that they are parties to this pledge.

Abraham had two sons, Ishmael and Isaac. God blessed Ishmael, promising that he would become the father of a great nation. But it was Isaac that God chose to inherit the covenant from his father, appearing to him directly. Isaac in turn handed down the covenant to his son Jacob, who in his turn received the name "Israel" from God and handed the covenant down to all his offspring.

Abraham, Isaac, and Jacob are known as Israel's patriarchs, because they represent the first three generations included in the covenant with God.

The covenant at Sinai
The Torah relates that when Canaan was struck by famine, Jacob and his sons migrated to Egypt, where their descendants were subsequently enslaved. Several generations later, when the Israelite population in Egypt had increased, God appointed Moses, an Israelite raised in the Egyptian court, to lead the people out of slavery and back to the land of Canaan. The Israelites' escape from Egypt (the Exodus) involved many miracles: God struck the Egyptians with plagues that included afflicting them with boils and turning the Nile to blood, and he split the Red Sea so that the Israelites could pass through. With these miracles, God demonstrated his power, and his loyalty to the covenant with the patriarchs.

After liberating the Israelites from Egypt, and before leading them into Canaan, God brought »

The Hebrew Bible

The Hebrew or Jewish Bible, the sacred scriptures of the Jewish people, is a collection of writings composed mostly in the Hebrew language and written over the course of the first millennium BCE. With some variations in sequence and content, these same scriptures make up the Old Testament of the Christian Bible.

Jewish tradition divides the Bible into three parts. The first, called the Torah or Pentateuch, describes God's creation of the world and his covenant with Israel, and outlines the commandments that were imposed on the Israelites. Tradition attributes the Torah to Moses, but modern scholars believe that it was written by many authors over several centuries.

The second part of the Bible, Prophets, includes a narrative of Israelite history. This runs from the people's entry into Canaan to the end of their kingdom, when their capital and temple are destroyed and their people exiled. It also contains the writings of the prophets.

The final part, called Writings, comprises a diverse collection of later literature.

them to a mountain called Sinai, or Horeb. Moses ascended the mountain to speak to God, and a new covenant was established between God and the entire people of Israel. The covenant at Sinai recalled God's salvation of Israel and promised the Israelites that they would be God's "treasured possession" if they observed the commandments that he had given to Moses on Mount Sinai.

According to the Torah, God spoke these commandments aloud from the top of Mount Sinai, which was covered by cloud and fire, while all the people of Israel listened from below. Tradition has it that these commandments were inscribed personally by God onto the two stone tablets that Moses brought down from the mountain, although the Torah is not consistently clear on this point. Moses broke the tablets in anger when he saw that the Israelites had built a false god, a golden calf, while he was on the summit. He returned to Mount Sinai to have a new set of stone tablets inscribed, and these were placed in a gilded chest called

> The whole land of Canaan... I will give as an everlasting possession to you and your descendants after you; and I will be their God.
> **Genesis 17:8**

the Ark of the Covenant. The ark was equipped with staves so that it could be carried by the Israelites as they continued to Canaan.

The commandments

The most famous commandments in the Sinai covenant are the "Ten Commandments," or the Decalogue. The Decalogue comprises the most fundamental rules of Israel's covenant. It prohibits the worship of other gods or the depiction of God in physical form; it says that each week the Israelites must observe a sacred day of rest, the Sabbath; and it prohibits certain actions, such as murder and adultery.

In addition to the Decalogue, the Torah includes numerous laws that God is said to have conveyed to the Israelites indirectly through Moses, both at Sinai and on other occasions. These laws also form part of the covenant. According to a calculation in the Talmud (rabbinic interpretation of

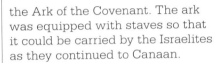

When the Israelites fled Egypt during the Exodus, God protected them and supplied them with food, as shown here in *The Gathering of the Manna*, a 15th-century work.

Jewish law) there are a total of 613 commandments in the Torah. They address many aspects of the Israelites' life in Canaan. Some constitute what we would consider civil law, describing systems of government, regulating property disputes, and setting guidelines for dealing with cases of murder and theft, among other matters. Others relate to the construction of a sanctuary for worshipping God, and establish sacrificial rites to be performed by a hereditary priesthood. Still others direct the behaviour of individual Israelites, instructing them on matters ranging from what they may eat, and whom they may marry, to the fair and charitable treatment of their fellows. Generally, the commandments aimed to establish a society that was just, by the standards of the day, and distinctive in its service of God.

The final book of the Torah, Deuteronomy, describes a third covenant between God and Israel, established in the land of Moab (in modern-day Jordan) before the Israelites entered Canaan. Deuteronomy tells that God commanded Moses to make this additional covenant with the people of Israel. It took the form of a final address from Moses, who was to die before he entered the promised land. Moses recalled God's salvation of Israel, relayed further commandments that God had given him at Sinai, and promised that God would bless the Israelites if they obeyed the commandments, and curse them if they disobeyed. The covenant at Moab reaffirmed the Israelites' loyalty to their God and his commandments.

The covenant in practice

In principle, traditional Jews consider the laws of the Torah eternally binding. However, the commandments have been subject to centuries of interpretation, and many are no longer applicable in practice. Certain laws pertaining to the rule of kings, for example, have not been applicable since the fall of the monarchy of Judah in the 6th century BCE, and the sacrificial rites have not been practised by mainstream Jews since the Romans destroyed their temple in Jerusalem in 70 CE. In addition, many of the Torah's

The rituals of Judaism, such as the lighting of candles for Shabbat, the Sabbath or day of rest, serve to remind Jews of the bond created by their covenant with God.

laws deal with agriculture and are considered binding only in Israel. In the present day, Jews maintain a range of approaches to the commandments and their interpretations. Traditional Jews observe the Sabbath, the festivals, and dietary laws (such as avoiding certain meats and not mixing meat and dairy), as well as »

Noah is not only an important figure in Judaism and Christianity, but also in Islam; his covenant with God forms part of the Qur'an.

The covenant with Noah

In addition to God's covenant with Israel, the Torah also tells of a covenant between God and all living beings. God made this covenant with Noah, whose family survived a primordial flood that wiped out most life on Earth. This covenant stipulated that God would never again destroy the world by flood. Like Israel's patriarchs after him, Noah was also promised many descendants who would fill the Earth. The sign of God's covenant with

Noah was the rainbow, which would thereafter serve as a reminder of God's promise of safety. Later Jewish tradition understood the Noahide covenant to include seven commandments, which were incumbent on all humankind. These "Noahide laws" forbade idolatry, murder, blasphemy, theft, sexual immorality (such as incest), and consuming forbidden flesh, and required courts of justice to be set up.

The Israelites' loyalty to God was tested by 40 years of exile in the desert. This is commemorated in the festival of Sukkot, in which fragile booths are built to resemble their desert homes.

other rules. But for many modern Jews, the essential laws are those that pertain to the love of one's neighbour and the just treatment of other human beings. Progressive Jews often cite a dictum attributed to Rabbi Hillel the Elder on the Golden Rule: "That which is hateful to you, do not do to your neighbour. That is the whole Torah; the rest is the explanation."

If you will obey Me faithfully and keep My covenant, you shall be My treasured possession among all the peoples.
Exodus 19:5

The promise of the land

In his covenant with Abraham, God granted the land of Canaan to the patriarch's descendants as an inviolable gift. Yet it is stated elsewhere in the Bible that the Israelites' hold on the land is conditional on observance of the commandments. This conditionality is said to explain why the Israelites were eventually conquered by their enemies and exiled from their land. Parts of the Torah include exile among the curses that would befall the Israelites if they violated the covenants at Sinai and Moab; many modern scholars believe that these passages were written in response to these events.

At the same time, the Torah asserts that God never abandoned his covenant with the patriarchs. While in exile, the Israelites had the opportunity to repent, and God led them back to their land, thereby upholding his covenant with Abraham. In this way

the promise of the land, although conditional, remains eternal: the Israelites might lose the land for a time due to their sins, but they need not lose hope of returning.

The "Chosen People"

The Torah offers little in terms of explanation as to why God chose the patriarchs and their descendants, yet it emphasizes that by virtue of their covenantal relationship with him, the Israelites are privileged above other nations. The authors of the Bible did not view the Israelites as inherently superior to other people – on the contrary, they often describe them as sinful and unworthy – but they clearly perceived Israel's status as special. As Jews came to believe that their god was the one God who ruled the whole world, their status as his chosen nation took on even greater significance.

Throughout history, Jews have struggled to understand why God chose them and what this choice implied about their place in the world. One ancient tradition suggests that, rather than God choosing Israel, Israel chose God. This tradition maintains that God offered the commandments to all the nations of the earth, but all except Israel rejected them, finding them too burdensome. In accordance with this view, the Israelites' status is not a result of choice on God's part, but a product of free will. At the same time, it seems to deny freedom of choice by holding individuals responsible for the decisions of their ancestors.

> The meaning of Jewish history revolves around the faithfulness of Israel to the covenant.
> **Abraham Joshua Heschel, Polish-born US rabbi**

Some Jewish mystical traditions with origins in the Middle Ages suggest a different perspective, asserting that the souls of Jews were chosen at the time of creation and are qualitatively superior to those of non-Jews. However, prominent thinkers from the major modern denominations of Judaism (Modern Orthodox, Conservative, and Reform) emphatically reject any claims of essential difference between Jews and non-Jews. Modern Jewish thinkers tend to view the covenant instead as imposing a mission on Jews to live in accordance with God's will and thereby convey God's truth to the world. Some have suggested that Israel is not unique in having been chosen by God, and that other peoples may have been chosen to fulfil other missions. Some liberal Jews reject the idea of "chosenness" on the grounds that it presupposes superiority over other people and encourages ethnocentrism.

Joining the covenant

Traditional Judaism maintains that status in the covenant is transmitted from parent to child through the maternal line; so the child of a Jewish mother is automatically Jewish and bound by the commandments. This inherited status cannot be forfeited: a Jew who does not observe the commandments has violated the covenant, but he or she remains a Jew. On the other hand, it is possible for a non-Jew to become Jewish through conversion. Under rabbinic law, a convert to Judaism must accept the Jewish commandments and be immersed in a ritual bath (and if male, be circumcised), at which point he, or she, assumes all the rights and duties of a Jew.

Traditionally, conversion to Judaism involved a commitment to a strict regime of observance. Today, progressive Judaism places greater emphasis on individual autonomy in determining Jewish identity and its obligations. In both Reform Judaism in the USA and Liberal Judaism in the UK, the children of Jewish fathers and non-Jewish mothers are accepted without formal conversion if they self-identify as Jewish.

In spite of varying beliefs and practices, the concept of the covenant remains central to all streams of Judaism. It represents and defines the individual Jew's purpose in the world, linking him or her to the Jewish people across the span of history, and to the Jewish God. ∎

How an individual joins the covenant depends on the faith, or otherwise, of his or her parents. Judaism does not actively seek converts, but accepts those who show commitment and sincerity.

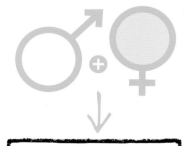

If your **mother is Jewish** and your father is not, then **you are Jewish**, and can never be not Jewish.

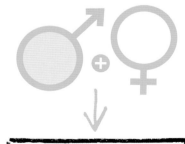

If only your **father is Jewish**, some modern denominations **will accept you** without conversion.

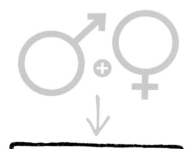

If neither of your parents is Jewish, **you may convert** to Judaism, following the correct rituals.

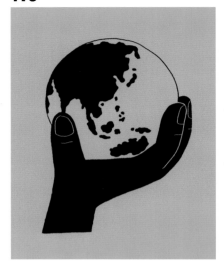

BESIDE ME THERE IS NO OTHER GOD

FROM MONOLATRY TO MONOTHEISM

IN CONTEXT

KEY SOURCE
Second Isaiah

WHEN AND WHERE
c.540 BCE, Babylon/Judea

BEFORE
1400–1200 BCE The prophet
Zoroaster forms a new religion
with one supreme god.

c.1000 BCE The "Song of the
Sea", a poem in the Bible's
Exodus, proclaims YHWH
supreme over other gods.

c.622 BCE King Josiah of
Judah abolishes worship
of gods other than YHWH.

AFTER
c.20 BCE–40 CE Philo of
Alexandria argues that biblical
monotheism had anticipated
later Greek philosophical
conceptions of God.

7th century Islam is revealed
to the Prophet Muhammad,
and monotheism supplants
polytheistic beliefs held
among the tribes of Arabia.

YHWH is the
greatest god; his power
is supreme, universal,
and eternal.

⬇

Because he is
omnipotent he needs
no subordinates.

⬇

No other being can
countermand his wishes.

⬇

Even **events** that harm his
people – the Israelites – are
orchestrated by him.

⬇

Both the **"evil"** and **"good"** of
the world are part of **his plan**.

⬇

**There are no other gods
but YHWH.**

The earliest authors of the
Jewish Bible seem to
have acknowledged the
existence of many gods, but
insisted that the one whose name
is rendered as YHWH was the
greatest among them, and that
the Israelites should worship only
YHWH. It appears, then, that at
some time during the biblical
period, the Jewish people moved
from this exclusive worship of
one god among many (known as
monolatry) to the belief that only
one god existed (monotheism).

YHWH rules all nations
In addition to the views of the
Bible's authors, archaeological
evidence suggests that the early
Israelites worshipped a variety
of regional gods. The prophets of
the god YHWH, whose writings
comprise a large portion of the
Bible, harshly rebuked the people
for this practice. It is not clear
whether the prophets were all
true monotheists, but they did
believe that YHWH was supremely
powerful and ruled over all nations.

In 722 BCE, the Assyrians
conquered the northern kingdom of
Israel and exiled its people. Around
130 years later, the Babylonians

See also: Beliefs for new societies 56–57 ▪ The battle between good and evil 60–65 ▪ God's covenant with Israel 168–75 ▪ Defining the indefinable 184–85 ▪ The unity of divinity is necessary 280–81

The people of Israel were vanquished by the Assyrians during the 8th century BCE and led away to exile, as shown on this relief from the palace of Sennacherib at Nineveh.

conquered the southern lands of the Jewish people, known as the Kingdom of Judah. In the ancient Middle East, such conquests were usually interpreted as victories by the conquering people's god over that of the defeated people – so the supremacy of YHWH appeared to be challenged. Yet the prophets insisted that these events were all, in fact, YHWH's doing: he was using the other nations to punish the Israelites for violating their covenant with him (pp.168–75).

No God but YHWH

The Jews returned from exile in Babylon to their homeland in 538 BCE, under the decree of Cyrus the Great, emperor of Persia, where the Zoroastrian faith predominated.

Around this time, the earliest clear articulation of monotheism in the Bible emerged, in a collection of writings known as "Second Isaiah". It emphasizes that YHWH created, and rules over, the world alone. Israel's restoration is a sign of YHWH's control over history, which is both transcendent and personal: he determines the actions of kings but also leads his people to salvation like a shepherd guiding his flock.

The problem of evil

Monotheism raises the "problem of evil": namely, if there is only one God, who is just and merciful, as the Bible insists, then how can he preside over a world in which the righteous suffer? This is the theme of the biblical book of Job, which tells of a righteous man who questions how God could have allowed his terrible misfortune. God's response suggests that there is no answer: his rule over the world is beyond human understanding. ▪

Second Isaiah

The biblical Book of Isaiah claims to be the work of a prophet by that name who lived in the late 8th and early 7th centuries BCE. However, the latter portion of the book deals with the Jews' return from exile in Babylon in the 6th century BCE. Modern scholars refer to this section as "Second Isaiah" or "Deutero-Isaiah" and attribute it to one or more 6th-century writers.

Second Isaiah echoes the language and themes of the first part of the book, while also introducing new ideas and motifs, including explicit monotheism. Like earlier prophetic works, it interprets Israel's exile as punishment for the people's sins, but proclaims that the punishment has ended and it will be followed by everlasting glory when Israel finally embraces YHWH alone.

Many scholars believe that the final portion of the book was written later still and constitutes a "Third Isaiah".

Before Me no God was formed, nor shall there be any after Me.
Isaiah 43:10

THE MESSIAH WILL REDEEM ISRAEL

THE PROMISE OF A NEW AGE

IN CONTEXT

KEY TEXTS
The Dead Sea Scrolls

WHEN AND WHERE
c.150 BCE–68 CE, Palestine

BEFORE
c.1005–965 BCE King David reigns over Israel as God's "anointed" one, or "Messiah".

586 BCE The Babylonian conquest and exile of the Jews ends David's dynasty.

AFTER
1st century CE Jesus is proclaimed the Messiah.

2nd century CE Simeon Bar Kokhba is hailed as the Messiah.

20th century CE Menachem Mendel Schneerson, leader of a Hasidic sect, promotes Jewish observance as a way to bring the Messiah; he is himself hailed as the Messiah by his followers.

Throughout much of their recorded history, the people of Israel were ruled by kings. A ritual called "anointing", in which oil was poured on the monarch's head, functioned much like a coronation and served to indicate God's election of the ruler, who was referred to as God's anointed one, or in Hebrew, "Messiah". Originally, the term Messiah was used for any anointed leader, but over time it came to refer to a specific ruler who would arise in the future and rescue Israel from its enemies, ushering in a golden age – the Messianic Era. Jewish tradition offers much speculation as to the events that

See also: God's covenant with Israel 168–75 ▪ Faith and the state 189
▪ The origins of modern political Zionism 196–97

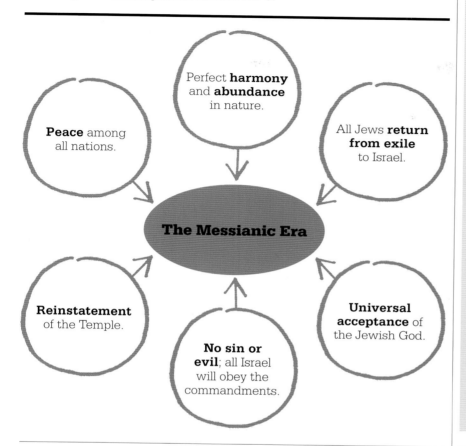

- Perfect **harmony** and **abundance** in nature.
- Peace among all nations.
- All Jews **return from exile** to Israel.

The Messianic Era

- **Reinstatement** of the Temple.
- **No sin or evil**; all Israel will obey the commandments.
- **Universal acceptance** of the Jewish God.

Israelites and Jews

Abraham's son Isaac fathered two sons, Esau and Jacob; the Bible relates that God changed Jacob's name to "Israel". The families of Jacob's 12 sons grew into the 12 tribes of Israel (Israelites), occupying an area roughly equivalent to the modern territory of Israel. In the late 10th century BCE, the Israelites were divided into two kingdoms – the southern tribes formed the Kingdom of Judah, while the northern tribes formed the Kingdom of Israel. These two kingdoms were subsequently conquered and broken up – Israel by the Assyrians in 722 BCE, and Judah by the Babylonians in 586 BCE. However, the people of Judah endured as a distinct group with a distinct religion. From this point, they were called "Jews" and their religion "Judaism", although they still thought of themselves as Israelites. Modern citizens of Israel are called Israelis.

would characterize the Messianic Era, but most agreed that it would be a period of brotherhood and glory on earth, when delicacies and miracles would be commonplace, swords would be beaten into ploughshares, and the wolf would live with the lamb.

Some traditions speculated that the Messiah would be an earthly ruler (with a close connection to God), others that he would be a heavenly figure appointed in a time before creation itself. Similarly, a number of traditions envisioned the Messianic Era to be part of the normal course of history, while for others it was a miraculous time when God's spirit would reign on earth.

A Messiah from David's line

One of the first kings of the united monarchy of Israel and Judah was a man named David, who reigned from around 1005 to 965 BCE. According to the Bible, David was instrumental in uniting the people of Israel and defending them against the Philistines. The Bible relates that God loved David, referring to him as his "son", and established an agreement, or covenant, with him, promising that his descendants would rule over Israel forever.

However, the Babylonians conquered Judah in 586 BCE, exiling most of its inhabitants and destroying the Temple, and »

They will beat their swords into ploughshares and their spears into pruning hooks. Nation will not take up sword against nation, nor will they train for war anymore.
Isaiah 2:4

David's dynasty came to an end. The fall of the kingdom might have suggested that God had broken his covenant with David. Yet the people of Judah continued to hold out the hope that, some time in the future, a descendant of David would once again rule over Israel as God's Messiah.

Foretold by prophets

Even before the fall of the monarchy, some of Israel's prophets predicted that a king descended from David would unite the two kingdoms and rescue them from their enemies. Although these prophecies were written in different periods and some referred to specific historical kings, later generations interpreted them as foretelling the advent of a future Messiah. After the Babylonian conquest, some prophets foretold that the people would eventually return to their homeland and rebuild their temple. A few envisioned that the nations of the world would one day recognize Israel's God and come to worship him in Jerusalem. These visions of a glorious future were not unconditional, however. The prophets believed that Israel's misfortunes were God's punishment for the sins of the people and its leaders and that future restoration would only be possible if Israel repented.

Foreign rule

The prophets' visions were partly realized when the Persian king Cyrus the Great defeated the Babylonians and allowed many Jews to return to their homeland and rebuild the Temple. Indeed, Cyrus is addressed in the Bible as the "Lord's Messiah". However, a lengthy period of domination by foreign powers, including the Greek and Roman Empires, followed the return of the Jews to the homeland. During this time, they turned again to biblical prophecies about the Messiah and an age of national restoration.

The Jews drew on prophetic traditions that envisioned a great battle between the forces of good and evil, in which God would emerge triumphant and sinners would be punished. Jewish apocalyptic works of this period, which include the Dead Sea Scrolls, offer elaborate descriptions of this battle and the accompanying

> My servant David will be king over them, and they will all have one shepherd. They will follow my laws and be careful to keep my decrees.
> **Ezekiel 37:24**

plagues and tribulations that would precede the advent of the Messiah: floods and earthquakes, the darkening of the sun and moon, and the falling of the stars from the sky. These events came to be known as the "birth pangs of the Messiah", since for all the agony that they would cause they were simply a precursor of the Messianic Era, when evil would be banished from earth, the rule of oppressive empires would be swept away, and people could live free of distraction and crime.

Biblical manuscripts make up almost half of the scrolls. Most are on parchment in Hebrew, Aramaic, Greek, or Nabataean.

The Dead Sea Scrolls

In 1947, a Bedouin goatherd discovered a cache of buried scrolls in a cave in Qumran, on the northwest shore of the Dead Sea. The scrolls are thought to be the writings of the Essenes – an ancient Jewish sect – that had been hidden when members of the sect fled the Romans during the Jewish revolt of 66–70 CE. The Essenes rejected the priesthood that was then in control of the Jerusalem Temple and formed a community in the desert, where they awaited the end times, apparently believing that they alone would be redeemed in the Messianic Era, which would usher in a new, purer temple and priesthood. The scrolls include the earliest known manuscripts of nearly every book in the Hebrew Bible as well as a wealth of later Jewish literature, and they have contributed greatly to our understanding of Jewish thought in the period.

Some Jewish thinkers maintain that the return of the diaspora and the rebuilding of Jerusalem will be the two most important preludes to the coming of the Messiah.

Appearance of the Messiah

Every so often throughout history, an exceptional individual would appear whom some people thought might be the Messiah. One such person was Jesus of Nazareth, known to his followers as "Christ", from the Greek word for "Messiah". Jesus's followers, who became known as Christians, continued to believe that he was the Messiah after his execution by the Romans, but most Jews rejected this claim.

Another messianic claimant was Simeon Bar Kokhba, who led a revolt against the Romans in 132 CE. His revolt was a colossal failure, which effectively brought an end to Jewish life in Jerusalem and the surrounding area. Those Jews who were not killed were dispersed throughout the Roman Empire, and many were sold into slavery.

The failure of this, and other, revolts against Roman rule and the loss, again, of the Jewish religious centre in Jerusalem brought new relevance to the prophecies from the Babylonian exile.

Resurrection and afterlife

The Messianic Era was originally envisioned by some traditions as a time of national restoration, when Israel would be redeemed and its oppressors would perish. Later, however, it was generally believed that it would also be a time of judgment for every person, living or dead, when the righteous would be rewarded and the wicked punished.

The Hebrew Bible says little about life after death. Most early biblical authors shared the ancient belief that the dead lived on in the underworld, but offered little detail on the subject. Many Jews came to believe that a person's ultimate fate depended on his or her conduct in life. Some said that the righteous lived on in Paradise while the wicked were condemned to a place of torment, called Gehenna. Others emphasized a final judgment in the Messianic Era, when the dead would be resurrected. Both ideas persisted in Jewish belief, and both the Messianic Era and the individual afterlife are commonly referred to as the "World to Come".

Jewish messianism today

Within Orthodox Judaism, the promise of messianic redemption remains a core belief. Many leaders state that if Jews, as a group, embrace God and obey his commandments, they can hasten the Messiah's arrival. Yet the idea of the Messiah has mostly flourished when Jews have been oppressed, and the relative freedom of Jews in much of the modern world has lessened the sense of urgency of the hope for national restoration. The Reform movement, in particular, rejected the ideas of a messianic king, a return to the Jewish homeland, and the rebuilding of the Temple, although aspects of these beliefs have been re-evaluated over the years. The one feature of messianism that remains central in all streams of Judaism is, however, the belief that humankind – and the Jewish people in particular – has the ability to bring about a better future through righteous action. ∎

King Messiah, the Son of Man, will arise in the future and will restore the kingship of David to its ancient condition.
Moses Maimonides

RELIGIOUS LAW CAN BE APPLIED TO DAILY LIFE
WRITING THE ORAL LAW

IN CONTEXT

KEY TEXT
The Talmud

WHEN AND WHERE
**2nd–5th century CE,
Palestine and Babylonia**

BEFORE
140 BCE –70 CE The Pharisees
espouse belief in an Oral Law.

2nd century CE Rebellions
against Roman rule prompt
the destruction of many of the
Yeshivot (places for the study
of the Torah); Rabbis write
down the Oral Law.

AFTER
11th century CE Rabbi
Solomon ben Isaac (Rashi)
produces a commentary on
the Talmud, which becomes
standard in printed editions.

c.1170–80 The Jewish
philosopher Maimonides
composes the Mishneh
Torah, a work describing
and reviewing the laws
mentioned in the Torah.

Each page of the Talmud holds
the **text of the Mishnah** – a
Hebrew account of the Oral Law.

↓

The text of the Mishnah is
explained and discussed in
the **surrounding Gemara**.

↓

Texts of the Mishnah and
Gemara are then **surrounded
by other layers of text**
and commentaries from
a later period.

↓

The text of the Talmud
is a **discussion**.

↓

Its arguments guide the reader
to the **kernel of the truth**.

J ewish tradition maintains
that God gave Moses a body
of laws and teachings, which
he passed on to the people of Israel
(pp.168–75). Many of these are
recorded in the first five books
of the Hebrew Bible, the Torah,
but some Jews also believe
that Moses received additional
teachings (transmitted verbally to
the community's leaders, and then
from generation to generation),
which became known as the "Oral
Law". This Oral Law included
additional details about, and
interpretations of, the biblical laws.

From the 2nd century CE, Jewish
rabbis (a word meaning "scholars"
or "teachers") set out to record the
Oral Law. The result was a large
new body of literature. Many of
the rabbis' writings are collected
in a set of books called the
Talmud which, for observant
Jews, is the most important and
authoritative religious text after
the Bible itself.

Part of the reason the Oral
Law is important is that the Bible's
laws are frequently ambiguous.
For example, the Bible prohibits
working on the Sabbath, but it
does not explain what kind of
work is prohibited. The Talmud

See also: God's covenant with Israel 168–75 ▪ Progressive Judaism 190–95 ▪ The pathway to harmonious living 272–75

The primary purpose of the Talmud is to record the analysis of Jewish traditions by the best intellects of previous generations, and to challenge new students to find their own truths.

resolves this ambiguity by specifying 39 types of activity (including building, cooking, and writing) that are forbidden.

In addition to recording the laws given to Moses, the Talmud includes extensive discussions between rabbis over interpretation. These discussions are considered part of the Oral Law too, because the authority to interpret the laws was handed down through Moses.

Each page of the Talmud is designed to reflect this debate: the earliest writings, or Mishnah, setting out the law, are surrounded by the discussions, or Gemara, so the book can be read a series of conversations between rabbis.

Acceptance of the Talmud

The concept of an oral law has not been universally accepted among Jews. Prior to the writing of the Talmud, the doctrine of the Oral Law was promulgated by a Jewish sect called the Pharisees. However, two sects – the Karaites and the Sadducees – rejected this doctrine. The Karaites originated around the 8th century in Baghdad and (unlike the Sadducees) still exist today. Karaites have their own traditions for interpreting the Bible, but they do not believe that any teachings were given to Moses besides those in the biblical text. Nonetheless, other branches of Judaism accept the Talmud as a sacred text, and Orthodox Jews continue to trace its origins to the Oral Law given to Moses by God. Many modern Jews do not take this idea literally, but rather view the Talmud as part of a living tradition that preserves and interprets Jewish law for every generation and encourages theological debate. ∎

Versions of the Talmud

A collective work of thousands of rabbis over hundreds of years, the Talmud is organized into six orders that deal with different aspects of law and tradition, then into tractates and chapters. There are two versions of the Talmud: the Jerusalem Talmud, which was compiled in the 4th century CE in the Land of Israel, and the Babylonian Talmud, which was compiled c.500 CE in Babylonia (modern-day Iraq).

Although there are many similarities between the two versions, the Babylonian Talmud, which is more than 6,000 pages in extent, is generally considered to be more authoritative and is used more widely by students of Judaism. The Jerusalem Talmud was never completed due to the persecution of the Jews in Israel, and is thus far shorter and more cryptic than the Babylonian Talmud.

Moses received the Torah from Sinai and transmitted it to Joshua, Joshua to the elders, and the elders to the prophets, and the prophets transmitted it to the men of the Great Assembly.
Ethics of the Fathers

GOD IS INCORPOREAL, INDIVISIBLE, AND UNIQUE
DEFINING THE INDEFINABLE

IN CONTEXT

KEY THINKER
Moses Maimonides

WHEN AND WHERE
12th century, North Africa

BEFORE
30 BCE–50 CE The Jewish philosopher Philo describes the God of the Bible in Greek philosophical terms, as lacking Aristotelian attributes.

933 CE Rabbi Sa'adia Gaon's *Book of Beliefs and Opinions* proposes several arguments for God's unity.

AFTER
13th century The Zohar, a Jewish mystical text, propounds the idea that an infinite and unified Godhead became manifest in creation and in ten "emanations".

c.1730 Rabbi Moshe Chaim Luzzatto's *The Way of God* states that God encompasses all perfections, but these exist in him as a single, essential attribute.

Since biblical times, belief in one God has been a central feature of Jewish religion. Yet the idea that God is "one" may be understood in a variety of ways: that is, God could be the greatest of many divine beings, or God could be a single being composed of several different elements. In the Middle Ages, a number of Jewish philosophers in the Muslim sphere of influence sought to demonstrate that the oneness of God, properly understood, excluded all of these other possibilities.

Moses Maimonides was a particularly influential philosopher of this school. He explained the

God has **no physical or mental attributes** that we can describe, as these cannot exist outside his oneness.

God is **all-powerful**, because there can be nothing over which he does not have control.

God has a **unity and nature** unlike anything that we can comprehend.

God is **infinite**, because we cannot imagine any limits to his presence and power.

God is **eternal**, because we cannot conceive of a time at which he did not exist.

See also: From monolatry to monotheism 176–77 ▪ Mysticism and the kabbalah 188 ▪ The unity of divinity is necessary 280–81

Jewish tenet of monotheism in terms of the classical Greek philosophical doctrine that God is "simple" – that is, not composed of parts or properties.

God's oneness, according to Maimonides, is different from the oneness of any other being: he is a single, unique, indivisible entity; he is also beyond human understanding and description, and therefore cannot be given specific attributes.

God cannot be categorized

God, Maimonides argued, is not "one of a species" – he is not a member of a group of beings that share certain characteristics. Three different men, for example, are each individuals, but they share the attribute of "maleness" and therefore belong to the category of males. God, on the other hand, has no attributes, and therefore cannot belong to a category of beings, divine or otherwise.

God's oneness also differs from that of a body, which is divisible. This means that God is not like

God is not two or more entities, but a single entity of a oneness even more single and unique than any single thing in creation.
Maimonides

a physical object, which can be broken into parts. But Maimonides went further, and argued that God is also intellectually indivisible: he cannot have any attributes (as defined by Aristotle), as he would then consist of both his essence and his attributes. If God were "eternal", for example, there would effectively be two gods: God and God's eternity.

Maimonides' belief that God has no attributes is a product of a school of thought called "negative theology", which maintains that it is inaccurate to characterize God in any affirmative way. Given the limits of human language, we may describe God as "eternal", but in truth we can only affirm that God is not non-eternal: that is, his essence is beyond comprehension. Maimonides included the doctrine of God's oneness among his 13 essential principles of Jewish faith, which also include such concepts as God's antiquity and the belief that the Torah comes from the mouth of God. Many regard these principles as the fundamental elements of Jewish belief. ▪

According to Maimonides, God existed before everything and is the creator of all things. His existence is independent of all other things but all other things need him in order to exist.

Moses Maimonides

Moses Maimonides (also known as Rambam) was born in 1135 in Cordoba, Spain, into a Jewish family. His childhood was rich in cross-cultural influences: he was educated in both Hebrew and Arabic, and his father, a rabbinic judge, taught him Jewish law within the context of Islamic Spain. His family fled Spain when the Berber Almohad dynasty came to power in 1148, and lived nomadically for 10 years until they settled first in Fez (now in Morocco) and then in Cairo. Maimonides began training as a physician due to his family's financial problems; his skill led to a royal appointment within only a few years. He also worked as a rabbinic judge, but this was an activity for which he thought it wrong to accept any payment. He was recognized as head of the Jewish community of Cairo in 1191. After his death in 1204 his tomb became a place of Jewish pilgrimage.

Key works

1168 *Commentary on the Mishnah*
1168–78 *Mishneh Torah*
1190 *Guide for the Perplexed*

GOD AND HUMANKIND ARE IN COSMIC EXILE

MYSTICISM AND THE KABBALAH

IN CONTEXT

KEY FIGURE
Isaac Luria

WHEN AND WHERE
16th century, Palestine

BEFORE
From 1200 BCE Zoroastrians believe that every act of right moral conduct by humans collectively aids the cosmic struggle of good against evil.

10th–15th century CE Christian mysticism flourishes in Europe in the Middle Ages.

AFTER
18th century In Europe, as the Haskalah ("Jewish Enlightenment") dismisses mysticism, Israel ben Eliezer founds Hasidic Judaism in Ukraine, based on Isaac Luria's exposition of kabbalah.

1980s In Los Angeles, the Kabbalah Centre attracts celebrity followers with teachings derived from the Judaic mystical tradition.

The texts of Judaism include, along with the Hebrew Bible (p.171) and the Talmud (a compendium of rabbinic interpretations), a body of mystical knowledge known as kabbalah. Originally an oral tradition, it was collected in the Zohar ("Divine Splendour") in the late 13th century in Spain. The Zohar and its kabbalistic ideas took on a special significance for exiled Jews – in particular for the scholars of Safed in Palestine – after their expulsion from Iberia (present-day Spain, Portugal, and Andorra) in the 1490s. Among them was the

Jewish men at penitential prayers, the Selichot, in Jerusalem. According to kabbalah, observance of the commandments will help lead people from exile to redemption.

teacher Isaac Luria, whose interpretation of the Zohar gave a unique description of the creation that was applicable to the experience of Jews in exile. It provided an explanation of good and evil, and the way to redemption.

In Luria's interpretation, before the creation only God existed. In order to make space to create the world, he contracted or withdrew into himself (*tzimtzum*): a form of self-imposed exile for the sake of creation. A divine light streamed into the created space in the shape of 10 *sefirot* – emanations of the divine attributes of God. Adam Kadmon (meaning "primordial man") formed vessels to contain the *sefirot*. But the vessels were too delicate to hold the divine light: the upper three were damaged, and the lower seven completely destroyed, scattering the divine light. This destruction of the vessels (known as *shevirat ha-kelim* or *shevirah*) upset the process of creation and divided the universe into those elements that assisted, and those that resisted, the creation: good and evil, and the upper and lower worlds.

This damage can be repaired, Luria explained, by detaching the "holy sparks" of divine light to which

See also: The promise of a new age 178–81 ∎ Man as a manifestation of God 188 ∎ Sufism and the mystic tradition 282–83

God contracted himself to **make a void** in which to **create the world** yet maintain his transcendence.

There then followed **10 emanations**, the *sefirot,* which together formed a **divine light** revealing God's purpose.

But the **vessels** containing the *sefirot* were not strong enough and **were destroyed** in a catastrophe, *shevirah.*

This is the **source of both good and evil**, and is embodied in the Fall of Adam.

The damage cannot be repaired until the **sparks of the divine light are reunited**, and until then…

… **God and humankind are in cosmic exile.**

Isaac Luria

Isaac ben Solomon Luria Ashkenazi was born in 1534 in Jerusalem. His German father died when Isaac was a child, so he moved with his mother to stay with her brother in Egypt. There he studied rabbinical literature and Jewish law with some of the foremost scholars of the day, including Rabbi Bezalel Ashkenazi, and traded as a merchant. He married aged 15, but continued his studies. Six years later he moved to an island on the Nile to study the Zohar and the early kabbalists, barely speaking to anyone, and then only in Hebrew. During this time, he said he had conversations with the long-dead prophet Elijah, who told him to move to Safed, a centre of kabbalistic study in Ottoman-ruled Palestine.

Working with Moses Cordovero, Luria became known for his teaching of the kabbalah, and his disciples dubbed him HaARI, "the Lion", from the initials, in Hebrew, of "holy Rabbi Yitzhak". He died in Safed in 1572.

the forces of evil in the lower world are clinging, and restoring them to their source in the upper world: a process of *tikkun olam* – repairing the world. The responsibility for this rests on the Jewish people, who rescue a holy spark each time they obey a holy commandment, and pass one back to universal evil when they sin. Until all the divine sparks are reunited in the world of the good, there can be no redemption, and humanity will live in cosmic exile.

Although Luria did not leave a record of his interpretation of kabbalah, his esoteric teachings were preserved by his followers. After his death, his ideas spread quickly throughout Europe. Because of the rational, comprehensive nature of Lurianic kabbalah, kabbalistic study became a mainstay of Jewish thought, and in the 18th century it formed the basis for the Hasidic movement (p.188), which places particular emphasis on a mystical relationship with God. ∎

The Torah is concealed. It is only revealed to those who have reached the level of the righteous.
The Talmud, Hagigah

THE HOLY SPARK DWELLS IN EVERYONE

MAN AS A MANIFESTATION OF GOD

IN CONTEXT

KEY FIGURE
Israel ben Eliezer

WHEN AND WHERE
1740s, Ukraine

BEFORE
16th century Isaac Luria
and other teachers reawaken
interest in the mystical
elements of the kabbalah.

AFTER
19th century Hasidism
gains adherents in reaction
to the intellectualization and
secularization of Judaism.

1917 The Bolshevik Revolution
in Russia breaks up many
Hasidic communities.

1930s With the rise of Nazism,
Jews from Germany, Eastern
Europe, and Russia flee to the
USA; all Hasidic communities
in Europe are destroyed during
World War II.

1948 The State of Israel is
founded. Many displaced
Hasidic Jews settle there.

Hasidic Judaism, founded by Israel ben Eliezer (known as Baal Shem Tov, or the Besht) in the 1740s, is characterized by enthusiasm and rituals of mass ecstasy, performed under the guidance of a spiritual leader, or *zaddik*. One of its main teachings is that the divine dwells within everyone. It is now one of the major branches of ultra-Orthodox Judaism.

The movement emerged from the Jewish communities of Central and Eastern Europe during the 18th century. These communities were often small and isolated, and their lifestyle was very different from that of urban Jews living elsewhere. Mainstream Jewish philosophy had, by then, become more intellectual, and theology more legalistic. This development was at odds with the needs of the inhabitants of small villages, or shtetls, especially in areas such as southern Poland.

To maintain cohesion in these communities, especially in the face of persecution by the Cossacks (East Slavic people), religious leaders travelled around from place to place. They offered worshippers not only guidance, but also an opportunity to participate more actively in religious observances. Where rabbinical teaching had become detached from the people, charismatic leaders such as Baal Shem Tov explained that the Torah was not the exclusive realm of the rabbis. Spiritual learning was available to all: the "holy sparks", or divine light – a manifestation of God – outlined in the mystical tradition of the Lurianic kabbalah could be found in everyone. ∎

Hasidic men dance at a wedding celebration. The distinctive clothing of Hasidic Jews, drawn from earlier styles of Eastern European dress, sets them apart from other branches of Judaism.

See also: Mysticism and the kabbalah 186–87 ▪ Mystical experience in Christianity 238 ▪ Sufism and the mystic tradition 282–83

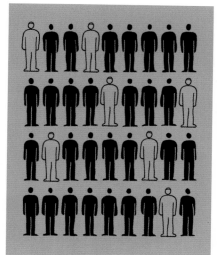

JUDAISM IS A RELIGION, NOT A NATIONALITY
FAITH AND THE STATE

F ollowing in the wake of the
Enlightenment in Europe,
the Haskalah movement, or
so-called "Jewish Enlightenment",
was inspired largely by the work
of the German Jewish philosopher
Moses Mendelssohn. He believed
that the persecution endured by the
Jews was largely a result of their
separateness from the societies
in which they lived.

His criticism of the separation
of Jews and Gentiles (non-Jews)
also raised the issue of what it
meant to be Jewish. In his opinion,
Judaism was a religion that should
be treated in the same way as any
other in a tolerant, pluralistic
society, and its followers should be
allowed freedom of conscience as
citizens of the country in which
they lived; conversely, being a Jew
did not imply belonging to a
separate nation or people.

In his book *Jerusalem: or On
Religious Power and Judaism* (1783),
Mendelssohn argued not only for
emancipation of the Jews, but also
that they should "come out of the
ghettoes" and play a more active

The state has physical power
and uses it when necessary;
the power of religion is
love and beneficence.
Moses Mendelssohn

part in secular cultural life. In
particular, he promoted the idea
of Jews learning the local language
– as he had done – to help integrate
themselves better into non-Jewish
societies, and published his own
translation of the Torah into German.

Although Mendelssohn was
himself a practising Orthodox
Jew, his ideas and the Haskalah
movement he inspired built the
foundation for Reform Judaism in
the 19th century. ∎

See also: God's covenant with Israel 168–75 ▪ Progressive Judaism 190–95
▪ The origins of modern political Zionism 196–97

DRAW FROM THE PAST, LIVE IN THE PRESENT, WORK FOR THE FUTURE

PROGRESSIVE JUDAISM

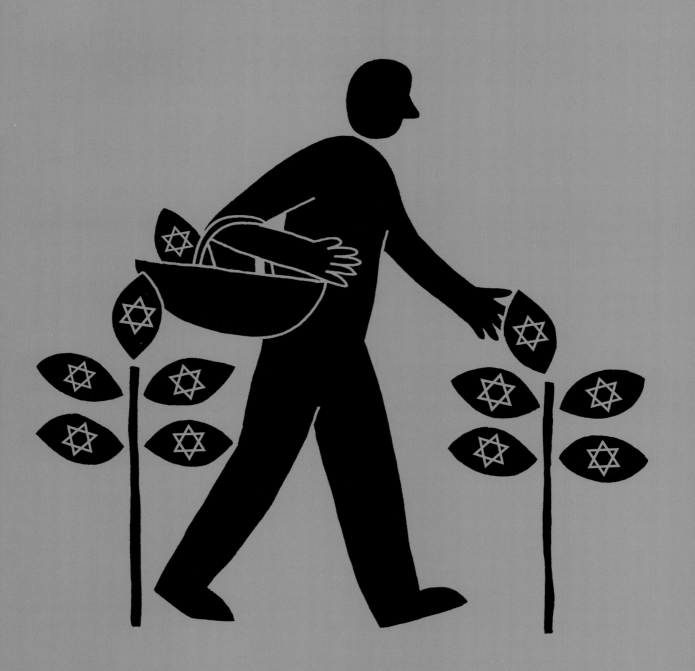

IN CONTEXT

KEY MOVEMENT
Progressive Judaism

WHEN AND WHERE
19th century,
Europe and USA

BEFORE
19th century The German
Enlightment offers Jews the
possibility of secular education
and participation in society.

AFTER
1840 The West London
Synagogue is established.

1872 The Reform Academy
Hochschule für die Wissen-
schaft des Judentums is
established in Berlin.

1885 Reform Judaism
flourishes in the USA. The
Pittsburgh Platform defines
the principles of Reform.

20th century Progressive
synagogues and communal
organizations are established
throughout the world.

Jewish emancipation in
Europe began in Germany in
the 18th century. Previously,
Jews had been restricted in where
they could live, and had been
barred from entering universities
and the professions, but the force
of European Enlightenment led to
them being given equal rights as
citizens. Yiddish-speaking Jews
learned German, became part of
the modern world, and began to
feel the freedom of individuality.
Many Jews started looking to
secular education – rather than
Jewish tradition – as a means
of achieving their potential.
Progressive Judaism, which
began with the Reform movement
in Germany, was a response
to these changes, to modernity,
and to the new freedoms.

The earliest and most visible
reforms emerged in Berlin and
Hamburg. They concerned the
synagogue service: the sermon
would be given in German, and
men and women would sit together
rather than being segregated. More
radically, the impact of modern
biblical scholarship led some Jews
to question the divine authority of
the biblical texts, and the traditions

> The Talmud speaks with
> the ideology of its own time,
> and for that time it was right.
> I speak for the higher ideology
> of my own time, and for
> this age I am right.
> **Extreme reformers in**
> **19th-century Germany**

that had kept them apart from
society. The authority of the classical
rabbis was now seen to be a
function of its time, and was
also called into question.

Some, faced with this new
insight and the opportunities
it gave rise to, abandoned their
Judaism in favour of secular
nationalism. Others sought instead
to modernize Judaism in the
light of historical, academic study
of the religion (*Wissenschaft des*
Judentums). The pace of change
was too rapid for some, and various

Abraham Geiger

Abraham Geiger was born in
Frankfurt-am-Main, Germany,
in 1810. He was educated in the
Jewish and German classics, and
studied Arabic for his dissertation,
"What Did Muhammad Take from
Judaism?". A passionate advocate
of *Wissenschaft des Judentums*,
the academic study of Judaism, he
set out to distil Judaism's eternal
spiritual and ethical core through
ground-breaking scholarship. He
sought to modernize Judaism
as a whole rather than to create
a separate movement, rejecting
practices if their historical reason
was no longer relevant. When he

was appointed as second rabbi
in Breslau, in 1838, Geiger found
his authority disputed by the
existing, traditionalist rabbi:
both were officially rabbis of the
whole community, but eventually
each served his own faction.
Geiger later presided as the
rabbi in Frankfurt and then in
Berlin, and also taught at the
new Reform Academy for two
years before his death in 1874.

Key works

1857 *The Original Text and*
Translations of the Bible

See also: The promise of a new age 178–81 ▪ The origins of modern political Zionism 196–97 ▪ The Protestant Reformation 230–37 ▪ The rise of Islamic revivalism 286–90 ▪ The compatibility of faith 291

groups seceded from the community, perhaps to be served by a more orthodox rabbi.

Questioning theology

Theological innovation led to liturgical reform and the publication of a new Reform prayer book in Hamburg in 1818. Scholars and rabbis, such as Abraham Geiger, now began to question key theological assumptions. Geiger recognized historical precedents for modifying Jewish tradition to adjust to new conditions, and suggested that some observances could be altered to be compatible with modern ways of living.

Some of Judaism's traditional theology was abandoned too. The German reformers no longer felt that they could pray for a messiah in the form of one person who would return the people to the Land of Israel to rebuild the Temple and restore the priestly sacrificial cult. Instead, they replaced the idea of the messiah with one of the messianic ideal – peace for every nation on earth – that every Jew

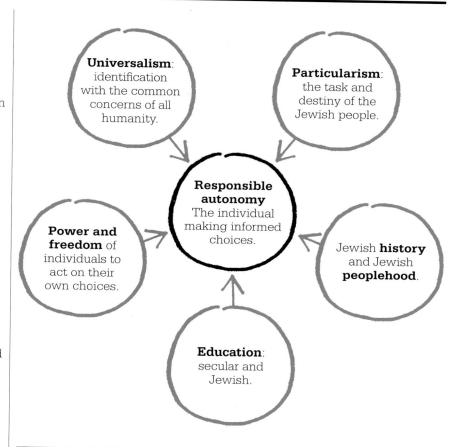

Universalism: identification with the common concerns of all humanity.

Particularism: the task and destiny of the Jewish people.

Responsible autonomy: The individual making informed choices.

Power and freedom of individuals to act on their own choices.

Jewish **history** and Jewish **peoplehood**.

Education: secular and Jewish.

A minority is always compelled to think. That is the blessing of being in the minority.
Leo Baeck, progressive rabbi

would work to bring about. Even more daring was the new idea that the Jews were no longer in exile but could realize their Jewish destiny as citizens of a modern nation.

This dream was in some ways short-lived. For many there was no real social integration without conversion to Christianity, and the Holocaust of Nazi Germany and World War II made clear the limits of hope for an enlightened humanity.

Religious autonomy

There is a tension in progressive Judaism, as in other strands of the religion today, between being part of a nation and community (universalism), and having a unique destiny (particularism). What differs for progressive Jews is probably the modern focus on autonomy – their freedom to determine how they live their Jewish lives. Progressive Judaism teaches that responsible autonomy requires making choices based on ethics, Jewish education, and commitment to the Jewish people, with reverence for the past and a commitment to the future.

Jewish theologies continue to develop. Although monotheism remains a fundamental tenet » of the faith, progressive Judaism's theology extends the notion of a "commanding" God to the idea of an ongoing relationship with God, in which each Jew exercises his or her individual freedom. The "mitzvot", or commandments, are expressions of this relationship.

The concept of monism

Another group of progressive thinkers believes God to be an inseparable part of the self, rather than an external divinity. Some have absorbed the views of Jewish mystics, who understand the entire creation as taking place within God, which means that everything *is* God. Monotheism, or the belief in one god, becomes monism, meaning that there is only one-ness, and that this one-ness *is* God. These theological transformations within progressive Judaism mean that the role of the individual and the commandments can no longer be seen as fixed. Along with the newly defined

relationship between individual, God, and the commandments, Jews in the progressive movement also came to review conventional interpretations of the Hebrew Bible. They now regard it as a composite text from different historical periods – a written record of a human encounter with the divine, rather than the recorded words of God, meaning that its authority is not straightforward. Since God's intentions were not fixed once in time, the revelation could be considered continuous.

In a similar way, progressive Judaism recognizes the impact of history and human authorship on the development of Jewish law, or Halachah, which is traditionally rooted in biblical commandments and the rulings of classical rabbis. Halachah has undergone transformation in both progressive and Orthodox communities. One progressive view sees Halachah as undergoing continual adaptation to respond to ethical and practical

problems in the contemporary Jewish world. This view takes account of modern scientific developments, such as stem cell research, and is strongly guided by contemporary ethics, tackling issues such as care at the end of life. Other progressives describe a post-Halachic Judaism, perhaps identifying more closely with the ancient Hebrew prophets and an ethically driven Prophetic Judaism.

Rituals and observances

Modern approaches to ritual practice also reflect the idea of Judaism's continuing evolution, stipulating that divine authority is not limited to the Torah. The Sabbath (Shabbat), for instance, is considered a day of rest and holiness distinct from the working week. Progressive Jews respect the Sabbath, and are still likely to begin it with lighting Shabbat candles on Friday evening, although not all will insist that this be done before sunset, if it occurs very early. They may also reject the traditional prohibition on driving a motor car to the synagogue on Shabbat.

Dietary laws

In matters of *kashrut* (dietary law), some progressive Jews might dismiss all the rules as antiquated, whereas others might avoid the meats that are forbidden in the Torah but not concern themselves with the later rabbinic prohibitions concerning the separation of meat and milk products and the utensils used in the preparation of each. Some might focus instead on the discipline of *kashrut* as a way of expressing consciousness of what they eat, perhaps extending this to eating organic, fair-trade products or food with low "food miles". Others might view vegetarianism as a proper or suitable (from the

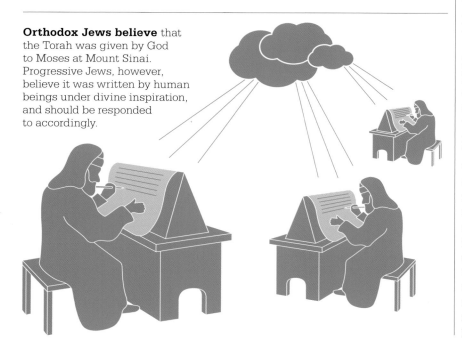

Orthodox Jews believe that the Torah was given by God to Moses at Mount Sinai. Progressive Jews, however, believe it was written by human beings under divine inspiration, and should be responded to accordingly.

Progressive communities mark the time when a girl becomes bat mitvah (a daughter of the commandment); traditional custom prohibited women from taking part in religious services.

meaning of the Hebrew word "*kashrut*") diet and therefore as a modern, progressive expression of the observance.

Liturgy for today

Historically, Jewish liturgy has tended to lengthen over the centuries as new prayers have been added. Progressive services retain the framework and core prayers, but remove some repetition; prayers, and their translations, reflect a reworking of concepts that do not accord with progressive beliefs, such as the resurrection of the dead, the restoration of the temple, and animal sacrifices. Many progressive liturgies avoid feudal and gendered language both for God and the community, referring, for example, to the "Eternal" instead of the "Lord", "ancestors" instead of "forefathers", and including the biblical matriarchs along with the patriarchs.

Novel liturgical compositions may sometimes be included, such as poetry or prayers of interfaith understanding, and a shorter weekly passage from the Torah read. In many congregations, services are conducted in Hebrew as well as the vernacular, and are often accompanied by music. Progressive Jews observe the Hebrew festival dates given in the Torah, as is the practice of all Jews in the Land of Israel. This is in contrast to Orthodox and Conservative Jews in the diaspora, who traditionally extend the duration of festivals by a day, as was the custom outside Israel before the Hebrew calendar was fixed in 358 CE.

Women and men in progressive communities generally enjoy full equality in communal leadership (including ordination as rabbis) and in ritual life, whether in the synagogue or home. Girls therefore celebrate their ritual adulthood at the age of 13 (becoming bat mitzvah) just as boys do (becoming bar mitzvah) by reading publicly from the Torah and even leading the congregation in prayer.

Progressive Judaism today

The core ideals of German Reform Judaism took root, and led to the growth of progressive Jewish communities in most countries in the world today. In the UK, Reform Judaism and Liberal Judaism emerged, and, with German Jewish immigration to the USA, an American Reform movement came into being there. This gave rise to other progressive communities in the US, such as Reconstructionist Judaism and Conservative Judaism, which is modern in its theology but traditional in its practices. Other progressive forms of Judaism are found worldwide, including in Israel, where the faith tends towards a more traditional expression of Judaism than in the diaspora.

A recent worldwide resurgence of interest in Jewish learning across the religious spectrum has led to an engagement with the study of classical texts in Hebrew for their spiritual, literary, and ethical value. Today's believers may draw from a wide range of Jewish and secular influences, and are therefore less likely to form a lifelong commitment to only one of the Jewish movements. ■

The past has a vote, but not a veto.
Dr Mordecai M. Kaplan, Progressive theologian

IF YOU WILL IT, IT IS NO DREAM

THE ORIGINS OF MODERN POLITICAL ZIONISM

IN CONTEXT

KEY FIGURE
Theodor Herzl

WHEN AND WHERE
1896, Austria-Hungary

BEFORE
586 BCE King Nebuchadnezzar of Babylon destroys the Temple in Jerusalem and drives the Jews into exile. From 538 BCE the Jews start to return to the Land of Israel, in accordance with a decree from Persian emperor Cyrus the Great.

70 CE The Romans destroy the second Temple; the Jews are exiled again.

635 The Islamic Caliphate conquers Palestine; in 1516 the Ottoman Empire takes control of the region.

AFTER
1882–1948 Jews from the diaspora immigrate to the Land of Israel in waves.

1948 The State of Israel is founded.

The solution to the "Jewish question" is not assimilation, but the **establishment of a Jewish nation state**.

Since being driven into exile, Jews have dreamed of **returning to Zion**, the Land of Israel.

This requires **lobbying** of the international community…

… and if there are sufficient numbers of Jewish people who want it, **it can be achieved**.

If you will it, it is no dream.

Ever since their expulsion from their homeland by the Babylonians and the Romans, many among the Jewish diaspora had dreamed of a return to Eretz Yisrael, the Land of Israel, also known as Zion after Mount Zion in Jerusalem. It was not until the late 19th century, however, that their hopes were consolidated into a political movement, Zionism, which aimed to establish a nation state in Palestine for the Jewish people.

During the Haskalah, or "Jewish Enlightenment", Jewish thinkers inspired by Moses Mendelssohn (p.189) had urged Jews to assimilate themselves

See also: God's covenant with Israel 168–75 ▪ Faith and the state 189
▪ Ras Tafari is our Saviour 314–15

> I consider the Jewish
> question neither a social
> nor a religious one…
> It is a national question.
> **Theodor Herzl**

into the culture of their adopted countries as a way to overcome the persecution they had suffered. In much of western Europe and the USA, emancipation had allowed middle-class Jews, in particular, to integrate into society.

One such Jew, the journalist and writer Theodor Herzl, firmly believed in Jewish assimilation, until he experienced extreme anti-Semitic feeling in France, an ostensibly liberal country. He came to realize that ghettoization and anti-Semitism were inevitable: Jews tended to gravitate to places where they were not likely to be persecuted, but once they had immigrated in significant numbers to these places, anti-Jewish feeling arose, and persecution followed. Similarly, even where Jews had tried to blend in with the local community and behave as loyal citizens, they were still treated as aliens and driven into isolation. He concluded that the solution to these problems lay not in assimilation, but in the large-scale separation of Jewish people into one place. Anti-Semitism could not be defeated or eradicated, but could be avoided by establishing a Jewish nation state.

A Jewish homeland

In Herzl's short book *The Jewish State*, published in 1896, which he described as a "proposal of a modern solution for the Jewish question", he set out the argument for establishing a Jewish homeland. The obvious choice for this was the Land of Israel, then a part of Ottoman-ruled Palestine. This proposal marked the beginning of modern Zionism as a political movement, rather than a theological aspiration. The following year, 1897, Herzl set up an international conference, the First Zionist Congress, at which it became clear that the political will for a Jewish state existed, and was achievable if Jews in suffcient numbers were to put pressure on the international community for its foundation. A phrase from Herzl's novel *Old New Land* was adopted as the Zionist movement's rallying cry: "If you will it, it is no dream". ▪

Israel's flag, adopted in 1948, is derived from a design produced for the First Zionist Congress. It is inspired by the tallit, or blue-bordered prayer shawl, and the Star of David.

Theodor Herzl

Theodor Herzl was born in 1860 in Pest, part of modern-day Budapest. He moved to Vienna with his family when he was 18. There he studied law, and, in 1839, after a brief legal career, he moved to Paris. Here he worked as a correspondent for the *Neue Freie Presse* (New Free Press) and as a theatre writer.

After reporting on the Dreyfus Affair of the 1890s, in which a Jewish officer was framed for treason by the military, he concluded that the establishment of a Jewish homeland in Zion, the Land of Israel, was essential. He outlined his arguments in *The Jewish State* and elaborated on them in his novel, *Old New Land*. Herzl worked tirelessly to promote the ideals of Zionism: he organized the first congress of Zionism in Basel, Switzerland, in 1897, and was president of the World Zionist Organization until his death in 1904. In 1949 his remains were moved from Vienna and reburied in Jerusalem.

Key works

1896 *The Jewish State*
1902 *Old New Land*

WHERE WAS GOD DURING THE HOLOCAUST?
A CHALLENGE TO THE COVENANT

IN CONTEXT

KEY MOVEMENT
Holocaust theology

WHEN AND WHERE
Mid-20th century, Europe

BEFORE
1516 The Republic of Venice establishes the ghetto, which becomes the model for ghettos created across Europe to isolate Jewish communities.

1850s Anti-Semitism in Europe takes on a more secular, racist stance.

1880s Beginning of a series of pogroms – violent anti-Jewish mob attacks – in Russia.

1930s Hitler becomes German Chancellor, and begins a campaign of harassment and genocide against Jews.

AFTER
1945 Jews are liberated from concentration camps at the end of World War II and resettled, many in the USA and later in the newly formed State of Israel.

E ver since their expulsion from Israel by the Romans in 70 CE, the Jews have endured exile and persecution. However, the Holocaust, or Sho'ah ("catastrophe") – the systematic genocide of around 6 million Jews, or two-thirds of the European Jewish population – was an event of unprecedented horror that tested the faith of the Jewish people in their covenant with God. This challenge raised an important question: was the Holocaust God's doing, or did he stand aside and allow it to happen? Jewish theology struggled to provide answers, and a number of Jews lost faith, believing God had abandoned his people.

The greatest test
Different groups of Jews offered a range of other interpretations of the Holocaust. Some saw it as being no different from the persecutions they had already suffered, except in scale. They defined it as an extreme example of suffering in the world, a test of faith, and a revelation calling for an affirmation of survival;

Never shall I forget those moments that murdered my God and my soul.
Elie Wiesel

others saw it as punishment for the sin of abandoning God and his laws, which God had responded to with his own temporary absence. A further group saw the Sho'ah as separate from God, an example of human free will and its fallibility, perhaps explained in kabbalistic terms as a stage of God's *tzimtzum*, or contraction, from the world.

A whole new field of "Holocaust theology" has since emerged, examining these various responses, and reappraising the covenant in the light of the Sho'ah. ∎

See also: God's covenant with Israel 168–75 ∎ Mysticism and the kabbalah 186–87 ∎ The origins of modern political Zionism 196–97

WOMEN CAN BE RABBIS
GENDER AND THE COVENANT

IN CONTEXT

KEY MOVEMENT
Feminism in Judaism

WHEN AND WHERE
Late 20th century, USA and Europe

BEFORE
19th century The Reform movement emerges in Judaism, and with it the question of women taking a fuller role in the covenant.

1893 The National Council of Jewish Women is founded after the World Parliament of Religions in Chicago.

1912 The Women's Zionist Organization of America, Hadassah, is founded.

1922 The idea of ordaining women rabbis is discussed at the Central Conference of American Rabbis, but no agreement is reached.

1935 The first woman rabbi, Regina Jonas, is ordained in Berlin, Germany.

Paradoxically, while Jewish identity is traditionally transmitted matrilineally (p.175), women have been excluded from participation in the observance of Judaism for much of its history. Until the 19th century, the idea of women reading from the Torah to a congregation, for example, or leading prayer as a cantor was considered heretical; the notion of a female rabbi was unthinkable.

However, with the foundation of liberal Reform Judaism, and especially in the progressive Reconstructionist movement, the subject of women's role in the covenant became an issue of increasing importance. The first woman rabbi was ordained in the Reform movement in Germany in 1935. In the USA, the UK, and elsewhere in Europe, real pressure for change came with the rise of feminism in the 1970s. The Reform movement in the USA ordained its first woman rabbi in 1972, and three years later a female cantor. Following this lead, other branches of Judaism began to initiate reforms, allowing women to participate in rituals and as witnesses, and bringing in bat mitzvah ceremonies (the female equivalent of the bar mitzvah). Women were finally admitted into rabbinical schools in the 1980s. Today, only Orthodox Judaism still holds out against the ordination of women rabbis, but in all branches of the faith, women are taking an increasingly active, if not leading, role in the synagogue. ∎

The festival of Hanukkah is celebrated here by Barbara Aiello, the first female rabbi in Italy. Granting girls equal access to religious education has transformed their role in Judaism.

See also: God's covenant with Israel 168–75 ∎ Writing the Oral Law 182–83 ∎ Progressive Judaism 190–95

CHRIST
FROM 1ST CENTURY CE

ANITY

Jesus is born in Roman Judea: he is believed by Christians to be the Son of God born to the Virgin Mary.

Jesus is crucified by Judea's Roman rulers. Christians believe that he rises again three days later and ascends to heaven.

The Roman emperor Constantine issues the Edict of Milan, allowing the **Christian faith to be freely practised**.

Christianity becomes the **official religion of the Roman Empire**; converts include Augustine of Hippo.

c.4 BCE   **c.30–36 CE**   **313 CE**   **380 CE**

c.26 CE   **CA. 44–68 CE**   **325 CE**   **1054**

Jesus is baptized by John the Baptist and his ministry begins.

All but one of the apostles, John, are **martyred**.

The **Nicene Creed** is established at the Council of Nicea and later ratified as the universal creed of the Christian Church.

During the **Great Schism**, Christianity is divided into Western (Roman Catholic) and Eastern (Orthodox) branches.

C hristianity takes its name from the Greek word *christós*, a translation of the Hebrew word for "messiah", or anointed one. This title was given to Jesus by a Jewish sect who considered him to be the Messiah – the saviour prophesied in the Tanakh, the Hebrew Bible – and the Son of God in human form. Christians believe that Jesus's arrival on earth heralded a "New Covenant" or New Testament with God that followed the Old Testament covenants between God and the Jewish people.

The main beliefs of Christianity are based on the life and teachings of Jesus as recorded by his followers in the 1st century CE in the Gospels (meaning "good news") and the Epistles (or letters) of the New Testament.

Christians give great significance to the story of Jesus's crucifixion, resurrection, and ascension to heaven. It is the central belief of Christianity that Jesus suffered, died, and was buried, before being resurrected from the dead – in order to grant salvation to those who believe in him – and that he then ascended to heaven to rule alongside God the Father.

Implicit in this belief is the acceptance that Jesus was, as the Son of God, God incarnate, both human and divine, and not merely a prophet. This led to the concept of the Trinity, that the one God exists in three distinct forms – the Father, the Son, and the Holy Spirit.

The life of Jesus also provides a framework for the rituals of Christian worship, the most important of which are known as

sacraments. Especially significant are the sacraments of baptism and the Eucharist – the taking of bread and wine, as Jesus instructed his followers at the Last Supper. Others include confirmation, holy orders (the ordination of ministers), confession, the anointing of the sick, and matrimony – although not all of these are accepted by every Christian denomination.

Persecution to adoption

From its beginnings in Roman Judea to its status as the religion with most adherents in the world today, Christianity has shaped the culture of much of Western civilization. The early Christians were persecuted by both Jewish authorities and the Roman Empire, and many were put to death. Nevertheless, the faith persisted

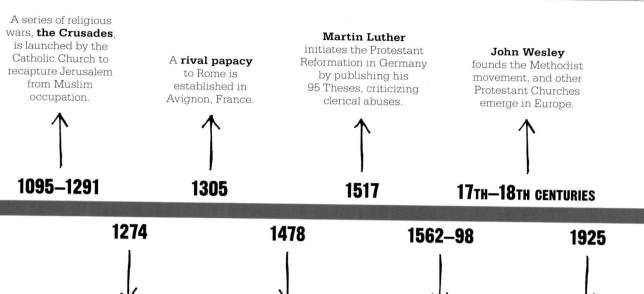

A series of religious wars, **the Crusades**, is launched by the Catholic Church to recapture Jerusalem from Muslim occupation.

A **rival papacy** to Rome is established in Avignon, France.

Martin Luther initiates the Protestant Reformation in Germany by publishing his 95 Theses, criticizing clerical abuses.

John Wesley founds the Methodist movement, and other Protestant Churches emerge in Europe.

1095–1291   **1305**   **1517**   **17TH–18TH CENTURIES**

1274   **1478**   **1562–98**   **1925**

Thomas Aquinas publishes *Summa Theologica*, which becomes the basis for official Catholic dogma.

The Spanish Inquisition, the most notorious of the inquisitions instituted to suppress heresy, is founded by King Ferdinand and Queen Isabella.

Catholics and Protestants wage war in France (known as the Wars of Religion).

The Scopes **Monkey Trial** pits evolutionary theory against the Biblical Creation.

under the leadership of the early Church. Gradually, Christianity came to be tolerated by Roman leaders, and, after the Council of Nicaea, where a universal Christian creed was agreed, it was eventually adopted as the official religion of the Roman Empire in 380 CE.

From then on, Christianity became a powerful force in the political and cultural life of Europe and the Middle East. Its influence spread rapidly and produced such thinkers as Augustine of Hippo, a convert to Christianity, who integrated Greek philosophical ideas into the doctrine. With the decline and fall of the Roman Empire, power in Europe moved to the popes, who were considered the natural successors of the apostles and the first bishops. In the 11th century, a split in the

Church over papal authority – the so-called Great Schism – divided Christianity into two distinct branches, the Western (Roman Catholic) Church and the Eastern (Orthodox) Church. Christianity also faced a challenge from the Islamic Empire from the 8th century on, and, through the 12th and 13th centuries, fought a series of Crusades to recapture Jerusalem from the Muslims.

Church power

The Catholic Church retained its influence in Europe, and its dogma dominated learning and culture throughout the Middle Ages. Philosophical and scientific ideas were often seen as heretical, and even the great Thomas Aquinas found his application of Aristotelian reasoning to Christian theology

initially condemned: only centuries after his death was it adopted as official Catholic dogma.

The Renaissance of the 14th–15th centuries heralded a new challenge to the authority of the Church in the form of humanism and the beginnings of a scientific Golden Age. The revival of interest in classical learning prompted criticism of the Catholic Church, and the Protestant Reformation was triggered by publication of Martin Luther's 95 Theses in 1517. Protestantism began to flourish in northern Europe and paved the way for new Christian denominations. Of the roughly 2.2 billion Christians worldwide today (around a third of the world's population), more than half are Catholic, roughly one third are Protestant, and the remainder are Orthodox. ■

JESUS IS THE BEGINNING OF THE END

JESUS'S MESSAGE TO THE WORLD

IN CONTEXT

KEY FIGURE
Jesus of Nazareth

WHEN AND WHERE
4 BCE–30 CE, Judea

BEFORE
c.700 BCE The Jewish prophet Isaiah foretells the coming rule of God.

6th century BCE During the exile of the Israelites in Babylon, the prophet Daniel has a vision of the end of oppressive earthly kingdoms.

c.450 BCE The arrival of the "day of the Lord" is a key theme for Jewish prophets.

AFTER
1st century CE The first Christians take Jesus's message throughout the Roman Empire.

20th century The kingdom of God becomes a major theme in Christian theology and ethics.

In 63 BCE, the Roman general Pompey conquered Jerusalem, putting an end to a century of Judean self-rule and turning the region into a Roman client state. Rome was the last in a long line of invading forces, which stretched back over 500 years and included Babylon, Persia, Greece, Egypt, and Syria. This repeated loss of sovereignty had dented national pride and caused religious consternation, challenging the Jewish concept of themselves as God's chosen people.

Key Jewish religious texts from previous centuries (such as the prophetic work of Isaiah) had promised that a time would come

See also: The promise of a new age 178–81 ▪ Jesus's divine identity 208
▪ Entering into the faith 224–27 ▪ Awaiting the Day of Judgment 312–13

There is a **lack of justice and peace** in kingdoms ruled by humans.

God **promised to fulfil our hopes** for justice and peace **at the end of time**, in a kingdom He rules.

Jesus has taught and shown us how to experience the **forgiveness, peace, and justice** that God promised.

Jesus's ministry therefore marks the beginning of the kingdom of God: the **beginning of the end**.

Jesus of Nazareth

Jesus was born in Bethlehem, in the Roman province of Judea, in around 4 BCE, with the extraordinary claim that his mother Mary was a virgin. Little is known about Jesus's early life, but it is most likely that he was schooled in the Jewish scriptures and religion. It is believed that he may have shared his father's occupation as a carpenter, and lived and worked in Nazareth.

When Jesus was around 30 years old, he embarked upon a ministry of teaching and healing across the area where he lived. According to the Gospels, he drew huge crowds with his engaging stories, radical teaching, and astonishing miracles, but paid special attention to 12 followers, or disciples. However, his message about God's kingdom soon attracted the censure of the authorities. He was betrayed by Judas, one of his disciples, and arrested and condemned to death on fabricated charges. Three days after Jesus had been crucified, reports were made that his tomb had been found empty and that he had appeared to his disciples, resurrected from the dead.

when Israel's God would be the acknowledged ruler of the whole world. He would bring in a system of justice and peace for all through his appointed representative, known as the Messiah (meaning "anointed one"). This would be the climax of world history, so the prophecy said: the end of the old, existing era and the beginning of God's era. However, given the new Roman occupation, this kingdom of God seemed a distant dream.

Announcing a new world

In around the late 20s CE, a Jewish rabbi called Jesus began a brief, but extraordinary, ministry throughout Roman-occupied Israel. »

Preaching to his band of disciples, Jesus gave the core message of his ministry: the awaited arrival of God's kingdom had become a reality.

Jesus's core message was that God's long-awaited kingdom was now arriving. Some people who heard his message thought that he intended to raise an army to expel the Romans. However, his goal was not Israel's political independence, but the liberation of the entire world from all evil. According to a collection of Jesus's teachings known as the Sermon on the Mount (found in the Gospel of St Matthew in the New Testament), Jesus announced that God's kingdom now held sway over both heaven and earth, and that under this new rule the distorted values of human kingdoms would be overturned. God's kingdom, he said, belonged not to the greedy, the self-assured, and the warriors, but to the poor, the meek, and the peacemakers.

All are welcome

Jesus's message was manifested in his actions. Centuries earlier, the Jewish prophet Isaiah had said that when God's kingdom came, there would be wonderful miracles of healing: the blind would be able to see, and the deaf able to hear that

God was now king, and the lame would jump for joy. The biblical accounts of Jesus's ministry are full of stories of healings just like these. In addition, Jesus said there was no longer any barrier to entering God's kingdom. Until that time, the Jewish faith had viewed non-Jews as beyond salvation, along with those people who failed to adhere to God's laws ("sinners"), but Jesus said that even these groups would be welcomed into the kingdom. Jesus demonstrated the forgiveness of sinners by sharing meals – one of the most intimate and meaningful of Jewish activities – with social outcasts and religious renegades. The future was likened to a banquet prepared by God, to which people from all over the world would be invited.

But people were confused: wasn't the kingdom of God supposed to be the climax of world history? If so, why did the world not end with Jesus's announcement? The answer that Jesus gave them was that the kingdom would not arrive all at once, as most people had expected. In one of his many

Jesus's miracles, such as the healing of the blind, affirmed that, just as Jesus went among the poor and the outcast, so God invited everyone, regardless of status, into his kingdom.

parables (stories used to illustrate his message) he compared God's kingdom to the yeast in a batch of dough. In another, he described the kingdom as acting like seeds sown in the ground. Both yeast and seeds take time to produce results, growing almost imperceptibly, but are slowly and surely at work.

A new religion

Jesus invited those who heard him to allow God's kingdom and its values into their own lives without delay. He taught that the kingdom of God is both now, and not yet, here, that it has begun and continues to grow whenever people choose to live by the rule of God, embracing his values and experiencing healing and forgiveness. However, Jesus also acknowledged that there would be a future moment when, at the climactic end of the present world order, God's rule would triumph over all other kingdoms. When this day of judgment arrived, it would be too late to decide to be part of

> Blessed are the poor in spirit, for theirs is the kingdom of heaven.
> **Jesus (Matthew 5:3)**

How can the end have a beginning? Jesus said that the final replacement of our present world with the kingdom of God would be delayed, giving people time to secure themselves a place in that kingdom by believing in him.

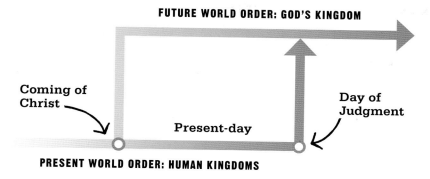

FUTURE WORLD ORDER: GOD'S KINGDOM

Coming of Christ

Present-day

Day of Judgment

PRESENT WORLD ORDER: HUMAN KINGDOMS

The time is fulfilled. God's kingdom is arriving! Turn around and believe the good news.
Jesus (Mark 1:15)

God's new world. This gave his message a note of urgency. People needed to make a decision now; far from being a distant dream, the end had already begun.

The idea that Jesus marked the "beginning of the end" led directly to the separation of Christianity from its Jewish roots. The early followers of Jesus claimed that they no longer had to wait to discover who God's Messiah would be, because Jesus was that Messiah – the one God had appointed to bring his kingdom to earth. However, Jesus's opponents refused to believe this and decided to silence him by killing him. When Jesus's followers did not give up their beliefs even after Jesus died, and in fact enlarged on them – by claiming that God had confounded Jesus's opponents by raising him from the dead – it became clear that their faith, led by a figure who could not be conquered by death, was something new and distinct within the catalogue of religions.

From the earliest days, Christianity has been defined by the conviction that Jesus's ministry was the beginning of the end. One of the key prayers of Christianity,

the Lord's Prayer, taught by Jesus himself, asks that God's kingdom come on earth "as it is in heaven." In offering this prayer, Christians are asking for the earthly advent of God's kingdom now, even as they wait for it to arrive in fullness at the end of present world history.

God's kingdom today
Historically, the Christian church has sometimes understood the "kingdom of God" or "kingdom of heaven" as a purely spiritual realm that leaves the physical world unaffected. But in the early 20th century, New Testament scholars began to take a new interest in the Jewish context of Jesus's ministry, and since then Jesus's message about the kingdom of God has had an especially prominent place in Christian theology. By paying closer attention to the background of Jesus's original message, the political and economic implications of the arrival of God's kingdom have become clearer. Christians now believe that the kingdom occurs wherever present reality and its values are transformed by the rule of God, a belief that has inspired many Christians to

champion movements for social change; for example, Martin Luther King and the civil rights movement in the United States, Gustavo Gutiérrez and the liberation of the poor in South America, and Desmond Tutu and the end of apartheid in South Africa.

The end of all things
The idea that Jesus's ministry marked the "beginning of the end" is known in theology by the term "inaugurated eschatology". Eschatology is a word that itself evolved from two Greek words meaning "last" and "study", and it refers to the study of the end of things, or the end of all things – the end of the world. To Christians, Jesus's message about God's kingdom gives Christianity an inaugurated eschatology: the end of all things was inaugurated (begun but not completed) by his message. The fact that the presence of God's kingdom today in the lives of Christians can still only be called the beginning of the end is a reminder that the Christian faith still looks towards a final, definitive action by God. ∎

GOD HAS SENT US HIS SON
JESUS'S DIVINE IDENTITY

IN CONTEXT

KEY BELIEVERS
Early Christians

WHEN AND WHERE
1st century CE, communities around the Mediterranean

BEFORE
From c.500 BCE Jewish scriptures use the term "son of God" to describe God's earthly representative.

c.30 CE Jesus is arrested and accused of blasphemy by the Jewish authorities for claiming to be the son of God. He is sent for trial by the Roman governor Pontius Pilate on charges of sedition, and condemned to death.

AFTER
325 CE The Nicene Creed states that Jesus is the divine Son of God, using the phrase "of one substance with the Father".

451 CE The Chalcedonian Creed affirms Jesus as both fully God and fully human.

Many ancient kings and emperors claimed that they had been adopted by the gods, thereby giving themselves divine legitimacy to rule. On their deaths, some, such as Julius Caesar, were elevated to divine status – a process that was known as apotheosis – and worshipped.

In the Gospels, Jesus calls God his Father many times, in ways that are open to many interpretations, from the broadest – that God, as the creator, is the "Father" of all

You are the Christ, the Son of the living God.
Matthew 16:15

humankind – through the symbolic to the literal. The last of these was claimed by the first Christians as the truth. They pointed to the extraordinary miracles of Jesus's ministry decribed in the Gospels, and especially to his resurrection from the dead, as evidence of his unique place in God's plan.

God has become human
The early Christians also claimed that Jesus's divine status was unlike that of other rulers. Jesus was not adopted by God as a reward for his obedience; rather, Jesus had always been God's Son, even from before his birth, and so he shared God's divine nature throughout his human life.

This idea, known as the incarnation, became a central belief of Christianity. It is the opposite of apotheosis; in the incarnation, the eternally divine Son of God took on humanity in the person of Jesus. God had sent his divine Son into the world as a human in order to bring his kingdom from heaven to earth. ∎

See also: Beliefs for new societies 56–57 ▪ The promise of a new age 178–81 ▪ A divine trinity 212–19 ▪ The Prophet and the origins of Islam 252–53

THE BLOOD OF THE MARTYRS IS THE SEED OF THE CHURCH
DYING FOR THE MESSAGE

IN CONTEXT

KEY DEVELOPMENT
Persecution of the early Christians

WHEN AND WHERE
c.64–313 CE, Roman Empire

BEFORE
c.30 CE Jesus is crucified, having told his followers to expect persecution in turn.

1st century CE In response to oppression by the Roman authorities in Jerusalem, Christianity becomes an underground movement, and Christians leave the city and spread out across the Empire.

AFTER
3rd century A breakaway Christian sect opposes readmitting to the Church those who had renounced their faith to avoid persecution.

16th century Catholic and Protestant factions in Europe persecute each other, each seeing their suffering as proof of their faithfulness.

O n 9 March 203 CE, two young mothers – a Roman noblewoman, Perpetua, and her slave Felicity – were led into the arena at Carthage with other Christians, where they were flogged, mauled by wild beasts, and finally executed. The story of these two female martyrs was recorded in *The Passion of Perpetua and Felicity*, in order to inspire other Christians to stay committed to their faith even when threatened with persecution and death.

Death brings life
The theologian Tertullian, writing in Carthage at that time, developed a Christian understanding of martyrdom, noting that "The blood of the Christians is the seed". The Roman emperors intended their waves of persecution to deter citizens from embracing a faith that put the authority of Jesus above that of the state. However, as Tertullian argued, far from being an obstacle to the growth of Christianity, persecution helped it to spread. The fact that Christians

The early martyrs went to their deaths willingly, believing that their example would "seed" Christianity's message into other hearts and minds.

were willing to be put to death, rather than renounce their belief that Jesus was the world's divinely appointed and rightful ruler, both intrigued and attracted non-believers.

This understanding of martyrdom assisted the growth of Christianity throughout history, because it gave Christians the confidence that even the most violent opposition to their message was not a sign of failure, but rather the seed of success. ∎

See also: God's covenant with Israel 168–75 ∙ Faith and the state 189 ∙ The Protestant Reformation 230–37 ∙ The rise of Islamic revivalism 286–90

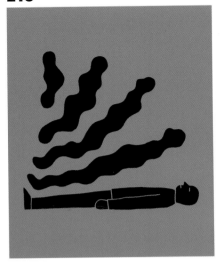

THE BODY MAY DIE BUT THE SOUL WILL LIVE ON
IMMORTALITY IN CHRISTIANITY

IN CONTEXT

KEY FIGURE
Origen

WHEN AND WHERE
3rd century CE, Egypt and Palestine

BEFORE
4th century BCE The Greek philosopher Plato popularizes Socratic teaching that death is the separation of the immortal soul from the mortal body.

c.30 CE At the time of Jesus's death, Jewish thought is divided: the Pharisees believe in an actual, bodily resurrection after death for God's faithful, while the Sadducee sect denies any form of afterlife.

AFTER
13th century Dante's *Divine Comedy* encapsulates the medieval view of the soul's journey after death.

1513 The Fifth Lateran Council of the Church declares the immortality of the soul to be orthodox Christian belief.

God **does not change**.

↓

God's relationship with humans therefore will not change.

↓

Human bodies die, so God's unchanging relationship cannot be with them.

↓

Humans must have **immortal souls**, so that their relationship with God can go on.

↓

The body may die but the soul will live on.

What happens when we die? Do we continue to exist in some form or does our entire being disintegrate like our bodies? Many thinkers in the ancient world considered these questions and the issues arising from them. Greek thought was influential in the Roman Empire, and Plato's ideas on these subjects gained widespread support in the centuries before Jesus's birth, death, and resurrection.

Plato's thinking was dualist. He believed there were two parts to human life: the physical body, which constantly changes and eventually dies; and the thinking soul, which exists eternally.

In the third century CE, the theologian Origen of Alexandria explained elements of the Christian message using terms from Greek philosophy. In particular, he developed Plato's thinking into a Christian understanding of the soul that would last for centuries.

Only souls matter
Like Plato, Origen believed that while human bodies are mortal and die, souls are immortal. For Origen, however, the immortality of the soul is a direct implication

See also: Physical and mental discipline 112–13 ▪ Man as a manifestation of God 188 ▪ The ultimate reward for the righteous 279

According to Origen, the soul is the part of us that returns to God after death. Artists found this hard to convey without giving the soul, and indeed God, a human appearance; this 16th-century panel shows St Paul and the Trinity.

of God's unchanging nature. Since God cannot change, the relationship he has with humans cannot end once their bodies disintegrate. Therefore there must be a part of the human that does not die, and this is the soul. A typical Platonist, Origen thought the soul was far more important than the body, which was a distraction from a spiritual life.

Hell and heaven
Origen's teaching shaped the popular Christian understanding of salvation from that moment on. Unlike the Platonists, the writers of the Hebrew Bible had not separated the soul from the body. If there was going to be any life after death at all, then a person's body would need to be raised from the dead to go along with its soul. Jesus's bodily resurrection from the dead

showed that this was possible for those who believed in him. However, after Origen, less emphasis was placed on bodily resurrection, and much Christian teaching focused exclusively on the state of the soul before death and its fate after death. The souls of those who had rejected God were considered to be spiritually dead, and would live out their immortality in hell. However, the souls of those who had embraced Jesus's message would ascend to a state of perfection with God in heaven.

A modern perspective
Recent Christian thinkers have suggested that Origen relied too heavily on Platonism. A growing movement in Christian theology rejects dualism (the separation of body and soul), teaching instead that the life of the soul after death is possible only if God also resurrects a person's body. Another widespread belief today is that of "conditional immortality": immortality is only given to those who have believed in Jesus, and not to everyone. ▪

…the soul, having a substance and life of its own, shall, after its departure from the world, be rewarded according to its deserts.
Origen

Origen

Origen was born to Christian parents in Alexandria, North Africa, in around 185 CE. When Origen was 17, his father was martyred, and Origen took up a life of disciplined study, becoming a respected thinker both inside and outside the Church. The bishop of Alexandria appointed him head of the catechetical school, instructing new Christian converts before their baptism. After a dispute with the bishop, Origen moved to Caesarea in Palestine, where his writings included an eight-volume defence of Christianity against one of its critics, the philosopher Celsus.

Around 250 CE, Origen was tortured by the Roman authorities in an attempt to make him renounce his faith. Origen refused, and was released. However, he died a few years later, in 254 CE, most likely as a result of injuries sustained while he was being persecuted for his faith.

Key works

c.220 *De Principiis (First Principles)*: the first systematic rendition of Christian theology
248 *On Prayer*; *On Martyrdom*; *Against Celsus*

GOD IS THREE AND GOD IS ONE

A DIVINE TRINITY

IN CONTEXT

KEY TEXT
The Nicene Creed

WHEN AND WHERE
**4th century CE, Nicea
and Constantinople**

BEFORE
500 BCE Jewish daily prayer
includes the Shema, affirming
that God is one (monotheism).

1st century CE Christians
worship Jesus and the Holy
Spirit with the God of Israel.

c.200 CE Tertullian explains
the Trinity as "three persons
of one substance".

AFTER
c.400 CE St Augustine's *The
Trinity (De Trinitate)*, gives an
analogy of the Trinity based on
three elements of human life:
mind, knowledge, and love.

20th century "Trinitarian
theology", starting with the
doctrine of the Trinity, thrives
with theologian Karl Barth.

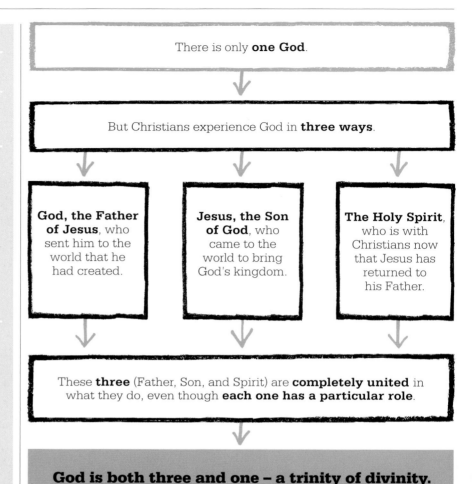

There is only **one God**.

But Christians experience God in **three ways**.

God, the Father of Jesus, who sent him to the world that he had created.

Jesus, the Son of God, who came to the world to bring God's kingdom.

The Holy Spirit, who is with Christians now that Jesus has returned to his Father.

These **three** (Father, Son, and Spirit) are **completely united** in what they do, even though **each one has a particular role**.

God is both three and one – a trinity of divinity.

In a maths test, it is safe to assume that 1 + 1 + 1 = 3, but not so in a theology exam. One of the most notorious conundrums of the Christian faith is that to describe God, 1 + 1 + 1 = 1, not 3. Some of the greatest Christian theologians have struggled to explain how God can be three distinct persons (Father, Son, and Holy Spirit) yet remain only one God. However, this idea, which is known as the doctrine of the Trinity, is a central plank in Christian theology, setting its understanding of God apart from other religions.

A standardised way of speaking about God, known as the doctrine of the Trinity, was settled upon by members of the early Church some 300 years after the death of Jesus. A range of ideas had emerged as the faith spread across the Roman Empire and beyond, so Church leaders articulated the doctrine as a response.

Rooted in Judaism
The roots of Christianity are in Judaism – the religion into which Jesus was born and of which he claimed to be the Messiah. Just as

Judaism is monotheistic, so is Christianity – Christians, like Jews, believe in just one God. But how could the first Christians claim to be monotheistic if they worshipped both Jesus as God and the God whom Jesus called Father? And how did this relate to the Spirit, whom Jesus said he would send, so that God's presence would remain with Christians? Since the Spirit was also worshipped as God, did this mean that Christians were "tri-theists" (believing in three gods) rather than monotheists? The doctrine of the Trinity is an

See also: From monolatry to monotheism 176–77 ▪ Jesus's divine identity 208 ▪ The unity of divinity is necessary 280–81

The Trinity is portrayed as Son, Father, and dove – inspired by Jesus' baptism, when the Holy Spirit "descended on him like a dove" – in this 17th-century fresco.

attempt to answer these tricky questions, with the assertion that Christians worship one God in three persons.

What Jesus taught

As the Gospel writers recorded, Jesus referred to God as his Father throughout his ministry. The implication of this teaching was clear, Jesus was God's Son and he claimed the same divinity as God. He also spoke about his close relationship to the Spirit: "the Holy Spirit, whom the Father will send in my name, will teach you all things and will remind you of everything I have said to you" (John 14:26). Jesus again hinted at the shared divinity of the three persons of God in the Great Commission, a statement in which he commanded his followers to "make disciples of all nations, baptizing them in the name of the Father and of the Son and of the Holy Spirit" (Matthew 28:19). In accordance with these teachings, the early Christians worshipped Jesus. After all, he had made it possible for everyone who believed to be part of God's family (a status previously only accorded to the Jews) forgiving their past rebellion against God, and assuring them that they would be included when God brought peace and justice to the world. Jesus had said and done things that only God could say and do: as he had implied during his life, Jesus was God.

Similar but not the same

The doctrine of the Trinity emerged in response to a series of other answers that the early Christians »

We believe in one God, the Father almighty … and in one Lord Jesus Christ, the only begotten Son of God … and in the Holy Spirit, the Lord and lifegiver…
Nicene Creed

The Nicene Creed

By the start of the 4th century CE, Christianity had spread across the Roman Empire. With such a wide appeal, it was increasingly difficult to establish a uniform understanding of the faith. The Emperor Constantine saw the problems these differences were causing, so he called a council of Church bishops from all over his empire to meet in Nicea in 325 CE. He encouraged the bishops to agree a statement of faith – in particular, to define the nature of the Trinity – that would be acceptable to all Christians. This creed would be recited in churches and would help steer Christians away from heretical beliefs, especially those of the Arians (see p.216). In 381 CE, Emperor Theodosius called another council, this time in Constantinople. The 325 CE creed was clarified and expanded, resulting in the "Nicene Creed", which is still recited today in churches all over the world.

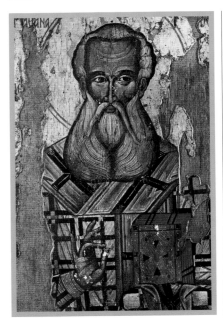

St Athanasius of Alexandria is remembered for his staunch theological defence of Trinitarianism against the teachings of Arianism. He had a key role in drafting the Nicene Creed.

judged to be wrong, or "heretical". One such idea was Arianism – the theology of Arius (c.250–336 CE), a Christian leader in Alexandria, Egypt – which emphasized monotheism so strongly that it denied the deity of the Son and, by implication, of the Spirit. For Arius, only the Father was truly God. Although the Son was to be honoured for having the closest possible relationship with the Father, the Son was still only a representative of the Father's deity, and did not share that deity.

This tallied with some aspects of accepted Christian thinking: one of the essential characteristics of God was that he was uncreated – he had no beginning as well as no end to his life. The Arians therefore argued that since children have to be born, the Son of God could not possess all the essential characteristics of God, because, as a Son, he must have been born. An Arian dictum about the Son of God stated that "there was once when he was not": there must have been a time before the Son of God was born, when God existed without him. In their view, this logic proved that only the Father was truly God. One of the words used to describe the Son was *homoiousios*, which is a Greek term meaning "of similar substance". The Son was "of similar substance" to the Father, but not the same.

The Arians had preserved monotheism, but at the expense of the Son and the Spirit. This was potentially disastrous for the Christian faith, as the central claim of Christians was that through the life, death, and resurrection of Jesus – the Son of God – God himself had saved them. If the Son of God was not truly God, then how could they be sure that God really did want to forgive them their sins and receive them in his kingdom?

At the Council of Nicea in 325 CE, Arianism was condemned when its central tenet, that the Son was *homoiousios* with the Father, was rejected. Instead, Jesus was declared to be *homoousios*, which means "of the same substance". This distinction made all the difference – it was agreed that the Son utterly shares the Father's deity. Consequently, it was accepted that the Son had no beginning – God has always been a Father and a Son, together with the Holy Spirit.

Persons, not masks

A second answer deemed heretical to the question of the Trinity was given by a 3rd-century CE priest in Rome, Sabellius, and his followers. Unlike the Arians, the Sabellians affirmed that the Son and the Spirit were truly God. They solved the problem of whether God is one or three by maintaining that Father, Son, and Spirit are three "modes" of the one God's being. This idea is known as modalism.

"Father", "Son", and "Spirit" can be thought of as masks available to an actor in a play. There is only one actor, but he can play three parts, simply by wearing three different masks. At first, this might seem like a good way to describe how God is experienced: sometimes Christians encounter him as the Father, at other times as the Son, and still other times as the Spirit.

However, if Christians only ever encountered God's three masks, how could they be sure that they had met God himself? After all, people can wear masks in order to hide their true identity. What if God wore the masks to pretend to be something he is not? And so, instead of talking about masks or modes, Christian theologians began to use the Greek term *"hypostases"*, which was translated into Latin as *"personae"*, or persons. They posited that God is three hypostases of one *ousia* (Greek for essence/being – in Latin, *"substantia"*, or substance),

God is divided without division, if I may put it like that, and united in division. The Godhead is one in three and the three are one...
Gregory of Nazianzus

> Every act which extends from God to the creation… originates with the Father, proceeds through the Son, and is completed by the Holy Spirit.
> **Gregory of Nyssa**

so three persons of one substance. Such theological reasoning involved stretching the meaning of human terms in order to express the magnitude of God appropriately. Some of the theologians who achieved this most successfully were the Cappadocian Fathers: Basil of Caesarea, Gregory of Nazianzus, and Gregory of Nyssa (Basil's younger brother), who lived in the late 4th century CE. They explained the difference between *ousia* and hypostases ("substance" and "persons") by giving an example: *ousia* is humanity as a general category, while each hypostasis is an individual human. Every person has their humanity in common with other people; but at the same time, each person has individual characteristics that make them who they are. Defining humanity accordingly would involve stating "we experience one common humanity in billions of persons", followed by listing every person who has ever lived, is living, and will live.

In this definition of the Trinity, the persons of the Trinity have their divinity in common, in the same way that people share their common humanity. There are just three persons of the one divine substance – Father, Son, and Spirit.

By using the language of hypostases or persons, Christian thinkers were able to avoid the problems of Sabellius and modalism. It was agreed that Father, Son, and Spirit were not three masks worn by a mysterious divine actor, just as there is no ideal human lurking somewhere behind all the humans who have ever lived. Instead, there are three persons (Father, Son, and Spirit) who, together, are God.

Understanding the Trinity

Why is it important to Christians that one God is worshipped in three persons, rather than as three separate gods? The easy answer is that if the Trinity was understood as three separate gods, Christians could not be certain that the God of the story of Jesus Christ had anything to do with the God who they believe created the world, or who is at work in the world today.

The idea of a Trinity safeguards the unity of God's relationship with the world. Traditionally, the Father is seen as the one who created the world, the Son is the one who came into the world to save it, and the Spirit is the one who transforms the world into the place God wants it to be. It is important that these are seen as one God working in three ways towards the same goal – to share God's love with the world – not »

The Trinity comprises three distinct persons that are not interchangeable, yet share the same divine substance, and this divine substance is present in only these three persons.

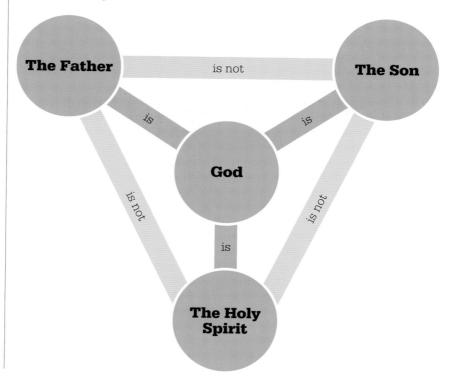

Red rose petals fall inside the Pantheon, Rome, at the end of Pentecost Mass, commemorating the descent of the Holy Spirit onto the disciples on the day of Pentecost.

three times, as if telling the same story from three different, but complementary, perspectives. This repetition, maintains Barth, reflects what God's existence is really like – whatever God does, he does as Father, Spirit, and Son.

Defining principle

The doctrine of the Trinity is often considered one of the most obscure and complicated aspects of Christian theology. Nonetheless, Christians hold to the doctrine because they believe it reflects a vital characteristic of God. Just as in the debates with the Arians and Sabellians in the 4th century CE, the idea of the Trinity is essential to orthodox Christian faith. Groups, such as the Jehovah's Witnesses and the Unitarians, who hold conflicting views on this issue are generally not considered authentically Christian by the mainstream Church.

One interesting development in recent times has been the notion of the "social Trinity", in which the cooperation of the three persons of

as three Gods pulling in three different directions. Augustine (p.221) explained that it is this love that binds the Trinity together.

Metaphors of the Trinity

Over the centuries, many people have tried to identify metaphors for the Trinity in order to explain how three can be one, and one three. For instance, St Patrick – a 5th-century CE missionary who took Christianity to Ireland – used the image of a three-leaf shamrock. Others have used the analogy of speech to explain the Trinity: the Father is the one who speaks, the Son is the word that is spoken, and the Spirit is the breath by which the word is spoken. By far the most influential Christian theologian of the 20th century was Karl Barth (1886–1968), a Swiss pastor and professor. He came up with a helpful guide for trinitarian thinking, which has been embraced by much contemporary theology. The doctrine of the Trinity means that whatever is said about the Christian God, has to be said

As Father, Son, and Spirit are three, they are three agents of what the one God does with creatures.
Robert Jenson

the Trinity is seen as a model for human community. Since God can only be God as long the relationships between Father, Son, and Spirit are maintained, so humans, made in God's image, can only be truly human as they maintain meaningful relationships with God and others.

The Trinity and the Spirit

The Spirit often seems like the forgotten person of the Trinity. Perhaps this is because the debates of the 4th century CE were primarily about the relationship between Jesus, Son of God, and God the Father, so the Spirit received only a brief mention in the creeds. It might also be because the Spirit seems the most difficult of the three persons to comprehend, a situation made more confusing by the use of the older English term "Holy Ghost" – from the word *gast*, meaning "spirit".

According to the Gospel of John, Jesus told his followers that he would send God's Spirit to be with them after he had left them and ascended into heaven. Because the Spirit was supposed to transform the lives of God's followers from the inside out, so that they would live the kind of holy lives that God wanted them to, the Spirit then became known as the Holy Spirit.

The name of Father, Son, and Spirit means that God is the one God in threefold repetition...
Karl Barth

While Christians of different denominations understand the Holy Spirit in different ways, the Pentecostal movement of the 20th century did much to raise the public profile of the Spirit. The movement was named after the day of Pentecost, when Jesus sent the Spirit to his disciples. On that day, the Spirit is said to have appeared as a flame above the heads of the disciples, who were filled with the Holy Spirit. This enabled them to preach in languages that had been previously unknown to them.

The idea of the Holy Spirit's transformative power is central to Pentecostal Christians. They believe that believers may be taken over by the Holy Spirit in the way in which the Spirit took hold of the disciples. This very intense, personal experience is called a "baptism" by the Holy Spirit, and worshippers actively seek this spiritual renewal over and above their normal Christian life.

Charismatic Christianity

Since the 1960s, the charismatic movement has introduced the Pentecostal enthusiasm for the Spirit into other denominations. The word "charismatic" comes from *charismata* (Greek for "gift of grace") and refers to the spiritual gifts which are evidence of the Spirit's activity among Christians, including gifts such as healing, prophesying, and speaking in tongues (or other languages).

The pronounced role of the Spirit in the Pentecostal and charismatic movements has prompted the Church to think through its understanding of all three persons of the Trinity, if it is not to inadvertently sideline one or more. The idea of the Trinity remains as vital now as ever, informing how Christians speak about the God they believe and worship. ∎

Gifts of the Holy Spirit

Many spiritual gifts are recognized in the Christian Church. For believers, these gifts are given by God to the Church to help it do the work of God's kingdom in the world. The gifts are for three main purposes: ministry, motivation, and manifestation.

Christians maintain that the Spirit enables some people to perform special roles within the Church. These ministry gifts include full-time callings to be a pastor or an evangelist. Motivational gifts are practical gifts that encourage the work of the church: these include prophecy, teaching, giving, leading or showing mercy.

Sometimes, the Spirit's activity is seen in a special way, such as in "tongues" (speaking with unlearned words in order to praise God), healing, or other miracles. These gifts are called manifestations, which show the Spirit is at work.

The Bible says that the Spirit helps to produce good fruit in the lives of Christians: Christians grow into "love, joy, peace, patience, kindness, goodness, faithfulness, gentleness, and self-control" (Galatians 5:22–23).

GOD'S GRACE NEVER FAILS
AUGUSTINE AND FREE WILL

IN CONTEXT

KEY FIGURE
Augustine of Hippo

WHEN AND WHERE
**354–430 CE,
present-day Algeria**

BEFORE
From c.1000 BCE The Jews
understand themselves to
be chosen by God because
of his grace, not by virtue of
their inherent goodness.

c.30 CE Jesus teaches his
followers about grace: "You
didn't choose me. I chose you".

AFTER
418 CE Augustine's teaching
on grace is accepted by the
Church and Pelagius is
condemned as a heretic at
the Council of Carthage.

16th century Calvin develops
Augustine's thought in his
doctrine of predestination,
which becomes a central
element of the theology of
the Protestant Reformation.

D o we choose God, or does
God choose us? This
question has troubled
Christian thinkers since the
earliest days of the Church. At its
heart is the tricky philosophical
issue of free will, translated into
the context of the Christian faith.
It took the brilliant mind of the
theologian Augustine to come up
with a way of explaining how God's
choice relates to human choice.

The Pelagian controversy
Augustine was propelled into the
debate over free will in the early
5th century when Pelagius, a Celtic
monk, arrived in North Africa. The

Salvation is by **God's grace**,
not human capability.

The **human** will is **weak**.

God's grace **cannot fail**.

The **weak human** will
always **choose sin**
over God.

God gives grace to
people to **enable them**
to choose him.

Humans are thus **not
free to choose** God.

See also: God's covenant with Israel 168–69 ▪ Why prayer works 246–47
▪ Striving in the way of God 278

In infant baptism, Christians believe that the stain of sin is washed away. Pelagius argued that because infants have not developed free will, they could not have sinned.

controversy was initially about the baptism of infants. Pelagius argued that there was no need for infants to be baptized to wash away the stain of sin, as was generally the belief of the time. He maintained that sin was a result of human free will, and since he believed infants had not developed free will, they could not have sinned. Moreover, if children chose to follow God's way as they developed free will while growing up, there would be no need for them to be baptized at all.

Augustine disagreed with nearly everything Pelagius said. He argued – based as much on experience as on logic – that it is impossible for humans to choose freely to follow God's way. From birth, the weak-willed human veers towards choosing what is wrong, an idea that became known as original sin. In order to choose God, Augustine believed that humans need God's help – which is precisely why baptism is so important. God chooses to give

humans his grace (his saving help), and because God is all-powerful, whatever he does must be effective. Those humans who receive God's grace are at liberty to make their own decision to choose God, rather than sin. Augustine maintained a careful balance: God's choice does not replace human choice, but rather makes it possible for humans to choose.

Predestination

Augustine's concept, which became known as the doctrine of predestination, was adopted by Protestant reformers, notably John Calvin. In some extreme statements of predestination, the idea that God's grace can not fail was emphasized at the expense of human freedom, reducing human decisions to inconsequential acts, because God has already decided what will happen – the so-called paradox of free will, by which, many argue, that predestination robs humans of free will. Augustine's idea of grace is a valuable way of maintaining the balance between God's choice and that of humans. ▪

God extends his mercy to humankind not because they already know him, but in order that they may know him.
Augustine of Hippo

Augustine of Hippo

Aurelius Augustine was born in 354 CE in Thagaste, North Africa. He was brought up as a Christian by his devout mother, but renounced his faith during his youth and led a dissolute life for several years. After studying Greek philosophy in Carthage, he embraced Manichaeism, a Persian religion, but returned to Christianity after being impressed by the sermons of Bishop Ambrose in Milan and the example of the desert hermit Anthony (p.223).

Augustine was baptized on Easter Day in 387, and by 396 he had been appointed Bishop at Hippo. He preached and wrote prolifically about theological controversies until his death in 430. He is rightly regarded as one of the great Christian thinkers, and his teaching has continued to influence Christian thought throughout the Western world. Recognized as a saint by the Anglican and Catholic Church, he was awarded the highly honoured title, Doctor of the Church, in the 13th century.

Key works

397–400 CE *Confessions*
413–427 CE *The City of God*

IN THE WORLD, BUT NOT OF THE WORLD

SERVING GOD ON BEHALF OF OTHERS

IN CONTEXT

KEY MOVEMENT
Monasticism

WHEN AND WHERE
From 3rd century CE,
Mediterranean

BEFORE
2nd century BCE–1st century CE Within Judaism, ascetic Essenes gather in monastery-like communities in order to live lives of purity and abstinence.

AFTER
529 CE St Benedict establishes a monastic community in Italy; in 817 his *Rule* becomes the authorized set of precepts for all monks in Western Europe.

11th century St Francis and St Clare found the Franciscan order of monks, and the Order of St Clare for nuns.

16th century Monasteries that are seen as too wealthy and corrupt are closed during the Protestant Reformation in Europe.

Christians have to live in **the world**.

↓

The world is full of **distractions from God**.

↓

By **retreating** from the world, monks and nuns can focus on their **spiritual life**.

↓

Without distractions, they can **pray for** and seek to better the **world around them**.

↓

Monasticism is about being in the world, but not of the world.

Nowadays, monasteries are sometimes thought of as relics from a bygone age. However, when they began to flourish in the early medieval period, after the collapse of the Roman Empire in the 5th century, they were at the forefront of society. In a Europe that, culturally speaking, was entering what we now know as the Dark Ages, monasteries became beacons of learning and innovation. These powerful institutions embodied a central idea in Christianity: that some people can be set apart from the demands of conventional living in order to focus on leading a spiritual life that will be of benefit to others as well as themselves. An important aspect of monasticism has always been praying for people in the wider world.

From caves to cloisters

Monasticism has its roots in the lives of the "fathers and mothers" who lived in the Egyptian desert, from the 3rd century CE. These early monks and nuns had retreated from the world in order to live simple lives of devotion and prayer. They took Jesus's words seriously – "What good is it to gain the whole

See also: Self-denial leads to spiritual liberation 68–71 ▪ Higher levels of teaching 101 ▪ The purpose of monastic vows 145 ▪ Immortality in Christianity 210–211 ▪ The Protestant Reformation 230–37

In the 3rd century CE, one of the first desert hermits, St Anthony, attracted thousands of followers, who settled in caves around him; this monastery was eventually built at the site in Egypt.

world but lose one's own soul?" – and so became ascetics, giving up worldly possessions and marriage to focus on their spiritual lives. The world was understood to be a place of many temptations, which could distract a person from the ways of God. As an antidote to the busyness of life, the ascetics sought quiet, contemplative prayer. It was said that, "Just as it is impossible to see your face in troubled water, so also the soul, unless it is clear of alien thoughts, is not able to pray to God in contemplation."

As monasticism spread out from the desert and into Europe, caves were superseded by specially designed buildings that became known as monasteries. Many were built around a cloister, an enclosed courtyard or garden used for meditation. Although monasteries had moved from the desert to more populated environments, the idea of retreating from the world in order to nurture spiritual life persisted.

A life for others
However, monasteries were not simply spiritual refuges from the outside world. At a time when most Christians were peasants, working long hours simply to survive, the monks and nuns worshipped and prayed on their behalf. Monastic groups such as the Benedictines (founded in the 6th century) and the Cistercians (12th century) offered hospitality and charity as well as prayer. Throughout the Middle Ages, monasteries remained centres of education. Monks and nuns copied and illuminated precious manuscripts, and passed on their knowledge. According to the monastic ideal, retreating from the world gave them the time and energy to serve the world, in God's name. ∎

In the Eastern Christian church there is only one monastic order, which follows the instructions for monastic life written by St Basil.

Eastern monasticism

While Western European monasticism is renowned for its great communal buildings, many Eastern monasteries follow an older tradition of monks and nuns living in relative isolation from each other, inspired by St Anthony. Another extreme early Eastern monastic tradition was practised by the Stylites, such as St Simeon, who lived on the top of pillars, fasting, praying, and preaching. Although Eastern monasteries have slightly different practices, they still embody the idea of separation from the world for the sake of a spiritual life, and for the benefit of others. One of the holiest places in Eastern monasticism is Mount Athos in Greece, the Holy Mountain, which has some of the oldest monastic buildings in the world. This isolated peninsula is completely autonomous and set apart from the world; women are not permitted access to the land.

THERE IS NO SALVATION OUTSIDE THE CHURCH

ENTERING INTO THE FAITH

IN CONTEXT

KEY MOVEMENT
The Fourth Lateran Council

WHEN AND WHERE
1215 CE, Rome

BEFORE
1st century CE The first Christian communities form.

313 CE The Roman Emperor Constantine publishes the Edict of Milan, allowing Christians to worship freely.

1054 The Great Schism divides the Roman Catholic and Eastern Orthodox Churches.

AFTER
1545–63 The Council of Trent reaffirms the seven sacraments against Protestant calls for two.

20th–21st century The ecumenical movement affirms that all Christians, regardless of denomination, are part of one worldwide Church.

I s it possible to be a Christian without also being a member of the Church? Many people today would answer "yes", pointing out that Jesus did not provide his disciples with instructions for setting up a religious institution. Some would contend that, in order to be a Christian, it is sufficient to have a personal belief in Jesus, without even belonging to the Church, in any of its denominations.

Despite this argument, being a member of the Church has been considered an essential element of Christian faith for most of its history. At first, in the years following Jesus's death and resurrection, Christians simply

See also: God's covenant with Israel 168–75 ▪ Faith and the state 189
▪ The central professions of faith 262–69 ▪ Awaiting the Day of Judgment 312–13

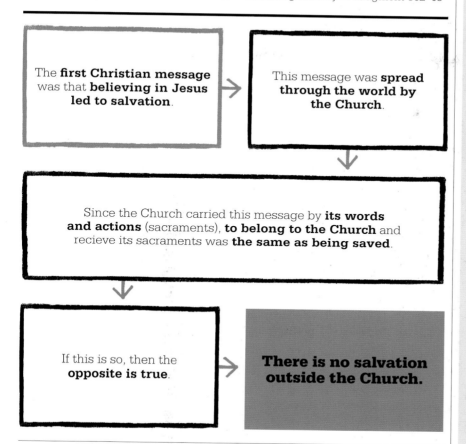

The **first Christian message** was that **believing in Jesus led to salvation**.

→ This message was **spread through the world by the Church**.

Since the Church carried this message by **its words and actions** (sacraments), **to belong to the Church** and recieve its sacraments was **the same as being saved**.

If this is so, then the **opposite is true**.

→ **There is no salvation outside the Church.**

The Christian hell

Throughout Christian history, ideas of hell have symbolized the threat of exclusion from God's salvation. In Jesus's teaching, the word used for hell, Gehenna, referred to a real place outside the walls of Jerusalem, the Valley of the Son of Hinnom. It is thought that sacrificial burnings of children once occurred here, and the place was considered cursed. This gave rise to the popular image of hell as a place of permanent fire.

During the Middle Ages, the horrors of hell became a regular theme in religious art, reminding people of their need to stay within the Catholic Church if they wanted to escape the threat of eternal torment.

More recently, Christian thinkers have suggested that Jesus did not mean that there was an actual place called hell where those who failed to accept his message would be punished forever. "Hell" was just his name for an existence without God. Since God is understood to be the author of life, to be without his presence is simply non-existence, or everlasting death.

adapted the religious gatherings at Jewish synagogues, from which many of the early believers were drawn. Like the Jews, Christians came together to pray and sing, share food, and read the Scriptures. For Christians, this meant the Hebrew Bible, which became known to them as the Old Testament, and a new collection of documents Jesus and his significance, known as the New Testament.

As the Christian message spread into the non-Jewish world, Christian gatherings developed their own identity and were named *ecclesia*, from the Greek, meaning "called out". This referred to the idea that the group had been called out by God to share the message of Jesus with the world.

Mother Church
By the mid-3rd century CE, the theologian Cyprian had made it clear that belonging to the Church was a non-negotiable element of Christian faith, not an optional extra. At this time many Christians were suffering intense persecution from the Roman authorities because of their faith; some had renounced their beliefs in order to save their lives. Church leaders were unsure what course they should take with such people. They questioned whether to »

readmit them to the Church if they truly repented, or whether to exclude them and let them form their own, separate communities. Cyprian was adamant that the Church should forgive them and allow them back, since in his understanding there could be only one true Church, and it was impossible for people to be saved outside it. He likened the Church to Noah's Ark in the Old Testament story of the flood, commenting that just as the only people who were saved were those on the Ark, so too the only people to be saved from God's judgment of evil were those in the Church.

By Cyprian's time, the Church had already developed a clearly defined structure. Deacons and priests led local congregations, while bishops and archbishops were responsible for slightly larger geographical areas. Partly due to the political and economic importance of Rome itself during this early period, the Bishop of Rome was increasingly seen as the leader of the whole Church, and by the 6th century was the only bishop called the "pope" (from a Greek word meaning "father").

Papal power increased during the medieval period. Although at first the Pope's preeminence was seen as a useful way to ensure the unity of the Church, by the start of the 11th century, Eastern Greek-speaking church leaders felt they were being unfairly dominated by the Western, Latin-speaking Pope. In 1054, in the Great Schism, the Church split into Eastern and Western branches, citing doctrinal differences as well as the issue of papal authority. However, the Pope in Rome still claimed to be leader of the worldwide Church, and at the

> You cannot have God for your Father, if you do not have the Church for your mother.
> **Cyprian, *The Unity of the Church***

Fouth Lateran Council of Church leaders in 1215, Pope Innocent III reasserted his authority over the powerful bishops in the Eastern Church at Constantinople, Antioch, Alexandria, and Jerusalem.

In Western Europe, the Roman Catholic Church, presided over by the Pope, was seen as the only true family of faithful Christians until the end of the Middle Ages. The dominance of the Roman Catholic Church in medieval life added weight to the idea that it was impossible to be saved outside the Church.

Seven sacraments

While the Church had established massive political and economic influence during the medieval period, its main power was spiritual. It understood that one of its main functions was to bring visibility to the spiritual union between God and his people. Because the Christian relationship with God seemed intangible by nature, it was more convenient to assess Christian faith by the state of a person's relationship with the Church.

Within the Church, special rites were used to mark different stages of the Christian life. Known as

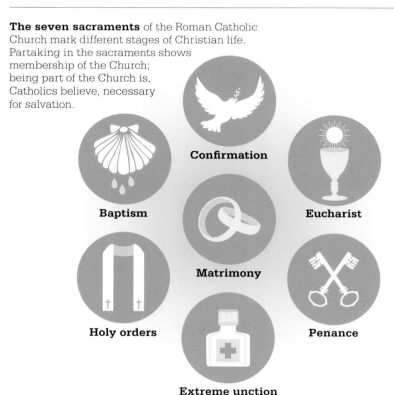

The seven sacraments of the Roman Catholic Church mark different stages of Christian life. Partaking in the sacraments shows membership of the Church; being part of the Church is, Catholics believe, necessary for salvation.

Confirmation

Baptism

Eucharist

Matrimony

Holy orders

Penance

Extreme unction

> There is one Universal Church of the faithful, outside of which there is absolutely no salvation.
> **Fourth Lateran Council**

sacraments, these rites were physical actions that had spiritual significance. Originally, the early Church celebrated only two sacraments – baptism and the Eucharist – tracing them back to the example and teaching of Jesus himself. However, during the Middle Ages, their number increased to a total of seven, all of which were offered with the authority of the Catholic Church. These were: baptism (the moment a person enters the Church and their sin is washed away); confirmation (the point at which a person receives the gift of God's Holy Spirit to help live a Christian life); the Eucharist (a regular celebration of the forgiveness achieved by the death and resurrection of Jesus); penance (the actions specified by a priest in order for a person to be reconciled with God after confessing sin); extreme unction, otherwise known as "the last rites" (anointing and giving comfort and the assurance of forgiveness to the dying); and holy orders (when a person decides to spend their life serving God within the Church). The last of the seven rites was marriage, which was considered a sacrament because the close relationship between a husband and wife was thought to mirror the close relationship between God and his people.

Receiving the sacraments was a clear indication that a person remained a member of the Catholic Church, and so could rely on being saved by God. Church legislation was therefore developed to guide both priests and lay people as to how the sacraments should be properly used. They were considered so important that the clergy were forbidden from making a profit out of doing their duties. At the Fourth Lateran Council, it was decreed that all Christians should receive the Eucharist at least once a year at Easter, and should also confess their sins and do penance at least once annually. The prayers of a priest at the bedside of a sick person were considered so essential that doctors were required to call a priest to attend to the patient before they did their own work. These important regulations ensured that the Church offered the sacraments freely and regularly, and that Church members received what was offered.

Avoiding damnation

Like other Church councils before and after it, the Fourth Lateran Council made it clear that to reject the sacraments of the Catholic Church, was to remove oneself from the Church and so also to lose the salvation offered on behalf of God. If the Church was to be seen as the "mother" of the faithful, then anyone who was not a "child" of the Church could not enjoy salvation.

Special condemnation was reserved for people who not only failed to receive the sacraments themselves, but also taught others to reject them. Since it was believed that the popes of the Roman Church had inherited and passed on true teaching from Peter, one of Jesus's closest disciples and considered the first pope, anyone who rejected the teaching of the pope was held to be rejecting the teaching of Jesus. Unrepentant heretics (believing in anything other than the teachings of the Catholic Church) faced the punishment of excommunication: they were removed from the Church and forbidden from receiving sacraments until they changed their minds. If they died before giving up their heresies, they could expect to miss out on God's salvation and to endure the horrors of hell.

At the end of the Middle Ages, the monopoly on salvation by the Catholic Church was challenged by the Protestant Reformation (pp.230–37). No longer could a single Christian institution claim that there was no possibility of salvation outside itself. However, the idea that salvation is not possible outside the wider Christian Church has persisted among many Christian groups. ∎

St Peter, close disciple of Jesus and martyred in Rome, is the source of papal prerogative. His authority is thought to be inherited by the popes, and so to reject their word is to reject Jesus.

THIS IS MY BODY, THIS IS MY BLOOD
THE MYSTERY OF THE EUCHARIST

IN CONTEXT

KEY FIGURE
Thomas Aquinas

WHEN AND WHERE
1225–74, Europe

BEFORE
From 300 BCE Jews add the drinking of a cup of wine that has been blessed to the eating of unleavened bread during the Passover meal.

1st century CE St Paul writes with instructions for the early Christians as they regularly celebrate Jesus's last meal with his disciples.

1215 CE The Fourth Lateran Council defines the Eucharist as one of seven essential sacraments for the Catholic faithful.

AFTER
16th century The Protestant Reformers reject the concept of transubstantiation, generally favouring a more symbolic understanding of Jesus's words.

In the **sacrament** of the Eucharist, Christians experience the **"real presence" of Jesus**.

But the elements in the Eucharist are **bread and wine, not flesh and blood**.

Aristotle distinguishes between **"substance"** and **"accidents"** (the form or attributes of something).

The **"accidents"** of the bread and wine are clearly **unchanged**.

So it must be the "substance" that is **converted** from bread and wine **into the body and blood of Jesus**.

This is the mystery of the Eucharist.

Before his arrest and eventual crucifixion, Jesus shared a Passover meal of bread and wine with his disciples, saying "This is my body" and "This is my blood". Since then, this ritual has been celebrated by Christians in an act of worship known variously as the Eucharist, Holy Communion, the Lord's Supper, and the Breaking of Bread. But over the centuries, the meaning and significance of his words have been the subject of huge controversy. In what sense does the bread and wine change into the body and blood of Jesus?

In the 13th century, the great medieval theologian Thomas Aquinas developed the theory of transubstantiation. He drew

See also: Beliefs for new societies 56–57 ▪ Entering into the faith 224–27 ▪ The Protestant Reformation 230–37

> The presence of Christ's true body and blood in this sacrament cannot be detected by sense, nor understanding, but by faith alone.
> **Thomas Aquinas**

on the recently rediscovered philosophy of Aristotle to clarify previous teaching about the Eucharist. Aquinas's teaching became the official doctrine of the Roman Catholic Church.

The purpose of Aquinas's teaching was to explain how the "real presence" of Jesus could be found in the elements of bread and wine. This was important because Christians believe that the Eucharist is a sacrament, a sacred act that is thought to embody a religious truth (p.226). If Jesus were not present when the bread and wine were shared, the sacrament would lose its meaning and significance.

When is bread not bread?

According to Aristotle, "substance" is the unique identity of an object or person – the "tableness" of a table, for example. "Accidents" are the attributes of the substance, and can change without its identity altering – a table might be wooden, and blue, but if it was metal and pink it would still be a table.

For Aquinas, this meant that it was possible for the substance or essence of an object or person (such as Jesus) to be found in the accidents or attributes of other objects (such as bread and wine). He said that it was also possible for one object to be converted into another object: so, as the priest prayed over the bread and the wine, the substance of bread and wine

Holy Communion is fundamental to the faith of nearly all Christians. Roman Catholic and Orthodox Christians believe in transubstantiation; others see it more as a symbolic act.

was converted into that of the body and blood of Jesus (hence the term transubstantiation – "to change from one substance to another"). However, the accidents or attributes of the bread and wine remained, so the "real presence" of Jesus in bread and wine was to be believed, but not physically seen. ▪

Thomas Aquinas

Thomas Aquinas is acclaimed as the greatest theologian in the medieval scholastic movement, which was characterized by a new method of contemplating the Christian faith in an academically rigorous way. Aquinas was born to a noble family in Roccasecca near Naples in 1225. While at university in Naples, Aquinas joined the recently established Order of Preachers (later known as the Dominican Friars). He continued his studies in Paris and Cologne, subsequently becoming a highly regarded teacher in the Catholic Church. His major contribution to Christianity was his use of Greek philosophy, notably the work of Aristotle, to explain and defend Christian theology. Known as "Thomism", his system of theology became the standard within Catholic thinking for centuries. Aquinas died at the age of 49 in 1274, while he was travelling to the ecumenical Council of Lyon.

Key works

c.1260 *Summa contra Gentiles*
c.1265–74 *Summa Theologica* (Sum of Theology)

GOD'S WORD
NEEDS
NO GO-BETWEENS
THE PROTESTANT REFORMATION

IN CONTEXT

KEY MOVEMENT
The Reformation

WHEN AND WHERE
16th century,
Western Europe

BEFORE
1382 John Wycliffe publishes the first major translation of the Bible into English.

1516 The Christian Humanist thinker Erasmus publishes a new edition of the Greek New Testament, which includes his new Latin translation.

AFTER
1545–63 The Council of Trent is convened. As representatives of the Catholic Church, the group condemns the Protestant movement.

1563 The Heidelberg Catechism is published, offering a Protestant statement of faith for both Calvinists and Lutherans. It becomes an influential Reformed catechism.

The Roman Catholic Church was a formidable institution in the late Middle Ages. From his palace in Rome, the Pope held sway not only over Europe's religious life, but also over its politics and economics. The Church was a major landowner, and, through the feudal system, many peasants found themselves indebted to it for their homes and livelihoods, as well as for the care of their souls. At the other end of the spectrum, it was in the best interests of nobles and rulers to maintain good relations with the Church, obeying its laws, and paying tithes and taxes.

However, in the first decades of the 16th century, a spiritual and social revolution shifted power away from the Catholic Church, initiating a new chapter in the history of Christianity in Europe. This revolution, now known as the Protestant Reformation, was based on the idea that God could be known and worshipped directly, without the need for an authorized hierarchy of priests to act as intermediaries. The reformers placed the teachings and traditions of the Church under the authority of Scripture, and maintained that salvation could only come from personal faith rather than from following the Church's decrees.

Renaissance Europe

By the 16th century, Europe had begun to shake off the old ideas of medieval life. The horizons of the known world were expanding rapidly, with Spanish, Portuguese, and French explorers following in the wake of Columbus's voyage to the Americas in 1492. Transport and trade were flourishing as a result of advances in seafaring, including a new route around Africa to India.

In Europe, the feudal system was being abandoned in favour of new kingdoms and city states controlled by rulers interested in improving the economic prosperity of their territories. Culturally, artists, philosophers, and scientists were rediscovering the classical learning of the past, in a loosely connected movement known as the Renaissance. In short, a new world was arriving and it seemed that the Church, with its ancient traditions and structures, was set to have a smaller role within it.

The Bible was written in the **common language** of the day (the Old Testament in Hebrew, the New Testament in Greek).

→

The first Christians were encouraged to **study the Scriptures** to make their own mind up about Christian faith.

→

Restricting the **Bible to Latin** during the Middle Ages meant that **most people could not make up their own minds** about what it said.

Translating the Bible into the vernacular meant that **everyone could read and hear** God's Word for themselves.

←

God's word needs no go-betweens.

See also: The power of the shaman 26–31 ▪ The personal quest for truth 144 ▪ Augustine and free will 220–21 ▪ Mystical experience in Christianity 238

Martin Luther preaches from the pulpit in this painting in the Church of St Mary in Wittenberg. The presence of the crucified Christ is a symbol of a direct relationship with God.

Misunderstanding God

Church services in the Middle Ages were held in Latin, a language that most people did not understand. The authorized version of the Bible – a 4th-century translation from the original Hebrew and Greek by St Jerome known as the Vulgate, meaning "commonly used" – was also written in Latin. As a result, most churchgoers relied upon their priests to explain the truths of Christianity to them. Priests held considerable power over the minds of their congregations and tended to advocate the traditions of the Catholic Church, rather than going back to the original texts.

Although this meant that there was a consistency to Catholic teaching across Europe, there were obvious dangers as well. For instance, how could people in the churches be certain that their priests were teaching them what the Bible really contained? How could they check the truth of what they heard?

Conflict with Rome

The Reformation began because a German monk, Martin Luther, believed that people were being deceived – sometimes unwittingly – by the priests and leaders of the Catholic Church of the day.

Luther was angered by the preaching of the Dominican Johann Tetzel, who had arrived in the villages near Wittenberg, Saxony, where Luther was a parish priest and university professor. Tetzel was essentially on a fundraising mission for the Church: in Rome, Pope Leo X was raising money to build a vast church, the Basilica of St Peter; and, closer to home, the German Cardinal Albrecht needed to repay a loan taken out to defray the expenses of his position. Tetzel had been authorized to sell certificates, called "indulgences", which claimed to release people from the threat of suffering for their sins in purgatory after their death. Indulgences had been available in the Catholic Church for many centuries, but Luther was appalled at Tetzel's blatant sales tactics, which frightened people with terrible images of how much their deceased loved ones were suffering in purgatory. "As soon as the coin in the coffer rings, the soul from »

A Christian is a perfectly free lord of all, subject to none. A Christian is a perfectly dutiful servant of all, subject to all.
Martin Luther

Pope Julius II is shown in this 19th-century painting in the process of instructing Bramante, Michelangelo, and Raphael to start work on the Vatican and St Peter's Basilica.

purgatory springs", Tetzel warned, and many of Luther's parishioners duly paid for the indulgences in the hope of purchasing salvation.

Luther had become firmly convinced, from his studies of the Bible, and especially the Book of Romans in the New Testament, that salvation was a free gift from God to those who have faith, not something to be bought. He recorded his objections to the sale of indulgences in 95 theses, or statements, which he sent to his bishop, the Prince of Mainz, and reportedly pinned to the door of the church in Wittenberg. A copy of the theses found its way to a printer, and the publication became an overnight bestseller.

Far more was at stake than the collection of funds for a pope's building project and an archbishop's pocket: Luther's protest raised the issue of authority within the Catholic Church. In 1520, Pope Leo X responded by publishing a document explaining how Luther had misrepresented the teaching of the Church, and declaring him and his followers to be heretics. Luther was invited to retract his views, but he refused, and even burned his copy of the Pope's document.

Authority of the Scriptures

Luther's meaning was clear: even though the Pope may have been the leader of the Church, he was not the final authority when it came to matters of faith. The final authority was God's word itself, as recorded in the Bible, otherwise known as the Scriptures. Luther held that it was not necessary for Christians to rely upon the traditions and teachings of the Church to come to a true knowledge of God and salvation. Instead, Christians could bypass these human traditions, which were often inaccurate anyway, and discover truth directly from the Bible. This would later be expressed by the Latin phrase *sola Scriptura*, "Scripture alone": the Reformers were convinced that people do not need "middle men" to interpret the meaning of the

Scriptures for them. Anyone could read the Bible and come to a clear understanding of God's way of salvation, which, for Luther, did not involve indulgences, popes, or many of the other practices of the Catholic Church.

Luther's rejection of tradition in favour of returning to original biblical sources fell on fertile soil in the early 16th century. The Humanist movement (not to be confused with modern, secular humanism) was already seeking to recover the classical learning that had been forgotten during the Dark Ages. Christian Humanists such as Desiderius Erasmus (1466–1536) encouraged their students to study the original languages of the Bible (Hebrew for the Old Testament and Greek for the New) and the writings of the very first Christians, the Church Fathers. The Reformation encouraged everyone to join in by reading the Bible for themselves.

Those who preach indulgences are in error when they say that a person is absolved and saved from every penalty by the pope's indulgences.
Martin Luther

> Luther has been sent into the world by the genius of discord. Every corner of it has been disturbed by him. All admit that the corruptions of the Church required a drastic medicine.
> **Erasmus**

A revolution in print

While the direct engagement of people with the Scriptures was a central plank of the Reformation, there remained a large obstacle. Many people were illiterate, and even if they could read, the Bible was available only in Latin, and only to a select few, because every copy had to be written out by hand. Earlier attempts to translate the Bible into the vernacular had been resisted strongly by the Catholic Church. As far back as 1382, John Wycliffe had translated the Bible into English, but it was not available to all.

By Luther's day, however, the printing press, which had been invented by Johannes Gutenberg in nearby Mainz in 1440, had revolutionized the publishing process. Luther harnessed this new technology: he set out to translate the Bible into the German language as it was spoken by ordinary people, publishing the New Testament in 1522 and the whole Bible in 1534. The combination of Luther's colloquial language and the relative cheapness of the printed Bible meant that Christians across Germany could soon read the Scriptures for themselves. Before long, both French and English translations were printed, and these fuelled the spread of Reformation ideas throughout Europe. Alongside Bibles, the printing presses of Europe churned out hundreds of pamphlets and books written by the Reformers, which were eagerly consumed by people thirsty for new ideas.

Protest and schism

At first, Luther and his followers simply wanted to bring about reform within the Catholic Church, hence their name, "Reformers". However, in a series of church meetings known as "diets" (similar to sessions of a parliament), it became clear that the Catholic Church would not accept the demands of the Reformers, which included independence from the Pope, services in the local language rather than Latin, and marriage for the clergy. Hopes for reform of the Catholic Church were finally dashed at the Diet of Speyer in 1529.

Luther's followers submitted a "Letter of Protestation", refusing to submit to the authority of the Church. From then on, they took on the new name of "Protestants", which expressed their rejection of Catholic authority in favour of their new-found confidence in interpreting the Bible themselves.

Political support

The Protestant movement was backed by a number of German princes who took advantage of Luther's religious revolt to secure the political independence of their states. They began suppressing the Catholic faith and Church influence within their territories, adopting the motto, *Cuius regio eius et religio* ("Whoever is the »

Martin Luther

Martin Luther was born in Germany, in 1483. He gave up law school in order to become a monk, after nearly being hit by a lightning bolt in a thunderstorm. By 1508 he was teaching theology at the University of Wittenberg, where he was also a priest. Luther's studies led him to his key insight, which would develop into the doctrine of justification by faith: God declares Christians to be righteous in his sight simply on account of their faith in Him, and not because of anything "good" they might do (or, in the case of indulgences, might buy). Luther's challenge to the pope's authority made him a wanted man, but he refused to recant. He spent the rest of his life preaching and writing, and by the time he died in 1546, the Lutheran Church was well established.

Key works

1520 *Appeal to the German Ruling Class,* calling for reform of the church.
1534 the *Luther Bible* (translation of Old and New Testaments).

ruler, his must be the religion"). In other words, they demanded the right to impose the Church of their choice upon their people.

Once established, the Protestant principle changed both the religious and the political landscape of Europe forever. It gave other rulers the grounds they needed to remove their kingdoms from the control of the Pope. The English Reformation, for example, began when King Henry VIII, a one-time opponent of the reformers, sought to curb the Pope's authority in order to divorce his wife, Catherine of Aragon, and marry Anne Boleyn.

Protestantism gave rise to a number of new branches of the Church, known as denominations. Whereas the Catholic Church had been the only Church in Europe for centuries, a whole host of denominations emerged following the Protestant Reformation. While Protestants were agreed that the authority of the Roman Catholic Church was to be rejected, they could not agree on a unified alternative system of thought. Disputes between some Protestant movements were at times as fierce as those between the Catholics and Protestants.

Protestant proliferation

Three main Protestant strands arose from these turbulent times: Lutherans, who followed the ideas of Martin Luther; Presbyterians, who were influenced by the work of John Calvin (see opposite); and Anglicans, moderate Protestants based in England who kept hold of many aspects of Catholicism the other movements rejected.

... Scripture, gathering together the impressions of Deity, which, till then, lay confused in our minds, dissipates the darkness, and shows us the true God clearly.
John Calvin

The Counter-Reformation

In a sense, the Catholics had been right about controlling the means of communication with their flock: without the regulation of papal authority, the Church was no longer united in its thinking. To try to stem discontent over corruption and worldly attitudes, and reclaim "lost souls" from the Protestants, the Catholic Church launched a Counter-Reformation. In 1545, Catholic leaders met in the Italian city of Trent, aiming to re-establish the superiority of the Catholic Church against the rising tide of Protestantism. By the end of the Council of Trent, which spanned 18 years to 1563, traditional Catholic doctrines had been reaffirmed, but reforms were also introduced addressing the unacceptable practices of the clergy that had sparked the Reformation.

An *Index of Forbidden Books* was published, naming 583 heretical texts, including most translations of the Bible and the works of Erasmus, Luther, and Calvin (the *Index* was enforced until 1966). A church-building

The Reformation depended upon the widespread dissemination of the Christian scriptures. The Bible was translated into the vernacular, printed in the presses, and distributed.

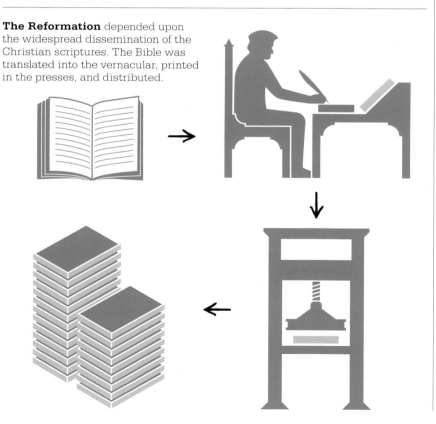

Churches built in northern Europe for Protestant congregations, such as this Lutheran church in Vik, Iceland, are often plain in design, eschewing any embellishment or decoration.

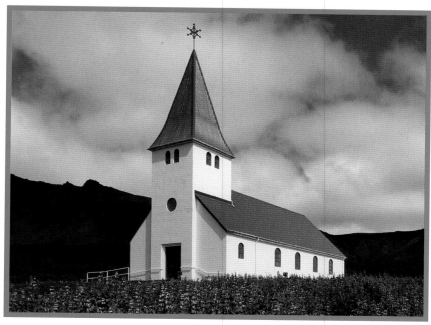

programme was started, with the intention of constructing great new churches with space for thousands of worshippers, and acoustics designed – for the first time – for vernacular sermons. Ignatius Loyola, a former soldier and the son of a Spanish nobleman, was charged with setting up the Society of Jesus, an order of missionaries also known as the Jesuits, who were willing to go anywhere without regard to their own safety, to spread Catholicism. The Church also used a process known as the Inquisition to reassert its authority, prosecuting people accused of heresy and using often brutal methods to extract the truth from the accused.

Exit from the Dark Ages

The Counter-Reformation was partly successful in Italy, Spain, and France, but changes made to the Catholic structures elsewhere were minimal, and certainly not

enough to entice the Protestants back to the fold. Henceforth, Europe was host to a marketplace of different churches, each vying for the hearts and minds of Christians. While Catholicism could claim a long and illustrious heritage, the idea of Protestantism seemed to match the spirit of the age. One of the mottos of the Reformation was *post tenebras lux*, "after darkness,

light". After the so-called Dark Ages, the Protestant spirit sought to shed the skin of medieval Catholicism and embrace a new world of ideas. It was especially confident that reading and hearing the Bible in a language that could be clearly understood would lead to a relationship with God that was uncluttered by priests, popes, and indulgences. ■

John Calvin

Born in northern France in 1509, John Calvin came into contact with Christian Humanism while at the University of Bourges, where he devoted himself to theological study. During this period, he experienced a religious conversion that caused him to break with the Roman Catholic Church and join the growing Protestant movement. Forced to flee France, Calvin became a minister in Geneva, Switzerland, from 1536 to 1538, then Strassburg (now Strasbourg) until 1541, before returning to Geneva, where he remained until his death in 1564.

Calvin stressed humanity's sinfulness and inability to know God without the study of Scripture; he emphasized God's sovereignty, which meant God could freely give the gift of salvation to whoever he chose. Followers of Calvin, known as Calvinists, established churches around the world that became known as presbyterian, from the Greek for "elder".

Key works

1536 *Institutes of the Christian Religion* (first Latin edition)

GOD IS HIDDEN IN THE HEART
MYSTICAL EXPERIENCE IN CHRISTIANITY

IN CONTEXT

KEY FIGURE
Teresa of Avila

WHEN AND WHERE
16th century, Spain

BEFORE
From 3rd century CE Monks and nuns adopt lives of solitude in the desert in order to escape worldly distractions and focus solely on God.

c.1373 The English mystic Julian of Norwich recounts her visions in *Sixteen Revelations of Divine Love*.

16th century A new emphasis on personal communion with God, instead of ritual, leads to the Protestant Reformation.

AFTER
1593 Teresa of Avila and fellow Spanish mystic John of the Cross, a major figure in the Counter-Reformation, establish the Discalced, or Barefoot, Carmelites, a more contemplative form of the monastic order.

From the earliest days of Christianity, Christians believed that Jesus had made it possible for them to have a direct relationship with God. However, some Christians struggled with worship in churches, finding it too ritualistic. A quest for an intensely personal experience of God emerged in the later Middle Ages, as a reaction to formalized worship. It became known as Christian mysticism. Rather than following the usual pattern of reciting authorized prayers, mystics advocated silent contemplation of God. This often led to overwhelming experiences of God's love. Mysticism has been embraced by many Christians because it requires neither priests nor prayer books to guide the believer, only a personal communion with God.

The interior journey
One of the classic works on mystical experience was written by Teresa of Avila (1515–1582), a Spanish Carmelite nun. In *The Interior Castle*, Teresa narrates the journey of the Christian soul through six rooms in a castle until it reaches the seventh, innermost room, where God dwells. Each room represents a more intimate level of prayer until the soul achieves the goal of perfect union with God's life, which Teresa described as "spiritual marriage". ■

In a male-dominated Church, some of the most renowned mystics were women, such as Teresa of Avila (left), Catherine of Siena (1347–1380), and Julian of Norwich (c.1342–1416).

See also: Self-denial leads to spiritual liberation 68–71 ▪ Man as a manifestation of God 188 ▪ Sufism and the mystic tradition 282–83

THE BODY NEEDS SAVING AS WELL AS THE SOUL
SOCIAL HOLINESS AND EVANGELICALISM

IN CONTEXT

KEY FIGURE
John Wesley

WHEN AND WHERE
18th century, UK

BEFORE
1st century CE Jesus preaches to open-air gatherings, which anyone may attend. He reportedly urges his followers to feed the hungry, clothe the naked, and care for the sick.

Late 17th century
The Pietist movement in Continental Europe stresses practical Christian living.

AFTER
19th century In the USA, the Wesleyan and Free Methodists are active in the anti-slavery abolitionist movement.

1865 William Booth, a Methodist minister, founds the Salvation Army with the mission of saving bodies as well as souls.

The Industrial Revolution posed a new challenge for Christianity. While a select few enjoyed unprecedented wealth, thousands of people in towns and cities endured perilous working conditions and suffered ill health and extreme poverty. In Britain, brothers John and Charles Wesley, both Anglican priests, responded to the needs of a changing society with a message of "social holiness". John Wesley described social holiness as a faith that was not just private and internal, but publicly engaged with the social issues of the day.

The Christian message
In May 1738 the Wesleys were deeply moved by reading the works of Martin Luther, and came to a new understanding of the necessity of faith for salvation. The experience had a profound effect on their ministry and caused them to join a growing number of "evangelicals" who took the Christian message out of churches, preaching in marketplaces, fields, and homes. Evangelicals fervently

By salvation I mean not barely deliverance from hell or going to heaven, but a present deliverance from sin.
John Wesley

believed that experience of Christianity could transform individuals and society. They were at the forefront of important movements, such as the abolition of the slave trade, the trade union movement, and the provision of free education for working-class children. The Wesleys' followers became known as Methodists, after the methodical, practical way in which they applied their faith to the needs of others. ∎

See also: Living in harmony 38 ∎ Let kindness and compassion rule 146–47
∎ The Sikh code of conduct 296–301

SCIENTIFIC ADVANCES DO NOT DISPROVE THE BIBLE

THE CHALLENGE OF MODERNITY

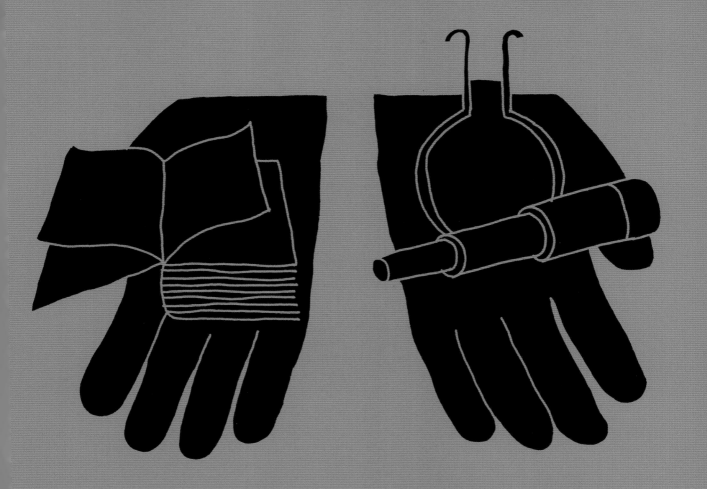

KEY MOVEMENT
Protestant Liberalism

WHEN AND WHERE
19th century, Europe/USA

BEFORE
From late 17th century
Pietism develops within the
Lutheran Church.

From 1780s Immanuel Kant's
philosophy champions reason.

1790s The Romantic
movement gains influence
in Europe as an alternative to
the Enlightenment.

AFTER
1859 Charles Darwin's
publication of *On the Origin
of Species* results in tension
between a conservative view
of the Bible and science.

1919 Theologian Karl Barth's
commentary on the Romans
marks the end of liberalism
and the beginning of neo-
orthodoxy (the new orthodoxy).

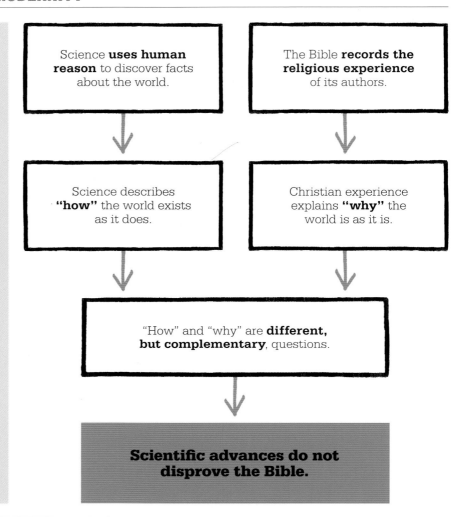

Science **uses human reason** to discover facts about the world.

The Bible **records the religious experience** of its authors.

Science describes **"how"** the world exists as it does.

Christian experience explains **"why"** the world is as it is.

"How" and "why" are **different, but complementary**, questions.

Scientific advances do not disprove the Bible.

The idea that the earth revolves around the sun, rather than the other way around, is today accepted as fact. However, in the early 17th century, this theory, which had been published by the Polish astronomer Copernicus in 1543, was in direct opposition to the teachings of the Catholic Church and sparked a controversy that embroiled the finest natural scientists of the day. Most notably, Galileo Galilei, a mathematician in Florence, was condemned as a heretic for supporting the theory.

The positions of the Church and of Galileo differed because of the different ways in which they arrived at "truth". According to the Church, truth was revealed by God, and was supported by passages in the Bible that suggested the earth was at the centre of the universe. Science, on the other hand, used experimental observations – Galileo was a pioneer of using the telescope in astronomy – to build theories about the workings of the world. Until well into the medieval period, these two methods had existed happily side by side.

In the 13th century, for instance, the medieval theologian Thomas Aquinas (p.229) had encouraged the systematic exploration of the natural world. He took it for granted that a deeper understanding of creation would lead to a better knowledge of the creator.

This mutual respect was conceivable as long as the results of scientific reasoning coincided with the concept of "divine revelation" (truth communicated by God to humans through Scripture) but not when the two thought systems reached different conclusions.

See also: The Protestant Reformation 230–37 ∎ The compatibilty of faith 291 ∎ Jewish Science 333 ∎ The Church of Christ (Scientist) 337

While both Catholic and Protestant denominations of the Church insisted that their faith in divine revelation was well placed, it seemed obvious to many that the results of experiment and reason were far more reliable. Difficult questions were soon being asked that would shake the foundations of Christian belief across the modern Western world, and by the end of the 18th century the Church was in danger of losing popular support as people increasingly doubted the rationality and relevance of the Christian faith. In response, Christian thinkers needed to articulate, in a radically new way, how religion and science, faith and reason, could coexist.

From facts to feelings

This new era of Christianity was heralded by the German theologian Friedrich Schleiermacher (see right). While working as a hospital chaplain in Berlin, he had come into contact with Romanticism,

a cultural movement that had been born out of a reaction against what was perceived as the soulless rationalism of the Enlightenment. The Romantics emphasized the importance of feelings and emotions in human life at a time when ideas and objects in the world were being valued purely for their scientific credibilty and usefulness. Schleiermacher realized that as long as Christian belief was assessed according to the same criteria and at the same level as scientific knowledge, it would be considered unreasonable. Instead of trying to prove the truth of Christianity as though it were a scientific theory (as many of his predecessors had), he translated it into the realm of feelings, as championed by the Romantics. »

Romanticism valued emotion above reason and the senses above the intellect. The movement found expression in the art, literature, and philosophy of the early 19th century.

Friedrich Schleiermacher

Friedrich Schleiermacher was born in 1768 in Breslau (then Prussian Silesia), the son of a reformed clergyman. He was educated by the Moravian Brethren, a strict Pietist sect, before moving to the more liberal University of Halle to study theology and philosophy (focusing in particular on the work of Kant). When he moved to Berlin in 1796, he was introduced to key members of the Romantic movement. Schleiermacher became a professor of theology at Berlin University in 1810. When he died in 1834, his radical reinterpretation of doctrine had given rise to a completely new form of theology known as theological liberalism, which would be a dominant intellectual force in Europe and the United States for a century.

Key works

1799 *On Religion: Speeches to its Cultured Despisers*, Schleiermacher's most radical work on theology.
1821–22 *The Christian Faith*, Schleiermacher's major work of systematic theology.

Friedrich Schleiermacher identified true religion with a specific type of "feeling". It was distinct from knowledge or activity and was an end in itself. Knowledge, action, and feeling were different but related realms.

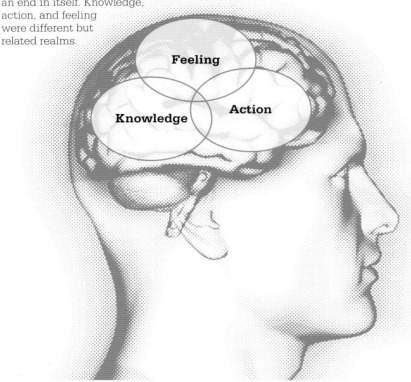

He emphasized that science and faith were not in competition: they should be seen as complementary because they each focused on different aspects of human life.

Redefining religion

Schleiermacher's most significant idea was his redefinition of the nature of religion. In his first important book on the subject, *Religion: Speeches to its Cultured Despisers* (1799), he discussed three realms of human life: knowledge, action, and feeling. Although he recognized that these three realms are necessarily related to each other, he was convinced that they ought not to be confused: according to him, knowledge belongs to science, action belongs to ethics,

and feeling belongs to religion. Schleiermacher believed that the problem facing Christianity was that it had often focused too heavily on knowledge and action, and too little on feeling. In doing this, Christianity was in danger of being undermined by the rationalism of the modern world. On the one hand, scientific reason disputed some of Christianity's fundamental beliefs, such as the miracles and resurrection of Jesus. On the other hand, the philosophy of Kant and others saw morality as based on universal principles, rather than on the contents of the Bible. The challenge to Christianity posed by science and philosophy did not, however, disturb Schleiermacher; on the contrary, it presented an

opportunity to recover what he considered to be at the very heart of the Christian religion, which was simply, "a sense and taste for the infinite". In his book *The Christian Faith* (1821–22), Schleiermacher systematically reinterpreted Christian theology as a description of Christian experience. For example, according to him, a statement such as "God exists" does not make any claim about the actual existence of God; instead, it describes a person's feeling that he or she is dependent upon something that is beyond him or herself.

A record of experience

In the mid-19th century, a number of scholars, primarily based in Germany, were using a form of analysis known as "historical criticism" to look at Biblical texts. They studied the Bible's original sources from the Middle East to reinterpret its content within a historical context. By focusing on the ways in which the Bible had been composed and compiled as a set of human documents, this analysis appeared to strip the sacred text of its supernatural

The self-identical essence of piety is this: the consciousness of being absolutely dependent, or, which is the same thing, of being in relation with God.
Friedrich Schleiermacher

origins (the belief that it was of divine authorship). The result was that, for many people, the Bible could no longer be referred to as the inspired word of God.

Friedrich Schleiermacher's view, however, helped to rescue the Bible from what some perceived to be irrelevance. He claimed that since religion relates fundamentally to experience, the Bible is supremely important as a record of religious experience. It can therefore be used as the ultimate guide to Christian experience, as believers compare their own feelings of dependence on God with those described within the sacred text.

This approach to the Bible became known as the "liberal" view, as opposed to the more "conservative" view, which insisted – in the face of this historical criticism – that the Bible contained facts about God, and not just facts about human experience. Tension between these two views has shaped Protestantism ever since.

Unintended consequences
Schleiermacher developed his idea of religious experience in order to protect Christianity from being

Christian doctrines
are accounts of
the Christian religious
affections set
forth in speech.
Friedrich Schleiermacher

relegated to history while science moved forward to shape the future of the world. By assigning religion and science to different spheres of human life (religion to feeling, and science to knowledge), he was successful in establishing a means by which they could coexist.

However, while many Christians embraced Schleiermacher's thesis as a solution to the friction between science and religion, others were dissatisfied with what they saw as the relegation of Christian faith to the sphere of "feelings". They also identified an unintended consequence: Christianity could no longer claim to have an authoritative voice in the public sphere if it was associated most strongly with an individual's feelings, as these are, in essence, personal. This seemed to be at odds with the original message of Christianity, which concerned the arrival of God's kingdom in the whole world (not just in private religious experience) and indicated an important societal role.

Taking a stand
In the 20th century, the liberal movement was strongly criticized by a new generation of scholars, including the eminent Swiss theologian Karl Barth. He was particularly appalled that his liberal theology teachers had failed to take a principled stand against the rise of Nazism in Germany in the 1930s, and claimed that this was because Schleiermacher's theology had been allowed to become far too influential within the Church. He maintained that a private Christian experience could be too easily indifferent to the needs of the world outside.

Barth argued that for Christianity to be successful in opposing some of the obvious

Clergymen carry a symbol of peace, indicating their opposition to nuclear arms. Critics of theological liberalism argued that an emphasis on personal feelings encouraged indifference to important issues in the world.

misuses of science and knowledge – such as genocide, the arms race, and nuclear armament – in the modern world, Christian theology would need to be based on more than private feelings.

Today, Christian thinkers still face the challenge of explaining to people how they can trust what the Bible says about God, when what it says about the world is often disputed by scientific reasoning. Many Christians would answer with a modified form of Schleiermacher's argument. The Bible talks about the same reality as that described by science, history, politics, and other social sciences. However, it simply answers different questions: not, "how did this come to be?", but "why did this come to be?". Science and faith – the "how?" and the "why?" – do not disprove each other, but complement each other. They help Christians to reach a more complete understanding of the universe that Galileo observed through his telescope. ∎

WE CAN INFLUENCE GOD
WHY PRAYER WORKS

IN CONTEXT

KEY MOVEMENTS
**Process theology
and open theism**

WHEN AND WHERE
**Late 20th century,
USA and Europe**

BEFORE
From prehistory Many
primal belief systems use
prayer and ritual to seek
the favour of supernatural
forces or beings.

First millennium BCE
The Bible tells that God
answered Moses's prayer
to change his mind about
destroying the Israelites after
they worship the golden calf.

AFTER
1960s The Liberation
Theology movement in
South America emphasizes
social and economic justice,
maintaining that God
responds especially to the
prayers of the poor and
oppressed in society.

F from the earliest times,
Jewish and Christian
theologians have
wrestled with complex issues
surrounding the nature of God
and the relationship of God to
humankind. To some he is a
vengeful God, who not only
stands in judgment at the end of
time, but also chooses whether or
not to respond to those who pray.
To others, he is perceived as an
all-knowing presence who has
decided the course of world history
and has reasons for all events, so
that every detail of the future is
mapped out in advance. In this
latter representation, God is
immune to appeals from humans
for help because he has absolute
prior knowledge of the outcome
of every situation.

The relevance of prayer
How the relationship between
God and the things that happen is
understood has deep implications
for the role of Christian prayer.
If God already knows the past,
present, and future, then prayer –

God knows everything that exists.	The **future** hasn't happened yet, so it **doesn't exist**.
We can **influence** what the future becomes **by our prayers and actions** today.	Therefore, the future is still **open to change**.

See also: The battle between good and evil 60–65 ▪ Divining the future 79 ▪ Devotion through puja 114–15 ▪ Jesus's message to the world 204–207 ▪ Augustine and free will 220–21

God… is so related to the world that there is between him and that world a "give-and-take"… He is influenced by what happens.
W. Pittenger

Theologians of hope

The rejection of traditional theological concepts such as God's foreknowledge (his awareness of future events), immutability (his unchanging nature), and impassibility (his freedom from emotion and independence from other beings) was not confined to any one school of theology during the 20th century. The ideas have been labelled in various ways, including process theology, the openness of God, and open theism. In the later 20th century, a group of theologians emerged who have been loosely termed the "theologians of hope". These include, in Germany, Jürgen Moltmann and Wolfhart Pannenberg, and in the USA, Robert Jenson. One of their principal arguments was that because the future does not yet exist – even for God – the essential characteristic of Christianity is hope.

communicating with God by offering verbal praise or requests, through thoughts and meditations, or in the form of deliberate acts of worship – seems irrelevant. Merely telling God what he already knows would carry no hope of changing what will happen. However, if the future is not already determined by God and is truly open, then prayer becomes an essential part of shaping that future.

Inside the mind of God
Although Christian theology has traditionally regarded God as omniscient, possessing a complete knowledge of all things past, present, and future, in the 20th century some theologians began to reject the idea of his "foreknowledge" (knowledge of the future). If God knows what will happen, then the future must already be set in stone, which, they argued, would remove true freedom and spontaneity from history. This would also raise questions about God's essential goodness, and whether he is complicit in evil if

he has prior knowledge of it, but takes no preventative action – as may be evident, for example, in his knowledge, even before the creation, that humans would bring suffering and wickedness into the world.

The future is open
The classic Christian view of God's foreknowledge depends upon the belief that God exists outside of time, so that what is in the future for human beings (and hence is nonexistent and unknowable) is in the past for God (and therefore both exists and is knowable). However, this view owes more to ancient Greek philosophy than genuine Christian thinking. The Bible describes a God who actively accompanies his people through time, not simply watching them from a distant position outside of time. Moreover, Christians believe that the coming of Jesus as a human being should be understood as the clearest indication that God is not outside of time or the reality of human life

on earth, since he lived a human life, with all its limitations. Consequently, if the future does not yet exist for either humans or God, then it can be truly open. Seen from this perspective, God is not a distant observer but an active participant in the historical process, a presence who listens to the prayers and appeals of people, responding to their needs and walking beside them in their journey through life. ▪

The misuse of weapons of war, such as nuclear bombs, indicates the human capacity for evil – in the future as well as the past. Does God know about this and choose to do nothing?

ISLAM
FROM 610 CE

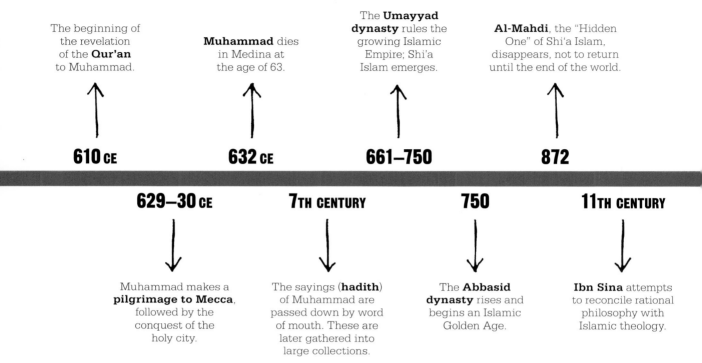

The beginning of the revelation of the **Qur'an** to Muhammad.

610 CE

Muhammad dies in Medina at the age of 63.

632 CE

The **Umayyad dynasty** rules the growing Islamic Empire; Shi'a Islam emerges.

661–750

Al-Mahdi, the "Hidden One" of Shi'a Islam, disappears, not to return until the end of the world.

872

629–30 CE

Muhammad makes a **pilgrimage to Mecca**, followed by the conquest of the holy city.

7TH CENTURY

The sayings (**hadith**) of Muhammad are passed down by word of mouth. These are later gathered into large collections.

750

The **Abbasid dynasty** rises and begins an Islamic Golden Age.

11TH CENTURY

Ibn Sina attempts to reconcile rational philosophy with Islamic theology.

Founded in the 7th century, Islam is nevertheless regarded by its followers as an ancient faith – one that has always existed as God's intended religion. Along with Judaism and Christianity, it is an Abrahamic religion, tracing its roots back to Ibrahim (Abraham), the first of a line of prophets sent to reveal the faith – a line that also includes Musa (Moses) and Isa (Jesus). Muslims believe the last in this line is the Prophet Muhammad, who received the revelations contained in the Qur'an and established Islam as it is known today.

Islam is a strongly monotheistic religion, emphasizing the oneness of an incomparable God, Allah (Arabic for "*the* God"), and people's duty to serve him. Islam teaches that human life is a gift from God, and the way a person lives their life will be assessed on the Day of Judgment. The central professions of the faith are summed up in the Five Pillars of Islam. Religious life revolves round the mosque, which, as well as being a centre of worship and teaching, acts as a focus for the social life of the community.

The last prophet

The revelation to Muhammad is considered the final and complete revelation from God. Memorized by Muhammad's immediate followers, it was written in the form of the Qur'an – Islam's holy scripture and the ultimate and unquestionable word of God. Beyond the Qur'an, there also exist sayings attributed to Muhammad, collectively known as the hadith. The scriptures have inspired a rich tradition of scholarly interpretation. From the judgments of theologians on the holy books and an examination of the life of the Prophet Muhammad, has emerged a system of religious law and moral codes known as shari'a, which informs the civil law of many Islamic countries.

From its origins, Islam has been entwined with civil and political life. Muhammad himself was as much a political as a religious leader and thinker. Because of his preaching of monotheism, he and his followers were forced to flee Mecca (an event known to Muslims as the Hijra, commemorated annually) for Medina, where he established the first Islamic city-state, with himself as spiritual, political, and military leader. He then led his people back to Mecca, conquering the city and establishing the beginnings of an

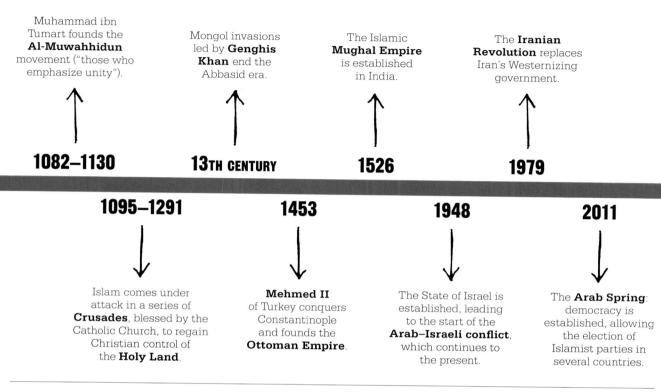

Muhammad ibn Tumart founds the **Al-Muwahhidun** movement ("those who emphasize unity").

Mongol invasions led by **Genghis Khan** end the Abbasid era.

The Islamic **Mughal Empire** is established in India.

The **Iranian Revolution** replaces Iran's Westernizing government.

1082–1130   **13TH CENTURY**   **1526**   **1979**

1095–1291   **1453**   **1948**   **2011**

Islam comes under attack in a series of **Crusades**, blessed by the Catholic Church, to regain Christian control of the **Holy Land**.

Mehmed II of Turkey conquers Constantinople and founds the **Ottoman Empire**.

The State of Israel is established, leading to the start of the **Arab–Israeli conflict**, which continues to the present.

The **Arab Spring**: democracy is established, allowing the election of Islamist parties in several countries.

empire to unite the disparate tribes of Arabia. Within a century of his death in 632, the Islamic Empire had expanded across northern Africa and into Asia. Despite disputes over who should succeed Muhammad, which led to the division between Sunni and Shi'a Islam, the Islamic Caliphate – the Muslim political and religious state ruled by a caliph – wielded great political unity and power.

The Islamic Golden Age
Soon, the Islamic Empire extended over a wider area than Christian Europe. However, in contrast to Christianity, which saw scientific thought to be a threat to its dogma, Islam saw no incompatibility between its theology and the disciplines of philosophy and science. Cities such as Baghdad

and Damascus became centres of scientific inquiry and learning. Islamic writing and poetry also flourished, along with decorative arts, including calligraphy.

The Islamic Empire eventually fragmented, but Islam remains one of the largest of all religions, practised by some 25 per cent of the world population. About three-quarters of adherents are Sunni and 10–20 per cent Shi'a. Around 50 countries have a Muslim majority: of these, a handful, including Saudi Arabia, Afghanistan, Pakistan, and Iran are considered Islamic states, based on religious law; a large number of other countries, mainly in the Middle East, have Islam as their official state religion; others still have secular governments, but predominantly Islamic

populations. Indonesia is the country with the largest number of Muslims, followed by Pakistan, India, and Bangladesh.

Approximately 25 per cent of Muslims live in the Middle East and North Africa, and there are now Muslim communities in almost every other country in the world.

Islam has come into conflict, both ideologically and politically, with the Christian world since the Crusades, and following colonial domination by the West. Recent tensions have given rise to a radical interpretation of jihad ("struggle") by some fundamentalist Muslims as a religious duty to defend their faith through conflict. However, Islam is essentially a peaceable religion, and most Muslims identify more closely with the compassionate principles of their faith. ■

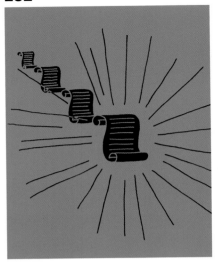

MUHAMMAD IS GOD'S FINAL MESSENGER
THE PROPHET AND THE ORIGINS OF ISLAM

IN CONTEXT

KEY FIGURE
Muhammad

WHEN AND WHERE
570–632 CE, Arabia

BEFORE
c.2000–1500 BCE In the Hebrew Bible, God makes a covenant with the patriarch Abraham; Islam will recognize this figure (in Arabic, Ibrahim) as one of the first prophets.

c.14th–13th century BCE In Jewish, Christian, and Muslim tradition, Moses, leading the Israelites, receives commandments from God on Mount Sinai.

1st century CE Jesus, later recognized by Muslims as a prophet, foretells the coming of a final prophet or messenger of God.

AFTER
19th century In India, Mirza Ghulam Ahmad claims to be a prophet bringing a new message that will reform Islam.

God **revealed** His Word to Moses and Jesus.

↓

Humanity **misinterpreted and corrupted** the message of the revelations.

↓

God now **transmits His Word** directly to Muhammad.

↓

The pure **message of Islam** is His final message to humanity.

↓

Muhammad is God's final messenger.

According to Islamic tradition, in around 582 CE a Christian hermit, Bahira, was living in the Syrian desert when, one day, a boy passing by with a camel train caught his attention. After talking with him, Bahira concluded that the sign of prophecy was upon the boy. He was destined for greatness, Bahira foretold, and should be cared for well.

The young boy was Muhammad ibn 'Abdallah, who became the prophet of Islam and, according to Muslims, God's final messenger. This implies, of course, that there were messengers sent by God (in Arabic, Allah) before Muhammad; these include notable figures such as Musa (Moses) and Isa (Jesus). To Musa, God revealed the Tawrat, or Torah, to guide the Jews. To Isa, God gave the Injil, a lost scripture with a name that translates as "Gospel", although it did not resemble in its form the four canonical Gospels of Christianity.

Muslims consider Jews and Christians to be "People of the Book", because, like Muslims, they are also monotheists with a holy scripture that was revealed to them by God. Muslims honour, in some ways, the revelations God gave to messengers

See also: God's covenant with Israel 168–75 ▪ Jesus's message to the world 204–207 ▪ The origins of Ahmaddiya 284–85

> Muhammad is… the Messenger of God and the Seal of the Prophets.
> **Surah 33:40**

before Muhammad, but they also believe that these revelations became corrupt. Jews introduced elements to the Torah that did not come directly from God. Likewise, Jesus's followers mishandled his message and distorted the Gospels, misrepresenting God's original intentions. Therefore, Islam teaches that the Jewish and Christian scriptures in their current form are no longer God's pure revelations, but corrupted by human error.

God's word uncorrupted

In order to overcome this corruption, God sent down his undefiled word one final time, in the form of the Qur'an, through Muhammad – his final messenger. Thus, Islam is not seen by Muslims as a new religion with a new holy book. Instead, Islam is considered the original, pure, and unique revelation of God. It supersedes those revelations that were given to Moses and Jesus and mishandled by their followers.

Now in Saudi Arabia, Mecca is the holiest city of the Islamic faith, as it is the birthplace of Muhammad; this is the Grand Mosque, the heart of the city.

Moreover, it marks an end to further revelation. Muhammad is the "Seal [last] of the Prophets": he marks a close in God's revelation and is the last of God's special messengers.

By the early 7th century, Muhammad claimed the authority of a prophet, whose mission was to preach the worship of the one, true God. Many Jews, Christians, and polytheists in his native Mecca believed his message. This fledgling community of Muslims was persecuted for its beliefs, and so Muhammad left Mecca for nearby Medina, where the Muslim community expanded.

Given Muhammad's eminent status in Islam, Muslims have always looked to his life and words as a model for Islamic living. Many of the things he said and did are recorded in the Sunna, which comprises authoritative collections of Muhammad's sayings (*hadith*) and actions (*sunna*). These serve as examples to Muslims seeking guidance on how to live their lives. ▪

Muhammad ibn 'Abdallah

Born near Mecca around 570, Muhammad ibn 'Abdallah was raised by his uncle, Abu Talib. The young Muhammad accompanied his uncle on many of his journeys as a camel-train merchant, meeting travellers from a wide variety of cultures and religions. He gained a reputation for being wise and trustworthy.

When in his early 20s, Muhammad was employed by a wealthy widow, Khadija, to manage her business. She, too, was a camel-train merchant. Khadija later proposed to him and they were married. After her death, Muhammad remarried and is said to have had 13 wives or concubines.

Muhammad would often retreat from business and family life to a cave in the desert, where he would meditate. In 610, during a moonless night of meditation, the angel Jibrail (Gabriel) appeared in a bright light to Muhammad, offering to him the first of many revelations that would eventually make up the Qur'an, Islam's holy book. Muhammad's career as a prophet lasted for 22 years. He died in 632 in Medina.

THE QUR'AN WAS SENT DOWN FROM HEAVEN

GOD REVEALS HIS WORD AND HIS WILL

IN CONTEXT

KEY TEXT
The Qur'an

WHEN AND WHERE
610–632 CE, Arabia

BEFORE
c.2000–1500 BCE Muslims believe Moses is given the Torah on Mount Sinai.

10th–9th century BCE Dawud (King David of Israel) receives the Zabur, a second holy book, from God; this may be the biblical book of Psalms.

1st century CE In Islamic tradition, God bestows a book of revelation and truth on Jesus.

AFTER
c.7th century CE The companions of the Prophet produce the first Qur'anic text.

8th–9th century CE The scholar al-Shafi'i enshrines the Qur'an as the primary reference for shari'a, or Islamic law.

According to the Islamic faith, God has revealed his will to humankind through nature, history, and, most importantly, his word. Nature, or God's creation, is a sign pointing to God's existence. In history, the rise and fall of empires are signs of God's sovereignty over humankind. But of greatest significance is that God's will is revealed through his word and conveyed by his messengers.

In Islam, God's ultimate word and will are contained in the Qur'an, the book that was revealed to the Prophet Muhammad, chosen by God as His final messenger (pp.252–53). Within it are *ayat* – verses, or "signs", that reveal to the world what God desires and commands. Another name for the Qur'an is *al-Tanzil*, "the Downsent". For Muslims, the Qur'an is God's literal word that has been sent down to humankind from heaven.

The recitation

According to Islamic tradition, Muhammad spent many days meditating in a cave on Mount Hira overlooking Mecca. One night the angel Jibrail (the Arabic name

Recite! In the name of your Lord who created, created man from a blood-clot. Recite!
Sura 96:1–5

for Gabriel) appeared to him in the cave, summoning Muhammad to prophethood and demanding that he "Recite!" (p.253). What followed was the first revelation of the Qur'an. The whole of the Qur'an was revealed to Muhammad at intervals over a prolonged period of time so that he could gradually recite it (the Arabic word *qur'an* means "recitation") to others. The revelations, many of which Muhammad was to receive in a trance-like state, began in 610 CE and continued over the next 22 years. At first, Muhammad memorized the revelations and

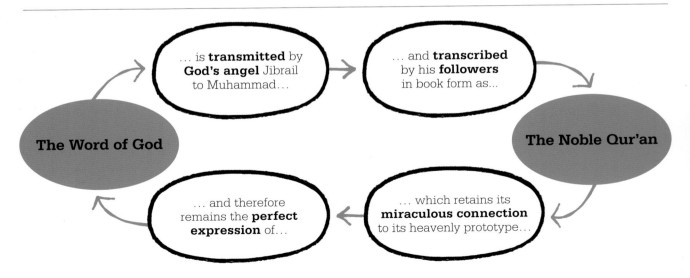

The Word of God ... is **transmitted** by **God's angel** Jibrail to Muhammad... ... and **transcribed** by his **followers** in book form as... The Noble Qur'an ... which retains its **miraculous connection** to its heavenly prototype... ... and therefore remains the **perfect expression** of...

See also: God's covenant with Israel 168–75 ▪ The Prophet and the origins of Islam 252–53 ▪ The central professions of faith 262–69 ▪ The pathway to harmonious living 272–75

The angel Jibrail appears to Muhammad and delivers the first revelation. Here, in accordance with Islamic tradition, a faceless figure represents the Prophet.

speaking, by length. The longer chapters are found at the beginning of the Qur'an, with shorter chapters arranged towards the end. As a whole, the chapters cover a wide range of topics, providing guidance on worship, politics, marriage and family life, care for the disadvantaged, and even matters of hygiene, community affairs, and economics.

In an attempt to classify and date the chapters of the Qur'an, modern scholars have created a system for identifying them. In this method of classification, revelations that appear to have been given to Muhammad early in his prophetic career, when he resided in Mecca, are known as the Meccan chapters. The earliest of these Meccan revelations are often very rhythmic and full of imagery. Many begin with oaths. »

passed them on orally. His followers memorized them in turn, but the revelations were eventually written down, sometimes by Muhammad's secretaries, at other times by his followers. Portions of the Qur'an have been found written on pieces of animal bone, leather, stones, palm leaves, and parchment.

A standardized version of the Qur'an in book form was compiled in the mid-7th century, soon after Muhammad's death. Muslims believe that this compilation, and the ordering of the 114 chapters and 6,000 verses that resulted, were divinely inspired.

Many sections of the Qur'an contain material that matches, or at least corresponds closely to, portions of the Hebrew Bible and Christian New Testament. However, according to the Muslim view, these holy books are corrupted (pp.252–53): the Qur'an is therefore believed to function both as a corrective to, and a progression beyond, previous revelations.

The ordering of the suras

The chapters (suras) and verses that make up the Qur'an are not arranged chronologically or according to topic but, broadly

[It is] a Qur'an which we have divided [into parts], in order that you might recite it to the people at intervals. And we have sent it down progressively.
Sura 17:106

For example, chapter 95 of the Qur'an is introduced with, "By the fig and the olive and by Mount Sinai and by this city of security!".

Later Meccan chapters are more serene and contain frequent illustrations of the truth of God's message drawn from nature and history. They are more formal than other chapters and often discuss matters of doctrine. God is frequently referred to in these chapters as "the Merciful".

Revelations accorded to Muhammad when he was living in the city of Medina are classified by scholars as the Medinan chapters. These chapters are quite different from the Meccan ones because, by this time, Muhammad was no longer leading a fledgling group of followers, but had become the head of a large, independent community of Muslims.

As a result, the Medinan chapters are characterized less by themes of doctrine and the proofs of God's signs. Instead, more time is spent in discussion of legal and social matters and how such rulings should be applied in order to regulate life within the growing Muslim community.

For example, in chapter 24 of the Qur'an, Muslims are told to bring four witnesses in order to corroborate an accusation of adultery. This was an important safeguard for women in a society in which even the sight of an unrelated man and woman together might be considered

> This Qur'an is not such as could ever be produced by other than God.
> **Sura 10:37**

cause for suspicion. The testimony of those who do not provide the necessary witnesses should be rejected and such persons dealt with harshly according to this Medinan chapter of the Qur'an.

Rote and recitation

Western scholarship has added numbers to the chapters and verses of the Qur'an for ease of reference. For Muslims, however, chapters are referred to by specific, distinguishing words that appear within each chapter. For example, the Qur'an's second and longest chapter is known as "The Cow". This chapter is named after a story it contains about a heifer that is reluctantly sacrificed by the Israelites. In the account, the flesh of the sacrificed animal is used to bring a slain man to life again in order to identify his murderer.

Muslims also rarely refer to individual verses by number, instead preferring to quote the beginning of a passage under discussion. This form of referencing of course requires not only great familiarity with the text of the Qu'ran but also considerable memorization skills. Nonetheless, many Muslims memorize large

The Qur'an is not arranged in any narrative or chronological order. Opened at any point, it will offer reassurance of God's will to the reader through suras (chapters) that often take their name from a story, theme, or truth that they contain.

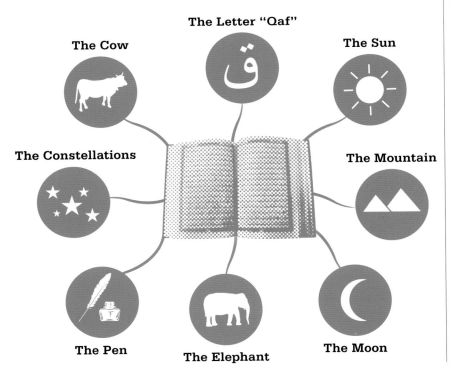

Reading, learning, and reciting
portions of the Qur'an are central to Islamic education, and remain an everyday activity for Muslims thoughout their adult lives.

portions of the Qur'an, and some are even able to commit the entire book to memory.

To learn the entire Qur'an by heart brings great prestige and blessing, and a Muslim who has achieved this is known as a hafiz or a "guardian" of the Qur'an. A hafiz keeps God's holy book alive, and is often called "*shaykh*", a mark of great respect. Such Muslims often become reciters of the Qur'an, a role that is undertaken during daily prayers and other important rituals and ceremonies. This skill is so highly prized that auditoriums are often filled to capacity for recitation contests.

The Qur'an has a pre-eminent place both in Islam and within God's plan for the world. It is considered the divine miracle brought by the Prophet Muhammad – the only miracle, in fact, as Muhammad himself did not perform them. Muslims believe that the Qur'an is based on a heavenly prototype, a book written in Arabic and existing with God in heaven.

This means that, even though the Qur'an was given to Muhammad in the form of oral recitations and only later written down, the physical book itself is regarded as sacred.

Respect for the Qur'an

The Muslim belief that the Islamic holy scripture exists in heaven makes the handling of its earthly representations a matter of great care and delicacy, and there are several guidelines regarding how Muslims should treat their sacred book. The Qur'an, and the Arabic text in particular, should never be left on the floor or in any unclean place. When displayed among a pile of books, it should always be positioned on top; and when placed on a bookshelf, it should rest on the highest shelf, with nothing else beside or above it.

In addition, before handling the Qur'an, Muslims should make certain that they are ritually clean by washing themselves, just as they would before worshipping God. The Qur'an should also be carried with care, and for this »

The Qur'an and the Bible

Readers of the Qur'an and both the Hebrew Bible and the Christian Bible will find many characters and stories in common. The words of the Qur'an appear to assume some familiarity with Jewish and Christian texts, while offering some gentle correctives in certain details. In the Qur'an, for example, Adam and Hawwa (Eve) are forgiven by God before being sent from paradise, because they begged for His mercy, rather than cast out and cursed as in the Bible. Jesus (as prophet, rather than divine figure) appears several times, but nowhere near as often as his mother Mary, spoken of in the Qur'an with especial fondness. In a miracle unreported in the Bible, the infant Jesus speaks up from the crib to defend his mother's honour when ill-wishers accuse her of fornication.

... recite the Qur'an in slow, measured rhythmic tones.
Sura 73:4

Printed and bound copies of the Qur'an are checked meticulously for accuracy before being distributed – here by a 600-strong team of readers at the King Fahd printworks in Saudi Arabia.

reason it is frequently carried in a bag to avoid damage. If it should accidentally fall, then it is honoured, sometimes with a kiss, and returned to safety. Some Muslims will make a charitable donation in cases where they have handled the Qur'an carelessly.

The sacred respect shown towards the Qur'an is maintained for old and worn-out copies as well, which may not be thrown away, but instead should be disposed of through a respectful burial. This can be done in any appropriate place for a burial, including at sea. Some Muslims will also allow a disposal by fire.

Stipulations for the disposal of the sacred text are also meant to apply to any paper, jewellery, decoration, or other material on which verses of the Qur'an have been written. For this reason, some Muslim-majority regions provide special disposal bins so that such material can be collected and disposed of properly.

Many of these rules of respect apply not only to the written text of the Qur'an, but also to its oral recitation. Since the Qur'an is perceived as God's literal word, it is thought to come alive when it is recited. As a result, many Muslims cover their heads when it is read aloud and sometimes even during their personal study of the Qur'an.

The role of language

The belief that the heavenly prototype of the Qur'an is written in Arabic makes Qur'anic Arabic not only the sacred language of Islam, but the language of God as well. For Muslims there is therefore a very real sense that the Qur'an loses its status as divine revelation when it is translated into other languages. Due to this belief, translations of the Qur'an are frequently accompanied by the Arabic text, and even then these texts are considered mere interpretations or translations of the meaning of the original Arabic. They are in no way substitutes or equivalents of the Arabic Qur'an.

Since Qur'anic Arabic is considered a divine language, other aspects of Muslim life and thought are further shaped around the language. For example, Muslims throughout the world memorize the Qur'an and their prayers in Arabic, regardless of whether or not they understand the language.

Perhaps most importantly, the text of the Arabic Qur'an, since it is holy, shares certain characteristics with God, its author. Thus, it is perfect, eternal, uncreated, and unchangeable. Known as *i'jaz al-Qur'an* (the "miraculousness" or "inimitability of the Qur'an"), this doctrine means that the language, literary style, and ideas revealed in the Qur'an are irreproducible and cannot be matched by any human

endeavour. Everything about it, from the grammatical constructions of the Qur'an's Arabic, to the sound of it when it is read and chanted, and the prophecies it foretells, is considered miraculous and matchless. According to Muslims, any attempt to equal or surpass the Qur'an will surely fail.

Another aspect of the Qur'an's miraculous nature is its unique repetition of basic themes. Opening the Qur'an at any section will often yield a treatment of the book's essential message. This formulaic, and almost abbreviated, style is challenging for non-Muslims, or those familiar with the narrative structure of other holy scriptures. For Muslims, however, this style is a mysterious testament to the Qur'an's unparalleled beauty.

The Qur'an is not only the most sacred book of Islam, but is also considered by Muslims, and even many non-Muslims, as the crowning achievement of Arabic literature. As such, the Qur'an is studied for its poetic prose as much as it is read for its divine guidance. But the respect,

Falsehood cannot come to it from any direction, it is preserved by God Who said: "Verily, We, it is We who have sent down the Qur'an and surely, We will guard it from corruption.
Sura 15:9

> ... a guidance for the people and clear proofs of guidance and the criterion [of right and wrong].
> **Sura 2:185**

appreciation, and matchlessness accorded to the Qur'an are not limited by Muslims to its message or its recitation. Even the Arabic script within the holy book has significant visual value and plays a central role in Islamic art.

The art of Islam

Motivated by a desire to avoid idolatry in all its forms, Muslim tradition forbade representational illustration within the Qur'an.

However, abstract images, such as patterns, were permitted, and the Arabic script itself developed into an elevated art form: beautiful Arabic calligraphy was used to write out the Qur'an, often in spectacular coloured inks and precious gold leaf.

As a result of the prohibition on portraying animals or human figures, artists also developed the Islamic arabesque style. This is a form of artistic decoration that consists of rhythmic lines, elaborate scrolling and interlacing foliage, and repeated geometric motifs. These artworks – which appear on mosaics, in the Qur'an, and inside mosques – also have an important spiritual message: the endlessly intertwining shapes and patterns, in which there appears to be no beginning or end, are intended to prompt reflection on the infinity of Allah. ∎

Islam does not allow representation in religious imagery; instead, beautiful calligraphy and patterning are used. The geometric designs reflect the order and harmony that Allah brings.

The transcribers of the Qur'an

In order to safeguard the integrity of the Qur'an, Zayd ibn Thabit, one of the Prophet's close companions, formed a group of scribes responsible for writing down revelations as they came to Muhammad. Eventually, Zayd and his scholars produced a full-length manuscript of the Qur'an, which was cross-checked with those who had memorized the revelations to ensure that there were no errors. The finished manuscript was presented to Hafsah, one of Muhammad's wives.

Since Arabic is written without vowels, a correct reading and pronunciation of the text depends upon the reader's familiarity with the language. When discrepancies cropped up, the dialect of the Quraysh, Muhammad's tribe, was given precedence. Even so, variations of the written Qur'anic text arose. Consequently, Uthman ibn Affan, one of Muhammad's companions, oversaw the production of an authorized version in the mid-7th century. The book of the Qur'an as it is known today is largely a result of this compilation.

THE FIVE PILLARS OF ISLAM

THE CENTRAL PROFESSIONS OF FAITH

IN CONTEXT

KEY SOURCE
**Hadith (sayings)
of Muhammad**

WHEN AND WHERE
Early 7th century, Arabia

BEFORE
From 1000 BCE The Torah, then
the Talmud, set down the rules
for Jewish life that form part of
God's covenants with Israel.

1st century CE Christianity
incorporates the Judaic
covenants, in particular the
Ten Commandments.

610 CE The Prophet
Muhammad starts to receive
the revelation of the Qur'an.

AFTER
680 CE Shi'a Islam introduces
additional "pillars" that guide
faith and observance.

8th century CE Schools of
Islamic law develop, offering
further interpretations that
guide Islamic life and practice.

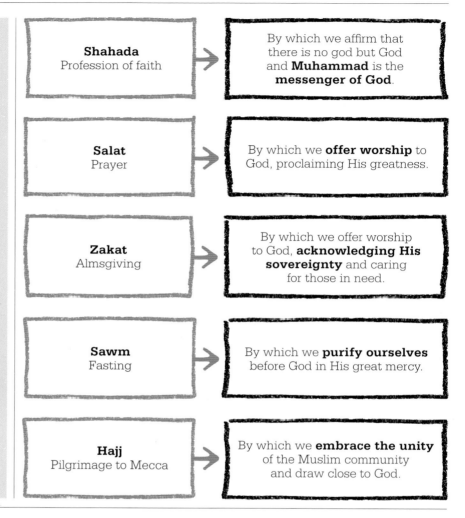

Shahada
Profession of faith

By which we affirm that there is no god but God and **Muhammad** is the **messenger of God**.

Salat
Prayer

By which we **offer worship** to God, proclaiming His greatness.

Zakat
Almsgiving

By which we offer worship to God, **acknowledging His sovereignty** and caring for those in need.

Sawm
Fasting

By which we **purify ourselves** before God in His great mercy.

Hajj
Pilgrimage to Mecca

By which we **embrace the unity** of the Muslim community and draw close to God.

According to a tradition narrated by Abdallah ibn 'Umar ibn al-Khattab, one of Muhammad's companions, the Prophet summarized Islam by saying that the religion is based on five principles: "To testify that there is no god but God and Muhammad is God's messenger; to offer the prayers dutifully and perfectly; to pay the obligatory alms; to perform the pilgrimage to Mecca; and to observe the fast during the month of Ramadan".

Known as 'ibadat ("acts of worship") to Muslims, and often referred to as the "pillars of Islam",

these five practices lie at the core of the faith, and all branches of Islam accept and perform them.

The profession of faith
While not summarizing the whole of Islam as a religion, the pillars serve as a kind of outline of minimal obligations for Muslims to abide by. Their simplicity and straightforwardness are intentional, for Muslims are intended to follow God unencumbered by the heavy burden of religious stipulations. As the Qur'an confirms, "[God] has not laid upon you in religion any hardship". With this in mind,

the first pillar, and central creed of Islam, is a simple acknowledgment of the distinctiveness of the one, true God and the unique place of his messenger, Muhammad. This profession of faith, known as the shahada ("witness"), is the only means by which a person may become a Muslim. The shahada is whispered in a Muslim's ear at birth and at death. It is also offered as a testimony throughout the day when Muslims are called to prayer. Although succinct, the shahada is made up of two significant parts. In the first part, Muslims bear witness to the absolute oneness

Each Muslim baby has the shahada, the profession of faith, whispered in his or her ear at birth; an earlier Arabic tradition still practised by many is to dab honey on the baby's lips.

of God. This affirms one of the core beliefs of Islam (*tawhid*, or God's unity), but it also functions as a reminder that polytheism (belief in more than one god) and the worship of any being or thing alongside, or in association with, God is the ultimate sin in Islam.

The second part of the shahada recalls that Muhammad is not just God's prophet, but his special messenger, surpassing other prophets before him. He is also honoured as the final prophet.

Commitment to prayer

The second pillar of Islam is *salat* (prayer). While Muslims may offer informal, personal prayers or requests to God as they wish, the main prayers of Islam are prescribed, quite formal and regulated, and are a designated opportunity to worship God.

Muslims are summoned to prayer five times every day: at dawn, noon, mid-afternoon, dusk,

There is no god but God and Muhammad is the messenger of God.
The shahada

and evening. In earlier times, and in some cases nowadays, a prayer leader, or muezzin, would ascend a minaret, a tall tower outside the mosque, and call local Muslims to prayer by chanting the shahada and urging them to come to the mosque. Today, muezzins often chant into a microphone, which projects the summons into the community via loudspeakers. Sometimes, a prerecorded call may be played. Often, Muslims do gather for prayers at a mosque, but when this is not possible, prayers can be performed alone or in groups in any location.

Prayers are preceded by purification, an act so important that Muhammad is thought to have said it was "half the faith". For the five prayers, Muslims begin by washing their hands, mouth, and nostrils with water. They wash their entire face and clean their forearms, also passing a wet hand over their heads, and cleaning their feet and ankles. The number of times each body part is cleansed varies in different schools of Islam. Having ritually cleansed themselves, Muslims »

Abdallah ibn 'Umar

Abdallah ibn 'Umar ibn al-Khattab was the oldest son of 'Umar I, the second leader of the Muslim community after Muhammad's death. He was born in the early 7th century and converted to Islam along with his father. As a close companion of Muhammad, Ibn Umar stood by the Prophet's side in several battles and was esteemed for his nobility and selflessness.

Most importantly, Ibn 'Umar is known as one of the most trustworthy authorities on the early history of Islam. Given his close relationship with Muhammad and other important figures in early Islam, he had extensive knowledge of the period. He also served as a credible source for many Hadith (sayings) of Muhammad. When he was approximately 84 years old, Ibn 'Umar made a pilgrimage to Mecca and died there in 693.

stand facing the direction of Mecca, the holiest city of Islam, and recite their prayers. In mosques, this direction is marked by a decorated niche known as a mihrab. Outside mosques, Muslims may find the exact direction of Mecca using specially marked compasses and even web-based applications. Those praying outside the mosque will usually perform their prayers on a special prayer mat, signifying that the act of prayer is performed in a clean place.

Prayer is begun with the declaration, "God is most great". Then Muslims recite a set of fixed prayers that include, among other passages, the opening chapter of the Qur'an: "In the name of God, the Most Gracious, the Most Merciful. All praises and thanks be to God, the Lord of the Universe, the Most Gracious, the Most Merciful, the Ruler on the Day of Judgment. You do we worship and You we ask for help. Guide us along the Straight Path, the way of those on whom You have bestowed Your grace, not of those who earned Your anger or who are lost." The profession of faith is then repeated

and an offering of peace to others is offered with the words: "May the peace, mercy, and blessings of God be upon you". These prayers are offered in Arabic and worshippers accompany them with prostrations and bows, together with raising and lowering their hands.

To non-Muslim observers, the Islamic prayer rituals may appear complex and overly regulated. For Muslims, however, participating in the habits of ritual purification and prescribed prayer allows them to worship God freely, unencumbered by the burden of their own agendas. As they join in unison with other Muslims to pray, they are also reminded of God's greatness, knowing that fellow believers all over the world are worshipping God in the same way.

The importance of charity

The third pillar of Islam is zakat (almsgiving). A central concern in the Qur'an is the treatment of the poor, marginalized, and disadvantaged. Consequently, Muslims are enjoined to care for the social and economic wellbeing of their communities, not simply

God is most great. I testify that there is no god but God. I testify that Muhammad is the messenger of God. Hurry to prayer. Hurry to success. God is most great.
Call to prayer

through acts of charity, which are encouraged, but also by paying an alms tax. All adult Muslims who are able to do so offer a percentage, not just of their monetary income, but of their entire assets for this tax. This percentage is traditionally set at 2.5 per cent, a figure arrived at by scholarly agreement, and drawn from references in the Sunna, for instance "one-quarter of one-tenth" of silver. In some cases, the offering may be as much as 20 per cent of farming or industrial assets.

Often, almsgiving is voluntary, but in some countries it has been regulated by governments. In such cases, stamps made specifically for sending alms are distributed. Otherwise, offerings can be placed in distribution boxes in mosques and at other locations.

Not only is the giving of alms considered an act of worship to God, but it is also thought to be something that is owed. If what

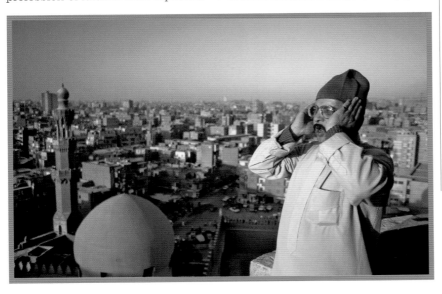

The call to prayer is made from the top of the mosque's minaret or tower by a chosen individual known as a muezzin, who may also indicate the prayer schedule to be followed.

> Righteous are those who… give the zakat.
> **Sura 2:177**

Muslims receive comes to them from God's sovereign blessing, then it is only right for them to give to those who have received less. With this in mind, almsgiving is not considered an act of charity for Muslims, but a duty they perform on behalf of those who require and deserve assistance. According to the Qur'an, worthy recipients of alms are the poor, orphans, and widows, as well as causes that aim to eliminate slavery, to help those who are in debt, and to spread Islam.

Observance of Ramadan

The fourth pillar of Islam is *sawm* (fasting), and in particular, the fast of Ramadan. This is the name for the ninth month in the Islamic lunar calendar. The penultimate night of this month-long fast commemorates the time when Muhammad received the first revelation of the Qur'an from the angel Jibrail. Pious Muslims may pray for the entire evening, hoping that their prayers will be answered. In general during Ramadan, all Muslims who are physically able abstain from food, drink, and sexual relations during daylight hours. Instead, they use this time for purifying themselves by reflecting upon their spiritual

The direction of Mecca from any location is determined using the "Great Circle" method – in other words, the shortest route (over one of the Poles if necessary). Calculating this was a preoccupation of Muslim scientists during the Golden Age of Islamic scholarship, from the 8th to the 13th centuries.

condition, considering any wrong committed, remembering God's great mercy, and contemplating the needs of their communities.

Each morning before daybreak, families gather for a small meal that must sustain them throughout the day. In the evening, after dark, families visit one another and take part in a larger meal that often includes special foods, such as dates, which Muhammad is believed to have eaten in order to break his fast.

Many Muslims go to their local mosque for evening prayer during Ramadan and recite a special

The direction of Mecca, or "Qibla" is commonly shown in public buildings in the Muslim world for purposes of prayer.

prayer said only during the month of fasting. Likewise, some Muslims use Ramadan for acts of piety, such as reciting the entire Qur'an.

Ramadan ends with a special feast, known as 'Id al-Fitr, which breaks the month of fasting. The feast is obligatory and is an »

The *hilal* or crescent moon that appears after the new moon announces the beginning and the end of the fasting month of Ramadan, although this period may also be calculated.

enormously joyous occasion. Families visit one another to share in special meals and to exchange gifts and sweets. Businesses often close for part of the celebrations, which can sometimes continue for several days.

Pilgrimage to Mecca

The fifth pillar of Islam is hajj: making a pilgrimage to the holy city of Mecca in Saudi Arabia, which begins after the month of Ramadan. Every adult Muslim who is physically able, and has the financial means to make the trip, should perform the pilgrimage at least once in his or her lifetime. To do so, Muslims travel by whatever means possible to Mecca. Many Muslim travel agencies even offer special hajj packages to groups and individuals to help ensure a memorable and problem-free experience. As pilgrims near the city, they often shout, "I am here, oh Lord, I am here!". The main focus of the pilgrimage is the Kaaba, the cube-shaped structure sitting at the centre of Mecca's Grand Mosque. According to tradition, the Kaaba was originally

built by Ibrahim (Arabic for Abraham) and his son Ismail (Arabic for Ishmael) in order to house a black stone given to Ibrahim by the angel Jibrail (Gabriel). The stone was meant to symbolize God's covenant with Ismail. In pre-Islamic times, the Kaaba was also a pilgrimage site for followers of polytheistic religions. At that time, the Kaaba was filled with shrines to various tribal gods. But under

Muhammad's guidance, it was cleansed of these shrines and restored as a symbol of worship of the one God, Allah.

Before arriving at the Kaaba, Muslim pilgrims must purify themselves. To do so, men wear seamless white robes and cut their hair, and some even shave their heads. Similarly, some women wear white robes, but many others choose to wear simple clothing that is traditional to their country of origin. In this state of purity, both men and women refrain from sexual activity, and from wearing jewellery or perfume. They also refrain from bathing, arguing, or anything that might taint their purity. In essence, everyone in their white robes represents not only purity, but unity and equality as well. On the one hand, the hajj is meant to be free of hierarchy and disunity, placing emphasis on total devotion to God and Muslims' special worship

… eat and drink until the white thread of dawn appears to you distinct from the black thread, then complete your fast until the nightfall.
Sura 2:187

Whoever performs hajj for the sake of pleasing God… shall return from it as free from sin as the day on which his mother gave birth to him.
**Hadith Sahih
Bukhari 26:596**

> I am here, oh Lord,
> I am here!
> **Pilgrim's prayer on
> reaching Mecca**

Permissible pilgrimage

Only Muslims may enter the holy city of Mecca and, in the very conservative form of Sunni Islam that is practised in Saudi Arabia, the Kaaba is the only permissible destination for pilgrimage. Under this orthodox form of Islam, known as Wahhabism, veneration of historical sites, graves, and buildings associated with Islamic history is strongly discouraged, as it might lead to worship of things other than God – the sin of idolatry, or shirk. As there is no concept of a "sacred" site or shrine, therefore, many old buildings in Mecca have been demolished to make way for new development, giving the city an almost entirely modern appearance. Not all forms of Islam follow this interpretation of shirk – Sufism, for example, holds the tombs of its saints and scholars in deep reverence.

during the pilgrimage. On the other hand, the great variety shown in female pilgrims' clothing reflects the diverse character of the global Muslim community coming together in spiritual unison at the Grand Mosque.

Rites of Mecca

Once pilgrims enter the Grand Mosque they perform the *tawaf,* walking around the Kaaba in an anticlockwise direction seven times. They will try to get as close as they can to the structure, and, if possible, will kiss or touch the black stone exposed in one of the Kaaba's corners. During the following seven days, pilgrims pray in the Grand Mosque and take part in other ceremonies. For example, pilgrims drink water drawn from the Zamzam well inside the mosque. According to Muslim tradition, this well was miraculously created by God in order to sustain Ismail as a baby when he was stranded in the desert with his mother, Hajar (Arabic for Hagar). Some pilgrims run between two hills, Safa and Marwa, to commemorate Hajar's search for water. They may also travel beyond Mecca, to Mina and Mount Arafat, where they pray to God, asking for forgiveness for the sins of the entire Muslim community. From here, pilgrims return to Mecca, to the Grand Mosque, where they circle the Kaaba again in a farewell *tawaf.*

The pilgrimage ends with a feast commemorating Ibrahim and his obedience to God. Even Muslims who have not made the pilgrimage celebrate this feast, which lasts for three days. Much food is eaten, with the leftovers distributed to the poor and needy.

Those who have made the journey to Mecca honour the faithfulness shown by Ibrahim by symbolically stoning the devil: they throw stones at three pillars representing evil. Finally, many pilgrims end their pilgrimage by visiting the city of Medina and the mosque in which the Prophet Muhammad is buried.

Lightening the burden

The five pillars of Islam may be seen to be representative of the faith as a whole, and to reflect the "light burden" that God places on his followers. However, although they show the simplicity of Islam, any number of practical difficulties may be encountered in attempting to follow the necessary stipulations. What if the direction of prayer cannot be established? What if a Muslim is unable to fast on one of the days of Ramadan? God offers a simple solution to such obstacles: "And to God belong the east and the west, so wherever you turn there is the face of God. Surely God is All-Sufficient for his creatures' needs, All-Knowing".

The essential point for Muslims is to turn towards God in worship in the best way that they know how, until such a point in time when they may worship him just as their fellow believers. ∎

The Kaaba in Mecca is a square, stone building that predates Islam by many centuries. The Grand Mosque was built around it.

THE IMAM IS GOD'S CHOSEN LEADER
THE EMERGENCE OF SHI'A ISLAM

IN CONTEXT

KEY FIGURE
'Ali ibn Abi Talib

WHEN AND WHERE
c.632–661, Arabia

BEFORE
From 1500 BCE The Hebrew Bible identifies Abraham and his successors as having been chosen by God to lead the Israelites.

1st century CE After his death, Jesus is known as Jesus Christ, the Messiah or anointed one. His mother Mary becomes a major devotional figure.

c.610 CE In Islam, Muhammad is chosen by God to receive the revelation of the Qur'an.

AFTER
c.1500 The Persian Safavid dynasty converts from Sunni to Shi'a Islam, and Iran develops as the major bastion of Shi'ism, while Arabia remains mainly Sunni.

When the Prophet Muhammad, founder of Islam, died in 632, he had established Islamic authority over the entire Arabian peninsula through a campaign of warfare and conquest. However, Muhammad had no sons who survived him, and on his death the Muslim community was divided over who was to succeed him as their leader.

Muhammad was considered to have a divine right to rule, but this prerogative ended with him. The majority of Muslims believed that the small group known as the Companions of the Prophet were best suited to leadership, as they were the people most closely guided by Muhammad and they were also the compilers of the Qur'an. They adopted one of Muhammad's

---

Who should **succeed the Prophet Muhammad?**

Many followers believe that **electing a leader** is in accordance with the Sunna – the teachings and sayings of Muhammad.	The Shi'a 'Ali party believe that God has indicated **a line of rightful succession** within the Family of the Prophet.
Sunni Islam is therefore headed by a **leader chosen by consensus**.	Shi'a Islam is therefore headed by an **imam who is chosen by God**.

See also: God reveals his word and his will 262–69 ▪ Striving in the way of God 278 ▪ The origins of Ahmaddiya 284–85

closest companions, Abu Bakr, as his successor. Abu Bakr was to be succeeded in turn by two more of the Companions, Umar and Uthman, as caliph, or ruler, of the Islamic territories. These caliphs were recognized as wise leaders and "the best of Muslims". Their followers believed that choosing a leader by community consensus best accorded with the ideas in the Sunna, Muhammad's teachings and sayings. These early caliphs were therefore appointed or elected, and the supporters of Abu Bakr and his two successors became known as Sunni Muslims.

An alternative choice

A minority group of believers disagreed with Abu Bakr's original appointment; they believed that the rightful leader should have been a close relative of Muhammad, and, in particular, a member of a special group known in the Qur'an as the Household (family) of the Prophet. This group claimed that Muhammad had suggested a successor: his

The first imam, 'Ali ibn Abi Talib, and his sons were members of the Household of the Prophet, so were seen to have divine knowledge, here depicted as shining down from heaven.

son-in-law and cousin 'Ali ibn Abi Talib, because Muhammad had publicly honoured 'Ali's ability to lead the community. Shi'a Muslims take their name from 'Ali, whom they see as the Prophet's rightful heir – they are known as the Shi'a 'Ali (Party of 'Ali).

'Ali was eventually appointed to lead the whole Muslim community in 656, after the death of Uthman, but when 'Ali died, Muslims were again divided; Shi'as supported 'Ali's son as successor, while Sunnis supported the election of Muawiyah I, a powerful governor of Syria. To this day, Shi'as remain a minority group within the Muslim community, dedicated to 'Ali and his successors. These descendants of Muhammad, known as imams, have absolute religious authority – their knowledge is considered to be divine and infallible. The largest branch of Shi'a Islam, whose imam is currently absent (see right), is led by proxy figures, or *marjas* – for example, Iran's Ayatollah Khomeini.

Since the dispute concerns the issue of leadership, Shi'a Islam is considered a movement within Islam, not a separate belief system. However, it does have its own emphases. To the Five Pillars of Islam Shi'as add another five: making offerings for the benefit of the community, commanding good, forbidding evil (all beliefs shared by many non-Shi'as), plus two unique to Shi'a Islam – loving the Household of the Prophet, and turning away from those who do not. ▪

Further divisions in Shi'a Islam

The succession from 'Ali, first imam of Shi'a Islam, has been marked by further divisions caused by disagreement over succession. Disputes after the deaths of the fourth and sixth imams led to the formation of, respectively, the Five-Imam Shi'as, or "Fivers", and Seven-Imam Shi'as, or "Seveners".

The Seveners, also known as Ismaelite Shi'as, divided yet again over the question of which Family member was the rightful successor in the eyes of God; their largest branch is known as Nizari Ismailism, currently led by the Aga Khan.

Twelve-Imam Shi'as, or "Twelvers", are by far the largest group within Shi'a Islam. They believe that their last imam, the six-year-old Muhammad al-Qa'im, did not actually die but went into a hidden existence in 874, and will eventually return as the messianic figure known as the Imam al-Mahdi. His reappearance will signal the beginning of the ultimate struggle for good that, in Islam, marks the end of the world.

God intends only to remove from you the impurity [of sin], Oh People of the [Prophet's] Household, and to purify you with purification.
Sura 33:33

GOD GUIDES US WITH SHARI'A

THE PATHWAY TO HARMONIOUS LIVING

IN CONTEXT

KEY FIGURE
Abu 'Abdallah Muhammad ibn Idris al-Shafi'i

WHEN AND WHERE
767–820 CE, Arabia

BEFORE
1500 BCE The Torah records the Ten Commandments: religious and ethical laws given to Moses by God.

7th century CE The Prophet Muhammad receives the revelation of the Qur'an; his sayings and actions are passed down by his followers.

AFTER
c.14th century Ibn Taymiyyah, an Islamic scholar, issues a fatwa against the Mongols for not basing their laws on shari'a.

1997 The European Council for Fatwa and Research is founded to assist European Muslims in interpreting shari'a.

I n Islamic thought, to submit oneself to God's guidance (*islam* means "submission") is the mark of a true Muslim. To help followers navigate life in ways that are pleasing to him, God has offered a pathway known as shari'a, meaning literally "the road to the watering hole". In the context of Arabia's deserts, a road to water is a great treasure and, similarly, shari'a is the pathway, by God's law, to harmonious living. It is a system of ethics and a science of law (*fiqh*) that is meant to govern humankind and guide everything people do.

This system required sources to refer to, and, early on, Muslims relied on Muhammad's revelations (the

See also: Living in harmony 38 ▪ Wisdom lies with the superior man 72–77 ▪ The personal quest for truth 144
▪ Writing the Oral Law 182–83 ▪ God reveals his word and his will 254–61

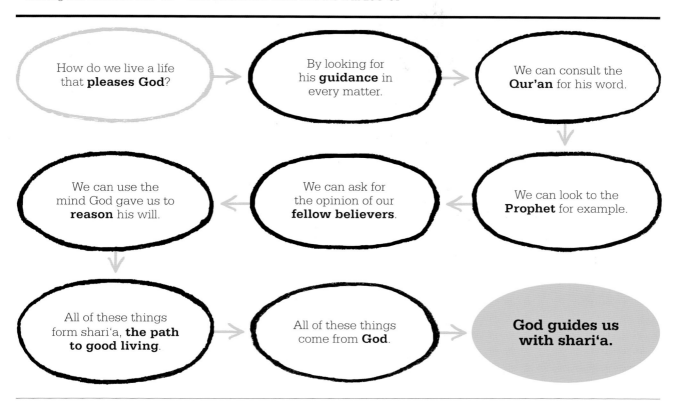

How do we live a life that **pleases God**?

By looking for his **guidance** in every matter.

We can consult the **Qur'an** for his word.

We can use the mind God gave us to **reason** his will.

We can ask for the opinion of our **fellow believers**.

We can look to the **Prophet** for example.

All of these things form shari'a, **the path to good living**.

All of these things come from **God**.

God guides us with shari'a.

Qur'an) and his example (Sunna) for direction. With his death, however, this guidance ceased. As it was, the question of how to apply existing revelations to everyday life, across the various cultures of the growing Muslim community, was a delicate matter. Despite the emergence of Islamic judges who could rule on public and private concerns, there was a call for more uniform and clearly defined shari'a.

Defining Islamic law

Scholars keen to standardize Islamic jurisprudence emerged in many Muslim communities, leading to disagreement over how to apply the law. Should its scope be restricted to the teachings of the Qur'an and the Sunna, or could jurists incorporate their own analysis and reason?

By the 8th century, Muslims differed widely on the application of shari'a. Scholar Abu 'Abdallah Muhammad ibn Idris al-Shafi'i, seen by many as the father of Islamic jurisprudence, came to the fore to offer unifying thought on the legal concerns of the day. According to al-Shafi'i, there were four sources of law: the Qur'an, the Sunna, the consensus of the community (*ijma*), and analogical reasoning (*qiyas*).

Believed to be the literal word of God, the Qur'an is the primary source for Islamic principles and values. In many passages, it directly addresses matters such as murder, exploitation of the poor, usury, theft, and adultery, clearly condemning them. In other instances, the Qur'an works to curb certain behaviour over time. For example, early ››

"The road to the watering hole" – the literal translation of shari'a – is a concept that has considerable resonance for believers who came from an unforgiving desert climate.

revelations on alcohol suggest that while some good may be found in it, it may also have a connection to sin (2:219). Later revelations prohibit Muslims from praying while drinking (4:43), and the latest plainly condemn the use of alcohol (5:93). The Qur'an also guides Muslims in personal and community affairs. For instance, while it does not expressly prohibit slavery, it does offer guidance on how to treat slaves. Marriage concerns such as polygamy, dowry, and inheritance rights for women are also governed.

Stipulations such as these are explicit in the Qur'an and offer clear guidance. However, while the Qur'an treats other matters of morality and civic duty in a similar fashion, much of its treatment of legal concerns tends to be generic. In these cases, the example of Muhammad given in the Sunna supplements the Qur'anic material. While the Sunna cannot replace the Qur'an's authority, the belief that Muhammad was inspired by God led to the acceptance of his example as authoritative. Al-Shafi'i refined the use of the Sunna in legal matters by restricting the use of the term Sunna to Muhammad. Doing so eliminated any confusion with local customs, and added greater authority to the traditions of the Prophet. However, collections of Muhmmad's sayings, actions, and what he prohibited and allowed grew in number, requiring the application of a strict process of validation. As a result of this, legitimate traditions of Muhammad – that is, those with a proper chain of authority and not contradicting the Qur'an – can be brought to bear on legal matters.

Legal interpretation

Even with al-Shafi'i's definitions, situations could arise that are not specifically addressed in either the Qur'an or Sunna. With Muhammad no longer alive to offer guidance on such legal matters, the role of interpretation became crucial. Al-Shafi'i therefore sought to give authority to legal interpretations reached by consensus among the Muslim community. Early on, this was a practical way for solving problems on which the Qur'an and the Sunna were silent; majority opinion would help in reaching decisions. Over time, however, "the community" came to be defined in legal terms as a collective body of legal scholars and religious authorities whose decisions would be made on

There has come to you from God a light and a clear book by which God guides those who pursue his pleasure to the ways of peace...
Sura 5:15–16

behalf of wider Muslim society. There remained some situations where no authoritative text existed, and when consensus could not be reached. Initially, jurists used their own judgment to arbitrate new legal concerns. This was known as *ijtihad*, or striving intellectually, and incorporated a judge's personal opinion or reasoning. Al-Shafi'i restricted the role of personal reasoning in *ijtihad* to the use of deductive reasoning to find analogous situations in the Qur'an or Sunna from which new legal rulings could be derived. For example, the Qur'an prohibits making a sale or a purchase during the call to Friday prayers: Muslims are instead urged to cease trading so that they may gather for worship (62:9–10). What about other contracts that might be made during the call to prayer? Should a marriage, for example, be arranged during this time? The Qur'an is silent on the matter, but analogical

Muslim scholars and religious leaders are relied upon to interpret original sources where guidance on certain matters is not explicit.

Analogical reasoning can be used to determine acceptable behaviour. The Qur'an makes no mention of drugs, but does forbid alcohol. So we can infer that other intoxicants are forbidden too.

reasoning can be used to derive a legal opinion. If the aim of the Qur'an is to discourage actions preventing Muslims from worship, then, likewise, restriction on business can be applied to other contracts, actions, or services such as a marriage. Instead of scholars merely offering a personal opinion on matters such as these, al-Shafi'i helped to ground creative thinking in the authoritative sources of Islam, the Qur'an and the Sunna.

Schools of law

Although al-Shafi'i's summation of the four sources of law – the Qur'an, the Sunna, community consensus, and analogical reasoning – did much to unify shari'a, different schools of law use these sources in different ways. From the 13th century, four schools have predominated in Sunni Islam, the largest branch of the faith. Each school is named for the individual who framed its main concerns: Shafi'i, Hanbali, Hanafi, and Maliki. The Shafi'i and Hanbali schools rely on evidence from the sources in interpreting law, while the Hanafi and Maliki encourage analogous reasoning as well.

Further schools of law developed in Shi'a Islam. Given the key role of the imam for Shi'a Muslims, these schools emphasize the traditions of 'Ali and the imams. Muhammad's cousin, 'Ali, is seen by Shi'as as the first imam – a point on which Sunnis and Shi'as disagree. Shi'as often favour the rulings of the imam, their supreme leader and highest authority on law, over analogical reasoning and community consensus.

The schools of law remain in Muslim society today. In regions where Muslims are predominant, scholars rule on legal matters in courts of law and issue fatwas (rulings). In turn, judges enforce and uphold the law. Muslims facing more mundane questions as to the best way to live a Muslim life may also ask for authoritative advice. In non-Muslim societies, local scholars offer guidance to their communities and, in a modern twist, Muslims can also consult (web-based) helplines run by international centres devoted to Islamic law. While there is still debate about how best to derive legal rulings, shari'a remains for many a straight path to the best life God can give to his followers. ■

Abu 'Abdallah Muhammad ibn Idris al-Shafi'i

Much legend has grown up around the life of al-Shafi'i. As a result, the details of his early years remain uncertain, but according to the oldest surviving accounts he was born in Gaza in 767. When he was young, his family moved to Mecca, where he studied Hadith (the words and deeds of Muhammad) and law. He is said to have memorized the Qur'an by the age of 10. He then moved to Medina, studying law under Malik ibn Anas, founder of the Maliki School of Islamic law. He taught in Baghdad, finally settling in Egypt. Through his work as a teacher and scholar, he became known as the father of Islamic jurisprudence, helping to shape Islamic legal thought. He died in 820 and was buried in al-Fustat (Cairo).

Key works

9th century *Treatise on the Foundations of Islamic Jurisprudence; The Exemplar*

My community will never agree on an error.
Hadith of Muhammad

WE CAN THINK ABOUT GOD, BUT WE CANNOT COMPREHEND HIM
THEOLOGICAL SPECULATION IN ISLAM

We are told that **all bounty is in the hand of God**.

We do not know how, or in what sense, this is true.

We must just **believe and accept it**.

Questioning it would **lead to innovation**, which is forbidden.

We can think about God, but we cannot comprehend him.

Islam teaches that God is transcendent, or beyond human comprehension. While this does not prevent Muslims from thinking about God, and reflecting on aspects of who he is and what he does, they must never do so in the expectation of being able to understand his nature or his actions. This was the conclusion reached by Abu al-Hasan al-Ash'ari in the 10th century, when Islam entered a controversy stirred up by philosophical speculation about the nature of God.

In the 8th century, caliphs (civil and religious heads of the Muslim state) of the Abbasid dynasty

See also: Defining the indefinable 184–85 ▪ The pathway to harmonious living 272–75 ▪ The unity of divinity is necessary 280–81

> God... is unlike whatever occurs to the mind or is pictured in the imagination...
> **'Ali al-Ash'ari**

had encouraged the development of scholarship and the arts in the Islamic world, and Arabic translations of works by Greek philosophers, such as Aristotle, became available to Muslim theologians. Some of these scholars applied the "new" Greek ways of thinking to the content of the Qur'an. They formed a group called the Mu'tazilites, which became a prominent force in Islamic theology in the 9th century.

Radical thinkers

The Mu'tazilites were inspired by the idea that Greek philosophical methods could be used to resolve apparent contradictions in the Qur'an. The Qur'an stresses the unity of God – he is indivisible, and so cannot have any kind of body, made up of parts, as humans have. Yet there are passages in the Qur'an that specifically refer, for example, to God's hands and eyes. To take descriptions such as these literally would lead to anthropomorphism (attributing human characteristics to God) and might be seen as comparing God with the beings he created,

which was the greatest sin. The Mu'tazilites proposed that such references are metaphorical. So, for example, a reference to God's hand could be interpreted as indicating his power. They then applied Greek logic to other theological issues, such as free will, predestination, and determining the nature of the Qur'an itself – whether it had existed eternally, or had been created by God at some point.

Before long, however, the wide-ranging speculation of the Mu'tazilites began to attract censure and turn public opinion against them. Theological and philosophical speculation about God is permissible and indeed important to Islamic thought, but seeking answers to questions not specifically addressed by the Qur'an or Muhammad is, according to Islam, not only unnecessary, but also a sin – bid'ah, the sin of innovation.

One Mu'tazilite thinker, al-Ash'ari, refused to reduce the Qur'an's descriptions of God to metaphors, but he also refused to anthropomorphize God. Instead,

he asserted that God might be described as having hands without Muslims knowing how this might be possible. Al-Ash'ari and his group of fellow-thinkers, known as the Ash'arites, left the words of the Qur'an intact, but also kept theological thinking about God pure, by refraining from speaking about him in human terms, as God is beyond comprehension. ▪

Islamic scholars are free to think about God and reflect on aspects of who he is and what he does, but they must never expect to understand his nature or his actions.

Abu al-Hasan al-Ash'ari

Abu al-Hasan al-Ash'ari was born in around 873 CE in Basra, in present-day Iraq. He is credited with much of the development of kalam (the science of discourse on divine topics), and taught many of Islam's greatest scholars. Through his thinking and the work of his pupils, Ash'arite theology became the dominant school of theology for orthodox Muslims. He remained a

Mu'tazilite theologian until the age of 40, when he abandoned much of Mu'tazilite thought. Some say this followed a theological dispute with his teacher, others that he realized there were contradictions between Islam and Mu'tazilite theology. He died in 935.

Key works

9th–10th century Theological Opinions of the Muslims; The Clarification of the Bases of the Religion

JIHAD IS OUR RELIGIOUS DUTY
STRIVING IN THE WAY OF GOD

IN CONTEXT

KEY FIGURE
Shams al-A'imma al-Sarakhsi

WHEN AND WHERE
11th century, Persia

BEFORE
7th century CE Muhammad's armies conquer and unite much of Arabia under the banner of Islam.

8th century Islamic expansion continues into Spain in the west and Persia in the east.

8th century Legal scholar Abu Hanifa argues that Islam only permits defensive war.

AFTER
12th century Ibn Rushd (Averroes), an Islamic philosopher, divides jihad into four types: jihad by the heart, by the tongue, by the hand, and by the sword.

1964 Egyptian author Sayyid Qutb argues for jihad as the mission to make Islam dominant in all the world.

Despite the guidance given by the Qur'an, Muhammad, and shari'a, maintaining a focus on God and a disciplined life remains a challenge to Muslims. Disobedience is always a temptation and evil is a constant presence. Muslims, therefore, must constantly strive to stay close to God and struggle against evil. This "striving" or "struggling" is known as jihad.

For most Muslims, jihad is used in two different ways. The "greater jihad" is the most common. This is the constant struggle against personal sin, involving repentance and seeking God's mercy, avoiding temptation, and pursuing justice for others. The "lesser jihad", although less common for Muslims, is the more widely known. It involves the legitimate use of force, sometimes militarily, against those who do evil.

In the 11th century, one of Islam's most noted legal scholars, Shams al-A'imma al-Sarakhsi, discussed lesser jihad as a four-stage process. He argued that in the first stage, jihad towards others should be peaceful and passive. In the second

Even the youngest students learn the importance of striving to be a good Muslim by upholding the faith, seeking God's mercy, avoiding temptation, and pursuing justice for others.

stage, Islam should be defended with peaceful argument. The third stage allowed for followers to defend the Muslim community against injustice. In the fourth stage, Muslims are called on to engage in armed conflict, within specific legal and Qu'ranic guidelines, when the Islamic faith is under threat. ∎

See also: Augustine and free will 220–21 ∎ The pathway to harmonious living 272–75 ∎ The rise of Islamic revivalism 286–90

THE WORLD IS ONE STAGE OF THE JOURNEY TO GOD
THE ULTIMATE REWARD FOR THE RIGHTEOUS

IN CONTEXT

KEY FIGURE
Abu Hamid Muhammad al-Ghazali

WHEN AND WHERE
1058–1111, Persia

BEFORE
500 BCE The Hebrew Bible describes humankind's first existence in a heavenly garden.

1st century CE Jesus announces the inauguration of "God's kingdom" on earth.

From 874 Shi'a Muslims believe that the "hidden imam" will return in the future to usher in the end of days.

1014–15 Muslim philosopher Ibn Sina (Avicenna) writes his most important work on eschatology, *Al-Adhawiyya*.

AFTER
1190 Muslim philosopher Ibn Rushd (Averroes) discusses the Day of Judgment in his *On the Harmony of Religions and Philosophy*.

According to the Qur'an, the end of the world will be accompanied by the Day of Judgment, when the fate of every person will be determined by the scales of justice. Those whose good deeds on earth outweigh their bad deeds will proceed to *jannah* (paradise), depicted in Islam as a luxurious garden; while those whose bad deeds outweigh their good deeds will be relegated to the fiery torments of *jahannam*, or hell.

This idea of divine judgment is set against the Qur'an's pervasive descriptions of God's mercy and forgiveness. Indeed, Muslims are distinguished clearly from non-Muslims as those who hope for God's mercy. They also hope for a meeting with God (the Day of Judgment is often referred to as this in the Qur'an), when they will receive his clemency.

Hope and paradise
The Muslim scholar Abu Hamid Muhammad al-Ghazali focused on the relationship between the Muslim concepts of hope and

paradise in a treatise entitled *The Book of Fear and Hope*. He argued that those who truly fear God will run towards him, longing for his mercy. Al-Ghazali likens the desire for a meeting with God to a farmer who sows seed in tilled ground, faithfully waters the seed, weeds the ground regularly, and rightly hopes for a harvest. Similarly, the Muslim who believes in God, obeys his commands, and pursues morality can expect both compassion from God and the rewards of paradise. ∎

And nothing but the reins of hope will lead to the vicinity of the Merciful and the joy of the Gardens.
Al-Ghazali

See also: Preparing for the afterlife 58–59 ▪ The promise of a new age 178–81 ▪ Jesus's message to the world 204–207

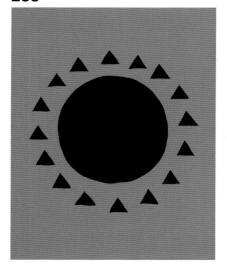

GOD IS UNEQUALLED
THE UNITY OF DIVINITY IS NECESSARY

IN CONTEXT

KEY FIGURE
Muhammad ibn Tumart

WHEN AND WHERE
1082–1130, North Africa

BEFORE
c.800–950 CE Aristotle's works are translated into Arabic.

10th century Muslim scholar al-Farabi discusses the First Cause (God).

1027 Persian philosopher Ibn Sina (known in the West as Avicenna) argues that reason requires God's existence.

AFTER
c.1238 Ibn 'Arabi, a prominent Sufi teacher, reflects on the "Oneness of Being".

1982 The Palestinian thinker Ismail al-Faruqi writes *Tawhid: Its Implications for Thought and Life*.

1990 Ozay Mehmet argues that *tawhid* is the basis for Muslim religious and secular identity.

Islam is a monotheistic religion and one of its central tenets is *tawhid* (literally "oneness") – the doctrine of divine unity. According to Muslim thought there is only one God, and he is single in nature; he is not a trinity, as Christians believe. The notion of *tawhid* features widely in the Qur'an and forms the first part of Islam's central creed, the shahada: "There is no god but God". Conversely, the doctrine of divine unity also forms the basis for the greatest sin in Islam, and one that is unforgivable:

Reason tells us that things in the world (including humans) are changing, impermanent, and were **created by something** that preceded them.

→

However, **at the beginning** of all events and beings, there must be something that was **not itself caused by any other thing**.

↓

The unique creator did not "begin" and will not end – **God has existed and will exist forever**.

←

This is God, the **unique creator**.

↓

The absolute creator is **the only being** that is unchanging, eternal, and the First Cause of everything.

→

God is one being, that has **no partners or equals**.

See also: Defining the indefinable 184–85 ■ A divine trinity 212–19 ■ The central professions of faith 262–69 ■ Theological speculation in Islam 276–77

High in the Atlas Mountains of Morocco, the Tin Mal Mosque became the spiritual centre of the Almohad creed in the 12th century.

shirk, which is the violation of *tawhid*. Literally meaning "to share", the sin of shirk is committed when a partner is attributed to God. This is because it suggests either a belief in many gods, or a belief that God is less than perfect and therefore requires a partner.

A creed of unity

Throughout the history of Islam, Muslims have reflected on the notion of divine unity. In the 12th century, this gave rise to a movement whose followers were known as Al-Muwahhidun ("those who emphasize unity"), or the Almohads. Founded by Muhammad ibn Tumart, this movement was based on its conception of divine unity, which came to be expressed in the Almohad *'aqida*, or creed.

The Almohad creed combined elements of *kalam* – theological speculation on God's nature – with direct interpretation of the Qur'an and the Sunna (the sayings and actions of Muhammad). One of its most significant characteristics is that it was meant to appeal not just to scholars, but to a wide audience that would be able to test its assertions against their own logic and personal experience.

Cause and effect

The Almohad creed begins with certain sayings of Muhammad that suggest the notion of divine unity was, to him, the most significant part of Islam. The creed then offers the unique assertion, largely derived from Aristotelian philosophy: that reason and logic – rather than faith – demand the truth of God's existence. As a result, those with reason can deduce whether or not God exists.

The Almohad creed uses deductive reasoning to argue for God's unity, building each of its assertions on the one before it. It argues that everything has a maker – something has caused each thing in the world to be made (whether that was a human making a tool, or an acorn growing into a tree). Humans themselves are creations of extraordinary complexity. And if everything in the world was made by something, there must be a being at the beginning of that chain of cause and effect that was not brought about by something before it – the initial cause of everything else. This being is God – who is unique and absolute (without a beginning or an end). If we acknowledge his absolute existence, then we must also acknowledge that no other god can share his power, and therefore, God alone is one and unequalled. ■

Muhammad ibn Tumart

Muhammad ibn Tumart was a Berber born in the Atlas Mountains of modern-day Morocco in around 1082. He travelled to the East to study Islamic theology and, growing in religious fervour, he formed a movement based on a desire to reform Islam along the lines of his vision of the oneness of God.

Ibn Tumart returned to Morocco around 1118; here his movement grew in strength and numbers. In 1121, he proclaimed himself the Mahdi (Guided One, or redeemer) who would restore purity to Islam. He died in around 1130, before his followers came to reign over large portions of north-western Africa and parts of Spain.

Ibn Tumart's movement receded in the 13th century. None of his texts survive, although writings about him and his followers (including those of the Almohad creed) are preserved in *Le livre de Mohammed ibn Toumert* (The Life of Muhammad ibn Tumart).

It is by the necessity of reason that the existence of God, Praise to Him, is known.
Almohad 'aqida

ARAB, WATER-POT, AND ANGELS ARE ALL OURSELVES
SUFISM AND THE MYSTIC TRADITION

IN CONTEXT

KEY FIGURE
Jalal al-Din Rumi

WHEN AND WHERE
13th century, Persia

BEFORE
8th century An early Sufi poet, Rabi'a al-'Adawiyya, from Basra, Iraq, fuses asceticism and devotion in her development of Sufism.

10th century Persian master al-Hallaj declares in a trance "I am the Truth"; his words are interpreted as a claim to be God, for which he is executed.

AFTER
13th century Some Sufi practices, such as reciting God's names, are incorporated into Jewish worship.

19th century Emir 'Abd al-Qadir, a Sufi scholar, leads the struggle against the French invasion of Algeria.

21st century More than a hundred Sufi orders exist.

If shari'a law is, for Muslims, an exterior pathway leading to the true worship of God, then Sufi mysticism is an interior path helping its practitioners not only to follow God, but to be closer to him. In the early stages of Islam's development, simple obedience to the will of God was not a strict enough doctrine for some Muslims. In response to the growing indulgence of the ruling

Revered for his ascetism and kindness, Sufi saint Nizamuddin Awlia's tomb is visited by thousands of Muslims and non-Muslims each day, where they light incense and pray.

Muslim elite as they gained in power, disenchanted Muslims wished to return to what they felt was the purity and simplicity of Islam during the time of Prophet Muhammad. They pursued an ascetic lifestyle by removing themselves from the material world and seeking a direct, personal experience of God. Some Sufi Muslims even declared that God was within them.

As Sufism developed, groups, or orders, were founded, in which religious masters taught the doctrine to students. At the heart of many of these orders lay the belief that the self must be renounced in order to fully abide in God. Accordingly, Jalal al-Din Rumi, a 13th-century Sufi master, wrote of an impoverished Arab and his greedy wife who live in the desert. The woman urges her husband to offer their filled water-pot to God, hoping they might receive something in return. Although reluctant, the husband succumbs to his wife's urgings and offers the pot – and, in return, it is filled with gold. This "treasure" is, however, of little use to them in the desert and therefore acts as a reminder that the pursuit of wealth and self-interest detracts from the correct focus on

See also: The performance of ritual and repetition 158–59 ▪ Zen insights that go beyond words 160–63 ▪ Mystical experience in Christianity 238

God **cannot fill a vessel** that is **already filled**.

We must **empty our lives** of material concerns.	We must **cleanse our minds** of selfish distractions.	We must **free our hearts** of earthly desires.

We must let ourselves be filled by **nothing but God.**

Thus we will **find God within ourselves**.

Jalal al-Din Muhammad Rumi

Jalal al-Din Muhammad Rumi was born in 1207 in Balkh (in modern-day Afghanistan). His family claimed descent from Abu Bakr, the Prophet Muhammad's Companion and successor. After travelling with his father throughout Persia and Arabia, he settled in Konya (in modern-day central Turkey).

In Konya, Rumi met the Sufi master Shams-i Tabrizi (of Tabriz). At the time, Rumi was a professor of Islamic sciences, but the Sufi master had such a deep impact upon him that he abandoned his studies in order to devote himself to mysticism. His followers founded the Mawlawi order of Sufis, known to many as the Whirling Dervishes.

Though known for his philosophy and scholarship, Rumi is best remembered for his mystic poetry. He died in Konya in 1273.

Key works

1258–1273 *Spiritual Couplets*
13th century *The Works of Shams of Tabriz*
13th century *What is Within is Within*

God. In the same parable, Rumi recounts the heavenly angels' jealousy of Adam. They, too, forsake their focus on God. The parable, for Rumi, describes humanity in general and the temptation to pursue the self. For Sufis, an individual's focus should be the denial of the self in the pursuit of an experience of God.

Renouncing the worldly

In Sufism, achieving a personal experience of God involves moving through successive stages of renunciation, purification, and insight. As a result, not only are Sufis ascetic – breaking ties to the material world through poverty, fasting, silence, or celibacy – but they also place great emphasis on devotional love of God, often through religious experiences or psychological states. This is often achieved through the repetition of God's names (for example,

God the merciful, God the great) or meditative breathing exercises. Becoming absorbed in these exercises helps the Sufi practitioner to forget worldly attachments and focus more fully on God.

Rumi placed particular emphasis on using both music and dance to pursue a direct experience of God's presence. The Whirling Dervishes, the Sufi order founded by his followers, use singing or chanting and bodily movements to enter ecstatic states to experience union with God. Their rhythmic spinning dance is said to symbolize the solar system, which they mimic by turning in circles around their leader.

In the view of many Muslims, some Sufis pressed the boundaries of Islamic orthodoxy, and Sufism was suppressed from the 17th century onwards. However, orders are still found worldwide, attracting both Muslims and non-Muslims. ▪

THE LATTER DAYS HAVE BROUGHT FORTH A NEW PROPHET

THE ORIGINS OF AHMADIYYA

IN CONTEXT

KEY FIGURE
Mirza Ghulam Ahmad

WHEN AND WHERE
Late 19th century, India

BEFORE
632 The Prophet Muhammad, the final prophet of Islam, dies in Medina.

872 The Mahdi, the Hidden One of Shi'a Islam, disappears, supposedly not to return until the end of the world.

19th century The anti-British Indian independence movement grows in strength, with some militant elements.

AFTER
1908 Hakim Noor-ud-Din assumes Ahmadiyya leadership.

1973 Ahmadiyya splits into Qadiani and Lahori groups.

1983 A Qadiani Ahmadiyya conference attracts 200,000 participants; the following year, restrictions are placed on the group in Pakistan.

There can be **no prophet after Muhammad**.

↓

But Islam's followers have **lost the pure message** from God that he brought.

↓

A **new message** is needed to steer Muslims back to the **pure path of the faith**.

↓

Mirza Ghulam Ahmad, as renewer and minor prophet, **brings that message**.

In 1882, Mirza Ghulam Ahmad declared himself to be a minor prophet, or divinely appointed reformer, of Islam. He had come, so he claimed, to rejuvenate Islam and to return it to its pure foundations. The movement that formed around him came to be called Ahmadiyya.

In orthodox Muslim thinking, the Prophet Muhammad is the final prophet of Islam, and anyone else claiming the status of prophet should therefore be denounced. But Ghulam Ahmad did not claim to bring a new revelation beyond the Qur'an. Rather, he simply offered a new interpretation, with the aim of bringing the Muslim community back to its roots. As such he was comparable with other, minor prophets who did not bring the law, but restored it: Aaron, for example, who is thought by Muslims to have been sent by God to revitalize the message given to Musa (Moses).

Ghulam Ahmad had previously developed some unorthodox teachings. Part of his message was that Isa (Jesus) did not die on the cross, nor was he – as Muslims traditionally believed – saved from death on the cross by being raised up to heaven by God. Ghulam Ahmad claimed that Jesus merely

See also: The Prophet and the origins of Islam 252–53 ▪ The emergence of Shi'a Islam 270–71 ▪ Striving in the way of God 278 ▪ The rise of Islamic revivalism 286–90

The Qadiani belief in Ghulam Ahmad's prophethood continues to incite strong feeling in orthodox Islam, even leading to occasional public protest against the movement.

swooned, subsequently recovered, and went to Afghanistan and Kashmir in search of the lost tribes of Israel. Ghulam Ahmad also challenged Islamic thinking concerning jihad, claiming that the only acceptable form was a spiritual jihad designed to peacefully spread the message of Islam. This was a particularly significant idea in the context of 19th-century India, where anti-British unrest was growing.

Controversial claims
Ahmad's claims evolved as his followers grew in number, and he declared himself not just to be Islam's prophetic reformer, but its redeemer – a messianic figure known to Muslims as the Mahdi – and the spiritual successor of Jesus. For many Muslims, these claims went too far and challenged the place of Muhammad and the revelation

given to him. For these reasons, Ghulam Ahmad and his followers were rejected by many Muslims.

Even within his own movement, Ghulam Ahmad's assertions caused controversy. After his death in 1908, the Ahmadiyyas split into two factions: Qadiani Ahmadiyyas, who maintained Ghulam Ahmad's teachings, and a new branch known as Lahori Ahmadiyya. The Lahori branch accepted Ghulam Ahmad as a renewer of the Islam faith, but this was as far

as they were willing to go. They, too, rejected his claim that he was a minor prophet.

In Pakistan in 1973, Qadiani Ahmadiyyas were legally declared non-Muslims, and, in 1984, an ordinance was drafted allowing for punishment of any Qadiani who claimed to be a Muslim, used Islamic terminology, or referred to his or her faith as Islam. The Qadiani Ahmadiyyas have since moved their international headquarters from the Indian subcontinent to London. ▪

Mirza Ghulam Ahmad

Mirza Ghulam Ahmad was born in 1835 in Qadian, a village near Lahore in India. His twin sister died shortly after their birth. In a society where the majority was illiterate, Ghulam Ahmad studied Arabic and Persian, and learned aspects of medicine from his father, a physician. As a young man, he took a position with the government, while continuing his religious studies.

He announced his divine mission in 1882, and in 1888 he asked his followers to formally pledge allegiance to him. Some 40 did so, and in 1889 he published

a set of rules to guide all who joined his movement. Ghulam Ahmad travelled widely across northern India, spreading his message and debating with Islamic leaders. He died in 1908, leaving the leadership of the Ahmadiyya movement to a companion, who eventually passed it to Ahmad's eldest son.

Key works

1880–84 *The Arguments of the Ahmadiyya*
1891 *Victory of Islam*
1898 *The Star of Guidance*

ISLAM MUST SHED THE INFLUENCE OF THE WEST

THE RISE OF ISLAMIC REVIVALISM

IN CONTEXT

KEY FIGURE
Sayyid Qutb

WHEN AND WHERE
20th century, Egypt

BEFORE
1839–97 Activist and writer
Jamal al-Din al-Afghani
criticizes the colonial presence
in Islamic countries.

1849–1905 Egyptian
scholar, jurist, and reformer
Muhammad 'Abduh decries
Western influence.

1882 British forces occupy
Egypt. The British presence
and influence grow with time.

AFTER
1903–79 Abul A'la Mawdudi,
a revivalist thinker, becomes
one of the most widely read
Muslim writers.

1951 Ayman al-Zawahiri, a
friend of Sayyid Qutb, plays
a major role in the militant
group al-Qaeda.

Islam grows weak under the influence of Western powers and ideas.

→

Islam must be strong to offer itself as **the best system of living** for the world.

↓

We must return to the example of Muhammad and the Qur'an to **regain Islam's purity**.

←

Muslim countries and communities must be **governed well, according to Islamic principles**.

↓

Such governance will **guide Muslims back** to the message of the Qur'an.

→

Islam must shed the influence of the West.

By the end of the 18th century, the world's great Muslim powers were in decline. The Ottoman and Mughal empires had lost political influence, and Western powers were colonizing the predominantly Muslim areas of northern Africa and parts of Asia – French North Africa, British India and the Middle East, and Dutch Indonesia. Some Muslims welcomed the changes and modernizations that came with the Western presence. For others, however, the influence of the West forced them to consider the place that science and technology, Western politics and economics, and even fashion had in their lives. Some wished simply to protect Islam against the secularization that came with modernization; others were more militant and anti-Western, seeking to overthrow imperialist governments; others still were prepared to accept a degree of Western influence, but sought clear dictinctions between what was Islamic and un-Islamic.

Out of this context emerged a number of very influential Islamic thinkers and reformers. Although each had their own contexts and emphases, they were all aware of the weakness of the global Islamic community at the time, and felt that Muslims straying from Islam under Western influence were responsible. As a result, they sought to revive the role of Islam as the dominant influence in their societies.

Many Muslim revivalists felt that the best way forward was to restore Islam by not only shedding the influence of the West, but by emphasizing the superiority of Islam as well. To do this, they argued for the central role of jihad

See also: God reveals his word and his will 254–61 ▪ The pathway to harmonious living 272–75 ▪ Striving in the way of God 278

Egyptian workers are searched by British soldiers during the Suez Crisis in 1956. Religious insensitivity and poor treatment by the British troops fed Islamic revivalism.

(p.278) in religious and political life. Taken in this sense, jihad became a revolutionary struggle against un-Islamic forces, eliminating perceived evil in pursuit of what revivalists believed was justice and righteousness. Likewise, the revivalists thought that immoral governments should be replaced by Islamic systems established according to divine principles. In many Muslim revivalists' minds, a government based upon the Qur'an and Islam would provide the perfect social system, and the best way to achieve it was by a jihad that expressed itself through militant action, resistance, and revolution.

Egyptian activism
Sayyid Qutb, a Muslim activist in 20th-century Egypt, became one of the most influential revivalist thinkers. From Qutb's perspective, Egypt had grown increasingly weak and corrupt under British colonial rule. Having become disillusioned by his experience of the West and its cultural influence, Qutb sought to lead fellow Muslims out from under foreign control and back to Islam. He wrote extensively on the Qur'an and its interpretation, as well as matters of religion and the state, and joined the Muslim Brotherhood, a group formed in Egypt in the 1920s, which aimed to use the Islamic faith as a means of "ordering the life of the Muslim family, individual, community… and state".

Ages of ignorance
Qutb's interpretation of jihad was consistent with the perception of Islam as a religion that provides the perfect model for living. He believed that Muslims had an obligation to establish their moral standards on earth so that everyone could benefit from them. Jihad, then, became a continual struggle against unbelief and injustice, or what Qutb called *jahiliyya*. This term was traditionally used to describe the age of ignorance – the period before the revelation of the Qur'an – but it was applied by Qutb to everything he considered »

I went to the West and saw Islam, but no Muslims; I got back to the East and saw Muslims, but not Islam.
Muhammad 'Abduh

Sayyid Qutb

Born in 1906 in Qaha, a farming town just north of Cairo, Sayyid Qutb attended a local school, where he memorized the Qu'ran by the age of 10. He went on to a British-style education in Cairo and began work as a teacher. At first enamoured with Western culture, he developed an interest in English literature and studied educational administration in the USA.

However, his experience of what he considered the irreligious culture of the USA, along with his view of British policies during World War II, soured his vision of the West. Back in Egypt, he joined the Muslim Brotherhood, began writing on Islamic topics, and advocated an Islamic ideology in place of Western influences.

In 1954, Qutb was arrested along with other Muslim Brotherhood members for conspiring to assassinate Egypt's president, Gamal Abdel Nasser. After serving a 10-year sentence, he was released, only to write his most controversial work, *Milestones*, in which he called for a re-creation of the Muslim world based on Qur'anic principles. In so doing, he rejected forms of government that were not truly Islamic. He was arrested and sentenced to death for plotting to overthrow the Egyptian state. In August 1966, he was executed and buried in an unmarked grave.

Key Works

1949 *Social Justice in Islam*
1954 *In the Shade of the Qur'an*
1964 *Milestones*

> We… believed once in English liberalism and English sympathy; but we believe no longer, for facts are stronger than words. Your liberalness we see plainly is only for yourselves…
> **Sayyid Qutb**

alien to Islam. For him, *jahiliyya* was not just a period of time, but a state of being that was repeated every time a society strayed from the path of Islam.

Islamic governance
Qutb applied the concept of *jahiliyya* to governments that he did not consider properly Islamic.

He strongly opposed any system of government in which people were in "servitude to others", considering this to be a violation of God's sovereignty. This included Communist nations (because of their state-imposed atheism) as well as polytheist nations, such as India, and Christian and Jewish states. Qutb also argued that many Muslim countries lived in a state of *jahiliyya* because they accepted alien – and in particular Western – ideas and tried to incorporate them into their governments, laws, and cultures. For Qutb, the only effective way to rid society of *jahiliyya* was by implementing an Islamic way of life with its superior strategies and beliefs for governing humanity.

Renewed jihad
This line of thinking about *jahiliyya* led Qutb and his followers to advocate the implementation of jihad. Understood this way, jihad might be necessary for each new generation of Muslims, at least as long as foreign, un-Islamic forces

> …Islam possesses or is capable of solving our basic problems… without doubt it will be more capable than any other system we may seek to borrow or imitate, to work in our nation.
> **Sayyid Qutb**

exerted their influence. This meant that Muslim scholars who interpreted the Qur'an in such ways as to suggest that its discussions of jihad were no longer applicable in the modern world were misled. Qutb argued that jihad was meant to be enforced in his day in the same way it was when the Qur'an was revealed; this might not mean eliminating every non-Muslim from power, but it did mean shedding the influence the West had upon the world. Muslims should do what was necessary to ensure that a pure Islam as a system of governance could flourish uninhibited by un-Islamic pressures. In this way, Qutb helped to shape not only how future Islamic revivalists would see the world, but how the people in the West would come to perceive Islam in the late 20th century. ■

Supporters of Mohamed Morsi, a prominent member of the Muslim Brotherhood, celebrate his election as President of Egypt in 2012. The Muslim Brotherhood remains a major force in Egyptian social and political life.

ISLAM CAN BE A MODERN RELIGION
THE COMPATIBILITY OF FAITH

IN CONTEXT

KEY FIGURE
Tariq Ramadan

WHEN AND WHERE
1960s, Switzerland

BEFORE
711 Muslims begin raids on the Iberian Peninsula.

827 Muslims begin conquest of Sicily and establish an Emirate in 965.

15th century Islamic Ottoman Empire expands in the Balkans.

AFTER
1960s Large-scale Muslim emigration begins from Turkey and northern Africa to Europe.

1979 The Iranian Revolution leads to the overthrow of Iran's Westernizing government.

2008 Rowan Williams, the Archbishop of Canterbury, states that the adoption of aspects of shari'a law is inevitable in the UK.

One of the most significant questions faced by Muslims today is how to relate Islamic faith to secular, modern life. This question becomes more pressing when people from Muslim countries move to the West, bringing with them not just their religion, but their religion as practised in a specific cultural context. As a result, many Muslims face a disjunction between what is Islamic and what is modern, secular, or Western.

The idea developed by Tariq Ramadan – an Islamic scholar, whose family went into exile from Egypt to Switzerland because of his father's membership of the Muslim Brotherhood (p.289) – is that it is possible to be at once a Muslim and an American or a European: religion and national culture are separate concepts, and it is the duty of a Muslim not only to respect the laws of the host country, but to "contribute, wherever they are, to promoting good and equity within and through human brotherhood". Ramadan encourages Muslims to

Tariq Ramadan advises European governments on Muslim relations; he is a prominent communicator and advocate of Muslim integration.

take the traditional sources referred to by Islamic scholars – the Qur'an and Sunna – and to interpret them in the context of their own cultural background, taking responsibility for their faith in the environment they inhabit. Ramadan's goal is to help Muslims contextualize many modern issues facing Islam, so that they are able to become Western Muslims whose culture and religion are compatible. ■

See also: Faith and the state 189 ▪ Progressive Judaism 190–95 ▪ The central professions of faith 262–69

MODERN
RELIGIO

FROM 15TH
CENTURY

NS

Guru Nanak founds Sikhism in the Punjab region of India during a time of tension between Hindus and the Muslim Mughal Empire.

Claiming guidance from God and the angel Moroni, **Joseph Smith Jr** translates the Book of Mormon and founds the Church of Jesus Christ of Latter-day Saints, USA.

Mirza Husayn 'Ali Nuri proclaims himself a messenger of God, adopts the title Baha'u'llah, and founds the Baha'i Faith in Persia.

Western trade in the Pacific region leads to the rise of the so-called **cargo cults** in Melanesia and New Guinea.

1499   **1830**   **1863**   **1885**

18TH–19TH CENTURY   **19TH CENTURY**   **1880S**   **1926**

Creole religions evolve within communities of African slaves in the Caribbean.

A number of new religions emerge in Japan, including **Tenrikyo, Oomoto, and Kurozumikyo**.

The Watch Tower Tract Society, part of the Bible Student Movement in the USA, lays the foundations for what becomes known as the Jehovah's Witnesses.

After a revelation from the **Supreme Being**, Ngô Van Chiêu founds the **Cao Đài** religion in Vietnam.

Most of the world's major religions evolved out of the ancient civilizations, with their foundations in the folk traditions that preceded them. The Abrahamic religions (Islam, Judaism, and Christianity), for example, trace themselves back to the stories of Noah and the Flood, long before any Middle Eastern civilizations, and, similarly, the various branches of Hinduism are based on beliefs that predate Indian civilization.

As philosophical and scientific thinking became increasingly sophisticated over the millennia, these faiths faced a choice: to adapt with the times and embrace change, or denounce anything new as heretical. Breakaway sects emerged, and – driven by events such as the Industrial Revolution in Europe, and the exploration and colonization of new lands – gave rise to a number of new religious movements fuelled by reluctance to compromise in the face of change.

New faiths

It is often difficult to determine whether a breakaway group is a branch of an older religion, or a completely new faith. Mormons and Jehovah's Witnesses, for example, both believe in the divinity of Jesus, but many of their other beliefs separate them from mainstream Christianity. Similarly, Tenrikyo and other new Japanese religious movements bear many similarities to both Buddhism and Shinto, and both the Hare Krishna and Transcendental Meditation movements are obviously derived from Hinduism.

Their status as "new" religions depends greatly on how much they are accepted or rejected by the "parent" religions.

In some cases, syncretic religions – amalgams of two very different faiths – have evolved, especially among displaced or oppressed people. For example, while Africans taken to the Caribbean as slaves were forced to adopt their masters' Christianity, they used it as a framework for practising the religions of their homelands, resulting in creole faiths, such as Santeria (also known as Regla de Ocha or Lukumí), Candomblé, Orisha-Shango, and Vodun (or Voodoo), depending on the tribe they had come from. In the 20th century, a Jamaican religion, the Rastafari movement, grew out of the Black

The **Rastafari** movement begins in Jamaica, after Ras Tafari becomes Emperor Haile Selassie I of Ethiopia.

Based on **L. Ron Hubbard's** theories of *Dianetics*, Scientology is developed as a religion in the USA.

Maharishi Mahesh **Yogi** founds the Transcendental Meditation movement, using traditional Hindu meditation techniques.

A.C. Bhaktivedanta Swami Prabhupada takes the Hindu tradition of chanting to the USA, where he founds ISKCON, the "Hare Krishna" movement.

1930

1952

1957

1965

1950s

1954

1961

1992

One of a number of neopagan religions, **Wicca** is founded in Britain after the repeal of the Witchcraft Act.

Sun Myung Moon establishes the Unification Church in Korea.

The "non-creedal, non-doctrinal" **Unitarian Universalist Association** is founded in the USA.

In China, **Li Hongzhi** combines meditative qigong practices with Daoist and Buddhist ideas in **Falun Dafa**, also called Falun Gong.

Consciousness movement, building a mythology around the Emperor Haile Selassie of Ethiopia, a country that Rastafarians consider to be Judah. Western influence in the Pacific region also led to new varieties of traditional folk religions, known as the cargo cults.

Many other new religions have emerged as specific to a particular location. Sikhism, for example, is associated with the Punjab region of Pakistan and India; the religion was founded as a reaction to the hostility between Hindus and Muslims in the area, and was based on a peaceful, democratic social foundation. The Church of Jesus Christ of Latter-day Saints in its Book of Mormon provided a specifically US addition to the Christian Bible, with a mythology of saints and angels among the indigenous American people. Other modern religions have been established with the aim of uniting all faiths, or at least recognizing the validity of other beliefs and embracing them in their own faith: these, which include Baha'i, Cao Đài, and Unitarian Universalism, have arisen in various areas of the world where a variety of major faiths have historically co-existed.

Search for the spiritual
A quest for mystical enlightenment produced the Hasidic movement in Judaism, and Sufism in Islam, and some Christian denominations have become more charismatic in recent years. Others in the West have drifted away from religious tradition: some to the past and neopagan religions such as Wicca; others to movements from the East such as ISKCON, Transcendental Meditation, and Falun Gong; while others, notably Scientology and some modern Japanese religions, have grown out of loosely science-based beliefs. Many of these new religions were founded by a charismatic leader or prophet who claimed divine revelation, and have been dismissed as "cults" designed for the glorification of their leaders. Some such faiths have declined in popularity, but others have gained a strong following and an eventual acceptance as "new religious movements" in their own right. Before dismissing them, it is as well to remember that Christianity was initially considered a "cult" by the Romans and Jews, and that Muhammad was driven out of Mecca with his small group of followers for his heretical beliefs. ∎

WE MUST LIVE AS SAINT-SOLDIERS

THE SIKH CODE OF CONDUCT

IN CONTEXT

KEY FIGURE
Guru Nanak

WHEN AND WHERE
15th–16th century, India

BEFORE
6th century BCE Jainism and Buddhism reject the Hindu concept of a just war, arguing for absolute non-violence.

7th century CE The Qur'an contains verses that suggest war in the defence of the faith and the faithful is righteous.

AFTER
1699 The Sikh Khalsa order sets out the conditions and principles justifying conflict.

18th century Sikh armies engage in war with the Mughal and Afghan empires.

1799 The Sikh kingdom of Punjab is established.

1947 The partition of India and Pakistan splits Punjab and sparks religious tension.

The Sikh religion was founded by Guru Nanak, a devoutly spiritual man who became disillusioned with the Hinduism that had surrounded him when he was growing up in a village near Lahore (in modern Pakistan) in the 15th century. Islam had also influenced this area since the 10th century, and its importance grew as the Mughal empire in India expanded.

Guru Nanak viewed the Hindu emphasis on ritual, pilgrimage, and reverence for prophets and holy men as a hindrance to what he considered most important – our relationship with God. Although he used many different names for God, he recognized him as one omnipresent, transcendent divinity, similar to the concept of Brahman in Hinduism. Following a revelation from God when he was around 30 years old, Nanak devoted his life to preaching the path to salvation. He argued that the way in which believers conduct their lives is an integral part of achieving unity with God and finding salvation. After accepting the title of "guru", or teacher, from his followers, he went on to become the first of a succession of 10 Sikh gurus, whose teachings are collected in the Sikh holy book, the Adi Granth. This book came to be considered as the 11th and final guru of Sikhism, and is known as the Guru Granth Sahib (p.303). Nanak's followers became known as Sikhs, from the Sanskrit word for learner or disciple, guided in their way of life by God and the gurus.

Finding God in a good life

Like Hindus, Sikhs believe in the cycle of death and rebirth. However, they take a different view of the purpose of human life. For the Sikh, the aim is not to attain a place in paradise, as there is no final destination of heaven or hell. Instead, Sikhism teaches that being born human is a God-given opportunity to take the path to salvation, which follows five stages, from sinning to achieving freedom from the cycle of death and rebirth. The five stages are: wrongdoing; devotion to God; spiritual union with God; attainment of eternal bliss; and freedom from rebirth.

To make the most of this opportunity, Sikhs follow a strict code of conduct and conventions,

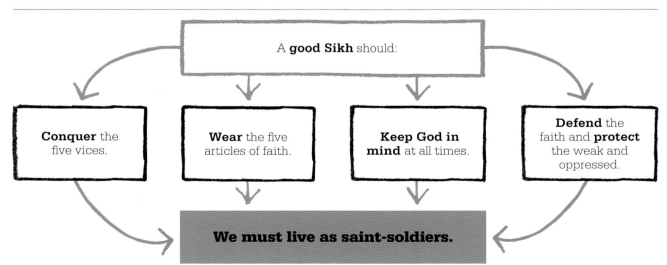

A **good Sikh** should:

| Conquer the five vices. | Wear the five articles of faith. | Keep God in mind at all times. | Defend the faith and protect the weak and oppressed. |

We must live as saint-soldiers.

See also: Living in harmony 38 ▪ The battle between good and evil 60–65 ▪ Selfless action 110–11
▪ Physical and mental discipline 112–13 ▪ Striving in the way of God 278 ▪ Class systems and faith 302–303

The Khalsa belongs to God, and Victory belongs to Him.
**Traditional
Sikh greeting**

The Khalsa order was founded in response to persecution of Sikhs under the Mughal empire, when Guru Gobind Singh called for Sikhs willing to lay down their lives in defence of the faith.

which was formally laid down by the 10th guru, Guru Gobind Singh, when he created the order of the Khalsa, the community of all Sikhs baptized into the faith, in 1699.

Virtue and courage
The idea of social justice lies at the heart of the Khalsa order (the name means "the pure" or "the free"). Members are encouraged not only to share with others, but also to protect the poor, the weak, and the oppressed. This was a crucial part of Guru Nanak's original philosophy, and it was reinforced during the period of the Ten Gurus, when Sikhs were persecuted both by their Muslim rulers and by Hindus, who regarded the Sikh faith as heretical. Guru Gobind Singh's intention in forming the Khalsa was to establish an order of Sikhs that embodied the twofold virtues of bhakti (spirituality, or devotion) and shakti (powerfulness). He envisaged an ideal of the *sant-*

sipahi, or "saint-soldier", who first and foremost led the life of a saint in his devotion to God, but would act as a warrior to defend his faith or prevent injustice, if necessary.
The Khalsa would protect the weak, and dedicate themselves to a virtuous lifestyle of chastity and temperance, ridding themselves of the five vices – lust (*kaam*), anger (*krodh*), greed (*lobh*), emotional attachment (*moh*), and egotism (*ahankar*) – and keeping God in mind at all times. Guru Gobind Singh codified a lifestyle that was appropriate to all Sikhs when he established the Khalsa order: not only did he prohibit rituals, pilgrimages, and superstitious practices, but he also outlined the virtues necessary to a life devoted to God, such as honesty, simplicity, monogamy, and avoidance of alcohol and drugs.
The Khalsa were not asked to renounce the world in their devotion to God, in fact quite the

opposite: they were asked to play an active part in it by commitment to family and community, and by demonstrating a social conscience, which is considered one of the highest of all the Sikh virtues.
Guru Gobind Singh stressed that a Sikh should act like a warrior only out of necessity in leading a saintly life: he should be a soldier-like saint rather than a saint-like soldier, and all Sikhs should act on the principle of "fear not, frighten not". Singh likened the courage needed to behave in this way to that of the lion, and suggested that Sikhs being baptized in the Khalsa order should adopt the surname Singh (lion) or Kaur (lioness).

Five articles of faith
After they are baptized in the Khalsa order, Sikhs are expected to wear the five articles of faith, commonly known as the "five Ks", as an outward expression of »

their status as saint-soldiers. Each of these – *kesh* (uncut hair), *kangha* (comb), *kara* (bracelet), *kachera* (undergarment), and *kirpan* (sword) – has a deep symbolic meaning, as well as distinctively identifying the wearer as a Sikh.

Hair is considered by Sikhs to be a gift from God, and *kesh* (the practice of leaving the hair and beard uncut) is seen, in part, as the avoidance of vanity. However, it is also a symbolic representation of the ideal of leading a life in a way that God intended, without interference, and in harmony with his will, and as such is an important outward sign of the Khalsa code of conduct.

Sikhs are expected to keep their hair clean and well-groomed, combing it twice daily with the *kanga*, a special comb that is also used to hold it in place under a turban. This regular grooming is a constant reminder of the Sikh's duty to lead a virtuous life devoted to God, which is why the *kanga* is also considered one of the five articles of faith.

The most easily identifiable aspect of a male Sikh, his turban, is not actually one of the five articles of faith. Nevertheless, it has become an essential item of Sikh clothing and has helped to give its wearers a strong sense of identity and social cohesion. The turban was adopted at the suggestion of Guru Gobind Singh, who pointed out that all the gurus had worn a turban, and that doing likewise would help the wearer to concentrate on following their example. The primary purpose of the turban, however, is to pull back and protect the uncut hair of male Sikhs.

Proofs against temptation

Just as important as the positive virtues is the avoidance of vice. The steel bracelet known as the *kara* is a symbol of the vows taken by a Sikh during baptism to refrain from the five vices. Because it is worn on the wrist it is often visible to the wearer, and therefore acts as a frequent reminder to consider carefully whether his or her actions will lead to evil or wrongdoing. The Jain faith uses a very similar device, in the form of its emblem of the raised palm (p.70): a reminder to stop and consider the intention behind

> God approves not the distinction of high caste and low caste. None has he made higher than others.
> **Sri Guru Granth Sahib**

any action. Similarly, the *kachera*, a cotton undergarment – worn by both men and women – that resembles loose-fitting shorts, ostensibly acts as a warning to control sexual passion and desire, but is also a symbolic reminder that Sikhs should strive to overcome desires of all kinds and lead a faithful life in a broader sense.

Defending the faith

The soldierly aspect of Sikhism is encapsulated in the *kirpan*, the ceremonial sword, which symbolizes courage and dignity. It encourages its wearer to be constantly determined to defend the Sikh faith and its moral values, and protect the downtrodden from tyranny.

Sikhism has at various times been associated with nationalist political movements in the Punjab, where it originated. The region has often suffered from religious conflicts, which Sikhs have

The Sikh turban is an important symbol of faith and dignity. By keeping the hair well groomed, it distinguishes the Sikh man's appearance from the matted locks worn by Hindu ascetics.

inevitably been drawn into. There was even a short-lived Sikh Empire formed in 1799 but dissolved by the British in 1849. After the formation of the Akali, a Sikh reform movement, in the 1920s, and the Akali Dal political party in 1966, there were calls for an autonomous Sikh state in the Punjab, where violent incidents between Sikhs and Hindus, along with tensions between Muslim Pakistan and Hindu India, have continued into modern times. Outside the Punjab, however, the Sikh diaspora has generally integrated into society.

An updated code of conduct for contemporary Sikhism is offered in the *Sikh Rehat Maryada*, published in 1950, which gives guidance on personal and public life, including ceremonies and worship. However, as Guru Nanak originally preached, devotion to God and a socially responsible lifestyle are more important in Sikhism than rituals and reverence. This is reflected in the institution of the gurdwara, which, as well as being a temple for worship, is also the hub of the Sikh community. Sikh worship is generally not prescribed by the gurus, other than the early morning prayer, which uses the Mul Mantra composed by Guru Nanak as a meditation on God's Name. This can be practised anywhere, not just in the gurdwara, and because there is no priesthood in Sikhism, this, alongside readings and hymns from the Guru Granth Sahib, can, in the spirit of Sikh egalitarianism, be performed by anyone. ■

Guru Nanak

The founder of the Sikh religion, Guru Nanak, was born in 1469 into a Hindu family in Talwandi, in the Punjab region of India (now known as Nankana Sahib, Pakistan). Tension was running high between the Hindus and Muslims there as the Mughal Empire spread south into the Indian subcontinent. As a young man, Nanak worked as an accountant, but was always fascinated by spiritual matters. According to Sikh tradition, after receiving a revelation, in which God gave him a cup of nectar and told him of his vocation to spread the message of his Name, Nanak embarked on a 25-year mission, travelling and preaching with his companion, the Muslim minstrel Bhai Mardana. In five long trips, he visited the major cities and religious centres of India and Arabia, where he set up *dharamshalas*, centres of worship. He was given the title "guru", or teacher, by his followers. After his final journey, to Baghdad and Mecca, he returned to Punjab, where he remained until his death in 1539.

The "five Ks" of the Sikh religion here surround the Sikh symbol of crossed swords. The sword or *kirpan* is one of the 'Ks", or articles of faith. The others are uncut hair and beard, comb, bracelet, and cotton shorts.

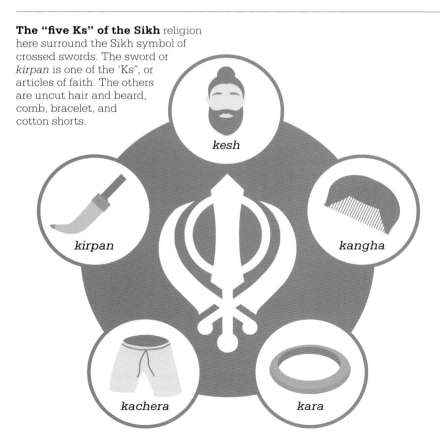

kesh

kirpan

kangha

kachera

kara

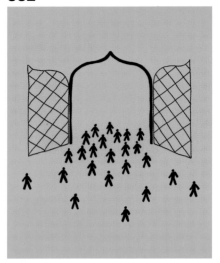

ALL MAY ENTER OUR GATEWAY TO GOD
CLASS SYSTEMS AND FAITH

IN CONTEXT

KEY FIGURE
Guru Nanak

WHEN AND WHERE
From 15th century, India

BEFORE
From 1700 BCE The Vedic
scriptures divide society into
four varnas, or classes, with
brahmins (priests) at the top;
this rigid social hierarchy
pervades Indian society to
the present day.

AFTER
c.1870 Indian sage Sri
Ramakrishna advocates
religious tolerance, stating
that all religions may lead to
God via a heightened state
of consciousness.

1936 Indian philosopher and
political leader Mahatma
Gandhi propagates the notion
of *sarvadharma samabhava*,
the equality of all religions,
and speaks out against the
Indian caste system.

Sikhism is one of the most
egalitarian of all religions,
quite free of division or
discrimination by race, class, or
sex. All are welcome in gurdwaras
(Sikh temples) regardless of faith;
there are no priests – decisions are
taken by the community – and
both men and women may read
from the Sikh holy book. This
inclusiveness can be traced to
Sikhism's origins, when Guru
Nanak (p.301) received a revelation
from God, and announced: "There
is no Hindu or Muslim, so whose
path shall I follow? I shall follow
the path of God."

Disillusioned about the existing
religions of India at that time, and
by the social divisiveness he saw in
all religions, Guru Nanak considered
that, from the divine perspective,
religious labels – such as "Hindu"
or "Muslim" – were irrelevant. In
their place, Guru Nanak offered
an alternative, all-embracing faith
based on devotion to God rather
than the observance of ritual and
reverence for individual holy men.

A legacy of equality
Guru Nanak's teachings were
consolidated by subsequent Sikh
gurus, and when the 10th guru,

Guru Gobind Singh, established
the Khalsa order, into which most
Sikhs are initiated (p.299), he
made the order open to everyone.
Controversially, for the time, he
denounced the caste system and
gender discrimination. He also
abolished the priesthood in
Sikhism, which he felt had become
corrupt and self-serving – guilty of
the very vices the faith seeks to
overcome. Instead, he appointed
custodians of the holy book, the
Guru Granth Sahib, at each temple,
while also permitting all Sikhs,
male or female, to read from it in
worship at the gurdwara or at home.

Both Sikhs and non-Sikh visitors
are welcome to join in communal meals
at Sikh temples. Everyone, whatever
their race, class, or sex, sits on the floor
to eat, to emphasize the equality of all.

See also: God-consciousness 122–23 ■ Gender and the covenant 199 ■ The Sikh code of conduct 296–301 ■ Cao Đài aims to unify all faiths 316

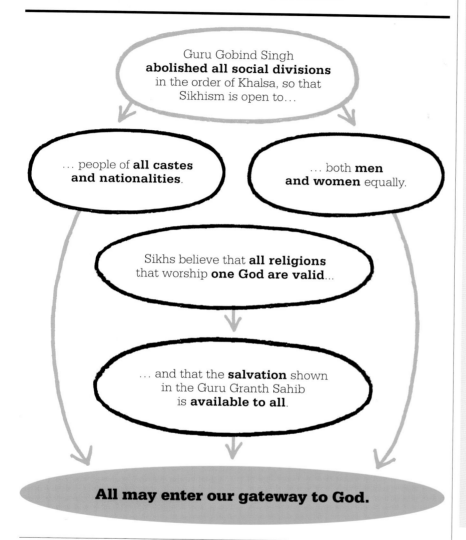

Guru Gobind Singh **abolished all social divisions** in the order of Khalsa, so that Sikhism is open to…

… people of **all castes and nationalities**.

… both **men and women** equally.

Sikhs believe that **all religions** that worship **one God are valid**…

… and that the **salvation** shown in the Guru Granth Sahib is **available to all**.

All may enter our gateway to God.

The Guru Granth Sahib

The central religious text of Sikhism is a collection of hymns and verses compiled and written by the succession of 10 Sikh gurus, the leaders of the faith, who lived between 1469 and 1708. This collection consists of some 1,430 pages, or *angs*, of their teachings. The first version of the book, known as the Adi Granth, was compiled by the fifth guru, Guru Arjan Dev, from the sayings and writings of his predecessors, and was added to by subsequent gurus. Guru Gobind Singh, the 10th guru, completed the text and nominated it, rather than another human leader, as his successor, calling it "the embodiment of the gurus", and giving it the title Guru Granth Sahib. Unlike its predecessors, this "11th guru" is available for all to consult, and a copy takes pride of place in every gurdwara, or Sikh temple. Originally written in a specially devised script, Gurmukhi, in a mixture of dialects collectively known as Sant Bhasha, it has since been translated into several modern languages.

Sikhs do not need to perform any particular rituals or undertake pilgrimages, but they are expected to show their devotion to God in their everyday lives. It is not even a requirement to worship at the gurdwara. These temples serve as "social centres" and exemplify the notion of community spirit that is such an important component of Sikhism. For Sikhs, anyone who believes in and worships one God follows the same path as Sikhism, and their faith deserves respect. Sikhs regard an individual's religion to be largely the result of the culture in which he or she was brought up: Hindus, Muslims, Christians, and Sikhs have a common inspiration, but the particular form this takes is determined by society. For this reason, Sikhs do not attempt to convert people of other faiths. ■

All beings and creatures are His; He belongs to all.
Guru Granth Sahib

MESSAGES TO AND FROM HOME

THE AFRICAN ROOTS OF SANTERIA

IN CONTEXT

KEY BELIEVERS
Displaced Yoruba people from western Africa

WHEN AND WHERE
From 16th century, Cuba

BEFORE
From prehistory African tribal mythologies incorporate strong links to the land and to the ancestors.

9th–6th centuries BCE The peoples of the kingdom of Judah maintain their faith while in exile in Assyria, Babylon, and Egypt.

15th–19th centuries European colonial conquests are accompanied by forcible conversions to Christianity.

AFTER
19th century The slave trade is abolished; Creole religions are practised more openly in the Caribbean and Brazil.

1970s Santeria becomes established in the USA.

S anteria is a religion that combines traditional western African religion with Catholicism. This blended, or syncretic, religion developed in Cuba between the 16th and 18th centuries. During this period, huge numbers of people from western Africa were enslaved and taken to work on the Caribbean plantations that were established following the Spanish colonization of the islands. The Yoruba people of present-day Nigeria and Benin formed the majority of those taken to the Cuban sugar plantations. These slaves came from the well-established Oyo Empire, which had a sophisticated religious tradition. This was outlawed by the Spanish.

Slaves taken from western Africa to the Caribbean

↓

...took their religion with them and **incorporated it into the Christianity** of their owners, initially to conceal its nature from them.

↓

However, they **retained the elements of communication** with their gods, spirits, and ancestors in Africa through trances and possession.

↓

In this way, believers continued to **transmit messages to and from home**.

See also: The power of the shaman 26–31 ▪ The spirits of the dead live on 36–37 ▪ Living the Way of the Gods 82–85 ▪ Ras Tafari is our Saviour 314–15

A Santeria altar often blends imagery from both Catholicism and western African beliefs, with particular saints identified with particular African deities, or orishas.

However, the Yoruba slaves soon learned to conceal the worship of their African gods by appearing to practise Catholicism. Unaware of this, the Spanish slave-owners dismissed the religious practices of their slaves as merely a simplistic form of Christian worship, and sarcastically dubbed it Santeria, the "way of the saints" (a term now viewed as pejorative by some).

The Rule of Osha

The Yoruba religion, known as Regla de Ocha or "Rule of Osha" (Regla Lucumí, in the Yoruba language), already had similarities to Catholicism. The Yoruba believe in one God, Olorun (or Olodumare), the source of all spiritual energy – analogous to Catholic worship of the one God. They also believe in a lesser pantheon of spirits known as orishas, each with an area of responsibility – akin to Catholic reverence of the saints. So, while ostensibly praying to a Catholic saint, the Yoruba slaves would communicate with an orisha with similar characteristics. This hybrid religion allowed the Yoruba to maintain contact with their culture and a link with their homeland, and, they believed, to communicate with their ancestors through the spirits.

Hybrid elements of the religion include the adoption of numerous Spanish words and the addition of images of Catholic saints alongside the traditional portrayals of orishas, and in some cases, the retention of the traditional framework of a Catholic service. Rituals are presided over by a priest or *santeros*. Hymns are replaced with drumming and chanting, with the aim of inducing a trance state. While in a trance, the believer may become possessed by spirits conveying messages from their ancestral home. The drums convey messages to the orisha.

Although there is a strong element of the supernatural and magic in Santeria, and some ceremonies call for ritual sacrifice (usually of a chicken), believers are insistent that "black magic" is not involved. They maintain that their beliefs are distinct from other syncretic religions of the Caribbean, such as Haitian voodoo.

The relationship between Santeria and Catholicism still exists today, although the need for secrecy no longer remains. Adherents of Santeria are often baptized in the Catholic faith and practise separate ceremonies for the saints and orishas. ▪

Hybrid religions

Santeria is just one of many Creole religions – hybrids of African and European faiths – that had their origins in slavery. Yoruba (the dominant culture of the area plundered by slave traders in western Africa) figures largely in many Creole religions: Candomblé in Brazil, Santeria in Cuba, and Orisha-Shango in Trinidad and Tobago. However, other African peoples, including the Igbo from Nigeria, added their cultures to the mix, in religions such as Umbanda and Obeah. Perhaps the best-known African-European faith emerged in Haiti, where French, rather than Spanish, Catholicism was incorporated into African *vodun* beliefs as voodoo. This also made its way into the southern United States. The religions of the African diaspora gained some political significance after the abolition of slavery, especially as Pan-African and black civil rights movements grew in the 20th century, giving rise to another hybrid religion in Jamaica: the Rastafari movement (pp.314–15).

I humble myself before the mysteries of Eshu-Elegba. You are the messenger of Olodumare and Orisha and the Ancestors.
Prayer to the orisha Eshu

ASK YOURSELF: "WHAT WOULD JESUS DO?"
FOLLOWING THE EXAMPLE OF CHRIST

After the **ascension** of Jesus and the **martyrdom** of the apostles…

… the original Church **turned away from the Gospel** in the Great Apostasy.

In a series of revelations, **priesthood authority** was **restored** to Joseph Smith and his successors, the Latter-day Saints…

… who take as **their model Jesus** himself, rather than the dogma of any existing church.

Ask yourself: "What would Jesus do?"

In reaction to the rationalism of the Enlightenment that spread from Europe to the American colonies in the 18th century, a Christian revival occurred in the United States at the beginning of the 19th century. Many breakaway Christian groups were formed at this time. They rejected the traditions of the established church and incorporated charismatic elements of the faith – "gifts of the spirit", such as prophecy and visions. There was also a move to "restore" Christianity to the principles of the New Testament.

It was against this background that Joseph Smith Jr had the first of a series of visions, in which God

See also: Jesus's message to the world 204–207 ▪ Jesus's divine identity 208 ▪ A divine trinity 212–19
▪ God reveals his word and his will 254–61 ▪ Awaiting the Day of Judgment 312–13

Mormonism is the pure doctrine of Jesus Christ, of which I myself am not ashamed.
Joseph Smith

and Jesus Christ came to tell him that he had been chosen to restore the true Church. How the "Church of Christ" would differ from the other restorationist groups was explained when Smith said an angel had guided him to find and translate a text, the Book of Mormon, which described how God had led his followers to the New World. He was told of the "Great Apostasy" that followed the ascension of Christ and the martyrdom of the Apostles,

when the original Christian Church became corrupted and diluted. God conferred on Smith the authority to re-establish the Christian Church.

Modern-day prophets

Smith, and his successors, are considered by their followers to be modern-day "prophets, seers, and revelators", who received guidance from God in the form of revelations from Jesus Christ. Church members believe that, rather than following the doctrine of any existing Church, they are living as Christ has taught them, as "latter-day saints" – a term adopted by Smith when he established the Church of Jesus Christ of Latter-day Saints, although the movement is more commonly called Mormonism. In addition to taking their lead from revelations, Latter-day Saints believe they should follow Jesus's example. The most important consideration for them is, "What would Jesus do?".

After Joseph Smith's death, the movement divided into several branches, with the majority following Brigham Young (1801–1877), who set

A Mormon family prays together in their living room during their "family home evening". These evenings are a Mormon tradition intended to reinforce and solidify family ties.

up a Mormon community in Utah. They hold to a strict moral code, "The Word of Wisdom", avoiding alcohol, tobacco, coffee, and tea, and extramarital sexual activity. Marriage is among the rituals they believe necessary for salvation, as are baptism and confirmation. Early Mormons practised polygamy, but this was renounced by the mainstream movement in 1890. ∎

Joseph Smith Jr

The son of tenant farmers, Joseph Smith Jr was born in 1805 in rural Vermont, but in 1820 moved with his family to western New York, a centre of the Protestant revival movement known as the "Second Great Awakening". Confused as to which of the numerous denominations he should follow, he prayed for guidance and had a vision in which God the Father and Jesus appeared to tell him all the Churches had "turned aside from the gospel". He later said he had been visited by the angel Moroni, who told him of scriptures inscribed on golden plates, written

by ancient inhabitants of America. With divine guidance, Smith supposedly located and translated the scriptures, the Book of Mormon, and published it in 1830, the year that he also founded his Church.

Persecuted for his heretical beliefs, he moved around frequently, establishing Latter-day Saint communities in Ohio and Missouri before finally settling in Nauvoo, Illinois. He was arrested for inciting a riot in Carthage, Illinois, in 1844, but was killed by an angry mob before he could stand trial.

WE SHALL KNOW HIM THROUGH HIS MESSENGERS

THE REVELATION OF BAHA'I

IN CONTEXT

KEY FIGURE
Baha'u'llah (Mirza Husayn-'Ali Nuri)

WHEN AND WHERE
From 1863, Persia

BEFORE
7th century Muhammad is hailed as God's final prophet, bearing the message of Islam. After his death, leadership disputes cause a split between Shi'a and Sunni Muslims.

1501 Shah Ismail I establishes the Safavid dynasty, ruling over a united Persia whose state religion is Shi'a Islam.

1844 Siyyid 'Ali Muhammad Shirazi claims he is the Mahdi, the redeemer predicted in Shi'a Islam. He adopts the title Bab ("Gate"), and founds a new religion to succeed Islam.

AFTER
1921 In Lahore (modern Pakistan), Mirza Ghulam Ahmad claims to bring a new message from God for Islam.

Different religions have been established in various places and at various times in history.

↓

These religions were **founded by "divine messengers"** such as Moses, Buddha, Jesus, and Muhammad.

Each of these divine messengers **revealed God** in a way that suited the time and place...

... and **prophesied messengers** yet to come.

Baha'u'llah is the most recent of these messengers, revealing **religious truth for modern society**...

... but will be followed by other divine messengers in a **continuing and progressive revelation**.

We shall know him through his messengers.

See also: The promise of a new age 178–81 ▪ The Prophet and the origins of Islam 252–53 ▪ The emergence of Shi'a Islam 270–71 ▪ Cao Đài aims to unify all faiths 316 ▪ A faith open to all beliefs 321

In Shi'a Islam, most followers believe that the Mahdi, the descendant of Muhammad who will come to restore the religion of God, is Muhammad al-Mahdi, the "Twelfth Imam", who lived on earth until 941. His return to bring peace and justice to the world is a cornerstone of the branch of Shi'a known as the Twelvers (p.271). This belief was especially prevalent in 19th-century Persia, where Shi'a Islam had for centuries been the state religion. It was here, in 1844, that Siyyid 'Ali Muhammad Shirazi (1819–50) declared that he was the Bab ("Gate"), and had come to establish a faith in readiness for the coming of "He whom God shall make manifest".

The Islamic authorities persecuted his followers, known as Babis, for their beliefs. Among them was Mirza Husayn 'Ali Nuri, who came to believe he was the one whose coming had been predicted by the Bab. He adopted the title Baha'u'llah ("Glory of God") in 1863, proclaiming that he was a messenger of God, the latest in a line of such messengers including Moses, Buddha, Jesus, and Muhammad. Throughout history, he explained, religions have been established by these messengers, with each one in turn bringing the religious truth in a manner that was well-suited to the time and place. Each messenger has also prophesied the coming of another messenger, in a progressive revelation, a continual unfolding of the message of God.

The nature of the message

In his writings, Baha'u'llah explains that God has two reasons for sending these prophets to the world: "The first is to liberate the children of men from the darkness of ignorance, and guide them to the light of true understanding. The second is to ensure the peace and tranquillity of mankind, and provide all the means by which they can be established."

Baha'u'llah's own mission, as the messenger prophesied by previous prophets, was to bring a message that was relevant to the modern world, one of worldwide peace, unity, and justice. Central to his message was the concept of unity of religion, acceptance of the validity of all the world's major religions, and respect for their prophets as messengers of God. With this teaching he hoped to avoid what had hitherto become a source of religious conflict, while promoting the unity of humankind and rejecting inequality, prejudice, and oppression. ▪

> All peoples and nations are of one family, the children of one Father, and should be to one another as brothers and sisters
> **Baha'u'llah**

Baha'u'llah

The founder of the Baha'i faith was born Mirza Husayn 'Ali Nuri in Tehran, Persia, in 1817, but is better known by his adopted title of Baha'u'llah ("Glory of God"). He was brought up as a Muslim, but became one of the first followers of the Bab, Siyyid 'Ali Muhammad Shirazi. In the 1850s, he came to believe that he was the fulfilment of the Bab's prophecies. He was imprisoned for his heretical beliefs, then banished to Baghdad and later to Constantinople (modern Istanbul), where, in 1863, he declared himself as Baha'u'llah, God's latest messenger on earth.

Most of the Babis believed his claims, and, as his followers, became known as Baha'is. In 1868, Baha'u'llah again fell foul of the Ottoman authorities, and was sent to a penal colony in 'Akka, in Palestine. He was gradually permitted greater freedom, but nevertheless remained a prisoner in 'Akka until his death in 1892.

Followers of the Baha'i faith consider it more respectful to depict Baha'u'llah not with an image, but with a stylized version of his name in Arabic calligraphy, as shown left.

BRUSH AWAY THE DUST OF SIN
TENRIKYO AND THE JOYOUS LIFE

IN CONTEXT

KEY FIGURE
Nakayama Miki

WHEN AND WHERE
From 1838, Japan

BEFORE
6th century Buddhism spreads to Japan, bringing with it ideas of reincarnation derived from Hinduism.

8th century In response to increasing Buddhist influence, traditional Japanese beliefs in gods and spirits are codified in the Kojiki and the Nihon Shoki, the first texts of Shinto.

AFTER
Late 19th century Tenrikyo believers attach themselves to a Buddhist sect to avoid persecution, but Tenrikyo is forcibly incorporated into the official state religion of Shinto.

1945 After World War II, State Shinto is disestablished and Tenrikyo is classified as a separate religion.

Tenrikyo is one of the so-called Japanese New Religions that appeared in the 19th century and were regarded as sects of Shinto. Tenrikyo was founded by a peasant woman, Nakayama Miki, following revelations to her from Tenri-O-no-Mikoto, "God the Parent", during a Buddhist exorcism ritual in 1838. She recorded the substance of these revelations in the Ofudesaki ("Tip of the Writing Brush"), Tenrikyo's sacred text, and became known to her followers as Oyasama (the Parent) or the Shrine of God.

Tenrikyo followers believe in a single, benevolent God, who wishes humans to find happiness in their lives on earth. A major part of Tenrikyo practice is to follow the "Joyous Life", avoiding what are seen as negative tendencies. What other religions consider as sins, Tenrikyo describes as "mental dust" that needs to be swept away by *hinokishin* – the performing of acts of kindness and charity. Believers identify eight mental dusts that need to be swept away

> Throughout the world, God is the broom for the sweeping of the innermost heart.
> **The Ofudesaki**

in order to follow the joyous life successfully: *oshii* (miserliness), *huoshii* (covetousness), *nikui* (hatred), *kawai* (self-love), *urami* (grudge-bearing), *haradachi* (anger), *yoku* (greed), and *koman* (arrogance). *Hinokishin* is also practised to give thanks to Tenri-O-no-Mikoto for allowing believers to "borrow" their bodies in a cycle of reincarnation based on the notion of *kashimono-karimono* ("a thing lent, a thing borrowed"). ∎

See also: Living the Way of the Gods 82–85 ∎ Escape from the eternal cycle 136–43 ∎ Let kindness and compassion rule 146–47

THESE GIFTS MUST BE MEANT FOR US

CARGO CULTS OF THE PACIFIC ISLANDS

IN CONTEXT

KEY BELIEVERS
Pacific islanders

WHEN AND WHERE
Late 19th century, Pacific

BEFORE
Pre-colonial times Tribes in Melanesia, Micronesia, and New Guinea hold a variety of beliefs involving ancestral spirits as well as deities.

1790s The first Christian missionaries arrive in the Pacific islands.

AFTER
1945 The term "cargo cult" is coined in the colonial news magazine *Pacific Islands Monthly*, and is popularized by anthropologist Lucy Mair.

1950s Some Tanna islanders in Vanuatu start to worship Prince Philip, husband of Britain's Queen Elizabeth II, believing him to be John Frum's brother, who "married a powerful lady overseas".

Western trade and colonialism during the 19th century brought modern goods in abundance to the islands of the Pacific and, despite the work of Christian missionaries, this had an unexpected impact on indigenous belief systems. Islanders came to believe that this material wealth, the "cargo" of the Western traders, was of supernatural origin, and had been sent to them as a gift from their ancestral spirits, but had been seized by the white men.

Followers of the John Frum cult figure "drill" with model weapons to attract well-stocked military vessels. Some say the name "John Frum" was originally "John From" America.

They developed the idea of a "golden age" to come, when – by propitiating their ancestors and deities with religious rites – the cargo would be restored to them, and the Westerners would be driven out of their lands.

These cults sprang up in parts of Melanesia and New Guinea, and proliferated in the 1930s as air transport increased. Their spread accelerated during World War II, when the islands were used as bases by American and Japanese forces, bringing in large quantities of equipment and supplies. The cult figure John Frum, revered on the island of Tanna in Vanuatu, is often depicted as an American serviceman. As well as developing special religious ceremonies that frequently mimicked military drills, with flags and uniforms, cult followers built wharves, landing strips, and sometimes even life-size models of aircraft to attract the bringers of goods.

Cargo cults persist in some remote areas of the Pacific, but have been largely superseded as Western influence has spread. ∎

See also: Making sense of the world 20–23 ▪ Social holiness and evangelicalism 239 ▪ The African roots of Santeria 304–305

THE END OF THE WORLD IS NIGH

AWAITING THE DAY OF JUDGMENT

IN CONTEXT

KEY FIGURE
Joseph Franklin Rutherford

WHEN AND WHERE
From 1931, USA and Western Europe

BEFORE
1st century CE Jesus announces the arrival of "God's Kingdom"; in the Book of Revelation, St John describes the apocalypse that will precede God's final judgment.

19th century According to the Plymouth Brethren's "Dispensationalist" view of Bible teachings, all who accept Jesus will be swept up into heaven by a "rapture" that will precede global tribulation.

1881 Charles Taze Russell founds what is originally called the Zion's Watch Tower Tract Society; his Bible Student movement predicts Christ's advent on earth.

The Jehovah's Witnesses emerged from the Bible Student movement in the United States in the 1870s. They see their faith as a return to the original concepts of 1st-century Christianity, and refer to this early interpretation of the Bible as "the Truth". The group believes that all other religions, and all forms of present-day government, are controlled by Satan, and face complete destruction in the battle at Armageddon with Satan, when only true Christians – Jehovah's Witnesses – will be spared.

According to the movement, the present world era is nearing its end, having entered its "last days" in October 1914. This was first thought to be the beginning of the battle at Armageddon, but is now accepted as the time when God, known as Jehovah, entrusted the

In 1914, Jesus Christ began his **rule of God's heaven** and **expelled Satan** to earth…

…where he has **corrupted** the world and **fights** the true believers, **Jehovah's Witnesses**.

God will establish his **kingdom on earth** after destroying the world ruled by **Satan**.

The world is now in its **"last days"** before the battle at Armageddon.

The end of the world is nigh.

See also: The battle between good and evil 60–65 ▪ The end of the world as we know it 86–87 ▪ Jesus's message to the world 204–207 ▪ A divine trinity 212–19 ▪ Entering into the faith 224–27 ▪ The ultimate reward for the righteous 279

Judgment Day is near, according to Jehovah's Witnesses, who believe that those not of their faith can soon expect a reckoning, as depicted here in John Martin's *The Great Day of His Wrath*.

rule of the Kingdom of Heaven to Jesus Christ, who then expelled Satan to earth. During this final phase, Jesus, aided by a "faithful and discreet slave" in the Governing Body of Jehovah's Witnesses, will maintain his invisible rule over earth. For Jehovah's Witnesses there is no literal second coming; rather, Jesus will at some unknown point begin the battle against Satan, after which God will extend the Kingdom of Heaven, creating an earthly paradise under Christ's Millennial Reign. They believe Christ to be God's representative ruler and not part of a Trinity. Similarly, the Holy Spirit is not part of the deity, but manifests in forces such as gravity.

During the thousand-year reign of Christ on earth – a prolonged "judgment day" – the dead will be resurrected and judged by Jesus, facing a final test when Satan is released into the world. Only true believers, a select 144,000 Jehovah's Witnesses, will remain when Jesus passes the rule of the Kingdom back to God.

Because of their dismissal of other faiths (even other Christian denominations) as corrupted by Satan, Jehovah's Witnesses have been rejected by most other religions. Public opinion has been adversely affected by their insistent door-to-door evangelizing and the selling of their publications *The Watchtower* and *Awake!* – which nevertheless command high circulation figures worldwide. But their rejection of "corrupt" government has had surprising results. Many Jehovah's Witnesses who would not fight for the Nazis ended up in concentration camps. Elsewhere, their refusal to engage in the wars of secular governments helped to bring about changes to the laws of conscientious objection, and their refusal to compromise their beliefs has led to many court cases and influenced civil rights legislation in several countries. ▪

Joseph Franklin Rutherford

Born in rural Missouri, USA, in 1869, Joseph Rutherford came from a poor farming family and was raised as a Baptist, but became disillusioned with religion after he left home. He studied law and had a successful legal career in Missouri and New York. His interest in religion was renewed in the 1890s by the work of Charles Taze Russell, founder of the Bible Student movement, and he became actively involved with the Watch Tower Society, becoming its second president in 1917, after Russell's death. Dramatic changes were made to the organization under his leadership, and the doctrines of present-day Jehovah's Witnesses were established. He remained president of the Society, increasing its membership by introducing door-to-door evangelizing, among other things, until his death from cancer in 1942.

The Lord declares he has entrusted his people with the privilege and obligation of telling his message.
The Watchtower

THE LION OF JUDAH HAS ARISEN

RAS TAFARI IS OUR SAVIOUR

KEY FIGURE
Haile Selassie

WHEN AND WHERE
From 1930s, Jamaica

BEFORE
18th–19th century Creole,
or syncretic, religions arise
among slave communities,
fusing African beliefs with the
Christian faith that slaves are
forced to adopt by their masters.

1920s Written in Anguilla, the
Holy Piby identifies Ethiopians
as God's chosen people, and
Marcus Garvey as a prophet;
it becomes an influential
Rastafari text.

AFTER
Mid-20th century In the
USA, the Nation of Islam
movement proclaims W. Fard
Muhammad to be the messiah
predicted by both Judaism
and Islam. While fighting for
African–American and black
Muslim rights, the movement
becomes heavily politicized.

The black peoples of Africa
have been **exploited for
centuries** by "Babylon",
the white men…

↓

… but it was prophesied that
a **saviour** from the family of
Judah would come to "Zion"
(Africa) to **free them
from oppression**.

↓

The saviour appeared in
the form of **Ras Tafari**,
God's chosen king on earth…

↓

… who became **Emperor
Haile Selassie I of Ethiopia**,
the Holy Land for Rastafarians.

↓

**The Lion of Judah
has arisen.**

Unlike the Creole religions
that developed among
the black slaves in
the Caribbean (pp.304–305),
Rastafari has little to do with
traditional African religions.
Instead, the movement is largely
based on the Christian Bible.
It nevertheless emphasizes its
binding links to Africa.

Rastafari (followers dislike the
term Rastafarianism, and indeed
all "isms") is as much a political
or social movement as a religious
faith. It emerged during a period
of increasing awareness of the
"African-ness" of the black
population of the New World.
Pan-Africanism – the movement to
unite and inspire people of African
descent – was also on the rise. This
movement had begun in the 19th
century, but gained momentum in
the 1920s and 1930s, particularly
through the work of the political
activist Marcus Garvey (1887–1940).
He was especially influential in his
native Jamaica, which at that time
was still under British rule.

Garvey's denunciation of
oppression and exploitation
chimed with many Jamaicans,
especially as large numbers lived
in poverty. The vast majority of

See also: Jesus's message to the world 204–207 ▪ Social holiness and evangelicalism 239 ▪ The African roots of Santeria 304–305 ▪ The Nation of Islam 339

Jamaicans were descended from African slaves, and had been forced to adopt the British slave-owners' mainly Protestant Christianity, while their own African-based religious beliefs and traditions had been largely quashed. What evolved was therefore a uniquely black Jamaican interpretation of

The Rastafari flag with its imperial lion is waved behind Damian "Jr Gong" Marley, son of reggae legend Bob Marley.

the Christian scriptures, rather than a synthesis of African and Christian beliefs.

A saviour in Zion

Inspired by black nationalism and Pan-Africanism, some Jamaicans claimed that much of the Bible had been changed by white men as part of their ongoing oppression of Africa and Africans. They interpreted the Old Testament's Zion as Africa, and believed that a saviour would come to rescue African peoples from oppression by "Babylon" – the corrupt Europeans. The saviour was prophesied to come to Zion from the family of Judah. When Ras Tafari came to the throne of Ethiopia with the dynastic title "His Imperial Majesty Haile Selassie I, Conquering Lion of the Tribe of Judah, Elect of God and King of the Kings of Ethiopia" the prophesy was seen as fulfilled, and the Rastafari movement was born. Most Rastafarians

believe Haile Selassie to be the second coming of Jesus, an incarnation of their God, Jah, but some see him as simply God's earthly representative and ruler.

Rastafari spread in the post-World War II years as Caribbean migrants left to seek work in Britain and America. Jamaican culture and music, especially reggae, became very popular in those countries in the 1960s and 1970s, and Rastafari gained a considerable following in its wake. ▪

Many discouraging hours will arise before the rainbow of accomplished goals will appear on the horizon.
Haile Selassie

Haile Selassie

Born Tafari Makonnen, inheriting the title "Ras" (analogous to "Duke") as the son of Ethiopian nobility, Haile Selassie became Regent of Ethiopia in 1916. He replaced the heir to the throne, Iyasu, whose links with Islam and general misconduct precluded his becoming head of state. On the death of the Empress Zewditu in 1930, Tafari, a devout member of the Ethiopian Orthodox Church, was crowned Emperor, and took the regnal name of Haile Selassie, "Might of the Trinity". He spent some years in exile in England following Mussolini's invasion of

Ethiopia, returning in 1941 after the British liberation. Although respected around the world, he became increasingly unpopular in his home country, and in 1974 was deposed and imprisoned by members of the armed forces calling themselves the Derg ("Committee"). Many members of his family and government were imprisoned or executed, and, in August of the following year, it was announced that the ex-Emperor had died of respiratory failure, although there was some controversy around the causes of his death.

ALL RELIGIONS ARE EQUAL
CAO ĐÀI AIMS TO UNIFY ALL FAITHS

IN CONTEXT

KEY FIGURE
Ngô Van Chiêu

WHEN AND WHERE
From 1926, Vietnam

BEFORE
6th century BCE In China, Confucius teaches a philosophy of morality, respect, sincerity, and justice.

3rd century BCE Buddhism, founded in India by Siddhartha Gautama, spreads to China.

1st century CE Jesus, revered as a saint in Cao Đài, promises to return to earth to complete God's purpose for humankind.

6th century Muhammad receives the Qur'an, and says it is a renewal of the message given to Moses and Jesus.

AFTER
1975 The Communist regime in Vietnam proscribes Cao Đài.

1997 Cao Đài is granted formal recognition by the Vietnamese authorities.

In 1920, a Vietnamese civil servant, Ngô Van Chiêu, stated that during a seance he was contacted by the Supreme Being, who informed him that the time had come to unite all the world's religions into one. Referring to himself as Cao Đài ("Supreme Palace" or "Altar"), God explained that in the past, his message had been revealed through prophets in two periods of revelation and salvation, which had given rise to all the world's major religions. He had now chosen, in a third period, to reveal his truth via seance ceremonies. Ngô Van Chiêu, along with others who had received similar revelations, founded the Đài Đao Tam Ky Pho Đo ("Religion of the Third Great Period of Revelation and Salvation"), commonly known as Cao Đài.

Combining elements of several religions, especially Buddhist and Confucian philosophy, Cao Đài reveres the prophets of all the major world faiths, along with more surprising figures such as Joan of Arc, Shakespeare, Victor Hugo, and Sun Yat-sen. In unifying the world's faiths, and removing the religious differences that lead to aggression, Cao Đài hopes to achieve world peace. Despite this ambition, Cao Đài became associated in the mid-20th century with the Vietnamese nationalist movement, and was involved in political and military resistance to French colonialism and, later, Communism. ∎

Because of the very multiplicity of religions, humanity does not always live in harmony. That is why I decided to unite all… into one.
God's message to Ngô van Chiêu

See also: God-consciousness 122–23 ▪ Jesus's message to the world 204–207 ▪ The origins of Ahmadiyya 284–85 ▪ The revelation of Baha'i 308–309

WE HAVE FORGOTTEN OUR TRUE NATURE
CLEARING THE MIND WITH SCIENTOLOGY

IN CONTEXT

KEY FIGURE
L. Ron Hubbard

WHEN AND WHERE
From 1952, USA

BEFORE
1950 L. Ron Hubbard sets up
the Hubbard Dianetic Research
Foundation and publishes an
article on Dianetics in the sci-fi
magazine *Astounding Science
Fiction*, followed by his book
*Dianetics: The Modern Science
of Mental Health.*

AFTER
1982 A Religious Technology
Center is established to oversee
Scientology technology; some
members see this as against
original Scientology principles
and form a breakaway group,
which they call the Free Zone.

1993 Scientology is formally
recognized as a religion
in the USA.

Scientology as a religious
philosophy evolved from the
work done by science-fiction
author L. Ron Hubbard in the 1930s
and 1940s on Dianetics. This was a
self-help system based on elements
of psychotherapy with an emphasis
on dealing with past traumatic
experiences to achieve spiritual
rehabilitation. This process of
counselling, known as "auditing",
is at the heart of Scientology.

Followers of Scientology believe
that man's true spiritual nature
is embodied in an eternal spirit
known as the Thetan, which has
been reborn continually in human
form, and has consequently lost
its true nature of spiritual purity.
By undergoing one-to-one auditing,
using an "E-meter" (an instrument
for detecting electric current,
designed by Hubbard), practitioners
can free their unconscious minds
of images of trauma, known as
engrams, and return to the state
of "Clear" – their true spiritual
identity. Progressing through
various levels of auditing, they
eventually reach the level of

Scientology headquarters in Berlin,
Germany, displays the eight-pointed
cross, representing the eight "dynamics
of existence" that are defined in the
movement's theology.

"Operating Thetan", and rediscover
their original potential. Hubbard
was keen to secure celebrity
endorsement for Scientology, and
this, along with the high cost of
one-to-one auditing sessions and
study materials, led to accusations
that Scientology was a money-
making cult. After protracted court
cases in the USA, and elsewhere,
Scientology now has tax-exempt
status as a religion in some parts
of the world, but is still not
recognized in many countries. ∎

See also: The ultimate reality 102–105 ∎ Escape from the eternal cycle 136–43
∎ Purging sin in the Unification Church 318

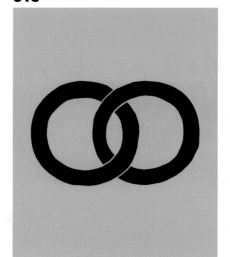

FIND A SINLESS WORLD THROUGH MARRIAGE

PURGING SIN IN THE UNIFICATION CHURCH

IN CONTEXT

KEY FIGURE
Sun Myung Moon

WHEN AND WHERE
From 1954, South Korea

BEFORE
1st century St Paul affirms that all humankind inherits sin from the Fall, and also that marriage is a sacred state.

From 2nd century The early Christian Fathers formulate the doctrine of original sin, but dispute whether Adam or Eve was more responsible for it.

4th century St Jerome uses the example of Jesus to argue that celibacy is the preferred state for a truly holy life.

7th century The notion that Mary, mother of Jesus, was herself conceived free from original sin gains ground.

16th century Martin Luther reasserts that all humans are born sinful, with the exception of Mary, mother of Jesus.

The Holy Spirit Association for the Unification of World Christianity, commonly known as the Unification Church, or more pejoratively as "the Moonies", was founded by Sun Myung Moon in Seoul, South Korea, in 1954. His family had converted from Confucianism to Christianity when he was ten years old, and, as a teenager, Moon had a vision of Jesus asking him to complete his mission of redemption.

To do this, Moon established the Unification Church, which he saw as a Christian denomination based on the Bible and on his own book the *Divine Principle*, but offering a radically different interpretation of the Christian story of the Fall that led to original sin: Moon believed that Eve's spiritual relationship with Satan before her sexual one with Adam led to all of her progeny being born with defective, sinful natures, and, crucially, that Jesus came to rectify this, but was crucified before he had the opportunity to marry – and therefore he only achieved a partial redemption.

"Wedding Blessing" ceremonies, often with hundreds of couples participating, are not legal marriages, but are believed to free the couple's offspring from original sin.

Children born without sin

The path to complete redemption for humankind, Moon maintained, would begin with his own marriage to Hak Ja Han in 1960, and be followed by the mass weddings and rededications that became characteristic of the Unification Church and are its core ceremonies. Children of these marriages, in which pre- and extra-marital sex are proscribed, would then be born without fallen natures, thus heralding the advent of a sinless world. ∎

See also: The battle between good and evil 60–65 ▪ Wisdom lies with the superior man 72–77 ▪ Augustine and free will 220–21

SPIRITS REST BETWEEN LIVES IN SUMMERLAND

WICCA AND THE "OTHERWORLD"

IN CONTEXT

KEY FIGURE
Gerald Gardner

WHERE AND WHEN
From 1950s, UK

BEFORE
Pre-Christian era Celtic and Norse mythologies include the idea of otherworlds such as Asgard, where the Norse heaven Valhalla is situated.

19th century Spiritualists and Theosophists coin the name Summerland to describe an astral plane where virtuous souls rest in bliss.

1920s Anthropologist Margaret Murray publishes work on the Christian persecution of witches in history, identifying witchcraft as a pagan religion separate from black magic cults.

AFTER
1970s In the USA, feminist politics is incorporated into Wicca by practitioners of Dianic Witchcraft.

Probably the best known of the 20th-century neopagan ("new pagan") religions, Wicca originated in England, and was popularized by a retired civil servant, Gerald Gardner, in the 1950s. Although he referred to the religion as witchcraft, and its adherents as the Wica, the version he founded and its various subsequent branches or traditions are today known as Wicca.

Wiccan beliefs are centred on the principles of masculine and feminine, as embodied in the complementary Horned God and Moon Goddess, and the existence of an "otherworld" known as Summerland where souls spend the afterlife. Many branches of Wicca also believe in reincarnation, and see Summerland as a resting place for souls between lives, where they can examine their previous life and prepare for the next. These souls are sometimes contacted by Wiccans in magic ceremonies similar to those of spiritualism, involving mediums or ouija boards, but this practice is not universal.

Although Wiccans believe in an afterlife, they emphasize making the most of the present life in nature-based rituals. These include celebrations of the seasons, and rites of passage such as initiation, wiccaning (similar to baptism), and marriage or sexual union.

Because of some apparent resemblances to Satanism (the Horned God, for example), Wicca has often been confused with black magic cults, and has, until recently, suffered prejudice and persecution, especially in Christian countries. ∎

I do not remember my past lives clearly; I only wish I did.
Gerald Gardner

See also: Animism in early societies 24–25 ∎ Man and the cosmos 48–49 ∎ The power of the great goddess 100

NEGATIVE THOUGHTS ARE JUST RAINDROPS IN AN OCEAN OF BLISS
FINDING INNER PEACE THROUGH MEDITATION

IN CONTEXT

KEY FIGURE
Maharishi Mahesh Yogi

WHEN AND WHERE
From 1958, Europe

BEFORE
From 1700 BCE Meditation techniques are found in early Indian Vedic practices.

From 6th century BCE Meditation is practised in Buddhism in India and Confucianism in China.

19th century European intellectuals discover Eastern philosophy and arouse general interest in Buddhist and Hindu meditation and yoga.

AFTER
1967 The Beatles meet Maharishi Mahesh Yogi in London and visit his ashram in India for TM training.

1976 TM promotes its "Siddhi" programme with the claim that it enables practitioners to levitate.

In 1958, Maharishi Mahesh Yogi travelled to the West to teach Transcendental Meditation (TM), with the original intention of founding a Hindu revival movement. His methods evolved from Hindu mantra meditation techniques, with the similar aim of transcending the confines of physical consciousness to tap into a creative force.

Cultivating inner peace
The practice of TM involves sitting in meditation for 20 minutes, twice a day, using a personal mantra. This is believed to result in improved psychological and physical well-being and increased potential for creativity, allowing the individual to experience "communion with the wellspring of life" and overcome negative thoughts, which become merely "raindrops falling into the ocean of your bliss".

At first, TM initiates were encouraged to give thanks to the Hindu deities for providing the knowledge behind the method and to study the Vedas and the

Maharishi Mahesh Yogi founded TM as the Spiritual Regeneration Movement. Today it is an organized international movement with its headquarters in the Netherlands.

Bhagavad-Gita. Today, proponents of TM offer it as a scientific method for self-development that is open to all. TM techniques have been adopted not only by individuals, but also by business institutions, and even in some medical practices, posing the question as to whether it should be considered as religion, or simply a form of therapy based on traditional Indian techniques. ∎

See also: Physical and mental discipline 112–13 ▪ Zen insights that go beyond words 160–63 ▪ Life-energy cultivation in Falun Dafa 323

WHAT'S TRUE FOR ME IS THE TRUTH

A FAITH OPEN TO ALL BELIEFS

IN CONTEXT

KEY MOVEMENT
Unitarian Universalism

WHEN AND WHERE
From 1961, USA and Canada

BEFORE
6th century BCE Confucius asserts that virtue is not sent from heaven, but can be cultivated in the self.

1st century CE Angering the Jews, who consider themselves the "chosen people", Jesus asserts that God's kingdom is open to all who accept him.

16th century In Protestant Christianity, the authority of Rome is replaced by spiritual self-examination.

19th century The Baha'i Faith emerges as one of the first "universalist" new religions, open to all.

20th century Cao Đài is founded on the principle that all religions are equal.

The Unitarian Universalist Association (UUA) was formed in 1961 by the merger of two movements founded in the 19th century: the Universalist Church of America and the American Unitarian Association. Although it emerged from a largely Christian tradition, and some members have beliefs that are Christian in nature, the UUA aims to be a "non-creedal, non-doctrinal religion which affirms the individual's freedom of belief". Members acknowledge the need for a spiritual and religious dimension to life and believe individuals can learn from all the world's religions. They place more emphasis on a humanist search for truth and meaning in this life than on belief in a supreme being and salvation in an afterlife. Some followers are in fact agnostic or even atheist.

For the Unitarian Universalist, personal experience, conscience, and reason form the basis for religious faith; the opinions and beliefs of all men and women should therefore be respected.

This notion of respect runs through the UUA philosophy and its "Seven Principles": the inherent worth and dignity of every person; justice, equity, and compassion in human relations; the acceptance of one another and encouragement to spiritual growth; a free, responsible search for truth and meaning; the right of conscience, and the use of the democratic process within congregations and in society at large; the goal of world community; and respect for the interdependent web of all existence. ∎

The freedom of the mind is the beginning of all other freedoms.
Clinton Lee Scott

See also: God-consciousness 122–23 ▪ Why prayer works 246–47 ▪ The revelation of Bahá'í 308–309 ▪ Cao Đài aims to unify all faiths 316

CHANTING HARE KRISHNA CLEANSES THE HEART
DEVOTION TO THE SWEET LORD

IN CONTEXT

KEY FIGURE
A.C. Bhaktivedanta Swami Prabhupada

WHEN AND WHERE
From 1960s, USA and western Europe

BEFORE
4th century BCE First evidence of worship of Lord Krishna, a key figure in the Hindu epics, appearing as an avatar of the god Vishnu in the *Mahabharata*.

6th century The bhakti tradition of devotional worship develops in Hinduism.

16th century The Gaudiya Vaishnava movement in India sees Krishna as the original form of God – the source of Vishnu, and not his avatar.

1920 Srila Bhaktisiddhanta Sarasvati Thakura Prabhupada founds the Gaudiya Math, an organization to spread the Gaudiya Vaishnava message around the world.

The Hare Krishna movement or International Society for Krishna Consciousness (ISKCON) is best known for the practice of chanting the Maha Mantra. ISKCON has its roots in the Gaudiya Vaishnava movement in Hinduism, founded by Chaitanya Mahaprabhu (1486–1534), in which believers use devotional practices known as bhakti to please and to develop a loving relationship with the god Krishna, believed to be the Supreme Personality of Godhead.

The Maha Mantra
The mantra is chanted as a means of clearing the mind and cleansing the heart. The repeated use of the holy name enables "Krishna consciousness" to emerge from the soul, free of the distraction of sensual or physical consciousness. The chant "Hare Krishna, Hare Krishna, Krishna Krishna, Hare Hare, Hare Rama, Hare Rama, Rama Rama, Hare Hare" calls upon the energy of God (Hare), the "all-attractive" (Krishna), and the "highest eternal pleasure" (Rama).

Chaitanya taught that by using this mantra anyone, even if born outside the Hindu class system, could achieve Krishna consciousness. In the 1960s, one of Chaitanya's followers, A.C. Bhaktivedanta Swami Prabhupada, travelled to the USA and founded ISKCON. Its ideas chimed well with hippy culture and a new interest in Eastern spirituality, and spread to Europe after being popularized by celebrities such as the Beatles. ∎

Lord Krishna provides everything we need to bring the spiritual world into our lives.
A.C. Bhaktivedanta Swami Prabhupada

See also: A rational world 92–99 ▪ Devotion through puja 114–15 ▪ Buddhas and bodhisattvas 152–57 ▪ The performance of ritual and repetition 158–59

THROUGH QIGONG WE ACCESS COSMIC ENERGY

LIFE-ENERGY CULTIVATION IN FALUN DAFA

IN CONTEXT

KEY FIGURE
Li Hongzhi

WHEN AND WHERE
From 1992, China

BEFORE
c.2000 BCE Various movement and breathing exercises are developed for meditation and healing in China, and are later collectively known as qigong.

5th century BCE Qigong exercises are incorporated into the philosophies of Daoism, Confucianism, and Buddhism in China.

1950s The Chinese Communist government adopts qigong techniques as part of a secular health-improvement programme.

AFTER
1990s Li Hongzhi moves to the USA; the Chinese Communist Party declares Falun Dafa a heretical organization, while in the West, the practice of qigong gains in popularity.

There was a revival of interest in the meditative exercises known as *qigong* (literally "life-energy cultivation") in China in the second half of the 20th century, and while the Communist authorities saw it as a way to improve public health, others found spiritual meaning in the practice. Among them was Li Hongzhi, who founded the Falun Dafa movement (popularly known as Falun Gong) in the early 1990s. He advocated the practice of Falun Gong ("Practice of the Wheel of Law") as not only a means of cultivating life-energy,

Qigong exercises aim to rebuild or rebalance *qi*, the esssential life force or energy, through controlled movement, breathing, and mental awareness.

but also a way to put practitioners in touch with the energy of the universe in order to elevate them to higher levels of existence.

In his book *Revolving the Wheel of Law*, Li describes five core exercises to cultivate the mind, body, and spirit. He explains that the Falun (the "law wheel") is situated in the lower abdomen, and its rotation – in sympathy with the revolving of the universe – rids the practitioner of negative influences, allowing access to cosmic energy. Complementing these exercises is a philosophy based on the virtues of *zhen-shàn-ren* (truthfulness, benevolence, and forbearance), similar to traditional Confucian, Daoist, and Buddhist ideas, which governs the conduct of Falun Dafa practitioners.

Viewed by some as a new religion, but by others as a practice continuing in the Chinese tradition of "cultivation" of the mind, body, and spirit, Falun Dafa has attracted many followers in China, where its religious overtones have, however, led to it being outlawed. ■

See also: Aligning the self with the *dao* 66–67 ▪ Physical and mental discipline 112–13 ▪ Escape from the eternal cycle 136–43

DIRECTO

RY

DIRECTORY

Despite the apparent prevalence of atheism in the West, the number of people professing some kind of religious belief is increasing worldwide. Christianity and Islam, both proselytizing religions, are now espoused by more than half of the world's total population. Other faiths, such as Hinduism, have also continued to attract followers into the 21st century. Religions spread for all kinds of reasons, such as the missionary activities of their adherents, population increases, and the need to fill "belief vacuums" that occur when primal or other local religions go into decline. So, while many people in Africa have left behind traditional beliefs to embrace new Christian churches, in Europe dissatisfaction with Christianity and interest in ideas from the East has led to a modest growth in Buddhism and other Eastern religions.

MAJOR WORLD FAITHS

NAME	FOUNDED	FOUNDER	GOD	ADHERENTS
Baha'i Faith	Tehran, Persia, 1863	Baha'u'llah	One God, revealed through various religions	5–7 million
Buddhism	Northeastern India, c.520 BCE	Siddhartha Gautama, or Buddha	Theravada is nontheistic; Mahayana involves devotion to the Buddha and bodhisattvas	376 million
Cao Đài	Vietnam, 1926	Ngô Van Chiêu	One God, and reverence for founders of other faiths (including Buddhism, Daoism, and Christianity)	8 million
Christianity	Judea, c.30 CE	Jesus Christ	One God, in the form of the Holy Trinity: Father, Son, and Holy Spirit	2,000 million
Church of Christ (Scientist)	Massachusetts, USA, 1879	Mary Baker Eddy	One God, no Holy Trinity	400,000
Church of Jesus Christ of Latter-day Saints (Mormons)	New York, USA, 1830	Joseph Smith	Three separate beings: God the Father; Jesus Christ the Son; and the Holy Spirit	13 million
Confucianism	China, 6th–5th centuries BCE	Confucius	None, although Confucius believed in the Great Ultimate, or *dao*	5–6 million

NAME	FOUNDED	FOUNDER	GOD	ADHERENTS
Church of Scientology	California, USA, 1954	L. Ron Hubbard	None	Not known
Daoism	China, c.550 BCE	Laozi	*Dao* pervades everything	20 million
Falun Dafa	China, 1992	Li Hongzhi	Many gods and spiritual beings	10 million
Hinduism	India, prehistoric	Indigenous	Many deities, all manifestations of one supreme reality	900 million
Islam	Saudi Arabia, 7th century CE	Muhammad, the final Prophet	One God, Allah	1,500 million
Jainism	India, c.550 BCE	Mahavira	No gods, but devotion to some divine beings	4 million
Jehovah's Witnesses	USA, 1872	Charles Taze Russell	One God	7 million
Judaism	Israel, c.2000 BCE	Abraham, Moses	One God, YHWH	15 million
Rastafari movement	Jamaica, 1930s	Haile Selassie I	One, Jah, incarnate in Jesus and Haile Selassie	1 million
Santeria	Cuba, early 19th century	None; a syncretic faith	More than 400 deities	3–4 million
Shinto	Japan, prehistoric	Indigenous	Many gods and spirits, known as *kami*	3–4 million
Sikhism	Punjab, India, 1500 CE	Guru Nanak	One God	23 million
Tenrikyo	Japan, 1838	Nakayama Miki	God the parent	1 million
Unification Church	South Korea, 1954	Sun Myung Moon	God, the heavenly parent of all humanity	3 million (official figure)
Wicca	Britain, 1950s, based on ancient beliefs	Gerald Gardner	Usually two: the Triple Goddess and the Horned God	1–3 million
Zoroastrianism	Persia, 6th century BCE	Zoroaster	One God (Ahura Mazda), but dualism embraced	200,000

BRANCHES OF HINDUISM

The Hindu faith is thought to have originated in the Indus Valley (Pakistan and northwest India) more than 3,000 years ago. Today, it has almost a billion followers, most of them in India. Hindus all worship a supreme being, though the identity of this deity differs according to sect. There are four principal denominations: Vaishnavites, for whom Vishnu is god; Shaivites, who are devoted to Shiva; Shaktis, who worship the goddess Shakti; and Smartas, who can choose their deity. These faiths, and other branches of Hinduism, share many beliefs; the Vedas (pp.94–99) are their most sacred texts, and central to Hindu belief is the idea that a person's deeds affect their future, in an endless cycle of birth, death, and rebirth.

VAISHNAVISM
c.600 BCE, India

The largest devotional sect within Hinduism, Vaishnavism focuses on the worship of Vishnu as the one supreme god. He is seen as the preserver of the universe, a figure unparalleled in his divine benevolence. Vishnu is said to give life to the Creator, Brahma, who sits in a lotus blossom at Vishnu's navel, and to sustain and protect all that Brahma creates. As well as inspiring devotion in his own right, he is also worshipped in the form of his avatars, Rama and Krishna. Followers, or Vaishnavas, emphasize devotion over doctrine. Their final goal is freedom from the cycle of birth and death, and spiritual existence in the presence of Vishnu.

SHAIVISM
c.600 BCE, India

One of the four major denominations, of Hinduism, Shaivism holds that Shiva is the supreme god. At the heart of Hinduism is the belief that dualities can be reconciled by a higher divinity. Shaivites (worshippers of Shiva) believe that Shiva embodies this coming together of opposites like no other deity. He embraces many dualities, such as life and death, time and eternity, and destruction and creation, and takes a multiplicity of forms. In one popular depiction he appears as Nataraja, Lord of the Dance. After destroying the universe, he dances its re-creation, carrying both fire (symbolizing destruction) and a drum (the first sound to be made at the beginning of creation). Shaivism encompasses many subsets, and is widespread in India, Nepal, and Sri Lanka today, and its influence is felt as far as Indonesia and Malaysia.

SHAKTISM
5th century CE, India

Shaktism is one of the main devotional branches of Hinduism. According to Hindu belief, Shakti is the divine power that creates and sustains creation; the great goddess (known as Devi or Mahadevi) embodies Shakti and is often referred to by the name Shakti; those who worship her are known as Shaktis (p.104). Although the roots of goddess worship in India extend to the earliest Indus Valley civilizations, Shaktism is thought to have arisen as an organized movement in the 5th century CE. The goddess of Shakti devotion has many names and can take many forms (fearsome, wrathful, benign, and homely), but all point to her as a manifestation of divine power and energy. The sacred texts of the faith are the Vedas, the Shakta Agamas, and the Puranas. Some devotees hope to come closer to the goddess by using yoga, puja, and Tantra (pp.112–15).

THE DARSHANAS
2nd–13th centuries CE, India

While the followers of theistic sects, such as Vaishnavism, Shaivism, and Shaktism, worship deities, Hinduism also encompasses six schools, or *darshanas*, which focus on philosophy rather than gods. These schools emphasize the ultimate reality or Brahman, the great "self" who must be realized to attain liberation from reincarnation.

The *darshanas* follow sacred texts written in early Indian history, and each branch relates to a different sphere. The six *darshanas* are Samkhya (cosmology), Yoga (human nature), Vaisheshika (scientific laws), Nyaya (logic), Mimamsa (ritual), Vedanta (metaphysics and destiny).

SMARTISM
9th century, India

One of the four major sects of Hinduism, Smarta derives its name from the Sanskrit word *smriti*, which refers to a group of sacred Hindu texts. This orthodox Hindu sect draws from Advaita Vedanta philosophy, which propounds the unity of the the self and Brahman, and the teachings of the monk-philosopher Adi Shankara, who is thought to have founded the movement in India in the 9th century. Followers uphold the rules of conduct outlined in the ancient texts, known as the sutras, and worship the supreme god in any form (Shiva, Shakti, Vishnu, Ganesha, or Virya); for this reason, they are considered liberal and non-sectarian.

LINGAYATISM
12th century, southern India

Followers of the Lingayat sect take their name from the linga, emblem of the god Shiva, which devotees wear around their necks. The movement is thought to have been established in southern India in the 12th century by the teacher and religious reformer, Basava. Lingayats are distinctive for their worship of Shiva as the sole deity; in their monotheistic belief, Shiva and the self are one and the same.

They reject the authority of the brahmin caste and of the sacred texts, the Vedas, promoting a message of social equality and reform. The movement retains a large following in southern India.

SWAMINARAYAN SAMPRADAY
Early 19th century, western India

Swaminarayan Sampraday was founded by the religious reformer Swami Narayan at the beginning of the 19th century, largely as a response to alleged corruption among other Hindu sects. Rituals, laws, observances, and prayers are based on Hindu tradition and the teachings of the movement's founder. By following these moral and spiritual codes in everyday life, the aim is to become an ideal *satsangi* (adherent) and thereafter attain ultimate redemption. The movement has several million followers throughout the world.

BRAHMOISM
1828, Calcutta, India

Brahmoism is a Hindu reform movement that can be traced to the Brahmo Samaj (Divine Society), founded by Ram Mohan Roy in Calcutta in 1828, which aimed to reinterpret Hinduism for the modern age. Brahmoism differs from orthodox Hinduism in its adherence to one universal and infinite deity. It rejects the authority of the Vedas (pp.94–99) and, in some cases, belief in avatars (incarnations of deities) and karma (effects of past deeds). One of its key features is social reform. Brahmoism has a following in Bengal, India, and in Bangladesh.

ARYA SAMAJ
1875, India

Arya Samaj is a modern religious and social reform movement founded by Swami Dayananda, a religious leader who sought to reaffirm the supreme authority of the ancient Hindu texts, the Vedas (pp.94–99). He built a number of schools throughout India in the late 19th century, designed to promote Vedic culture. Similar projects continue today, including the establishment of colleges and orphanages, and activities that focus on social reform and the alleviation of injustice and hardship. The sect is opposed to the caste system, but has been criticized for intolerance of other faiths. Arya Samaj upholds the doctrines of karma and samsara, and the centrality of rituals connected with major events in life. The movement is popular in northern and western India.

SATHA SAI BABA SOCIETY
1950, India

Sathyanarayana Rajuin (born 1926) is thought to have performed numerous miracles. Aged 14 he was stung by a scorpion and went into a trance; on waking he claimed to be a reincarnation of the guru Shirdi Sai Baba, and was henceforth known as Sathya Sai Baba. His fame spread in the 1950s due to his miracles; he attracted several million devotees who are guided by four principles: truth, *satya*; duty, dharma; peace, shanti; and divine love, *prema*. Unlike many Hindus, he did not attach a specific dharma to each social class – all are said to be equal.

BRANCHES OF BUDDHISM

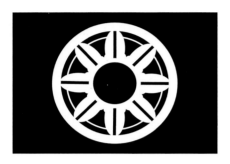

Now followed in many parts of the world, Buddhism originated in northern India over 2,500 years ago, with the teachings of Siddhartha Gautama. Buddhism arose within Hinduism, which, at the time, was producing some of its most deeply philosophical and abstract texts, and Buddhism is dominated by ideas, not deities and doctrines. It has one aim – to guide the individual on to the path that leads to enlightenment, or spiritual liberation from the worldly self. Buddha himself taught that any means by which this aim could be achieved was valid, and as Buddhism spread geographically, it also diversified to suit local traditions of worship. It now takes several forms, from the ascetic to the highly ritualized.

THERAVADA BUDDHISM
6th century BCE, Northern India

Theravada Buddhism is, with Mahayana Buddhism, one of the two main forms of Buddhism. The oldest surviving branch of Buddhism, it is generally considered the form closest to the dhamma – the original teachings of Buddha. It is practised today in Thailand, Laos, Cambodia, and Burma. Central to Theravada is the concept of the *sangha* or monastic community. Theravada monks (and sometimes nuns, although they have a lesser status) have few possessions and live in basic accommodation. They follow the Eightfold Path and the Five Precepts (pp.136–43), travel around villages, and teach the dhamma and the scriptures of the Pali Canon. Their most important activity is meditation, which they practise to empty their minds of the self and move closer to nirvana (perfect enlightenment). Although a full-time monastic existence is the ideal, there is also a place in Theravada Buddhism for lay people. They play an important auxiliary role in helping to sustain the monks in their pursuit of an ascetic way of life; for example, supplying them with food in return for blessings and teachings.

MAHAYANA BUDDHISM
3rd–2nd century BCE, Northwestern India

Mahayana Buddhism, which, with Theravada Buddhism, is one of the two main forms of Buddhism, spread eastwards from India and is today practised in large areas of Asia, including China and Korea. Unlike Theravada Buddhists, who believe that total enlightenment represents a departure from this existence, adherents of Mahayana Buddhism believe that Buddha has remained eternally present in this world, guiding others to enlightenment. In this tradition, there is no purpose to enlightenment unless it is used to assist other people on their spiritual path. Mahayana Buddhists believe other people may become buddhas, and revere those who have come close to nirvana as bodhisattvas (wisdom or enlightenment beings), and who possess, in addition to their compassion, six perfections: generosity, morality, patience, vigour, meditation, and wisdom.

PURE LAND BUDDHISM
7th century CE, China

Arising in China out of the Mahayana tradition, Pure Land Buddhism now consists of several sects based in China and Japan. All are centred on devotion to Amitabha, the Buddha of Infinite Light, said to rule a paradise known as the Pure Land. By means of various spiritual techniques focused on Amitabha, the faithful may avoid the cycle of death and rebirth, go to dwell with him in the Pure Land, and thereafter achieve enlightenment. The main Pure Land text is the 1st-century Lotus Sutra, which states that devotion to Amitabha is the one true way.

TIBETAN BUDDHISM
7th century, Tibet

Buddhism was introduced to Tibet by Indian missionaries in around the 7th century CE. Although derived from the Mahayana tradition (see opposite), Tibetan Buddhism evolved quite differently from Buddhism in other countries. It has its own orders of monks and its own religious practices, including devotion to a guru and the use of mandalas, or symbolic diagrams, as meditation aids.

One of Tibetan Buddhism's most distinctive features is its nomination of lamas. These spiritual teachers are the most revered of all the monks, and several are believed to have been spiritual leaders in a previous life. Succession is by reincarnation. When a lama nears the end of his life, he gives a series of clues as to the identity of his next incarnation. His followers then search for the child who best matches these clues.

TANTRIC BUDDHISM
7th century, India

Tantric Buddhism takes its name from the texts known as Tantras, which became powerful tools in the quest for buddhahood. The texts describe how a person can realize their "Buddha nature" more quickly than in other forms of Buddhism. The techniques involved include the use of rituals, meditation, mandalas, and even magic. The Tantras seek to reconcile all states and emotions, recognizing that all are part of the essential Buddha nature of all people.

Tantric Buddhists revere many buddhas and bodhisattvas (including Amitabha, the Buddha of Infinite Light), seeing each as a manifestation of buddha nature. Today there are schools of Tantric Buddhism in Tibet, India, China, Japan, Nepal, Bhutan, and Mongolia.

ZEN BUDDHISM
12th century, Japan

The Chinese version of Buddhism (Ch'an) took root in Japan in the 6th century, where it became known as Zen. The religion has also had a significant impact in countries influenced by Chinese culture, such as Vietnam, Korea, and Taiwan. Zen Buddhism emphasizes devotion to meditation, the attainment of enlightenment, the value of experience over scripture, and the belief that human beings are identical with the cosmos and share an identity with all that is in it.

For its followers, Zen pervades every aspect of life – the physical, intellectual, and spiritual realms. Composing poetry and creating minimalist rock gardens are considered particularly expressive activities. The best-known schools of Zen are Rinzai and Soto.

NICHIREN BUDDHISM
13th century, Japan

The Japanese monk Nichiren founded this school of Buddhism based on the passionate faith he placed in the supreme spiritual power of the Lotus Sutra, a collection of Buddhist teachings from around the 1st century CE. He encouraged his followers to chant from the text: "I take refuge in the Lotus of the Wonderful Law Sutra". Rejecting all other forms of Buddhism, he believed that only the study of the Lotus Sutra could lead to buddhahood. Many Nichiren Buddhist sects still flourish in Japan and a number of new religious movements take his teachings as their basis, for example, Soka Gakkai (see right).

SOKA GAKKAI
1937, Japan

In 1937, two Japanese reformers, Tsunesaburo Makiguchi and Josei Toda, founded an education society inspired by the teachings of the Japanese Buddhist monk Nichiren. Following Makiguchi's death in 1944, Toda refounded the organization as a religious sect, naming it Soka Gakkai. Like Nichiren Buddhism, it places strong emphasis on the Lotus Sutra, and on the ritual chanting of the words of its title. The movement has attracted some 12 million followers in Japan and around the world, partly as a result of determined recruiting.

TRIRATNA BUDDHIST COMMUNITY
1967, United Kingdom

Formerly the Friends of the Western Buddhist Order (FWBO), the Triratna Buddhist Community was founded by the English-born Buddhist monk Sangharakshita. After studying in India he returned to the UK to form the movement in 1967, with the aim of explaining how Buddhism's basic teachings can be applied to life in the West today. Members are ordained, but may choose a monastic or a lay lifestyle. They commit to a number of core principles: taking "Triple Refuge" in the Buddha, the dhamma, and the *sangha*; the ideal of buddhahood; and belief in other teachings of the Buddhist tradition. These combine a balance of moral precepts, study, and devotion. The movement has affiliations with groups in Europe, North America, and Australasia.

BRANCHES OF JUDAISM

Judaism is the religion of the Jews. Dating back to around 2000 BCE, it is the oldest of the three main monotheistic faiths (the others being Christianity and Islam), all of which have roots in the Middle East. According to Moses, the patriarch to whom God revealed the tablets of the law, the Jews were God's chosen people and received his guidance in the form of the Torah. For much of their history the Jews were exiled from their homeland, so followers of Judaism may be found far beyond the Jewish state of Israel, giving rise to geographical branches of the faith. Jews interpret their faith in different ways, with varying emphasis on the centrality of the Torah and Oral Law to their beliefs and observances.

ORTHODOX JUDAISM
c.13th century BCE, Canaan

Orthodox Judaism sees itself as the continuation of the religious tradition developed in Canaan 3,000 years ago and practised by the Jews in the time of Moses. It is not a single movement, but is made up of many branches that share a set of core beliefs. At the heart of the faith is the belief that the Torah – the first five books of the Hebrew Bible – contains the actual words of God, and provides guidance on every aspect of life. From the Middle Ages, Orthodox Judaism was deeply rooted in Central and Eastern Europe. These communities of Jews were known as Ashkenazim, from the name of a patriarch. They were persecuted and frequently ghettoized over the centuries, and millions of Orthodox Jews in Europe died during the Holocaust. After World War II, many Jews travelled to the USA, and later to the State of Israel, which was established in 1948, and where Orthodox Judaism is the state religion. More than 50 per cent of practising Jews consider themselves to be Orthodox.

SEPHARDIC JUDAISM
10th century BCE, Iberia

The name Sephardic Judaism refers to the Jews who lived in Iberia (modern-day Portugal and Spain) from as early as the 10th century BCE, and their descendants. Despite some restrictions, Jews coexisted peacefully for centuries with Christians and then Muslims in Iberia. However, following the Christian conquest of Spain in 1492, and of Portugal in 1497, the Sephardim who resisted conversion to Christianity were expelled by Christian decree and fled to North Africa, Italy, France, England, the Netherlands, the Ottoman Empire, and even the Americas. Today there are thriving Sephardic communities in Israel, France, Mexico, the USA, and Canada. Many of the fundamental beliefs of Sephardic Judaism are consistent with those of Orthodox Ashkenazi Judaism, though there is more emphasis on mysticism, and some notable differences in culture and practice, including those relating to language, diet, holidays, prayer, and worship.

HASIDIC JUDAISM
c.1740, Mezhbizh (now in Ukraine)

Hasidic Judaism (from *hasid*, meaning "pious one") is a branch of Orthodox Judaism that stresses a mystical relationship with God. Followers believe the Torah is made up of words that are in some sense realignments of the name of God, YHWH. A true Hasid is cut off from the world and meditates, prays, and studies the Torah to become closer to God. A core belief of Hasidism is that God is both the centre of the cosmos and infinite.

NEO-ORTHODOX JUDAISM
Late 19th century, Germany

The Neo-Orthodox movement arose out of the persecution of Jews in the West in the late 19th century. It provided a middle ground for those who wished neither to withdraw completely into Orthodox communities nor to wholly renounce them. Although adhering to the teachings of the Torah, Neo-Orthodox Judaism attempted to accommodate, and adapt to, the demands of the modern world. Followers consider it vital that Jews engage with non-Jewish peoples.

REFORM JUDAISM
1885, Pittsburgh, Pennsylvania, USA

Popular in western Europe and North America, Reform Judaism has its origins in 19th-century efforts to update liturgy and worship in Europe. Reform Jews tend to see the Torah as written by a number of different writers inspired by God, rather than as God's actual words. They have adapted their beliefs and practices to be more consistent with modern lifestyles and are accordingly less strict in their observances than Orthodox Jews. For example, Reform Jews have abandoned many traditional dietary laws and adopted new traditions, such as the ordination of women rabbis.

CONSERVATIVE JUDAISM
1887, New York City, USA

Many Jews felt that the Reform movement in the late 19th century went too far in rejecting the traditional tenets of their faith. As a result, in 1887, the Jewish Theological Seminary was founded to foster a branch of the faith that preserved the knowledge of historical Judaism as exemplified in the Hebrew Bible and the Talmud. This form of Judaism, now known as Conservative or Masorti Judaism, holds that the Torah and Talmud do have a divine origin, and that their laws must be followed; however, rabbis have a freer hand in interpreting those laws than their Orthodox equivalents. Many of the rulings of Conservative rabbis have been rejected by Orthodox Jews, but the movement has proved popular, especially in the USA.

JEWISH SCIENCE
1920s, Cincinnati, Ohio, USA

The Jewish Science movement was founded in the early 1920s in the USA by Alfred G. Moses, Morris Lichtenstein, and Tehilla Lichtenstein. It is often considered to have been a response to the growing influence of Christian Science, as developed by Mary Baker Eddy (p.337) at the end of the 19th century. Adherents are encouraged to cultivate a sense of personal contentment and a positive attitude towards themselves and others. Rather than being regarded as a paternal figure, God is seen as an energy or force that permeates the universe, and as the source and restorer of health. Self-help, visualization, and affirmative prayer (focusing on a positive outcome) are central to the faith and are believed to promote both physical and spiritual wellbeing. Jewish Science acknowledges modern medicine and, unlike Christian Science, permits conventional medical treatment.

RECONSTRUCTIONIST JUDAISM
1920s–40s New York City, USA

The Reconstructionist movement was founded by Mordecai Kaplan, a Lithuanian-born American. He proposed a progressive approach to Judaism, which he regarded to be an appropriate response to modernity. This branch of Judaism considers the laws of the Torah to be useful only if they have a clear purpose for the Jewish people, or for humanity as a whole, and that the laws therefore require continuous reinterpretation. Some of the changes that have been effected in Reconstructionist Judaism are quite radical. For example, their Sabbath Prayer Book includes no mention of the Jews as a "chosen people", and does not look forward to the coming of a Messiah. In place of such doctrines, Reconstructionism strives for a better world for all, populated by better people.

HUMANISTIC JUDAISM
1963, Michigan, USA

Rabbi Sherwin T. Wine founded Humanistic Judaism in the USA in the 1960s to offer nonreligious Jews a nontheistic alternative to the traditional religion. Humanistic Jews hold that Judaism is an ethnic culture formed by the Jewish people, with no connection to God. The tradition's humanistic, egalitarian philosophy is reflected in its uplifting celebration of Jewish culture: nontheistic rituals and ceremonies are open to all, Jew and non-Jew, regardless of gender and sexual orientation. Participation in religious festivals is considered important, although all references to God are omitted from services, and religious passages have been rewritten from a secular perspective. Adherents are encouraged to focus on self-determination, self-help, and reason to shape their lives, rather than on the intervention of divine authority.

BRANCHES OF CHRISTIANITY

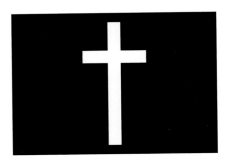

The world's largest religion, with more than two billion adherents, Christianity is based on the teachings of Jesus Christ, which are chronicled in the Gospels – four books in the New Testament of the Bible. Christianity is a monotheistic religion that has common roots with Judaism. However, Christians believe that Jesus was the Messiah promised in the Old Testament. For centuries the main religion of Europe, Christianity spread around the world with European colonization from the 15th century. Political and doctrinal differences saw Christianity diversify into Eastern and Western branches in the Great Schism of 1504, and then into numerous denominations following the Reformation, which began in the 16th century.

ROMAN CATHOLIC CHURCH
1st century CE, Rome, Italy

The Roman Catholic Church is the original, and still the largest, Christian Church. Its leaders, the popes, claim to be the descendants of St Peter, who founded the first Christian Church in Rome in the 1st century CE. This lineage is seen to connect the Pope directly with Christ's first followers, and therefore to give him a unique authority: he is considered infallible when ruling on key articles of faith.

ORIENTAL ORTHODOX CHURCHES
3rd–4th centuries CE, various

The Oriental Orthodox Churches, which include the Coptic Church and those of Syria and Ethiopia, as well as Armenia (right), share the view that Christ has one nature (inseparably human and divine). All Oriental Orthodox Churches trace their origins directly to the early centuries of Christianity. The Coptic Church is Egypt's national Christian Church, dating to the 3rd century CE. The Ethiopian Orthodox Church was founded around 340 CE as a branch of the Coptic Church. It follows several Jewish-influenced practices, such as observing a day of rest on the Sabbath, circumcision, and certain dietary rules that link it to its Middle Eastern origins. The Syrian Orthodox Church has members in southern Turkey, Iran, Iraq, and India, as well as in Syria itself. The Syriac language is used in worship, and the liturgy is one of the richest of all the Christian Churches.

ARMENIAN CHURCH
c.294 CE, Etchmiadzin, Armenia

Armenia was the first country to make Christianity its state religion: St Gregory converted its ruler, King Tirirdates III, in the late 3rd century CE. The Armenian Church was at first close to the Eastern Orthodox Churches, but around 506 CE they split over definitions of the nature of Christ. Like the Oriental Orthodox Church, of which it is part, the Armenian Church sees Christ as having one nature, simultaneously human and divine. Armenian Christians worship in their own language using a 5th-century translation of the Bible. Their churches are plain and they have two kinds of priests: parish priests who, unless they are monks, must marry before ordination; and doctors, who are celibate and may become bishops.

EASTERN ORTHODOX CHURCHES
1054, Constantinople (Istanbul)

The Eastern Orthodox Churches of Eastern Europe, the Balkans, and western Asia arose from a split between the Western Catholic Church and the Churches of the Byzantine Empire in the Great Schism of 1054. This split was caused by differing views about the Holy Trinity (pp.212–19). In addition, the Western Church tends to stress humankind's sinful nature, while the Eastern Church recognizes its essential goodness; the Western Church focuses on dogma, whereas the Eastern is more centred on worship. All Orthodox Churches celebrate seven sacraments, like those of the Catholic Church, but they are referred to as mysteries. The mystery at the heart of the faith is emphasized by the fact that large parts of the Eastern Orthodox service take place behind a screen, out of sight of the congregation.

LUTHERANISM
1520s, Germany

The Lutheran Church traces its origins to German reformer Martin Luther (p.235). Lutheranism spread across northern Europe during the 16th and 17th centuries. Followers see the Bible as the only guide to doctrine and believe that people come to God through faith in Jesus Christ, not good works. There are now around 70 separate Lutheran Churches, all under the umbrella of the Lutheran World Federation.

ANGLICANISM
1534, London, England

The Anglican Church separated from the Roman Church in the 16th century due to ecclesiastical and political conflicts surrounding King Henry VIII's petition to the Pope for a divorce from Catherine of Aragon. It retained many Catholic features at first, but was later influenced by Protestant reformers. Today, the Anglican Church embraces those who favour elaborate ritual, known as "Anglo-Catholics", as well as those termed "Evangelical" who hold simpler services. The Anglican Church includes 30 autonomous Churches around the world, known as the Anglican Communion. All believe in the importance of Scripture, accept an unbroken line of bishops (traced back to the Apostles), and celebrate two sacraments: baptism and the Eucharist (p.228).

MENNONITE CHURCH
1540s, The Netherlands

The Dutch preacher Menno Simons, originally a Catholic who joined the Anabaptists – a radical Reformation group – in 1536, believed in Church reform, pacifism, and the baptism of adult believers only. His followers, known as Mennonites, spread throughout Europe. German Mennonites were among the early settlers of America, and many Russian Mennonites migrated to the USA after World War II. Today, the majority of Mennonites live in North America and pursue a Bible-based faith. They anticipate the Second Coming of Christ and live a life of holiness and prayer. Missionary and relief work is important to believers.

PRESBYTERIANISM
16th century, Scotland

Presbyterianism originated with 16th-century reformers, such as French theologian John Calvin (p.237). As well as his influential ideas on predestination, Calvin believed Christian groups should be governed by elders. This appealed to Church leaders in Scotland, keen to increase community involvement in religious affairs. Presbyterians are so named for being governed by presbyters (ministers or elders) and have no bishops. Congregationalism developed for similar reasons, especially in England, and was the religion of the Pilgrim Fathers in America. In the late 20th century, the Presbyterians and Congregationalists joined to form the World Alliance of Reformed Churches, whose members see salvation as the gift of God.

BAPTISTS
Early 17th century, The Netherlands and England

The first Baptists were English Protestants; their Church was founded in England in 1612 by Thomas Helwys. Baptist beliefs include the primacy of the Bible and that baptism should be reserved for adult believers who can profess their faith. Baptist churches spread across the USA and are especially popular with the black community there; they have gained ground internationally and are one of the world's largest Christian groups today.

QUAKERS
c.1650, Great Britain

The Quaker movement began in the 17th century, led by George Fox. The name originated when Fox told a magistrate to quake at the name of the Lord. Fox and his followers had no clergy, no sacraments, and no formal liturgy, believing that the Friends – as they called themselves – could communicate directly with God. They opposed warfare and refused to take legal oaths. Although widely persecuted, they are now admired for their campaigns for peace, prison reform, and abolition of slavery. Modern Quakers still emphasize direct contact with God, gathering together in silence until the Spirit moves a member to speak.

AMISH
Late 17th century, Switzerland

The Amish are members of a strict Protestant group that originated in Switzerland under the leadership of a Mennonite minister, Jacob

Amman, but now mostly live in the eastern USA. Of several groups of Amish that exist today, the most distinctive is the Old Order, who adopt traditional clothes, shun recent developments such as motorized transport, and run their own schools, preferring to help each other than to accept state benefits. Worship takes place in their homes, with different householders taking it in turn to host the Sunday service.

MORAVIAN BRETHREN
1722, Saxony, Germany

In 1722, German Count Nikolaus von Zinzendorf invited a group of Protestants from Moravia (now in the Czech Republic) to form a community on his estate in Saxony. Owing their origins to the earliest Protestants, the followers of reformer Jan Hus, who was burned at the stake in 1415, they became known as the Moravian Brethren. Their Church looks to the Scriptures for guidance on faith and conduct, with little emphasis on doctrine. A key part of their worship is the sharing of a communal meal called a lovefeast. They are evangelical, sending missionaries throughout the world.

METHODISM
1720s–30s, England

Methodism was founded by John Wesley in England in the 18th century. It is now one of the four largest Churches in Britain and has more than 70 million adherents worldwide. Methodists believe that Christians should live by the "method" outlined by the Bible, and place major emphasis on scripture and little on ritual. Preaching is considered especially important.

SHAKERS
c.1758, Great Britain

The Shakers' name is derived from the trembling experienced by members in religious ecstasy. Their founder, Ann Lee, claimed she had revelations that she was Christ's female counterpart. Persecuted in England, she and her followers emigrated to America, where they held their possessions in common and were celibate. Although the group was popular in the 19th century, membership declined in the 20th century, and today there are few members. However, the Shakers are still respected for their austere lifestyle and the simple furniture they created.

UNITARIANISM
1774, England

Unitarians believe in one God but not the Holy Trinity (pp.212–19), and they seek truth based in human experience rather than religious doctrine. Unitarian ideas began to emerge in Poland, Hungary, and England in the 16th century, but the first Unitarian Church was founded in England only in 1774, and in the USA in 1781. Numbers declined in the 20th century, but there are still thriving congregations in the USA and Europe. Congregations are independent of one another and there is no Church hierarchy.

MORMONISM
1830, New York, USA

The Church of Jesus Christ of Latter-Day Saints was founded by American Joseph Smith. He claimed to have been guided to a set of gold tablets bearing the word of God by an angel. He translated them as *The Book of Mormon* (1830), which, together with other Mormon texts, and the Bible, form the religion's writings. Smith claimed the right to guide the Church through further revelations, including permission for polygamous marriages and the possibility for all men to become gods. After his death in 1844, the Mormons followed a new leader, Brigham Young, to Utah, where the Church remains strong.

PLYMOUTH BRETHREN
1831, Plymouth, England

The Plymouth Brethren began as a group of Christians who rejected the sectarian nature of the existing Protestant churches, seeking a less formal religion. They believed that all should have equal access to their faith, and did not ordain priests. Enthusiastic preachers, they emphasized the importance of regular worship, Bible study, and missionary work. In 1848, they divided into two broad groups, the Open and the Exclusive Brethren, differing in their interpretation of certain theological issues and their attitudes towards outsiders. Today, there are an estimated two million members of the group around the world.

CHRISTADELPHIANISM
1848, Richmond, Virginia, USA

The name Christadelphians ("Christ's brothers") reflects a desire of the Church's English founder, John Thomas, to return to the faith of Jesus's first disciples. He rejected the term "Christianity", believing that the Christian Churches had distorted Jesus's true message. Followers adhere to Jesus's teachings but reject the doctrine of the Holy Trinity and look forward to the Second Coming of Christ. The Church does not ordain priests, and its members do not vote or take part in politics, and reject military service.

SEVENTH-DAY ADVENTIST CHURCH
1863, Battle Creek, Michigan, USA

Adventists are Protestant Christians who believe in the imminent Second Coming of Jesus Christ. At this time, known as the Advent, Christ will return to earth, destroy Satan, and create a new world. The American Adventist William Miller claimed this process would begin around 1843. When it did not, he blamed people's refusal to keep the Sabbath (hence the term Seventh-Day Adventist) and founded the Church in 1863. Adventists follow the dietary rules of the Old Testament, eschew worldly pursuits (such as gambling and dancing), and observe the Sabbath on Saturday.

THE SALVATION ARMY
1865, London, England

Methodist preacher William Booth founded the Salvation Army in London in 1865. His beliefs were strongly influenced by his religious background, but the sect's organization was inspired by the military. The church leader is its general and its ministers are officers and wear uniforms. Booth's aim was to do missionary and social work on a large, organized scale, and the denomination gained a reputation for helping the poor.

JEHOVAH'S WITNESSES
1872, Pittsburgh, Pennsylvania, USA

The Jehovah's Witnesses (pp.312–13) have their roots in the International Bible Students' Association. They believe that Jesus Christ was not, himself, God, but God's first creation. They anticipate the coming of the kingdom of God, reject nationalism, and dispute doctrines such as the Trinity. The Church aims to convert others by door-to-door proselytizing.

CHURCH OF CHRIST (SCIENTIST)
1879, Boston, Massachusetts, USA

Mary Baker Eddy dedicated her life to reviving the early healing ministry of Jesus after she was cured without medical treatment following an injury. Eddy claimed to be able to heal the sick, and believed that those who understand the link between God and love can also become healers. She founded the Church of Christ (Scientist) in 1879. Eddy's own writings and the Bible form the basis of the religion. Services feature readings from both but have no sermons. Christian Science is today established in more than 80 countries.

PENTECOSTALISM
1900–1906, Topkepa, Kansas; Los Angeles, California, USA

Pentecostal churches are prevalent in the developing world, and in poorer communities in the developed world. They take their name from the first Pentecost, (p.219) when the Holy Spirit is said to have descended on the Apostles

as tongues of flame. The Churches' roots are in the work of the preacher Charles Parham. These Churches emphasize spiritual experiences, such as healing, exorcism, prophecy, and speaking in tongues after baptism in the Holy Spirit. Parham's student, William J. Seymour, founded the Apostolic Faith Gospel Mission in Los Angeles, which inspired the founding of Pentecostal churches worldwide.

CHARISMATIC MOVEMENT
1950s–60s, various

The Charismatic movement is a worldwide movement of Christian revival. At its heart is the belief in the charismata, or gifts of the Holy Spirit (p.219). Worship tends to be informal and the Second Coming of Christ is often seen as imminent. The movement stresses the importance of the Holy Spirit, which is said to enter believers during baptism.

NEW AFRICAN CHURCHES
20th century, Africa

The last hundred years have seen the rapid rise of a specifically African form of Christianity south of the Sahara. In the late 19th century, Africans began to reject the Christianity imported by Western missionaries, creating independent African Churches. The largest include the Kimbanguists, founded in the Democratic Republic of the Congo, with some 10 million members; and the similarly sized Celestial Church of Christ in Benin. Many of these Churches arose in times of persecution and have a strong sense of sacred places.

BRANCHES OF ISLAM

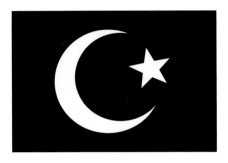

The most recently founded of the three great monotheistic religions, Islam spread quickly from its roots in the Middle East and has been hugely influential in scholarship and politics all over the world. The most significant division within Islam is that between Sunni and Shi'a, two branches that developed when the early Muslim community disagreed over who was to succeed their first leader, Muhammad. Later conflicts over leadership led to further subdivisions, but there are also groups within Islam that are set apart by doctrinal differences: Sufism, or mystical Islam, for example, is vigorously opposed by some more orthodox Muslim groups that consider its practices un-Islamic.

SUNNI ISLAM
7th century CE, Arabian Peninsula

More than 85 per cent of the Muslim population of the world is Sunni. In most Islamic countries, the majority of Muslims are Sunni, with the exception of Iran, Iraq, Azerbaijan, and Yemen, as well as some of the Gulf States. The founders of this form of Islam were the group of Muslims who believed that Abu Bakr, Companion and father-in-law of Muhammad, should succeed the Prophet as the first leader or caliph (literally, "successor"). Sunni Muslims take the Sunna, or tradition of Muhammad, as the model for Muslim conduct and have a further allegiance to one of four schools that interpret Islamic law, or shari'a (p.273): Hanafi, Maliki, Hanbali, and Shafi'i.

SHI'A ISLAM
7th century CE, Arabian Peninsula

Shi'a Islam is named after the Shi'a 'Ali, or Party of 'Ali, the group within the early Muslim community that claimed that Muhammad had nominated his cousin 'Ali to lead the faith as his successor. Its largest branch identifies 'Ali and a continuous line of 11 descendants as the imams, or spiritual leaders, of Islam, whose authority is divinely sanctioned. This branch is known as Twelve-Imam Shi'a, or the Twelvers. Another group of Shi'a Muslims, the Seveners, does not recognize the last five imams in this lineage. Both groups also have doctrinal differences with Sunni Islam: for example, they hold that God may change his decisions (a concept called *bada'*).

KHARIJITES
7th century CE, Middle East

The assassination of the third caliph, 'Uthman ibn 'Affan, in 656 CE sparked a bitter conflict that split the Islamic world. At its centre was a group of rebel Muslims responsible for the assassination, who later became known as the Kharijites, a name deriving from the Arabic for "to leave" or "exit". They did not believe that the position of caliph should be inherited, but rather that it should be won by election. The sect gained a reputation for their extreme militancy and opposition to established authority; however, some Islamic scholars have interpreted their actions as an attempt to uphold justice. The Kharijites maintained a literal and unswerving observance of the Qur'an, lived puritanical lives strictly according to Islamic rule, and held that anyone who committed a major sin could not remain a Muslim. The early Kharijites were almost wiped out in their frequent uprisings, but members of a more moderate group survive today in North Africa, Oman, and Zanzibar.

ISMAILISM
7th century CE, Arabian Peninsula

Ismailism is a sect of Shi'a Islam and itself has numerous subsects, including the Druze (see opposite). The movement has its origins in the late 7th century CE, following a conflict within Shi'a Islam over who should succeed Jaafar al-Sadiq as the sixth imam.

Those who considered his son Ismail to be the rightful successor established a breakaway group, and became known as Ismailis. Although there are variations within Ismailism, its followers generally uphold fundamental Muslim belief with respect to the unity of God, the Prophet Muhammad, the Qur'an, and shari'a law. However, among their principal doctrines is a belief that the religion has exterior and interior aspects, and that the exterior features hold hidden, inner truths that will be made clear via the imams. The imams' interpretations of the Qur'an's hidden truths are regarded as binding in the community.

DRUZE
11th century, Middle East

The beliefs of the sect known as the Druze developed out of Ismailite doctrine. This small sect is characterized by extreme secrecy: many of its teachings and practices have been withheld, not only from the outside world, but also from its own members. The Druze community is divided into the *ukkal* (initiated) and the *juhhal* (uninitiated); only the *ukkal* have access to the faith's sacred texts and may participate fully in rituals and ceremonies. The majority of Druze now live in Lebanon, with smaller groups in Syria and Israel.

SUFISM
13th century, Turkey

The mystical and ascetic branch of Islam is known as Sufism (pp.282–83). Devotees follow a spiritual teacher and seek a direct and personal experience of God, which is often characterized by intense, ecstatic experiences, including trance-like states. The spinning of the Whirling Dervishes, a Sufi order, is an expression of this attempt to experience God. Because Sufism involves such practices, which are thought to lead to the union of the individual with God, Sufis have been accused of turning their backs on Islam. However, they insist that their experience of the love of God is the anchor of their Islamic faith, and that adherence to shari'a law (pp.272–73) is as vital to them as it is to other Muslims.

AHMADIYYA
1889, Punjab, India

Controversy has surrounded the Ahmadiyya movement since its establishment in Punjab towards the end of the 19th century. The founder of the movement, a Sunni Muslim named Mirza Ghulam Ahmad, claimed not only to have been divinely inspired, but also to be a messiah figure (pp.284–85). This conflicted with the accepted idea of Muhammad as the last true prophet, and as a result most other Muslims regard followers of the Ahmadiyya movement as heretics. The movement does, however, share many traditional beliefs of Sunni Islam and accepts the Qur'an as its holy text. Adherents believe that the message about their version of Islam should be conveyed to non-Muslims as well as Muslims, and the movement has spread throughout the world, building centres of worship and learning in Africa, North America, Asia, and Europe.

SALAFISM
Late 19th century, Egypt

Salafism is a modern, conservative movement within Sunni Islam that looks to the Salaf, or "predecesors", the earliest Muslims, for guidance on exemplary Islamic conduct. The movement is considered to have emerged as a reaction to the spread of Western, specifically European, ideology in the late 19th century; Salafists believe in eliminating foreign influence to ensure a return to the pure faith. They have a strict interpretation of the sins of shirk (idolatry) and *bida'h* (innovation), and reject *kalam*, or theological speculation. Followers uphold the precedence of shari'a law (pp.272–73) and the literal truth of the Qur'an. Salafism is said to be Islam's fastest-growing movement worldwide.

THE NATION OF ISLAM
1930, USA

Arising out of the Depression of the 1930s in African-American areas in the USA, the Nation of Islam was founded by Fard Muhammad, to whom some have ascribed divinity. Other key figures have included the civil rights activist Malcolm X and Louis Farrakhan. The theology of the movement combines core Islamic beliefs with a strong political agenda focused on African-American unity and rights. The Nation of Islam has been accused of being both black supremacist and anti-Semitic, but has nevertheless been effective in spreading ideas about faith and equality among black people, and upholds a strict code of ethics.

GLOSSARY

Key
(B) Buddhism
(C) Christianity
(D) Daoism and other
  Chinese religions
(H) Hinduism
(I) Islam
(J) Judaism
(Jn) Jainism
(S) Sikhism
(Sh) Shinto
(Z) Zoroastrianism

Adi Granth (S) See **Guru Granth Sahib**.

Advaita Vedanta (H) A school of Hindu philosophy developed in the 9th century, which gives a unified explanation of the **Vedas**, and focuses on the idea of **Brahman**.

Ahadith (I) See **Hadith**.

Ahimsa (B, H, Jn) A doctrine of non-violence of both thought and action.

Akhand path (S) A complete and uninterrupted oral rendition of the **Guru Granth Sahib**.

Allah (I) The name of the one God.

Amrit (S) Sweetened holy water used in religious ceremonies; the specific Sikh ceremony of initiation.

Analects (D) The collected sayings of Confucius and his contemporaries, written by his followers.

Ananda (H) A state of bliss.

Anata (B) A state of freedom from ego to which Buddhists aspire.

Anicca (B) The impermanence of existence.

Arhat (B) A perfect being who has attained **nirvana**.

Artha (H) The pursuit of material wealth, one of the duties of a person in the "householder" stage of life, the second phase of the **ashrama**.

Ashkenazim (J) Jews from Eastern and Central Europe, and their descendants around the world.

Ashrama (H) The stages of life, of which there are four, in the Hindu social system: student; householder; retiree; and ascetic.

Atman (H) The individual self.

Avatar (H) An incarnation of a Hindu deity; especially the various incarnations of the god Vishnu.

Avesta (Z) The principle sacred texts of Zoroastrianism.

Ayat (C) The smallest entries in the Qu'ran, which are short verses or "signs".

Baptism (C) The sacrament that admits a person to the Christian Church in a ritual that involves being sprinkled with, or immersed in, water.

Bar/bat mitzvah (J) The ceremony marking a Jewish boy's or girl's admission to the adult religious community; the state of having reached religious adulthood.

Bhakti (B, H) An active religious devotion to a divinity leading to **nirvana**.

Bible (C) The collection of books that constitute the sacred text of Christianity. The Christian Bible comprises the Old Testament, which includes the Jewish books of the law, Jewish history, and the prophets; and the New Testament, which deals with the life and work of Jesus, his followers, and the early Church. See also **Hebrew Bible**.

Bodhisattva (B) Someone on the path to becoming a **buddha**, who puts off final enlightenment to help other people to reach the same state.

Brahma (H) The creator god, one of the Hindu **Trimurti**.

Brahman (H) The impersonal and unchanging divine reality of the universe. All other gods are aspects of Brahman.

Brahmin (H) A priest or seeker of the highest knowledge; the priestly class and custodians of **dharma**.

Buddha (B) An enlightened being.

Canonization (C) The process by which the Christian Church declares that a person is a saint.

Charismata (C) "Spiritual gifts" conferred by the Holy Spirit of God on believers, manifesting in forms such as the ability to heal, or speak in tongues.

Christ (C) Literally, "anointed one"; title given to Jesus.

Confirmation (C) A ritual in which those who have been baptized confirm their Christian faith.

Covenant (J) An agreement between God and the Jewish people in which the Jews are identified as the group he has chosen to play a special role in the relationship between himself and humanity.

Dao (D) The path or way that an individual aims to follow; the underlying way or pattern governing the working of nature.

Darshan (H) The worshipping of a deity by means of viewing an image of the god or goddess.

Dhamma (B) A variant of **dharma**, most commonly used in Buddhism.

Dharma (H) The underlying path or pattern that characterizes the cosmos and the earth; it also refers to the moral path that a person must follow.

Dukkha (B) Suffering or dissatisfaction; the idea that all life is suffering, the first of the **Four Noble Truths** defined by Buddha.

Eightfold Path (B) The path of disciplined living that Buddhists follow in the hope of breaking free from the cycle of death and rebirth. Followers aim to achieve correct understanding, intention (or thought), speech, conduct, occupation, effort, mindfulness, and concentration.

Enlightenment (B) Discovery of the ultimate truth, and the end of **dukkha**.

Eucharist (C) One of the main sacraments, involving the taking of wine and bread as the blood and body of Christ; it is known as Mass in Catholicism, Holy Communion in the Anglican Church, and the liturgy in the various Orthodox churches.

Fatwa (I) A non-binding judgment on a point of Islamic law given by a recognized religious authority.

Four Noble Truths (B) A central teaching of Buddhism, explaining the nature of **dukkha**, its causes, and how it can be overcome.

Fravashi (Z) A guardian angel who protects the souls of individuals as they struggle against evil.

Gathas (Z) The most sacred texts of Zoroastrianism, supposedly composed by Zoroaster himself.

Gentile (J) A non-Jew.

Gospels (C) The four books of the New Testament of the **Bible**, attributed to the apostles Matthew, Mark, Luke, and John, which tell of Jesus's life and teachings; "gospel" can also refer to the content of Christian teaching.

Granthi (S) An official who takes care of the **Guru Granth Sahib** and the **gurdwara**. A granthi is also a skilled reader of the sacred book.

Gurdwara (S) A Sikh temple; the place where the **Guru Granth Sahib** is housed.

Guru (H) Teacher; **(S)** One of the 10 founder-leaders of Sikhism.

Guru Granth Sahib (S) The Sikh sacred book, also known as the **Adi Granth**.

Hadith (I) Traditional accounts of the deeds and teachings of the Prophet Muhammad; the second source of Islamic law and moral guidance after the **Qur'an**.

Hafiz (I) A term of respect for a person who has memorized the **Qur'an**.

Haggadah (J) The body of teaching of the early **rabbis**, containing legends, historical narratives, and ethical precepts.

Hajj (I) The pilgrimage to Mecca, the fourth of the five pillars of Islam; all Muslims hope to make this journey once in their lives.

Halal (I) Conduct that is permitted; specifically, the correct method of slaughtering livestock, and the meat from correctly slaughtered animals.

Haram (I) Conduct that is forbidden; something sacred or inviolate.

Hasid (J) A member of a Jewish group founded in the 18th century which places a strong emphasis on mysticism.

Haskalah (J) The Jewish Enlightenment, a movement among European Jews in the 18th–19th centuries.

Hebrew Bible (J) A collection of sacred writings that form the basis of Judaism, including the **Torah**, revelations of prophets, and other sacred texts; the equivalent of the Old Testament in the Christian **Bible**.

Icon (C) A sacred image, usually depicting Christ or one of the saints, which is used as a focus for devotion, especially in the Orthodox Churches.

Imam (I) Leader of prayers in a mosque; or, one of the great leaders of the Muslim community in the Shi'a branch of the faith.

Incarnation (C) The belief that in the person of Jesus Christ, divine and human natures were made one.

Jihad (I) A religious duty to struggle against evil in the name of God, whether spiritually or physically.

Jina (Jn) A spiritual teacher. See **tirthankara**.

Kaaba (I) One of Islam's most sacred buildings, sited in Mecca inside the Masjid al-Haram mosque; a principal destination for those on **hajj**.

Kabbalah (J) An ancient Jewish mystical tradition based on an esoteric interpretation of the Hebrew Bible.

Kaccha (S) Long shorts worn under other garments by Sikhs; one of the distinguishing "five Ks" of Sikhism.

Kalam (I) Discussion and debate, especially relating to Islamic theology.

Kami (Sh) A spirit or deity in Shinto religion. There are many thousands of kami in the Shinto pantheon.

Kangha (S) A small comb worn in the hair by Sikhs; one of the "five Ks" of Sikhism.

Kara (S) A steel bangle worn by Sikhs on the right wrist. One of the "five Ks" of Sikhism.

Karma (B, H) The law of moral cause and effect that influences our rebirth after death.

Kesh (S) Uncut hair; one of the "five Ks" of Sikhism.

Khalsa (S) The community of initiated Sikhs, founded by Guru Gobind Singh.

Khanda (S) A two-edged sword of the kind used by Guru Gobind Singh in a ritual that marked the founding of the Khalsa; now a symbol of Sikhism.

Kirpan (S) A sword worn by Sikhs; one of the "five Ks" of Sikhism.

Kirtan (S) Hymn-singing that forms an important part of Sikh worship.

Koan (B) In Zen Buddhism, a problem or riddle without logical solution, which is intended to provoke an insight.

Kojiki (Sh) The sacred text of Shinto.

Kosher (J) Sanctioned by religious law; especially food deemed fit to eat, according to Jewish dietary laws.

Kundalini (H) Life force or energy that is coiled at the base of the spine.

Lama (B) An adept spiritual teacher in Tibetan Buddhism, specifically one who has undergone particular **yogic** or other training, or one who is considered to be the reincarnation of a previous spiritual leader.

Mandala (B) A sacred diagram, usually depicting a conception of the cosmos, used as a focus for meditation and in other rituals, especially in Tibetan Buddhism.

Mantra (B, H) A sacred sound or word used to bring about a spiritual transformation; in Hinduism, the metrical psalms of **Vedic** literature.

Matha (H, Jn) Monastic and similar religious establishments.

Matsuri (Sh) A festival or ritual in Shinto. Many feature processions of shrine-bearing worshippers.

Maya (H) The illusion of the world as experienced by the senses.

Mihrab (I) A niche in the prayer hall of a mosque, indicating the **qibla**.

Mishnah (J) The first major written redaction of the Jewish oral traditions and also the first major work of rabbinic Judaism.

Mitzvah (J) A commandment from God; specifically, either one of the 10 principal commandments, or one of the 613 instructions found in the **Torah**.

Moksha (H) The release from the round of life, death, and rebirth; also known as mukti.

Mool mantra (S) A statement of Sikh belief in the oneness of God, composed by Guru Nanak; also called the mool mantar.

Mudra (B, H) A symbolic gesture, usually with the hands.

Mullah (I) An Islamic religious scholar, who may also preach and lead prayers in a mosque.

Murti (H) An image or statue of a deity, seen as the dwelling place or embodiment of the deity.

Nirvana (B) The state of liberation from the round of death and rebirth.

Puja (H) Worship through ritual.

Puranas (B, H, Jn) Writings not included in the **Vedas**, recounting the birth and deeds of Hindu gods and the creation, destruction, or recreation of the universe.

Pure Land (B) The paradise where, according to some forms of Buddhism, the souls of believers go after death; known in Japanese Buddhism as jodo.

Purusha (H) The eternal and authentic self that pervades all things in the universe.

Qi (D) The life force or active principle that animates things in the world, according to traditional Chinese philosophy.

Qibla (I) The direction that a Muslim should face when praying – that of the **Kaaba** in Mecca.

Qigong (D) A system of breathing and exercise for physical, mental, and spiritual health.

Qur'an (I) The words of God as revealed to the Prophet Muhammad and later written down to form the sacred text of Islam.

Rabbi (J) A teacher and spiritual leader of a Jewish community.

Rabbinical (J) Of, or relating to, rabbis.

Ramadan (I) The ninth month of the Islamic calendar; a month of daily fasting from dawn until sunset.

Ren (D) Benevolence or altruism in Confucianism.

Sabbath (J) The rest day of the Jewish week, lasting from sunset on Friday to sunset on Saturday.

Sacraments (C) The solemn rites of Christianity. The Catholic and Orthodox Churches recognize seven: **baptism**, **Eucharist**, penance, confirmation, ordination, extreme unction (last rites), and marriage. Most Protestant Churches recognize only two: baptism and the Eucharist.

Sadhu (H) A holy man who has dedicated his life to seeking God.

Salat (I) Prayer; the second of the five pillars of Islam. Muslims are expected to pray five times each day.

Samsara (B, H) The continuing and repeating cycle of birth, life, death, and rebirth.

Samskara (H) Imprints left on the mind by experience in current or past lives; Hindu rites of passage.

Sawm (I) Fasting, especially during the month of **Ramadan**; the fourth of the five pillars of Islam.

Sangha (B) An order of Buddhist monks and nuns.

Satya (H) Truth, or what is correct and unchanging.

Sefirot (J) The 10 emanations, the attributes of God in **kabbalah**.

Sephardim (J) Jews who come from Spain, Portugal, or North Africa, or their descendants.

Seva (S) Service to others, one of the important principles of Sikhism.

Shahada (I) The Muslim profession of faith, translated as, "There is no God but God; Muhammad is the messenger of God"; the first and most important of the five pillars of Islam.

Shari'a (I) The path to be followed in Muslim life and, therefore, Islamic law, based on the **Qur'an** and on the **Hadith**.

Shi'a (I) One of the two main groups of Muslims, consisting of those who believe that Muhammad's cousin 'Ali was his rightful successor as caliph. See also **Sunni**.

Shirk (I) The sin of idolatry or polytheism.

Sruti (H) The **Vedas** and some of the **Upanishads**.

Sufi (I) A member of one of a number of mystical Islamic orders, whose beliefs centre on a personal relationship with God. Sufi orders can be found in **Sunni**, **Shi'a** and other Islamic groups. Sufism is associated with the ecstatic whirling dances of the dervishes.

Sunna (I) Muhammad's way of life, taken as a model for Muslims and recorded in the **hadiths**.

Sunni (I) One of the two main groups of Muslims, followers of those who supported an elected caliphate. See also **Shi'a**.

Sutra (B, H) A collection of teachings, especially sayings attributed to Buddha.

Talmud (J) Text made up of a body of discussion and interpretation of the **Torah**, compiled by scholars and rabbis, and a source of ethical advice and instruction, especially to Orthodox Jews.

Tantra (B) Text used in some kinds of Buddhism (mainly in Tibet) to help users to reach enlightenment, or the practices based on such a text.

Tirthankara (Jn) One of the 24 spiritual teachers or **jinas** who have shown the way of the Jain faith.

Torah (J) The first five books of the Hebrew **Bible**, seen as representing the teaching given by God to Moses on Mount Sinai.

Trimurti (H) The trio of principal Hindu gods – Brahma, Vishnu, and Shiva – or a threefold image of them.

Trinity (C) The threefold god, comprising Father, Son, and Holy Spirit in a single divinity.

Upanishads (H) Sacred texts containing Hindu philosophical teachings; also known as the Vedanta, the end of the **Vedas**.

Vedas (H) Collections of hymns and other writings in praise of the deities.

Wa (D) Harmony, in which the group takes precedence over the individual.

Wuwei (D) Uncontrived and effortless doing.

Yin–yang (D) The two principles of the cosmos in Chinese philosophy, seen as opposite but complementary and interacting to produce a whole greater than either separate part.

YHWH (J) The four letters that represent the name of God in Judaism, considered to be too holy to utter, but pronounced "yahweh".

Yoga (H) A form of physical and mental training. One of the six schools of Hindu philosophy.

Zakat (I) The giving of alms in the form of a tax to help the poor; the third pillar of Islam.

Zazen (B) Seated meditation.

Zurvan (Z) The God of time; in some forms of Zoroastrianism, the primal being, from whom were derived the wise lord Ahura Mazda and the hostile spirit Angra Mainyu.

INDEX

ACKNOWLEDGMENTS

Dorling Kindersley and cobalt id would like to thank Louise Thomas for additional picture research, and Margaret McCormack for the index

PICTURE CREDITS

The publisher would like to thank the following for their kind permission to reproduce their photographs:

(Key: a-above; b-below; c-centre; l-left; r-right; t-top)

21 Corbis: Anthony Bannister/Gallo Images (tr). **22 Getty Images:** Per-Andre Hoffmann (bl). **23 Corbis:** Ocean (tr). **25 Getty Images:** Time & Life Pictures (tr). **29 Corbis:** Michel Setboun (tr). **31 Alamy Images:** Horizons WWP (tl); Getty Images: Apic/Contributor (br). **33 Corbis:** Nathan Lovas/ Foto Natura/Minden Pictures (cr). **35 Corbis:** Giles Bracher/Robert Harding World Imagery (tr). **37 Getty Images:** Maria Stenzel (tr). **39 Getty Images:** Juan Carlos MuÃ±oz (cr). **43 Alamy Images:** Pictorial Press Ltd (tl). **44 Alamy Images:** Emiliano Rodriguez (br). **45 Getty Images:** Richard I'Anson (tl). **47 Corbis:** William Henry Jackson (tr). **48 Getty Images:** David Sutherland (br). **50 Corbis:** Michele Westmorland/Science Faction (bc). **57 Alamy Images:** Imagestate Media Partners Limited - Impact Photos (tl). **59 PAL:** Peter Hayman/The British Museum (tr). **63 Corbis:** Kazuyoshi Nomachi (tr); Paule Seux/Hemis (bl). **64 Getty Images:** Religious Images/UIG (tl). **65 Corbis:** Raheb Homavandi/Reuters (br). **67 Fotolia:** Pavel Bortel (tl); Corbis: Liu Liqun (tr). **69 Corbis:** Werner Forman/Werner Forman (tr). **71 Alamy Images:** John Warburton-Lee Photography (bl); Stuart Forster India (tr). **75 Getty Images:** (bl); Keren Su (tr).

76 Mary Evans Picture Library: (tr). **77 Corbis:** Imaginechina (br). **78 Getty Images:** De Agostini Picture Library (br). **81 Corbis:** (bl). **84 Corbis:** Michael Freeman (bl). **87 Getty Images:** Universal Images Group (tl); Corbis: Kieran Doherty/Reuters (bl). **95 Alamy Images:** Franck METOIS (br). **97 Getty Images:** Gary Ombler (tr). **99 Corbis:** Nevada Wier (bl). **100 Corbis:** Godong/Robert Harding World Imagery (cr).**103 Getty Images:** Comstock (br). **108 Corbis:** Hugh Sitton (br). **111 Corbis:** Stuart Freedman/In Pictures (br). **112 Alamy Images:** Emanuele Ciccomartino (br). **114 Alamy Images:** World Religions Photo Library (cr). **119 Corbis:** Juice Images (br). **121 akg-images:** R. u. S. Michaud (tr). **123 Getty Images:** The Washington Post (bc); akg-images: R. u. S. Michaud (tr). **125 Alamy Images:** Lebrecht Music and Arts Photo Library (bl); Corbis: Bettmann (cr). **132 Corbis:** Pascal Deloche/Godong (bl); Pascal Deloche/Godong (tr). **134 Corbis:** Jeremy Horner (bl). **135 Fotolia:** Benjamin Vess (tr). **138 Getty Images:** Chung Sung-Jun (br). **140 Getty Images:** Oli Scarff (tl). **142 Getty Images:** SuperStock (bl). **143 Corbis:** Earl & Nazima Kowall (tr). **145 Corbis:** Nigel Pavitt/JAI (cb). **147 Alamy Images:** Mary Evans Picture Library (bl); Corbis: Peter Adams (tr). **149 Getty Images:** DEA / V. PIROZZI (bl). **150 Getty Images:** Andy Ryan (tr). **155 Getty Images:** Godong (br). **156 Corbis:** Peter Turnley (tl); **157 Alamy Images:** Mark Lees (tr); Fotolia: Oliver Klimek (bl). **159 Corbis:** Alison Wright (bl); Alison Wright (tr). **162 Getty Images:** Kaz Mori (tl). **171 Getty Images:** DEA / G. DAGLI ORTI (bl); Corbis: Peter Guttman (tr). **172 Getty Images:** The Bridgeman Art Library (bl). **173 Corbis:** Christophe Boisvieux (bl); Getty Images: PhotoStock-Israel (tr).

174 Corbis: Nathan Benn/Ottochrome (tl). **177 akg-images:** Erich Lessing (tl). **178 Corbis:** Dr. John C. Trever, Ph. D. (bl). **179 Corbis:** Richard T. Nowitz (tr). **183 Getty Images:** Philippe Lissac/Godong (tr). **185 Corbis:** NASA, ESA, and F. Paresce /handout (bl); Getty Images: Danita Delimont (tr). **186 Corbis:** Kobby Dagan/Demotix (bc). **188 Getty Images:** Uriel Sinai/Stringer (cr). **192 Alamy Images:** INTERFOTO (bl). **195 Alamy Images:** Israel images (tl). **197 Getty Images:** Steve McAlister (bc); Alamy Images: World History Archive (tr). **199 Corbis:** Silvia Morara (br). **205 Corbis:** Massimo Listri (cb); Chris Hellier (tr). **206 Corbis:** Francis G. Mayer (tl). **209 Corbis:** The Gallery Collection (tr). **211 Getty Images:** De Agostini Picture Library (tl); Universal Images Group (tr). **215 The Bridgeman Art Library:** Clement Guillaume (tr). **216 Getty Images:** Universal Images Group (tl). **218 Corbis:** eidon photographers/Demotix (tl). **219 Alamy Images:** van hilversum (tr). **221 Corbis:** Tim Thompson (tl); Getty Images: Mondadori Portfolio/UIG (tr). **223 Corbis:** Hulton-Deutsch Collection (br); Jose Nicolas (tr). **225 Getty Images:** Conrad Meyer (tr). **227 The Bridgeman Art Library:** AISA (br). **229 Getty Images:** DEA / VENERANDA BIBLIOTECA AMBROSIANA (bl); Scott Olson/Staff (tr). **233 Getty Images:** Lucas Cranach the Elder (t). **234 Corbis:** Alfredo Dagli Orti/The Art Archive (tl). **235 Corbis:** Bettmann (tr). **237 Getty Images:** (bl); Corbis: Paul A. Souders (tr). **238 Corbis:** Heritage Images (cb). **243 Alamy Images:** The Protected Art Archive (bl); INTERFOTO (tr). **244 Corbis:** Matthias Kulka (tl). **245 Getty Images:** Ron Burton/Stringer (tr). **247 Corbis:** (br). **253 Getty Images:** Muhannad Fala'ah/Stringer (cb); Alamy Images:

Rick Piper Photography (tl). **257 Getty Images:** Leemage (tl). **259 Corbis:** Howard Davies (tr). **260 Corbis:** Kazuyoshi Nomachi (tl). **261 Getty Images:** Patrick Syder (bl); Insy Shah (tr). **265 Corbis:** Alexandra Boulat/VII (tr). **266 Corbis:** Christine Osborne (bl). **267 Alamy Images:** Philippe Lissac/Photononstop (br). **268 Corbis:** Tom Morgan/Demotix (tl). **269 Getty Images:** AHMAD FAIZAL YAHYA (br). **271 The Bridgeman Art Library:** Christie's Images (tl). **273 Corbis:** Bertrand Rieger/Hemis (br). **274 Getty Images:** Wathiq Khuzaie (bl). **277 Corbis:** Owen Williams/National Geographic Society (cr). **278 Getty Images:** Rozikassim Photography (cr). **281 Getty Images:** Walter Bibikow (tl). **282 Corbis:** John Stanmeyer/VII (cb). **283 Alamy Images:** Peter Horree (tr). **285 Alamy Images:** ZUMA Press, Inc. (tr). **291 Corbis:** Hulton-Deutsch Collection (tl). **299 Corbis:** ETTORE FERRARI/epa (tr). **300 Corbis:** Christopher Pillitz/In Pictures (bl). **301 Alamy Images:** Art Directors & TRIP (tr). **302 Corbis:** Christopher Pillitz/In Pictures (bl). **305 Alamy Images:** Alberto Paredes (tl). **307 The Bridgeman Art Library:** (bl); Corbis: James L. Amos (tr). **309 Alamy Images:** Art Directors & TRIP (bl). **311 Corbis:** Matthew McKee (bc). **313 The Art Archive:** Tate Gallery London / Eileen Tweedy (tl). **315 Getty Images:** Ethan Miller (tl); Henry Guttmann (bl). **317 Getty Images:** travelstock44 (cl). **318 Corbis:** Bettmann (cr). **320 Alamy Images:** Pictorial Press Ltd (cr). **323 Getty Images:** China Photos (cl).

All other images © Dorling Kindersley.

For further information see: **www.dkimages.com**